LANGUAGE AND REVOLUTION

The Cummings Center for Russian and East European Studies
The Cummings Center Series

LANGUAGE AND REVOLUTION
Making Modern Political Identities

Edited by
Igal Halfin

 THE CUMMINGS CENTER
FOR RUSSIAN AND EAST EUROPEAN STUDIES
TEL AVIV UNIVERSITY

The Cummings Center is Tel Aviv University's main framework for research, study, documentation and publication relating to the history and current affairs of Russia, the former Soviet republics and Eastern Europe. The Center is committed to pursuing projects which make use of fresh archival sources and to promoting a dialogue with Russian academic circles through joint research, seminars and publications.

THE CUMMINGS CENTER SERIES

The titles published in this series are the product of original research by the Center's faculty, research staff and associated fellows. The Cummings Center Series also serves as a forum for publishing declassified Russian archival material of interest to scholars in the fields of history and political science.

EDITOR-IN-CHIEF

Gabriel Gorodetsky

EDITORIAL BOARD

Michael Confino
Igal Halfin
Shimon Naveh
Yaacov Ro'i
Nurit Schleifman

MANAGING EDITOR

Deena Leventer

LANGUAGE
and
REVOLUTION
Making Modern Political Identities

EDITED BY
IGAL HALFIN

FRANK CASS
LONDON • PORTLAND, OR

First published in 2002 in Great Britain by
FRANK CASS PUBLISHERS
Crown House, 47 Chase Side
London N14 5BP

and in the United States of America by
FRANK CASS PUBLISHERS
c/o ISBS, 5824 N.E. Hassalo Street
Portland, Oregon, 97213-3644

Website: www.frankcass.com

Copyright collection © 2002 Frank Cass & Co. Ltd.
Copyright articles © 2002 individual contributors

British Library Cataloguing in Publication Data

Language and revolution: making modern political
identities. – (The Cummings Center series)
1. Language and history – Europe 2. Revolutions – Europe –
History 3. Revolutions – Social aspects – Europe 4. Europe –
Languages – Political aspects 5. Europe – History – 18th
century 6. Europe – History – 20th century
I. Halfin, Igal II. Cummings Center for Russian and East
European Studies
302.2'094

ISBN 0-7146-5304-7 (cloth)
ISBN 0-7146-8307-8 (paper)
ISSN 1365-3733

Library of Congress Cataloging-in-Publication Data

Language and revolution: making modern political identities/
edited by Igal Halfin
   p. cm – (The Cummings Center series, ISSN 1365-3733; 16)
Includes bibliographical references and index.
ISBN 0-7146-5304-7 (cloth) – ISBN 0-7146-8307-8 (paper)
1. Languages and languages–Political aspects. 2
Revolutionaries–Europe–History–20th century 3.
Nationalism–Europe–History–20th century. I. Halfin, Igal. II.
Series
   P119.3 .L314 2002
   907'.2–dc21
                                                            2002025988

All rights reserved. No part of this publication may be reproduced, stored in or introduced into a retrieval system or transmitted in any form or by any means, electronic, mechanical, photocopying, recording or otherwise, without the prior written permission of the publisher of this book.

Typeset in 10.25/12pt Garamond by Cambridge Photosetting Services
Printed in Great Britain by MPG Books Ltd, Bodmin, Cornwall

Contents

Acknowledgements ix

Introduction 1
Igal Halfin

1. Liberty and Unanimity: The Paradoxes of Subjectivity and Citizenship in the French Revolution 27
David Andress

2. The Desacralization of the Monarchy: Rumors and 'Political Pornography' during World War I 47
Boris Kolonitskii

3. Making Cossacks Counter-Revolutionary: The Don Host and the 1918 Anti-Soviet Insurgency 83
Peter Holquist

4. Modernity and the Poetics of Proletarian Discontent 105
Mark D. Steinberg

5. Working, Struggling, Becoming: Stalin-Era Autobiographical Texts 135
Jochen Hellbeck

6. On Being the Subjects of History: Nazis as Twentieth-Century Revolutionaries 161
Peter Fritzsche

7. Intimacy in an Ideological Key: The Communist Case of the 1920s and 1930s 185
Igal Halfin

8. Grigorii Aleksandrov's *Volga-Volga* 215
Katerina Clark

9. The Symphony as Mode of Production: Shostakovich's
   Fourth Symphony and the End of the Romantic Narrative   235
   Boris Gasparov

10. Regarding the Modern Body: Science, the Social and the
    Construction of Italian Identities   249
    David G. Horn

11. Bodies of Knowledge: Physical Culture and the New Soviet
    Man   269
    David L. Hoffmann

12. Discourse Made Flesh: Healing and Terror in the
    Construction of Soviet Subjectivity   287
    Eric Naiman

13. Death in Auschwitz as 'Ugly Death'   317
    Boaz Neumann

14. A French Great Man's Last Rites: The National Funeral of
    Léon Gambetta and the Transfer of His Heart to the
    Panthéon   341
    Avner Ben-Amos

15. Enshrined Oblivion: The POW Memorial Church in
    Bochum, Germany   365
    Elisabeth Domansky

16. Varieties of Interpretation: The Holocaust in Historical
    Memory   379
    Dan Diner

Notes on Contributors   393

Index   397

Acknowledgements

It was a thrilling experience to run an international conference in Tel Aviv in January 1999 – especially for me, a junior faculty member with a very short stint of service in my department. I must extend here my gratitude to Professor Gabriel Gorodetsky and Professor Shulamit Volkov who placed their trust in me and offered me this extraordinary opportunity. It is indeed unusual for established scholars to so generously allocate authority and funds to promote young upstarts, eager to commit intellectual patricide. Thus, we were able to run a conference predominated by historians who had only recently left the study bench, and who were in the process of articulating a new historiographical paradigm. As a result, some of the work presented in this volume may be a bit raw, perhaps even speculative, but it bears unmistakable signs of excitement and enthusiasm.

Of course, there were difficulties along the way. My intention was to bring together scholars from Russia, western Europe, the United States and Israel who were interested in language and subjectivity. It became apparent that the historiographical traditions in the various countries did not necessarily converge, and that if we wanted to have a productive conference we would have to invite literary scholars with historical interests and not just historians proper. Before I set out to organize this conference, I did not know, for example, that French historians do excellent work on the Self, but do not travel. Nor was I aware that German historians travel willingly, but do not care much for the Self. Ultimately, we had the most pertinent traditions represented, and the older generation had a chance to comment on (and criticize) the weaknesses in the work of the younger generation.

I would like to express my deep gratitude to the real organizers of this project, Tali Nevo, Deena Leventer and Beryl Belsky. Without their indefatigable efforts in meeting the logistical challenge, and more important, in helping me edit this book, it would all have remained on paper. Of course, it still has, but in a different and much more fulfilling sense.

Introduction

Quintus: As I understand it, then, my dear brother, you believe that different principles are to be followed in history and in poetry.

Marcus: Certainly, Quintus; for in history the standard by which everything is judged is the truth, while in poetry it is generally the pleasure one gives; however, in the works of Herodotus the Father of History, and in those of Theopompus, one finds innumerable fabulous tales.

Cicero, Laws *I, i–ii*

Tenuous as the definition of historical writings may have been and much as the ancient historical text was unreliable, some would say even baseless, it seems that history, as a unique field of human inquiry first conceived of by the Greeks, was based on some sort of distinction between truth and fiction. All writing had to be coherent to carry meaning, but history alone was shouldered with the task of describing what truly happened. Poetry could conjure up an endless number of possible worlds. History alone set itself the task of reconstructing the real world, its genesis and transmutations.

And yet, this seemingly fundamental distinction – what seemed to be the unassailable core of self-understanding of the historical profession – seems now to be unraveling. More and more people claim that the fantastic is as much a fact as the real. History, in this view, addresses a chain of poetic inventions that have a reality of their own, sometimes more important, as it were, more real, than bare facts. Are dreams less real than real events? Are the conceptions which nations or population groups have of each other, phantasmogorical as they may be, less worthy a subject of historical inquiry than political or social realities? Should historians criticize human perceptions – measuring them against an objective truth – or should they carefully reconstruct them, seeking their own internal truth? And finally, does this mean that the historian always finds himself implicated in his materials, unable to mold his data into an objective, independently verifiable narrative?

Most observers would agree that the linguistic turn, which began in France sometime in the early 1970s, came to dominate Anglo-Saxon historiography toward the mid-1980s. Few, however, would agree on what exactly 'the linguistic turn' means. Some analytical terms lost much of their former allure, for example, 'cause', 'production', 'class', 'freedom', etc. Others, for example 'effect', 'narrative', and, of course, 'discourse' and the 'self', became highly fashionable. The new terminology bears the marks of a shift in the main influences on the historical craft: economics and, to a degree, sociology were forsaken, and with them quantification. Anthropology and literary criticism took their place, bringing the omnipresent 'culture', and 'language', to the fore. But what exactly do these terms mean? Once we look deeper and attempt to unravel the clichés somewhat, we realize that we have to address sophisticated bodies of theorizing, often at odds with each other. Indeed, terms that appear to the outsider as meaningless jargon generate endless debates among insiders: 'language' and 'discourse' or 'culture' and 'discourse' suddenly appear far from interchangeable, pointing to the heterogeneous intellectual origins of the linguistic turn.

This volume does not purport to introduce order into this chaos, only to present it and, one hopes, to indicate its more promising potential. The essays collected here – the fruit of an international historical conference in Tel Aviv in January 1999 – can be read as representing a united stance against the old historiography, which tended to focus on social and political history. At the same time they can also be read against each other, as representing an ongoing attempt, if not to articulate a common interdisciplinary agenda in humanistic studies, at least to bring its various branches under one roof, enabling a beginning of a dialogue.

The essays in this volume assume the horizon of modernity, where 'meanings' are not given and where legitimization is a perennial need. Hence the question of identity (yet another cliché appearing in our title) is not something self-evident, or related to our station in life, but an open-ended inquiry. The question of identity is not as basic as one tends to think, however. If we focus on the answer to this question, if we explore the menu of identities the modern world offers its inhabitants, we easily lose sight of the revolutionary movement that changed the context in which questions of identity were posed, catapulting them into their current pre-eminence.

In this context, the French Revolution has to be our starting point. It was this event that paved the way to modernity, for it was 1789 that secularized meanings and allowed salvation to be construed in a secular idiom. Secularization does not stand here for the total elimination of traditional religious ideas, but for their appropriation and reinterpretation as essential, meaning-giving elements, in a world view based on secular premises. Meanings were not secularized in the sense that the world had become somehow atheistic: binaries such as sacred/profane, religious/Godless, ethical/scientific, etc., conceal more than they reveal (as the success of the various attempts to read modern ideologies through a Christian prism suggests). Thus it is easy to show that Reason was venerated by the Jacobeans as a divine value and that their iconoclastic rituals shifted the locus of the sacred rather than completely desacrilized politics. Furthermore, it has been frequently pointed out that the modern timeline retained an eschatological structure: even today most political narratives presume that humanity moves from darkness to light, from bondage to freedom, however defined. The Judeo-Christian concept of linear time and the belief that perfection can be obtained at the end of a historical process unites almost all modern ideologies, certainly liberalism and Marxism, and arguably even Nazism.

The birth of modernity should be sought elsewhere: in the fact that not God but Man was crowned as the driving force of history, in the confidence that he could bring about his own salvation according to a timetable he controlled, instead of sitting idly and waiting for divine intervention. Of course, the study of a narrative by which a given society lives is a historical methodology applicable to all times and periods. What makes modernity special is that its narrative is self-aware, presenting itself as a problem, not as a solution. Modernity is based on a myth and operates with abstractions no less than Christianity. The radical departure should be sought not in narratives but in matters of attitude, in the roles assigned to the various historical agents. What strikes us in the period following the French Revolution is the strong emphasis on activism, on the call not to wait but to begin changing the world here and now. No longer content with perfecting their individual souls, meekly awaiting the Judgement Day, men now believed in organized political action. Acting collectively, they demanded the transformation of everybody and everything.

From 1789 on, the history of the world and the history of the individual were inexorably linked. History was to arrive at its End with humans gaining knowledge of themselves as active participants in the collective emancipation of humanity. To prove himself a true republican, each citizen had to bring about in himself a revolution equal to the one which had transformed France. What in the Christian civilization surfaced only occasionally, during sporadic upheavals of a messianic kind, and was usually condemned by the Church as an impermissible and vain attempt to interfere with God's handiwork, became a perennial phenomenon with the modern ideologies which sought to change the world. The revolutionary subject was creative and enterprising, not God-fearing and reactive. He was self-assured because Reason replaced belief. This human trust in the mind was known in the ancient world but delegitimized by the Christian Fathers who denounced the 'sin of curiositas', thus establishing knowledge as a dangerous form of vanity. Activism requires awareness of the story, confidence in an ability to discern who we are, where we came from and where we are heading. Modernity, then, gave birth to a specific type of political discourse, one that construed humans as masters of nature and society. Certain ways of construing the world and oneself, and certain forms of political institutions, followed.

A number of the essays here expose the discursive solidarities within the revolutionary camp, both within a given country and between countries. Paying attention not only to what separated political groups and movements but also to what united them, the authors take some important steps toward unearthing the basic grammar of the modern revolutionary phenomena. The present inquiries attempt to amend traditional historiography, which tends to be preoccupied with revolutionary debates – missing in the process the general field of reference all revolutionary actors shared. Many studies of modern revolutions have focused on a particular social group, gender or ethnicity. Sharing the outlook of the historical subjects, they rehash issues predicated on the social theory of representation: inquiring as to the identity of the social group deserving representation, and whether the political practices implemented in the name of this group truly represented it. In place of this axis of questioning, we may ask how groups subject to representation were constituted in the first place. Representative organs of various types all sought to structure individuals into movements they had already posited as existing. The Russian Revolution was a 'social revolution' not so much due to the social groups participating in it or because the social order was changed as a result of 1917, but because all historical actors sought to employ the language of class as a tool to transform the body politic.

Rather than replicating the claims of this or that political movement on behalf of its preferred social constituency, this volume critically examines the discursive premises that underpinned modern political debates and endowed them with meaning. An attempt is made to assess the meaning and impact of the tendency of revolutionaries to practice a form of politics predicated on scientific theories of social representation and justify their actions by claim to popular legitimacy. For what unites modern regimes – be they Western liberal democracies, east European people's democracies or Third World dictatorships – is that they all seek legitimacy in the 'people' and not in divine grace.

The sources of modern identity reside in the new, demanding role ascribed to men and women in history. In wresting agency from the hands of God and placing it into the hands of man the French Revolution paved the way to the contemporary politics of identity. Instead of asking who they were meant to be and what was their true place in the universe, men began asking themselves who they wanted

INTRODUCTION

to become and what they wanted to be known for. Identity became malleable – a project, not a given. This does not mean that conversion is a modern invention, of course. But in shedding his old self and taking another, the Christian convert assumed a self already molded for him by tradition. The modern convert, by contrast, faces a double task: he is busy not only fitting himself into a new mold but in actually designing it as well.

It was in this very unsettling configuration of questions – where humans had to judge themselves against a constantly contested set of standards – that the question of the Self arose. A project of self-recreation had begun in earnest: New German, New Jew, New Man, New Woman became charged political notions. Somewhere in the late eighteenth or early nineteenth century individuals began asking themselves how they could transcend the gap between their concrete selves and whatever notion of Man the savants of their time had proposed to them. To become oneself meant to take a stance – self-consciously so – on a variety of philosophical issues. Self-awareness may have been an elusive goal, but it was required, for without it no personal journey could be regarded as complete. It is little wonder, then, that the moderns flaunted 'self-awareness', or 'consciousness'.

This volume pays special attention to the role of language in forging the modern self: the poetics of modern identity is the subject of our concern here. While social historians regard language as a pragmatic tool, as an instrument of power, intellectual historians treat language as a supra-human force which somehow grips men and turns them into brainwashed automatons. Taking issue with both approaches, scholars contributing to this book treat language as a force that provided the historical protagonist with the horizon of meanings: language constricted his field of vision, on the one hand, and invested him with a tool to creatively reshape his identity, on the other. During the momentous reconfiguration of political and social identities brought about by the advent of modernity, individuals were relocated within new sets of discursive relations. Focusing on the idea of the New Man that animated all revolutionaries, these essays ask what it meant to define oneself in terms of one's class origins, gender, national affiliation or racial origins. Whether they write about the construction of class identity during the Russian Civil War, the transformation of Germans into Nazis or the making of citizens out of the king's royal subjects in revolutionary France, contributors ask in what way revolutionary language shaped the realm of the possible during the momentous events that changed the face of Europe in the nineteenth and early twentieth centuries.

Was the modern notion of man, and consequently of politics, radically different from the traditional one? Could man, at last rational and self-assured, attempt to eradicate evil from himself and from the world around him? The question of secularization reappears here. Christian civilization maintained that the individual was sinful and could thus, at best, achieve a conditional degree of perfection, always dependent on God's ultimate grace. By contrast, an entire historiographical tradition posits that, deriving from the Enlightenment, modern social thought believed in the inherent plasticity of man. Voltaire, Rousseau and their followers regarded human imperfections as a result of evil social influences, arguing that once these influences were extirpated, man would recover his intrinsic purity and goodness. According to this reconstruction of the modern tradition, the direct heirs of the Enlightenment, be they Jacobean republicans or Soviet Communists, stand on one side of the historical barricade; its antipode, nationalism, and certainly the irrational, myth-oriented Nazism, on the other. A number of chapters in this volume question this dichotomy, however, as being perhaps too comfortable in its assumption, against considerable evidence, that the morbid component of modernity can easily be desegregated from the progressive one.

The inclusivist side of Nazism cannot be ignored even if the price casts a certain cloud over the Enlightenment. Thus it emerges that Nazism saw itself as a revolutionary ideology, self-consciously so, in so far as it believed in the self-transformation of man and in his capacity to rediscover himself (Jews not being considered human, of course); hence, its considerable appeal to many sectors of German society. In this context, Nazism appeared as progressive and life-giving. Despite its universalist credentials, Communism never posited that all men would be saved. Evil had a presence in the Communist universe: it characterized those who understood the Party gospel and yet deliberately refused to follow it. The apotheosis of Communist history – humanity holding hands and marching toward a classless paradise – cannot thus be disassociated from Stalin's systematic attempt to eliminate those who reached the Marxist well but refused to drink from it.

There are additional affinities between Communism and Nazism. Thus it is not easy to uphold the dichotomy between the future-oriented Communists and backward-oriented Nazis: Hitler's regime was forward-looking in so far as it denounced the old Germany, despised Wilhelmine conservatives and constantly called for a transformative movement forward. Paradoxically, only the Nazi drive ahead was able to clear the way to the mythical Germanic Middle Ages. Much to the consternation of many twentieth-century leftist radicals, Goebbels, too, prided himself on being a revolutionary. The Communists, to inverse the terms of our comparison for a moment, may be presented as backward-looking in the sense that their own notion of classless society had much to do with the Marxist anthropology positing a primitive paradise inhabited by peaceful men leading good and collective lives. To be sure, according to Engels, humanity had to exit its primitive stage to become conscious and thus worthy of itself. But the Nazis were also eager for Aryan pride, and their bucolic utopias were a matter of the future and not the past.

Finally, there is an embarrassing uniformity in the means to salvation advocated by the Nazis and the Communists, namely science (and the practices of reshaping the bodies politic accordingly). To be sure, science is the crown of modernity, ubiquitous in contemporary Denmark and Great Britain as well as in Germany and Russia. But only in the latter two countries did science also function as a discourse of legitimation, the very stuff from which politics was made. Known from fairly widespread political slogans in the nineteenth century, 'class' and '*volk*' were turned here into scientific concepts. Their legitimizing quality came not from their popularity but from their scientific basis. Communists were reshaping their souls in accordance with the new psychological guides issuing from the printing shops of the state, and the Nazi project of self-discovery was impossible to implement without new discoveries in the theory of race – on the cutting edge of anthropological theory of the time. It is unclear whether such conflation between knowledge and politics marks Nazism and Communism as deviations from the modern legacy, or its best expressions, but it points to important similarities between these two political systems – that the proponents of Enlightenment have difficulties coming to terms with.

While painting with a very wide brush, it is not my intention to present the various modern political discourses as somehow interchangeable, only to suggest that the essays contained here open interesting vistas into the commonality, and not only the dissimilarities, between them. We should certainly not ignore crucial differences between Hitler's Germany and Stalin's Russia: thus it is debatable to what extent the Communist notion of a perfect society has a corollary within Nazism. Many historians would argue that the Nazis were more interested in the process rather than in the telos (that would preclude us from describing the Nazi concept of time as a secularized Christianity). Was the Third Reich perceived as an existent utopia on earth, or only a stage toward an Aryan paradise? In other words, was there in Nazism a calculus of time similar to the Marxist one, a calculus based upon endless distinctions between the various transitional epochs toward a classless society (for example, state capitalism, developed socialism, building blocks of communism, etc.)? Was a '*Judenfrei* Poland' somehow similar to Russia relieved of its bourgeoisie? These are risky questions, encumbered with enormous ethical weight, but it is perhaps time we asked them.

Another key question which moves us from the preoccupation with the macro (how in history, writ large, notions of time and space were conceived) to the micro (how the Self was conceived) concerns the shape of the enemy, the inverse side of the New Man, as it were, and the means to destroy him. The belief in irredeemable human wickedness and in the imperative to eliminate it by political means seems to be another bridge between Nazism and Communism. An active, destructive agenda that inspired a forward-looking set of state-sponsored practices cannot be dismissed as some sort of atavism. It seems that Stalin and his henchmen believed in irredeemable, hopeless individuals who had to be eliminated no less than Hitler did. Yet in Stalinism these were discrete individuals – those who saw the light and yet refused to follow it – and not racial or social groups that had to be extirpated. The victims of the Great Purge (1937–38) died as people with names and faces, not as vermin. While NKVD archives are filled with personal folders including names, photographs and confessions, only indirect evidence enables us to establish who exactly died in Auschwitz. Beyond the fact that he was a Jew or a Gypsy, the Nazis simply did not care about the life stories of the people they killed. Communists 'executed' individuals, Nazis 'exterminated' racial categories.

But let us get back to where it all started. David Andress shows how the French Revolution released men from the dense signifying network in which they were immersed during the *ancien régime*. For the first time, the individual was liberated from the corporate bodies that marked his niche in society, and from the Church which ascribed to him divine grace or sinful error. He, or even she, could release himself/ herself from his/her marked personhood and fuse with the body politic. The preconditions for work on the Self were thus established.

At the same time, Andress cautions us not to assume that the modern individual immediately emerged as a project with clear-cut contours – rather, such an individual seems to have been reinscribed into the events of the French Revolution by subsequent historiography. The French revolutionary discourse inserted the individual into the nation, directly attempting to dissolve him in the collective whole. In terms of Robespierre's or Saint-Just's teaching, a strong sense of individuality was more a sin than a virtue: reason was a unifying, not an individualizing faculty – every rational agent was expected to behave in the same way. In Rousseau's famous theory of the General Will, individual citizens were not sovereign; only the collective abstraction called the Nation was. Andress persuasively shows that, disassociated from the nation, private citizens were believed to be susceptible to greed and corruption.

The fact that, during the French Revolution, practices of self-realization paradoxically involved elaborate programs of self-abnegation and abandonment of the Self should not obscure the fundamental point that the Revolution introduced a new strategy of self-interrogation and self-

INTRODUCTION

deciphering. While the liberal subject with a strong sense of individual uniqueness and autonomous selfhood was perhaps nowhere to be found in those days, 1789 opened horizons for work on the Self. We must not confuse a sense of self with a sense of individuality. If the Self of the French Revolution was illiberal, many other more recent selves shared its properties. In many ways, the illiberal self Andress is talking about reminds one of the Communist self, for example, in the eagerness to remove all selfishness and seclusiveness and anxiousness to secure its fusion with the collective. The cardinal question 'Who should I be?' and the techniques of working on the Self predicated upon that question had emerged.

While Boris Kolonitskii deals with a much later period – the beginning of the twentieth century – he also captures a country making its entrance into modernity. His study of the desacrilization of the Russian monarchy explores a problematic well known to students of the French Revolution who have recently drawn attention to the ways in which pornographic rumors circulating in Versailles on the eve of 1789 contributed to delegitimization of the Bourbon dynasty. Depicted as an impotent, who was unable to satisfy the voracious sexual appetites of his wife Marie Antoinette, Louis XVI symbolized the loss of potency of the French crown as such. The Russian plot is quite similar, and not unknown. Here it is Rasputin, the proverbial 'lover of the Russian queen', who occupies center stage. This travesty of a 'holy man' was perceived at one and the same time as a German spy and the tsarina's seducer. Kolonitskii shows that stories about betrayals and conspiracies amplified the already impressive array of rumors about the court's religious, medical and erotic experiments. Of course, myths of conspiracy, xenophobia and sex accompany every deep crisis in government, facilitating iconoclastic mass movements. It would be a mistake to disengage the material presented in Kolonitskii's chapter from its direct context – the fact that the tsar was married to a German and that the Russian empire happened to be at war with that country. At the same time, the author warns us against trivializing the cultural situation. He alerts us to the fact that the country was undergoing a profound change and that the transition to modernity is impossible unless the traditional sources of legitimation – royal blood and holy oil – are somehow profaned.

What was changing was not only the political language itself but also the means of disseminating it and the identity of the speakers. The year 1917 represented not only the demise of the myths the Romanovs relied on for three hundred years to legitimize their rule but also the paternalistic system that disseminated symbolic goods. These were replaced by a modern news machine with its endless signifiers, a system that was seldom structured hierarchically and whose sources were unclear. Indeed, Kolonitskii shows that it would be a simplification to erect a social base under the rumor mill and relegate pornographic rumors to the realm of popular culture: if at times high society turned away from political pornography, it also facilitated the dissemination of these very rumors, 'which then made possible the appearance of corresponding texts, images and theatrical productions'. It appears that the 'élites' and the 'masses' alike created a more or less homogeneous space where different versions of the rumors could circulate creating new archetypes of political consciousness, which made the Russian Revolution possible. In desacrilizing the Romanov court, rumors dismantled the very notion that some men are more entitled than others and that what is traditional is moral and good. Russia's old, paternalistic culture was never to recover from these blows.

It was only seldom, however, that the New Man could be worked on directly. Modern ideologies usually posed a variety of intermediary categories that mediated between the universal and the particular. Offering us an indispensable treatment of such concepts as 'social group', 'class' and 'population', Peter Holquist debunks the sociological approach that attempts to derive meanings out of the social base they supposedly represent. Language, the old historiography tells us, is secondary because it only expresses (and often distorts) the interests hiding behind it. But, as Holquist masterfully shows, on the Don during the Russian Civil War, it often worked the other way around. Discourse – the vision of the body politic and the techniques used to realize it – was primary; 'objective social reality', if we must use such terms at all, was secondary. In other words, the course of events was dictated not by real interests stemming from people's life conditions and social standing but by contemporary politicians' perceptions of those interests.

Class analysis serves Holquist better not as an analytical tool but as a historical force in its own right: the Cossacks were supposed to support the Whites because this was widely alleged to be inherent in their social nature, and toilers were supposed to support the Reds because this, again, was supposed to be their true class interest. Eventually, both sides complied with what was expected of them: neither side was able to break out of the prison of revolutionary language. The Whites and the Reds – and this seems to me to be Holquist's main point – were constituted as political agencies not by virtue of their true location in society but by a complex interaction between symbols, practices and institutions upholding them – an interaction that was creative and open-ended, and not deterministic and somehow preordained as the social historian tends to argue.

Speaking of the image of the city in revolutionary discourse, Mark

INTRODUCTION

Steinberg continues the account of how revolutionary agency was created in Russia. The city, he shows, is perhaps the key emblem of modernity – it is there that the individual encounters the machine and the intellectual, the core agencies of enlightenment that enable him to extricate himself from the village life style with its parochialism and religion, and begin his ascent toward political consciousness. If previous chapters decried social determinism, this essay resists the complete dictatorship of symbols. Rejecting post-structuralist claims about the 'death of the subject', Steinberg makes room for historical indeterminacies and a self-generating subjecthood. While he agrees that the human Self is not a supra-historical given, he sees little value in the idea that the Self is somehow completely interpolated, compelled to realize cultural stereotypes to the letter. Admitting multiple voices and allowing for the ambiguities of discourse, Steinberg highlights the spaces where individuals could not only appropriate but also interpret and often subvert the regnant one.

Exploring the dialogue between the individual and the new world in the Russian cities during the Civil War, Steinberg analyzes the force of emotional and moral sentiment in constituting meaning and action. He shows that workers tended to appreciate the city as a symbol and promise of a better future, a location where their sense of solidarity and common consciousness was forged. The machine – the emblem of the city in the socialist world view – brought them together and taught them to reason and speak alike. In the Marxist mytho-poetic imagination, mechanisms of the mind and the small cogs of the machine echoed each other, forging workers into supermen of the future. Much as they venerated the machine, workers also despised it, however, for the machine threatened to disenchant their lives, to strip them of their individuality and deprive them of spirit. Ultimately, then, the city was an ambivalent symbol: it was not only the locus where sadness and longing were replaced by the pathos of struggle and overcoming but also a place where filth, drunkenness and loss of Self were a distinct possibility.

The chapters by Hellbeck and Fritzsche are best read together as they offer comparable studies of the new individual identities offered by Communism and Nazism respectively. In his study of Stalinist diaries, Hellbeck shows that the Communist regime not only did not annihilate the sense of self among the citizenry but actually encouraged and proliferated a variety of personal vehicles of self-transformation. Individuals treated their diaries as laboratories of the self where they met their doubts, struggled with their inner resistance and evaluated their progress in the process of becoming new men and women. Calling upon the populace to become engaged in the program of building socialism of their own will, the Party expected it to comply with revolutionary projects proceeding from personal conviction. Hellbeck shows how members of Soviet society applied to themselves a fundamentally modern notion of the subject as a political agent seeking to comprehend his personal role in the unfolding of History by means of his life chronicles. The skill with which diarists creatively wove themselves into the loose matrix of subjectivization produced by the Revolution is remarkable, as is their inability and unwillingness to relieve themselves of the mechanisms of self-realization designed by the regime.

Peter Fritzsche shows that Nazism was another cultural movement which appealed to emotions and proposed a blueprint for regeneration. Positing a correspondence between an individual life and the course of German history, Hitler's regime urged the citizen to become involved with the larger movement of history. For 'true Germans', personal participation in politics was not only possible but mandatory – regardless of sex, age or social standing. The highly self-conscious transformation of the Self provided the central pivot to privately and sometimes publicly constituted autobiographical narratives – a genre known to be prevalent in Communism but one seldom noted in National Socialism where the idea of self-transformation, in the religious or the secular key, was expected to be rejected as anti-scientific. When Fritzsche points to a peculiar equation between historical time and intimate time in Nazi ideology, the parallel with the diarists of the Stalin era becomes especially striking. Both Fritzsche and Hellbeck strongly object to the preoccupation with an historical, liberal self which is then construed as simply beset in the twentieth century by illiberal calamities. Both their chapters suggest that to argue for an ontological priority of such a self is to neglect the massive participation of individual citizens in the mechanism of larger political projects.

The foregoing does not serve to deny that the axes along which the Nazi self was supposed to be articulated were in many ways unique. To be sure, the urge to create a new sense of a collective, one that transcended the limiting horizons of the local community, was common in Communism and Nazism. But if Communists talked about a proletarian collective, one international in scope, the Nazis had in mind a specifically biological collective, a hidden nation of regenerated Germans. In the former case, the Self fashioned itself after class theory, in the latter after race theory.

But then again, we must note the considerable resemblance between the Nazi call for self-awakening and self-transformation, and parallel rhetoric in the Soviet Union. Despite the determinism one could expect from a Nazi self, a self supposedly rooted in immutable laws of nature, Fritzsche demonstrates that the Nazi autobiographer embraced the active voice – 'I became', 'I found', 'I came to National Socialism', various autobiographers kept reiterating – clearly drawing on voluntarist tropes not unknown to the students of Bolshevism. The movement away from tradition, the village and the old vocation were experienced as a personal rebirth by Nazi autobiographers. Choosing the outbreak of World War I as the cataclysmic event (and not the 1918–19 revolutions, as the German Communists would), they also sought to emphasize turning points in their personal narrative, events that awakened them to their responsibility to the collective and the need to establish communion with the Nation.

In passing, Fritzsche observes that the Nazi autobiographers had seriously considered Marxism, had attempted to articulate its alleged shortcomings, and that they read Adolf Hitler against Karl Marx. This enables a comparison of the discourses of Nazism and Communists, based on their respective convictions that they, and they alone, were the bearers of spirituality whereas all competing ideologies were driven by interest and deeply corrupt. It is well known that Marxism regarded all fascist and liberal ideologies as representatives of capital. Comintern spokesmen depicted Nazism as the last stance of the besieged international bourgeoisie. But it is fascinating to observe that the early Nazis made a parallel argument in claiming that Marxism, with its constant emphasis on economic motivations behind human action, pulled men back to the gold-thirsty kingdom of the Nibelungen, while Nazism alone transcended narrow interests and spoke for genuine human regeneration.

Citizens of the Third Reich reconsidered their relations with friends, neighbors and biological 'others' in light of the regime's racial guidelines. Fritzsche demonstrates how the Nazis 'nationalized' their families, recruiting younger brothers, but also fathers and occasionally sisters and mothers, into the movement. In dwelling on how the revolutionary subject shattered private life, Fritzsche emphasizes that the disintegration of the family was not a by-product of official policy but an official aim of the regime, a practice with strong ideological moorings. In my own chapter, I attempt to show the Communist parallel of this idea. The Bolshevik party inserted itself between the individual and his loved ones, turning intimacy into a political matter. In the Communist case, the very notion of family love was reconstructed to fit the image of society where family loyalties were ideological in their inspiration. Thus sons had to denounce their fathers and family members had to spy on each other, searching for the omnipresent Trotskyist interlopers in their own homes.

Here, too, however, comparison has its limits. Though both Stalin and Hitler wiped out whole families of would-be 'enemies', biological determinism with its perception of man as fully shaped by nature was alien to the Soviet legal system. If in Nazi Germany people were wiped out because their blood was of the 'wrong type', in Stalinist Russia the court of the NKVD troika was obliged to prove that the relative of a convicted Zinov'evist or Bukharinist was, even when taken as a discrete moral persona, also an irredeemable enemy.

In designing their new selves, Soviet citizens of the 1930s could not rely on their own imaginations alone. The New Man was a cultural artefact, and his construction required inspiration and considerable intellectual effort. Here, the chapters by Katerina Clark and Boris Gasparov are especially pertinent. Relying on Foucault's key distinction between 'repressive power', emanating from the state, operating through law and prohibiting the individual from acting in certain ways, and 'productive power' that prompts the individual to obsess with forbidden language, constantly multiplying and expanding its meanings, Katerina Clark suggests we look at Soviet cinema through the prism of the Ministry of Illusion and not the Ministry of Fear. This scholar alerts us to the possibility that Soviet cinema provoked the individual into enriching meanings inherent in the Stalinist myth rather than constraining him to a rote repetition of the official, immutable truths. In examining one of the classics of the Soviet cinema from the 1930s, *Volga-Volga,* Clark surveys the cast of characters whose moral features and political loyalties Soviet citizens were supposed to emulate. Explicitly stating she is interested in the 'formation of the Stalinist subject', she offers a reading of contemporary fantasies – the social-psychological level of reality that, in her definition, encompasses and transcends ideology. Even though Clark studies a comedy – a seemingly innocuous form of art – she shows that *Volga-Volga* contained important ideological coordinates, presenting before the viewer a 'politicized parable of subject formation'. Praising enthusiastic Stakhanovists and condemning ossified bureaucrats, the movie pointed to the superiority of the Russian over the German, the Romantic over the modernist. In fact, the movie went even further: it showed that utopian society must fuse the high with the low, the individual and the collective, the spontaneous and the self-controlled. Clark concludes that the eschatological journey the movie outlines is that of the Russian individual from the spontaneous (unconscious) province to the omniconscious center, a journey which took the Soviet citizen 20 years to accomplish (the movie was filmed in 1937).

Boris Gasparov is another pathfinder in the study of Stalinist culture. His chapter, too, breaks away from the notion of a subtext, so popular among the historians of the totalitarian regimes in the 1950s and the 1960s, according to which one must ignore the poetics of the cultural artefact, be it a movie, a novel or a piece of music, in favor of the political context in which the work of art was created and/or the biography of the man behind it. Dmitrii Shostakovich, perhaps the most celebrated

INTRODUCTION

of Soviet composers, is a case in point. A score of historians and musicologists tried to understand his music in terms of his political attitudes, his personal relations with the Stalinist élite, his Russian patriotism and so on. Some depicted Shostakovich as a man of conscience, someone who did all he could to preserve the traditions of the Russian intelligentsia under impossible circumstances. Others pointed to the fact that the same Shostakovich signed a letter condemning Sakharov, a major physicist and a leading conscientious objector of the 1960s, thus, according to some, casting serious doubt over his commitment to freedom.

Be that as it may, Gasparov tells us, such an approach assumes a natural, immutable self – in this case Shostakovich's – and tries to examine how this self responded to events around it. The self is taken for granted here; only circumstances change. But – and this seems to me to be the essay's key point – what if the Self is subject to a historical change? Gasparov invites us to distance ourselves from speculation about who exactly Shostakovich really was (there is no way to answer this question for certain, and, even if there was, it is doubtful how the answer would deepen our historical understanding) and move toward the image of the man the composer tried to conceive. Rather than being posed outside the text (or rather, in this context, the score) as a given, the Self is turned into an object of investigation. Gasparov shows that Shostakovich's symphonies were construction sites attempting to realize the New Man. There was little that was accidental or idiosyncratic in the composer's quest: the Self he proposed, his blueprint for the New Man, turns out less a reflection of his bottomless genius and more similar to what we know to be the subjecthood of socialist realist novels and painting so persuasively analyzed by Katerina Clark.

We are now perhaps in a better position to appreciate the subtle provocation in the title of Gasparov's essay: the author invites us to regard the composer not only as a producer but also as a product. Shostakovich's symphonies mold the listener and the composer alike; they tell them how to think (or rather, feel), and thus recreate them in their own image. The relation between man and his product becomes two-dimensional: in creating our cultural artefacts, Gasparov suggests, we recreate ourselves. Here we might recall Hellbeck's point that not only did the Stalinist subject compose his ideal self and safely deposit it in his diary, but he actually tried to reform himself according to the image he himself had created.

Deepening this move away from the mind of the New Man to the other, more elusive layers of the Self, Hoffmann and Horn show that modern regimes were also interested in how people were experiencing life. The New Man turns out not only to be a cerebral creature but also a feeling and moving organism. Indeed, most strands in modernity take a stand *vis-à-vis* the body/mind problem and posit a certain body without which a new personality would be impossible.

Positions that sought to legitimize this notion of the New Man in a return to nature – and here fascism must be our prime example – laid special stress on the body and pointed to the corruption it underwent in recent centuries. In examining Italian fascism, David Horn focuses not only on its notions of health but also of sickness and degeneration. Horn points out that the body – in everyday perception assumed to belong to nature rather than history – turns out to be an entity that can be 'modernized'. The body is shaped, disciplined and acted upon, not something that is born, grows and decays according to a natural rhythm; in other words, it is produced to meet certain social expectations. Horn points to a number of studies that investigated the history of the Western body in the period between the two world wars, a period of sustained interest in the making and remaking of bodies in relation to particular understandings of 'the modern'. In very different nations such as the liberal United States, the Communist Soviet Union, fascist Italy and Nazi Germany, 'reworking of the body was tied to the production of new types of male and female citizens', and to the protection of the body politic.

Foucault's power/knowledge dyad is brought to bear here with great effectiveness: the way bodies were described and construed as an object of intervention was directly linked to the elaboration of various sciences: biomedicine, social analysis, race theory and other bodies of knowledge diagnosing pathologies and pointing the road to individual and social rejuvenation. In order to understand the cultural preconditions of the demographic campaign taking place in Italy in the 1920s (and also known from the Nazi and the Communist cases), Horn has examined the ways in which nineteenth-century Italian criminology, a young but self-assured science, suggested new ways of talking about deviants and criminals. Emphasizing the interdependence between normal and pathological bodies, Horn explains that it was only toward the beginning of the twentieth century that criminology learned to interfere with authority in this domain of the seemingly natural, and turn the body into an object of systematic management, into a source of hope for a national and racial regeneration.

Surprisingly, David Hoffmann is able to show that the Communists, despite their almost proverbial emphasis on consciousness as a body-transcending force, were also very interested in yoking the body to the tasks of socialism. The young Soviet regime, and the Red Army especially, elaborated various ways of disciplining and strengthening the physique of the worker. In widespread programs that emphasized bodily health, Hoffmann finds plenty of evidence to the centrality of what Foucault called 'anatomo-politics' – the attempt to create a body machine by optimizing the capabilities of human movement and instilling individuals with new capacities. In Stalin's Soviet Union, no less than say in Mussolini's Italy or Hitler's Germany, physical culture satisfied the aestheticizing impulse inherent in the ambition to create man endowed with a pure, muscular body that moved effortlessly and rhythmically and exuded perfect harmony. Of course, there were also specific, socialist components to the Soviet sport programs: non-competitive exercises were supposed to promote a sense of cooperation and collectivism, unity in strength, and political mobilization against class enemies.

Hoffmann's evidence points to the bizarre modality in which power appeared in the Soviet Union. On the one hand, lavish parades of physical culture emerged as 'rituals of discipline' and 'controlled movement', thus calling to mind the anatomo-power familiar to the West since the seventeenth century. In this connection, we should note Hoffmann's excellent discussion of regularizing techniques, among them the establishment of norms for the physical development of youngsters, the elaboration of complex theories of physical conditioning, and establishment of norms for exercise and leisure. On the other, in so far as physical culture parades were almost always militarized, appearing under the paternal gaze of elevated and thus heavily marked Party leaders, they resembled pre-modern court ceremonies rather than what we know from, say, French or British modernity.

It seems that any serious discussion of power in the Soviet Union would have to begin with the crucial distinction Michel Foucault makes between juridical power and disciplinary power. In the case of juridical power, coded sets of representation are used to instill in the compliant subject the certainty of reward and in the transgressive subject an equal certainty of punishment. A regime based on juridical power penalizes to prove the axiom that deviation does not pay. Thus every observer of the Soviet scene is familiar with the huge posters and slogans hanging on the walls of official buildings or displayed on parades which juxtaposed positive images of Communist glory with ghastly representations of the fate befalling oppositionists and wreckers of every sort. Disciplinary power, on the other hand, while preventive, does not base its effectiveness on a sign system. Instead, it operates around a set of training activities designed to produce what Foucault calls 'normalized individuals' whose everyday life, be it in school, in the factory or in the office, is completely routinized. United in the Communist society in ways that are not easy to determine, both types of power were geared to bringing about the conditions necessary to transform the body of the individual such that he would become an active and enthusiastic participant in the construction of a classless society. To be sure, the Soviet self was prescribed not only as a certain body but also as a certain mind. If liberals sculpted the body alone (hence discipline), Communists also took the mind as a subject of intervention (hence propaganda).

How power operated in Communist regimes is a problem historians have only begun to posit. The strategies and modalities involved in the operation of bio-power in the West, theorized so masterfully by Michel Foucault, cannot be simply applied to twentieth-century Russia. Unless we want to plunge into hopeless conceptual confusion, Foucault's thinking has to be applied to civilizations he did not study with utmost care. No discussion of Communist power can be equated with 'disciplinary spread' alone for it invariably contains elements of the symbolic. Communist regimes were based on explicit ideology, something imbued with semantic contents, not just normalizing techniques, that is, sets of ideologically blind disciplinary practices permeating the liberal world.

How are we to understand the kind of power deployed in the labor camps, for example? In a sense, it can be argued that the camp – usually viewed as the epitome of the Stalinist repressive mechanism – was not only the Other of Soviet society – a place where all the violators of norms were sent, but also its cultural model. Viewed along the axis of juridical power, the labor camp may be seen as a powerful negative symbol. The peculiar wedding of discipline and representation it effected ensured that those inside the labor camp would be trained and those outside the labor camp terrorized. Disciplining individuals through work and enlightenment, the labor camp indeed produced docile individuals submitting to, if not cooperating with, the Stalinist project. What is striking here, however, is that the organization of a positive Communist space, a factory or a university, for example, was not necessarily so different. In a sense, the discipline within these institutions, with their minute regulation of what was said and done, can be presented as an instance of the same logic underlying the operation of the labor camp. Foucault's notion of 'disciplinary swarming' – the piecemeal adoption of carceral methods in a variety of non-punitive sites – could in our context characterize the ways in which the disciplinary regime underlying life in the labor camp became an indefinitely generalizable mechanism permeating the Stalinist polity.

Such analysis would explain why Hoffmann's findings in a totalitarian country are not so different from those of Horn in a liberal country. But if disciplinary power was as effective in the Soviet Union as it was in the West, why terror? Why did the Soviet regime have to kill and enslave if it could simply drill? Why parades, show trials, endless propaganda campaigns, and so much rhetoric? When a Soviet general extruded his decorated chest for everyone to see, this was certainly a display of

INTRODUCTION

juridical power emanating from the state and designed to awe, to overwhelm, to impress, but not to control and discipline. Disciplining power, juridical power, perhaps something in the middle? Or do we need a more refined analytical tool to approach Soviet history?

According to the old historiography, the Soviet subject never entered into a creative dialogue with ideology. The subject was either completely taken in by it, becoming a 'true believer', or remained indifferent, only adjusting his lips and his body, to comply with what the regime required. Undertaken from the point of view of discourse analysis, the recent controversial focus on the body enables historians to examine the interaction between words and acts, between the concrete and the discursive, in less absolute terms. Thus Eric Naiman sets out to examine the ways in which contemporaries approached the corporeal in constructing their personal selves. Unearthing a bizarre story about Zamkov, a doctor who injected people with the urine of pregnant women in order to rejuvenate them, Naiman traces a fascinating dialogue between the body as an object of a medical intervention and the official ideological narrative about the miraculous qualities of Soviet science. In failing to produce immortality, the hero of Naiman's chapter calls attention to the limits of the symbolic in its attempt to penetrate the organic and make it as timeless as the Communist ideology purported itself to be. This is in direct contrast to his wife, Mukhina, who actually turned the body into steel, creating perhaps the most famous Stalinist sculpture of all, which depicted an iron strong man and a woman holding a hammer and sickle. Naiman alerts us to the suppressed aspects of modernity, which actually reveal some of the less-than-obvious motivations animating both the scientific community and those who worship it. A mega-project for the rejuvenation of human tissues appears perhaps eccentric to us today, though it was not far from the mainstream of Soviet science of the 1930s. But then, if we look again into the uses of technology today, and study, for example, the ways in which science is utilized to clone humans or to freeze cadavers in the Utah deserts until sufficient knowledge is available for reanimation, we realize that the modern project is interested in immortality no less than, for example, pre-modern Christianity was.

Offering an especially provocative study of the Nazi world view generally, and the Nazi view of the body more specifically, Boaz Neumann shows that even seemingly natural, ahistorical notions have to be re-examined, since different discursive regimes use them differently and mean by them very different things. Thus Neumann argues that 'life' and 'death' – apparently self-evident concepts – were reconstructed in Hitler's Germany. Furthermore, and here his claim is especially fascinating, unless we carefully decipher the ways in which these concepts were deployed, we will fail to understand such borderline, barely comprehensible events as the Holocaust. Neumann shows that the meaning of Auschwitz was lost on many historians because – fearing that to explain would mean to somehow justify – they refrained from serious conceptual work, preferring to focus on empirical evidence only. The incredible amount of research invested in the study of the Nazi death camps over the years precludes insight if, as often happens, it comes to replace the startling, the almost unbearable, with the familiar. Neumann's point is not that historians should do theoretical rather than solid empirical research – a charge many proponents of the linguistic turn have to face daily – but that they should be imaginative in how they construe the object of historical research.

Perhaps more than any other public activity, practices of commemoration were heavily regulated in modern countries, liberal and totalitarian alike. Indeed, much was omitted from public memory, sometimes intentionally, sometimes not. There is no denying that collective memory is a fierce field of contestation – more than one generation of historians has invested considerable effort into unearthing the truth behind it. Commemoration is very often related to oblivion – an attempt to remember one thing and obliterate another. This feature of commemoration, however, should not be confused with forced oblivion, as the repressive hypothesis understands them. Rigid standardization of public memory, as Avner Ben-Amos's study of the treatment of the heroes of the Third Republic suggests, had to do not with the authoritarian demand by the men currently in power to suppress memory, but with the need to create significations that would fit into the contemporary field of meaning – into the way in which a given regime conceived of the past of France and its future.

In emphasizing the narrative nature of historical memory, Ben-Amos links up with the general problematics of the present volume: it is a certain emplotment, he argues, that always leads the story to a culmination, eventually endowing memory with its collective sense. This chapter is attentive not only to what the official practices of selective memory expunged, but also to the substitutes they offered. What is striking about portrayals of the heroes of the French Revolution or the Prussian War of 1870–71 is not the taboos, but the richness of practices regarding who was to be remembered, when and how.

Sharing Ben-Amos's interest in memory, Domansky explores an event which is difficult for the German public discourse to remember – the Second World War. Her chapter examines the creation of a Thanksgiving Church in Bochum in the 1950s celebrating the return of POWs from Soviet captivity – a rare memorial indeed for a society that could not openly mourn its dead during Nazi rule. Eluding almost any concrete reference to the recent war, this strange memorial transposed German suffering into a Christian key, presenting the war as a divine ordeal all of humanity had to face, Germany included. Here German soldiers metamorphosed from Nazi perpetrators into generic men, almost accidental exponents of a suffering humanity. Inserting remembrance of the war into the heart of a parish community and transcribing Germany's war experience into the sacred Christian story of human sin and salvation, the Church was thus normalizing the nation's suffering. Domansky documents and examines the way in which a specific national community suppressed a historical event, while, at the same time, distorting it in order to allow the national collective to at least try to come to terms with the events that transpired. Much like Ben-Amos, she shows that memory always operates in a specific political environment: normalization of World War II was followed by recontextualization and insertion of the POW episode into recent history. If, in the immediate post-war years, the soldiers' return was read against the background of a clash between two antagonistic and equally problematic ideologies, Nazism and Communism, in the 1950s it was understood against the background of the struggle of the free world with Soviet Russia; in this scenario, Germany was on the 'right' side, the side of Christian humanity and Christian ethics suffering at the hands of the East (read: Soviet Union or East Germany, depending on the context), where people lived in a society that resembled one large labor camp.

Concluding this volume, Dan Diner's chapter also engages the question of memory and commemoration. Here, we return to the fundamental gambit of historians subscribing to the linguistic turn: the insistence on questioning the boundary between reality and its representation. How things are reconstructed after the fact is no less important than how they really happen. The claim here is more radical than it perhaps first appears: moving beyond platitudes about the futility of human memory and the unavoidable politicization of history, Diner suggests that the truth/myth dichotomy does not contribute to our understanding. Humans always construe their knowledge in accordance with certain rules of storytelling and there is no truth to be distilled when the 'distortions' introduced by these 'obstacles' are removed. Demonstrating that historians of the Holocaust are unable to establish an objective ground from which to view their data, Diner does not criticize them for their biases and idiosyncrasies, arguing that this 'failure' is unavoidable. A certain way of approaching the world, the type of memory one deploys, affect how one reconstructs the past. The dream of objectivist historiography about a convergence of narratives becomes a fallacy supported by those who remain indifferent to the syntax of human apperception. Diner's challenge is considerable for he implicitly questions the very distinction between history and historiography. Unable to hide behind fetishes such as science and objective procedure, the historian eventually has to concede that his own stories bear the mark of the stories of the protagonists he is studying. The two sets of narratives, our own and that of our protagonists, turn out strangely intertwined. The historian loses something – his sense of objectivity; but he also gains something – he can now account for his 'situatedness', his complicity in the human endeavor.

A word should be said at this point about the status of the historical narrative as it appears in the essays collected in this book and its relation to historical thinking of contemporaries. (I am aware that not all contributors would fully agree with my discussion here.) The reader might be struck by a certain confluence between the Jacobean or the Bolshevik meta-history and our own reconstruction of French or Russian history, for example. What contemporaries were talking about and what the historian is presenting as his key evidence appear strangely identical. Should we not be critical toward our source material, distancing ourselves from the language of the period we study? A historian who ascribes to the linguistic turn indeed does not employ principles of historical causality absolutely extrinsic to the ones he is studying; not a single chapter in this volume attempts to explain what historical protagonists were saying or doing in terms of underlying economic interests or political struggles. Such interpretative strategy is at risk of being mistakenly identified as historical naivety: taking what he finds in the archive at face value, the scholar, so the charge goes, fails to approach sources critically; focusing on what the archive candidly reveals, he remains blind to what it conceals.

I wholeheartedly accept the observation that instead of establishing a radical distance from the source base the contributors to this volume betray a good measure of intimacy with the material (intimacy that is easily misconstrued by their antagonists as sympathy). By reading the lines and not between the lines, by remaining at the level of language itself, they are trying to understand how language operates and with what consequences. The analyses presented here do, however, transcend the self-understanding of contemporaries in so far as they show that these consequences were unknown to the contemporaries who spoke the language they did. Penetrating the pores of the language we study, we force language, as it were, to testify against itself.

The analysis does not posit a multi-layered social structure where language expresses the truth that lies underneath it, hidden in the interests lurking in society, but treats language as a constitutive force that brings society into being in the first place. In fact, a question must be raised regarding the notion of 'society' itself – the sacred cow of so much traditional historiography. For society is too often understood to be something fixed, saturated, a field where blind social agents vie for power and privilege. No matter how 'fluid' and 'heterogeneous' society is, how 'complex' and 'conflicted' its constitutive components are believed to be, society remains in the last account a totality. The historian, in such accounts, is supposed to place himself outside society and, observing it dispassionately, speak from an external vantage point. While such historiography ignores the fact that society is not a reality but an idea or, rather, a set of notions – a discursively mediated entity which is never stable – we attempt to show that many imaginary societies coexist within a single political discourse, all hoping to be realized. Politics is not about the 'real', lurking behind the linguistic screen, but about the realization of a particular scenario emplotted in a particular language.

Language is always in the making; it is never simply there. This is why it would be a misreading to say that this volume substitutes the study of the real with the study of the imaginary. Always steeped in the symbolic, the Self is not as concrete as we take our concrete 'I', the locus of our corporeal identity, to be. Indeed, the reader must be urged not to confuse the notion of the Self deployed throughout this book with first-person pronouns familiar to him from commonsensical language. The Self is a theoretical construct that presents the subject not as a natural 'I' but as something reflective and therefore mediated through language. When Peter Fritzsche or Jochen Hellbeck speak of the Nazi or the Stalinist self they do not pretend to give an exhaustive description of what people really thought or felt in the 1930s. They simply point out that these spheres of human life were an object of the regime's intervention, that individuals were supplied with a new language to describe their thoughts and feelings, and that we have to study what individuals were expected to feel and think if we want to understand the sweep of the ambition to create a New Man. Language could be modified and even subverted but it could not be ignored without risk of the protagonist becoming a social outcast.

In any event, the agenda here is not sociological. The essays in this volume do not study a population – in itself not a neutral and objective term but one invented during the revolutionary epoch to describe an object of government intervention (Peter Holquist) – but a language individuals were taught to employ in their everyday life. Gasparov and Clark do not claim that Stalinist subjectivity exhaustively characterized the individual's self-understanding and Neumann would probably say the same about the Nazis. Russians and Germans may well have had alternative ways of describing themselves and we should not be surprised that those Soviets citizens who found their way to the West after

World War II, or those Germans who successfully reached the other shore of the Allies' denazification campaign of the late 1940s, proved to be adepts of liberal language. A historical subject articulates itself along a number of axes, taking part in a plurality of identity games. The point is, rather, that as long as individuals lived in a certain discursive system they had to take its language seriously and that this language merits careful study.

Heretofore, I tried my best to squeeze the essays in this volume into the Procrustean bed of something like a school, although the participants of the Tel Aviv conference (as those who attended it certainly remember) did not always agree on methodology. I would like to conclude then with a few remarks about the problems which plague adherents of the linguistic turn. It would perhaps be futile to dwell here on the inner tension between terms such as 'structure' and 'conjuncture' or 'language' and 'discourse', though the choice of one over the other is never naive. Let me just say a word about the use of psychoanalytical vocabulary, a subsidiary theme here but one that I believe reveals interesting nuances of opinion.

Indeed, whether they are aware of it or not, historians often speak about something akin to symptoms. For, in choosing what evidence to present and what to omit – the amount of detail that can be cited in reference to a certain problem is, of course, limitless – historians present the evidence they select as somehow 'symptomatic'. It is as if they are telling the reader: look how I arranged the symptoms of this historical epoch! Now I can 'diagnose' it for you. In that broad sense, all historians appear to be adherents of psychoanalysis. But here it is interesting to return briefly to the French origins of the linguistic turn. For it is a French intellectual tradition, from de Saussure through Lacan to Derrida, which, exhibiting strong influences of French rationalism, places such heavy emphasis on words. Lacan is very important here: recall that for him even the 'unconscious is structured like a language'. In other words, everything is linguistic. Not in the sense that there is only language (historians need the concept of a 'trauma' for example, something that cannot be put into words) but in the sense that everything has a linguistic dimension.

Far from denying the importance of language, Anglo-Saxon historiography, on the other hand, steeped as it is in British empiricism, clings to 'experience' as something that precedes the concepts we live by. Here we may recall the Aristotelian definition of 'experience' as precisely a state where we are reduced to the soma, unable to account for how we got into this situation or whether we will ever emerge from it. (The 'experience of pain' is a prime example here.) Note in this connection how Mark Steinberg structures his argument. Subscribing to the linguistic turn, he nevertheless regards workers' poetics as only one aspect of their world. Workers' experiences in the factory, in his view, are no less important for the understanding of their world view and behavior. Steinberg is no reductionist; for him, 'culture' (and language) is not a superstructure that can be simply deduced from relations of production. But traces of social history, with its strong preference for the 'real' over the 'imaginary', are evident in his analysis.

In clinging to the category 'workers', Steinberg retains the basic ontology of social history, and it does not matter in the present context that he refashions this ontology, à la Gramsci, in cultural terms. If, for someone like Jochen Hellbeck, 'workers' are a discursive construct, a word and a strategy that allow one to enroll himself in the 'messianic' class and make sense of that choice, for Steinberg 'workers' are as real as the industrial morphology of the factory in which they work. In fact, this almost tangible entity, not language, is perceived here as something that comes to make sense of the labor process, which constitutes the Russian working class in the first place. Psychoanalysis – and Steinberg does deploy Freudian terms, 'anxiety' probably being the most prominent among them – is used in his chapter as a methodology that explains language rather than as one that studies it in its own right (not *how* this language operates, but *why* that language and not another). I presume that Steinberg would accept the 'relative autonomy of language' but not the more radical contention that 'there is nothing outside language'.

This would hold as well for Elisabeth Domansky and Dan Diner – two scholars who reflect the encounter between the German intellectual tradition and the linguistic turn. Their approach – a curious combination of phenomenology and psychoanalysis – is interested in how language is experienced. Unlike Lacan's, this is a more accurate return to Freud, where language characterizes consciousness, and the unconscious is explicitly described as somatic and preverbal. Diner speaks about linguistic constructs people apprehend more than comprehend – a move that transcends intentionally and expands the notion of language while not moving beyond it. And Domansky, who in her study of the memory of World War II in Germany makes frequent excursions into psychoanalysis, distinguishes between the neurosis and psychosis of memory. In her eyes, memory certainly has the structure of a narrative, but what makes this narrative interesting — in contrast to what Fritzsche tacitly suggests, for example – is not so much its surprising coherence and/or versatility as its fissures, distortions and actual caesuras. Thus if Andress, Gasparov and I are interested in symptoms as moments that tell us something about the structure of the narrative, Domansky is keen to move beyond the narrative to the experience that it tried, usually unsuccessfully, to express and make sense of.

It seems that each position loses something and gains something. Thus, in the final account, Steinberg and Domansky might be charged with trivializing language in that they eventually seek reality outside it. In so far as language is something that should be explained rather than something that does the explaining, their argument is almost self-defeating. However, an exclusive focus on language precludes historians from explaining change, for example – and is that not what historians are supposed to do, first and foremost? Obsessed with showing that language is a coherent whole, some supporters of the linguistic turn find it difficult to explain how this whole modified itself over time. It is no wonder that historians strongly influenced by literary theory tend to study synchronic structures, slices of historical time, as it were, and not diachronic processes. Though, to turn the argument against itself one last time, they can always argue that the 'what' has to come before the 'why'; in other words, we have to understand what Communism is and what Nazism is, precisely, as meaningful structures, before we can ask how they came about, developed and eventually dissolved.

1

Liberty and Unanimity: The Paradoxes of Subjectivity and Citizenship in the French Revolution

DAVID ANDRESS

INTRODUCTION

The French Revolution is frequently presented as the originary point of a distinctively modern world view, in which autonomous subjects wrestle with the issues of individual and collective existence. The Revolution, which engendered the Declaration of Rights, wherein political liberties, at once individual and universal, were for the first time enshrined in a European constitution, and which was based on a perceptibly 'democratic' struggle against aristocracy and tyranny, has long stood as the foundation of progress toward self-realization in politics.[1] Undoubtedly, nineteenth- and twentieth-century representations of revolutionary change relied heavily on such images, but this chapter will question whether such an account can be wholly applied to the French Revolution itself. To be more precise, these self-realizing processes may have been retrospectively inscribed into the French Revolution as a historical event, but were not necessarily present in the events which made up the decade of the 1790s in France. As historians, it is vital for us to be able to distinguish between the contemporary awareness of an event and its subsequent re-inscriptions, which are also part of history, but the history of a later era.

The modern age of politics has been posited on the identity of the autonomous individual political actor struggling to assert her/his subjectivity in the public sphere. However, in the late eighteenth century, the idea of such a subjectivity was a delicate issue within the more-or-less enlightened intellectual polity. The revolutionary decade was at the turning-point of European thought, from strict rationalist forms of perception and psychology, toward the Romantic-individualist model in which the Self is a much more complex, and self-constructing, identity.[2] One of the central paradoxes of revolutionary political culture is the vision of the revolutionary process as one of collective social self-recreation, without a clear perception of any implications of that process for individual development. It is certainly the case that in trying to make 'citizens' out of 'subjects', the revolutionaries believed that they were formulating a 'new man', but it is doubtful whether the intellectual baggage they carried into the revolutionary decade would actually permit that to happen. In its vision of how people should be, the French Revolution remained tied very closely to originary models – that what had been, or always was, needed only rediscovery. The central revolutionary metaphor of *régénération* embodies this – that is, regeneration, as an atrophied limb might miraculously return to its proper function for which it was originally designed. To cite Robespierre:

> What is the goal toward which we are heading? The peaceful enjoyment of liberty and equality; the reign of that eternal justice whose laws have been inscribed, not in marble and stone, but in the hearts of all men ...[3]

Where they are going is somewhere that already exists – thus, logically, a truly new man need not be created to get there; one need only rediscover that which is already inscribed in the hearts of men. The Revolution, throughout its development, was almost entirely wedded to notions of the natural, and thus pre-existent, as its grounding justification for action. The shining future that would animate so much later revolutionary activity is largely absent from the actual political discourse of the French Revolution.

The French revolutionaries' underlying concepts of selfhood and subjectivity were likewise turned away from the individualistic, self-creating mode of later re-inscriptions. The psychological heritage of the late eighteenth century, going back to Locke, was based on 'sensationism', or the notion that the mind as such was the product of sense-impressions acted upon by reason. Reason was taken to be a uniform faculty – to the extent that one possessed it, it would reflect on a given set of impressions in the same fashion as any other reasoner would. This is in itself a strongly anti-individualist conception. Although it liberates human reason from the thrall of divine grace and sinful error, it holds human reason to be indivisible.[4] For later writers such as Horkheimer and Adorno, this would render the Enlightenment responsible for much of our own century's evils, but we may also see the more immediate consequences of this issue. The revolutionary self would have to be molded out of a stuff that was allegedly uniform, and yet subject to a bewildering array of differing priorities. The selfhood of women, of workers, of peasants, not to mention the selfhood of priests or aristocrats, would be challenged when it did not meet revolutionary criteria.[5] The primary discourse of the revolutionary period would rely on unanimity as its underlying criterion, and that unanimity would draw on universal reason to construct itself, unaware of the particularity of its claims.

The Self is of course a specifically modern concept, and one that is always gendered and embodied, thus rendering its alleged universality within the revolutionary discourse paradoxical.[6] Of course, we must note that it is paradoxical only for us, from our present subject-position. The thinking of the eighteenth century on such subjects both obeyed rules deemed consistent to their users, and served powerful purposes in taking the forms that it did. We might equally well take Bourdieu's expression of 'practical sense' as accounting for why some of the operations of Enlightenment reason took the paths they did, to answer the needs of their users; or adopt the Foucaultian language of discourses of power.[7] Whichever forms of approach we take, there is a variety of aspects of late eighteenth-century thought, both in its guise as sophisticated theorization and in its broader sense of a less reflexive 'political culture', that require exploration, in order to see and analyze these discourses in action.

As we shall see below, power, influence and position in the Old Regime were personal, but not individual: they depended not on the individual identity, or 'selfhood', of a person, but on that identity in so far as it was formed from and represented by a series of interpersonal networks and associations, grids of status which tied individuals into relationships. Revolutionary and post-revolutionary perceptions of social position would attempt to unhitch the individual from such networks, creating a politics of the impersonal, and challenging the prevalent perceptions of representation as it operated across a range of registers of possibilities for 'public selves'. In so doing, however, these constructions were working with conceptions of the individual which explicitly denied the autonomy that later generations would seek to place at the heart of the Revolution's achievement.

SELF AND IDENTITY IN ABSOLUTIST CONCEPTIONS

There was very little place for the individual in Old Regime patterns of thought. Society was defined, in the terms used by the theorists who had rescued monarchical power from *ligueur* and *frondeur* challenges in the sixteenth and seventeenth centuries, as a hierarchy of corporate bodies. The individual male adult had a recognized identity only in so far as he fitted clearly into one of those bodies, be they large groups such as the aristocracy or clergy, institutions such as the various law courts and municipal corporations, economic structures such as artisan guilds, or merely the inhabitants of a specific village or district. All of these were seen to be collectivities defined by the differences between them, rather than agglomerations of individuals with definable independent, and equal, civil status. Women and children had no independent status at all, acquiring it only in relation to their male relations or wider propertied family. The alternative to this structure of difference, in the eyes of theorists such as Loyseau, was chaos. Equality, and the freedom for unrestricted social intercourse, would license the collapse of society. In a world view sharply focused by the perspectives of the Catholic religion, individuality, or selfhood, was an essentially dangerous quality: outside the grace of the Church and its secular equivalents, obtained by conformity and obedience on the part of the individual, there lay only sin and damnation.[8] Only the king, whose body incorporated all of society into itself through his representative nature, could exist as a 'public individual'.[9]

Close beneath the surface of this corporate society there functioned another, equally anti-individualist, apparatus – that of the family. Patriarchal structures persisted strongly in the legal and cultural frameworks of the eighteenth century, and continued to dictate the trajectories and life choices of substantial groups within the population – women of property in particular, but in general any heirs, assumptive or prospective.[10] Pressure, or simply expectation, to make life choices with regard to familial rather than individual social strategies also influenced those who experienced the tug of paternal authority less strongly, including those who themselves wielded such authority, and this of course was a self-replicating system across the generations. Family authority was sufficiently 'real', and sufficiently invested in the state structure, to be one of the principal mechanisms of the system of administrative detention by royal order (the famous *lettres de cachet*) so feared by philosophers and revolutionaries: far more wayward sons or drunken husbands spent time in dungeons through this system than did seditious authors.[11] Such seditious authors as did experience the heavy hand of the state were stigmatized by another aspect of its familial frame of reference: in the police records they are classed as 'boys', lacking the stable position in a household that would entitle them to recognition as full adults.[12]

The system of identity-by-relation that made up the Old Regime perception of Self made itself felt at the lowest possible levels as well. For the urban populations that had to negotiate their lives under the gaze of the police, only a network of relations could protect them from suspicion – one had to be 'known', to be able to find someone to make an *aveu*, an 'avowal' of one's honesty, to escape suspicion. And of course that avower himself needed to be 'known' to others as honest, or at least rooted in the community, to make the avowal effective.[13] In the economic sphere, such interpersonal dependence was also essential to existence. The artisan economy of the towns depended for its continued functioning on systems of informal credit so wide-ranging and complex that only the continual careful negotiations of trust and personal contact, the maintenance of a fragile social honor, were able to keep workers in work, masters in supplies and families in food.[14]

In the big city, it was all too easy to be anonymous, but such anonymity was less a refuge for personal autonomy than the start of a slide into oblivion. Literature and the archive both attest to the requisites for successful life in the city, which meant adapting oneself to the demands and expectations of others. The alternatives were crime and prostitution, acts placing oneself outside the body corporate, and frequently steps on the path to that other quintessentially individual act, suicide.[15]

OPINION AND REPRESENTATION IN THE OLD REGIME

At first glance, the rise and acknowledgement, by commentators and authorities alike, of a rational 'public opinion' in the 1770s and 1780s has nothing in common with the anti-individualist, corporatist definitions of public identity otherwise operating in the Old Regime, and indeed posed a central challenge to them. Yet, through the problematic qualities of rationality, this phenomenon would raise equal, if not greater, barriers to assertive individuality. Rationality, as discussed above, was indivisible for the *philosophes*. Rationality was also a quality widely felt to be intruding to an ever-greater extent into the public realm during the later eighteenth century. In so doing, as has been widely remarked, rationality and opinion, specifically 'public opinion', became conjoined as forces to be reckoned with in the political calculations of the élite.[16]

The force of public opinion, as it evolved in the later eighteenth century, came to be expressed as a tribunal: a neutral, disinterested and above all correct judge of public actions. This tribunal, which was of course a purely abstract concept, has been argued to function as an acknowledgement of the place of public opinion – the views of a 'reading public' assumed to be educated, rational and propertied – as an increasingly potent force in political calculations, while also maintaining the unity of the political sphere. Public opinion was formed, in this model, through rational contemplation of texts, and discussion in strictly private forums. The privacy of opinion-forming processes was seen as critical in order to avoid what were seen as the excesses of the 'reign of opinion' in British politics. The result in the British model, where politics was a matter of free public debate, and where the interaction of self-interested factions was legitimized in the elections and debates of the House of

Commons, was, according to the French, endemic disorder of a type intolerable to the French body politic.[17] The French model of public opinion, in essence, came down to individual readers absorbing texts, and bowing down to the 'reason' to be found in them, thus taking part in an implicitly unanimous process which obviated any need for public, collective displays of opinion.

In order to envisage public opinion as rational, to render it safe within their intellectual and cultural frame, French thinkers had to envisage it as unanimous. This of course entirely begs the question of the contours that such opinion was to adopt. By the end of the Old Regime, a field of public opinion that was at once moralizing and salacious, concerned with sentimentality and eager to condemn immorality (while hearing about it in detail), was leading court society to its destruction. Writings that appealed to this public opinion, such as the self-consciously melodramatic *mémoires* published in judicial proceedings, frequently used the device of the defenceless individual faced by hostile collective forces to raise sympathy.[18] However, in order to do so, such 'individuals' were characterized in stereotypical ways, made into examples of a 'type' which would supposedly induce sympathy in certain kinds of audiences. The patterns of such sympathy were, to modern eyes, highly artificial, and leant to a considerable degree on Rousseau's sentimental moralizing in *Emile* and *La Nouvelle Héloïse*.[19] They also leant, in a different fashion, on a pornographic, and highly-gendered, discourse about state power, publicity and the role of sexuality in the perceived decline of the French state. Here, deviance – individuality – however embodied, was held up as a powerful negative force within the state. The reader saw, or was held to see, in the obscene descriptions of court life that circulated with remarkable freedom in the 1770s and 1780s a 'representative public sphere' (Habermas's phrase) that produced only degeneracy, reinforcing the tension between that sphere and the more abstract 'public', and damning the artificiality of representation.[20] Representation, however, would be the key to the evolution of the Revolution, while remaining highly problematic.

Political action in the later eighteenth century was seen as a field of representation, and, for the thinkers of this time, representation was a very dubious concept indeed. The master-metaphor of the Baroque era for dealing with notions of representation in the political sphere was the theater, and this can be seen as still operating with considerable force from 1789.[21] During the early years of the Revolution, political actors were continually compared to theatrical actors, sometimes in the sense of spectators' feelings of watching a 'great drama' unfold, at other times in ironic or satirical commentary on their oratorical bluster or ineptitude. An orator such as Mirabeau could be criticized for 'stagy' rhetoric and gestures, or alternatively praised for infusing his speech with 'male eloquence' and vehement emotion, according to the critic's taste. Even at the most naive level, however, it was sensed that such a conflation of the 'national representation' with fictional performance was unsettling.[22]

Representation presented for late eighteenth-century metaphysics the problem of something that at once was, and was not, what it appeared to be. The person of the actor itself was troubling, and not merely for the conventional reasons that associated actresses with prostitution, and denied socially marginal theater companies a civic voice. The prolific author and commentator Restif de la Bretonne, for example, examined the nature of the individual, the actor, who takes on another's identity to play a role. This was dangerous for society, according to Restif, creating a space where selfhood was unfixed, and a group of people to whom duplicity was second nature. His suggested solutions to this problem offered two alternatives: either actors should be slaves of the state, and thus possessing no identity as citizens they would be freed to act as a blank canvas for their roles, or actors should be citizens, but ones trained from early youth to perform only one role (presumably in a predetermined classical repertoire). This single 'alter ego' would then be publicly recognized, and outside its regulated performance the actor-citizen could have a 'normal' civic life.[23]

The pre-revolutionary public sphere was considerably agitated about the nature of acting and the actor, in ways which conveyed quite explicit underlying political themes. The influence of writers such as Diderot and Sedaine had brought into prominence in the later decades of the century the theory that, in the first place, the content of drama should relate much more directly to the lives of the audience – the so-called *drame bourgeois* – and, second, that the actors should no longer strive to 'inhabit' their roles absolutely, but should aim to stimulate imagination in the audience through gesture and declamation. Thus the stage should exist to represent 'real life' to the audience, and to simultaneously distance them from it and encourage their identification with it. Distance is created by the overt tactic of gestural acting, an attempt to indicate essential emotional attitudes rather than to convey direct identity with the character. Identification then comes through the audience's reflection, investing the artificial scene before them with 'real' emotion drawn from their real or imagined experience.

This mode of thought set itself up against earlier models of the actor's representation, which saw the role as 'filling' and potentially transfiguring him, just as the substance of Christ transubstantiates the host. This was felt, by authors such as Diderot, to leave the audience too passive in the face of the presented spectacle, both in the basic experience of watching, and in the subject matter of stylized court or antique dramas. While older drama projected itself toward an ideal, unchanged spectator, the *drame bourgeois* sought to draw the spectator into a transforming process. It would not be an exaggeration to see these forms as 'absolutist/monarchical' and 'republican' in their basic conceptions.[24]

However, if the gesture of the actor and the reflective activity of the audience could have been taken for granted, the Revolution would not have had the problems with representation that it did. We have already seen the anxiety that Restif felt about the 'civic' identity of actors *per se*, and other critics challenged the whole basis of Diderotian theater. The most well known, of course, was Rousseau, who in his *Lettre à d'Alembert sur les Spectacles* denounced modern theater as a school of corruption and dissimulation, cutting citizens off from their real collective existence by substituting alluring illusions. Rousseau preferred to think of spectacle as something that should consciously bind a community together by abolishing the distinction between actor and audience: a model of participatory festival lifted from ancient semi-mythical examples that, directly or indirectly, was to play a large part in the Revolution.

The conflict between Diderot's and Rousseau's views is an example of a wider tension that ran through pre-revolutionary and revolutionary practices in regard to representation, identified by one author as the tension between abstractionism and anti-abstractionism. Abstractionism, in this sense, indicates the practice of extracting certain features or qualities of a situation, and using them to represent the whole – whether in theater, or in politics, for example, where the king represents the nation. Anti-abstractionism, as espoused most clearly by Rousseau, saw this form of practice as a threat to the body politic, dividing Self from representation in a fashion which made room for deceit and manipulation.[25] For Rousseau, both politics and theater should be a realm of public, collective self-representation. To allow oneself to be represented was to sanction rule. Thus anti-abstractionism attributed to abstractionism (which here includes the forms of theater favored by Diderot) just the 'monarchist' tendencies that the latter had held against older forms of representation. There was no obvious way out of this bind: the body politic either includes representative organs, or it does not, and this dilemma was to tear at the heart of every project of revolutionary reconstruction.

PLOTS AND THE FEAR OF THE INDIVIDUAL IN THE EIGHTEENTH CENTURY

The problem of how to deal with representation in the public sphere was compounded by further consequences of the psychological models prevalent in the late eighteenth century. Although the French recoiled from the thought of admitting British-style 'party politics' into the operations of the public sphere, this was at least in part due to their belief that many pernicious effects of such activity were already visible in France. Explanations for public catastrophe tended toward the baroque, and inevitably involved conspiracy of some kind. One of the most noteworthy examples of this form of explanation was the so-called famine plot persuasion. France, although avoiding general famine in this period, continued to succumb periodically to local and regional food shortages, with accompanying short-term price inflation. A variety of problems connected to the highly regionalized nature of the French economy, and the relative lack of sophistication in both transportation and agriculture itself, can largely account for these in the view of the historian. To the French, however, there could be nothing wrong with their agriculture – this was an article of public faith – and thus the dislocations in food supply were posited as the consequence of deliberate conspiracy. The assumption of wrongdoing permeated the normal functioning of the market in eighteenth-century France. Police regulations insisted on publicity for all market transactions, especially in the wholesaling of food, precisely because the merchant was feared as an inherently dishonest and anti-social individual. Private profit would, if unchecked, ruin the public good.[26]

At the larger level of the kind of crises induced by grain shortage, conspiratorial explanations evolved that frequently went to the highest levels of power in their search for the hidden levers of famine. In one of the greatest ironies of eighteenth-century public life, the well-intentioned, extremely expensive but highly inefficient attempts of local and central authority to alleviate difficulties of supply rebounded into further ramifications of plot. Large-scale shipments of grain, and stockpiling in warehouses, the locations of which were suppressed to avoid pillage, could only be interpreted by the contemporary culture as part of a plot to drive prices sky-high with artificial dearth.

One can account for the 'famine plot persuasion' through specific cultural and institutional influences, but it can also be seen as an example of something wider: a concern shared by much of eighteenth-century European society with plot as an explanation for misfortune. This was a tendency, moreover, which had been nurtured and reinforced by the changes in perception of cause and effect that were central to the developing Enlightenment. The emphasis on a rationalist/mechanist view of the universe, developing from the Newtonian revolution of the later seventeenth century, had removed the force of Providence, or Fate, or indeed God, from the mental repertoire of the educated. In this way, Europeans seemed to lose sight of the possibility of unintended consequences, and resorted to the idea of deliberate action as necessarily accounting for events in the social and political realm. Whereas in previous ages conspiracies had taken the form of identifiable plots of individuals for specific ends – from Catiline to the Gunpowder Plot – now shadowy tendrils of unspecified malevolence were seen as extending from the powerful to thwart whichever group feared or propagated the notion of plot.[27]

Toward the 1780s, the mushrooming growth of competing scientific and pseudo-scientific explanations for natural phenomena can only have reinforced such concerns. As common conceptions of reality were challenged on all sides by individuals and groups, each of which claimed to have discovered the secret motive force of the universe, it is not to be wondered at that simple human intention stood out as an explanation for human actions.[28] The consistency of such views, and the evidence that could be produced for them, withstood every challenge, and every appeal to calm and reason, that both Old Regime and revolutionary authorities would make. The 1780s were an age of credulity, when almost anything could be believed of nature. On the operation of the human mind, however, only reason stood out as providing causes. This clarity, amidst scientific disorder, only reinforced the conviction that political or social evils were the product of evil designs.

Thus the plot-paranoia of the late eighteenth century extended in several directions. First, it targeted those who already had, or who openly sought, power, on the assumption that such positions and projects automatically involved manipulation. Second, it enveloped the sphere of what we might call coincidence and socio-economic circumstance, rejecting either mode of behavior decisively in favor of conspiratorial explanations. Third, in line with more general corporatist prejudices, it targeted the individualist, particularly in economic affairs, as an antisocial figure who manipulated the weak to his own ends. François Furet has claimed this form of thought as a product of Revolution itself: 'It [the Revolution] inaugurated a world that attributes every social change to known, classified and living forces; like mythical thought, it peoples the world with subjective volitions ... In such a world, human action no longer encounters obstacles or limits, only adversaries, preferably traitors.'[29] However, it is clear that in fact such an attitude pre-dated, and to a degree determined, the shaping of a 'revolutionary' consciousness.[30]

IDENTITIES AND COLLECTIVITIES IN REVOLUTION AND REPUBLIC

When the political condition of France deteriorated in 1789 to the point that reconstruction of the basic relations of state power became inevitable, all the conceptual tensions that had built up over the previous decades came, overtly or covertly, into play. What had been achieved, on the surface, by the end of 1789 was a fundamental socio-political restructuring, and one which was based around the autonomous individual citizen. Below the surface of political pronouncements, however, a field of other forms of judgement restrained and restricted the application of the apparently clear revolutionary principles. Elements of this observation are, of course, commonplace. The revolutionaries themselves, in later years, would repudiate many of the social divisions put in place in the early stages of the Revolution, while the writings of Karl Marx, to say nothing of his followers, dwelt on the disjuncture between egalitarian aspiration in the political field and maintenance of the structures of economic inequality.[31] What is less commonplace is the observation of the very many differing levels of discourse and organization on which revolutionary citizenship posed political and conceptual dilemmas.

In the short-term environment of the storming of the Bastille, efforts to conceptualize the crowds participating in this event either as 'the people' or as 'citizens' had already become problematic. The distinction between the two groups was evident to contemporary observers. The journalist Loustalot's account of these events in his *Révolutions de Paris* opened with an exposition on the aimless destruction carried out by 'the people' in contrast to the determined and disciplined action of 'the citizens'.[32] An Assembly *député* went further in distinguishing 'the seditious armed by license' from 'the citizen armed for liberty'. Colin Lucas has demonstrated that this type of discourse was used to 'free' the revolutionary import of collective violence from its more brutal aspects. By palming these off on to brigands and vagabonds, 'the revolutionary contribution of the crowd could remain uncontaminated by frightening violence'. Meanwhile, this did not stop commentators slipping into an assimilation of all the poor with the untrustworthy rabble, or even those that Lucas describes as 'potentially more radical', laying the blame for crowd violence on the 'ignorance and gullibility of the poor', who were led by 'others' into their acts.[33] This returns us to the perspective of manipulations and conspiracies. Mona Ozouf has observed that revolutionary thought was never able to rid itself of a conviction that individuals were easily manipulated. Their models of psychology continued to rest on those we have observed earlier in the century: 'a sensationism which privileged heteronomy over autonomy and tended to consider men primarily as sensitive and impressionable beings'. Thus such individuals required leadership above all.[34]

Arguably, although the Revolution trumpeted its individualism, its political institutions actually projected revised forms of corporatism, of which there were two main types. The first, expounded from the center and visible, for example, in the writings of the Abbé Sieyès, projected France as 'one and indivisible'. Thus political sovereignty was not the possession of individual citizens, but only of them when they came together as a national body. Citizens were not sovereign; only the abstraction called the Nation was.[35] A second, countervailing form of corporatism was that which resulted from cutting the Gordian knot of local administration, and effectively licensing the self-creation of communes at the end of 1789. Allowing claims to corporate existence to be put forward by any and every small community produced a corporatist vision of local autonomy that was radically at odds with Sieyès' version of citizenship, but also at odds with an individualist pattern of political participation.[36]

The confusions of revolutionary political thought over the place of individual autonomy were embodied in the contradictory arrangements made, on the one hand, for eligibility to the electoral process, and on the other, in the mechanics of the process itself. The criteria for eligibility straightforwardly prescribed political activity as the domain of the independent individual: on which grounds domestic servants joined women in the ranks of those categorically excluded from such participation. Adult males were then categorized on their tax-paying abilities for admission as basic electors, candidates for local office and for national office. However, this straightforward property franchise was then exercised in a fashion reminiscent of Rousseau's ideal in the *Social Contract*, where the General Will was sought through individual communion with the good of the Nation. The General Will was not, as such, any kind of drive or urge, as one might otherwise construe the notion of 'will', and certainly was not supposed to emerge through any kind of open public debate. Rather it functioned in Rousseau's thought as an expression of the collective good, and its recognition was seen to be a condition of, and conditional upon, the individual's recognition of the primacy of the public good over individual concerns – a characteristic inscribed by Rousseau, following Montesquieu, as 'virtue'.[37]

Thus, in the particular example of the voting system, declared candidacy was prohibited, as was public discussion of individuals' suitability. Rather, voters listed all those they thought worthy of office, and out of these, through multiple rounds of voting, were sifted overall majorities for each of the vacant places, which might number from a handful to over 50.[38] In such a straightforward issue of electoral mechanics, it might be stretching a point to see anti-individualist political philosophy in action, but why then could not men propose themselves as candidates? Such an 'individualist' act was clearly deemed inappropriate for the management of the revolutionary polity, which sought to entrench private reflection in place of public debate, precisely to restrict the opportunity for self-interested individualism to have public expression. Nonetheless, the political rhetoric of the Revolution continued to insist on the citizen as an individual, in the sense of having no other connections but those to the state. The 'shadow' of former corporatist identities was viewed with great suspicion, by authorities and radicals alike.[39]

As the political rhetoric of the Revolution evolved, the process whereby it labeled groups, factions and tendencies as having meaningful identities followed a logic that was geared almost exclusively to external perceptions, and not to self-articulated identities. This is most evident in the constitution of the group defined as *sans-culottes*, a political neologism deriving from stage farce, and initially used as a term of low abuse against radicals. According to the work of various historians, this group identity was constituted from several sources and directions, none of which directly reflected definable characteristics of the group that *sans-culotte* would be most consistently applied to, namely the urban working classes. The label carried with it a set of assumptions and behaviors defined within the political sphere, in terms of disinterest, honesty, patriotism and republicanism, that then were alleged to carry over to a social identity. This identity, however, served to distance those who followed the model of *sans-culotte* behavior from what might have been more realistic concerns of an urban lower class, such as their relations with higher groups, their power in the sphere of production, and so on. Moreover, the group constituted as *sans-culottes* was misidentified in the political discourse at two levels, at least, because further research identifies its leading components as quite clearly comprising sections of the urban bourgeoisie.[40]

Beginning from the point of misidentification of *sans-culottes*, it is possible to elaborate a whole series of spurious socio-political identities that were acted upon during the period of the Terror, and that have largely been accepted since that point as being meaningful. Within the Parisian polity, for example, the opponents of the *sans-culottes*, labeled as 'moderates', were and have been largely characterized in terms of an identity as a higher social group than the *sans-culottes*, despite their superficially political label. Moving from the urban to the national political arena, we find the radical 'Jacobins' or 'Montagnards' defined in opposition to the 'Girondin' grouping by the spring of 1793. Here there is a conflation of social and moral rhetoric in play, as the latter group appears as an 'aristocracy of wealth' attempting to tear the body politic apart in pursuit of narrow sectional interests in the mercantile cities of France.[41] In the case both of the *sans-culotte*/moderate and Jacobin/Girondin divides, there is little in fact that can be held to distinguish between these groups, wherever social analysis is possible. Perhaps most intriguingly, we find characterized as *enragés*, madmen, those spokespeople for popular concerns about the food supply that contradicted the Jacobin line in the summer of 1793. All the issues that one would have supposed to animate the *sans-culottes* are here condemned as 'objectively counter-revolutionary' by those groups themselves.[42]

The establishment of group labels and identities in the French Revolution was tied to questions about loyalties and relationships which were in themselves constantly in flux. By the climax of the period of Terror, this had resulted in an atmosphere of pure conformism in the political sphere. Identities and interests that might otherwise have been articulated were suppressed in favor of views which simply echoed the lead given by those who orchestrated Terror. Ironically, one of the clearest examples of this emerged after the fall of Robespierre. The exaggerated accusations of personal dictatorial ambition leveled against him were echoed from all corners of the nation, as organizations and officials competed to demonstrate loyalty to those they would just as swiftly have denounced, had the thermidorian coup failed.[43] At one level, these forms of behavior are clearly subject to overtly political pressures in their production, but they also bear the marks of the wider philosophical-psychological currents of this period.

THE COLLECTIVE BODY AND THE LOSS OF SELF

One such wider issue, and a further area where the revolutionary demand for unanimity was put into dramatic effect, was in the acting-out of moralizing discourses on gender-identity, typified by the works of Rousseau, that had come to dominate public discussion by the 1780s.[44] Through these discursive mechanisms, individuality was highly constrained. This is of course most evident for women, whose brief association with political rights and social free expression was always precarious, and cut off violently and definitively in the late autumn of 1793 by a range of measures, from the prohibition of female political societies to the regulation of women's dress, the symbolic deletion of female figures from republican imagery, and the very real executions of leading female 'enemies of the Revolution'.[45]

However, for men too, the constraints of the particular revolutionary constructions of gender-identity were far from negligible. In particular, it has been argued that a conflation of beliefs about gender-role performance and self-presentation through bodily rigor helped to facilitate the passage to the guillotine, demanding from men a rigid stoic demeanor and inhibiting protest – in short, that the revolutionary political culture created a kind of body that went uncomplaining to the scaffold.⁴⁶ If such an interpretation is valid, then it shows the formation of selves which are in practice almost entirely self-effacing, a theme that will be returned to below.

Wider study of the role of corporeal metaphor in the revolutionary political culture has revealed it to be effectively ubiquitous. As such, use of bodily imagery contributed to a thoroughgoing collectivization of political imagination in revolutionary France. The body of the Nation took over from the body of the king as the representation of political authority, and of political activity in general, and this metaphor was elevated to a central structuring concern on a variety of levels.⁴⁷ It was the organization of this body and its unity which underlay the systems and patterns of political activity designed by thinkers such as Sieyès, and it was the self-transparency of this body which prompted the growing waves of licensed and encouraged denunciation of political and social deviance which marked the course of the Revolution.⁴⁸

In this pattern of denunciation, we can see joined some of the themes of political culture that had emerged from the eighteenth century. The actions of isolated individuals were feared, and at the same time expected, to lead to disunity and conspiracy. Individuals alone were too subject to the temptations of wrongdoing. The conviction that transparency was required in social relations, stripping away the veils of representation to expose 'true' identities and intentions, derived from a terror that concealment and dissimulation were endemic, led to plots, and undermined a desired, and essential, unity. This, of course, would tear apart the Jacobin movement in the spring of 1794, as the circle of acceptable opinions grew ever narrower.

Robespierre, in his 'Report on the Principles of Political Morality' delivered in February 1794, set out the desirable qualities of a democratic or republican polity: 'a state in which the sovereign people, guided by laws which are of their own making, do for themselves all that they can do well, and by their delegates do all that they cannot do for themselves'.⁴⁹ However, this is immediately qualified by recognizing that the 'war of liberty against tyranny' continues, and that the 'spirit of revolutionary government' is still required. This will lead Robespierre to his famous pronouncement on the interdependence of Terror and Virtue. Quite clearly, in the realm of Terror, individual self-realization is at something of a discount, but problems with individual identity lie deeper within Robespierre's discourse than that. For him, the 'mainspring' of a republican or democratic government is the virtue which he takes from Rousseau's philosophy: 'which is nothing other than the love of the nation and its laws'. This 'nothing other', however, on closer examination is a whole program of self-abnegation. 'That sublime sentiment [virtue] supposes the preference of public interest to all particular interests', Robespierre goes on, and observes, 'how, for example, can the slave of avarice or ambition be made to sacrifice his idol for the good of the country?'[50]

As the rest of the speech makes clear, Robespierre's vision of self-realization under a democratic polity is essentially one of the abandonment of self. Although the speech of Robespierre and his colleagues proclaims the desire to establish 'a people who are magnanimous, powerful and happy' in place of the misery of the Old Regime, there is very little in any of their program which suggests where such happiness may be drawn from, except in the joy of fusion with the Nation. The undercurrent of much of this discourse continues to be a fundamental distrust of individualism and non-conformity. There is heavy irony in the fact that in a previous decade Rousseau had been outraged by Diderot's remark that 'only the wicked man is alone', taking it as a slight on himself, and yet one of his most faithful disciples, Saint-Just, would require all men in his projected ideal Republic to declare their friendships publicly, and, if they had none, they would be disbarred from citizenship.[51]

With the politics of Rousseauism, as expressed in the period of the Terror, we find issues of political philosophy and psychology inextricably intertwined. It is wickedness in its various forms which pervades the closing pages of Robespierre's report on political morality, often a wickedness associated plainly with weakness, the inability to resist the superficial temptations of individual enrichment or 'aristocratic' depravity. Psychologically, the revolutionaries cannot believe in autonomy; the individual is subject to the impressions which fall upon him, and to the influences of his surroundings (and this is, by their own creation, an all-male polity now). Ideally, the Jacobin Republic would have remolded the entire social world, remaking public life as a series of festivals, and inscribing public buildings to stand as civics lessons in stone.[52] Citizens of the new France would not have been left alone to succumb to their weaknesses, nor left idle so that their thoughts might drift toward selfishness. Wickedness would be ascribed to the individual, and only in the uniformity of collectivity was there safety.

CONCLUSION

We have observed here the kaleidoscopic extent of the anti-individualist tendencies operating in the period of the French Revolution. From beliefs about basic psychology, to social functioning, to gender, to the nature of representation and social action, many factors combined to present the revolutionary period as a difficult one for individual autonomy. Of course, after Thermidor, such individualism would become all the rage, and 'high society' would rediscover itself, economic liberalism licensing gain as it provoked starvation. The Thermidorians and the Directory invented a Republicanism that abandoned the vision of reconstructing humanity, settling for repression and political manipulation as they trod on a knife edge between vengeful royalists and unrepentant Jacobins.[53] Generations to come would endure the police dictatorship of Napoleon and the fumbling reactionaries of the Restoration, but, in those new circumstances, they would look back to the Revolution, and build out of it something that had only existed as a dream at the time.[54]

The free individual was the Revolution's greatest invention, but it was a political concept that could only come to fruition after the turmoil of the 1790s had passed. The Revolution itself offered chances for political participation that revealed how hard it was to involve a whole population in politics to the degree that the revolutionaries' preconceptions demanded. The uncaring liberalism of the Directory began the process of untangling the demands of liberty and unanimity that would finally, paradoxically, allow the Revolution's achievement to be seen. During the Romantic period, the radicals of Europe discovered their 'selves' far more fully than the revolutionaries had been able to, and built new revolutionary movements on foundations that had been formed in a different era. Individual liberty and autonomous selfhood, like the owl of Minerva, flew only in the dusk of Revolution.

NOTES

1. François Furet's account, *Interpreting the French Revolution* (Cambridge: Cambridge University Press, 1981), implicitly endorses this view of the Revolution as the birth of modern politics, although presenting a rather pessimistic view of the politics of the Revolution itself. For the extent to which overtly 'optimistic' views of the nature of the revolutionary event were on display in 1989, see Steven L. Kaplan, *Farewell Revolution*, 2 vols (Ithaca, NY: Cornell University Press, 1995). For a sideline on the 'modernity' of the event, and a claim for it as the starting-point of 'modernism' in Western culture, see T.J. Clark, 'Painting in the Year Two', *Representations* 47 (1994), pp. 13–63.
2. See Norman Hampson, *The Enlightenment: An Evaluation of Its Assumptions, Attitudes and Values* (Harmondsworth: Penguin, 1968), esp. Chs 4, 6, 7.
3. Maximilien Robespierre, 'Report on the Principles of Political Morality', 17 pluviôse II (5 Feb. 1794), translated in Keith M. Baker (ed.), *The Old Regime and the French Revolution* (Chicago, IL: University of Chicago Press, 1987), *Readings in Western Civilisation* 7, pp. 369–84, citation p. 370. On *régénération*, see Antoine de Baecque, *The Body Politic; Corporeal Metaphor in Revolutionary France, 1770–1800* (Stanford, CA: Stanford University Press, 1997), pp. 131–56.
4. The simplest recent introduction to this is Dorinda Outram, *The Enlightenment* (Cambridge: Cambridge University Press, 1995), pp. 1–14.
5. For the persistent misconstruction and neglect of peasant viewpoints in the Revolution, see Peter Jones, *The Peasantry in the French Revolution* (Cambridge: Cambridge University Press, 1988), and John Markoff, *The Abolition of Feudalism; Peasants, Lords and Legislators in the French Revolution* (University Park, PA: Pennsylvania State University Press, 1996). The misconstruction of women's identities in this period is by now an established fact of revolutionary historiography. For a relatively recent

examination, see Olwen Hufton, *Women and the Limits of Citizenship in the French Revolution* (Toronto: University of Toronto Press, 1992).
6. See the recent discussion of Voltaire's troubled and evolving sense of 'self' in David Wooton, 'Unhappy Voltaire, or "I Shall Never Get Over It As Long As I Live"', *History Workshop Journal* 50 (2000), pp. 137–55.
7. For the former, see Pierre Bourdieu, *The Logic of Practice* (Stanford, CA: Stanford University Press, 1990), esp. pp. 66ff.; for the latter, a starting point must be Michel Foucault, *Discipline and Punish; The Birth of the Prison* (New York: Vintage Books, 1979).
8. Charles Loyseau published his masterwork, the *Traité des ordres et simples dignitez*, in 1610. It remained a standard text into the reign of Louis XIV and beyond. See the extracts translated in Baker (ed.), *Old Regime and French Revolution*, pp. 13–31.
9. Study of this phenomenon begins with Ernst Kantorowicz, *The King's Two Bodies: A Study in Medieval Political Theology* (Princeton, NJ: Princeton University Press, 1957). For some recent observations on this theme, see Sara Melzer and Kathryn Norberg (eds), *From the Royal to the Republican Body: Incorporating the Political in Seventeenth- and Eighteenth-Century France* (Berkeley, CA: University of California Press, 1998), esp. Introduction and Chs 1–3 and 6.
10. See Sarah Hanley, 'Engendering the State: Family Formation and State Building in Early Modern France', *French Historical Studies* 16 (1989), pp. 4–27.
11. See Arlette Farge and Michel Foucault, *Le Désordre des Familles: lettres de cachet des Archives de la Bastille* (Paris: Julliard, 1982).
12. See Robert Darnton, *The Great Cat Massacre and Other Episodes in French Cultural History* (New York: Vintage Books, 1985), p. 168. This characterization included, for example, the married Diderot, 37, and a father, and another writer aged 57.
13. See David Garrioch, *Neighbourhood and Community in Paris, 1740–1790* (Cambridge: Cambridge University Press, 1986), and David Andress, 'Social Prejudice and Political Fears in the Policing of Paris, January–June 1791', *French History* 9 (1995), pp. 202–26.
14. See Michael Sonenscher, *Work and Wages: Natural Law, Politics and the Eighteenth-Century French Trades* (Cambridge: Cambridge University Press, 1989).
15. See the impressionistic but wide-ranging works of Richard Cobb on social marginality in this period: *Reactions to the French Revolution* (Oxford: Oxford University Press, 1972), and *The Police and the People: French Popular Protest 1789–1820* (Oxford: Oxford University Press, 1970). On suicide in particular, see his *Death in Paris; The Records of the Basse-Geôle de la Seine, October 1795–September 1801, Vendémiaire Year IV–Fructidor Year IX* (Oxford: Oxford University Press, 1978).
16. See Keith Michael Baker, *Inventing the French Revolution* (Cambridge: Cambridge University Press, 1990), and Mona Ozouf, '"Public Opinion" at the End of the Old Regime', in T.C.W. Blanning (ed.) *The Rise and Fall of the French Revolution* (Chicago, IL: University of Chicago Press, 1996), pp. 90–110.
17. See Daniel Gordon, 'Philosophy, Sociology and Gender in the Enlightenment Conception of Public Opinion', *French Historical Studies* 17 (1992), pp. 882–911.
18. See Sarah Maza, *Private Lives and Public Affairs: The Causes Célèbres of Prerevolutionary France* (Berkeley, CA: University of California Press, 1993).
19. See Darnton, *Great Cat Massacre*, Ch. 6, 'Readers Respond to Rousseau; the Fabrication of Romantic Sensitivity', pp. 209–45.
20. See Robert Darnton, *The Literary Underground of the Old Regime* (Cambridge, MA: Harvard University Press, 1982), and *The Forbidden Best-Sellers of Pre-revolutionary France* (New York: W.W. Norton, 1996); see also Benjamin Nathans, 'Habermas's "Public Sphere" in the Era of the French Revolution', *French Historical Studies* 16 (1990), pp. 620–44. The works in nn. 15–17 above also discuss Habermasian interpretations.
21. See Yaron Ezrahi, 'The Theatrics and Mechanics of Action: The Theater and the Machine as Political Metaphors', *Social Research* 62 (1995), pp. 299–322, for a brief overview. Melzer and Norberg (eds), *From the Royal to the Republican Body*, Chs 4, 7 and 8 also address various forms of 'performance' in eighteenth-century France and their links to public representation.

22. See, for two rather different perspectives, Angelica Goodden, 'The Dramatising of Politics: Theatricality and the Revolutionary Assemblies', *Forum for Modern Language Studies* 20 (1984), pp. 193–212; and Susan Maslan, 'Resisting Representation: Theater and Democracy in Revolutionary France', *Representations* 52 (1995), pp. 27–51.
23. See the discussion of Restif's *Mimographe* in Scott S. Bryson, *The Chastised Stage: Bourgeois Drama and the Exercise of Power* (Saratoga, CA: Anma Libri, 1991) (Stanford French and Italian Studies 70), pp. 84–7. Bryson also notes Restif's plans to regulate prostitution, remarkably close in form to the 'panoptic' vision Foucault has dissected.
24. An accessible introduction to this theme is given in Sarah Maza, 'Luxury, Morality and Social Change: Why There Was no Middle-Class Consciousness in Prerevolutionary France', *Journal of Modern History* 69 (1997), pp. 199–229; and Maza, *Private Lives and Public Affairs*.
25. The terms abstractionism and anti-abstractionism are used to define the argument in Paul A. Friedland, 'Representation and Revolution: The Theatricality of Politics and the Politics of Theater in France, 1789–1794', PhD Thesis, UC Berkeley, 1995.
26. See Steven Lawrence Kaplan, *The Famine Plot Persuasion in Eighteenth-Century France* (Philadelphia, PA, 1982), Transactions of the American Philosophical Society, Vol. 72, Part 3.
27. See Gordon S. Wood, 'Conspiracy and the Paranoid Style: Causality and Deceit in the Eighteenth Century', *William and Mary Quarterly* 39 (1982), pp. 399–441. Norman Hampson, *Will and Circumstance; Montesquieu, Rousseau and the French Revolution* (London: Duckworth, 1983), discusses, though less specifically, this reliance on human will to provoke action.
28. See Robert Darnton, *Mesmerism and the End of the Enlightenment in France* (Cambridge, MA: Harvard University Press, 1968).
29. Furet, *Interpreting the French Revolution*, p. 26. See also pp. 53ff.
30. See Timothy Tackett, 'Conspiracy Obsession in a Time of Revolution: French Elites and the Origins of the Terror, 1789–1792', *American Historical Review* 105 (2000), pp. 691–713.
31. On such writings, see François Furet, *Marx and the French Revolution* (Chicago: University of Chicago Press, 1988), notably the distinction drawn between political and real equalities in works such as 'On the Jewish Question'.
32. See C. Lucas, 'Talking about Urban Popular Violence in 1789', in A. Forrest and P. Jones (eds), *Reshaping France: Town, Country and Region during the French Revolution* (Manchester: Manchester University Press, 1991), pp. 122–36; p. 124.
33. Ibid., pp. 129–31.
34. Mona Ozouf, 'La Révolution française et l'idée de l'homme nouveau', in Colin Lucas (ed.), *The French Revolution and the Creation of Modern Political Culture*, Vol. 2, *The Political Culture of the French Revolution* (Oxford: Pergamon Press, 1988), p. 229.
35. See Ran Halévi, 'La Révolution constituante: les ambiguités politiques', in Lucas (ed.) *Political Culture of the French Revolution*, pp. 73–4.
36. See Isser Woloch, *The New Regime: Transformations of the French Civic Order, 1789–1820s* (New York and London: W.W. Norton, 1994), pp. 26–36; and Ted W. Margadant, *Urban Rivalries in the French Revolution* (Princeton, NJ: Princeton University Press, 1992), pp. 84–140.
37. Montesquieu's original discussion of 'virtue' as the animating principle of the republican or 'democratic' form of government occurs in *The Spirit of the Laws*, Vol. 1, Book 3, Section 3 (pp. 20–2 of the Hafner edition, New York, 1949). Rousseau's discussion can be found in *The Social Contract*, Books II and IV, and the association of General Will and virtue is clarified by his *Discourse on Political Economy*, which originally appeared in the *Encyclopédie* of the 1750s (pp. 128–68 of the Everyman edition of *The Social Contract and Discourses* (London, Knopf, 1973)).
38. See Malcolm Crook, *Elections in the French Revolution: An Apprenticeship in Democracy* (New York: Cambridge University Press, 1996), esp. pp. 60–75. For Rousseau's pronouncements on voting, see *Social Contract*, Book II, Chs 1–4, and Book IV, Chs 1–3, (Everyman edn, pp. 200–7 and 274–80).

39. See David Andress, 'Economic Dislocation and Social Discontent in the French Revolution: Survival in Paris in the Era of the Flight to Varennes', *French History* 10 (1996), pp. 30–55.
40. See Sonenscher, *Work and Wages*, Ch. 10; and Sonenscher, 'Artisans, Sans-Culottes and the French Revolution', in Forrest and Jones (eds), *Reshaping France*, pp. 105–21. Richard M. Andrews, 'Social Structures, Political Elites and Ideology in Revolutionary Paris, 1792–4: A Critical Evaluation of Albert Soboul's *Les Sans-Culottes Parisiens* ...', *Journal of Social History* 19 (1985–6), pp. 71–112, addresses questions of material or 'class' identity.
41. See 'Forum on the Girondist Faction in the French Revolution', *French Historical Studies* (1988), pp. 506–48, and Patrice Higonnet, 'The Social and Cultural Antecedents of Revolutionary Discontinuity: Montagnards and Girondins', *English Historical Review* (1985), pp. 513–44. See also Paul R. Hanson, 'The Federalist Revolt: An Affirmation or Denial of Popular Sovereignty?', *French History* 6 (1992), pp. 335–55.
42. See R.B. Rose, *The Enragés: Socialists of the French Revolution?* (Sydney: Sydney University Press, 1968), and Albert Mathiez, *La Vie Chère et le Mouvement Social sous La Terreur* (Paris: Payot, 1927).
43. See B. Baczko, *Ending the Terror: The French Revolution after Robespierre* (Cambridge: Cambridge University Press, 1994), esp. Chs 1–2.
44. See Carol Blum, *Rousseau and the Republic of Virtue; The Language of Politics in the French Revolution* (Ithaca, NY: Cornell University Press, 1986), for one useful introduction to this area.
45. A process outlined in L. Hunt, *Politics, Culture and Class in the French Revolution* (Berkeley, CA: University of California Press, 1984), Ch. 4, and in D.G. Levy, H.B. Applewhite and M.D. Johnson (eds), *Women in Revolutionary Paris, 1789–1795, Selected Documents* (Urbana, IL: University of Illinois Press, 1979).
46. See Dorinda Outram, *The Body and the French Revolution: Sex, Class and Political Culture* (New Haven, CT: Yale University Press, 1989).
47. See de Baecque, *Body Politic*.
48. Ibid., Chs 2–3, 6. See also C. Lucas, 'The Theory and Practice of Denunciation in the French Revolution', *Journal of Modern History* 68 (1996), pp. 768–85.
49. Baker (ed.), *Readings in Western Civilisation* 7, p. 371.
50. Ibid.
51. See Blum, *Rousseau and the Republic of Virtue*, pp. 58–9, for Rousseau's umbrage, and Norman Hampson, *Saint-Just* (Oxford: Blackwell, 1991), for the *Institutions Républicaines*.
52. See Mona Ozouf, *Festivals and the French Revolution* (Cambridge, MA: Harvard University Press, 1988), and James A. Leith, *Space and Revolution: Projects for Monuments, Squares, and Public Buildings in France, 1789–1799* (Montreal: McGill-Queen's University Press, 1991).
53. For general accounts of this period, see Martyn Lyons, *France Under the Directory* (Cambridge: Cambridge University Press, 1975), and Denis Woronoff, *The Thermidorean Regime and the Directory* (Cambridge: Cambridge University Press, 1984). For a discussion of the 'abandonment' of citizenship, see Howard G. Brown, 'From Organic Society to Security State: The War on Brigandage in France, 1797–1802', *Journal of Modern History* 69 (1997), pp. 661–95.
54. On the revolutionary tradition within France, see Pamela M. Pilbeam, *Republicanism in Nineteenth-Century France, 1814–1871* (Basingstoke: Macmillan, 1995). For the politics of the revolutions of 1848 and the mid-century 'democratic' movement, see Jonathan Sperber, *The European Revolutions, 1848–51* (Cambridge: Cambridge University Press, 1995). Michael Broers, *Europe After Napoleon* (Manchester: Manchester University Press, 1996), discusses systematically the various political ideologies of the early nineteenth century, which are all linked, by affinity or opposition, to the revolutionary tradition, as they saw it.

2

The Desacralization of the Monarchy: Rumors and 'Political Pornography' during World War I

BORIS KOLONITSKII*

The February Revolution of 1917 is impossible to imagine without a whole range of rumors. The mixture of fact and fantasy – myths of betrayal and conspiracy cast in xenophobic tones, fused with hearsay about religious, medical and erotic experiments performed by the élites – became an important part of the pre-revolutionary milieu. As A.I. Spiridovich, a well-informed general of the gendarmes, recalled: 'what was "said" in the capital, and what was passed on to the provinces, together with other rumors and gossip, created, in the end, an atmosphere conducive to revolution ... Here everything was simplified, made more comprehensible, vulgar and vile.'[1]

The police were aware of this mood on the eve of revolution. The November 1916 report of the Okhrana noted: 'Rumors fill the gaps in everyday life: they are believed more than the newspapers, which for reasons of censorship can not reveal the whole truth ... Society ... thirsts for debates on "political" topics, but has no material for such discussions. Anyone who takes any interest spreads rumors on the war, peace, German intrigues and so forth. There is no end in sight to the daily dose of rumors upon which the capital thrives.'[2] Rumors about the betrayal of the 'Old Regime' were a call to action in February 1917. Many of the leaders of the February days wrote about them, Aleksandr Kerenskii being no exception.[3]

All of this is common knowledge. However scholars still face the task of compiling a register of such rumors, studying the history of their development and dissemination, tracking down their sources and determining their political significance.

---
*Translated by Nathaniel Knight.

RUMORS, THE DEFAMATION OF THE IMPERIAL FAMILY AND MASS CULTURE

One well-known reflection of the dissemination of rumors was the increase in court cases brought against people accused of slandering the imperial family. The Imperial Penal Code stipulated relatively harsh punishments for crimes of this type: individuals daring to 'pronounce, even indirectly, impertinent, insulting words against the Sovereign Emperor, or who intentionally harm, distort or destroy portraits, statues, busts or other images of Him displayed in official or in public places', could be sentenced to the deprivation of all rights and privileges and to exile with hard labor for a period of six to eight years. Other articles laid down similar punishments for affronts to other members of the Imperial family. To be sure, if the offense was committed 'without direct intent to evoke disrespect', then the period of incarceration was reduced to between 8 and 16 months. If the offense was committed 'through a misunderstanding, out of ignorance, or in a state of intoxication', then one could expect to serve a prison term of two to eight months, or be detained for seven days to three months.[4]

It was precisely defamation of the Imperial family that constituted the highest percentage of state crimes. In 1911, for instance, 62 per cent of convictions of such crimes were based on the corresponding articles in the Penal Code. The majority (1,167 out of 1,203) got off with detention. While other types of crimes against the state were committed for the most part by members of the intelligentsia, charges for defaming the Imperial family were brought primarily against day laborers, miners and agricultural workers (in 1911, 80 per cent of individuals brought to trial for defamation of royalty were peasants). As a rule, this particular type of crime was committed in a state of drunkenness. Therefore criminologists believe that 'during 1914–1915 the number of convictions for state crimes should decrease significantly, both in light of wartime conditions and as a result of the prohibition on the sale of alcoholic beverages. Moreover, the latter factor should have a particular impact on the decrease in the number of indirect incidents of defamation of royalty.'[5]

However, these predictions proved to be incorrect. The police report for Riazan Province (October 1915) indicated that crimes related to defamation of royalty were becoming more frequent. In the digest of the Moscow Department of the Okhrana, dated 29 February 1916, it was noted: 'We must conclude with anguish, that if we were to react to all cases of brazen and blatant defamation of royalty, then the number of cases brought under article 103 would reach an unprecedented level ... Such is the mood of the lower classes and of the middle and upper bourgeoisie.'[6]

The very fact of the increase in the number of sentences under the articles in question came to be a rather alarming indicator of the instability of the regime. Apparently, it was precisely for this reason that, in February 1916, a Supreme Decree was issued limiting the imposition of such charges only to the most vicious of 'defamers'. However, the rise in defamation of persons of the Imperial family, in and of itself, need not be regarded as evidence of the growth of anti-monarchist sentiment. On the contrary, at times it testified to the preservation of monarchist views. For example, informers sometimes considered it a crime to swear in the same room in which a portrait of the Imperial family hung. They might inform even on a person who refused to remove his hat under such circumstances.

Even before the February Revolution, the rumor mill provoked the appearance of obscene caricatures and rhymes which were passed from hand to hand. For example, a rhyme appeared called the 'Woe-Cabinet (Woebegone Russia turned tail and went astray)' (*Gore-kabinet: Goremychnaia Rossiia isprokhvostilas' i rasputnoi stala*) the title of which in Russian plays upon the names of Rasputin and ministers Goremykin and Khvostov.

Griadushchii den' nash ser i muten.	Our coming days are grey and muddled
Kontsa Rasput'iu net kak net	No end to the confusion is in sight
Vot pochemu odin Rasputin ves' zameniaet kabinet.[7]	This is why Rasputin alone Is taking the place of the entire cabinet.

'Ode to the Newly Arisen Sycophant Grigorii, the Horse', another widely distributed work, was sold in typescript copies. The copy preserved in the Russian National Library bears the inscription: 'Purchased for one ruble in 1916'.[8] The demand created a unique kind of market for new texts and depictions. Members of the intelligentsia were engrossed in typescript versions of the anti-Rasputin book *The Holy Devil* by S. Trufanov (formerly Hieromonk Illiodor). References to the book could be found in the legal press, and the more 'piquant' pages of the work were read in manuscript form. In Moscow, for example, they appeared no later than February 1916.[9]

The murder of Rasputin provoked the appearance of new rhymes, which were often quite uncouth:

... A na mogilu zhe ego, molva tak govorit	And on his grave, as rumor has it
Prikazano sazhat lish' lilii, I nadpis' sdelat': Zdes' lezhit	It was ordered to plant only lilies And to include the inscription: 'Here lies

Chlen IMPERATORSKOI familii[10]   a member of the IMPERIAL
                                    family'

Amateur artists produced every imaginable type of postcard illustrating rumors and rhymes of this sort. Photographic techniques were also employed. In early February 1917 in Moscow there was talk of front-line soldiers who had openly cursed the tsaritsa and showed indecent photographs of her. Right-wing political figures also noted the dissemination of obscene images of the empress. On the eve of the February Revolution, a well-known member of the Black Hundreds, N.N. Tikhanovich-Savitskii from Astrakhan, complained to Minister of Internal Affairs A.D. Protopopov that 'pictures dishonoring royal persons' were being circulated openly.[11]

During the days of the February Revolution, rhymes on the death of Rasputin were sold at auctions which raised money for 'freedom fighters' and defense funds.[12] Following the overthrow of the regime, the protagonists of these rumors became heroes of the gutter press, theatrical presentations and cinema. Underground culture became a part of mass culture.

The 'Ode to Rasputin' was reprinted in the daily newspapers and in other periodical publications in the capitals and the provinces, and new versions continually surfaced. The naked tsaritsa was depicted alongside Rasputin on postcards. In a typical caption to a caricature, a scantily clad beauty, responding to a remark concerning her 'daring attire', responds: 'That's ridiculous! I have seen a picture postcard of Alice [the Empress Aleksandra] where she wasn't wearing anything at all, and, moreover, she was with Grishka Rasputin!'[13]

'Serious' readers could familiarize themselves with Illiodor's book published by S.P. Mel'gunov in the journal *Golos minuvshevo*. (The issue quickly became a bibliographic rarity.) Two additional editions followed. The publishers omitted 'fantastic' claims and 'salacious' details. (The omissions were not noted in the text.)[14] Thus, readers may well have assumed that the publishers were confirming the reliability of those portions of this dubious source that they had chosen to print. Even some contemporaries commented on the obvious faults of the publication.[15] However, this had no effect whatsoever on its popularity in 1917 nor in subsequent years.

Documentary evidence, some of which was obviously fabricated, appeared in the press as well. For instance, a certain journalist rewarded his lady friend, a telegraph operator, with a cake for helping to fabricate the 'traitorous' 'telegrams of the empress' to one Arnold Rosenthal. He then published this 'document' in the Petrograd newspaper *Rossiiskaia respublika*. The authorities launched an investigation immediately and quickly learned the truth; however, public opinion continued to be influenced by the sensational publication.[16]

The ordinary public engrossed themselves in pamphlets with titillating titles: 'Secrets of the House of Romanov', 'Secrets of the Russian Court', 'Secrets of the Tsarist Court and Grishka Rasputin', 'The Secret of the House of Romanov, or the Adventures of Grigorii Rasputin', 'The Secret of the Influence of Grigorii Rasputin', 'The Life and Adventures of Grigorii Rasputin', etc. A 'historical novel' was even produced in record time.[17] Some booklets were issued in large print runs. For example, Svobodnaia izdatel'stvo of Petrograd put out two editions of the book *The Whole Truth about Rasputin* and the pamphlet 'The Tsaritsa and Rasputin', in editions of 25,000 and 50,000 copies.[18] At times the publications were of an overtly obscene nature; the Kiev Executive Committee even ordered the confiscation of 'Rasputin's Manifesto' and 'Letters of the Tsar's Daughters to Rasputin'.[19] However, literature of this sort was in demand. One contemporary described life in his village thus: 'The mood of the people was light-hearted. They spoke little about serious matters, and read for the most part about the amorous adventures of the tsars and the "Ode to Rasputin". This literature was delivered to us in great abundance by our young people living in the city.'[20]

On 11 March, following the overthrow of the regime, private theaters were opened in the capitals. The play *Tsarskosel'skaia blagodat'* (Good Times at Tsarskoe Selo) opened and was performed twice a day in the Trinity Lampoon Theater for a run of almost two months. The repertoires of other theaters came to include the spoofs *The Fall of the Romanov and Co. Trading House*, *Rasputin's Happy Days*, *The Tsar's Slaves*, *Rasputin's Nighttime Orgies* and *The Fallen Woman of Tsarskoe Selo*. Some old plays were redone to include 'scenes with Rasputin': 'They take an old French farce, rearrange it a little, rename the main characters Rasputin and Anna Vyrubova and present it in the guise of some sort of "Grace at Tsarskoe Selo".' Many, including members of the intelligentsia, considered Vyrubova to be Rasputin's lover and a dominant figure in 'Rasputin's entourage'. A.A. Blok, who was present during the interrogations of Vyrubova after the February Revolution, noted: 'She considers herself *orthodox*, she firmly believes this. What an interesting combination, if she really, as people say, slept with Nicholas [too].' A portrait took shape in the mass consciousness of a dissolute, 'subtle and sensuous' beauty, and people who observed Vyrubova for the first time during the February Revolution were astonished to see a flabby elderly woman on crutches.[21]

Some contemporaries from among the intelligentsia dismissed such performances as 'the offspring of the revolutionary boor' *(porozhdenie khama revoliutsii)*. But Aleksandr Blok, on 1 July 1917, wrote the following remark in his diary: 'Yesterday at the Miniature Theater – a show on Rasputin and Anna Vyrubova. A harsh crowd. Despite its ineptness and stupidity there was a measure of truth. The audience (many soldiers) was ecstatic.'[22] It is curious that the author, who worked in the Extraordinary Investigative Commission created by the Provisional Government to examine the crimes of the 'old regime', saw 'much truth' in a play of this type.

Such productions were often perceived as 'pornography', and appeals were made in the press to repudiate them. A large segment of the public viewed them as highly improper. However, the passion for plays of this sort did not subside until the autumn of 1917 when, for example, a front-line soldier requested the actors of a touring company to present 'How Rasputin Lived in the Tsar's Palace'. Occasionally disturbances arose during such shows. In October, during the performance of *Tsarist Sins* in one of the Petrograd theaters, members of the audience got up on the stage and demanded that the play be expunged at once from the repertoire.[23]

Films screened in the cinemas included *Secrets of the House of Romanov* (produced by the Obnovlenie partnership), *Traitors to Russia* (Miasoedov and Company) (Orel partnership), *The Secret Romance of the Ballerina Kshesinskoi* (Kleo Producers), *The Romanov, Rasputin, Sukhomlinov, Miasoedov and Company Trading House, The Life and Death of Rasputin, The Shame of the House of Romanov* (A.L. Savva Co.). The I.G. Libkin Joint Stock Company put out several films of this sort: *Dark Forces (Grigorii Rasputin)* and *Slaves of the Tsar (Dark Forces,* Part II).[24] Colorful, flamboyant posters drew audiences to the showings. Trashy spectacles often enjoyed considerable success – even among young audiences. A contemporary poet wrote:

Plodit'sia merzosti kak krysy	Vileness is breeding like rats
I zvonko khvalit detvora	And the kids are loudly praising
'Roman razvratneishei Alisy'	'The Romance of Wanton Alice'
I 'Tainy Grishkina Dvora'.[25]	and the 'Secrets of Grisha's Court'.

The 'Rasputiniada' was perceived by contemporaries as 'pornography' (and it would appear that certain aspects of it corresponded to contemporary notions of pornography as well). Attempts to synthesize politically relevant subjects with the 'Parisian genre' appeared, it would seem, quite early. As early as 6 March 1917, at a meeting of Cinematography Labor Activists, I.N. Perestiani spoke out against pornography and exploitation of the Revolution. Those assembled appealed to Minister of Justice A.F. Kerenskii, asserting that 'shameless entrepreneurs, misunderstanding the full majesty and joy of the freedom won by the people, are churning out films in two or three days on obscene themes concerning the Old Regime'. The minister was called upon to 'stop those who are ready to unload a stream of muck and pornography on the populace'. Censorship of films and film producers was introduced outside the capital. For example, representatives of the Provisional Committee for the Regulation of Theater in the city of Moscow recommended that the I.G. Libkin Joint Stock Company cut from the film *Dark Forces* those scenes in which Rasputin 'preached humility'. The question of the struggle against 'pornography' was discussed in the press, where the creation of a special 'theatrical police' was recommended.[26]

The characters depicted in politicized post-revolutionary mass culture, at times, differed from the heroes of the pre-revolutionary rumors; however, it is impossible not to see a connection between them. Many of the storylines of rumors provided the foundation for screenplays and publications. Certain rumors were refuted; others spread in new directions. After the February Revolution rumors were reproduced and disseminated. But even more significant was the fact that, by appearing in print, without any refutation, they attained almost an official status. Pamphlets and postcards, films and theatrical shows provoked the appearance of new, still more monstrous, rumors, rhymes and jokes.

KEY CHARACTERS

The tsaritsa was never a particularly popular figure. Long before the Revolution, gossips had christened the daughter of the Duke of Hesse and Rhine, the 'Hessian fly', comparing her to a pest that destroys fields of grain. It was believed, notably by many officers at the beginning of 1917, that she did not speak Russian.[27] However, it was during the war years that the empress became the main focal point of pernicious rumors: 'Gossip attributes all failures, all shifts in appointments to the empress. It makes one's hair stand on end: what don't they accuse her of – each stratum of society from its own point of view, but with a common concerted outburst of hatred and mistrust.'[28]

Even in the early stages of the war Aleksandra Fedorovna was suspected of Germanophilia. On 3 March 1915, Robert Bruce Lockhart, the British consul in Moscow, wrote in his diary: 'There are several good stories going around about the Germanophile tendencies of the empress. Here is one of the best: The tsarevich is crying. The nurse says "Why are you crying, dear?" "When our side gets beaten, Papa cries, when it's the Germans, Mama cries, and when am I supposed to cry?"'[29] The very fact that anecdotes of this sort were passed around in the British consulate shows how widespread they were. Grand Duke

Andrei Vladimirovich wrote in his diary: 'It is astonishing just how unpopular poor Alix is. It can be affirmed unconditionally that she has definitely not done anything to give grounds for suspicion of German sympathies, but this is precisely what everyone is asserting. The only thing she could be rebuked for is that she wasn't able to be popular.' A persistent rumor emerged about the existence of a 'pro-German' party centered around the young empress. Accusations of this nature even sounded from the tribune of the State Duma. The leader of the Constitutional-Democratic Party Pavel Miliukov made a now famous speech in the State Duma on 1 November 1916 in which he denounced the regime and made the empress his primary target. Miliukov spoke of activities which aroused public indignation and punctuated every denunciation with the rhetorical question of whether this was a case of 'stupidity' or 'treachery'? The speech was banned for publication, but thousands of typed copies circulated around the country. The vast majority of readers were disposed toward the explanation that it was a case of 'treachery' rather than 'stupidity'. Thus, for example, a Russian general reportedly remarked to British officers in early 1917: 'What can we do? We have Germans everywhere. The empress is a German.'[30]

But if initially the tsaritsa was suspected 'merely' of sympathy for the Germans, later she came to be accused of 'active Germanophilia'. Some considered Aleksandra Fedorovna to be an 'unconscious tool of German agents'. That, for example, was how British ambassador Sir George Buchanan assessed the situation.[31] Others accused her of outright treason: 'The German woman-tsaritsa' was betraying state secrets to Germany or preparing for the conclusion of a separate peace that would enslave Russia. A.N. Rodzianko, wife of M.N. Rodzianko, chairman of the State Duma, wrote to Z.N. Iusupova on 1 December 1916: 'The ambassadors of France and England complained to Misha [her husband] that they are received [at court] with difficulty and that Germany, through Aleksandra Fedorovna, is trying to turn the tsar against the allies.' And in a letter dated 12 February 1917, she reports: 'On the Riga front they say openly that she supports all of the German spies, whom the division heads allow to remain free on her orders.'[32]

Indeed, in a special report of the military censor devoted to the mood of the Russian army at the start of 1917, it was noted that the officers attribute all the disorder to the 'German party'. Moreover, many were hostile toward the tsaritsa, considering her an 'active Germanophile'. A naval officer wrote in his diary in the beginning of 1917: Aleksandra Fedorovna 'is the de facto ruler. There is talk about her distinct German sympathies. Scoundrels! What are they doing to my motherland!' Officers did not always conceal their sentiments from the lower ranks. Soldiers spoke outright about the uselessness of fighting while the

Germans were 'powerful in Russia itself'. They regarded with mistrust anyone bearing a German last name, and they considered Aleksandra Fedorovna a 'pure-blooded German woman playing into the hands of Germans'. (At the same time, it was asserted that the soldiers 'loved' the tsar, but thought that 'he is kept in the dark, otherwise he would have rooted out the German influence'.[33])

Among the soldiers the most fantastic rumors circulated. Hunger was explained by the fact that grain was being secretly shipped out to Germany. It was also asserted that German prisoners of war were being sent home and that they were returning to the ranks of the army. The tsaritsa was also accused of shipping food to the enemy. A reference to this is contained in caricatures from the post-revolutionary period. A hungry German woman declares: 'Now that our ally, the Russian tsaritsa, has been arrested, we will have to eat all sorts of rubbish.' It can be surmised that these rumors were provoked by publications in *Novoe vremia* in January and July of 1915. Many in the country were convinced that German merchants sent weekly trainloads of grain to Germany through Riga. The tsaritsa was perceived not only as the protector, but also as the outright leader, of the smugglers. This motif appears in a leaflet published by the Kostroma Social Democrats in June of 1915: 'They say there is no grain. Then where is it? Surely the Russian land doesn't bear fruit for the Germans alone?' In the autumn of 1915 it was said that the shortage of sugar was caused by the fact that Aleksandra Fedorovna sold 80 train carriages of sugar abroad.[34]

Even staff generals and guard officers passed on the most improbable rumors. During the visit of the tsaritsa to General Staff Headquarters extraordinary measures were taken: secret documents were hidden from the empress because it was alleged that after every visit of this sort the Russian Army lost a battle. General M.V. Alekseev declared that the tsaritsa possessed a secret map with the location of forces, which was supposed to exist only in two copies – one held by himself and the other by the emperor. It was said that General A.A. Brusilov supposedly declined to answer a direct question from the tsaritsa about the timing of an attack on the grounds that he also feared a 'leak' of information.[35] As early as 1915, a colonel of the guards claimed that the Germanophilia of the bureaucracy and of the court itself made victory impossible, and that treason should be rooted out. In December 1916, it was said in Petrograd high society that the empress was pandering to the Germans, that she wanted peace and was creating in Russia a party which would help Kaiser Wilhelm. Even many officers of the Joint Guards Regiment that protected Tsarskoe Selo were sympathetic to speeches 'unmasking' the empress.[36] After the February Revolution the significance of the dissemination of rumors among the officers of the guard, and, consequently, the disloyalty of the latter, was exaggerated. In one 'anti-Rasputin' pamphlet it was reported that 'the officers of one of the Petrograd guard regiments received documentary evidence that negotiations with the German staff about the retreat of our forces from Riga were being carried out through individuals close to Empress Aleksandra Fedorovna'. And the tsar not only did not take the necessary measures, but he ordered that the Duma be dissolved. This supposedly influenced the decision of the officers of the Petrograd Garrison to unite 'with the people'.[37]

In society, the tsaritsa was named as the culprit in the death of the British war minister Lord Kitchener who was on a cruiser sunk by the Germans in May 1916: she supposedly informed Germany about the route and schedule of his voyage. It is possible that Rasputin gave grounds for this rumor when he claimed that the death of Kitchener was good, since he might have later caused harm to Russia. The empress considered it necessary to inform the tsar of the 'holy man's' opinion.[38]

The belief of many representatives of the Russian political élite in the treachery of the empress was passed on to diplomats, who informed their governments in the appropriate manner. British Member of Parliament Major D. Davies, who visited Petrograd in the beginning of 1917, noted in his report (read by the king and members of the cabinet): 'The tsaritsa, justly or not, is considered an agent of the German government.' He recommended 'all possible measures' to convince the empress to leave the country and stay until the end of the war in an allied country. Davies also wrote: 'there is no doubt that the enemy is constantly informed of every movement and operational plan. As a result, no serious information can be kept secret and this should constantly be kept in mind during negotiations with the Russian authorities.'[39]

Among the Russian public, rumors also circulated about plans to exile the tsaritsa, kidnap her and confine her in a monastery. Conversations of this sort supposedly were carried on in the salons of high society, in army headquarters and in regiments of the guards.[40]

Lord Bertie, the British ambassador to France, who had his own informants in Russia, wrote soon after February about the former tsaritsa: 'She is a Boche not only by birth but in her sentiments. She did everything she could to attain mutual understanding with Germany. She is considered a criminal or a criminal lunatic, and the former emperor is likewise considered a criminal owing to his weakness and servile consent to follow her prompts.' Such views were, apparently, widespread in the allied countries. A.A. Argunov, a Socialist Revolutionary (SR) who returned in 1917 from emigration, recalled how the French official in the prefecture repeated (rolling the whites of his eyes), 'Something has to be done about that Alice.'[41]

The figures of the 'traitors' – the tsaritsa and Rasputin – became part of the folklore of the pre-revolutionary period.[42] Kerenskii directed the

Extraordinary Commission, created by the Provisional Government for the investigation of the crimes of the old regime, to search for evidence of criminal ties between the Romanovs and Germany – an accusation which Kerenskii seems, at first, to have believed. N.K. Murav'ev, chairman of the commission, was initially convinced that the empress intended to open the front to the Germans, and that the tsaritsa gave the kaiser information about the movements of Russian forces. The 'respectable press' reported this as well. *Russkaia volia*, for example, related that the tsaritsa and the 'German lady's husband' (*nemkin muzh*) built a 'nest of treachery and espionage'. Certain interviews given by former grand dukes facilitated the spread of these rumors. Kirill Vladimirovich stated to a journalist: 'On more than one occasion I asked myself whether the former empress was not a collaborator of Wilhelm II, but each time, I forced myself to drive away this horrible thought.' Pre-revolutionary rumors and post-revolutionary publications even claimed that a secret radio-telegraph station was located at Tsarskoe Selo, which continually passed on reports to Germany. Counter-intelligence, when it tried to discover this station, was supposedly thwarted and the investigation closed. At the same time, it was claimed that the famous holy fool Mitia Koliaba, who had once had access to the court, had seen the 'apparatus'. After the February Revolution, searches were carried out which, of course, yielded no results.[43] However, sketches of the 'radio-telegraph station' continued to appear in illustrated journals. Many years later, tourists visiting the palace-museums in the former imperial residences still asked to be shown 'that' apparatus.

In certain rumors, the empress was portrayed as a long-time 'agent of influence': Bismarck supposedly specially organized her marriage so that she could head German espionage in Russia.[44]

During the war years, the interference of the tsaritsa in state affairs increased. This violated established tradition and diminished the authority of Nicholas II. Even Aleksandra herself acknowledged this at times.[45] However, rumors endowed her with absolute power: 'The tsar reigns, but the tsaritsa rules.' In his report of 5 (18 old style) February 1917, the British ambassador, Buchanan, noted that in actuality it was the tsaritsa who governed the country.[46] In post-revolutionary pamphlets she was dubbed 'autocrat of all Russias, Alice of Hesse'.[47] Friends of the empress supposedly named her the 'new Catherine the Great', a term used after February in various satirical texts:

Akh planov ia stroila riad	Oh, I made a load of plans
Chtob 'Ekaterinoiu' stat'	to become 'Catherine'
I Gessenom ia Petrograd	and I dreamed in time
Mechtala so vremenem zvat.'[48]	of calling Petrograd Hesse.

The very comparison with Catherine II could give rise to other historical parallels. In society it was claimed that the empress was preparing a coup in order to become regent. Many people believed this rumor since it came from a lady close to the chairman of the Council of Ministers, B.V. Strumer, who, supposedly, dreamed of seeing him as 'her majesty's premier'.[49] Even the authorities were compelled to pay heed to this rumor. In September 1916, A.A. Mosolov, head of the chancellery of the Imperial Court, wrote a letter to his chief, Minister Baron V.B. Frederiks. He deemed it impossible to apply sanctions to the press which was printing various reports about Rasputin. 'Given the current nervous state of both the press and public opinion, any repressive measures would impart an undesirable air of importance to this matter and only strengthen assumptions about a regency of the Sovereign Empress.'[50]

According to some rumors, reflected in the gutter press and cheap novels, the tsaritsa even planned to murder her husband. It was also claimed that the empress was planning to carry out a coup 'with the help of German bayonets'.[51] Peasants asserted simply that Nicholas had gone off to a monastery, and that the country was being ruled by the 'German woman' and 'Grishka' Rasputin to whom the tsar had 'signed over his kingdom'.[52]

Finally, the tsaritsa was accused of conjugal infidelity. She, supposedly, 'spread such debauchery that the most profligate philanderers and wantons known to man paled in comparison'. Various names were mentioned: 'Cuirassier Orlov', Aide-de-Camp Rear Admiral N.P. Sablin II.[53] At times rumors about the debauchery of the tsaritsa bordered on the fantastic:

V tsarskom temnaia 'malinka'	In tsarskoe [Selo] a dark 'raspberry' [slang for den of thieves]
S udovol'stviem tsvela	bloomed with pleasure
V tsarskom tereme Aliksa	In the tsar's palace Alix
S tseloi gvardiei zhila.[54]	Lived with an entire regiment.

But the most common accusation was that the tsaritsa was Rasputin's lover. Rumors of this liaison were recorded by military censors. In cinemas it was forbidden to screen a film in which the tsar was shown placing upon himself the St. George Cross because a voice inevitably sounded out in the dark: 'The tsar is with Egor (George) and the tsarina is with Grigorii.'[55] On a postcard depicting Grand Duke Dmitrii Pavlovich, a participant in the assassination of Rasputin, an inscription by a contemporary is preserved: 'He put an end to the shameful behavior of the tsaritsa, wife of Nicholas II. He killed the crony (*vremenshchik*) Rasputin, that disgrace to Russia.'[56]

Such rumors were believed not only by simple folk. They were widespread among the intelligentsia as well.[57] In her diary, Symbolist poet Zinaida Gippius wrote: 'and Grisha himself rules, drinks and f..ks the frauleins, including [Aleksandra] Fedorovna as is his wont' (entry for 24 November 1915; in the published version this phrase was omitted).[58] Even in the traditionally loyal strata of society there was talk about the tsaritsa's debauchery. A.N. Mandel'shtam, an official in the Ministry of Foreign Affairs, claimed to possess 'reliable' information confirming the liaison of the empress with the 'holy man'. None of his colleagues expressed any objections or doubts. When the historian S.P. Mel'gunov decided to publish excerpts from his manuscript *The Holy Devil*, he had to deal with the censors. After completing their formal inquiry, uniformed and decorated officials began a lively conversation about the content of the book. 'The gentlemen censors were especially interested in the question of the tsaritsa's relations with Rasputin.'[59]

After February, this topic became a favorite theme of 'gutter' literature: 'Alice wanted to find out herself about the miraculous powers of the holy man, and after the first soul-saving conversation, found this so much to her liking that she sent Nicholas packing forthwith and proposed that Grigorii occupy his place.' Some authors even 'reconstructed' the scene of the seduction.[60] Vyrubova figured as a regular participant in the 'orgies'.[61]

Aleksandra Fedorovna was also accused of corrupting her children. Rasputin, supposedly, seduced the tsar's daughters (in the 'Exaltation on the Death of Rasputin' he is called the 'tsarevnas' delight', the 'deflowerer of the tsarevnas' and the 'debaucher of the tsarevich').[62] The development of this rumor was influenced by actual meetings of the 'holy man' with the grand duchesses.

But it can also be posited that a patriotic initiative of the empress played a role here as well. Together with the elder tsarevnas, she had completed medical courses. The tsaritsa and tsarevnas worked in a hospital and even assisted during operations. This in and of itself evoked condemnation at times, both among the simple people and in society. The mere fact that young women were caring for naked men was considered highly indecent. In the eyes of many monarchists the tsaritsa had lost her dignity: 'in washing the feet of soldiers', she had forfeited, in their eyes, her royal majesty and descended to the level of a simple 'nurse', or even an ordinary hospital orderly. Some court ladies declared that 'the ermine mantle fit the tsaritsa better than the dress of a sister of mercy'.[63]

Many, nonetheless, took a fond view of the new image of the empress and her daughters. In photographs and patriotic pictures they were often depicted as sisters of the Red Cross. The allied press wrote:

'the visage of the tsaritsa in the white kerchief of the sisters of mercy did more to bring about the unity of the people with the tsar than all the decrees granting the people freedom'.[64]

However, perceptions of the sisters of mercy during the war years underwent a change. The reverent attitude evoked by a woman patiently bearing her patriotic and Christian burden faded away. For the front-line soldiers, the sister of mercy became a symbol of decadence, 'filth from the home front'. Terms such as 'sisters of comfort' and 'sisters without mercy' appeared. Staff automobiles were dubbed 'sister wagons' (*sestrovtsy*). In certain hospitals and medical trains, morals were actually quite loose; orgies involving officers and nurses were sometimes played out before the eyes of soldiers. At the same time, professional prostitutes, imitating the patriotic fashion of high-society ladies, sometimes used the popular uniform of the Red Cross. (German sisters of mercy working in Russia were actually ashamed of their uniform.) The soldiers themselves said that 'their lordships drank their way through the Japanese war and they're carousing their way through this one with the merciful sisters'. The sister of mercy became the central figure of sexual fantasy and hatred of the front-line soldier: 'You begin to feel hatred for women. The cross, the Red Cross, once the symbol of mercy, of caring for your loved ones, of self-sacrifice, now cries out loudly and crudely: for sale to the highest bidder. Oh the contempt with which wounded soldiers regard them.' The reaction of some peasants to the information that the tsar was awarding medals to sisters of mercy is indicative: 'He gives them [medals] because he lives with them at headquarters and he gives crosses to the ones he makes love to ... It would be better if the sovereign pinned them to the sisters of mercy on the ... because he made love to them.'[65]

According to the testimony of contemporaries, rumors and gossip about the tsaritsa and the grand duchesses, as the personification of the image of the sisters of mercy, 'corrupted' the consciousness of the broad masses in the capital.[66] As early as December 1915, a certain clerk declared, 'The old empress, the young empress and her daughters, build field hospitals for their debauches and travel from one to another.'[67]

By summer and autumn of 1917, the fall in the popularity of the tsaritsa led many doctors, wounded men and patients to openly demonstrate their lack of respect for her.[68] The empress became an object of contempt. It is indicative that before the Revolution rumors circulated in society about attempts on her life. It was claimed that a certain officer recovering in the hospital had taken a shot at her. The date was even given: 26 December 1916. It was reported on occasion that the bullet intended for the tsaritsa wounded Vyrubova.[69] A.N. Rozdianko wrote to Z.N. Iusupova on 12 February 1917: 'There is even a story that an officer shot at her and wounded her in the hand.' This rumor was recorded by the French ambassador as well.[70]

Hatred of the traitor-tsaritsa flared up during the February events: demonstrators cried out: 'Down with Sashka!' When the striking workers were reprimanded for 'aiding the enemy', the response rang out: 'But what about Sukhomlinov, Miasoedov. The empress herself is a German spy.'[71] Rumors about the 'betrayal of the empress' had no serious foundation but, in that situation, conjectures became the most important facts of political life. After the Revolution, the myth of the conspiracy of the tsaritsa was treated as a proven fact. In official sources she was named as someone 'implicated in treason'.[72]

The anti-dynastic, anti-monarchist mood was directed above all against the dissolute traitor, the 'German tsaritsa', against 'that woman' who ruled the country. This is extraordinarily important – we can sense here the patriarchal underpinning of mass political consciousness, bringing together xenophobia and misogyny.

The other leading character in the rumors was Rasputin. His influence during the war years grew significantly, yet rumors exaggerated it even further. In hearsay, the 'holy man' was dubbed 'chancellor of the Russian Empire', the 'uncrowned monarch, Grigorii the First'. Illiodor called him 'the unofficial Russian tsar and patriarch'.[73] Rasputin himself made no small contribution to the spread of these embellishments: in boasting of his influence, he too exaggerated.[74]

In meetings organized by the liberals, it was noted that the growth of an anti-dynastic mood was particularly noticeable in the lower ranks of society, where it was fed by the most absurd and wild rumors about the role and influence of Rasputin.[75] However, these were confirmed, it would seem, by the testimony of prominent dignitaries and bureaucrats, generals and politicians. War minister A.A. Polivanov, in November 1915, said that Rasputin and Prince Andronnikov 'rule Russia', and General of the Gendarmes M.S. Komissarov, giving evidence before the Extraordinary Investigative Commission of the Provisional Government, confirmed that Rasputin 'was the chancellor'.[76] General I.G. Erdeli, in a private letter (November 1916), cites General D'iakov: 'I see that Russia will perish, everything is leading to decay and internal destruction. The German organization is playing its role … In St Petersburg there is wholesale robbery, looting and bribery. There is nothing surprising in these misdeeds if Grigorii Rasputin is ruling the country.' Deputy of the State Duma G. Vostrotin wrote in December 1916: 'Grishka Rasputin continues to direct internal policy.' In December 1916, literally on the eve of the 'holy man's' death, O. Voeikova wrote from Petrograd to Countess E.L. Ignat'eva: 'Something truly incredible is going on when the Synod, before acting on papers approved by the *Tsar* demands the additional confirmation of Grishka.'⁷⁷ Certain incredible rumors were repeated later by memoirists: Kerenskii, for example, wrote that Rasputin 'yelled at the tsar'.⁷⁸

The image of the all-powerful 'holy man' was used widely in opposition and revolutionary journalism. V.I. Lenin, for example, in his articles from 1917, even named Rasputin the head of the 'tsar's gang', claiming that the union with the Anglo-French billionaires was concluded by the tsar and Rasputin.⁷⁹

After the February Revolution, the notion of an 'all-powerful' Rasputin was confirmed in numerous caricatures. In one of them, the tsar, the tsaritsa and Rasputin are depicted clad in an ermine mantle under a single crown. The caption reads: 'Three heads are better than one.' In the caricature, 'The Last Autocrat', Rasputin is presented with the tsar's orb upon which a tiny Nicholas II is perched. In another, Rasputin the Spider has trapped the tsar and tsaritsa in his web.⁸⁰

It is known that Rasputin initially was an opponent of the war, and the press openly accused him of carrying out propaganda in favor of a separate peace and enjoying the protection of the 'German Party'. In certain rumors Rasputin was even said to be blackmailing the tsar's family: 'If the war continues then the heir will die.'⁸¹

Rasputin was accused of being a direct German agent: 'Everyone considers Rasputin to be an individual who sold out to the Germans', the military censor reported in the beginning of 1917. Even many Russian politicians and foreign diplomats believed this – after all, the source of these rumors was the former minister of internal affairs himself, A.N. Khvostov. Unfortunate individuals who bore the same last name as the 'holy man' were also suspected of treason. L. Rasputin, a gunner from the 80th Siberian Regiment, decided to change his name. On 21 March 1917, he sent a petition to this effect: 'no one will trust me in battle, since my comrades do not trust me now to stand guard in front of our trenches, to observe the activities of the enemy.'⁸²

No evidence, however, of conscious collaboration of the 'holy man' with the German Secret Service was found, although his circle numbered more than a few suspicious persons. S. Hoare, who headed the British military intelligence mission in Petrograd, carried out a special investigation in an attempt to reveal the ties between Rasputin and the enemy, but to no avail.⁸³ Even after the February Revolution, Rasputin and the tsaritsa continued to 'sell out Russia', on the pages of numerous publications, on theater stages and cinema screens. Years later rumors of Rasputin's alleged espionage were repeated in memoirs. For example, Kerenskii wrote that Rasputin was the pivot around which the activities of the German agents revolved. And M.V. Rodzianko wrote about the 'cooperation' of the German General Staff and 'Rasputin's circle'.[84]

The periodic appearance of rumors about Rasputin's murder further stressed how contemptible he had become. A foreign press report noted that he 'is a constant candidate for eternal rest. Just as soon as a murder attempt of an unidentified victim is uncovered in Russia, that victim becomes Rasputin.'[85]

The rumors also included secondary figures – ministers B.V. Strumer and A.D. Protapopov, V.A. Sukhomlinov and V.B. Frederiks, Grand Duchess Maria Pavlovna and the ballerina M.F. Kshesinskaia. (The latter was accused of passing secrets of Russian artillery to the enemy.)[86] Vyrubova was also a frequent source of gossip.

The most important of the secondary characters, however, was the tsar himself, although sometimes he figured as an 'active' villain who 'sold out Russia' and engaged in debauchery.[87] The 'treason' of the tsar was spoken of both by simple people and by denizens of Petersburg salons. A September 1915 entry in Zinaida Gippius's diary reads: 'The government, in the end, doesn't even fear the Germans (it doesn't give a damn about Russia at all. The tsar is, after all, a traitor first and foremost, and he's stubborn as a mule, and a psychopath).'[88] A.N. Rodzianko wrote on 12 February 1917: 'Now it is clear that it is not only Aleksandra Fedorovna who is guilty of everything. As the tsar of Russia, he is even more of a criminal.'[89] Academician V.A. Steklov characterized the tsar in his diary as 'a German lackey and a traitor'. The tsar is also dubbed a traitor in the petitions of certain individuals who shared his name and who wished after February 1917 to change it because it was 'indecent'. Bombardier P. Romanov wrote on 9 April: 'it became clear even to us (who know little of state affairs) who it was that led Russia to the edge of destruction, i.e., all those in positions of power, and at their head, the traitor-monarch Romanov ... To bear the same last name as a man who betrayed his people, from whom he took payment to support his dissolute lifestyle, is extremely undesirable, and even, as a soldier and as a citizen who served in the army for two years – insulting.'[90]

The emperor was accused of intentionally keeping the army hungry, cold and without ammunition, of sending grain to Germany, releasing enemy prisoners of war, and initiating talks about a separate peace with Germany. German propaganda officers who fraternized with the Russians in 1917 recorded several rumors circulating among the Russian soldiers. Some sincerely believed that the war was the result of an agreement between Nicholas II and Wilhelm II, while others were certain that Germany had rejected a separate peace proposed by the Russian tsar.[91]

The Extraordinary Investigative Committee quickly concluded that the accusations of Germanophilia on the part of the tsar and tsaritsa had been false and presented a report to this effect to the Provisional Government. But the Russian press continued to claim the opposite. Even the respectable *Russkie vedomosti* wrote in July 1917 that Nicholas II had been overthrown for 'dealings and secret agreements with the enemy'. Some contemporaries considered the emperor to be an 'inhuman monster'.[92]

But more often in the rumors Nicholas appears as a passive tragic-comic character – suffering, weak-willed and effeminate. The image of the tsar as a limited, feeble and spineless person, who became a toy in the hands of self-serving underlings, was not new.[93] However, during the course of World War I this image was reinforced. The tsar was accused, above all, of inactivity and unpreparedness for war. He was contrasted with the often energetic and militaristic Wilhelm II. The latter, it was said, had spent 40 years preparing for war, while our 'sot' (*probochnik* – literally corkscrew) didn't do anything but sell vodka (in some cases, 'he only opened churches', or 'he only opened schools'). A Siberian peasant, for example, stated in July 1915: 'We must pray for the soldiers and Grand Duke Nikolai Nikolaevich. But why pray for the monarch? He didn't supply ammunition and apparently spent his time carousing and whoring.' Even a priest stated during a sermon in church in November 1915 that Germany was building fortresses and iron works while Nicholas II was opening taverns.[94]

Claims such as 'the emperor reigns but the empress rules ... under the direction of Rasputin' were taken literally, and vulgarized and simplified even further. Passing into mass literature these stereotypes gave rise to the image of Nicholas as a degenerate, a hereditary alcoholic and reprobate, putty in the hands of a decadent *muzhik* and a haughty German woman.'[95]

The emperor is being deceived and manipulated. His wife is cheating on him with a dirty *muzhik*. And Nicholas sees nothing. A front-line soldier wrote: 'Life is hard in this world for the father-tsar, who is like Gania the Blind because the German put dark glasses on him and made his eyeballs burst.' (A portrait of Nicholas with the eyes poked out was attached to the letter.[96]) In some rumors the weak-willed tsar almost voluntarily turns over his spouse to Rasputin: 'He demeaned himself and his power to such an extent that he shared it with the drunken, dirty, ignorant rogue Grishka Rasputin. But was it only his power? He shared with Rasputin his wife as well and all of his family.'[97]

The spineless 'hen-pecked husband' is plied with drink and narcotics, with court physician Badmaev's potions, by foreigners, criminals, traitors and possibly even his own wife.[98] Such fantastic rumors appeared even in the reports of ambassadors. George Buchanan, for example, reported to London that Rasputin allegedly influenced the tsar with the help of some kind of medicines and narcotics. (The rumors came from Grand Prince Dmitrii Pavlovich and F.F. Iusupov; the latter having informed journalists of this after the February Revolution.) The recipient of the ambassador's letter, Lord Hardinge, permanent deputy minister of foreign affairs, assessed the report as 'extremely interesting'. The rumor is repeated by Kerenskii in his memoirs.[99]

In some rumors, the empress simply terrorizes Nicholas: in her presence he maintains a persecuted silence. In the gutter press a phrase, reportedly uttered by F.F. Iusupov, is mentioned: 'When Aleksandra Fedorovna, spurred on by Rasputin, appears in the office of the monarch, he – I'm not exaggerating – literally hides from her under the table.'[100]

The premise of subordination and 'unmanliness' of the emperor is important for understanding the mood on the eve of the Revolution. The pathetic character depicted in these rumors did not correspond in the slightest to the patriarchal ideal, presented by official propaganda, of a great and all-mighty tsar-autocrat. He was no tsar, but a mere 'tsarling' (*tsarishka*).[101] It was precisely his 'weakness' that constituted his guilt: 'Nicholas walks around headquarters (*stavka*) like he's been hit with a ton of bricks.' On 3 February 1917 the workers at the Putilov Plant cried: 'Down with autocratic regime, since the monarch doesn't know who is ruling the country and is selling it out.'[102]

In the diary of D.A. Furmanov, we encounter analogous examples of peasant attitudes toward the 'boozer' (*butylochnyk*) Nikolashka:

> Attitudes toward him are for the most part either mocking or pitying, rarely are they malevolent, but they are always sharply negative toward Nicholas as a ruler. The mocking was for the most part on account of liquor, on account of his drunkenness, or on account of Rasputin. And the pity – such as it was – was sympathy for a stupid little man who was bewitched and led astray by the 'mean and clever German woman'. She managed everything with her ministers and didn't say a word to Nicholas. And if he ever did find out anything – it was no matter – they would get him drunk and he would sign. In the end, what we have is an image of Nicholas as an unfortunate, dim-witted, perpetually drunken person who was confused, deceived, even frightened, despite his ostensible power. Nicholas was particularly dispirited by his wife's unfaithfulness with Rasputin, and this is the main reason why he drank himself into oblivion.[103]

Such an image of 'Nikolashka the fool' did not correspond at all to the conception of a 'true', 'righteous' and powerful sovereign. At the base of the anti-monarchical sentiments of many contemporaries lay a patriarchal, essentially monarchist, mentality: the emperor was held to blame because he was not a 'real' tsar. The core of his 'malfeasance' consisted of 'professional incompetence'.

SOURCES OF RUMORS

The question of the sources of the anti-dynastic rumors has been touched upon by many authors, usually as part of an effort to determine the causes of the Revolution. Supporters of the overturned regime claimed frequently that the rumors were consciously fabricated and spread by the opposition, by revolutionaries and liberals.[104]

There is a measure of truth to this – the revolutionary underground used various rumors in its propaganda. For example, a pamphlet of the Petersburg Bolshevik Committee proclaimed: 'What has long been foretold by the leaders of the working class has come to pass: the autocratic government has committed a monstrous crime – the betrayal of the Russian people ... it has traded and sold the Russian army to the German bourgeoisie.'[105] What is astonishing, in fact, is how little use the underground made of rumors. The Rasputin theme, for example, is poorly developed in its propaganda.

The liberal opposition, on the other hand, was less restrained. The Progressive Bloc led a campaign to discredit the 'dark forces' and 'Rasputinites'.[106] Moreover, many figures in the opposition sincerely believed the most fantastic rumors.

Some contemporaries believed that Rasputin was specially selected by 'internationalists', 'dark forces' or 'enemies of Christianity' for anti-Russian activities. 'He was sent', wrote Archpriest V.I. Vostokov, 'by internationalists with the task of driving the imperial couple out of the hearts of the people, in preparation for the triumph of the revolution planned for Russia.' Others, such as N.D. Zhevakhov, revealed an even more complex plot: anti-Christian 'dark forces', Jews and 'agents of the International' specially selected the candidacy of Rasputin, built his fame and brought him to power in order to use him as their tool, but, when this did not succeed, they began to agitate against him in an attempt to smear the tsar's family – notably by getting Rasputin drunk, initiating orgies, fabricating photographs and so forth.[107]

There are no data at the disposal of scholars which would allow definitive confirmation that anti-monarchist rumors had been fabricated by the Masons. And even if one takes into consideration the fact that the identity of many Russian Masons has yet to be revealed, one could hardly suppose that there existed some kind of main nerve center for the creation and dissemination of rumors. It is indicative that, in the unmasking of Rasputin, a significant role was played not only by radicals but also by conservative, even far-right public figures, for example, V.M. Purishkevich and V.I. Vostokov.

In any event, mass consciousness should not be seen as a mere 'object' of propaganda. Not only did it interpret propagandistic reports in its own way, it also influenced their content. Thus, the term 'dark forces' can evoke completely diverse associations. For decades it was broadly used both in revolutionary and in official Russian state propaganda. Consequently, it was completely impossible to foresee the result of agitation: criticism of 'dark forces' directed against the Rasputinites would be interpreted either as anti-dynastic and anti-monarchic, or as anti-semitic, anti-German or even anti-bourgeois propaganda. It is not surprising that the term 'dark forces' was used both by socialists and by the Black Hundred leader V.M. Purishkevich.[108]

According to one viewpoint, the appearance of rumors was the result of enemy propaganda. Grand Duke Gavriil Konstantinovich recalls: 'These rumors were fabricated in Germany to draw Russia into turmoil.'[109] There are also specific grounds for such claims. In October 1914, a 'suspicious Russian' – Hieromonk Illiodor (S. Trufanov) – appeared in the German embassy in Norway. He proposed that the German authorities buy the manuscript of his book. Illiodor claimed that Rasputin was the true father of the tsarevich, that he practically controlled the government and that the war was started on his initiative. The German diplomats were skeptical about Illiodor's proposition; however, the manuscript caught the eye of the General Staff, and in February 1915 Illiodor was sent to Berlin.[110] The history of Illiodor's subsequent contacts with the Germans is unknown, but rumors reached Russia that Illiodor wanted to publish his book and drop it from airplanes along the front.[111]

In March 1916, enemy leaflets were distributed among Russian troops, showing the kaiser supported by the German people and the tsar leaning with his elbow on Rasputin's sexual organ. It is possible that this was the same caricature mentioned by M. Lemke in his diary entry from 21 February 1916: it depicted Wilhelm measuring the length of a German shell and Nicholas 'on his knees measuring with a yardstick Rasputin's member'. The author mentions that the leaflets were dropped from Zeppelins.[112]

In camps for Russian prisoners of war in Germany, anti-monarchist literature was widely distributed, including a collection of anecdotes about the Russian court. But on the front, German propagandists tried to rely upon the authority of the tsar's power. For example, at Christmas 1916, leaflets were scattered in the Russian trenches with the rhyme:

Tsar' batiushka khotel uzhe	The little-father tsar has long desired
Mir zakliuchit'	to conclude a peace
Chtob naroda svoego	so that his people
Bol'she ne gubit' ...	would no longer perish.
I skoro by mir	And there would soon have been peace

I konchili b voinu	and the war would have been over,
Nachal'niki-izmenshchiki Meshali tomy ...[113]	but the traitor bosses prevented this.

It was as if the enemy command were confirming the veracity of rumors about the preparation of a separate peace. After the February Revolution German leaflets claimed that the overthrow of the tsar was the work of the British, who wanted to foil the conclusion of a peace treaty between Russia and Germany: 'Stay true to your tsar! Now, when he wanted to give you your honorable peace, he has been killed or arrested by English spies.'[114]

Many anti-Rasputin rumors came from monarchist and Black Hundreds circles. The influence of the 'holy man' was intentionally exaggerated. In order to absolve the regime of any responsibility, certain Black Hundreds 'explained' political decisions that they found incomprehensible, by asserting that the court had been 'hypnotized by the holy man', who was surrounded by 'foreigners [*inorodtsy*] and spies'. At times this position was tinged with anti-Semitism: 'Our sovereign is as stupid as a calf', a certain shopkeeper asserted in June 1915, 'he is surrounded only by Yids and Germans, who are his officers and commanders.'[115] It is indicative that in certain rumors and anti-Rasputin texts particular members of the Imperial family figure as positive characters – Nikolai Nikolaevich, Dmitrii Pavlovich, Maria Fedorovna and Mikhail Aleksandrovich.[116] This also serves as indirect evidence that the rumor-mongers were well versed in the ins and outs of the court and that the rumors therefore had emerged in a monarchist milieu. High-society salons frequently generated gossip. The tsaritsa herself complained, not without justification, that this Fronde remained unpunished. Grand Duke Aleksandr Mikhailovich recalled high-society ladies 'who spent entire days going from house to house spreading vile rumors about the tsar and tsaritsa'. Government minister V.I. Gurko wrote about the revolutionary impact of these rumors as they filtered into mass consciousness: 'What was uttered in high society was eventually passed on to other social circles in both capitals and then, via grimy footmen and butlers, it filtered down to the popular masses where decidedly revolutionary work was carried out.'[117] We might add that the very fact that rumors were circulating among the élite served as a guarantee of their reliability to the masses. At the same time, it can hardly be said that the rumors always spread in one direction – some, for instance, arose among the peasantry.

During World War I, it was the regime itself which sparked the emergence of rumors: the teaching of Germanophobia and spy hysteria prepared the ground for the most fantastic concoctions.[118] While the main enemy was perceived to be Germany, the ethnic German Russians came to be viewed as the 'the enemy within'. Generals and officers 'explained' defeats by betrayal 'at the top', and soldiers suspected everyone bearing a German last name.

Public opinion rationalized military defeats and shortages of arms, ammunition and food in terms of enemy intrigue. The removal of several generals with German last names confirmed, it would seem, these suspicions. The arrest and execution in March of 1915 of police colonel S.N. Miasoedov, who had been unjustly accused by headquarters of spying, induced many skeptics into believing these rumors.[119] After the arrest of war minister V.A. Sukhomlinov even cautious contemporaries were prepared to believe the most fantastic rumors. Society proclaimed him a 'traitor' long before the completion of the investigation, as did certain memoirists including Kerenskii. The foreign press wrote that: 'if his case is investigated publicly, it will uncover horrible things'. Sukhomlinov was accused even of participation in the assassination of P.A. Stolypin.[120] Thus, his release intensified suspicion toward the authorities. The reason for military failures was sought in the tsar's entourage, and it was the tsaritsa and Rasputin who were the first to be blamed.[121]

Speeches in print and in the State Duma were often based on conjecture and the censoring of such publications. The censorship was perceived as proof of their veracity, sparking a new wave of rumors. Especially influential was the speech given by Pavel Miliukov on 1 November 1916, which was perceived as a charge of treason directed at the 'young empress'. In numerous apocryphal renditions of his speech disseminated throughout the country, these and other accusations were formulated in extremely strong language.

It was even presumed that the organizers of events aimed at oppressing the 'German spirit' did so with the conscious goal of discrediting the empress.[122] However, the tsaritsa herself contributed to the spread of these rumors. She suspected prominent officials at headquarters of treason and informed Nicholas II, fearing that the 'spies' would 'let the Germans know'.[123] Germanophobia arose during the February Revolution when many officers were fired, and ultimately killed, merely for the fact that their last names sounded German to the soldiers. The Revolution itself was perceived by many contemporaries as an anti-German coup, as liberation from the age-old foreign yoke and as a victory over the 'internal German', in the interest of victory over the 'external German'.[124] New exposés made during the days of revolution were treated as revelations. Soldiers of the First Guard Division stated to German propagandists: 'Now we know that the purpose of the old regime was to give aid to Germany.'[125]

The 'patriotic' mood affected mass culture as well, endowing detective novels and stories of the life of 'high society' with a xenophobic hue. A flood of publications such as *Secrets of the House of Hollenzollern* and *Secrets of the Viennese Court* created a defined genre, foreshadowing the appearance of *Secrets of the House of Romanov*.[126] The laws of the market prompted the authors of cheap literature to take into account the interests and inclinations of the potential audience; therefore rumors influenced the texts. The very same publishing house followed the release of the book *The Secret Powers of Love*, with the publication of *Secrets of the House of Romanov*.

Anti-German propaganda during the war years was often intertwined with revolutionary propaganda and usually contained an element of xenophobia – above all Germanophobia (this theme can be traced from the time of the Decembrists).

As we have seen, revolutionaries of various sorts often wrote about 'treason from on high', using to their advantage the atmosphere of espionage hysteria and xenophobia. While the police tried to accuse worker and socialist organization activists of collaboration with the enemy, the 'leftists' were using this tactic as well. A letter from Aleksander Kerenskii addressed to Duma Chairman M.V. Rodzianko claiming that 'treason has nested in the Ministry of Internal Affairs' was widely circulated in 1915.[127]

Even the 'patriotic' anti-German pogrom of May 1915 in Moscow was partially directed against the regime, and especially against the empress: the crowds headed toward the residence of her sister, Grand Duchess Elizaveta Fedorovna, on the assumption that she was hiding 'German princes', and had secret telephone links with Germany. While some internationalist organizations wanted to prevent the anti-German pogrom, others tried to steer it in the direction of political protest.Contemporaries perceived the unrest as the 'beginning of the revolution'.[128]

The majority of rumors had no basis in reality, but in the context of the growing crisis they became factors of political significance. While German propaganda claimed that actual power in Russia belonged to 'British agents', many influential Russian politicians and certain diplomats sincerely held that Russia was already secretly governed by German agents. Foreign journalists for their part believed that an enemy agency was controlling Russian censorship.[129] Political decisions were made on the basis of such assessments. Both the regime and the opposition found themselves at times victims of their own propaganda campaigns. This was characteristic, moreover, not only of Russia. An epidemic of paranoia seized all the belligerent countries. In Germany, for example, leaflets were spread claiming that the chancellor ... had been bought by the British.[130]

The psychological state of Russian society on the eve of February is reminiscent of the era of the French Revolution: rumors about the queen galvanized the country.[131] The 'decadent Austrian woman' was accused of marital infidelity and treason. Countless pamphlets in the genre of 'political pornography', decorated with openly obscene illustrations, flooded France. The queen was held accountable in court not only for crimes against the nation, but also for corrupting her own son. Her real and assumed lovers (both men and women) were sought out and executed. In those rumors Marie Antoinette completely overshadowed the figure of the 'weak-willed' king who was considered by popular hearsay to be impotent. The rumors were directed against the supposed influence of women at court, and the exquisite decadence of the élite was juxtaposed to the health and morals of the 'common folk'.

Still, the tone of Russian political pornography was more subdued than that of eighteenth-century France. Images classified as 'pornography' would have appeared quite innocent to Frenchmen during the era of the Great Revolution (and to Russians in the 1990s). S.P. Mel'gunov quite rightly notes that even Russian 'gutter literature did not reach the level of vileness and slander that can be seen in the demagoguery of the "Great French Revolution"'.[132]

Nonetheless, in the Russian and French situations there was much in common, and this did not escape the attention of contemporaries. S. Hoare recalled that the main disseminators of rumors and the most vicious critics of the regime were representatives of Russian high society. They reminded him of French courtiers in the era of Louis XVI who spread rumors about the royal family.[133] There are even more strikingly substantive parallels. It is unlikely that the enemies of the regime consciously based their activities on the French model. It would be more reasonable to suppose that myths of conspiracy, xenophobia, sex and religion are universal ingredients in the explosive ideological mixture inevitably created in times of deep crisis, without which a spontaneous mass movement cannot occur. Both in France and in Russia, we might note that, through their incompetence and tactlessness, the main figures in the rumors actually promoted their emergence and development.

***

A study of rumors makes it possible to offer certain observations with regard to the political and cultural situation in an era of revolution. In the given case we cannot in any way counterpose 'high' and 'low' cultures, the culture of the educated 'élites' and the dark 'masses'. Of course, many well-bred contemporaries rejected the coarse pornographic and so-called pornographic mass culture. But they also, at times, facilitated the dissemination of these very same rumors, which then made possible the appearance of corresponding texts, images and theatrical productions. Both the 'élites' and the 'masses' here appear as bearers of different versions of the same authoritarian patriarchal political culture.

Anti-monarchist rumors were an indicator of the severity of the crisis of the regime, but they themselves became a factor exacerbating this crisis. On the eve of the Revolution, rumors united a heterogeneous society, bringing together seemingly irreconcilable forces – monarchists and republicans, socialists and liberals, supporters and opponents of the war. The image of the tsar and the tsaritsa in 'reliable' rumors contradicted the official conception of patriotism. The characters in the rumors posed a challenge, as it were, to the religious and political convictions of many confirmed monarchists, who, in this atmosphere, quickly became radicalized. State Duma member I.V. Godnev received a report from Kazan: 'Those formerly on the far right are now sliding to the left, passing by the center. I have personally heard from both members of the intelligentsia and simple people on the far right the admission that they were not praying to the right gods, as well as requests to obtain Miliukov's speech from somewhere and so forth.'[134] Evidence of the radicalization of the right can be found in some letters sent to the leader of the Kadets. One correspondent calls Miliukov 'the savior of society', who struggles with people 'openly loyal in their hearts to German influence'. The author mentions Sukhomlinov, Rasputin, Trepov, Protopopov and Kurlov. But at the same time, these particular enemies of Russia are described with the help of terms characteristic of the vocabulary of the far right: 'people of hell', 'satanic forces', 'dark, unclean forces'.[135] In a short time, yesterday's antagonists found a common enemy in the face of the elusive and all-powerful 'dark forces'.

The rumors, which were 'confirmed' after the overthrow by numerous publications and productions, made the restoration of the monarchy impossible. They also provoked an unusually hostile, merciless attitude toward 'traitors'. The well-known mathematician V.A. Steklov wrote in his diary of 10 March:

> Gradually the vile picture of filth and decadence at court is being uncovered! ... Just like Rome during the renaissance – only worse! Such a mass of bloody villainy, deceit, provocation ... words fail me. These are monsters in human form and not people. And they still stand on ceremony with them! They've abolished the death penalty. They should have been told that they were sentenced to death, locked up in Tsarskoe Selo and held in perpetual anticipation, so as to bring them to the brink of insanity. And then string them up like no-good vermin later! And even executing them would not be enough of a punishment!

It should be noted that the author of these lines adhered to quite moderate, at times conservative political views,[136] which influenced the attitude toward the unfortunate Imperial family: thus, even the news of their murder in Ekaterinburg for a time did not evoke indignation.[137]

Memory of the rumors influenced the development of political consciousness after February. The myth of a conspiracy of 'dark forces', German agents and spies was drawn upon in attempts to compromise the Bolsheviks. Thus, dwelling on the theme of Rasputin carried a certain propagandistic weight: the tsar, tsaritsa and Rasputin were the main supporters of peace with Germany, and therefore all opponents of the war could be added to the 'dark forces'. In November, for example, the Kadets compared Lenin and Trotsky to Shtiurmer and Rasputin.[138]

However the experience of desacralization of monarchy was especially palpable in rumors about Kerenskii in the autumn of 1917. Here we find literally the same ideological configuration, and, above this, the myth of conspiracy. Internationalists accused Kerenskii, together with British and the French imperialists, of conspiring against the Revolution. On the right it was claimed that German agents had long been manipulating the revolutionary premier, that he had actually already negotiated a truce and was secretly collaborating with the Bolsheviks.[139] At the same time, rumors were spread about his nationality and moral character: Kerenskii the 'Jew', 'the syphilitic' and 'drug addict' who arranged orgies in the Winter Palace. An analyst in the British Ministry of War wrote: 'power has gone to Kerenskii's head. He has divorced his wife, found himself a ballerina and sleeps in the empress' bed.'[140]

Moreover, a certain resemblance in the fates of the former emperor and Kerenskii was emphasized. A *chastushka* (peasant rhyme) from 1917 exclaimed:

Na stole stoit tarelka	On the table lies a plate
A v tarelke vinograd	And on the plate there lie some grapes
Nikolai prodal Rossiiu	Nicholas sold out Russia
A Kerenskii – Petrograd.[141]	And Kerensky, Petrograd.

While the anti-dynastic patriarchal rumors emphasized in every way the unmanliness of the tsar, the 'leftist' and 'rightist' rumors in the autumn of 1917 draw exactly the same feminine image of 'Aleksandra Fedorovna' Kerensky, sleeping in the empress's bed, dressed in women's clothing (the uniform of a sister of mercy!) and so forth.

Naturally, in this and other cases, such rumors contain much more information about the bearers of the rumors than about their central characters. A study of rumors and the mass culture that permeated them make it possible to better understand the archetypes of political consciousness. To all appearances they were held in common among many political antagonists. Various, often hostile, ideologies overlie deep structures of authoritarian patriarchal consciousness. Thus, among many participants in the democratic revolution, an anti-monarchist consciousness could be combined with monarchist mentality. Dissatisfaction with the 'pseudo' tsar often served as the starting point for the radicalization of consciousness.

The rumors remained deeply entrenched in mass historical consciousness and were utilized in politicized historical works of the most diverse sorts. For example, in Stalin's USSR they created an atmosphere of spy hysteria necessary for mass repression. 'Sukhomlinov fulfilled the task of German espionage', proclaimed Stalin's *Short Course*, 'to disrupt the supply of shells to the front, not to send cannons, not to send rifles to the front. Certain tsarist ministers and generals themselves quietly aided the success of the German army: together with the tsaritsa, who was connected with the Germans, they gave out military secrets to the Germans.'[142] Here, as we see, rumors from the period of World War I are 'validated' after the February Revolution by mass culture.

NOTES

1. A.I. Spiridovich, *Velikaia voina i Fevral'skaia revoliutsii, 1914–1917 gg.* (New York: Vseslavianskoe izdatel'stvo, 1960), Vol. 2, p. 123.
2. B.B. Grave (ed.), *Burzhuaziia nakanune Fevral'skoi revoliutsii* (Moscow/Leningrad: Gos. izd., 1927), pp. 125–6.
3. A.F. Kerensky, *The Catastrophe: Kerensky's Own Story of the Russian Revolution* (New York/London: D. Appleton, 1927), p. 3.
4. *Ulozhenie o nakazaniiakh ugolovnykh i ispravitel'nykh 1885 goda*. 18th edn, revised and enlarged (Petrograd: N.S. Tagantsev, 1916), pp. 338–9.
5. E.N. Tarnovskii, 'Statisticheskie svedeniia ob osuzhdennykh za gosudarstvennye prestupleniia v 1905–1912 gg', *Zhurnal ministerstva iustitsii* 10 (1915), pp. 43, 47, 63–4.
6. Rossiiskii gosudarstvennyi istoricheskii arkhiv (RGIA), f. 1405, op. 521, d. 476; *Burzhuaziia nakanune Fevral'skoi revoliutsii*, p. 77.
7. RGIA, f. 1101, op. 1, d. 1140, l. 9 (verso). The document is dated 13 Dec. 1915.
8. The call number is 34.106.8.188.
9. *Burzhuaziia nakanune Fevral'skoi revoliutsii*, pp. 77–9.
10. RGIA, f. 1101, op. 1, d. 1140, l. 20 (verso). The theme was developed in the satirical literature of 1917. There were even proposals for an epitaph to the 'Imperial family's member' Aiaks (A. Ia. Sip-s'), 'Son starogo biurokrata', *Moriak* 8 (1917), p. 188.
11. E. Kuskova, 'Liudi Fevralia i Oktiabria', *Novoe russkoe slovo*, 24 March 1957; *Pravye partii: Dokumenty i materialy*. (Moscow: Rosspen, 1998), Vol. 2, 1911–1917 gg., p. 645.
12. *Russkoe slovo*, 4 March 1917.
13. *Amurskoe ekho* (Blagoveshchensk, 29 March 1917); Morglis Umora, 'Akafist Grigoriiu Rasputinu – Novykh, pamiat' koego prazdnyetsia v 17-i den' dekabria mesiatsa', *Trepach* 1 (1917), p. 14; *Vsemirnyi iumor* 14 (1917), p. 2.
14. Illiodor (Sergei Trufanov), *Sviatoi chert: Zapiski o Rasputine*, 2nd edn. (Moscow, 1917), p. IX.
15. See *Istoricheskii vestnik*, Vol. 148, 1917, pp. 609–11.
16. 'V pogone za sensatsii', *Rech'*, 7 May 1917; S.P. Mel'gunov, *Sud'ba imperatora Nikolaia II posle otrecheniia* (New York: Teleks, 1991), pp. 147–8; A. Ia. Avrekh, 'Chrezvychainaia

RUMORS AND 'POLITICAL PORNOGRAPHY' DURING WWI

Sledstvennaia Komissiia Vremennogo pravitel'stva: Zamysel i ispolnenie', *Istoricheskie zapiski* 118 (1990), pp. 72–101; E. Fon Maidel', 'Roman Romanovich fon Raupakh', p. 41, Columbia University, Bakhmetieff Archive, Raupakh Papers, Box 1: this particular publication specialized in exposing the empress. See Evgenii Novyi, 'Rossiiskoe pozorishche', *Rossiiskaia respublika* 1 (1917); Evgenii Novyi, 'Tsentral'naia stantsiia shpionazha', *Rossiiskaia respublika* 2 (1917).

17. S. Kshesinskii, *Sviatoi chert (Imperatritsa Aleksandra i Grigorii Rasputin: Istoricheskii roman v 2 chastiakh)* (Moscow, 1917).
18. Information on print runs is taken from *Knizhnoi letopisi*, 1917.
19. *Russkoe slovo*, 7 April 1917.
20. Rossiiskii gosudarstvennyi arkhiv literatury i iskusstva (RGALI), f. 131, op. 3, d. 483, l. 14.
21. OR IRLI (Otdel rukopisei instituta russkoi literatury), f. 654, op. 5, d. 6, l. 10; L. Zhdanov, *Nikolai 'Romanov' – poslednyi tsar': Istoricheskie nabroski* (Petrograd, 1917), p. 95; G.P. [Colonel G.G. Perets], *V tsitadeli russkoi revoliutsii (Zapiski kamendanta Tavricheskogo Dvortsa, 27 fevralia–23 marta 1917 g.)* (Petrograd: Prosveshchenie, 1917) (1997 reprint edn), p. 109. In May 1917 a medical commission conducted a special examination of Vyrubova and confirmed her virginity. Mel'gunov, *Sud'ba imperatora Nikolai II posle otrecheniia*, p. 130.
22. V. Bezpalov, *Teatry v dni revoliutsii* (Leningrad: Akademia, 1927), p. 38; *Russkaia muzykal'naia gazeta* 25/26 (1917), column 420; *Petrogradskaia gazeta*, 14 June 1917; A.A. Blok, *Dnevnik*, A.L. Grishuni (ed.) (Moscow: Sov. Rossii, 1989), p. 211.
23. Mel'gunov, *Sud'ba imperatora Nikolaia II posle otrecheniia*, p. 67; Blok, *Dnevnik*, p. 211; A.L. Bardovskii, *Teatral'nyi zritel' na fronte v kanun Oktiabria* (Leningrad, 1928), p. 61; E. Svift (Anthony Swift), 'Kul'turnoe stroitel'stvo ili kul'turnaia razrukha? (Nekotorye aspekty teatral'noi zhizni Petrograda i Moskvy v 1917 g.)', *Anatomiia revoliutsii: 1917 god v Rossii: Massy, partii, vlast'* (St Petersburg: Glagol, 1994), p. 402–3. *Rampa i zhizn'* 10/11 (1917), p. 1; 13 (1917), pp. 1, 5; 22 (1917), p. 9.
24. V. Rosolovskaia, *Russkaia kinematografiia v 1917 g.: Materialy k istorii* (Moscow/Leningrad, 1937), p. 57. *Sine-fono* 11/12 (1917), pp. 16–17, 28–9, 35, 39, 74, 119; *Proektor* 7–8 (1917), pp. 9–10. The contemporary press gives a sketch of such screenings. See Zriachii, 'Grishka na ekrane', *Vsemirnaia nov'*, 21 (1917), p. 15.

In the early 1890s Matil'da Feliksovna Kshesinskaia (1872–1971), a ballerina, was the lover of the heir to the throne and future Tsar, Nikolai Aleksandrovich. During WWI rumors circulated that Kshesinskaia was passing Russian military secrets to the enemy. Sergei Nikolaevich Miasoedov (1865–1915) was a police colonel. In December 1914 he was tried in the field by a military court for espionage and looting. The court found Miasoedov guilty and sentenced him to hang. GHQ applied considerable pressure to convict: faced with an indignant public, the defeat of the Russian Army was attributed to machinations by spies. Vladimir Aleksandrovich Sukhomlinov (1848–1926) was a general and minister of war from 1909 to 1915. The public viewed Sukhomlinov as the primary culprit in Russia's lack of preparedness for war. (Many even felt that he was in cahoots with the enemy.) He was subjected to an inquest to answer charges of 'criminal negligence', 'exceeding authority', 'fraud', 'extortion' and 'high treason' and subsequently arrested. The trial, which took place after the February Revolution, did not uphold the majority of the charges. However, Sukhomlinov was found guilty of failing to prepare the army for war. He was sentenced to an indefinite period of forced labor. Following the Bolshevik rise to power on 1 May 1918, Sukhomlinov was given amnesty on the grounds that he had reached the age of 70. He later emigrated.

25. A.M. Flit, 'Ee velichestvo poshlost', *Russkaia stikhotvornaia satira 1908–1917 godov*, I.S. Eventov (ed.) (Leningrad: Sovetskii pisatel', 1974), p. 582.
26. *Proektor* 7/8 (1917), p. 12; 9/10 (1917), pp. 14–15; 13/14 (1917), pp. 7–8; 17/18 (1917), p. 4; Teatral, 'Kak borot'sia s pornograficheskimi p'eskami', *Petrogradskaia gazeta*, 10 June 1917; 'Tsenzura zrelishch', *Petrogradskaia gazeta*, 1 Aug. 1917.
27. N.A. Epanchin, *Na sluzhbe trekh imperatorov* (Moscow: Nashe nasledie, 1996), p. 226; 'Russkaia armiia nakanune revoliutsii', *Byloe* 1 (1918), p. 153. It should be noted that, before being presented to the empress, the Samara Provincial Marshal of the Nobility, future Minister of Agriculture A.N. Naumov, specially asked a courtier: 'Can a Russian

Marshal of the Nobility being received by the Russian tsaritsa speak in Russian?' A.N. Naumov, *Iz utselevshikh vospominanii, 1868–1917* (New York, 1954), Vol. 2, p. 40.
28. V. Chebotareva, 'V dvortsovom lazarete v Tsarsom Sele', *Novyi Zhurnal*, Book 182 (1990), p. 205.
29. RGIA, f. 1405, op. 521, d. 476, l. 97 (verso); 106; House of Lords Record Office, Historical Collection 313. This excerpt was not included in the published diary of Lockhart: Sir Robert Bruce Lockhart, *The Diaries of Sir Robert Bruce Lockhart*, Vol. 1: 1915–1938, Kenneth Young (ed.) (London: Macmillan, 1973).
30. V.P. Semennikov (ed.), *Dnevnik b[yvshego] velikogo kniazia Andreia Vladimirovicha* (Leningrad: Gos. izd., 1925), p. 84–5; A.W.F. Knox, *With the Russian Army* (London: Hutchinson & Co., 1921), Vol. 2, p. 515.
31. Sir George Buchanan, *My Mission to Russia and Other Diplomatic Memoirs* (London/New York: Cassell and Co., 1923), Vol. 2, p. 56.
32. P. Sadikov (ed.), 'K istorii poslednykh dnei tsarskogo rezhima (1916–1917)', *Krasnyi arkhiv* 14 (1926), pp. 242, 246.
33. Ibid.; G.N. Mikhailovskii, *Zapiski: Iz istorii vneshnopoliticheskogo vedomstva, 1914–1920 gg.*, Book 1: Avgust 1914–oktiabr' 1917 g. (Moscow: Mezhdunarodnye otnosheniia, 1993), pp. 142–3; 'Russkaia armiia nakanune revoliutsii', *Byloe* 1 (1918), p. 152, 155–6; 'Oktiabr'skaia revoliutsiia v Baltiiskom flote (Iz dnevnika I.I. Rengartena)', in A. Drezen (ed.), *Krasnyi arkhiv* 25 (1927), p. 34; P.G. Kurlov, *Gibel' imperatorskoi Rossii* (Moscow: Sovremennik, 1991), p. 243.
34. A. Maksimov (ed.), *Tsar'skaia armiia v period Mirovoi voiny i Fevral'skoi revoliutsii (materialy k izucheniiu istorii imperialisticheskoi i grazhdanskoi voiny)*, (Kazan', 1932), pp. 150–2; *Vsemirnyi iumor* 12 (1917), p. 11; J.W. Long, *From Privileged to Dispossessed: The Volga Germans, 1860–1917* (Lincoln, NE/London: University of Nebraska, 1988), p. 229; F. Koch, *The Volga Germans in Russia and the Americas* (London: University Park, 1977), p. 240; O. Chaadaeva *et al.* (eds), *Bol'sheviki v gody imperialisticheskoi voiny, 1914–fevral' 1917: Sbornik dokumentov mestnykh bol'shevistskikh organizatsii* (Moscow/Leningrad, 1939), p. 48; RGIA, f. 1405, op. 521, d. 476, l. 146 (verso).
35. R. Messi (Robert Massey), *Nikolai i Aleksandra* (Moscow, 1992), pp. 301–2; Epanchin, *Na sluzhbe trekh imperatorov*, p. 471; On the hostile relations between officers and the empress see also V. Chebotareva, 'V dvortsovom lazarete v Tsarskoe Selo', *Novyi zhurnal* Book 181 (1990), p. 239.
36. Otdel rukopisei Instituta russkoi literatury (Pushkinskii dom) (OR IRLI), f. 654, op. 5, d. 2, l. 4; d. 9, l. 1.
37. *Tainy russkogo dvora: Poslednie chasy tsarstvovaniia Nikolaia II* (Khar'kov, 1917), p. 1. However, part of the Guards Officer Corps was actually caught up in the ferment. The Menshevik A.E. Diubua recalled that several regular officers of the Pavlov Regiment met with him and reported their unwillingness to participate in the suppression of the popular uprising. They requested that the leaders of the revolutionary organizations be informed of this. A.E. Diubua, 'V bol'nitse i v kazarme', *Arkhiv Amsterdamskogo Instituta sotsial'noi istorii*.
38. Spiridovich, *Velikaia voina i Fevral'skaia revoliutsiia*, Book 2, pp. 92, 106, 169; *Perepiska Nikolaia i Aleksandry Romanovykh*, Vol. 4, 1916 (Moscow/Leningrad: Gos. izd., 1926), p. 289.
39. Wren's Library (Trinity College, Cambridge), Lawton Papers, Box 28-14. Allied Conference at Petrograd, January–February 1917. Report on Mission to Russia by Major David Davies, MP, pp. 1–3.
40. V.V. Shul'gin, *Dni* (Leningrad, 1926), p. 108; V.N. Voeikov, *S tsarem i bez tsaria: Vospominaniia poslednego dvortsovogo komendanta gosudaria-imperatora Nikolaia II* (Moscow: Rodnik, 1994), pp. 166–7; A.F. Kerensky, *Russia and History's Turning Point* (New York: Duell, Sloan and Pearce, 1965), pp. 147, 150, 159, 160.
41. Lord Bertie to Lord Hardinge, Cambridge University Library, Manuscript Room, Hardinge Papers, Vol. 31, pp. 165; A. Argunov, *Iz proshlogo*, p. 38, Columbia University Library, Bakhmetieff Archive, Kovarsky Papers, Box no. 1. The text in brackets was crossed out.

42. V.N. Sidel'nikov, 'Narodnoe poeticheskoe tvorchestvo predoktiabr'skogo desiatiletiia (1907–1917 gody)', *Russkoe narodnoe poeticheskoe tvorchestvo* (Moscow/Leningrad, 1956), Vol. II, Book 2, p. 440.
43. Knox, *With the Russian Army*, p. 577. E. Fon Maidel', 'Roman Romanovich fon Raupakh', p. 40; I. Trufanov, *Tainy doma Romanovykh* (Moscow, 1917), pp. 53, 128–31; Mel'gunov, *Sud'ba imperatora Nikolaia II posle otrecheniia*, pp. 68, 69, 146–7; Messi, *Nikolai i Aleksandra*, pp. 308–9.
44. I. Kovyl'-Bobyl', *Tsaritsa i Rasputin* (Petrograd, 1917), pp. 5–6.
45. Messi, *Nikolai i Aleksandra*, pp. 300–1.
46. Buchanan, *My Mission to Russia*, Vol. 2, p. 56.
47. *Tainy Tsarskosel'skogo dvortsa* (Petrograd, 1917), p. 15; Trufanov, *Tainy doma Romanovykh*, p. 88.
48. *Chto teper' poet Nikolai Romanov i ego Ko* (Kiev, 1917), p. 1.
49. Spiridovich, *Velikaia voina i Fevral'skaia revoliutsiia*, Book 2, p. 106; M. Paleolog, *Tsarskaia Rossiia nakanune revoliutsii* (Moscow, 1991), pp. 208–9, 228.
50. RGIA, f. 472, op. 40, d. 47, l. 9.
51. Kshesinskii, *Sviatoi chert*, pp. 25, 159; S. Iakovlev, *Poslednie dni Nikolaia II (Ofitsial'nye dokumenty, rasskazy ochevidtsev)*, 2nd edn (Petrograd, 1917), p. 24.
52. Mikhailovskii, *Zapiski: Iz istorii Rossiiskogo vneshnepoliticheskogo vedomstva*, Book 1, p. 149.
53. *Taina doma Romanovykh* (vyp 1): *Favoritki Nikolaia II* (Petrograd, 1917), p. 16; Trudanov, *Tainy doma Romanovykh*, p. 83; *Tainy russkogo dvora* (Vol. 2), p. 2; *Tsar' bez golovy* (Petrograd, 1917), p. 1; *Tainy doma Romanovykh* (Petrograd, 1917) (Al'manakh svobody, Vol. 2), p. 12.
54. *Trepach* 1 (1917), p. 11.
55. Shul'gin, *Dni*, p. 108. The awarding of medals to the tsar often elicited a sharply negative response. A shell-shocked veteran was put on trial for these words: 'Hah! Why did they not give four crosses right away instead of just one.' RGIA, f. 1405, op. 521, d. 476, l. 26.
56. Private collection of A.M. Lutsenko, St Petersburg. The author is indebted to Mr Lutsenko for granting him access to these documents.
57. A.A. Blok, after a conversation with an investigator of the Extraordinary Investigative Commission, wrote in his diary: 'He [Rasputin] didn't sleep either with the empress or with Vyrubova.' Blok, *Dnevnik*, p. 213. We can assume that up to this point the author did not perceive rumors about the liaison of the tsaritsa and the 'holy man' as manifestly absurd.
58. Z.N. Gippius, 'Sovremmenaia zapis'', Otdel rukopisei Rossiiskoi natsional'noi biblioteki (OR RNB), f. 481, op. 1, d. 1, l. 62 (verso).
59. Mikhailovskii, *Zapiski: Iz istorii Rossiiskogo vneshnepoliticheskogo vedomstva*, Book 1, p. 149; S.P. Mel'gunov, *Vospominaniia i dnevniki* (Paris: Réunis, 1964), Vol. 1, pp. 201, 214.
60. Al'bionov, *Zhitie nepodobnogo startsa Grigoriia Rasputina* (Petrograd, 1917), p. 7; *Grishka Rasputina* (Al'manakh svobody, Vol. 1) (Petrograd, 1917), p. 2; Zhdanov, *Nikolai 'Romanov' – poslednyi tsar'*, pp. 99–100.
61. 'The tsaritsa engaged in debauchery with Vyrubova and Rasputin.' *Nikolai II-oi Romanov: Ego zhizn' i deiatel'nost', 1894–1914 gg. (Po inostrannym i russkim istochnikam)* (Petrograd, 1917), p. 70.
62. *Kazn' Grishki Rasputina* (Almanakh svobody, Vol. 1), p. 16.
63. A.A. Mosolov, *Pri dvore poslednogo imperatora (Zapiski nachal'nika kantseliarii ministerstva dvora)* (St Petersburg, 1992), pp. 98–9; Spiridovich, *Velikaia voina i Fevral'skaia revoliutsiia*, Book 3, p. 74.
64. RGIA, f. 1470, op. 2, d. 102, l. 158.
65. RGIA, f. 1405, op. 521, d. 476, l. 390.
66. S. Rafal'skii, *Chto bylo i chego ne bylo* (London: Overseas Publication Interchange, 1984), pp. 21, 37, 48–9; *Tsarskaia armiia v period Mirovoi voiny i Fevral'skoi revoliutsii ...*, pp. 36, 42, 43, 166; RGIA, f. 1470, op. 2, d. 102, l. 473. In a typical episode, a group of indignant officers went to the general: 'The chiefs are at a picnic with the sisters of

mercy, and they're all whores!' The general objected that his own wife also worked in the hospital. The officers were somewhat taken aback, but held their ground. F.I. Rodichev, *Vospominaniia i ocherki o russkom liberalizme* (Newtonville: Oriental Research Partners, 1983), p. 119.
67. RGIA, f. 1405, op. 521, d. 476, l. 481–481 (verso).
68. Messi, *Nikolai i Aleksandra*, p. 301.
69. 'Oktiabr'skaia revoliutsiia v Baltiiskom flote (Is dnevnika I.I. Rengarten)', A. Drezen, (ed.), *Krasnyi arkhiv* 25 (1927), p. 34; *Tainy doma Romanovykh*, Vol. 2, p. 6; *Tainy russkogo dvora*, Vol. 2; *Tsar' bez golovy*, p. 1; Trufanov, *Tainy doma Romanovykh*, p. 92.
70. 'K istorii poslednykh dnei tsarskogo regima (1916–1917 gg.)', *Krasnykh arkhiv*, 14 (1926); Paleolog, *Tsarskaia Rossiia nakanune revoliutsii*, p. 298.
71. Knox, *With the Russian Army*, p. 558; H. Pitcher (ed.), *Witnesses of the Russian Revolution* (London: John Murray, 1994), p. 24; I. Markov, 'Kak proizoshla russkaia revoliutsiia', *Rassvet*, 27 Nov. 1937.
72. V.E. Burdzhalov, *Vtoraia russkaia revoliutsiia: Vosstanie v Petrograde* (Moscow: Nauka, 1967), pp. 373–4; T. Hasegawa, *The February Revolution: Petrograd, 1917* (Seattle, WA: University of Washington Press, 1981), p. 220.
73. Burdzhalov, *Vtoraia russkaia revoliutsiia*, p. 67; Trufanov, *Tainy doma Romanovykh*, p. 135; *Kazn' Grishki Rasputina*, p. 13; Illiodor, *Sviatoi chert: Zapiski o Rasputine*, p. 94.
74. S. S. Ol'denburg, *Tsarstvovanie imperatora Nikolaia II* (St Petersburg, 1991), pp. 577–9.
75. *Buzhuaziia nankanune Fevral'skoi revoliutsii*, p. 64.
76. A. Iakhontov, 'Pervyi god voiny (Iiul' 1914–Iiul' 1915 g.): Zapisi, zametki, materialy i vospominaniia byvshego pomoshchnika upravliaiushchego delami Soveta ministrov', R.Sh. Ganelina, M.F. Florinskogo (eds), *Russkoe proshloe: Istoriko-dokumental'nyi al'manakh* (St Petersburg, 1996), Book 7, p. 326; P.E. Shchegolev (ed.), *Padenie tsarskogo rezhima: Stenograficheskie otchety i pokazaniia, dannye v 1917 g. v Chrezvychainoi sledstvennoi komissii Vremennogo pravitel'stva* (Leningrad, 1925), Vol. 3, p. 166. A.A. Blok, who worked in the commission, wrote down the works of Komissarov as such: 'Rasputin was the chancellor. The Minister of Internal Affairs, Shtiurmer, was subordinate to him in all matters.' OR IRLI, f. 654, op. 5, d. 13, l. 1 (verso).
77. RGIA, f. 1282, op. 2, d. 1983, ll. 17, 44, 48. It is possible that the text is referring to S.V. Vostrotin, the Kadet deputy from Yenisei Province.
78. Cited in Mel'gunov, *Sud'ba imperatora Nikolaiia posle otrecheniia*, p. 148.
79. V.I. Lenin, *Polnoe sobranie sochinenii*, 5th edn (Moscow: Gos. Izdatel'stvo polit. Literatury, 1958), Vol. 31, pp. 12, 297.
80. V.V. Lapshin, *Khudozhestvennaia zhizn' Moskvy i Petrograda v 1917 godu* (Moscow: Sovetskii Khudozhnik, 1983), p. 88; A.M. Lutsenko collection, St Petersburg.
81. *Dnevnik byvshego velikogo kniazia Andreia Vladimirovicha*, p. 75; *Blagorodnaia zhertva Fevral'skoi revoliutsii 1917 g. student V.I. Khlebtsevich* (Syzran, 1918), p. 60.
82. 'Russkaia armiia nakanune revoliutsii', *Byloe* 1 (1918), p. 154; Spiridovich, *Velikaia voina i Fevral'skaia revoliutsiia*, Book 2, c. 47, 48; RGIA, f. 1412, op. 16, d. 103, l. 2–2 (verso).
83. S.A. Hoare, 'A Watchman Makes His Rounds', Cambridge University Library, Manuscript Room, Templewood Papers, XXI:I, p. 52.
84. Kerensky, *Russia and History's Turning Point*, pp. 159–60; M.V. Rodzianko, 'Gosudarstvennaia Duma i Fevral'skaia 1917 g, revoliutsii', *Arkhiv russkoi revoliutsii* (Berlin, 1922) (reprint edn, Moscow: Sovremennik, 1991), Vol. 6, p. 44.
85. Buchanan, *My Mission to Russia*, p. 48; RGIA, f. 1470, op. 2, d. 101, l. 37.
86. *Taina doma Romanovykh*, vyp 1: *Favoritki Nikolaia II*, p. 16.
87. A village clerk from a village in Tambov Province declared in October 1914 he was in the 'democratic party' and therefore he knew for sure how the emperor spent his time: 'He, the tsar, goes to his museum; there they stand women up on chairs and do them from the rear, and when there are none of these women to be found, the sovereign mother goes there and everyone who wants to does her.' RGIA, f. 1405, op. 521, d. 476, ll. 83 (verso)–84.

88. Gippius, 'Sovremennaia zapis", OR RNB, f. 481, op. 1, d. 1, l. 55. The text in brackets was not included in the published 'Diary'. Compare: Z.N. Gippius, *Siniaia kniga: Peterburgskii dnevnik, 1914–1918* (Belgrade, 1929), p. 246.
89. *K istorii poslednikh dnei tsarskogo rezhima (1916–1917gg)*, P. Sadikov (ed.), *Krasnyi arkhiv*, 14 (1926), p. 246.
90. Sankt-Peterburgskoe otdelenie Arkhiva Rossiiskoi Akademii nauk, f. 162 (Steklov, V.A.), op. 3, d. 168, l. 58, entry for 17 March; RGIA, f. 1412, op. 16, d. 531, l. 1. Former Grand Duke Dmitrii Pavlovich wrote on 23 April 1917: 'Just the name "Romanov", has become a synonym of all sorts of filth, mischief and indecency', *K istorii poslednikh dnei tsarskogo rezhima (1916–1917 gg)* P. Sadikov (ed.), *Krasnyi arkhiv* 14 (1926), p. 229.
91. *Burzhuaziia nakanune Fevral'skoi revoliutsii*, p. 78; *Tsarskaia armiia v period Mirovoi voiny i Fevral'skoi revoliutsii*, pp. 150–1, 152; Bayerisches Hauptstaatsarchiv (Munich), Abt. IV: Kriegsarchiv. 2 Bay. Landw. Div. Bande 5, Akt 9, 11.
92. This was how, for instance, Kerenskii regarded him. This attitude changed after personal acquaintance with the former tsar. Cited in Mel'gunov, *Sud'ba imperatora Nikolaia II posle otrecheniia*, pp. 60, 159–60.
93. A. Tyrkova-Vil'iams, *Na putiakh k svobode* (New York: Chekhov, 1952), p. 193. Compare the impressions of a peasant deputy to the Duma: 'He's a kind of unfortunate, a miserable looking wretch. What kind of sovereign is he?' P. Garvi, *Vospominaniia: Peterburg – 1906 g., Peterburg – Odessa – Vena – 1912 g.* (New York, 1961), p. 20.
94. RGIA, f. 1405, op. 521, d. 476, ll. 53, 513.
95. M. Paleolog, *Rasputin (Vospominaniia)* (Moscow, 1923) (1990 reprint edn), p. 85; L. Zhdanov, *Sud nad Nikolaiem II* (Petrograd, 1917), pp. 28–9, 31, 33, 42 and *passim*. An anecdote recorded in November 1915 is indicative: In a Moscow court a case is being tried for defamation of royalty. The peasant witness is confirming the grounds for the indictment: 'The way he carries on! I said to him myself "you're always swearing at him, the fool, but you're better off going after her, that no-good bitch".' M. Lemke, *250 dnei v tsarskoi Stavke (25 sent. 1915–2 iiulia 1916)* (Petrograd: Gos. izd, 1920), p. 261.
96. *Tsarskaia armiia v period Mirovoi voiny i Fevral'skoi revoliutsii*, pp. 108–9. The practice of poking out the eyes on portraits of the royal family was quite common. Gania the Blind was presumably the village idiot.
97. *Nikolai II-oi Romanov: Ego zhizn' i deiatel'nost', 1894–1914 gg. (Po inostrannym i russkim istochnikam)* (Petrograd, 1917), p. 72.
98. *Tainy tsarskogo dvora i Grishka Rasputin* (Moscow, 1917), pp. 4, 5.
99. Sir G. Buchanan to Lord Hardinge, Cambridge University Library, Manuscript Room, Hardinge Papers, Vol. 31, p. 214; Vol. 32, p. 249; Kerensky, *Russia and History's Turning Point*, p. 161.
100. *Tainy tsarskogo dvora i Grishka Rasputin*, p. 12; Illiodor, *Sviatoi chert: Zapiski o Rasputine*, p. 93.
101. O. Chaadaeva, *Armiia nakanune Fevral'skoi revoliutsii* (Moscow/Leningrad, 1935), p. 64.
102. A.P. Prusakov, 'Fol'klor moskovskikh rabochikh v predoktiabr'skoe desiatiletie', *Sovetskaia etnografiia* 4 (1970), p. 112. 'Fevral'skaia revoliutsiia i okhrannoe otdelenie', *Byloe* 1 (1918), p. 160.
103. P.V. Kupriianovskii, *Neizvestnyi Furmanov* (Ivanovo, 1996), pp. 51, 100.
104. See, for example, Kurlov, *Gibel' imperatorskoi Rossii*, p. 160.
105. A.G. Shliapnikov, *Kanun semnadtsatogo goda. Semnadtsatyi god.* (Moscow: Izd. polit. literatury, 1992), Vol. 1, p. 160. See also pp. 170, 173.
106. V.S. Diakin, *Russkaia burzhuaziia i tsarism v gody pervoi mirovoi voiny (1914–1917)* (Leningrad: Nauka, 1967), pp. 251–3.
107. V. Vostokov, 'Tochnye dannye k posluzhnomu spisku mitrofornogo protoieriia Vl. Vostokova', p. 4; idem, 'Izbraniia o. Vostokova v Uchreditel'noe sobranie', Columbia University Library, Bakhmetieff Archive, Vostokov Papers, Box no. 1; [N.D. Zhevakhov], *Vospominaniia tovarishcha ober-prokurora Sv. Sinoda kniazia N.D. Zhevakhova. t.*

1: *Sentiabr' 1915–mart 1917.* (Moscow, 1993), pp. 184, 207, 240, 242–3, 246–53 and *passim.*
108. Diakin, *Russkaia burzhuaziia i tsarism v gody pervoi mirovoi voiny,* p. 251. Even relatives of the tsar denounced the 'continual intrusion of dark forces in all affairs' (from a letter of Grand Duke Nikolai Mikhailovich to Nicholas II dated 1 Nov. 1916). V.P. Semennikov (ed.) *Nikolai II i velikie kniazia (Rodstvennye pis'ma k poslednemu tsariu)* (Moscow/Leningrad, 1925), p. 68.
109. V.A. Maevskii, *Na grani dvukh epokh (tragediia imperatorskoi Rossii)* (Madrid: Rafael Tara Villa Paul, 1963), p. 11; Gavriil Konstantinovich, *V mramornom dvortse: iz khroniki nashei sem'i* (New York: Chekhov, 1955), p. 285.
110. Politisches Archiv des Auswärtigen Amts (Bonn), Der Weltkrieg, Russland, 104, No. 11c, R. 20984, A. 2587, R. 20985, A. 981, R. 20986, A. 3657, 3885, R. 20987, A. 6370.
111. *Padenie tsarskogo rezhima,* Vol. 1, p. 40.
112. K.K. Zvonarev, *Agenturnaia razvedka,* Vol. 2: *Germanskaia agenturnaia razvedka do i vo vremia voiny 1914–1918 gg.* (Moscow, 1931), p. 146; M. Lemke, *250 dnei v tsarskoi Stavke (25 sent. 1915–2 iulia 1916),* pp. 561, 683.
113. Bayerisches Hauptstaatsarchiv (Munich), Abt. IV: Kriegsarchiv, Bay. Kav. Div. Abt. 1c, Band 30, Akt 4.
114. Knox, *With the Russian Army,* Vol. 2, pp. 600–1.
115. Burdzhalov, *Vtoraia russkaia revoliutsiia,* p. 67; Maevskii, *Na grani dvukh epokh,* pp. 131, 220; RGIA, f. 1405, op. 521, d. 476, l. 1.
116. See, for example, *Tainy Tsarskosel'skogo dvortsa,* p. 14; Trufanov, *Tainy doma Romanovykh,* pp. 23, 24.
117. Velikii kniaz' Aleksandr Mikhailovich, *Kniga vospominanii* (Moscow, 1991), p. 163; V.S. Diakin (ed.), *Krizis samoderzhaviia v Rossii, 1895–1917* (Leningrad, 1984), p. 639; V.I. Gurko, *Tsar' i tsaritsa* (Paris, 1927), pp. 70–1.
118. The well-known military lawyer R.R. fon Raupakh recalled that after every serious defeat of the Russian army orders came down from headquarters to the military field court to begin a new search for spies and traitors. E. fon Maidel', 'Roman Romanovich fon Raupakh', p. 33, Columbia University Library, Bakhmetieff Archive, Raupakh Papers, Box no. 1.
119. See K.F. Shatsillo, 'Delo' polkovnika Miasoedova', *Voprosy istorii* 4 (1967), pp. 103–16.
120. RGIA, f. 1470, op. 2, d. 101, ll. 9, 256, 336, 498–9; Kerensky, *The Catastrophe,* p. 39.
121. See, for example, A.F. Peshekhonova, 'Byloe: Vospominaniia 1905–1919 gg.', Otdel rukopisei Rossiiskoi natsional'noi biblioteki (OR RNB), f. 581, op. 1, d. 70, l. 99.
122. *Dnevnik b[yvshego] velikogo kniazia Andreia Vladmirovicha,* pp. 84–5.
123. *Perepiska Nikolaia i Aleksandry Romanovykh,* Vol. III: *1914–1915 gg.* (Moscow/Petrograd, 1925), pp. 212, 223, 243.
124. As early as September 1915 at an assembly of Moscow lawyers it was asserted that 'it is precisely the internal German that is not allowing us to smash the external German'. *Burzhiaziia nakanune Fevral'skoi revoliutsii,* p. 44. See also p. 129.
125. Bayerisches Hauptstaatsarchiv (Munich), Abt. IV: Kriegsarchiv, Bay. Kav. Div. Abt. 1c, Band 30, Akt 2.
126. Often, the authors who had specialized previously in the 'unmasking' of the enemy, after the February Revolution switched over to exposing the fallen regime. Compare V.I. Albanov, *Shpiony i shpionazh* (Petrograd, 1914) with idem, *Zhitie nepodobnogo startsa Grigorii Rasputina* (Petrograd, 1917). The same can be said of the writers of popular songs. Compare F. Shkulev, 'Chto ty kaizer ...', *Spite orly boevye* (Moscow, 1916) with idem, 'Chem Rus' slavilas'", *Pesni Velikoi Russkoi revoliutsii* (Moscow, 1917), p. 8.
127. RGIA, f. 1405, op. 530, d. 1127, l. 3–3 (verso). The actual author of the letter was D.V. Filosofov. The letter was used in a leaflet of the Kadet Party published in February 1915. Shliapnokov, *Kanun semnatsatogo goda,* Vol. 1, p. 168.
128. 'Ulichnye besporiadki i vystupleniia rabochikh v Rossii po dokumentam Departamenta politsii (1914–1917 g.), *Istoricheskii arkhiv,* no. 5/6 (1995), p. 68; I. Menitskii, *Revoliutsionnoe dvizhenie voennykh godov (1914–1917)* (Moscow, 1925), p. 420; Mel'gunov, *Vospominaniia i dnevniki,* Vol. 1, pp. 194, 196, 197.

129. Letter of R. Wilton, *Times* correspondent in Russia, to Lord Northcliffe, dated November 1915. The British Library Manuscript Collection, Northcliffe Papers, Add. 62253, p. 161.
130. RGIA, f. 1470, op. 2, d. 82, l. 193.
131. See Lynn Hunt (ed.), *Eroticism and the Body Politic* (Baltimore, MD/London: Johns Hopkins University Press, 1984); Lynn Hunt, 'Pornography and the French Revolution', in Lynn Hunt (ed.), *The Invention of Pornography: Obscenity and the Crisis of Modernity, 1500–1800* (New York: Zone Books, 1993), pp. 301–22. It seems that the Russian empress felt some kind of connection with the executed queen; her portrait hung in Aleksandra Fedorovna's study, and one of the rooms in her suites was decorated in the style of the era of Louis XVI. Naumov, *Iz utselevshikh vospominanii*, Vol. 2, p. 39. The tsaritsa's sister, Grand Duchess Elizaveta Fedorovna, said to her during their final meeting: 'You will end up like Marie Antoinette.'
132. Mel'gunov, *Sud'ba imperatora Nikolaia II posle otrecheniia*, p. 67. Apparently, in pre-revolutionary Russia, French pornographic items were predominant. It is indicative that works of this sort were known as the 'Parisian genre'.
133. S. Hoare, 'Three Missions: Russia, Italy, Spain', Cambridge University Library, Manuscript Room, Templewood Papers, XXI: (A)2, p. 24.
134. RGIA, f. 1282, op. 2, d. 1983, l. 19.
135. Arkhiv Doma Plekhanova, Rossiiskaia natsional'naia biblioteka, f. 482, d. 224, l. 1.
136. Sankt-Peterburgskoe otdelenie Arkhiva Rossiskoi Akademii nauk, f. 162 (Steklov, V.A.), op. 3, d. 168, l. 47 (verso).
137. M.M. Novikov, *Moia zhizn' v nauke i politike* (New York, 1952), p. 282.
138. *Oktiabr'skoe vooruzhennoe vosstanie: Semnadtsatyi god v Petrograde* (Leningrad, 1967), p. 146. The socialist press rarely turned to the topic of the intimate life of the Imperial family. Mel'gunov, *Sud'ba imperatora Nikolaia II posle otrecheniia*, p. 67. W.G. Rosenberg, *Liberals in the Russian Revolution: The Constitutional-Democratic Party, 1917–1921* (Princeton, NJ: Princeton University Press, 1974), p. 270. For an example of the merging of anti-monarchist and anti-Bolshevik propaganda see Iu. Ia. Gombart, *Predateli Rossii ili bol'sheviki Nikolaia Romanova (Etiud iz semeinoi zhizni Romanovykh v 4-ikh kartinakh)* (Petrograd, 1917).
139. Gossip of this sort reached the British Ministry of Foreign Affairs, where it was dismissed outright. Record Office (London), Foreign Office (PRO FO), 371, 3016, N 205925, pp. 544–5; N 208373, pp. 577–8; N 210021, p. 582; 3017, N 209501, pp. 10–11. For more details, see B. I. Kolonitskii, 'Britanskie missii i A.F. Kerenskii (mart–oktiabr' 1917 goda)', in A.A. Fursenko (ed.), *Rossiia v XIX–XX vv.: Sb. Statei k 70-leniiu R.Sh. Ganelin* (St Petersburg, 1998), pp. 67–76.
140. PRO, War Office, 158/964, p. 6.
141. V. Bilyi, 'Koroten'ky pisni ('chastushki') rokiv 1917 1925', *Etnografichnyi visnyk* (Kiev, 1925), Book 1, p. 30.
142. *Istoriia Vsevoiuznoi Kommunisticheskoi partii (bol'shevikov): Kratkii kurs* (Moscow, 1946), pp. 166–7. In a book intended for the command staff of the Red Army, the accusations directed at Sukhomlinov were intensified: 'With his help, the War Ministry of Russia turned into a sort of den of spies, into an organ which paralyzed the military might of the Russian Army.' D. Seidametov, N. Shliapnikov, *Germano-avstriiskaia razvedka v tsarskoi Rossii* (Moscow, 1939), p. 13. It is curious that the authors, while citing the gutter press of 1917 word for word, did not repeat the accusations directed at the supreme authority. Compare: 'During the imperialist war, at the Russian court, under the patronage of the Tsaritsa Aleksandra a group of German spies who held high-ranking posts in the Tsarist army and government was active. Among those exposed as agents carrying out espionage for the Germans were War Minister Sukhomlinov, Colonel Miasoedov, the Police official Freitag and others.' O. Chaadaeva *et al.* (eds), *Bol'sheviki i gody imperialisticheskoi voiny, 1914– fevral' 1917: Sbornik dokumentov mestnykh bol'shevistskikh organizatsii* (Moscow/Leningrad, 1939), p. 214.

3

Making Cossacks Counter-Revolutionary: The Don Host and the 1918 Anti-Soviet Insurgency

PETER HOLQUIST

In spring 1918 an insurgency carried out in the name of the Cossacks overthrew Soviet power in the Don Territory. It has become a historiographical truism that this defeat of Soviet power resulted from a Cossack uprising, in defense of Cossack privileges and in response to Bolshevik excesses. This narrative is largely a recapitulation of the account set forth for the uprising by the All-Great Don Host (AGDH), the reconstituted anti-Soviet Host government. The AGDH claimed legitimacy as the capstone of this selfsame anti-Soviet Cossack movement.[1] To cement its authority, the AGDH arrogated to itself the primary role in this insurgent narrative. In place of a diffuse rebel movement, arising in many areas without any knowledge of the Cossack leadership's existence, the Host literature portrayed the insurgency as radiating out from Novocherkassk, the Host capital.[2]

The Host's account, of course, was not simply a description of events. It inevitably encoded its own conception of who constituted the narrative's social actors, while simultaneously functioning as justification for the Host's claim to power in the region. Both at the time and in the later historiography, such narrative control was itself an effective device for consolidating the Host's claim to speak for all liberated Cossacks. Pavel Kudinov, who headed an important local insurgent movement against Soviet power one year later, in 1919, bitterly charged in his memoirs that the official AGDH histories written in emigration passed over local insurgencies in silence, because they were headed by people not tied to the Host and who held a more egalitarian ideology.[3] Western and subsequent Russian historical literature, however, has largely replicated the Host's account of the movement because it was confirmed by Cossacks; they, seeking to protect their lifestyle, arrayed themselves against the peasants, who envied their prosperity.[4]

Despite the Host's own account, the 1918 anti-Soviet insurgency on the Don was really several spontaneous uprisings. Most erupted without any central coordination and their leaders had no knowledge of the Host leadership's own struggle around Novocherkassk. When Soviet forces occupied the Don, groups of officers had gone into hiding. By April 1918 these officers were conducting a low-intensity guerrilla war against the new order. At first Cossacks treated these officers with hostility, and even fired upon them when they tried to attack local soviets.[5]

This small-scale raiding became full-scale rebellion in late April and early May, when officers managed to find a base of support in many Cossack communities. Still, it was almost exclusively officers and students rather than ordinary Cossacks who initiated it. One participant later recalled that the uprisings were originally led by 'youthful officers who had once been teachers and agronomists ... we *frontoviki* extemporized for a long time ... there was talk of neutrality and the like ... One can't hide it. In a word, officers began the thing, and the community elders fostered it. And then we began to pull our weight.'[6]

The sea change in attitudes among ordinary Cossacks is usually attributed to arrival in their communities of marauding Red Guard detachments retreating from the German advance. However, many of the insurgents' own accounts of the origins of their movement belie this description. While there was undoubtedly some pillaging in the southern districts, one observer commented that the Cherkassk *stanitsy* (Cossack communities) generally 'did not experience the Red Guards; there were no seizures of property or requisitions'. In Sal' district as well, contrary to paradigm, one writer noted that 'the Bolsheviks who occupied [the district capital Velikokniazheskaia] conducted themselves tolerably – they robbed and arrested a few people, but they did not engage in any executions or terror'.[7] Likewise, in the north, 'there were no violent occurrences: everyone knew one another and were acquainted from childhood. There were almost no cases of "confiscations"'. Soviet forces established a military revolutionary tribunal in Ust'-Medveditsa, but only four members of the previous court were brought before it, three of whom were acquitted. The former chairman received a one-month prison sentence. In short, 'things were generally quiet'.[8] By their own account, Cossack insurgents, pressed by officers and hard-liners in their midst, ambushed passing Red Guard detachments that were behaving 'properly' and seeking to accommodate Cossack communities.[9]

Why then did these rebellions all break out so suddenly in late April? Participants and subsequent historians have recognized the cardinal role of German intervention to the success of the 'Cossack' insurgency. No one less than Ataman Krasnov, who was brought to power by the insurgency, attested that 'without the Germans, the Don would not have been freed from the Bolsheviks'.[10] German forces helped both indirectly, by driving back Red Guard detachments, and directly, by aiding Cossack insurgents in overthrowing Soviet power. The German involvement is usually discussed in terms of Krasnov's 'pro-German orientation'.[11] In fact, however, such behavior was widespread, and did not derive solely from Krasnov's policy. Local insurgents, who had no knowledge of Krasnov's activities in Novocherkassk, began cooperating of their own accord with German forces. As German forces moved into Donets district, they drove off Red detachments and engaged in joint operations with rebel Cossack units. They provided Cossack insurgents with logistical and intelligence support (including aerial reconnaissance), all at the invitation and request of local insurgent commanders. German forces not only helped repel Red Guard detachments, but became even more closely involved in the 'Cossack movement' by disarming peasant communities while simultaneously arming Cossack ones.[12] Prior to coming into contact with the Host authorities in Novocherkassk, district and *stanitsa atamany* received their sanction from local German military authorities.[13] On the very day that Krasnov's Circle for the Salvation of the Don came into existence in Novocherkassk, the Donets district *ataman* – oblivious to its existence – issued an appeal to the neighboring districts (First Don, Upper Don) to send delegates to form a Host government in his district capital Kamenskaia. In his letters, he indicated the desirability of constituting such a regional authority, since 'the commander of the German division in Kamenskaia has indicated that he can take upon himself the liberation of the entire Don region from the Bolsheviks [*sic*], if a delegation from the districts, furnished with definite instructions, requests this.'[14]

But the German advance provided only an opportunity that the insurgents seized. What then caused the rebellion to sweep throughout the Don in April 1918? The disparate uprisings were the product not so much of Bolshevik marauding, but of the 'Great Fear' similar to that generated by the French Revolution.[15] In both cases the rural population was animated by *fears* of politically motivated brigandage, fears testifying more to how rural inhabitants perceived a novel and volatile political environment than to the *actuality* of what they were perceiving. As Lefebvre writes, 'an explanation of the Great Fear is not so much the actual truth, as what the people thought the aristocracy could and would do'.[16]

In addition to the disconcerting revolutionary situation, new legislative organs – both the national congresses of soviets and the First Don

Congress of Soviets – propagated disturbing visions of a new ordering of the polity. In particular, two Soviet decrees concerning the symbolically weighty land issue (the 26 December 1917 guidelines on land committees and the 19 February 1918 decree on socialization of the land) fanned Cossack apprehensions that their distinctive lifestyle would be eliminated. One insurgent leader testified that until April 'it was a difficult task to involve the Cossacks of Ust'-Medveditsa district in overthrowing Soviet power, but the "General Regulations" made the task much easier'. The paragraphs granting land committees the authority to seize land particularly unsettled Cossacks.[17] Berezovskaia *stanitsa* expelled from the community its delegate to the First Don Congress of Soviets, an outlander, only when he began advocating the land socialization decree.[18]

Whereas French rural dwellers saw the ubiquitous and malevolent aristocrat lurking behind every shadow in the French countryside, so insurgents projected all their fears about the new order on to real or imagined 'Bolsheviks', reducing any actual foes to this Manichaean paradigm. Despite the fact that many local pro-Soviet activists on the Don were Left Socialist Revolutionaries (SRs) whose affiliation was quite well publicized, Cossack insurgents routinely depicted all local Left SRs as 'Bolsheviks'. For instance, an insurgent intelligence report about the ill-fated conscription expedition led by Krivoshlykov and Podtelkov, two Cossack leaders of the Don Soviet Republic, almost all of whose members were captured and executed by the insurgents, reported that Podtelkov, who had balloted for the Constituent Assembly as a Left Socialist Revolutionary, was in 'Bol'shinskaia sloboda, where he is conducting *Bolshevik* agitation'. Despite the fact that this expedition numbered many of the most prominent Left SRs in the Don Soviet Republic – Podtelkov, Krivoshlykov, Alaev, who had publicly balloted as members of that party – its agitation is nevertheless perceived as 'Bolshevik'.[19] Anti-Soviet insurgents similarly depicted Soviet land decrees as 'Bolshevik', even though the decrees reflected Left SR views at least as much as Bolshevik ones.[20] This collapsing of all support for soviets into the category of 'Bolshevik' in fact unwittingly contributed to the Bolsheviks' own attempts to aggrandize for themselves the role of sole party of the Soviet state.

If the Cossack insurgents imagined their foe in political terms as 'Bolshevik', they imagined him even more so in sociological terms as 'peasant'. Cossacks virtually obsessed about the threat they imagined neighboring peasant communities presented to their lifestyle. One Cossack insurgent recalled:

> The Cossacks feared the surrounding peasants, whose settlements were located throughout the Upper Don district ... Cossack communities con-

tinued to worry, and to insist on disarming the neighboring peasant communities. Rumors stubbornly circulated that the Ukes [*khokhly*] had not just rifles, but also machine guns. The Cossacks were very cautious, fearing massive arms caches and machine-guns in the peasant settlements. However, upon searching them, it transpired that nothing, other than a few rifles, was found.[21]

In fact, the peasants, aroused by rumors of shadowy 'Kadet' and 'Cossack' bands, did take to arming themselves. In one instance, a peasant community formed a detachment and dispatched it to confront a rumored 'counter-revolutionary band'. When they encountered it, they found it was a Cossack detachment from the neighboring community, itself mobilized to face a supposed Red Guard detachment. Upon this welcome discovery, both sides dispersed.[22]

Violence was not always avoided, however. Under the pretext of forestalling an assault by 'Kadets', local peasants pillaged both Gundorovskaia and Mechetinskaia *stanitsy* and arrested several leading members of the Cossack communities. Predictably, these two *stanitsy* soon joined the insurgency, and were quick to equate all peasants with 'Bolsheviks' and 'Red Guards'. Once they had the upper hand, the Cossacks of Gundorovskaia expelled all peasants from the neighboring community.[23] One peasant recalled that 'in April 1918 a civil war of local magnitude flared up, the so-called war of Cossacks against peasants, and peasants against Cossacks'.[24] As some peasant communities armed, they provided an empirical nexus for Cossacks' inchoate fears.

Petr Krasnov, who as *ataman* of the AGDH had access to intelligence reports with much evidence to the contrary, nevertheless defined the conflict in purely estate terms:

> At that time the Don divided into two camps, Cossacks and peasants. The peasants, with small exception, were Bolsheviks. Where there were peasant settlements, uprisings against Cossacks did not cease. The Don Host's entire north, where peasants predominated over Cossacks; Taganrog district; Orlovka and Martynovka Slobodas of the First Don district; the cities of Rostov and Taganrog; Bataisk Sloboda – all were awash in Cossack blood in the struggle with peasants and workers ... War with the Bolsheviks on the Don had already taken on the character not of political or class struggle, not of a civil war, but rather of a people's war, a national war. Cossacks defended their Cossack rights from the Russians [i.e., peasants].[25]

As noted above, this is essentially the prevailing historiographical view of the rebellion. Political attitude was neatly, if erroneously, based upon sociological contours. Indeed, Krasnov's geographic characterization ('The Don Host's entire north, where peasants predominated over Cossacks') is an ideal example of sociological data following political lines. While Krasnov might have wished to suggest that the rebellion succeeded in the south simply on account of a greater Cossack presence, the northern districts were, in point of fact, more Cossack in sociological terms than the southern ones. (Krasnov would have been correct in noting that while the southern districts overall had a lower Cossack presence, the Cossack officers and leadership were concentrated there.[26])

Of interest here is not so much the veracity of the Host narrative, but how the Cossack leadership came to perceive the conflict as one between anti-Soviet Cossacks and pro-Bolshevik peasants. From the very first, leaders of the insurgency reported, even if they did not see, the variegated response of the peasantry. The Don Government's own intelligence reports documented how peasants frequently shunned Bolshevik attempts to mobilize them, a far cry from Krasnov's portrayal of virtually all peasants as 'Bolsheviks'.[27] Some native peasants in fact embraced the anti-Soviet Cossack insurgency.[28] There were reports that even outlanders, peasants who were not native to the Don Territory and who were reputed to be the most monolithically Bolshevik, fought 'side by side' with the Cossacks against 'the common foe' (Raspopinskaia); that 'almost all outlanders are in the ranks of the Cossacks' (Nagavskaia); that 'the outlander population is arming against the pillagers' (Nizhne-Chirskaia); and that 'the outlanders are participating in the struggle against the Bolsheviks' (Kamenskii Brod).[29] Public reports also contained abundant testimony regarding non-Cossack participation in the 'Cossack' insurgency.[30] Indeed, when a full Host circle convened in August 1918, the Cossack authorities delegated several seats to those outlanders serving alongside Cossacks in certain insurgent regiments.[31]

To be sure, there was protracted peasant support in Orlovka and Martynovka for Soviet power, as well as in Efremevo-Stepanovka, Skasyrskaia and Chistiakovo. But a review of the sources, which the Cossack leadership also used, demonstrates that these communities were the exception. Nevertheless, on the strength of the sociological perceptual grid, these cases came to be seen as paradigmatic of 'peasant' behavior.[32]

This perceptual categorizing of political support by estate criteria ('the Don divided into two camps, Cossacks and peasants'), did not so much synthesize 'facts', as order them. Despite the demonstrably non-monolithic response of 'the peasants' and 'outlanders', a near-universal conviction emerged nevertheless 'that "outlander" and the "Bolshevik" were synonyms'.[33] Hence this schematicization entered the historiography.

The perceptual tools for understanding the insurgency led the Cossack leadership to align its opponents into social categories, specifically as 'peasants' or 'outlanders'. To what degree was the rebellion itself a 'Cossack' movement? The vast majority of participants in the 1918 anti-Soviet uprising belonged without doubt to the Cossack estate. This social topography is attributable, however, as much to the political ideology of the uprising as to the sociology of its political support. Mass participation by Cossacks demonstrated not so much freely given consent by a like-minded collective social group, as expressed the Cossack leadership's drive to recruit Cossacks, forcibly if need be, to serve the 'Cossack cause'. Thus the movement's ideology prefigured as much as it described its base of support, by forcibly enlisting Cossacks to participate in their own 'liberation'.

The Cossack leadership's own account of the insurgency, and much of the subsequent historiography, affirm that Cossacks rose up almost monolithically. One non-Cossack participant, Belogorskii, describes how Cossacks resisted 'to the last man' (*pogolovno*) in defense of their distinctive lifestyle.[34] This version was both a legitimizing myth for the Cossack leadership and a way to conceptualize the rebellion.[35]

The link between the rebellion and the Cossackry, then, became entirely tautological. Support for the rebellion was 'Cossack', and failure to do so marked one as 'non-Cossack'. Officers who led the movement gained a foothold in the Cossack *stanitsy* when a segment of the Cossack community acceded to their calls for mobilization against the wraithlike 'Bolshevik bands'.[36] Such action was invariably proclaimed in the name of defending the Cossackry and its interests, and quickly provided the orthodox standard for what (and who) was 'Cossack'.

Far from all Cossacks, however, favored mobilization against the pillaging hordes reputed to be threatening them. Indeed, among Cossacks the preference for 'neutrality' was at least as widespread as wholehearted adherence to the insurgency, a fact widely attested to in various memoirs.[37] Within Cossack communities, a hard-line faction pressed all Cossacks to adhere to the 'Cossack cause', branding as 'traitors' those who refused to share their vision. Cossack community resolutions ordering mobilization invariably directed all members of the community to enter the ranks, or to face courts martial for 'treason'. Those considering deserting were warned they would be executed.[38]

The spread of the rebellion in Ust'-Medveditsa demonstrates how political opponents of the new order fashioned a 'Cossack movement'. Throughout the early spring of 1918, Cossacks in this northern district had offered little support to several officer detachments seeking to overthrow Soviet power.[39] In April, however, inflammatory rumors began to circulate that 'the Russians' planned to confiscate the Cossacks' land and deport them all to Siberia, leading a segment of the Cossack communities to turn to the officers they had previously spurned.[40]

Ust'-Khoperskaia *stanitsa* emerged as the center of the insurgency. The community convened a *stanitsa*-wide 'congress of soviets' for 25 April (OS). With Cossacks already uneasy about land legislation, news that armed peasants from the town of Chistiakovo had attempted to free captured Red Guard prisoners set the rebellion's spark. The *stanitsa* 'congress of soviets' passed a resolution declaring that it no longer recognized 'existing Soviet power' and sanctioning all measures to detain Red Guards. The congress then decreed a compulsory mobilization (*prinuditel'naia mobilizatsiia*) of the community's entire male Cossack population, from ages 17 to 50. Command posts were reserved for officers alone, and overall command of the insurgency's forces was entrusted to General Golubintsev. Anyone avoiding mobilization would be subject to military law, up to and including execution.[41] The *stanitsa*'s outlying Cossack settlements then passed analogous resolutions, some ordered by the settlement *ataman*, others passed by the settlement's 'soviet'.[42] Some Cossack settlements, however, were reluctant. Bobrovskii *khutor* had to intercede on behalf of four of its members who had been arrested at the *stanitsa* assembly (including a father and son, both NCOs), offering a collective guarantee for their future behavior.[43]

Two days after the *stanitsa* assembly, the rebel leadership convened a 'soviet of free Cossack settlements and communities', with participation from neighboring *stanitsy*. (The adjective 'free' in the title is derived from the term for Cossack liberties (*volia*), rather than the word for egalitarian, civic freedom (*svoboda*).) The insurgent command, headed by Golubintsev, intentionally selected a 'soviet' to head the movement in order to keep its appeal as broad as possible. Many Cossacks at this stage proclaimed outright that, while they opposed Red Guards, they had no quarrel with local soviets. These views were common not only among soldiers who had served at the front, but equally among officers who had advanced through the ranks during the war.[44] The composition of the five-person committee elected by the 'soviet' reflected the republican sympathies to which Golubintsev hoped to appeal. (Golubintsev made sure to retain de facto control as commander of insurgent forces.) Its chairman, Lieutenant Vedenin, had been a teacher at the local secondary school before advancing to officer rank during the war. He openly expressed doubts about Golubintsev's agenda. Another member, Sergeant Alferov, confided to Golubintsev that he was 'a Bolshevik, but one with principles'.[45] The insurgents borrowed more than revolutionary rhetoric. They also formed a 'political department' for the purpose of 'informing distant Cossack settlements about the movement and the character of the popular uprising'.[46]

To uphold its cause, the insurgent assembly also proclaimed the universal mobilization of all Cossack males.[47] Far from all communities voluntarily embraced this measure. One week after the decree, Bukanovskaia *stanitsa* informed the insurgent leadership that it had convened an assembly to 'discuss' it. Three days later the local authorities reported that the *stanitsa* proper had mobilized its menfolk, but that the outlying settlements still had not. Two weeks later most settlements still had not mobilized, leading the *stanitsa* to call an assembly. The insurgent leadership tartly instructed the Bukanovskaia authorities that they should confiscate the land allotments of any Cossack who failed to support the insurgency immediately. (In July, six mounted militiamen seeking draft dodgers in one of Bukanovskaia's settlements were fired on by one fugitive Cossack's relatives.[48])

As its control spread, the soviet of free settlements continued to issue menacing mobilization orders, soon extending their claims to the entire Ust'-Medveditsa district.[49] By this time, Cossack settlements in areas not yet controlled by the anti-Soviet insurgents convened their own, pro-Soviet congress of soviets, which in turn issued its own mobilization orders for all of the district.[50] Communities now had to proclaim their unambiguous allegiance to one side or the other. Skurshinskaia *stanitsa* found itself inundated by mobilization orders from both sides. The *stanitsa* informed its outlying settlements that it had joined with the insurgents, but assured them that the rebels would not seek to wage war against the whole of Russia. This assurance did not sway several settlements, which begged their *stanitsa* leadership to try to seek a negotiated resolution.[51] Settlements in Arzhenovskaia *stanitsa* expressed similar sentiments. The *stanitsa* leadership showed little patience for such views, though: 'those guilty of non-fulfillment of the above-cited order, and of failure to appear at the muster-point, will be subject to harsh punishment, up to and including trial by court martial. Arzhenovskaia *stanitsa* is under martial law.'[52]

The Cossack leadership raised its revolt in the name of the entire Cossack estate, and it was fully prepared to compel Cossacks to participate in their own liberation. It expended a great deal of violence, in the form of both overt force and judicial coercion, to bring Cossacks into proper alignment with an imagined collective Cossackry. In the words of the captured commander of the 24th Cossack Horse regiment during his interrogation by the Red Army, Cossacks had originally armed to defend their homes, with little thought to the Host government. But soon the Don government 'began to demonstrate a desire to subordinate the Cossacks to it'.[53] This Cossack pointedly distinguished between Cossacks and the government seeking to speak for them.

But to explain how the Cossack leadership's view became a veritable orthodoxy, both at the time and in the subsequent historiography, we must study the means by which it subsumed the widespread but disparate opposition to 'Bolsheviks' under the rubric of the 'All-Great Don Host'. The insurgency's base was the area in Cherkassk district around the Don Host's administrative capital of Novocherkassk. A rebel detachment of 300–400 men (mostly officers), under the command of Colonel Fetisov, had briefly seized Novocherkassk in mid-April, just as the First Don Congress of Soviets was meeting in Rostov. Upon occupying the capital, the insurgents appointed K.S. Poliakov commander and S. Denisov as chief of staff of a not-yet-existent 'Don Army'. While forced to retreat soon afterwards, the brief occupation allowed many officers trapped in Novocherkassk to withdraw with the insurgents to Zaplavskaia *stanitsa*, where they set up a defensive position. From there they held out for nearly two weeks, growing to a force of nearly 6,500 men, which subsequently formed the core of the 'Don Army'.[54]

Kenez writes that the 'uprising spread rapidly and Cossacks came from nearby *stanitsy* to join the army'.[55] Yet the increasing number of Cossacks in the insurgent ranks did not testify to spontaneous social support for a Cossack agenda. Indeed, the struggle to fit them within the insurgent mold required considerable effort even in what were reputed to be the more conservative and loyal southern districts. In his memoir, Poliakov, the commander of the Don Army, observed that 'Cossack communities rose of their own accord against the Bolsheviks'. This observation must be contrasted with Poliakov's order of the time, cited below, in which he dispatched a punitive detachment to Starocherkasskaia to coerce its Cossack inhabitants into 'defending the Don', threatening merciless punishment for neutrality.[56]

The memoirs of Denisov, the Don Army's chief of staff, provide a detailed record of how ordinary Cossacks were brought into the insurgency's ranks.[57] Early on, the embryonic Host leadership resorted to a tool that it would soon extend to other regions: the punitive detachment (*karatel'nyi otriad*). As Denisov himself testifies, 'the command's firmness caused outbreaks, and the campaign *ataman* was forced to dispatch detachments for pacification, and even to equip repeated punitive expeditions'. Around mid-April the insurgency faced its own rebellion among Cossacks pressed into service in its ranks. The insurgent command took stern measures. On 26 April Poliakov issued an order reading:

> Today from Razdory a punitive detachment is being dispatched by steamboat to Starocherkasskaia, in order, by force of arms, to put an end to the harmful propaganda, and to force the deluded to come to the defense of their native region at this critical moment. Announcing this, the campaign *ataman* has ordered me to warn that any deviation or demonstration of neutrality will be mercilessly punished by military force.[58]

The Cossack leadership thus explained away Cossacks who did not share its agenda by referring to their 'delusion', a condition which a punitive detachment could soon cure. Nor was Starocherkasskaia an isolated case. On 27 April, the command ordered a garrison to occupy the 'politically unreliable' *stanitsa* of Melikhovskaia. Gunboats were dispatched up the Don river to press recalcitrant Cossack communities to join the cause. Not surprisingly, these measures worked: 'after the arrival of the punitive detachment, the mood is very firm'.[59]

As German units moved into Rostov, Taganrog and Donets districts and with local insurgencies elsewhere undermining Soviet power, the insurgent forces in Zaplavskaia succeeded in seizing Novocherkassk a second time from the disorganized Soviet forces. With the Don Territory's capital city in their hands, they could now present themselves as the authority representing the whole Don. Two days after they had seized the city, the insurgents convened a 'Circle for the Salvation of the Don', which sat for one week (11–18 May). Petr Krasnov, who was elected *ataman* by this gathering, extolled it as a true representative of Cossack sentiments, a direct and unmediated reflection of the Cossackry. He termed it 'gray', on account of its humble composition and its lack of the 'cowardly', meddling intelligentsia who claimed to speak on the Cossackry's behalf.[60] This characterization poorly describes the Circle's composition, but it reveals much about Krasnov's views of the Cossackry.

The portrayal of the assembly as an authentic representative of the humble Cossackry relies entirely on the insurgency's own tautological definition of 'Cossack'. Representation was weighted toward those serving in insurgent detachments, which sent two delegates, whereas *stanitsy* under the insurgency's control sent only one. Consequently, of the Circle's 130 delegates, only 33 were elected from the *stanitsy*, a further 48 came from insurgent Cossack units, and the remainder were officers and officials from Novocherkassk.[61] Cossacks who did not support the insurgency were not represented, precisely because such behavior was a priori not Cossack.[62] Conversely, those fighting the 'Bolsheviks' became, *mutatis mutandis*, impeccably 'Cossack'. Thus when V.V. Svechin, who had served in the headquarters of the Russian army and had then been appointed to represent Kaledin's Host government in Kiev, returned to the Don in this period, chairman Georgii Ianov immediately registered him as a member of the Circle.[63] By virtue of his support for the insurgency alone, Svechin had come to represent the 'gray' Cossackry.

Humble Cossacks, however, did not necessarily share Krasnov's sense of what they supported. One White intelligence report noted that:

Among the officers, as well as among the Cossackry's rank and file, a hostile attitude is evident toward both the *ataman* and the Circle for the Salvation of the Don, as well as toward those who elected it. Among simple Cossacks the Ataman has the reputation, earned while he was commander, of being too strict, and they see in his current measures a manifestation of this excessive harshness. Rumors are also circulating among Cossacks that the Circle for the Salvation of the Don elected General Krasnov *ataman* on account of behind-the-scenes intrigues – and even due to almost nothing more than a good dinner.[64]

Several months later, a commander in the Don Army noted that 'a sense of duty before the entire Host is poorly developed among Cossacks', who suffer at times from 'selfish interests'. By 'selfish interests', he meant that Cossacks stubbornly failed to recognize the Host as their collective representative.[65] These evaluations would not necessarily trouble members of the Circle or Krasnov. In their view, they represented the Cossackry as a corporate entity (hence their formulaic use of the term 'Cossackry' (*kazachestvo*), rather than simply 'Cossacks' in the plural), and, as such, they were responsible not to the plurality of individual Cossacks, but to the good of the estate as a whole, which was perhaps not as evident to 'simple Cossacks' as it was to its foremost caretakers and representatives.

The Circle translated its estate-based conceptualization of political affiliation into concrete legislation. It passed a law granting Cossack status to all those who sided with the Host leadership against 'the Bolsheviks'. Conversely, it also passed a law expelling from the Cossack estate all Cossacks 'participating in the Soviet forces and Bolshevik organizations'.[66] The AGDH later officially confirmed this practice with a law calling for the expulsion of all individuals, with confiscation of their property, for opposing 'the Cossackry' (meaning the AGDH), and for admitting as Don Cossacks all those who fought for the 'native Don'.[67] These measures, in fact, bore a similarity to those of the Imperial regime during World War I against German subjects, and extended the Host's 1917 claim to define who was and who was not Cossack on the basis of political allegiance.[68]

'Cossack' support for the Host was thus not a sociological description of its supporters but an ideological projection. One need only look at the numerous resolutions granting Cossack status to non-Cossack participants of the insurgency, or those expelling Cossacks for their failure to embrace it, to see that political allegiance determined 'social' identity, rather than vice versa. On the strength of the Circle's resolution, Cossack communities (*stanitsy*) purged those who did not share the insurgency's view of the Cossackry and its interests: Kumshatskaia *stanitsa* (First Don district) excluded 282 of its own members from the

Cossack estate for serving in Soviet forces; Nagavskaia *stanitsa* (First Don district) expelled 201, representing one-quarter of all Cossacks in the community.[69] Newspapers regularly published other *stanitsa* resolutions expelling hereditary Cossacks from the Cossack estate for their political views. In their petitions, communities employed the insurgency's own categorization for Cossacks. The assembly of Krylov *khutor*, Esaulovskaia *stanitsa*, twice asked the Host government to expel their co-villager Vasilii Samsonov from the Don 'as an individual harmful to the Don Cossackry'.[70]

At the same time as these communities were depriving hereditary members of the Cossack estate of their Cossack status, they were granting it to dozens and sometimes hundreds of non-Cossacks who had participated in the insurgency. Over a five-month period, the Host officially registered as Cossacks 1,400 'outlanders', only 150 of them officers, for their 'active participation in the Don's defense'.[71] The Cossack leadership's estate-based conceptualization of political support transformed the category of 'Cossack' from that of estate into that of acceptance of the Host leadership and its cause.

Punitive detachments could secure Cossacks for the insurgency's ranks, but to be effective, such violence required that its goals be clearly enunciated. The 'Court for the Defence of the Don' and local courts martial delineated for the population the insurgency's expectations, and more broadly, its world view.[72] The Court for the Defense of the Don was no abstract threat. Cossacks who deviated from the leadership's standard of 'proper' Cossack behavior were likely to find themselves facing either this court or its local equivalent, a court martial. The court punished Cossack parliamentarians who, contrary to the leadership's firm line, sought to negotiate with Soviet forces; it imprisoned other Cossacks for neutrality; and it tried Cossack soldiers for holding meetings in the ranks.[73] The Cossack leadership thus employed its courts to redefine desertion or neutrality into acts of treason 'to the entire Cossackry and the native Don'.

Judicial coercion was effective not simply as an instrument of repression. The courts did not merely punish the recalcitrant, but also explained the nature of their violation. It was in this sense that the courts martial were particularly effective in communicating the insurgency's tautological identification of 'Cossack' as meaning support for the anti-Soviet insurgency. The courts punished some for straightforward crimes such as pillaging, robbery and murder while in the service of 'Bolshevik bands'. Others it condemned for the simple charge of 'agitation on behalf of Soviet power'. However, the courts martial also handed down sentences against individuals charged with participation, not in the Red Army or even in the 'Bolshevik bands', but in '*organizations which pursue as their goal the destruction of the Cossackry*.[74] The courts even prosecuted individuals under the charge of 'threats and a hostile attitude to the Don Cossackry'.[75]

In addition to outright sentencing, the Cossack leadership forced the populace to employ the insurgency's own rhetoric in formulating petitions for amnesty. Entire communities sought to assure the Novocherkassk authorities that any complicity with 'Bolshevism' on their part had been coerced, and hastened to swear their allegiance.[76] A formulaic component of even individual requests for clemency or amnesty was the petition from the accused's community, requiring it to compose a resolution requesting pardon. Pavel Kadykov, along with his community, affirmed that his son had been forcibly mobilized by the Bolsheviks: 'our whole *khutor*, as represented by its best citizens, mourns for my son, *a true Cossack and defender of his native region*'.[77] The machine-gunners of the 1st Khoper foot regiment likewise appealed their conviction:

> Earlier we were unaware that there was an order and directive of the Large Circle that all orders from the commanders must be obeyed without fail and without any discussion ...Therefore we have the honor to request your directive to annul our punishment, and to return us to our positions, so that we may once again fight the Red Guards, as we did earlier, disregarding our own lives for the sake of the Cossackry and our Don state, a desire we express all as one, and give our oath to return to positions and fulfill our commanders' orders without question.[78]

The power both to sentence and to amnesty thus forced the populace to be conversant in the Cossack leadership's language, and to orient themselves to its world view.

With the western border secured by the German Army and with Soviet forces in disarray, the Don Army pushed northward, linking up with insurgent movements in other districts. As the AGDH expanded, it subsumed local authorities that had been established by their own rebel movements. The Donets district *ataman* placed all locally raised insurgent units under the command of his appointee Popov, instructing him to execute 'all officers and Cossacks who resist existing authority and conduct agitation against the command'.[79] One week later, he ordered all locally raised units to join General Fitskhelaurov's expeditionary force, which was extending the Host's authority into the northern districts. With the arrival of Fitskhelaurov's expeditionary force, Golubintsev's insurgent units of the 'soviet of free Cossack communities and settlements' were incorporated into the Don army.[80]

But the disparate and diffuse unrest against 'socialist measures' and 'Bolshevik bands' that had motivated many local insurgencies was not synonymous with the program of the Novocherkassk authorities. In *stanitsy* where the independent insurgent congresses had reinstated *atamany* who were prepared to recognize the legitimacy of the Host organs, the AGDH had little problem; if they were acceptable to the Host, they were officially reappointed by Krasnov. These district *atamany* then submitted the names of community *atamany* to Krasnov for approval. If *stanitsa atamany* proved unwilling to pursue the Host's agenda, military commanders were granted the authority to remove them. Where entire communities proved uncooperative, such as in Bukanovskaia, the Don command instituted direct military rule.[81]

But while all insurgents may have been 'anti-Soviet' (that is, opposed to the policies of the national Soviet government), many remained committed to some form of elective authority at the local level. In fact, in many places 'Soviet power' had been overthrown in the name of local congresses of soviets. Golubintsev was more calculating than most, but even he recognized the appeal of local soviets. The AGDH proved unwilling, however, to accept even local soviets that had rebelled against Soviet power. The Host insisted that all Cossack communities return to a system of *atamany*, not soviets. Golubintsev secretly corresponded with the Host leadership, plotting how to choreograph recognition of the Host government. While informing the population that he was postponing a congress to discuss how to constitute authority so as to focus all efforts on the armed struggle with the Red Guards, he simultaneously wrote Krasnov to immediately dispatch Host delegates so that, when the congress did meet, it would not 'diverge from the program of the Host government'. Such Host delegates, suggested Golubintsev, could '*direct* the congress to follow the line of the Host government'.[82] When a congress of insurgent communities finally met, it was chaired by Pavel Ageev, the leading pro-Host Cossack leftist who had taken refuge in Ust'-Medveditsa after the Soviet seizure of power. The congress dutifully voted to pass authority to an *ataman*.[83] So ended the 'soviet of free Cossack communities and settlements'.

Cossack insurgents, of course, did not unthinkingly reinstate their 'traditional' *atamany* and embrace the Host's claim to represent their collective interest. Against those who did not share the AGDH orthodoxy, the Novocherkassk authorities did not hesitate to employ the tools that had proved so successful in the lower Don. The expansion of their authority was invariably accompanied by both the use of punitive detachments and the intensive activity of courts martial. The gunboats used so successfully against the Cherkassk *stanitsy* moved up the Don to Romanovskaia and Kargal'skaia *stanitsy*.[84] Esaul Gavrilov's punitive detachment secured Khoper district, in the north, for the Cossack leadership. Gavrilov did so by 'pulling the population out of its neutrality'. He presented *stanitsa* assemblies with a categorical choice:

'for us or for the Reds'. When the populace still expressed a desire to be neutral, Gavrilov threatened to open fire: 'either you are for the Cossacks, or against them'.[85] This ultimatum was of course made to a community of Cossacks. To be 'for or against the Cossacks' was to be for or against the authorities behind Gavrilov. Similarly, Lieutenant Lazarev's punitive detachment secured Ust'-Medveditsa district for the AGDH. The detachment 'quickly arrived and reimposed order in the Cossacks' disorganized ranks'. The AGDH department of intelligence noted the punitive detachment's salutary effects: 'the mood of the Cossacks, formerly unsteady, has improved with the arrival of Lieutenant Lazarev's punitive detachment. Incidents of disobedience and desertion have ceased'.[86]

The arrival of the Don Army was followed soon afterward by the establishment of regional courts martial. The central Court for the Defense of the Don had been created in May 1918, and later that same month local court martial branches were operating in both the Donets and First Don districts; by June one was operating in Khoper; in July, in Ust'-Medveditsa.[87] As the Don Army drove Soviet forces out of the Second Don district in August, courts martial opened in Novogrigor'evskaia, Golubinskaia and Morozovskaia *stanitsy*, soon followed by a regional one in Tsymlianskaia. Sal' district entered the competence of the Tsymlianskaia court martial until it acquired its own branch in October. Through the activity of these organs, the Novocherkassk authorities instructed the populace in its discourse and expectations.

As the AGDH extended its control over other insurgent regions, punitive detachments and courts martial were only the most blunt instruments for shaping public discourse and ordering life. To regularize its control (courts martial and punitive detachments were necessarily considered extraordinary measures), the command ordered the formation of 'watch detachments' (*karaul'nye komandy*) in each *stanitsa* and *khutor*, numbering 30 men for the former and 10 for the latter. District officials were to approve the commanding officers, and they were to be staffed by Cossacks who were 'politically reliable'. (The watch commands in fact were analogous to the militia detachments proposed but never instituted by the Provisional Government in October 1917.[88]) Control was also consolidated through shaping the boundaries of public discussion. Prior even to the convocation of the Circle for the Salvation of the Don, the insurgent leadership established an 'information department' (*osvedomitel'nyi otdel*), responsible both for informing the population about the government's activity and for informing government organs about conditions throughout the Territory.[89] Consequently, the Ust'-Khoperskaia defense commander directed all *khutor atamany* that, since 'the headquarters for liberation forces releases operational reports daily, truthfully depicting the situation', those spreading rumors will be arrested.[90] (Such directives closely paralleled similar decrees from the period of World War I, and mirrored Soviet measures.[91]) Both by its presentation of an official interpretation of reality (through the information department) and by its punishment of public speech and behavior deviating from this representation (through courts martial), the AGDH established the boundaries of public expression. Having done so, the leadership could propagate its image of the rebellion as 'Cossack', a conception which was increasingly realized by the insurgency's institutions.

NOTES

1. For contemporary formulations, see *Ocherk politicheskoi istorii Vsevelikogo voiska Donskogo* (Novocherkassk, 1919), pp. 71–3; 'Kratkii istoricheskii otchet osvobozhdeniia zemli voiska Donskogo ot bol'shevikov: otchet upravliaiushchego voennym i morskim otdelom i komanduiushchego Donskoiu armeiu', reproduced in *Kazaki Rossii: donskoe kazachestvo v grazhdanskoi voine* (Moscow, 1993), pp. 165–77; and the historical newspaper-journal *Donskaia volna* (Rostov). This approach entered the historiography primarily through the publications of émigré members of the Don government, first and foremost *Donskaia letopis'*, 3 vols (Belgrade, 1923–24) (henceforth *DL*), edited by former members of the Host government. Other influential treatments, shaping the subsequent historiography, are: Petr Krasnov (the former leader of the AGDH), 'Vsevelikoe voisko donskoe', *Arkhiv russkoi revoliutsii*, Vol. 5 (1922), pp. 191–321; [S.V.] Denisov (commander of the Don Army through January 1919), *Zapiski: Grazhdanskaia voina na Iuge Rossii* (Constantinople, 1921); [V.] Dobrynin (head of intelligence and from February 1919 chief of staff of the Don Army after Poliakov's dismissal), *Bor'ba bol'shevizmom na Iuge Rossii* (Prague, 1921); and I.A. Poliakov (chief of staff of the Don Army through February 1919), *Donskie kazaki v bor'be s bol'shevikami* (Munich, 1962); as well as émigré journals such as *Kazach'i dumy* and *Rodimyi krai*. Even Anton Denikin, no friend to the Cossack leadership, nevertheless replicates the Host's view of the insurgency as emanating from the lower Don to 'other, distant districts' where 'more or less significant militias formed'; Anton Denikin, *Ocherki russkoi smuty*, 5 vols (Paris, 1921–26; reprint edn, Moscow, 1991–), 2, p. 320.
2. Both the *Ocherki politicheskoi istorii* and the 'Kratkii istoricheskii ocherk' portray the Don command as the entity which organized and extended the Cossack insurrection.
3. Pavel Kudinov, 'Vosstanie verkhne-dontsov', *Vol'noe kazachestvo* 101 (1932).
4. William Chamberlin, *The Russian Revolution*, 2 vols (Princeton, NJ: Princeton University Press, 1989), 2, pp. 134–5; Evan Mawdsley, *The Russian Civil War* (Boston, MA: Allen & Unwin, 1987), p. 86; Peter Kenez, *Civil War in South Russia, 1918* (Berkeley, CA: University of California Press, 1971), pp. 122–5; Richard Pipes, *Russia under the Bolshevik Regime* (New York: Knopf, 1993), p. 19.
5. G. Ianov, 'Don pod bol'shevikami', *DL*, Vol. 3, pp. 21, 34, 37; *Donskie vedomosti*, 18/31 (March 1919); *Donskaia volna* 40 (March 1919); *Kazach'i dumy* 12 (Oct. 1923), pp. 6–12 and 16 (Dec. 1923), pp. 2–7.
6. *Donskie vedomosti*, 13/26, Jan. 1919 (interview with participant by Fedor Kriukov, the Cossack movement's poet laureate).
7. 'Cherkasskoe vosstanie', *Donskaia volna* 11 (Aug. 1918), p. 9; 'Sovetskaia vlast' v Sal'skom okruge', *Donskaia volna* 35 (Feb. 1919), p. 6.
8. 'Bol'sheviki v Ust'-Medveditse', *Donskaia volna* 13 (Sept. 1918), p. 6. For Khoper district, see 'Na rodine Kaledina', *Donskaia volna* 20 (Oct. 1918), p. 7; also A.V. Golubintsev, *Russkaia vandeia: ocherki grazhdanskoi voiny na Donu, 1917–1920* (Munich: Alexandra Arciuk, 1959), p. 20.

9. Kozhin, 'V verkhov'iakh Dona', *Donskaia volna* 47 (May 1918), and 49 (June 1919); and A.I. Tret'iakov, 'Iz bor'by donskikh kazakov', *Rodimyi krai* 72 (1967). (These two accounts corroborate each other.) For a similar event in Novonikolaevskaia *stanitsa*, see *Priazovskii krai*, 20 May/2 June 1918.
10. Krasnov, 'Vsevelikoe voisko donskoe', p. 206; also p. 191. See also Dobrynin, 'Vooruzhennaia bor'ba', *DL*, Vol. 1, p. 101; Ianov, 'Don pod bol'shevikami', *DL*, Vol. 3, p. 26; Poliakov, *Donskie kazaki*, p. 240; Golubintsev, *Russkaia vandeia*, p. 62. Kenez, *Civil War in South Russia*, provides a fine analysis of the German role.
11. Krasnov, 'Vsevelikoe voisko donskoe', Ch. 4 is devoted to Krasnov's defence of his policy; Chapter 31 of Denikin's *Ocherki russkoi smuty* provides an extended critique of it.
12. Gosudarstvennyi arkhiv Rostovskoi oblasti (GARO), f. 856, op. 1, d. 3, ll. 69, 72; d. 4, ll. 1, 17, 25, 35, 55.
13. *Priazovskii krai*, 10/23 May 1918; 20 May/2 June 1918.
14. GARO, f. 856, op. 1, d. 3, ll. 69, 73. Such support was obviously in line with the more general German policy of dismembering the former Russian empire by invoking the principle of self-determination to establish proxy states. (Fritz Fischer, *German War Aims in the First World War* (New York: Norton, 1967); Wiktor Sukiennicki, *East Central Europe during World War One*, 2 vols (Boulder, CO: East European Monographs, 1984).
15. Georges Lefebvre, *The Great Fear of 1789* (Princeton, NJ: Princeton University Press, 1973).
16. Ibid., p. 60.
17. For the effect of the 'general guidelines on land committees' see G. Markov, 'Epopeia generala Golubintseva', *Donskaia volna* 49 (June 1919), quote on p. 15; and Golubintsev, *Russkaia vandeia*, p. 21. For the impact of the land socialization decree, Gosudarstvennyi arkhiv rossiiskoi federatsii (GARF), f. 393, op. 2, d. 30, l. 52 and 'Beseda s P. Ageevym', *Priazovskii krai*, 28 June/12 July 1918. The guidelines can be found in *Sbornik dekretov i postanovleniia po narodnomu khoziaistvu* (Moscow, 1918), pp. 465–70; excerpts from the land socialization decree can be found in James Bunyan and H.H. Fisher, *The Bolshevik Revolution, 1917–1918* (Stanford, CA: Stanford University Press, 1934), pp. 673–8.
18. GARF, f. 393, op. 2, d. 30, l. 52 (delegate's letter to CEC (Central Executive Committee)).
19. GARO, f. 856, op. 1, d. 4, l. 25 (my emphasis).
20. Bunyan and Fisher, *Bolshevik Revolution*, pp. 673–8.
21. Kozhin, 'V verkhov'iakh Dona', *Donskaia volna* 49 (June 1919), p. 13.
22. GARF, f. 1235, op. 82, d. 6, l. 74. Officers in the Cossack detachment, however, tried to keep the men mobilized.
23. GARO, f. 213, op. 3, d. 1041, l. 4 (Gundorovskaia *stanitsa* resolution); GARO, f. 46, op. 1, d. 4159, ll. 4–5 (Mechetinskaia *stanitsa* resolution).
24. Tsentr dokumentatsii noveishei istorii Rostovskoi oblasti (TsDNIRO), f. 12, op. 3, d. 1041; see also d. 1355, ll. 1–2.
25. Vsevelikoe voisko donskoe', p. 221. Cossacks often distinguished themselves from non-Cossacks in ethnic terms. They described native peasants as 'Russians' (indeed, most were ethnic Russians); non-native peasants (*inogorodnie*), among whom Ukrainians predominated, were often called *khokhly* (a derogatory term for Ukrainians).
26. V.V. Lobachevskii, *Voenno-statisticheskoe opisanie OVD* (Novocherkassk, 1908), p. 323.
27. GARO, f.856, op. 1, d. 4, ll. 25, 35; GARO, f. 856, op. 1, d. 3, l. 25; GARO, f. 856, op. 1, d. 15, ll. 90, 106; Rossiiskii gosudarstvennyi voennyi arkhiv (RGVA), f. 39456, op. 1, d. 60, ll. 42, 72, 95. These accounts also generically describe all opposition as 'Bolshevik'.
28. The settlement of Pronin, Chistiakov county, passed a resolution requesting that the commander of the insurgent forces accept them into the 'ranks of the Cossack liberation detachments' to drive the Red Guard from the region, and that they be accepted into the Cossack estate (GARO, f. 856, op. 1, d. 76, l. 63); the peasant proprietors (*sobstvenniki*) of the 30th department of Solonovka county petitioned the commander of insurgent forces for arms so they could defend themselves – not from Red Guards – but from peasants of neighboring Solonovka *sloboda*, with whom they had long lived in animosity (GARO, f. 856, op. 1, d. 15, l. 196); in addition to electing county elders, 'the

peasants of certain *slobodas* are expressing a desire to enter the ranks of the Cossack forces' (GARO, f. 856, op. 1, d. 15, l. 127).
29. RGVA, f. 39456, op. 1, d. 60, ll. 6, 61, 86, 118 (summary from Don Government's department of information for 24 June/6 July, 14/27 July, 23 July/5 August, 5/18 August).
30. *Donskoi krai* (Novocherkassk), 1/14 May 1918; *Priazovskii krai*, 12/25 May 1918, 27 May/9 June 1918.
31. *Postanovleniia Bol'shogo voiskovogo kruga VVD 4-ogo sozyva*, p. 17; GARO, f. 856, op. 1, d. 15, ll. 14, 38.
32. In his memoirs, Poliakov, at that time commander of the Don Army, engages in precisely such a reading. In discussing the outlander response to the insurgency, he argues that the actions of Martynovka and Orlovka, the same 'typical examples' cited by Krasnov, 'serve as a graphic illustration' of the general response of outlanders (*Donskie kazaki*, pp. 231–2).
33. RGVA, f. 39456, op. 1, d. 60, l. 104 (report of Don information department on attitudes of Cossacks of Starocherkasskaia, 2/15 August 1918). For identical formulations, see: *Proletarskaia revoliutsiia na Donu* 4, p. 5 ('during the civil war of 1917–1918 the word "outlander" became a synonym for the word "Bolshevik"'); Eduard Dune, *Notes of a Red Guard* (Urbana, IL: University of Illinois Press, 1993), p. 140; and esp. N. Belogorskii (*sic*), 'V dni Kaledina', *Beloe Delo* 4 (1928), pp. 43–4.
34. Belogorskii, 'V dni Kaledina', p. 43.
35. For the 'Cossack ideology' in the Civil War, see Peter Kenez, 'The Ideology of the Don Cossacks in the Civil War', in *Russian and East European History* (Berkeley, CA, 1984), pp. 161–83; and Carsten Goehrke, 'Historische Selbststilisierung des Kosakentums: ständische Tradition als Integrationsideologie', in *Osteuropa in Geschichte und Gegenwart* (Cologne, 1977), pp. 359–75. Neither, however, describes how this ideology operated in prefiguring descriptions of Cossack support for the insurgency.
36. In Migulinskaia *stanitsa*, a hard-core faction acted despite the doubts of many in the *stanitsa*: see the accounts in Kozhin, 'V verkhov'iakh Dona', *Donskaia volna* 49 (June 1919), p. 11 ('the Cossacks became very reluctant and began to curse the officers') and A.I. Tret'iakov, 'Iz istorii bor'by', *Rodimyi krai* 72 (1967), p. 35. (The hard-liners began the assault despite an order from the *ataman* to hold negotiations.) Similarly, when the Ermakovskaia *stanitsa ataman* attempted to enter into negotiations with Red Guards, a hard-line faction attacked nevertheless (I. Fomin, 'Nashe vosstanie', *Rodimyi krai* 98 (1972), pp. 14–15).
37. On neutrality, see Ianov, 'Don pod bol'shevikami', *DL*, Vol. 3, pp. 14–17; I.N. Oprits, *Leib-gvardii kazachii E. V. polk* (Paris, 1939), p. 116.
38. Among numerous examples, see: GARO, f. 856, op. 1, d. 76, ll. 19, 51–2; RGVA, f. 1304, op. 1, d. 480, l. 19; RGVA, f. 1304, op. 1, d. 478, l. 10.
39. M.N., 'Ust-Medveditskie partizany', *Donskaia volna* 54 (July 1919); P. Vetov, 'Alekseevskii partizanskii otriad', *Rodimyi krai* 65 (1966); Host intelligence report, reproduced in *Kazaki Rossii*, p. 172.
40. GARF, f. 1235, op. 81, d. 2, l. 200.
41. Golubintsev, *Russkaia vandeia*, pp. 20–2; GARO, f. 856, op. 1, d. 76, l. 1 (*stanitsa* congress resolution).
42. GARO, f. 856, op. 1, d. 76, ll. 11, 18, 19, 21, 26, 28, 51–2.
43. GARO, f. 856, op. 1, d. 76, l. 25. A *khutor* is a Cossack settlement within a *stanitsa*.
44. Golubintsev, *Russkaia vandeia*, pp. 40–1.
45. Ibid., pp. 41–2; TsDNIRO, f. 910, op. 3, d. 606, l. 38 (memoir of Cossack who participated in negotiations with the 'soviet of free Cossack settlements and communities').
46. GARO, f. 856, op. 1, d. 73, l. 3.
47. GARO, f. 856, op. 1, d. 73, l. 1.
48. GARO, f. 856, op. 1, d. 76, ll. 55, 61, 90 (*stanitsa* resolutions and correspondence with insurgent leadership); GARO, f. 856, op. 1, d. 15, l. 296 (militia report).
49. RGVA, f. 1304, op. 1, d. 480, ll. 14, 29.
50. GARO, f. R-4071, op. 1, d. 5, l. 131.
51. RGVA, f. 1304, op. 1, d. 480, ll. 5–6, 13.
52. RGVA, f. 1304, op. 1, d. 480, ll. 18–19.
53. RGVA, f. 100, op. 3, d. 334, l. 8 (interrogation form, 17 Dec. 1918).

54. Kenez, *Civil War in South Russia*, pp. 122–32; Ianov, 'Don pod bol'shevikami', *DL*, Vol. 3, pp. 23–5.
55. Kenez, *Civil War in South Russia*, p. 123; similarly, p. 141.
56. Poliakov, *Donskie kazaki*, p. 226; cf. GARF, f. 1257, op. 1, d. 5, l. 2 (order, 26 April 1918, signed by Poliakov).
57. Denisov, *Zapiski*, pp. 78–85.
58. GARF, f. 1257, op. 1, d. 5, l. 2 (order signed by Poliakov).
59. *Donskoi krai: organ donskogo vremennogo pravitel'stva* (Novocherkassk), 1/14 May 1918.
60. Vsevelikoe voisko Donskoe', Ch. 1. Kenez follows Krasnov in terming the Circle 'gray' (Kenez, *Civil War in South Russia*, p. 139).
61. K.A. Khmelevskii, *Krakh krasnovshchiny* (Rostov, 1965), p. 53.
62. In constituting itself, the Circle for the Salvation of the Don declared itself to represent 'military units and *stanitsy* which have taken part in driving out the Soviet forces' (my emphasis). (GARF, f. 1257, op. 1, d. 2, l. 5). Those who did not share this agenda were simply not represented.
63. V.V. Shapkin, Unpublished manuscript (Bakhmetieff Archive, Columbia University), section two, p. 13.
64. TsDNIRO, f. 910, op. 3, d. 677, l. 11 (materials gathered by Istpart member on situation on Don, citing TsGAOR, f. 446, op. 2, d. 28, ll. 5–7).
65. RGVA, f. 40116, op. 1, d. 6, l. 16 (operational report for Tsaritsyn front, July 1918).
66. See the *Postanovlenie obshchego sobraniia chlenov Vremennogo voiskovogo pravitel'stva i delegatov ot stanits i voiskovykh chastei (28 aprelia 1918)*; Postanovleniia 'Kruga spaseniia Dona', 28 aprelia po 5 maia 1918 (Novocherkassk, 1918), p. 8.
67. 'Zakon o priniatii v donskie kazaki, ob izkliuchenii iz donskogo kazachestva i vyselenii iz predelov Donskogo voiska' (passed 19 Sept. 1918), *Sbornik zakonov priniatykh Bol'shim voiskovym krugom Vseveilikogo voiska donskogo chetvertogo sozyva, v pervuiu sessiiu, 15-e avgusta po 20-e sentiabria 1918* (Novocherkassk: Donskoi pechatnik, 1918), pp. 51–2.
68. On First World War legislation, including confiscation and expulsion of imperial subjects of German origin, see Eric Lohr, 'Enemy Alien Politics in the Russian Empire during World War One' (Ph.D. dissertation, Harvard University, 1999). On the Host's 1917 measures regarding Golubov, see Ch. 3.
69. Host orders confirming earlier *stanitsa* resolutions both expelling Cossacks and granting Cossack status are printed in *Donskoi krai*, 24 July 1918; *Donskie vedomosti*, 6 Sept. 1918; 27 Sept. 1918; 4–5 Oct. 1918; 9 Oct. 1918; 19 Dec. 1918; 10–12, 16, 20, 24 Jan. 1919. The Host bureaucracy took some time to process these resolutions. Throughout the summer of 1918 communities granted Cossack status to those who sided with them: see RGVA, f. 39456, op. 1, d. 60, ll. 6, 86 (reports of Don department of information: Raspopinskaia registered over 60 cases of outlanders accepted as Cossacks, 24 June 1918; Kumshatskaia expelled 232 Cossacks, and accepted 28 outlanders, 23 July 1918).
70. GARO, f. 46, op. 1, d. 4154, l. 36 (*khutor*'s petition to the *ataman*).
71. *Donskie vedomosti*, 16 Jan. 1919. The use of 'outlanders' is ambiguous: it could be used either in the narrow sense of those not native to the Don, or more broadly for all non-Cossacks. This figure probably under-represents the total for those granted Cossack status, since it reflects only those officially processed by the Host administration.
72. For Order no. 2 of the Circle for the Salvation of the Don, laying out the Court's competence, see GARF, f. 1257, op. 1, d. 3, l. 2. For an excellent overview of the activity of courts martial in the south, and particularly for the Don Host, see the memoir of I. Kalinin, *Russkaia vandeia* (Moscow/Leningrad, 1926), esp. Ch. 17. In the Civil War, Kalinin had served on the Don district military court.
73. GARF, f. 1257, op. 1, d. 5, l. 3 (request from Don Army commander to Don provisional government to punish parliamentarians); *Priazovskii krai*, 8/21 May 1918; Krasnov, 'Vsevelikoe voisko donskoe', p. 232.
74. GARO, f. 46, op. 1, d. 4156, ll. 89–90 (my emphasis) (sentence by Tsymlianskaia court martial against colonist Ivan Kronberg, sentenced to ten years' hard labor; and petition from his community on his behalf, claiming he was forcibly mobilized, a plea rejected by the *ataman*); GARO, f. 46, op. 1, d. 4154, l. 6 (petition from merchant Egor

Kovalenko, sentenced by Tsymlianskaia court martial to one-year incarceration, with documentation from court).
75. GARO, f. 861, op. 1, d. 84, l. 32 (charge made by Morozovskaia investigative commission); also GARO, f. 46, op. 1, d. 4156, l. 15 (woman sentenced for outburst against Cossackry).
76. GARO, f. 46, op. 1, d. 4156, ll. 4–6 (amnesty petition from Podgornyi *khutor*, Ternovskaia *stanitsa*, to Ataman Krasnov, assuring him that inhabitants cooperated with Bolshevik authorities only under compulsion, and swearing to remove this guilt by recognizing the AGDH government and serving it loyally); GARF, f. 1257, op. 1, d. 5, l. 36 (resolution from Aleksandrovskaia *stanitsa* affirming that, while a 'Soviet organization' had indeed existed in the *stanitsa*, it had been forced upon them); *Donskoi krai*, 1/14 May 1918 also reports the Aleksandrovskaia appeal. One of the Circle for the Salvation of the Don's very first acts was to receive a delegation from Mariinskaia *stanitsa*, which conveyed its greetings to the Circle and hurriedly set forth the reasons for its failure to join the struggle against the Bolsheviks (*Postanovleniia ... Kruga spaseniia Dona*, p. 2).
77. GARO, f. 46, op. 1, d. 4156, l. 49 (my emphasis).
78. GARO, f. 46, op. 1, d. 4156, l. 50. Similar petitions, d. 4153, l. 13; d. 4154, ll. 15, 17; d. 4156, ll. 10, 90, 129, 167.
79. GARO, f. 856, op. 1, d. 4, l. 44.
80. Golubintsev, *Russkaia vandeia*, p. 67.
81. GARO, f. 856, op. 1, d. 15, l. 42; GARO, f. 46, op. 1, d. 4139, ll. 2–4, 11; *Donskie vedomosti*, 6 Sept. 1918; GARO, f. 36, op. 1, d. 4136, l. 2; GARO, f. 856, op. 1, d. 3, l. 36.
82. GARO, f. 856, op. 1, d. 73, ll. 6, 8 (directives postponing congress); GARO, f. 861, op. 1, d. 65, l. 1 (Golubintsev's letter to Krasnov) (emphasis in original).
83. GARO, f. 856, op. 1, d. 73, ll. 27–28 (resolutions and protocols of congress); GARF, f. 1260, op. 1, d. 15, l. 25 (Ageev's report to the Host on the congress's proceedings); *Priazovskii krai*, 29 June/12 July 1918.
84. GARO, f. 856, op. 1, d. 15, ll. 203–4 (telegrams from Upper Don *ataman* and military commander).
85. Khmelevskii, *Krakh krasnovshchiny*, p. 60; Ianov, 'Don pod bol'shevikami', *DL*, Vol. 3, p. 30.
86. RGVA, f. 39456, op. 1, d. 60, ll. 51, 65.
87. My account of the expansion of the courts martial is based on copies of sentences and petitions from the collection of the Don *ataman* (GARO, f. 46, op. 1, dd. 4153, 4154, 4156, 4174). Documentation is thus purely arbitrary, fixing the *latest* date a court martial might be operating, and possibly not even encompassing all branches. What is indisputable is their extensive activity.
88. GARO, f. 856, op. 1, d. 60, l. 3 (Order no. 4 for Cherkassk district, transmitting Campaign *ataman*'s 3/16 May order, 4/17 May); d. 4, l. 39 (Donets district *ataman*'s directive to *stanitsy* communicating order, 7/20 May). For the Provisional Government's orders to establish local militias staffed by politically reliable veterans, see the Interior Ministry's 7 October 1917 circular (*RPG* 3, p. 1649) and the War Ministry's 11 October 1917 order (*RPG* 3, pp. 1650–51).
89. *Donskoi krai*, 1/14 May 1918. Here, too, the Host was establishing institutions earlier proposed by the Provisional Government (see Ch. 5). On the origins of the practice of state surveillance of the population through such organs, see Peter Holquist, 'Information is the Alpha and Omega of Our Work', *Journal of Modern History* 69 (1997), pp. 415–50.
90. GARO, f. 856, op. 1, d. 76, l. 139; and d. 15, ll. 261, 264 (*stanitsa ataman* summoned to answer for his 'agitation' against mobilization); GARO, f. 46, op. 1, d. 4153, l. 17 and d. 4156, l. 8 (individuals sentenced for spreading 'rumors').
91. For bans on 'rumors of whatever sort' concerning military developments, see: point 20 of the 1914 'Temporary Statute on Military Censorship', a prohibition reiterated in the 1915 revision of the law; point 22 of the Provisional Government's 'list of information not subject to distribution'; for White laws banning rumors, see *Donskoi krai*, 1 May 1918 and GARO, f. 46, op. 1, d. 4153, l. 17 and d. 4156, l. 8 (individuals sentenced for 'spreading rumors'); for similar Soviet decrees, see Irina Davidjan, 'Voennaia tsenzura v Rossii, 1918–1920', *Catiers du Monde russe*, 1–2 (1997), pp. 117–25.

4

Modernity and the Poetics of Proletarian Discontent

MARK D. STEINBERG

> Others ... relished the feeling that the modern world was heading toward catastrophe. Most of the latter group were artists, conscious promoters of an aesthetic modernity that was, in spite of all its ambiguities, radically opposed to the other, essentially bourgeois, modernity, with its promises of indefinite progress, democracy, generalized sharing of the 'comforts of civilization', etc. Such promises appeared to these 'decadent' artists as so many demagogical diversions from the terrible reality of increasing spiritual alienation and dehumanization.
>
> Matei Calinescu, *Faces of Modernity*

The idea of modernity was a compelling, but also conflicted and unstable presence in revolutionary Russia's political culture: an ideological model with pretensions to hegemony, but also a marker of difference, ambivalence and even resistance. The revolutionary project of making a new world and new selves provided powerful metaphors and trajectories, shaping understanding and action. But this rhetoric was riven and volatile, producing – as frustrated Bolshevik cultural leaders of the time complained – misusages, ambiguities and subversions. These departures were signs of difference and deviation behind the facade of a discourse that claimed to be the 'proletarian' point of view. They were also signs of encounters with the recalcitrantly material world of modern structures and relationships of which discourses had to make plausible sense. Not least, they were signs of deep subjectivities: of the specific gravities of sentiment, emotion and imagination.

These generalizations reflect partly the particular empirical inquiry in this chapter: the intellectual handling of the idea of modernity in the imaginative and critical writings of working-class authors[1] during the first years of the Russian Revolution – individuals negotiating a brittle and unstable social boundary at a brittle and unstable time. But entwined with this empirical investigation is also an effort to grapple with more general and theoretical problems about modern subjectivity and about the construction of cultural meaning: often-debated questions about the force of discourse in the world, the weight of the world on discourse, the place of the thinking and acting subject, the power of emotion and sentiment, and the indeterminacy and ambiguity of human subjectivity. For all these questions, modernity is useful to think with and about. Indeed, in seeking to understand the making of modern identities, 'modernity' must be treated as a problem; as an object of human imagination and manipulation as much as a given setting or as a category of our own definitional analysis. The Russian case is especially illuminating of these questions, with its dynamic compressions of time, its heated conflicts and its revolutionary preoccupations with meaning, transformation, enthusiasm and activism.

It is by now a truism to argue that the social and material is constituted by language. Cultural fields of meaning, especially discourse – and, even more especially, politically powerful discourses (such as the correct 'proletarian' view of the modern) – have been repeatedly shown to have the power to rearrange the givens of experience, to shape vision and purpose, to structure the 'realm of the possible'.[2] In the writing of Russian history, much greater attention has been paid in recent years to the influence that language, images, symbols, rituals, myths and other discursive forms have had in shaping the world people see and the actions they take in it. The loosely materialist view of human consciousness and behavior that once tended to predominate in studies of modern Russian history, and especially of the Russian Revolution, has been eroded – at the hands, partly, of those who helped construct it – by greater emphasis on the cultural creation of identities, meaning, purpose and action.[3]

While history writing has benefited from this linguistic or cultural turn, many of these historians at the same time have resisted the tendency – though less innocently than in the past – to lose context and active subjectivity in the disembodied and subjectless play of texts and signifiers. Along with many anthropologists and sociologists and some literary theorists, historians have tended to remain attentive to the ways people make and use cultural forms and to how this making and using has been shaped, constrained and provoked by the harder surfaces of people's lives – material conditions and objects, social location, relative power, the process of cultural practice itself – even as these cultural forms influence how these more tangible experiences are perceived and are made meaningful. This complicating approach has been theorized, for example, around a notion of 'practice' (or 'action', 'social energy' or 'sensuous human praxis') that focuses on the intersections and mutual invasions of structure and agency and of the material and the cultural; around 'power' as a relational field of both social and discursive determinations; around the 'micro-historical' contexts in which culture, power and the everyday are entwined; around notions of a 'dialogue' between the word and the world, of 'fields of cultural production' or of the 'circularity' of language and the material in constituting experience; and around the idea of 'post-materialism' that transcends both materialist and cultural reductionism.[4] For all this dialogism, however, there remains a recognition that there exists an experiential, practical dynamic in which the physical and social world retains a power to pattern, limit and disrupt discourse.

These arguments – as I have made use of them in this inquiry – also point toward arguments about subjectivity. To put it bluntly, I view individuals and groups as having the power and the space (not unlimited, of course) to actively appropriate, rework, misuse and subvert available cultural forms. My understanding of this active subjectivity (and of its limits), however, also entails a recognition (though this is an interpretive terrain full of hazards) of the force of emotion, imagination and moral sentiment in constituting knowledge and meaning, and in shaping action. Finally, I find it necessary to admit into any theory of the thinking and acting subject, recognition of the deep indeterminacy of human response to the world and to discourse. In the face of a widespread tendency to treat discourse as a coherent system, as a web of orderly and stable meaning and signification shared by cultural communities (or imposed by hegemonic authority), I have come to share the views of those who have argued for recognizing the multiplicity, instability and even ambiguity of discourse. This is a theoretical argument: about agency and the subject, about the possibilities of deviation and even resistance as well as willed conformity. This is a historical argument: about the flux of modernity, and especially about those years of war and revolution when history itself, to use Peter Fritzsche's felicitous phase, went 'delinquent'.[5] This is also, frankly, an ontological argument: a recognition of the inherent disorder and contradictoriness of human life, of the fractured and fluid character of any social totality.

Questions of modern identity, politics and history run through all of these matters. If modern politics, as has been suggested, is the effort to 'domesticate the infinitude of identity', to 'hegemonize identity',[6] – for example, to forge a revolutionary movement or a new society – then modern history may be the space where the indeterminate variety and inconsistency of identities are sustained. It is this historical story that I investigate. Poetry, the genre of workers' writing I look at most closely in this essay, is useful (and was appealing to these writers) precisely because it most readily admits instabilities of meaning, encompasses multiple voices and tries to concretize imagination and feeling. And in using images and objects to convey ideas and feeling, poetry tends to display the dialogue of word and world most visibly.

THE REVOLUTIONARY PATHOS OF FACTORY AND CITY

In the ideological vocabulary of revolutionary Marxism in Russia, city, factory and machine quickly acquired a nearly hegemonic force as emblems of political value and as markers of the new modern identity, and 'proletarian' writers were said to exemplify this pathos for urban and industrial modernity. The communist revolutionary ideal vigorously pushed aside widespread views in Russian culture of the modern city as, at best, a simultaneously vital and sinister place of interwoven virtue and vice, creativity and vulgarity, awakening and alienation – an ambiguous symbol of the possibilities and hazards of modern progress – in favor of a fully confident modernism in which city, factory and machine were extolled as the womb and soul of the new society, and as touchstones of value and meaning in the making of a new modern identity. The capitalist factory and city, for all their horrors (indeed, dialectically, because of them), were lauded as the setting for the technical progress and heroic class struggle that would beget revolutionary progress. And, looking forward, the future Communist civilization was imagined as the epitome of an urbanized, technologically empowered and culturally advanced modernity. The metropolis – indeed, the cosmopolis, the 'universal city' – was the imagined landscape of Communism.

This positive modernism was especially visible in the first years after 1917, as state leaders, journalists, social activists, writers and artists spoke constantly of the values of urban and industrial modernization. The press featured stories on global developments in science and technology. Lenin and other Communist leaders regularly argued for the economic and cultural benefits of mechanization, rationalization and, in Lenin's famous slogan, 'electrification of the whole country'. Lenin, in particular, frequently and bluntly insisted that, in social life and politics as in war, 'those who have the best technology, organization, and discipline and the best machines, will gain the upper hand'.[7] Revolutionary writers and artists filled their works with invocations of city streets, factories, electric pylons, radios, telephones, airplanes, bridges, trains, skyscrapers and, of course, machines. Indeed, the machine, one scholar has written, became 'the dominant cultural symbol' in early Soviet Russia, standing for the official, and, one must add, stereotypically masculine virtues of efficient rationality, relentless drive, iron discipline and solidarity.[8]

MODERNITY AND THE POETICS OF PROLETARIAN DISCONTENT

Working-class writers, especially radical poets and authors associated with the 'proletarian culture' movement, were generally said to have embraced, indeed to have exemplified, this positive modernist imagination. Pavel Lebedev-Polianskii, one of the most powerful figures on the early Soviet cultural scene as national chairman of the movement of proletarian cultural organizations known as the Proletcult and later head of the state agency responsible for overseeing literature and publishing (Glavlit), was one of a number of leading Marxist intellectuals to declare repeatedly that worker-writers, in the wake of October, had finally awakened to the progressive dynamism of urban modernity and recognized the apparent evils of city life to be necessary contradictions in an unfolding historical dialectic. Previously, Lebedev admitted, 'the worker's muse' saw in the city 'the celebration of gluttony beside want, of the blinding gleam of shop windows, fancy restaurants and advertisements beside the lopsided hovels of the workers' neighborhoods, of flamboyantly chic ladies and idle fops of the bourgeoisie beside the prostitute and the unemployed'. Now, he argued (in 1918), 'the city seems quite different. The worker loves it',[9] admiring the creative and progressive power in the city and in industry.[10] Other Marxist intellectuals writing on proletarian culture similarly emphasized the positive urbanist and industrial consciousness of worker-writers, especially younger, urban-reared ones. Worker-writers, they argued, quoting appropriate examples, renounce nostalgia for the country, infuse their writings with the rhythms and objects of the city, and voice 'the pathos of a poetry glorifying the iron and concrete city, love ... of things and products and factories'.[11]

Examples of such canonically correct appreciation of the modern industrial city did indeed become increasingly noticeable after the October Revolution, especially among the politicized majority of worker-writers, many of whom were or became party members and almost all of whom joined – and often helped organize – local Proletcults. The modern city, but also the politically powerful language about the proletarian and the city, fascinated and attracted most worker-writers. Almost every major worker-writer after 1917 wrote, and wrote increasingly often, about the city and its significance. Most wrote at least one major poem focusing explicitly on the city and, to emphasize the universality of their arguments, usually titled these simply 'The City' (*Gorod*) or 'To the City' (*Gorodu*). These writings often describe the enchanting *physical* beauty of the city: its street corners, squares, sidewalks, posters, rooftops, electric lights, noise, factories and granite.[12] These everyday charms, however, paled in their imagination before more hyperbolic images of the physical city. Often, and increasingly so, the city appeared as an animate but supernatural hero: 'a fire-faced Colossus',[13] a 'great iron-stone giant',[14] a striding and talking creature made 'entirely of steel and fire ... breathing out cascades of light'.[15] When in the mood, as they had rarely been before October, these writers could revere the physical city with sensual passion, as in Vasilii Aleksandrovskii's blunt profession of love, 'Oh, I love you, I love your stones'.[16]

Such declarations of love for the physical city were, however, less common than a rather more theoretical love – a historical, dialectical love. This allowed them to admit the ugliness, evil and cruelty of the actual city (which they described at length), but to interpret these as prerequisites to achieving a higher good – as part of a necessary dialectic of self-transcendence. Influenced by Marxist ideology, worker-writers wrote of the city as the 'cradle of the commune'.[17] More generally, the city was often seen as the foundation of human civilization and progress, as the place where 'science and art develop, dreams and thoughts mature',[18] as the 'great bridge to the liberation and exaltation of man'.[19]

Even more abstractly, the city was appreciated as a symbol and promise of a better future, of a different and purified city. As in much utopian literature – from the biblical millenarian vision of a 'Holy City, the new Jerusalem, coming down out of heaven from God' (Rev. 21:2),[20] through Renaissance architectural and philosophical treatises on the Città felice, to Marxist futurology[21] – the future sometimes appeared in the imaginations of these worker-writers as an urban utopia. This might be a city to be found and reached: 'a bright city along an untraveled pathway'.[22] But more often this was a 'New City' to be built.[23] And unlike the city of the present – but much like the utopian cities of Revelation and the Renaissance and echoing the growing preoccupation in Soviet culture with purifying lives and landscapes[24] – the Communist New City of the Future would be 'gracefully elegant and crystalline in cleanliness'.[25]

Whether viewed in the present or in the future, the idealized city was properly imagined as a modern city, a city of factories and machines. Marxist cultural intellectuals pointed, with satisfaction, to the evidence that worker-writers – especially those associated with groups such as the Proletcult and the association of proletarian writers around the journal *Kuznitsa* (The Smithy) – saw the factory as a positive force and symbol, and even felt a special 'love and passion'[26] for the factory. In this ideal, the factory was a source of much good: of useful products made by workers' hands; a means of overcoming the country's backwardness (the 'cradle of the new Russia'); the social environment where solidarity, striving and struggle are nurtured and sustained; a spiritual force dispelling sadness and longing, replacing them with the pathos of struggle and overcoming the herald of the future, and a symbol of everything alive, dynamic and creative in life.[27]

MODERNITY AND THE POETICS OF PROLETARIAN DISCONTENT

There is no doubt that the Revolution and the establishment of organizations devoted to promoting a new 'proletarian culture' stimulated many worker-writers, if not ordinary workers themselves, to see the factory and machines in new, more positive ways. Giving voice to their political convictions, worker-writers mobilized a metaphoric language in which objects from industrial life were emblems of the Revolution. Thus, for example, the factory smokestack was envisioned as the spire of a 'temple' exhaling 'incense to the new god-man',[28] as a great torch, casting sparks of light into the hearts of workers and peasants, and as a scepter of power in the 'iron fist' of a worker-giant.[29] Airplanes were described as 'proud iron machines' that could fly along 'solar traces' and 'intersect the vortices of orbits', and which 'sing our victory',[30] or, in a rare literary contribution by Aleksandr Shliapnikov (the trade unionist and leader of the Workers' Opposition), as a means enabling an aspiring worker to transcend the everyday grind.[31] Revolutionaries were viewed as 'mechanics' making a new modern world,[32] the Revolution as standing for 'the power of machines',[33] and Soviet Russia as a giant with 'machine muscles'.[34]

That this was often only an abstract, purified and symbolic appreciation of machines was noticed and it worried some critics. Workers' poems and stories were undoubtedly filled with 'traditional' images of industry – furnaces, hammers, sparks, iron and smokestacks – but, as some critics noted with concern, workers should have featured images of *modern* industrial techniques: finely calibrated lathes, for example, or the quiet hum of an electric motor.[35] Indeed, the most common images of labor and industry were the least modern: the 'blacksmith' (*kuznets*) and the 'foundry' (*kuznitsa*). This, of course, was in accord with an emerging Bolshevik iconography of work, and reminds us of the abstract and ideological nature of these songs of industry. Like other Bolshevik artists, worker-writers employed images of the blacksmith and his workshop not as realistic pictures of modern industry, much less of their own work experience (none had worked in foundries), but as increasingly canonical, and abstract, images representing the struggle to 'forge' a new life.[36]

Intellectually and emotionally, however, factories and machines often represented more than abstract metaphors for social transformation. Worker-writers also found here, as in the city, a certain alluring beauty, a new modern aesthetic. Writers associated with the Proletcult movement, especially – encouraged by Soviet cultural officials and critics[37] – deliberately and insistently proclaimed a new modernist aesthetic. Proletarians, Vladimir Kirillov declared in his early and influential post-revolutionary manifesto in verse entitled 'We', 'destroy museums, and trample the flowers of art', in order to 'breathe a different beauty'.[38]

Others wrote of 'iron flowers',[39] and even an aesthetically defiant 'machine heaven' graced by glistening birds of steel and iron.[40]

For most of these social and cultural proletarians, this new sense of beauty was wrapped up with a new emotional orientation to the modern world – a great love and even a sensual passion for the objects of modernity: for electricity, railroads, airplanes, dynamos, smokestacks, iron, steel, and for the songs and dances of pulleys, belts and machines.[41] For some, this was an intellectual and political passion. Il'ia Sadof'ev, for example, declared that the Revolution helped him to see and hear the 'carnival' beauty and truth of the factory: in the 'peals and roars', and in 'joyful, drunken dance of pulleys' he discovered 'striving', 'liberty' the 'secrets of the world', the 'wisdom of the word', and 'inspiration'. Now, to be in the factory every day, 'to understand this iron tongue, to hear the mystery of the revelation', is 'ecstasy'.[42] But, most often, this was both a more abstract (less tied to specific political ideas) and a more physical passion. Thus, Aleksei Gastev found in cranes, girders, molten metal, factory whistles, hammer blows and the noise and 'whirl of fire and machines' a 'soul' and even an 'alluring passion'.[43] Others were similarly entranced by the beautiful 'singing of steel' as it was hammered and worked, by the 'wild choir' of screaming chisels, droning saws, and turning nuts and bolts, by the 'dance of maidens' in the movements of pulleys and cranes, and even by the inspiring 'growl of boilers'.[44]

This passion for iron and machines involved, for some, even more than aesthetics and emotion, much less fleshed-out political ideas: it was also part of a mythic psycho-cultural identity in which proletarians merged with machines. Most famously, Gastev wrote of the revolutionary worker growing into a mythic giant, reaching the height of smokestacks, as iron blood flows into his veins.[45] Into the early 1920s, Gastev continued to write about fusing man and machine, but less metaphorically and more literally through a new revolutionary engineering, which would produce factories operated by a 'great anonymity' in which the 'will of machinism and the will of human consciousness' would be 'unbreakably conjoined'.[46] In time, these self-regulating factories would evolve into 'gigantic machines' and these factory-machines would fuse into 'machine cities'.[47] As the power of this machinism grew, Gastev imagined, in a voice less of scientific manager than of modernist seer, the mentality and culture of the proletariat would also be transformed. The emerging proletariat would come to work, think, react and gesture identically throughout the world. The result, the apex of proletarian culture, would be a 'mechanized collectivism' in which 'there are no individual features', but 'a face without expression, a soul devoid of lyricism'.[48]

Although Gastev was unique among worker-authors in his practical devotion to promoting economic and psycho-cultural 'machinism' – as he was in his student-turned-worker social biography – other worker-writers were inspired by the same ideal of a new iron and machine personality. In 1918, for example, Kirillov declared, 'We have grown close to metal and fused our souls with machines'.[49] Aleksandrovskii predicted that the new people would be 'like machines'.[50] Similarly, Gerasimov described himself as such a new, modern man: 'My mother gave birth to me in a clamorous factory / Beneath a machine... / I greedily sucked an electric pacifier, / I was rocked in a steel cradle, / And the bold factory whistle sang my lullabies.'[51] This proletarian personality, Gerasimov maintained, needed to be extended to all Russians, especially peasants, who would be saved only when each shepherd carried an 'iron lash', farmers were awakened by a 'bronze rooster', electric lights overcame the darkness of peasant huts, and the very 'soul' of the peasant was 'electrified'.[52]

It bears noting that amidst all of this symbolic, aesthetic, sentimental and psychological romanticism about factory and machine we find little argument for the practical uses of modern technology. Mikhail Volkov's story expressing hope that Lenin's modernizing plan of 'electrification of the whole country' would eradicate rural backwardness and ignorance,[53] and an occasional literary use of the cliché of electricity bringing light to the countryside,[54] stand out for their atypicality.

THE AMBIGUOUS CITY

These hints of deviance point to deeper-running streams. Like a good deal of modernist writing and art in Russia, the enthusiastic embrace of modernity was ambivalent in its relation to the actual modern world. Modern objects were often displayed more as appealing fragments than as parts of a whole reality, a utopian metonymy suggesting a vision of modernity attracted less to systematic and orderly coherencies than to abstractions, aestheticized fragments and the vital flux of modern life, and, especially, to a modernity purged of the realities of the everyday. Admired and beloved urban and industrial spaces tended to be purified modern spaces: clean and bright, abstracted from everyday contexts, and often displaced into the future. In part, this was a modernist deviation – an echo of the 'dream of purity' that was central to the idealism of modernity,[55] and a reflection of revolutionary aspirations to create a new and dialectically different modern world out of the contradictions of modernity. But a closer look at these writings reveals deeper currents of anxiety and ambivalence that persistently undermined whatever ideological enthusiasms led these writers to view city, factory and machine as the aesthetic, social and psychological cradle of the future. Like many modernists – but intensified by their own experiences and memories as industrial workers – these proletarian writers found their faith in and identification with modernity difficult to sustain. Frequently, and increasingly, they admitted to feeling neither at home in the modern landscape nor certain that there was any way out.

At the very least, many worker-writers acknowledged, proletarians had to struggle to appreciate the city. In a poem published by the Moscow Proletcult in 1919, Nikolai Poletaev described the daily urban ugliness and coldness workers had to endure and admitted difficulty in learning to love such a place. The discordant language with which Poletaev describes his conversion to the city is revealing. The city 'bewitches' him with its 'potent, shadowy beauty', with a beauty that was, literally, lethal and ghostly (*postepenno okoldovan / smertel'no prizrachnoi krasoi*). As a result, he becomes 'forever welded' (*prikovan*) to the city – an ambiguous love suggesting as much compulsion as union.[56] Similarly, Ivan Eroshin tells us that he tried to flee urban life, but was inexorably drawn back to the city. In the end, he confesses an urbanist love, but cannot conceal his ambivalence: 'I am your captive [*toboiu ia plenen*] /... again I strive toward you, now more strongly, more in love, / Into your furious jaws!!!'[57] Vasilii Aleksandrovskii similarly described a weary wanderer in the countryside inescapably forced back toward the compelling but painful city, 'beyond the peace of the steppe', where suffering and struggle were intertwined, where the 'victims' feel at home only there.[58]

The metaphors and modifiers these worker-writers often chose to describe the city embodied their ambivalence. For Aleksandrovskii, the city was a 'fire-faced ... city-giant'.[59] Others similarly expressed admiration mixed with implicit dread in describing the city as a 'sleepless iron-stone dragon',[60] a 'captivating-commanding' giant (*plenitel'no-vlastnyi*), an 'unwearying, proud and wrathful protestant', a 'many-headed, bright-eyed dragon'.[61] Many of these writers would have agreed with the statement that the city was 'mighty, filthy and drunken', but having a beauty of its own.[62]

Sustaining this ambivalence was these writers' persistently moral and aesthetic way of looking at the city. Familiarity with the Marxist historical dialectic helped worker-writers, in theory, to glorify the city without romanticizing it, to admit the obvious horrors of city life without this lessening their passion for the modern. But these writers tended to see the city in a more essentializing way. While they often described and condemned class inequality and oppression, they viewed the harmfulness of the city as emerging less from its social relationships – which could be corrected by social reform or revolution

– than from its nature and spirit. And this was seen often to be a hostile spirit.

Thus, even when they recognized that the contradictions of the city were theoretically resolved in a teleological dialectic in which the city was necessarily a contradictory place of suffering and salvation, they often dwelled more on the suffering (which they were certain of) than on the salvation (which remained theoretical). For example, Sergei Obradovich, in 1921, offered the metaphor of two cities: the 'sorrowing' city of today, which had 'blood in every stone', and the city of the future whose 'stone legs' could already be heard 'thundering in the distance', and which would replace the city of today with a city of marble streets and glistening palaces of labor.[63] Less confidently, Aleksandrovskii suggested that the blood and suffering of urban life held the promise of redemption: 'We have been crucified by you, city / ... suffering is always holy / Love is always in blood.'[64]

The physical and visual spaces of the city were seen to reflect its alien and hostile nature, to signify a dark and menacing sentience. Thus, Kirillov wrote of the 'gloomy stones of the capital',[65] Poletaev of 'malicious' smoke from factory chimneys, Aleksandrovskii of factory smoke hurrying 'with the guile of Cain / to fill the tears in black clouds',[66] and Obradovich of the city's 'coiled snake-like body' and its 'satiated laugh and triumphant howl'.[67]

The city, of course, was viewed not only as a physical site, but as a *human* space. Its social relationships and its effects on the human personality evoked a deep moral skepticism about urban life. Sometimes, to be sure, descriptions of city life make it clear that these authors were describing a capitalist city and that the critique was a class one. Narratives often end, for example, with the outbreak of class struggle or Revolution.[68] Most often, however, the social nature of the city, its particular structure of class relations, was secondary if indicated at all. As noted above, scores of poems were simply titled 'The City', and few markers were inscribed to suggest that these writers had in mind only the pre-revolutionary capitalist city. Nor was there much reason to make such a distinction. After all, the Bolsheviks did not, before the 1930s (except briefly and ineffectively during the civil war), uproot capitalism in Russia. Least of all did they do much to deliberately remake the face of the city, except in their imaginations. If anything, the revolution, by stimulating millenarian desires to transform the world, may also have intensified moral dismay with the persistent realities of modern urban life.

In dozens of published poems, stories and essays, worker-writers dwelled on human suffering in the modern, industrial city, with little mention made of the particular structure of class relations that, any

Marxist would insist, generated these wrongs. The city, as portrayed, for example, by Vladimir Kirillov in his 1918 contribution to the genre of poems titled 'The City', was a cold, alienating and destructive place:

> O, how many unknown people,
> How many uncomprehending gazes!
> They go, they hurry, they run,
> They all wear masks on their souls ...
> Here is a look shining with mad torment,
> And that one, so vainly happy,
> Might not meet a new day ...
> And all pass by without a trace.[69]

A few years later, he predicted fatalistically that such a life – now symbolized by the sexual parading of 'cocks' and 'hens' (*samtsi i samki*) beneath the gaze of 'melancholy Pushkin' – would be just the same a thousand years hence.[70]

The city was also seen as alien and destructive in its moral character. Sergei Obradovich's poem 'The City', published in *The Smithy* in 1920, and reprinted several times during the 1920s as part of Obradovich's cycle of poems about the city, is filled with images of moral decadence: the mad 'café-*chantant* crowd', the mass genuflecting before the gods of money, 'the lending trade in wretched souls', the 'bawling' of advertising and of the 'bazaar', the depressing sight of prostitutes in the night gloom, and the sight and smells of the 'crowd, stinking and drunken'. The poem begins with declarations of love for the City (always capitalized): as a place 'of great Beginnings and Journeys', and, slightly more ambivalently, as a place workers made and grew up with, whose 'iron and stones we strengthened / with the cement of our sweat and tears'. The poem concludes with a vision of salvation through struggle and revolution, but this message is far from consistent. Like so many proletarians, Obradovich found it difficult to reconcile his political certainties with his emotional and moral perceptions. The horrors of the city, like the 'moans' of his father, Obradovich would 'remember [his] whole life'.[71]

The appearance of women in these imaginative commentaries on the city underscores the personal, sentimental and moral nature of these writers' judgements of the modern landscape, particularly about a landscape traditionally interpreted as deeply masculine – and especially their growing ambivalence. Women appeared most often in these writings, according to a familiar cultural formula, as innocents cast into the pit of urban temptation and degradation. Poets described, for example, the 'sadness and longing' of innocent and beautiful young women from the countryside who came to the cities to work.[72] And women's fall into prostitution – a traditional image of urban debasement – was still most often viewed as a crime *against* women (not as willful acts by women, for which they could be blamed morally, much less appreciated as assertive actors). Filipchenko's description was typical, indeed clichéd, in its hyperbole and tone of outrage: 'Mothers with tears of pain and shame in their eyes send their daughters into the streets to sell their bodies. Mothers, driven mad with hunger, sell themselves. Husbands send our their wives. Fiancés – their brides-to-be.'[73]

However, images of women in the city in the hands of some of these worker-writers were becoming increasingly complex. Most tellingly, the image of the prostitute was changing. A number of worker-writers now voiced a certain kinship with the city's 'fallen women', both as human beings and as symbols.[74] It was with a mixture of pity, irony and a new sympathy that Kirillov acknowledged that amidst the cold crowds of the city, 'Only prostitutes here and there / Openly proffer tenderness'. They also shared with him his urban loneliness.[75] Aleksandrovskii, in his 1920 ode to Moscow, even more explicitly treated the prostitute as a sign of both the city's evil and its allure. The poem explores familiar themes of nostalgia for a rural childhood and anguish at the ugliness, hardships and decadence of city life. In a central moment in this evidently autobiographical poem, Aleksandrovskii yields to the immoral pleasures of the city:

> I plunge my body into shame.
> I toss out the last scraps of decency,
> And wait like a proper husband,
> In the leer of boulevard puddles,
> For painted Beatrice.
> I don't know which pain is greater –
> The sores on the body of my lover,
> Or that I became a man in that fire,
> In the inescapable longing of night.

The ambivalence with which Aleksandrovskii viewed this encounter with a city prostitute – pleasure and anguish, self-degradation and self-becoming – paralleled his view of the city itself:

> Moscow!
> O, let me, let me
> Kiss
> Your swarthy street hands
> For the sake of deep, secret torments,
> For the sake of great, sweet pain.[76]

There is no simple moral formula here. Aleksandrovskii remained on the uneasy ground of ambivalence.

These writers were not alone among post-revolutionary authors, of course, in writing about women in the city nor in treating this theme ambivalently. The image of the woman was a major trope in early Soviet literature and journalism and served as a means of exploring diverse ideas, ideals and anxieties. Women in the city appeared in these writings as inspiring and troubling objects of passion, as icons of virtue and tenderness as well as of sexual depravity and danger, as signs of purity and pollution, as figures representing backwardness but also emancipation and freedom, as markers of natural equality and of essential physical and spiritual difference.[77] Worker-writers shared this deepening ambivalence in thinking about women in the city (and, by extension, about men and masculinity) – and in using this image.

With particular complexity and ambiguity, Mikhail Gerasimov meditated on women and city life in his 1918 poem, 'Mona Lisa'. At the heart of the poem are three female figures. The first two are familiar tropes: factory girl and city prostitute. The first, to whom the poem is dedicated and partly addressed, is a young woman 'who came to us at our factory', a weapons factory, filled with the joy and laughter of innocence. But her spirit was inevitably crushed: 'You, like all of us, have bound your wings / And covered your sorrowing eyes / With the dust of gun powder.' Prostitutes are the second female figure. They are, in Gerasimov's words, 'injured wingless seagulls' (a likely reference to Chekhov's symbol of female innocence victimized by men). Staring into the Ekaterininskii canal in Petrograd, the narrator ponders the reflections he sees of prostitutes standing nearby. Thoughts of suicide, sexuality, injury and sacred purity intertwine. To the poet, these prostitutes are 'sinless Madonnas', victims 'nailed up' by city life, but also 'poison-yellow flowers' in the 'Petrograd muck'. The third, and most important, figure is another 'Madonna' – Leonardo da Vinci's *Mona Lisa* and especially her sad, enigmatic, 'secret' and 'bewitching' smile, which appears on all of the surfaces of city life: in smoke pouring from factory chimneys, in factory windows, in the reflections of machines, on workers' blue shirts, in the 'granite of my prison', in the factories' 'iron fires', on the upturned dirty faces of workers, on graves. 'Crowned in the glow of dusk, / The face of the Gioconda shines, / A garland of roses and a garland of thorns, / Borne on her clear brow.'[78]

In this deliberately ambiguous and enigmatic poem, Gerasimov drew a complex picture of women (and male feelings about women) in the city. The clichéd – and hence, for readers, easily understandable – image of the innocent country girl whose vitality and dignity wither in the city and factory, is combined with ambivalent sympathy and revulsion before prostitutes, with sensual desire and fears of pollution, and, most complexly, with images of a transcendent universal feminine

– hints of which are in each figure portrayed. Indeed, this poem is pervaded with echoes of mystical ideas (familiar among Russian intellectuals) of the Eternal Feminine as the embodiment of both spiritual wisdom and sensuality, as well as of the related religious idea (widely held) of the purity, loving-kindness and suffering of the Mother of God. Here, as in other reworkings of the image of the urban woman, long a touchstone for judging the moral meaning of city and factory life, meanings were ambivalent.

An unresolved argument was constant in the writings (and presumably in the minds) of these worker-intellectuals. The young factory poet Nikolai Kuznetsov tried to capture this ambivalent perception – though simplifying it more than many could – by describing himself as living with his 'mind in the city but the country in my heart'.[79] I would emphasize and generalize this point. The definition of ambiguity, as an analytical concept, is language that is unstable and even contradictory in meaning, that calls for a choice between alternative meanings but provides no ground for making a choice, and that refuses resolution.[80] This applies here. Just as it would be mistaken to conclude that these accounts were only a social critique of the capitalist city, it would also be simplistic to speak only of an absolute anti-urbanism. Discordant ambiguity remained persistent. Anti-urban and anti-modern perceptions, values and sentiments intertwined and often clashed with formal and rational notions (though no less real for that) about the positive value of city and factory. Concerns with the immediacy of moral and spiritual problems intertwined with awareness of dialectical teleologies and intellectual abstractions. Indeed, as Kuznetsov tried to suggest about himself, this unresolved dialogue between rationalized ideas and emotional and moral perceptions may be precisely the intellectual practice that most nurtured ambivalence. In this unstable and unresolved interplay between reason (willful cognition) and sensibility, ambiguity and heteroglossia thrived.

MACHINE HELL

It was, of course, the *modern* city that so disturbed and alienated these workers just as it was the modern city that so enraptured them. Factories and machines were at the heart of this troubling modernity. Valerian Pletnev, writing in 1922 when he was head of the Proletcult, noticed a certain 'psychological Luddism' in the Russian working class.[81] Conversely, Nikolai Liashko spoke of the 'solitude of those who sing of iron'.[82] But this was a solitude not limited to that of a conscious vanguard among the backward masses. Such 'backwardness' remained strongly evident among even radicalized proletarian writers. Judging the world mainly in aesthetic and ethical terms, these writers tended to see industry as an infernal place animated by a malevolent spirit. The Revolution intensified these perceptions as these writers raised their voices ever more resoundingly against the evils of the old world. But it also intensified their ambivalence as they simultaneously embraced the now official ideology of scientific and rational progress and worried about its alienating, dehumanizing and destructive effects.

The most outright and old-fashioned hostility to factories and machines appeared in the writings of older workers such as Egor Nechaev, ideological anti-urbanists such as Petr Oreshin (who, though an urban-born son of urban workers, organized a 'peasant section' in the Proletcult), and among beginner worker-writers (especially from provincial cities).[83] But we find much the same in the writings of the most prominent Proletcult and Communist writers from worker backgrounds living in the capital cities. In a poem entitled 'In the Factory', published in 1918 in the journal of the Petrograd Proletcult, Aleksei Mashirov ('Samobytnik') portrayed the factory as a 'hell' (a common image in which the physical and the moral were by definition intertwined), where 'labor thunders and groans like a demon', where workers gaze with 'emaciated dull looks', and every movement of their exhausted muscles is torment, while the furnace blazes and the metal gleams.[84] Likewise, Mashirov and other worker-writers described the terror felt by a young worker (whether fresh from the countryside or from a working-class home) as he faces the fearsome appearance of the factory, the machines hellishly 'knocking, screeching and whistling all around', the drive belts slithering overhead like snakes, while even the factory air 'buzzed and rang'.[85] Similarly, almost all of the leading Proletcultists wrote of the factory as an infernal place: as a 'machine hell', where 'even the black stones [of the factory] wept' and whose 'poisonous smoke' was 'eating away at the stars' golden lashes' (Gerasimov),[86] as a 'malicious devil' (Aleksandrovskii),[87] and as a place of groans and prayers where even the screams of death could not be heard, but 'where everything human was drowned in the thick lava of the iron roar, and the whole factory seemed to thunder apathetically over man perishing in toil' (Gastev).[88] Death and torment were ever present. For Obradovich, the smoke of the factories was the 'black mourning dress' worn by a suffocating city.[89]

These images did more than *contradict* quite different portraits by the same authors: they were part of a pervasive ambivalence in how these workers viewed the modern landscape of cities, factories, machines and metal. Some of these writers explicitly recognized that this vision reflected the ambivalence of modernity itself. In a 1921 essay in *The Smithy*, Nikolai Liashko defined modernity with an industrial metaphor that evoked its chaos and flux, its simultaneously inspiring and terrifying nature:

> Modernity [*sovremennost'*] is a factory boiler trembling at full steam. There is not a moment's rest: it whistles, wheezes and shudders. Many are afraid: the deposits inside the boiler are eating away at its walls, boiling lava surges forth and flows over the stokers and machinists – and with them perish both crew and helmsman. It seems to many that this is just what is happening. Bang! – the abyss. For some it is heaven in the abyss, for others – hell. But no one is indifferent. Everyone trembles, listens, looks about. All seems quiet. But then appear new operators running the geographic map, new claimants to throne, knout and barge. Into the furnace are cast anew tons of terrible passions [*strasti*] and blood, and again the boiler trembles, whistles and wheezes. And in the midst of its roaring occurs only displacement and change and the opening up only of dizzying perspectives! Wonders grow into horrors and horrors into wonders. To enumerate the changes would fill thousands of pages, and to describe them would fill millions of pages. Unexpected pains and joys ... appear at every step.[90]

In the face of the 'contradictoriness and complexity' of modern times, Liashko argued, worker-writers, who 'stand close to life', necessarily view this life complexly and critically. Least of all could they write – as some thought they did or wished they would – about: 'factories, factories and nothing else'.[91]

Mikhail Gerasimov, perhaps Soviet Russia's most renowned 'poet of iron', was also deliberate in arguing that industrial modernity itself was imbued with ambivalence and indeterminate meaning. In his 1918 'Poem on Iron', which appeared in the national journal of the Proletcult, Gerasimov insisted on iron's many voices: 'groans / the cry of fetters / the wail of the guillotine blade', and shrapnel, but also movement, 'purity', 'light', 'the trill of a flute', tenderness, love and power.[92] Similarly, and still more complexly, Gerasimov portrayed the factory as a sexually and spiritually alluring and painful place – where factory stoves 'expose their hellish mouth / Burning and crudely caressing the body'.[93]

These arguments about modernity's ambivalence were often part of a dialectical vision of transcendence, of the necessary linkage between present sufferings and impending salvation, but its was a vision focused mainly on the suffering. Often, this was constructed as an argument about sacrifice and suffering for the sake of the future. Many of these writers described workers as 'crucified' on the 'iron cross', or buried in the 'factory crypt', only to be 'resurrected'.[94] A better future would arrive, most of these writers seemed to believe, though its coming was likely to be brutal. Aleksei Kraiskii, for example, imagined the future as a striding 'iron giant', tearing through the cold fields and darkness with roars and whistles. When this fearsome saviour runs short of water and fuel, workers feed it with their own blood and bodies.[95]

Gastev went even further and defined 'catastrophe' as essential to the very nature of modern life, as central to the existence that defined the emerging new psychology of proletarianized humanity.[96] He illustrated his theory of catastrophe in his prose-poem of 1917, 'The Tower' (*Bashnia*), a poetic tale, often reprinted and publicly declaimed after October, that describes the endless intertwining of heroic striving with catastrophic failure and death.

> Let there be still more catastrophes.
> Ahead are still more graves, still more collapses!
> So be it!
> Against the bright sky, the tower appears black, for iron knows no smiles: there is more misery in it than happiness, thinking more than laughing. Iron, covered with the rust of time, is the most serious thought, the gloomy thought of the age and epoch.[97]

Gerasimov similarly explored images of cruel and harsh aspiration when he imagined the factory as a titanic giant, whose great iron horns, thrust into the sky, pierce the heavens and God himself, drawing bloody 'red rays from the wounded God', who falls from his soft cloudy perch into the '"machine hell" below'.[98]

A dark ambivalence was especially characteristic of the writings on factory and machines of Andrei Platonov during these years. In pondering the forces and landscapes of modernity, Platonov interwove ideas about human mastery over nature with skepticism about triumphant human consciousness and will, and a sentimental and even erotic love of physical things with a fear and attendant abhorrence of matter.[99] According to the literary scholar V. Eidinova, Platonov viewed the world as embodying the opposing principles of spiritual and material, rational and emotional, nature and machines,[100] regarding modern technology, in particular, as Thomas Seifrid described it, with 'an ambivalent mixture of ecstasy and terror'.[101] Platonov's first story, published in the Voronezh railway workers' journal in 1918, was set in a smelting shop in a large metal plant, which the narrator, a new worker, enters 'almost joyfully'. Platonov describes the factory in conflicted terms. He admires the 'obedient machines' and flowing metal for their 'mighty pulse' and metallic 'song'. But his descriptions continually imply something evil and dangerous in this might: the 'rafters shudder', the 'engine whirs derisively and inexorably', the 'endless drive belts crack treacherously', and somewhere in the factory 'something whistles and smiles', 'something locked up, strong and cruelly ruthless' that 'wants its freedom, but cannot tear itself loose, and so wails and squeals, and furiously pounds and whirls in solitude and ceaseless rancor. It begs and threatens, and again shakes, with tireless muscles, the cunningly interwoven body of stone, iron and copper.' In this setting, workers toiled 'happily' and 'time passed unnoticed' until this innocent and vain joy was shattered by an accident – a 'whip' of burning metal tears itself free and kills a young worker. But after a period of silence and some shedding of tears the machines again are in motion.[102]

Catastrophe was never far from the surface in Platonov's world of modern achievement. His stories often portrayed engineers and workers filled with self-confidence in their abilities to control matter through will and consciousness and with faith in modern technique and science. In two short stories published in 1921 and 1922, Platonov described the efforts of the worker Markun and the engineer Vogulov to build machines that could harness vast amounts of energy for transforming the physical world. Both stories conclude with mighty catastrophes – at once appealing and horrifying. When Markun, standing before his mighty turbine, slips into a thoughtless rapture, his machine races to a higher and higher speed and then explodes, sending pieces flying destructively. Even more dramatically, the engineer Vogulov creates a high-energy power – which he calls 'ultra-light' [*ul'tra-svet*] – that is used to remake the world's natural landscape for human use, to help individuals (through injections of the stuff) to overcome the normal physical and mental limitations of ordinary human life, and then to remake the entire universe. The ultimate victory of technology over matter is paradoxical: treated humans die after only a few days (though these are days of greatness) and the entire physical universe is obliterated,[103] achieving with a vengeance the modern dream of purity. In a poem published in 1922, Platonov similarly envisions the current earth and universe being 'murdered by machines' and 'killed by iron', to be replaced by a 'new iron universe' in which 'we transgress all boundaries and laws'.[104] As in many proletarian writings, ecstasy and terror, good and evil, death and salvation are combined in these images of modern factories and machines and of modern change and progress.

MODERNITY, REVOLUTION AND AMBIVALENCE

Questions of theory are persistently at stake here, and no less for contemporaries than for our own analysis. In first place stands the problem of defining modernity itself. After all, as an imaginative construct, modernity has always stood in complex relation to the actual structures, objects and values of modernization and modern civilization. Matei Calinescu, for example, has written of 'two modernities' – one characterized by 'the doctrine of progress, confidence in the beneficial possibilities of science and technology, the concern with time', and 'the cult of reason'; the other an aesthetic modernity that found the contemporary bourgeois applications of science, time and reason repellent, embracing instead a modernity characterized by defiant rebellion, emotional passion and, often, an ambiguous and pessimistic vision of modern progress and the future.[105] Marshall Berman has similarly argued that modernism in literature, art and intellectual life embraced less the rationalizing and reordering drive of modernization than its dynamic disruption, chaos and flux, though tempered by an essential, if sometimes faltering, faith that a new and better life (and beauty) would emerge from the maelstrom.[106] Postmodernist theories have offered related but more complex readings of this dualistic modernity. Zygmunt Bauman, in particular, has explored the false and unsettling relationship of modernity to its own contingency, flux and uncertainty. Modernity, he argues, characteristically denied its own self and nature. Inherently critical, restless and insatiable, modern culture paralleled a modern society that was in a constant state of upheaval, destruction and instability. But it simultaneously struggled to overcome all of this: to disenchant the world by imposing the artifice of 'meaning-legislating reason'; to embark on a never-ending escape from the natural wilderness; to struggle constantly for universality, homogeneity and clarity, to 'problematize contingency as an enemy'; to define skepticism as ignorance; to 'purge ambivalence'. In short, it was in the very nature of modernity to 'live in and through self-deception', to engage in constant denial – in the name of necessity, universality, scientific truth, certainty and natural order – of the contingency, artifice, undecidability, provisionality and ambivalence of its own making.[107]

These contradictions within modernity and modernism were present with a particular intensity in Russia, where the Revolution was driven by an aspiration to race ahead of history to create a new world in the undeveloped and unpropitious space of the collapsed Russian empire. Marxist ideology encouraged this with its own paradoxical vision of modernity, its recognition of both the brutalities of urban, industrial modernity – the oppression, the disenchantment of the world, the decadence, the painful disorder – and modernity's dynamic energy, productive power, emancipating change and dialectical self-transcendence. At the same time, Marxism struggled to resolve contingency and uncertainty in order to construct a new order. Indeed, in its post-revolutionary Soviet stance, Marxist political theory placed increasing emphasis on the modernism of scientific rationalism and progress, and left less and less space for the modernism that stood in defiance of the materialism and rationalism of bourgeois modernity much less to question progress, modern order, and the cult of science and reason.[108] To borrow Bauman's phrase, Soviet modernity struggled to 'purge ambivalence'.

MODERNITY AND THE POETICS OF PROLETARIAN DISCONTENT

The modernist embrace of a world in flux – of ambiguity, multivalence and indeterminacy – was clearly uncomfortable for many Soviet Marxist theorists. Influential cultural officials such as Pavel Lebedev-Polianskii were openly and explicitly intolerant of ambiguity. Repeatedly, Lebedev-Polianskii reminded writers who claimed to be proletarian in mentality as well as in social origin that there was no place in the proletarian outlook for 'doubt' or 'imprecision',[109] that Soviet culture required 'clarity, precision, solidity and a forged shape, not endless indeterminacy'.[110] The communist literary theorist Semen Rodov similarly proclaimed bluntly that workers, especially when contemplating the central Marxist values of city, factory and machine, 'cannot and must not know ambivalence [*razdvoenie*]'.[111]

In fact, Marxist intellectuals admitted with various degrees of dismay, one found precisely such 'agonizing ambivalence' (*muchitel'naia razdvoennost'*)[112] among many proletarians. In the opening address to the first All-Russian Conference of Proletarian Writers in May 1920, Aleksandr Bogdanov, speaking in the name of the presidium of the Proletcult, complained that some proletarian poets continued to write in 'too foggy' a manner. (To illustrate his point, Bogdanov pointed to Gerasimov, one of the organizers of the conference, citing his poem 'Mona Lisa' as an example of such obscure and imprecise writing.) He advised writers to 'beware of modernist poets' and to pay more attention to the 'simplicity' (*prostota*) of such 'coryphaei of literature' as Pushkin, Lermontov, Byron, Goethe and Shakespeare. Gerasimov shrewdly responded that even Pushkin was not always clear. (He might have said the same for the other coryphaei.)[113]

As here, some worker-writers themselves – in moments that were as remarkably insightful as they were daring – argued for the greater truthfulness of their ambivalent perspective on modern life. The trouble with so many educated Communist critics of real proletarian literature, Vladimir Kirillov commented in 1921 (in a widely read essay that provoked much controversy), is that they have plenty of Marxist theory and dialectical method but have never 'tasted factory air'. Ironically, he continued, these 'theoreticians' tended to blame errors in workers' attitudes on 'bourgeois influence' and inadequate 'cooking in the factory boiler'. In fact, 'as in former times, the theoretician sits upon his high throne on Olympus' while the proletarian poet 'remains below in the gloom of Hell'. Though such critics may be 'the very best Marxists', he concluded sarcastically, they cannot 'understand deeply and multifacetedly the nature of the artistic creativity of the proletarian writer'.[114] Nor, he implied, could they understand the modern world these writers were portraying.

Other articulate worker-intellectuals similarly warned – and defended themselves – against the false simplicities of the increasingly official paradigm of revered modernity and the increasingly hegemonic epistemology of 'clarity, precision and solidity'. In recent years, complained Nikolai Liashko in 1920, a 'falseness' and 'forced intentionality' (*narochitost'*) has crept into proletarian writing under the effective pressure of demands by intelligentsia leaders that a 'true worker-writer' write only about 'the life of iron, furnaces, cranes', and sing only about how 'they are in iron, made of iron, made of steel'. This is a lie, Liashko argued. It is a lie partly because it is so at odds with the reality of the present: collapsed industry and silent factories. But the main error of this 'metal theme' runs deeper, Liashko insisted, for it clashes with the more subtle understanding that 'true' worker-writers have of the world. It is false and dangerous 'to reduce the whole gamut of life to one or two chords'. Truth, Liashko implied, is always what Mikhail Bakhtin would later call *raznorechivyi* (heteroglossic, polyphonic). To deny this complexity not only is coercive but, in the long term, threatens 'to atrophy perception'. The 'metal theme', in this light, is false not only because workers cannot forget that cities of iron and smoke are 'hells for working people'; most importantly, it is false before workers' more complex judgements and dreams:

> Hatred of the stagnant countryside and irresistible love for it, enmity toward the machine, which drains their strength, and tender feelings toward it, exist side by side in the soul of the worker. A great spaciousness opens up before the worker-writer: all of the heterogeneity of life, its light and its shadows.

This complex perception went well beyond any simply dialectical appreciation of progress emerging from contradictions. At stake, Liashko implied, were questions of the sources and nature of knowledge and truth. Rationality alone does not suffice: simplified and one-dimensional perception occurs when writers 'stop consciousness at that which is often borne only in the head'. But workers cannot stop here: 'too much lies in the heart of the worker-writer'.[115]

The 'heart' – and the darkness we often see there – marks a terrain of which historians and social scientists are normally (perhaps wisely) wary. But if ambivalence is to be understood beyond its formal structure as a type of conflicted cognition, it must be taken into account. It is difficult not to notice in the writings of these worker-authors a certain – and growing – anxiety, unease and even despair intertwined with the most passionate declarations of determination, hope and faith. Together with fervent hope that city and factory were indeed, as Vladimir Kirillov put it, 'a great bridge to the liberation and exaltation of man',[116] these proletarian intellectuals seem increasingly to have felt that there was no escape from the infernal machinery of industrial modernity, no dialectical transcendence, no satisfaction even in the recognition of ambiguity's truth. Ideological exhilaration, as we have seen, alternated with aesthetic and moral panic, and with thoughts about catastrophe and death.

Writing in 1918, Vladimir Kirillov described being so depressed by modern life that he had been tempted 'to beat [his] head against the stones' of the city, until he was saved by ideology in nature's form: the sun 'literally spoke' to him, reminding him of the joys of life and struggle.[117] But this revolutionary epiphany did not last long. By 1920, he was again (and now responding to the present rather than describing memories of the past) openly imagining his death and burial: dying 'amidst the noise of the trams' in his 'grey, stone building', and being buried amidst the 'same vanities and noise on the streets of the capital', the same drunken love and drunken sorrow, and the same newspapers being hawked – only now, he added, joined by an 'absurd' and trite mention of a dead poet. He admitted a slight possibility of happiness, however. Not in the joy of struggle, but in the unseen and private pleasures of a specter, smoking cigarettes, strolling and, in the evening, stroking the hair of his beloved.[118] By the early 1920s, as the transformative promises of the Revolution remained largely unfulfilled, thoughts about urban life were generating darker and darker thoughts. Critics of Aleksandrovskii's poems of this period, for example, noted with dismay that notwithstanding his efforts to 'constantly be bold' (*postoianno bodritsia*) and his insistence that his earlier anguish about city life had passed, a mood of despair was more and more 'interwoven' with deliberately bold, revolutionary songs.[119] Aleksandrovskii was not alone. Well into the 1920s, critics found, as we have seen, a pervasive 'agonizing ambivalence'.[120]

We might speak of this ambivalence as resistance – as refusal to accept an oppressive model of modernity, of the persistence of alternative visions of the world. But this was a compromised resistance, limited by an opposing enthusiasm for the modern, and grounded more in anguish and moral sensibility than in anger or committed dissent. Thus, these writers spoke not of defiance but of 'anguish' in the 'soul' of those 'born in granite',[121] not of opposition but of the multiplicities of the creative imagination, not of an ideological alternative but of the complicating (and discursively elusive) influence of what lies beyond the 'mind' in the 'heart'. Nor was this an embryonic postmodern consciousness: these proletarian intellectuals evidently found no pleasure in ambivalence, ambiguity or indeterminacy, no comfort in paradox or irony. They were almost all socialists and Marxists and they shared the earnest world-transforming idealism of the October Revolution. They could not embrace 'a life without truths, standards and ideals',[122] even when they could not fully embrace the available 'truths'. In this sense, perhaps, theirs was a deeply modern anxiety about modernity.

LANGUAGE AND REVOLUTION

NOTES

1. These individuals were 'authors' in the loose sense of people who did more than occasionally pen a few lines of poetry or prose, but who wrote with a deliberateness and determination that usually led to their being published regularly and, in most cases, becoming professional writers after 1917. They were 'working class' in that they began writing while employed as wage earners. They were employed in a variety of industries and trades, especially, for the authors mentioned most often in this essay, metalworking, printing, railroad shops, baking and leatherwork. Many were itinerants who often changed jobs as they moved about the country.
2. Particularly influential has been the work of philosophers, literary critics and interpretive cultural anthropologists and sociologists such as Mikhail Bakhtin, Pierre Bourdieu, Michel de Certeau, Jacques Derrida, Michel Foucault, Clifford Geertz, Stuart Hall, Reinhart Koselleck, Iurii Lotman, and Paul Ricoeur, and the work of cultural historians, notably Roger Chartier, Robert Darnton, Natalie Zemon Davis, Carlo Ginzburg, Lynn Hunt, Dominick La Capra, Jacques Rancière, David Sabean, Joan Scott, Gareth Stedman Jones, William Sewell and E.P. Thompson.
3. There are already far too many authors and publications to list here. Although already outdated, a relatively recent bibliography of cultural studies on pre-revolutionary Russian history can be found in Stephen F. Frank and Mark D. Steinberg (eds), *Cultures in Flux: Lower-Class Values, Practices, and Resistance in Late Imperial Russia* (Princeton, NJ: Princeton University Press, 1994). A useful collection on the early Soviet period that partly marks, at least within labor history, this shift toward cultural history, is Lewis H. Siegelbaum and Ronald Grigor Suny (eds), *Making Workers Soviet: Power, Class, and Identity* (Ithaca: Cornell University Press, 1994). In July 1996, *The Russian Review*, edited by the late Allan Wildman, devoted an issue to the linguistic turn in Russian history. Also illustrative is the shift within the work of almost all the leading 'social historians' in the field, for example Victoria Bonnell, Laura Engelstein, Sheila Fitzpatrick, Diane Koenker, Lewis Siegelbaum, Ron Suny and Reginald Zelnik.
4. See, for example, Clifford Geertz, *The Interpretation of Cultures* (New York: Basic Books, 1973); Pierre Bourdieu, *Outline of a Theory of Practice* (Cambridge: Cambridge University Press, 1977); Michel de Certeau, *The Practice of Everyday Life* (Berkeley, CA: University of California Press, 1984) and *The Writing of History* (New York: Columbia University Press, 1988); William H. Sewell, Jr, 'Toward a Post-materialist Rhetoric for Labor History', in Lenard R. Berlanstein (ed.), *Rethinking Labor History: Essays on Discourse and Class Analysis* (Urbana, IL: University of Illinois Press, 1993), pp. 15–38; Alf Lüdtke (ed.), *The History of Everyday Life* (Princeton, NJ: Princeton University Press, 1995); M.M. Bakhtin, *The Dialogic Imagination*, ed. Michael Holquist (Austin, TX: University of Texas, 1996). For useful summary discussions and evaluations of many of these theoretical issues, see the introduction to, and articles by Sherry Ortner and Stuart Hall in Nicholas Dirks, Geoff Eley and Sherry Ortner (eds), *Culture/Power/History: A Reader in Contemporary Social Theory* (Princeton, NJ: Princeton University Press, 1994) and Roger Chartier, 'Intellectual History or Social-Cultural History? The French Trajectories', in Dominick La Capra and Steven L. Kaplan (eds), *Modern European Intellectual History* (Ithaca, NY: Cornell University Press, 1982).
5. See Chapter 6 in this volume.
6. Dirks *et al.*, 'Introduction', *Culture/Power/History*, p. 31.
7. V. Lenin, 'Zakliuchitel'naia rech', 15 Marta, Chetvertyi s"ezd sovetov', *Pravda* 19(6), March 1918, reprinted in V.I. Lenin, *Polnoe sobranie sochinenii*, 5th edn, Vol. 36 (Moscow: Gos. izd. polit. literatury, 1962), p. 116.
8. Katerina Clark, *The Soviet Novel: History as Ritual* (Chicago, IL: University of Chicago Press, 1985), p. 94. On the overwhelming 'masculine ethos' in early Soviet culture, and on its tensions and contradictions, see Eric Naiman, *Sex in Public: The Incarnation of Early Soviet Ideology* (Princeton, NJ: Princeton University Press, 1997) and especially Elliot Borenstein, *Men Without Women: Masculinity and Revolution in Russian Fiction, 1917–1929* (Durham, NC: Duke University Press, 2000).
9. V. Polianskii [P.I. Lebedev], 'Motivy rabochei poezii', *Proletarskaia kul'tura* 3 (Aug.

1918), p. 9.
10. See also V. Polianskii, 'Dve poezii', *Proletarskaia kul'tura* 13–14 (Jan.–March 1920), p. 47.
11. V.L. L'vov–Rogachevskii, *Ocherki proletarskoi literatury* (Moscow/Leningrad, 1927), pp. 110–11; A. Voronskii, 'O gruppe pisatelei "Kuznitsa"', in A. Voronskii, *Iskusstvo i zhizn': sbornik statei* (Moscow/Petrograd: Krug, 1924), pp. 128–32 (originally published in *Krasnaia nov'* 13 [1923]). For similar statements, see S. Rodov in *Kuznitsa* 1 (May 1920), pp. 24–5; P. Bessal'ko in *Griadushchee* 1 (1919), p. 15; S. Rodov in *Gorn*, Book 6 (1922), p. 118–19; I. Pchelintsev in *Rabochii zhurnal* 3–4 (1924), p. 211; L. Kleinbort, *Ocherki narodnoi literatury (1880–1923 gg.)* (Leningrad, 1924), pp. 266–85.
12. I. Eroshin, 'V derevne', *Zavod ognekrylyi* (Moscow, 1918), p. 69; I. Sadof'ev, 'Ritm granita (Posviashchaiu Krasnomy Piteru)', *Griadushchee* 4 (1919), pp. 1–3; N. Poletaev, 'Chadilo chertova kadilo', *Gorn* 2–3 (1919), p. 4; S. Obradovich, 'Gorod (Poema)' (1919–20), *Kuznitsa* 5–6 (Oct.–Nov. 1920), pp. 17–23; Ia. Berdnikov, 'Gorod', *Griadushchee* 12–13 (1920), p. 1; V. Aleksandrovskii, 'Iz tsikla "Moskva"', *Tvori* 1 (Dec. 1920), p. 4, and 'V granite', *Kuznitsa* 4 (Aug.–Sept. 1920), pp. 8–9.
13. Aleksandrovskii, 'Iz tsikla "Moskva"'.
14. V. Kirillov, 'Gorodu', *Griadushchee* 2 (May 1918), p. 6.
15. Berdnikov, 'Gorod'.
16. Aleksandrovskii, 'Iz tsikla "Moskva"'. See also Kirillov, 'Gorodu'.
17. I. Sadof'ev, 'Ritm granita'. See also Sadof'ev, 'Petrogradu', *Dinamo–Stikhi* (Petrograd: Proletkul't, 1918), p. 38. For other examples of this theme, see Eroshin, 'V derevne'; and V. Aleksandrovskii, 'Putnik', *Gorn* 1 (1918), p. 10.
18. N. Liashko, 'Dukhovnye iady goroda i kooperatsiia', *Rabochii mir* 7, 23 June 1918, p. 24.
19. Kirillov, 'Gorodu'.
20. See also Revelation 3:12 and all of Chapter 21; also Psalms 46:4 (45:5 in the Russian Orthodox Bible), which sees God living in a divine 'city' (*grad*).
21. See Frank E. Manuel and Fritzie P. Manuel, *Utopian Thought in the Western World* (Cambridge, MA: Belknap Press of Harvard University Press, 1979).
22. I. Eroshin, 'Po doroge', *Tvorchestvo* 5 (Sept. 1918), p. 19.
23. A. Platonov, 'Mai' (1920), in *Golubaia glubina* (Krasnodar, 1922), p. 16.
24. See Katerina Clark, *Petersburg, Crucible of Revolution* (Cambridge, MA: Harvard University Press, 1995), esp. pp. 3, 84, 141, 209–11, 252.
25. I. Filipchenko, 'Lenin', *Rabochii zhurnal* 1 (1924), p. 65.
26. V. Kremnev, 'Poema Velikoi Revoliutsii', *Kuznitsa* 5–6 (Oct.–Nov. 1920), p. 65.
27. Kremnev, 'Poema Velikoi Revoliutsii'; Polianskii, 'Dve poezii'; S. Rodov in *Gorn*. 6 (1922), pp. 116–20; Voronskii, 'O gruppe pisatelei "Kuznitsa"', pp. 130–35.
28. Kirillov, 'Gorodu'. Ivan Eroshin also portrayed the factory as a 'temple'. Eroshin, 'Iz tsikla "Pesni truda"', *Zavod ognekrylyi* (Moscow, 1918), p. 48.
29. M. Gerasimov, 'Zavodskaia truba', *Tvorchestvo* 3 (July 1918), p. 3.
30. M. Gerasimov, 'Letim', *Zavod ognekrylyi* (Moscow, 1918), p. 17.
31. A. Shliapnikov, 'Aviatory', *Proletarskaia kul'tura* 7–8 (April–May 1919), pp. 59–62. See also S. Obradovich, 'Vzlet' (1922), in Rossiskii gosudarstvennyi arkhiv literatury i isskustv (RGALI), f. 1874, op. 1, d. 7, l. 66.
32. Sadof'ev, 'Ritm granita'; Iv. Ivanov, 'Ia – mashinist', *Molot* 1 (Nov. 1920), pp. 16–17.
33. V. Aleksandrovskii, 'Krylia', *Gorn*, Book 5 (1920), pp. 7–9.
34. M. Gerasimov, 'Iz poema "Oktiabria"', *Kuznitsa* 3 (July 1920), pp. 10–11.
35. For such criticism, see S. Grigor'ev, 'Novaia fabrika', *Gorn* 6 (1922), pp. 113–16.
36. For example, V. Aleksandrovskii, 'Kuznets', *Zavod ognekrylyi* (Moscow, 1918), p. 35; M. Gerasimov, 'Zarevo zavodov', *Zarevo zavodov* 1 (Jan. 1919), pp. 8–10. On the iconographic importance and significance of the blacksmith in Bolshevik culture, see Victoria E. Bonnell, *Iconography of Power; Soviet Political Posters under Lenin and Stalin* (Berkeley, CA: University of California Press, 1997), Ch. 1.
37. For example, see A. Lunacharskii, 'Nachalo proletarskoi estetiki', *Proletarskaia kul'tura*, 11–12 (Dec. 1919), pp. 8–10; and E. Bogdat'eva, 'Poeziia zolota i poeziia zheleza', *Griadushchee* 3 (June 1918), p. 13.

38. V. Kirillov, 'My', *Griadushchee* 2 (May 1918), p. 4.
39. M. Gerasimov, 'Zheleznye tsvety', *Zavod ognekrylyi* (Moscow, 1918), p. 16.
40. Samobytnik [A. Mashirov], 'Mashinnyi rai', *Griadushchee* 1–2 (1920), p. 1.
41. In addition to the examples below, see Pavel Bezsal'ko in *Griadushchee* 7 (Oct. 1918), p. 13.
42. I. Sadof'ev, 'V zavode', *Dinamo-stikhi* (Petrograd, 1918), pp. 44–5. Sadof'ev wrote many similar poems.
43. Aleksei Gastev, 'Zelezyne pul'sy', *Poeziia rabochego udara* (Petrograd, 1918), pp. 116, 123 (this was the first publication of this story); 'Kran', *Vooruzhennyi narod*, 6 Sept. 1918; 'Rel'sy', *Zheleznyi put'* (Voronezh) 1 (1918), p. 11; and other writings in *Poeziia rabochego udara*. See also the discussion of Gastev's writings by Kurt Johansson, *Aleksej Gastev: Proletarian Bard of the Machine Age* (Stockholm: Almqvist & Wiksell International, 1983); and Richard Stites, *Revolutionary Dreams: Utopian Vision and Experimental Life in the Russian Revolution* (New York: Oxford University Press, 1989), pp. 149–55.
44. I. Ustinov, 'Pevuchaia stal'', *Tvorchestvo* 3 (Aug. 1918), p. 12; RGALI, f. 1641, op. 1, d. 36 (notebook of published and unpublished poems by I.G. Ustinov); M. Gerasimov, 'Vesennee utro', *Zarevo zavodov* 2 (1919), p. 8; A. Sh. (a female member of a proletarian literary circle), review of N. Tikhomirov, *Krasnyi most': stikhi 1914–18* (Petrograd, 1919), in *Revoliutsionnye vskhody* 3–4 (Oct. 1920), p. 10; Fekuz, 'Liub'vi rabochego', *Rabochee tvorchestvo* (writings by 'worker correspondents' in Nizhnyi Novgorod) 1 (Dec. 1923), p. 35; *Rabochee tvorchestvo* 8 (Nov. 1924), p. 13.
45. I. Dozorov [A. Gastev], 'My rastem iz zheleza', *Metallist*, 16 Dec. 1917, p. 4. The poem was written, according to Gastev's preface to the fifth edition of his *Poeziia rabochego udara* (Moscow, 1924), in 1914. It was reprinted frequently after it first appeared in December 1917.
46. Aleksei Gastev, *Industrial'noi mir* (Khar'kov, 1919), pp. 50–5, 68, 70; 'O tendentsiiakh proletarskoi kul'tury', *Proletarskaia kul'tura* 9–10 (June–July 1919), p. 42.
47. A. Gastev, 'Novaia industriia', *Vestnik metallista* 2 (1918), cited in Johansson, *Aleksej Gastev*, p. 62.
48. Gastev, *Industrial'noi mir*, pp. 74–7; Gastev, 'O tendentsiiakh', pp. 44–5.
49. Kirillov, 'My'.
50. V. Aleksandrovskii, 'Moi muskuly – pruzhiny', *Zavod ognekrylyi* (Moscow, 1918), p. 36.
51. M. Gerasimov, 'Ia ne nezhnyi', *Tvori* 2 (1921), p. 3. Similar themes and phrases appeared in 1918 in 'Zheleznye tsvety', *Zavod ognekrylyi* (Moscow, 1918), p. 16.
52. M. Gerasimov, 'Derevnia', *Griadushchee* 11 (1920), p. 4. Later reprinted as the opening stanzas of 'Elektrifikatsiia', *Elektrifikatsiia* (Petersburg [sic], 1922), pp. 3–5.
53. M. Volkov, 'Letropikatsiia' (allegedly a peasant's ignorant mispronunciation of eletrofikatsiia), *Kuznitsa* 8 (April–Sept. 1921), pp. 22–8.
54. For example, M. Gerasimov, 'Iz poemy "Elektrifikatsiia"', *Griadushchee* 1–3 (1921), p. 6; *Elektrifikatsiia*.
55. Zygmunt Bauman, *Postmodernity and Its Discontents* (New York: New York University Press, 1997), Ch. 1. For the larger Soviet elaboration, see Clark, *Petersburg*.
56. Poletaev, 'Chadilo chertova kadilo', p. 4.
57. Eroshin, 'V derevne'.
58. Aleksandrovskii, 'Putnik'.
59. Ibid.
60. Quoted, along with other similar statements, in P. Bessal'ko, 'O poezii krest'ianskoi i proletarskoi', *Griadushchee* 7 (Oct. 1918), p. 13.
61. I. Sadof'ev, 'Ritm granita'.
62. A. Sh., review of N. Tikhomirov, *Krasnyi most'*.
63. S. Obradovich, 'Griadushchee', RGALI, f. 1874, op. 1, d. 7, l. 38 (this item is noted as a clipping from *Pravda*, 6 Dec. 1921, though I did not find it there).
64. V. Aleksandrovskii, 'Toboi my raspiaty, gorod' (1918), in V. Aleksandrovskii, *Zvon solntsa* (Moscow, 1923), pp. 19–20.
65. V. Kirillov, 'Vesna v stolitse', *Stikhotvorenie* (St Petersburg, 1918), p. 25.
66. Poletaev, 'Chadilo chertova kadilo', p. 4; V. Aleksandrovskii, 'Okraina', *Zavod ognekrylyi* (Moscow, 1918), p. 73.

67. S. Obradovich, 'Gorod', p. 18.
68. For example, Aleksandrovskii, 'Okraina', pp. 73–4; Obradovich, 'Gorod', pp. 19–21.
69. V. Kirillov, 'Gorod', *Stikhotvoreniia 1914–1918* (Petersburg [sic], 1918), p. 26 (not previously published).
70. V. Kirillov, 'Byl vecher, kak vecher', *Kuznitsa* 7 (Dec. 1920–March 1921), p. 9. Aleksandrovskii was similarly disturbed by posters along the streets that addressed sexual questions. V. Aleksandrovskii, 'Budni', *Kuznitsa* 9 (1922), p. 8.
71. Obradovich, 'Gorod'. Similar themes may be found in Petr Oreshin, 'Gorod', *Krasnyi zvon: sbornik stikhov* (Petrograd, 1918), pp. 69–70.
72. P. Arskii, 'Devushka, prishedshei v gorod', *Griadushchee* 7–8 (1920), p. 1.
73. I. Filipchenko, 'Lenin', *Rabochii zhurnal* 1 (1924), p. 58.
74. Incidentally, Baudelaire regarded the urban poet as spiritual cousin to the urban prostitute in their common identification with 'all the professions, rejoicings, miseries' that confront them. Quoted in Carl Schorske, 'The Idea of the City in European Thought, Voltaire to Spengler', in Oscar Handlin and John Burchard (eds) *The Historian and the City* (Cambridge, MA: MIT, 1963), p. 110.
75. Kirillov, 'Gorod'; 'Stolichnoe', *Stikhotvoreniia 1914–1918*, p. 24 (first published in *Krasnaia gazeta*, 25 June 1918).
76. V. Aleksandrovskii, 'Moskva (otryvki iz poemy)', *Kuznitsa* 5 (Oct.–Nov. 1920), pp. 12–16.
77. See Richard Stites, *The Women's Liberation Movement in Russia* (Princeton, NJ: Princeton University Press, 1978), Chs 10–11; Wendy Z. Goldman, *Women, the State, and Revolution* (Cambridge: Cambridge University Press, 1993); Catriona Kelly, *A History of Russian Women's Writing, 1820–1992* (Oxford: Clarendon Press, 1994), Ch. 9; Elizabeth Waters, 'The Female Form in Soviet Political Iconography, 1917–1932', in Barbara Clements, Barbara Engel and Christine Worobec (eds), *Russia's Women* (Berkeley, CA: University of California Press, 1991), pp. 225–42; Naiman, *Sex in Public*; Bonnell, *Iconography of Power*, Ch. 2; Borenstein, *Men Without Women*.
78. M. Gerasimov, 'Monna Liza, Poema', *Gorn* 1 (1918), pp. 11–16.
79. A. Kosterin, 'Nikolai Kuznetsov', *Rabochii zhurnal* 1–2 (1925), p. 232.
80. Shlomith Rimmon, *The Concept of Ambiguity: The Example of James* (Chicago, IL: University of Chicago Press, 1977); William Empson, *Seven Types of Ambiguity* (New York: New Directions, 1947 [1st edn London, 1930]); Donald N. Levine, *The Flight From Ambiguity: Essays in Social and Cultural Theory* (Chicago, IL: University of Chicago Press, 1985); Timothy Bahti, 'Ambiguity and Indeterminacy, the Juncture', *Comparative Literature* 3 (Summer 1986), pp. 211–13.
81. V. Pletnev, 'Sovremennyi moment i zadachi proletkul'ta', *Gorn*, Book 6 (1922), p. 23.
82. N. Liashko, 'Solntse, plechi, i gruz' (1920–22), *Rabochie rasskazy* (Moscow: Izd-vo VTsSPS, 1924), p. 95.
83. See, for example, *Glukhar': rasskaz* (Samara, 1920), pp. 3, 5–7; E. Nechaev, 'Iz pesen' o zavode (proshloe)', *Kuznitsa* 1 (May 1920), p. 7; P. Oreshin, 'Smychka', *Zheleznyi put'* 7 (1923), p. 1; I. Doronin, 'Na rabotu', *Rabochaia vesna*, Vol. 2 (Moscow, 1923), pp. 24–6; S. Khaibulin (a 15-year old member of a 'children's Proletcult'), 'K 25–mu Oktiabria', *Detskii proletkul't* 1 (7 Nov. 1919), p. 3.
84. Samobytnik [A. Mashirov], 'V zavode', *Griadushchee* 3 (1918), p. 11.
85. Samobytnik, 'Siluety iz zhizny rabochikh (etiud)', *Griadushchee* 1 (Jan. 1918), p. 6; Ivan Eroshin, 'Detstvo (rasskaz rabochego)', *Tvorchestvo* 4 (Aug. 1918), pp. 13–14.
86. M. Gerasimov, 'My', *Zarevo zavodov* 2 (1919), p. 9; also 'Kochegar' and 'Zavodu', *Zavod ognekrylyi* (Moscow, 1918), pp. 43, 54.
87. Aleksandrovskii, 'Okraina'.
88. A. Gastev, 'Vesna v rabochem gorodke', *Griadushchee* 7–8 (1919), p. 8.
89. Obradovich, 'Gorod', p. 18.
90. N. Liashko, 'O byte i literature perekhodnogo vremeni', *Kuznitsa* 8 (April–Sept. 1921), p. 29.
91. Ibid., p. 34.
92. M. Gerasimov, 'Stikhi o zheleze', *Proletarskaia kul'tura* 4 (Sept. 1918), p. 31 (p. 30 in another printing of the same date).
93. M. Gerasimov, 'Zavodskoe', *Sbornik proletarskikh pisatelei* (Petrograd [1917]), p. 4.

94. N. Liashko, 'Zheleznaia tishina', *Kuznitsa* 2 (June 1920), p. 16; M. Gerasimov, 'Krest' and 'Letim', *Zavod ognekrylyi* (Moscow, 1918), pp. 17, 47. Images of holy suffering and transcendence are documented and discussed in Ch 8 of my forthcoming book, *Proletarian Imagination*.
95. A. Kraiskii, 'Navstrechu griadushchemu', *Ponizov'e* 5 (1922), pp. 3–4.
96. Gastev, 'O tendentsiiakh', p. 44.
97. A. Gastev, 'Bashnia', *Metallist* 4 (18 Oct. 1917), pp. 4–6. Also printed in *Griadushchee* 2 (May 1918), pp. 11–12, and in editions of Gastev's *Poeziia rabochego udara*. See the discussion in Johansson, *Aleksej Gastev*, pp. 83–8.
98. Gerasimov, 'My'.
99. Thomas Seifrid, *Andrei Platonov: Uncertainties of Spirit* (Cambridge/New York: Cambridge University Press, 1992), Ch. 1. See also V.V. Eidinova, 'K tvorcheskoi biografii A. Platonova', *Voprosy literatury* 3 (1978), pp. 213–28, and Thomas Langerak, 'Andrei Platonov v Voronezhe', *Russian Literature* 23–4 (1988), pp. 437–68.
100. Eidinova, 'K tvorcheskoi biografii A. Platonova', p. 222.
101. Seifrid, *Andrei Platonov*, p. 53.
102. A. Platonov, 'Ocherednoi', *Zheleznyi put'* 2 (5 Oct. 1918), pp. 16–17.
103. A. Platonov, 'Markun', *Kuznitsa* 7 (Dec. 1920–March 1921), pp. 18–22, and 'Satana mysli (Fantaziia)', *Put' kommunizma* 2 (March–April 1922), pp. 32–7.
104. A. Platonov, 'Vecher mira', *Golubaia glubina: kniga stikhov* (Krasnodar, 1922), p. 17.
105. Matei Calinescu, *Five Faces of Modernity* (Durham, NC: Duke University Press, 1987), esp. pp. 10, 42, 48, 89, 90, 162. For discussion of Western models of modernization, see Michael Adas, *Machines as the Measure of Men: Science, Technology, and Ideologies of Western Dominance* (Ithaca, NY: Cornell University Press, 1989), esp. pp. 409–15.
106. Marshall Berman, *All That Is Solid Melts Into Air: The Experience of Modernity* (New York: Simon & Schuster, 1982).
107. Zygmunt Bauman, *Modernity and Ambivalence* (Ithaca, NY: Cornell University Press, 1991), and *Intimations of Postmodernity* (London/New York: Routledge, 1992), esp. Introduction and Ch. 9.
108. For evidence of these divergent modernisms in early Soviet culture and ideology, see Clark, *The Soviet Novel*, pp. 93–7; Stites, *Revolutionary Dreams,* esp. Ch. 7; René Fülöp-Miller, *The Mind and Face of Bolshevism* (London/New York: G.P. Putnam's sons, 1927); Jeffrey Brooks, 'The Press and its Message, Images of America in the 1920s and 1930s', in Sheila Fitzpatrick, Alexander Rabinowitch and Richard Stites (eds), *Russia in the Era of NEP* (Bloomington, IN: Indiana University Press, 1991), pp. 239–42; John Milner, *Vladimir Tatlin and the Russian Avant-Garde* (New Haven, CT: Yale University Press, 1983); Christina Lodder, *Russian Constructivism* (New Haven, CT: Yale University Press, 1983); Margarita Tupitsyn, *The Soviet Photograph, 1924–1937* (New Haven: Yale University Press, 1996), Ch. 1. Work that appeared in Mayakovsky's journal *Lef: zhurnal levogo fronta iskusstv*, was typical. See, for example, *Lef* 1 (March 1923), pp. 61–4, 69, 105–8, 172–9; 2 (April–May 1923), pp. 65–8; 4 (Aug.–Dec. 1924), pp. 40–4, 58–62, 89–108.
109. V. Polianskii (Lebedev-Polianskii), review of *Gorn*, in *Proletarskaia kul'tura* 5 (Nov. 1918), pp. 42–3.
110. V. Polianskii, review of *Pereval*, in *Rabochii zhurnal* 1–2 (1925), p. 262.
111. S. Rodov, 'Motivy tvorchestvo M. Gerasimova', *Kuznitsa* 1 (May 1920), p. 23.
112. A. Voronskii, 'O gruppe pisatel'ei "Kuznitsa", Obshchaia kharakteristika', *Iskusstvo i zhizn'*: *Sbornik statei* (Moscow and Petrograd, 1924), p. 136. See also P.I.M., Review of Aleksandrovskii, 'Shagi', *Rabochii zhurnal* 1–2 (1925), p. 277.
113. 'Protokoly pervogo Vserossiiskogo Soveshchaniia proletarskikh pisatelei' (10 May–12 May 1920), RGALI, f. 1638, op. 3, d. 1, ll. 1 (verso)-2.
114. V. Kirillov, 'O proletarskoi poezii', *Kuznitsa* 7 (Dec. 1920–March 1921), pp. 23–4.
115. N. Liashko, 'O zadachakh pisatelia-rabochego (zametka)', *Kuznitsa* 3 (July 1920), pp. 27–9.
116. Kirillov, 'Gorodu'.
117. V. Kirillov, 'Zov zhizn'', *Stikhotvoreniia 1914–1918* (Petersburg [sic], 1918), pp. 28–9.

118. V. Kirillov, 'Moi pokhorony', *Kuznitsa* 8 (April–Sept. 1921), p. 10. See also Kirillov's melancholy portrait of the unchanging crassness of city life ('so will it be for a thousand years'), 'Byl vecher, kak vecher'. For a story focused on an urban suicide, see Liashko, 'Stoiashchim na mostu, kriki i dumy', *Kuznitsa* 3 (July 1920), p. 25. A posthumous (though unhappy) specter, of course, features in Gogol's famous urban critique, the 'Overcoat', and Belyi's St Petersburg teems with spectral figures.
119. Voronskii, 'O gruppe pisatelei "Kuznitsa"', pp. 135–6; P.I.M., Review of Aleksandrovskii, 'Shagi'. This collection of poems is a good example of such deepening ambivalence. V. Aleksandrovskii, *Shagi* (Moscow, 1924).
120. Voronskii, 'O gruppe pisatelei "Kuznitsa"', p. 136.
121. S. Obradovich, 'Rozhdennomu, kak ty, v granite', *Kuznitsa* 4 (Aug.–Sept. 1920), p. 11.
122. Bauman, *Intimations of Postmodernity*, p. ix.

5

Working, Struggling, Becoming: Stalin-Era Autobiographical Texts

JOCHEN HELLBECK

One of the assumptions most deeply ingrained in the Western imagination of the Stalinist regime is that, in their core, members of Soviet society resided externally to state policies and Bolshevik ideology.[1] Though the 'system' succeeded, through a combination of propaganda and coercion, in enforcing a degree of outward popular compliance, individuals were able to mitigate these pressures by retreating into private spheres unaffected by 'official' ideology. In search of Soviet citizens' concealed or repressed selves, scholars have placed high hopes on the newly available 'hidden transcripts' (James Scott)[2] of Soviet society: secret NKVD reports and interrogations, unpublished correspondence and diaries. It is in this body of unofficial sources that the authentic scripts of individual selfhood, the essence of their subjectivity, are expected to be uncovered. Subjectivity in the Stalinist context is thus regarded as a quality that manifests itself in opposition to, and in spite of, the policies of the Soviet state.[3]

A related, but more pessimistic, view casts doubt on Soviet citizens' ability to develop any notion of individual subjectivity at all, if subjectivity is defined as a capacity for thought and action derived from a coherent sense of self. According to this theory, all political initiative was monopolized by the revolutionary state, and revolutionary politics by their very nature undercut the creation of stable identities. As a consequence, Soviet citizens were jolted out of traditional frames of self-definition and kept suspended in a climate of recurrent rupture, insecurity and disorientation.[4] What links these two interpretations is the notion that the Soviet regime sought to subjugate individuals' sense of selfhood, forcing them to conceal their subjectivity or obliterating it altogether. This chapter highlights an opposite dynamic: it argues that the primary effect on individuals' sense of self of the 1917 Revolution and of Soviet revolutionary practice was not repressive, but productive.

Revolutionary politics centered on creating revolutionary selves, on making Soviet citizens think of themselves and act as conscious historical subjects.[5] The activities of autobiographical reflection, writing and speech formed an important medium through which the creation of revolutionary subjectivity was to be achieved. Soviet citizens living through the first decades of Soviet power were intensely aware of their duty to possess a distinct individual biography, to present it publicly and to work on themselves in search of self-perfection. Most importantly, they were forced to acknowledge the political weight of their biography. The intense politicization of acts of talking and writing about oneself also influenced the writing of diaries in the 1930s – the source body investigated in this essay.

As a textual genre, the diary, along with other autobiographical narratives, was markedly shaped by the Soviet Revolution. In prerevolutionary times, writing an account of one's life or keeping a journal was limited to a relatively small segment of educated Russian society. Following the 1917 Revolution, the autobiographical domain expanded dramatically, both in absolute numbers and in sociological terms. It was not just that many more individuals became engaged in writing and talking about themselves but that the autobiographical range extended to entirely new layers of the population, thereby creating a new, specifically Soviet, sub-genre of sorts: of authors groping for a language of self-expression at the same time as they learned to read and write.[6] The Civil War accounts of Isaak Babel and Andrei Platonov record the awkward, earnest and intense attempts by barely literate peasant-soldiers to cast themselves as revolutionary subjects.[7]

In part this obsessive concern with the Self was a direct offshoot of the Revolution itself, an immediate articulation of the revolutionary ideas of human liberation, social emancipation and the dignity of the personality, all of which had made an explosive appearance in 1917.[8] But it is important to consider how this humanistic discourse was, from the outset, appropriated by the Soviet regime and integrated into an agenda of individual activation and mobilization in the service of strengthening the revolutionary state. With its stress on subjective involvement in the revolutionary cause, the Bolshevik regime was pursuing a quintessentially modern agenda of *subjectivization*, of fostering conscious citizens who would become engaged in the program of building socialism of their own will.[9] Soviet revolutionaries sought to remove all mediation between the individual citizen and the larger community, so that the consciousness of the individual and the revolutionary goals of the state would merge. In the process, individuals were expected to refashion their very selves, by enacting revolutions of their souls, paralleling the revolution of the social and political landscape.

What made this discourse of rearing conscious revolutionary subjects so potent was the fact that it was actualized through a host of *subjectivizing practices*, including political agitation, educational policies and re-educational measures aimed at 'reforging' class aliens. Even gulag camps, staffed with large libraries and other educational facilities, were conceived as construction sites of the New Man. Within this transformative framework, the Soviet state attached particular significance to the practice of autobiographical writing and speaking, both as a manifestation of the state of consciousness a given individual had achieved, and as a tool for raising this consciousness further. The most widespread type of formalized self-presentation in the Soviet system was the *avtobiografiia* – a short account of an individual's life, submitted in prose and presented orally, listing this person's educational and professional achievements, but at its core focusing on the formation of his or her personality. This form of self-presentation originated in the Communist Party milieu, as a means of assessing a given candidate's level of political consciousness. Yet, it was practiced also in the Komsomol and in non-Party institutions, such as universities and organs of state administration. In applying for membership to one of these institutions, any applicant had to compose and recite such an autobiography.[10] Significantly, Soviet citizens were required to resubmit their autobiography at recurrent intervals throughout their lives. It is therefore safe to assume that individuals were familiar not only with this genre of self-presentation and its attendant rules, but also with the underlying assumption that their biographies were subject to rewriting, in accordance with the progression of the Revolution along with the development of their own, subjective political consciousness.

During the first decades of Soviet power, state and Party agencies poured considerable energy into the production of large-scale autobiographical projects involving thousands of Soviet citizens.[11] Workers and soldiers wrote their recollections of the 1917 Revolution, and labor collectives in various branches of Soviet industry narrated the epic tale of their construction campaigns at the Stalinist 'industrialization front'. In all of these cases the plot operated on two levels: relating how individuals *made* the Revolution, *constructed* a factory, *built* the Metro, etc., and, at the same time, how they themselves *were* made by the Revolution and how they *were forged* as subjects in the course of the Stalinist industrialization drive. This dual theme was especially pronounced in the case of class enemies, criminals and social outcasts, who were to be refashioned into conscious and socially useful citizens through the combined tools of labor and autobiographical writing. The accounts of their lives describe the full trajectory of self-transformation, from 'human weed' or 'bad raw material', living in a similarly unformed or polluted social environment, to conscious, self-disciplined beings residing in the well-ordered socialist garden created to an extent by themselves.[12]

Alongside other autobiographical genres, Soviet revolutionaries also promoted the diary as a subjectivizing technique. Consider the case of the 'Red Army notebook' (*knizhka krasnoarmeitsa*) of the Civil War period, a booklet designed for each Red Army soldier to record the ammunition, food and clothing supplies distributed to him. The booklet contains a blank page at the end bearing the heading 'Personal Notes'. A caption below reads: 'If possible, keep a diary of your service in the Workers' and Peasants' Red Army'.[13] Yet notwithstanding this prominent case, the diary never received the same official support as the production of complete autobiographical narratives.[14] Soviet activists were deeply ambivalent about the diary's suitability as a catalyst of socialist self-transformation. They acknowledged that it had traditionally served as an inherently bourgeois medium that tended to further individuals' selfish, narcissistic drives, or at best produced 'empty talk'. There was also the suspicion that a diary, if written on one's own and concealed from the gaze of the collective, could undermine a Communist's socialist consciousness and become a breeding ground of counter-revolutionary sentiment.[15] This fear was poignantly expressed in the fact that diaries were among the materials most coveted by NKVD officers during searches of apartments belonging to 'enemies of the people'. Some literary specialists expressed not so much suspicion as disdain towards the diary medium: they expressly favored the production and publication of memoirs over diaries because the memoir had the educational advantage of presenting a cohesive, unified narrative of self-development. The diary narrative, by contrast, was uneven and resonated with competing voices in the process of self-constitution. The memoir represented a finished piece of work – a monument of the completed self – whereas the diary functioned as a mere construction site of the Self, conceived of as a work-in-progress.[16] As a disillusioned literary editor in charge of publishing a collection of workers' self-narratives put it: '[Diaries] can give great results, yet these results won't come overnight. The diary demands time, but we need material now.'[17]

It is important to bear official ambiguities towards the diary in mind when studying the existing diary literature of the 1930s, since such a perspective allows us to understand these diaries as far more than an unmediated product of Soviet state policies of subjectivization. Only in a few cases did diaries originate as clear assignments prescribed by Soviet officials; for the most part, they were kept on the initiative of their authors, who in fact often deplored the absence of official precepts of self-transformation according to which they could pattern their lives.

An investigation of this diary literature thus highlights the extent to which individuals, acting on their own, creatively wove themselves into a loose matrix of subjectivization produced by the Revolution, and how these individuals themselves supplied some of the core categories and mechanisms of self-realization in a Soviet vein.

The following discussion is based on an extraordinarily wide range of diaries from the 1930s, most of which have become available to researchers following the opening of the Soviet archives. Diarists comprise professional writers, artists, teachers, workers, peasants, engineers and scientists, state administration employees, Party workers, journalists, professors and scholars, university students, schoolchildren and a housewife. The group includes both urban and rural residents, members of all generations, men and women.[18] The discussion of these diaries is broken down into three parts. I begin by focusing on diaries as chronicles of socialist construction, before moving to an investigation of the introspective and self-transformative functions of Stalin-era diaries. The third section discusses the utility of a distinction between public and private spheres for an understanding of Soviet diaries and notions of Soviet subjectivity.

Excluded from the present investigation are diaries lacking an autobiographical orientation. This chapter thus does not explore the diaristic genre as a whole, nor does it seek to deduce from diaristic texts how their authors actually experienced the Stalin period. This latter point needs to be stressed, in view of the intuitive popular tendency to view the diary as an experiential sanctuary of sorts, as a repository of individuals' innermost thoughts and feelings. Yet no autobiographical text, however intimate and confessional it claims to be, is able to provide an immediate answer to the question of experience. Self-narratives can be fully understood only if located in the context of historically specific conventions of how to conceive of and present oneself. With respect to the Stalin era, this context was shaped by the language of the Russian Revolution, the rise of a new mode of universal self-expression, the politicization of the Self in the wake of 1917, and the absolute insistence on universal self-transformation and self-disclosure on the part of the Soviet regime. This framework goes a long way to explaining why the Self is such a prominent theme in Stalin-era diaries and why there is a remarkable scarcity of non-Soviet modes of self-realization in these texts. Not all diaries from the 1930s are autobiographical in character, but to the extent that they invoke the Self, most of them move within distinctly Soviet parameters of selfhood, by stressing the themes of work on reworking the Self, social utility and integration, and historical orientation.

CHRONICLES OF SOCIALIST CONSTRUCTION

Soviet diaries from the 1930s bespeak an extraordinary involvement of their authors in the development of the Soviet system. Diarists were often aware of participating in an exceptional historic period, which it was their obligation to record. 'When will I finally write my memoirs about the 1930s?' one of them asked.[19] The fact that this author posed the question in 1932, when the actual '1930s' had barely begun, illustrates the extent to which there existed at the time a notion of the Stalinist industrialization campaign as a distinct epoch in the making. Another diarist, a Party activist involved in the collectivization campaign, wrote his autobiographical record as a chronicle of class struggle. He began to keep the diary following his appointment as chairman of a village soviet. The first entry summarizes his achievements at his former workplace, which had also been at the collectivization 'front':

> There were many victories and defeats. The class enemy, the kulak, did not sleep, organizing the backward mass of poor peasants [*bedniaki*] and peasants of average means [*seredniaki*] against the kolkhozes. [...] Thus, in a bitter skirmish with the obsolete and dying capitalist elements, our kolkhozes have been born, reared and strengthened. A lot of struggle still lies ahead, especially at the new location, the Pirogov village soviet, where I have been transferred by the *raikom* of the Party.[20]

Significantly, the narrator begins by setting up a macro framework, the collectivization campaign in the Soviet countryside, in which he then places events from his own personal life. The same strategy is visible in the diary of Masha Scott, who expands the ideological framework structuring the narration of her personal life to its utmost extent – the epic of international class struggle. Masha Scott, one of the builders of the city of Magnitogorsk, related in her diary her first encounter with John Scott, a visiting American engineer, whom she would later marry. She described her disappointment upon seeing this fabled American visitor in person – an emaciated young man, dressed in rags and covered with blast-furnace dust:

> The first American I had ever seen, he looked like a homeless boy [*bezprizornik*]. I saw in him the product of capitalist oppression. I saw in my mind's eye his sad childhood; I imagined the long hours of inhuman labor which he had been forced to perform in some capitalist factory while still a boy; I imagined the shamefully low wages he received, only sufficient to buy enough bread so that he could go to work the next day; I imagined his fear of losing even this pittance and being thrown on the streets unemployed in case he was unable to do his work to the satisfaction and profit of his parasitic bosses.[21]

Ideological tenets, in the sense of projections of a world to be realized, also informed diaries that were produced explicitly as chronicles of everyday life (*byt*). Nikolai Zhuravlev, an archivist from Kalinin, began his diary with the following introductory remark:

> *6 January 1936* I am a local historian [*kraeved*] and an archivist. I know the significance for the historian of a document which deals with the everyday. I understand that a document, an ordinary document filed in an office, narrates primarily extraordinary facts and remains silent about all that has firmly become an attainment of everyday life. Which office will describe for you a normal day in the life of a normal person? ... This is why, in support of the historian of the city of Kalinin (the future will tell whether this will be myself or someone else), I have decided to begin these notes in which I will try, as far as possible, not to talk about the turns of my heart, but will concentrate more on facts.

Notably, the author's purported desire to write a chronicle of everyday life was motivated by an extraordinary event – the 800th anniversary of the founding of Kalinin (Tver'): 'The day on which my notes begin is an extraordinary one in the chronicles of the city. [...] It is a big holiday ... You feel this when you look at the faces of the people walking by. Among them are many kolkhoz workers who have come to the regional centre to celebrate yet another victory of socialist agriculture.' The following day, Zhuravlev summarized his impressions of the city festival: 'Celebrations like this can take place only in the land of socialism! I remember these official "festivities" under tsarism. [...] But our holiday is a genuine mass holiday, a genuine holiday of the people' (7 January 1936).[22]

Zhuravlev's diary illustrates the political significance of *byt* in the Soviet system. In view of the stated goal of the Bolshevik regime to revolutionize all aspects of traditional daily life, a diarist's description of living conditions under Stalinism was a profoundly ideological gesture.[23] It is in this light that the following diary of the Leningrad worker and student Arkadii Man'kov should be read.[24] Man'kov's account also focused on the *byt* of the Stalin era, but it emphasized solely the misery and despondency suffered by the working population. Man'kov's express purpose in keeping his diary of the 1930s was diametrically opposed to Zhuravlev's, since he sought to denounce the achievements claimed by the Stalinist regime. The contemporary social structure in the Soviet Union, Man'kov wrote, was 'purely capitalist'; to refer to it as a Marxist state was blasphemous (30 January 1933). All the while, however, Man'kov called for the realization of Marx's revolutionary goals – the end of exploitation and the arrival of material plenty. Like Zhuravlev, he referred to his diary as raw material for a history of daily life of the Stalin period that historians would have to write one day (24 July 1933), and, as was also the case with Zhuravlev, Man'kov's account was embedded in a vision of the socialist society of the future.[25] In spite of their radically different diagnoses, these two authors thus expressed themselves within a shared horizon of meaning defined by the campaign of building socialism.[26]

A diarist's mention of extreme material hardship in itself did not have to stand in the way of his or her ideological commitment. On the contrary, Galina Shtange, a 50-year-old housewife married to a leading Soviet engineer, deliberately mentioned the adverse conditions of contemporary life in order to underscore the heroic sacrifice assumed by herself and her generation in the building of socialism.

> *1 January 1937* ... It's just horrible when you think about how people live these days, and engineers in particular. I heard about one engineer, who lives with his wife in a 9-[square-]meter room. When his mother came to visit, there was absolutely no place for him to do his work. So he put the lamp on the floor and lay down (on his stomach under the table) and worked that way. He couldn't put it off; he had a deadline. I wrote down this example so that those who come after us will read it and get a sense of what we went through.[27]

The unstated assumption motivating this entry was that future generations of Soviet citizens, living in a materially plentiful Communist world, would have difficulty imagining the hardships borne by those who sacrificed themselves for the building of this future.

The sense that a diary kept in the 1930s, to be legitimate, had to be ideological in character, is also reflected in the laments of two diarists that their chronicles *failed* to reach such a level of interpretation. Repeatedly the Komsomol activist Anatolii Ul'ianov voiced his frustration at his own writings in his diary:

> *12 April 1933* I've just read through a couple of pages. How much emptiness, and how little reflection of life. The life about which people write books ... They rear heroes. But what do I have? I will try to be more detailed and more prosaic in writing about myself at home and at work.

> *7 May 1933* The end of the [diary] notebook is approaching. This notebook spans almost eight months, i.e., two-thirds of a year. But life is very incompletely illuminated. It is even very, very slightly illuminated. There are a lot of thoughts in there, but little on the essence of existence.

Firmly intent on devoting his diary to the essence of life, Ul'ianov intermittently produced a series of entries exclusively on his labor activities, summarizing production targets and results of the factory at which he worked, Komsomol meetings and his work as a social activist.[28] But he soon fell back into his habitual diaristic mode again. As late as in 1937 he complained:

> *15 January 1937* ... About the diary. What kind of stupid trumpery I have been writing over the last days (no, all the time!) in my diary. There is no life in it, only nonsense about womenfolk. From today on, I have decided to write only about what is real, what has happened as an accomplished fact, and I'll discard the rest. Yeah, and my life is somehow petty; in my 23 years, I haven't done anything intelligent, anything heroic; I'm only groping around like an idiot. A diary should reflect only the truth – live, heroic truth – but everything that I have written to date is some kind of nonsense. Under no circumstances will I keep writing like this.

Especially intriguing in this entry is how Ul'ianov's observation on the trivial character of his diary notes brings him to conclude that he is leading a petty life. There seems to be hardly any difference in the author's mind between 'writing like this' and 'living like this'. The boundary between writing and actual life is blurred, and there is a palpable sense of the diary's power to literally write its author's life: the more disciplined and consistently heroicizing his autobiographical narrative unfolds, Ul'ianov implies, the more real and heroic his actual life will become.

Another diarist, the writer A.V. Peregudov, realized only from the distance of a quarter century that his diary project had failed. In an entry of 1961 he remarked:

> It's been almost 25 years since I've opened this diary. I reread my notes and was amazed about how petty they are. But where are all the great things [*to velikoe*] that took place in our country, changing its face and strengthening its might? My explanation for this is that the diary was not destined for such a high purpose, but was kept for small, 'intimate and lyrical' notes which revolved only around my family life and nature and were of great interest only to myself and Mariia. How I regret now that I did not keep a different, a great diary, devoted to the great events. I tried frequently, but I never wrote it ...[29]

How widely the diaristic genre was deployed for chronicles of socialist construction is also illustrated in the case of numerous travel diaries left behind by foreign visitors to the Soviet Union in the 1920s and 1930s. Whether enthusiastic or skeptical in their responses, these authors invariably shared an impulse to witness and record in their personal chronicles the building of the New World.[30]

Beyond their ideological nature, another remarkable feature of many diaries from the 1930s is their emphasis on the narrator's personal involvement in the development of the Soviet system. Vsevolod Vishnevskii, the playwright, wanted his diaristic record to serve as historical testimony, so that future generations would judge his own and his contemporaries' actions:

> *22 January 1942* Our task is to preserve for history our observations, our present point of view – the point of view of the participant. You see, a year from now, or ten years from now, from the perspective of time, everything will become clearer. Possibly, there will be another point of view, another judgement. Therefore let us leave our story for the grandsons and great-grandsons. Our mistakes and victories will be the lessons for tomorrow.[31]

The urge to write oneself into the Soviet revolutionary trajectory can even be observed on the part of a potential victim of socialist construction, notably the campaign to collectivize agriculture. The diarist Tikhon Puzanov was a peasant youth from the Don region, who was still living in his parents' uncollectivized household in early 1933. The family could not meet the grain delivery quotas mandated by the local soviet and was threatened with expropriation and exile. While narrating in the diary his and his family's harsh 'struggle for existence' under the conditions of spreading famine, Puzanov also dreamt about the happy future promised by collectivization, emphasizing his active personal involvement in the realization of this future:

> All that I think about is how we will attain the happy future. Others think in a contrary way – they wait for it to happen [*zhdut gotovogo*]. And they are the majority; they are not a bit interested in their work. They don't care about how they work, as if they were serving a sentence. They aren't involved in the present world [*Oni ne zhivut nastoiashchim*]. For them it is all difficult and torturous, since collective labor has not yet entered the consciousness, the blood of the young; and the people are dreaming about a smallholder's existence [*mechtaiut o edinolichnoi zhizni*].[32]

Although himself a member of a kulak family, Puzanov took part in the collectivization campaign, joining activist raids on uncollectivized peasant households. On the pages of his diary he emphasized his 'genuine loyalty to the kolkhoz system', taking issue with those who suspected that he was working in the kolkhoz only to 'save [his] skin'.[33]

Most tangibly the subjectivizing effect of revolutionary ideology – the sense of the self coming to fruition through joining the socialist campaign – is evoked in the case of the kolkhoz activist Zhelezniakov. On the occasion of the sixteenth anniversary of the October Revolution, he noted:

> *10 November 1933* How good it is to feel, live and win in struggle! There is not, was not, and will not be in world history a generation happier than ours. We are participants in the creation of a new epoch! Do you remember, enemies, you who are encircling us from all sides, that only 20 years ago we were puny insects, crawling on the masters' floors, and then this paltry person, strangled by capitalism, comprehended himself as a class and shattered the whole world to its foundations on 7 November, 16 years ago ... There is nothing greater than to be a member, a citizen of the Soviet

land and to belong to Lenin's Communist Party, hardened in battle and led in our times by the beloved leader Comrade Stalin, with whom we are celebrating together *today the day of the great victories* of technical progress. Had the October Revolution not happened, could I have conceivably understood life in this way, and could I have conceivably forgone my personal life for the struggle for common goals? No! I would have remained half-animal, but now I am happy. I was raised by Lenin's party, and I have become ideologically hardened! I am prepared to confront any difficulties and to bear any sacrifice in the name of the great goals of the building of Communist society.[34]

LOGBOOKS OF THE SOVIET SELF

To be sure, passages like the one just quoted, celebrating the merging of the Self with the collective, appear to have been rare moments of rapture erupting from the generally less spectacular flow of the diary narrative. More typical of Soviet diaries was a mode of doubt, insecurity and intense self-criticism, coupled with admonishments not to give up work on oneself. In these cases the diary acted as a normalizing technique, a medium through which the mind observed and controlled psychic and bodily processes. The inward gaze provided by the diary enabled its author to embark on an extended struggle in battling weaknesses and impurities of the Self.

A large number of diaries from the 1930s functioned as both records and tools of psycho-physical training. They worked as an introspective, controlling and regulating device, enabling their authors to monitor the physiological and intellectual processes at work in them, in the service of controlling and perfecting them. To document this self-transformative project, diarists repeatedly invoked the concepts of 'planning', 'struggle' and 'consciousness', core Communist values of the period, highlighted especially during the first Five-Year Plans.[35]

In her diary the young schoolteacher Vera Shtrom repeatedly voiced the need to control and rationalize her life. She sought to achieve this by analyzing her soul and bringing to light the realm of her 'subconscious feelings'.[36] Shtrom also confided her dreams and fantasies, all her 'crazy' thoughts, to the diary, but expressly in a desire to 'systematize [her] impressions' and, ultimately, to live her life in a 'planned and systemic' fashion.[37] Similarly, Anatolii Ul'ianov, a Moscow worker and Komsomol activist, mobilized the diaristic medium to bring order to his life and increase his work productivity:

> *23 March 1930* I want to establish exact regulations of spending money and daily planning. I already did this today (it will be difficult, but I'll succeed). But I want to introduce a work plan [*planovost' raboty*] into my daily life, for both my mental-physical and leisure [activities]. I will try to

make my work more manageable this way. Fewer of the usual tricks (walks with the 'perfidious' Katia, etc., etc.).[38]

To fight the 'disorder in [her] soul', which she repeatedly diagnosed in her diary, the writer Vera Inber advocated what she called '"technicizing the soul" ..., in other words, constructivism'. In keeping with this mechanistic imagery she remarked elsewhere: 'Man is a factory. And his mind is the director of this factory' (9 July 1933).

Diarists established a variety of related dichotomies to describe the composition of their Self and the work attendant to change it. These included the opposition between the mind and the body, individuals' 'ideology' and their 'psychology', or, in the words of one diarist, the 'will' and the 'heart'.[39] In all conflicting pairs the will played a central role in the project to raise or remake the Self. The will appeared as coterminous with an individual's subjectivity. It was described as an autonomous power residing within the Self that, once activated, raised the Self to the level of a historical agent. In this context the diary functioned as a catalyst shaping and strengthening the diarist's will.

Leonid Potemkin, a student at the Sverdlovsk Mining Institute, repeatedly reflected in his diary on the duality of mind and body. He described how his mind, or conscious will, challenged and eventually overcame the sluggishness of the body, which hitherto was controlled by physiological, natural and hence unconscious forces, thus enabling him to merge with the laboring collective.[40]

Vladimir Molodtsov, a coal miner, observed that his will (or ideology – he used the two terms interchangeably) was engaged in a battle with his 'psychology':

> *17 November 1930* It is interesting how there is a lack of harmony between psychology and ideology. Ideologically, I myself mobilized myself [*sic*] to catch up with the plan, and, although I am working actively, my psychology still draws me back home, to my hearth. This is evidenced by the increasing numbers of dreams over the past two days, in which I saw my mother. But ideology will elevate psychology; this has to occur.[41]

In the pages of his diary, Stepan Podlubnyi, a young Moscow worker of kulak origins, elevated will-power to a moral ideal: '*5 January 1934* For a long time already, I have liked people with a strong will. No matter who this person is, but if he or she has great will-power, this is a good person.'[42]

Podlubnyi assiduously recorded all the instances when he felt that his own will-power had increased,[43] but, for the most part, his diary was a record of his failures – both at the workplace and in his personal life

– which Podlubnyi perceived to be rooted in his weak will.[44] But for Podlubnyi, his diary amounted to more than a bulletin of the 'sickness of [his] will' (31 October 1935); writing in it was also a cure, since he reasoned that by forcing himself to record regularly he would also strengthen his will-power (29 January 1933).

Will-power was attained through struggle. Diaries of the 1930s abound in references to life as a continuous struggle. Aleksandr Zhelezniakov, the Vologda kolkhoz activist, described a hay-harvesting campaign conducted under his initiative. To take advantage of a brief spell of dry weather, he coerced the recalcitrant kolkhoz women workers into staying in the field until all work was finished:

> We mowed until eleven at night, and the field was mown. The moon played a big role and helped me resolve this difficult task. Thanks to the Party. It reared in me firmness and resolve in struggle, to win in the most difficult conditions. What great happiness! Great, limitless happiness! I remember the words of Marx and Engels: 'Struggle is happiness!' The next morning it rained again. (12 October 1935)[45]

In their journals, diarists waged a struggle not just against an Other – recalcitrant kolkhoz workers, or the forces of nature – but also against themselves. Ul'ianov once noted in his diary that he had already improved somewhat in terms of his manners and his education. But he remained critical about certain aspects of his personality: 'In spite of my literacy, sometimes it is scandalous how coarse I am. Of course I don't want to turn into a sickly-sweet [*slashchaven'kii*] intellectual. But what I want is not to be an animal.' The diary entry concluded with the resolution: 'Struggle against coarseness, inconstancy and lies' (9 December 1932). Or, to cite from Podlubnyi's diary: 'I don't know where, I think it was Gorky who said that "life is a struggle". A very apt observation. A life without struggle – that is not the life of a human being, it's an animal's life. As far as I can remember about myself, all of my life has evolved as an inner, emotional struggle' (2 May 1933).

So far our discussion has focused on the role of the diary as a self-disciplining technique. Yet some of these diary narratives also evolve in a spiritual register. They describe a movement directed towards self-renewal, proceeding rarely in a straight line, and more often as an uneven process marked by intense struggle. The specific role of the diary in staging this journey of self-becoming is expressed in the case of the playwright Aleksandr Afinogenov, who referred to the daily entries of his journal as 'strict roadmarks of every single day that I have lived' (7 October 1937). One of Afinogenov's principal goals in keeping a diary was the production of a visible trace of self-development. For him, interrupting this journey was tantamount to a retraction into his present, imperfect self. To this extent, reviewing past diary entries enabled Afinogenov to monitor and sustain his journey towards salvation:

> *16 November 1937* Right now, today ... I got up with the desire to somehow move on: not to stop *thinking* and *accumulate* what I've already begun to accumulate, always *looking back and examining myself, not allowing myself to become my former self,* if even only a tiny bit.

Elsewhere Afinogenov vowed never to

> rest content with myself and my road. *Look up your notes more often,* look up the pages written on days of expectation and re-evaluation of yourself. May what you wrote back then serve you as a *permanent reminder.* Never depart from these notes (always collate them and check: what you wrote comes from the very depths of your heart's sensitivity) (6 November 1937).[46]

The sense that life for a citizen living in the Soviet system evolved as a journey is also graphically expressed in the autobiography of Heinrich Vogeler, a German Communist who emigrated to the Soviet Union in the 1930s. His memoir, written shortly before his death in 1942, was entitled *Becoming (Werden)*. In a diary note of that period, Vogeler explained his principal purpose in writing his autobiography: 'Perhaps this book will be read by people who are looking for paths to reach the new life. My story will allow them to recognize wanderings which they can avoid for themselves.'[47]

As these last examples illustrate especially well, Soviet diaries from the 1930s were characterized not just by an agenda of self-transformation, but, more basically, by a quest for self-expression. Expression, not repression, appears to be the principal theme of diary self-narratives from the period. The desire to fuse with the collective, to secure integration in Communist, collectivist values, was not a self-effacing dynamic; it did not diminish the private self, but, on the contrary, allowed it to grow.

PUBLIC AND PRIVATE

Historians of the Soviet system often assume that only privately voiced statements are reliable indicators of individuals' 'real' beliefs. They therefore endow the diary, understood as a private record *par excellence,* with a unique potential to express the individual self in undistorted fashion. Accordingly, diaries originating in the public realm – such as production or brigade diaries, or records written for the public eye – are dismissed as inauthentic records, especially in view of the pressures applied by the Soviet state which forced diarists to practice self-censorship. Yet this exclusive correlation of the authentic self with the private sphere would leave researchers with preciously few 'real' diaries to work with. Moreover, such a rigorous selection would risk missing the essential meaning of the diary in the context of the Stalinist order.

Our discussion thus far has shown that many diaries from the 1930s were kept as work projects of the Self. Class aliens, in particular, had a great desire to eventually publish their individual accounts of self-transformation, as visible proof, to others and to themselves, that they had successfully reworked themselves. Stepan Podlubnyi, the son of a kulak mentioned above, already knew the title of the autobiographical novel which he wanted to produce from his diary notes: 'The Life of an Outlived Class, Its Spiritual Rebirth and Adaptation to New Conditions' (25 September 1934). The writers Marietta Shaginian and Vera Inber, both of impure, non-Soviet origins and therefore threatened with social marginalization, published their diaristic accounts of self-transformation during their lifetimes.[48] Although the published versions of the diaries were censored, this does not mean that the diary manuscripts themselves were kept as publishable records. On the contrary, Podlubnyi was painfully aware that many passages in his diary would cost him dearly if they were to be revealed to state organs, but he still believed that one day censorship would be eased and his memoir would see the light of day (25 September 1934). His diary was at the same time an account of self-transformation addressed to the public, as well as a secret 'soulmate', to whom he confided the problems he encountered while seeking to transform himself. A number of other diarists kept their self-records secretly, while simultaneously entertaining thoughts of literary publications to be based on the diary material. Thus, multiple diverging impulses appear to have been at work in these diaries, making it extremely difficult to categorize them as private, semi-private or public records.

It is standard practice among literary theorists to treat the private literary voice as a fictional device. Even the most privately conceived self is staged, using available discursive conventions, as soon as it enters the literary realm.[49] Rather than inferring a private, and, by implication, authentic, self from a given diary, it would be more fruitful to define the diary in terms of a *genre* of private discourse, as a medium through which diarists could cultivate – rather than simply express – a private self. But complicating the issue further is the problem of employing the notion of the private for analytical purposes in the context of the Soviet state, which regarded it as one of its principal tasks to eliminate all traces of the bourgeois order, and chief among them, the public–private division. In the eyes of Soviet Marxists, bourgeois privacy was a beguiling yet utterly disingenuous concept which promised individual self-realization, but in fact only deceived the working class over the state of its social alienation. Once the illusory fusion of the individual with the partial private sphere propagated by the bourgeois order was broken, the formerly oppressed subjects would regain their nature as social beings. Their inner being and outer function would become one.[50]

Keeping in mind the particular status of the private realm in a Marxist state, it may be useful to consider the categories employed by Soviet diarists themselves to conceptualize their social existence, rather than to distinguish a priori between private or public spheres and purposes of diary-writing. The case of Galina Shtange, a 50-year-old housewife who joined the newly founded movement of housewife activists (*obshchestvennitsa*) in 1936, is salient. Her diary shows an inversion of the hierarchy of the public and private spheres, to be found in liberal thought.[51] Liberal discourse represents family life as the principal domain of the private. It is the realm of the individual's unfettered self-realization, outside of the encroachments of market relations and state authority. While also contrasting her family existence to the public sphere, Shtange, however, sought individual fulfillment in the latter. Torn between her duties as a housewife and a social activist, between the exigencies of her family and the Revolution, she subordinated the former to the latter.[52] This is how she described her enrollment in the Soviet women's movement:

> *13 May 1936* I was sitting at home, preoccupied with my own narrow little family affairs, when Zabelina came over and invited me to take part in an informal meeting with several other ladies from the PCCT[53] who wanted to join the movement. Naturally I agreed ...

A few months later, already an activist, she complained that her family prevented her from realizing herself:

> *27 August 1936* So much for my community work! ... I was completely engrossed in my work for two months. I found my element and felt wonderful, in spite of being so tired ... So I decided to give up the work that I love so much, and take up cooking, dishwashing and diapers again.

And in her end-of-year summary she decried her need for a 'personal life':

> *27 December 1936* The year is drawing to a close. It was a painful one for me. The family is upset that I spend so little time at home. I'm sorry for them, but what can I do? I'm not old yet; I still want to have a personal life. Now that I've fulfilled my obligations to my family, in the few years that remain to me *I want to live for myself.* I will always be sincerely glad to help them [emphasis added].

Shtange represented the private–public divide in the form of two different self-trajectories. Her narrow, petty household duties stood in the way of her self-realization which she hoped to achieve by serving the Revolution. Seen in this light, Shtange's diary, which is almost exclusively a record of her public activities, emerges as a catalyst of her Soviet self. In 1938, forced to give up her work as an activist and return to the household, she observed that she had 'suddenly aged by many years' (2 April 1938). The implication was that working for the Revolution had a rejuvenating effect. Elsewhere Shtange noted in her diary:

> Our work should be joyful, it's only natural; man is a social animal. He can be happy and joyful only in a collective. Leave a man alone, even in a golden palace, and his joy for living will just fade and die. Only an awareness of his usefulness to society can bring joy and satisfaction.[54]

The statement Shtange makes about herself applies to her diary as well: precisely because she cannot remain alone cut off from the collective, her diary, in so far as it is to reflect her sense of self, cannot possibly remain a fully private record. To be significant and satisfying it has to be devoted to public life. In this light it appears only logical that Shtange pasted her diaries with numerous news clippings, other documents from the public world, as if to underscore that her personal voice could come to fruition only in the framework of the Soviet collective.[55] Shtange's case thus illustrates once again that self-expression in the Soviet context does not stand in the way of, but on the contrary thrives on, public deeds and texts.

Stepan Podlubnyi conceptualized the relation between the private and the public realm in terms of an inner and an outer self. In his diary he often mentioned the feelings of his 'inner being' (*vnutrennost'*), using this expression synonymously with his 'soul' (*dusha*). His goal was to activate the inner self so that it would merge with the revolutionary agenda of the Soviet state. As he understood it, the soul of a Soviet citizen was to be filled with a distinctly political spirit and should form a realm of enthusiasm. He was dissatisfied when noticing that 'all the inside' was 'asleep' or when he felt himself to be in an 'idiotic and non-political mood' (7 June 1932).

To be sure, Podlubnyi did develop a distinct notion of the private, and he identified this sphere with parts of his diary. The diary represented his 'only friend', the only partner to whom he confided those thoughts that he knew would be dangerous to voice to anybody else, even to close friends. But he regarded these thoughts to be illegitimate. He possessed no positive notion of a private sphere in which to anchor a sense of self and personal values diverging from public norms. He therefore did not conceive of his diary as a record of a private sphere to be remembered. Rather, it served him as a 'rubbish heap' on to which he could discard all the 'garbage' accumulating in his mind (23 January 1933). He envisioned writing as a struggle from which he would ultimately emerge cleansed, fully identical with public values and thereby rid of any alternative selfish, and hence impure, private sphere.

Stalin-era journals are replete with private thoughts – private in the sense of being confidential and certainly not written for the public eye – but more often than not their authors viewed them as expressions of weakness, as tokens of their lack of will-power, not as a source of pride or a kernel of their selfhood. The public–private binary is thus not very helpful for an understanding of Soviet subjectivities if we assume the private realm to be the exclusive locus of positive identity. As such, privacy has no obvious meaning. It acquires positive or negative valence depending on the discourse in which the Self articulates itself. In the Soviet case, given the radically public and collectivist ethos promoted by the revolutionary state, it may not be so surprising after all that practically none of the 1930s diaries known to me were kept to cultivate a private existence, as distinct from the public one. The type of self-realization pursued by diarists was to be reached through techniques of purification and remaking the Self. Rather than using the dichotomy of private and public, diarists located their personal, and particular, existence with respect to the general public interest. These descriptions evoke two trajectories – the life of the individual and the life of the collective – which, ideally, were to merge into a single whole. Time and again, diarists wrote of their efforts to merge their personal lives with the 'general stream of life' of the Soviet collective.[56] A private existence in distinction from, or even in opposition to, the life of the collective, however, was considered inferior and unfulfilled.

Iuliia Piatnitskaia described in her diary a sense of personal regression arising from her inability to participate in the forward-thrusting life of the Soviet people. An engineer by background, she had lost her job following her husband's arrest in 1937, and now spent much time at a public library, leafing through technical journals:

> I looked through *Mechanical Engineering*. Every day that I live through pushes me further back. New machines are being built: lathes, agricultural tools, machines for the Metro, for bridges, etc. Work has been organized in new ways ... Engineers are raising in new ways questions of organization and/or the technology of tool-production. All in all, there is no doubt that life is moving forward, regardless of any 'spokes in the wheel'. The wonderful Palace of Culture for the *Zisovets* plant. I'm getting really jealous: why am I not in their collective? (26 March 1938)

One of the strategies employed by Piatnitskaia to deal with the calamity of her husband's arrest, which was also suggested by the state procurator to whom she turned for help, was to 'stand above [her] personal life' (9 April 1938). Piatnitskaia was 'tortured' that she could not bring herself to hate her husband, an enemy of the people. She urged herself to 'prove, not for others, but for myself', that she could overcome her personal doubts and distance herself from him: 'You will prove with this that you stand higher than a wife, and higher than a mother. You will prove with this that you are a citizen of the Great Soviet Union. And if you don't have the strength to do this, then to the devil with you.'[57]

CONCLUSION

This chapter has sought to introduce a historically contextualized notion of subjectivity for the early Soviet period (1917–41). Contrary to the ubiquitous habit of portraying the Soviet regime solely as an oppressive power that strove to subjugate Soviet citizens' sense of their selves, the discussion has recognized the Revolution as a tremendous subjectivizing force. This was due not only to the language of individual and social emancipation which burst on the scene in 1917 and provided people with entirely new registers of self-expression. More important even was the fact that subjectivity became an intensely political and, indeed, redeeming category practically from the outset of the Revolution. The questions of who one was, whether one was for or against the Revolution, whether one could change and how one could demonstrably transform oneself into a revolutionary subject were central, arguably the most pressing, questions of the period of early Soviet rule – questions that the Soviet regime pursued in the name of the Revolution, but, of course, also for the purpose of molding a loyal popular following. As a consequence, Soviet citizens had no choice but to be aware of their 'selves' as a distinct political category, as a personal identity subject to public scrutiny and as an entity to be shaped and perfected through work on oneself. The Revolution thus underscored – or in many cases actually created – the sense that one possessed, and had to be able to present, a distinct personal biography. Undoubtedly, the uninterrupted chain of social and personal ruptures caused by war, revolution and intense Soviet social engineering had a shattering effect on the individual's pre-existing sense of self, but it would be wrong to infer from this a social landscape of fractured, atomized individuals, as has been suggested,[58] because at the same time (and as never before) Soviet citizens were urged to comprehend themselves in terms of coherent self-narratives and thus to sculpt themselves as autobiographical subjects. From the outset, Soviet revolutionary policies had a strong subjective corollary, whereby individuals were to weave their subjective voices into the collective project of building a socialist society. This subjective stance, which gained even more political weight in the 1930s as compared to the preceding decade, has to be taken into account when studying autobiographical statements of the age.[59]

It is equally important to consider how the Soviet policies of subjectivization (notably the inquisitorial practices of the Stalinist state) supported, and lent legitimacy to, a discourse of the soul.[60] Here the diary perspective is particularly valuable because it shows how individual authors constructed relationships of interiority through the domain of their personal diaries. Their diary narratives illustrate how the Revolution came to be apprehended as an inner quality, in terms of the formation of their consciousness and the purity of their souls. The diaries also reveal a striking proximity between the obsessive desire on the part of Soviet leaders to probe into the essence of their social following, to study the soul of each Soviet citizen, and of individuals' own wondering about their very identity.[61] In many of these cases we observe a striking concordance of intimate and official 'transcripts', which only suggests how rich in meaning the 'official' Stalinist discourse on the Self was for contemporaries and how unjustly it has been neglected by scholars in search of the 'real' meaning and experience of the age.[62]

Conceivably one of the most lasting effects of the pre-war Soviet regime was the creation of coherent and purposeful individual biographies on a mass scale. Hence, one can observe a recurrent desire on the part of surviving Soviet citizens to emphasize a sense of historic purpose and personal fulfillment when recounting their experience of the pre-war Stalin period. Antonina Berezhnaia, formerly an engineer from Sverdlovsk, surprised her Western interviewers who kept asking her about the shortages and difficulties of her youth. Instead, all she wanted to do was talk about 'production and work for the public good over personal life and private satisfaction'.[63] And Leonid Potemkin, author of the remarkable self-expressivist Stalin-era diary mentioned above, was adamant in his old age to combat the notion that Stalinism meant just sacrifice, just evil and just repression. In his own words: 'I categorically reject the slanderous claim that our generation allegedly lived its life in vain.'[64]

NOTES

1. I want to thank Igal Halfin and Peter Holquist for their valuable comments and suggestions. I am grateful to the workshop and conference participants at the University of Michigan, Michigan State University, University of California Berkeley, Stanford University, University of California Riverside, Tel Aviv University, and the Maison des Sciences de l'Homme, Paris, for their stimulating comments and criticism. I also want to thank Véronique Garros, Natalia Korenevskaya and Thomas Lahusen for generously

sharing with me a great number of diaries from the Stalin period. Support for the writing of this essay was provided by the Michigan Society of Fellows.
2. James Scott, *Domination and the Arts of Resistance: Hidden Transcripts* (New Haven, CT: Yale University Press, 1990).
3. See Jochen Hellbeck, 'Speaking Out: Languages of Affirmation and Dissent in Stalinist Russia', *Kritika* 1 (2000), pp. 71–96. The latest to invoke James Scott's dichotomy of official and hidden transcripts are J. Arch Getty and Oleg V. Naumov, *The Road to Terror: Stalin and the Self-Destruction of the Bolsheviks, 1932–1939* (New Haven, CT, and London: Yale University Press, 1999); for a critique of this essentially liberal conceptualization of the Self, see Anna Krylova, 'The Tenacious Liberal Subject in Soviet Studies', *Kritika* 1 (2000), pp. 119–46.
4. Stefan Plaggenborg recently formulated this view from a cultural anthropological standpoint (Stefan Plaggenborg, 'Grundprobleme der Kulturgeschichte der sowjetischen Zwischenkriegszeit', *Jahrbücher für Geschichte Osteuropas* 1 (2000), pp. 109–18, esp. 115–16). This viewpoint in part echoes Moshe Lewin's earlier notion of the Stalinist 'quicksand society' (Moshe Lewin, *The Making of the Soviet System: Essays in the Social History of Interwar Russia* (New York: Pantheon, 1985), p. 221). The loss of the Self is also a central theme in Hannah Arendt's analysis of totalitarian regimes, *The Origins of Totalitarianism* (New York: Harcourt Brace Jovanovich, 1973).
5. When talking about the self-creating effects of the Russian Revolution, I certainly do not want to imply that selves, as self-conscious beings, did not exist prior to the Revolution. My argument is rather that the Revolution deployed on a massive scale a new thinking about the Self as both a problem and a political project. For a model of this approach to the Self as a problem, see Michel Foucault, *The History of Sexuality*, Vol. 1, *An Introduction* (New York: Pantheon Books, 1978), Ch. 1; Vol. 2, *The Use of Pleasure* (New York: Pantheon Books, 1985), Introduction.
6. Bibliographic evidence as well as what is known on state-sponsored efforts at autobiographical writing suggest that – both numerically and in terms of sociological breadth – the early Soviet regime engendered the largest collective autobiographical project undertaken in modern history. Only the Chinese Communist case may have rivaled the Soviet autobiographical project in terms of the sheer number of individual autobiographies sponsored by the regime. For a bibliography of published autobiographical material relating to the Soviet period, see the ongoing publication project, *Sovetskoe obshchestvo v vospominaniiakh i dnevnikakh. Annotirovannyi bibliograficheskii ukazatel' knig, publikatsii v sbornikakh i zhurnalakh*, ed. V.Z. Drobizhev, 4 vols (Moscow: Kniga, 1987–95). A Soviet literary encyclopedia notes that the production of autobiographical literature increased significantly after 1917 ('Memuarnaia literatura', in *Literaturnaia entsiklopediia*, Vol. 7 (Moscow: Izd-vo Kommunisticheskoi akademii, 1934), cols. 131-49). The popularity of the diary genre in Soviet Russia is underscored by a bibliography of recent journal publications of archival documentation, which lists more than two hundred diaries or diary excerpts, *Otkrytyi arkhiv. Spravochnik opublikovannykh dokumentov po istorii Rossii XX-go veka iz gosudarstvennykh i semeinykh arkhivov* (po otechestvennoi periodike 1985–1995 gg.), ed. I.A. Kondakova (Moscow, 1997).
7. See Isaak Babel, *Red Cavalry* (New York: A.A. Knopf, 1929); Andrei Platonov, *Chevengur* (Paris: YMCA, 1972).
8. Mark Steinberg, 'The Language of Popular Revolution in Russia, 1917', draft introduction to *Voices of Revolution, 1917* (New Haven, CT: Yale University Press, 2001); the humanist theme is strongly expressed in Maksim Gorky's serialized commentary in *Untimely Thoughts: Essays on Revolution, Culture, and the Bolsheviks, 1917–1918* (New York: P.S. Eriksson, 1968).
9. The ethos of social activation associated here with the Soviet regime was in fact already implemented in the course of World War I. But the Bolsheviks' approach was distinct in that they transposed the spirit of total wartime mobilization to post-war conditions and introduced a much broader set of practices to realize this goal (Peter Holquist, '"Information is the Alpha and Omega of Our Work": Bolshevik Surveillance in Its Pan-European Context', *Journal of Modern History* 69 (1997), pp. 415–50).

10. On the poetics of self-fashioning in Soviet autobiographies, see Igal Halfin, *From Darkness to Light: Class, Consciousness, and Salvation in Revolutionary Russia* (Pittsburgh, PA: University of Pittsburgh Press, 2000), especially Chs 4 and 5. The genre of the Soviet autobiography bears striking parallels to the Puritan mode of self-constitution, as at least once in their lives all Puritan converts were required to write and publicly recite their own spiritual histories. These autobiographical texts were shaped against the texts of predecessors and fellow believers. 'To be a pilgrim was to travel in the "Way" of such texts within the Puritan culture ...' (Kathleen M. Swaim, *Pilgrim's Progess, Puritan Progress. Discourses and Contexts* (Urbana and Chicago, IL: University of Illinois, 1993), p. 137).
11. S.V. Zhuravlev, *Fenomen 'Istorii fabrik i zavodov': Gor'kovskoe nachinanie v kontekste epokhi 1930-kh godov* (Moscow: Institut rossiiskoi istorii RAN, 1997); Frederick Corney, 'History, Memory, Identity and the Construction of the Bolshevik Revolution, 1917–1927', Ph.D. dissertation (Columbia University, 1997), especially pp. 273–8, 316–20.
12. See the final chapter, 'Gorky Sums Up', in *Belomor: an Account of the Construction of the New Canal between the White Sea and the Baltic Sea* (New York: H. Smith and R. Haas, 1935); A.S. Makarenko, *The Road to Life: an Epic of Education* (Moscow, 1951). The highest form of subjectivity, however, the role of progenitor of the New Soviet Man, was reserved for Stalin himself, who was likened to 'a gardener rearing his beloved fruit tree'. 'Otchetnyi doklad tov. Molotova o rabote pravitel'stva VII S''ezdu Sovetov SSSR', *Pravda*, 29 Jan. 1935.
13. *Knizhka krasnoarmeitsa* (Ekaterinoslav: Tipografiia gubernskogo voennogo komissariata, 1919). I thank Peter Holquist for pointing out this source to me.
14. See Note 10 on Puritan diary-keeping. Also, Charles E. Hambrick-Stowe, *The Practice of Piety: Puritan Devotional Disciplines in Seventeenth-Century New England* (Chapel Hill, NC: University of North Carolina Press, 1982). For the scattered initiatives of Soviet pedagogues, psychologists and literary activists to mobilize the introspective and self-transformative powers of the diary in their efforts to create the New Man, see Ch. 2 of Jochen Hellbeck, *Revolution of the Soul: Diaries from the Stalin Era* (Cambridge, MA: Harvard University Press, forthcoming).
15. Oleg Kharkhordin, 'Reveal and Dissimulate: A Genealogy of Private Life in Soviet Russia', in Jeff Weintraub and Krishan Kumar (eds), *Public and Private in Thought and Practice* (Chicago, 1994). In Il'ia Erenburg's novel, *Second Day* (Den' vtoroi), the chief villain, Vasia Safonov, keeps a diary shielded from the collective, to which he confides his counter-revolutionary thoughts. Transposed to real life, the same scenario could be observed in the case of Kirov's murderer, Leonid Nikolaev, whose diary the state prosecution used to provide evidence for his anti-Soviet disposition (Robert Conquest, *The Great Terror: A Reassessment*, (New York: Oxford University Press, 1990), p. 56). To counter possible individualistic effects of diary-keeping and foster the development of a collectivist consciousness, Soviet pedagogues also assigned collectively kept 'brigade diaries' in factories and schools. The Nazi regime in Germany produced a racialized version of the collective diary, with Nazi ideologues calling for the writing of 'clan diaries' (Tagebuch der Sippe), from which future generations were to 'draw power and knowledge and obtain insights into the character and fate of their blood relatives [*Blutsverbundenen*]' (Peter Boerner, *Tagebuch* (Stuttgart: Metzler, 1969)).
16. 'Memuarnaia literatura', p. 132.
17. Josette Bouvard, 'Le moi au miroir de la société nouvelle: les formes autobiographiques de l'histoire' (unpubl. ms.), p. 85.
18. The sociological breadth and variegated textual nature of this corpus of diaries (numbering about one hundred in total) defy simple classification. It is safe to say, though, that the majority of the diaries were written by members of a younger generation (born between 1895 and 1920). In terms of the provenance of these diaries, a good number of them, authored by members of the state bureaucracy, or the technical and artistic intelligentsia, had been deposited in Soviet state archives and were accessible to researchers already before the collapse of the Soviet Union. Others, belonging to the same group of people, had been locked away in *spetskhrany* until the late 1980s.

A third group of diaries is derived from non-state archives established during the perestroika period (e.g., Memorial and the Narodnyi arkhiv) or from private archives. Numerically, diaries from the latter two groups prevail strongly. Although impressive in number, these diaries scratch only the surface of the total of surviving diaries from the early Stalin period. The greatest as-of-yet untapped repositories of diaries from the 1930s are the central and regional archives of the KGB, to which foreign researchers still have virtually no access. Innumerable other diaries are preserved in private households throughout the post-Soviet territory. There is reason to fear that many diaries from the early Soviet period might get lost or never be made available to researchers, for the simple reason that their current owners are unaware of the historical significance of this genre. For a detailed survey of diaries from the 1930s, see Hellbeck, *Revolution of the Soul*, Ch. 3. Several of these previously unknown diaries from the 1930s have already been published in the West. See especially Veronique Garros, Natalia Korenevskaya and Thomas Lahusen (eds), *Intimacy and Terror: Soviet Diaries of the 1930s* (New York: New Press, 1995); Jochen Hellbeck (ed.), *Tagebuch aus Moskau 1931–1939* (Munich: Deutscher Taschenbuch Verlag, 1996).

19. Stepan Podlubnyi, diary entry of 2 Feb. 1932, in Hellbeck, *Tagebuch aus Moskau*, p. 92.
20. '1933–1936 gg. v griazovetskoi derevne (Dnevnik A.I. Zhelezniakova)', *Vologda. Istoriko-kraevedcheskii al'manakh*, vyp. 1 (Vologda, 1994), pp. 454–521 (p. 455, entry of 30 May 1933).
21. John Scott, *Behind the Urals. An American Worker in Russia's City of Steel* (1942), enlarged edn prep. Stephen Kotkin (Bloomington, IN: Indiana University Press, 1989), pp. 118–19.
22. In spite of Zhuravlev's intention to keep an impersonal diary of everyday life in Kalinin, his chronicle did turn largely into a confessional genre, recording intrigues at the workplace and problems with his adulterous wife at home (Diary of Nikolai Zhuravlev, Gosudarstvennyi arkhiv Kalininskoi oblasti, f. r-652, op. 1, ed. khr. 2).
23. On Soviet designs to revolutionize *byt*, see Eric Naiman, *Sex in Public: the Incarnation of Early Soviet Ideology* (Princeton, NJ: Princeton University Press, 1997), pp. 185–8; Katerina Clark, *Petersburg: Crucible of Cultural Revolution* (Cambridge, MA: Harvard University Press, 1995, pp. 242–60; Michael David-Fox, *Revolution of the Mind: Higher Learning among the Bolsheviks, 1918–1929* (Ithaca, NY: Cornell University Press, 1997); and Christina Kiaer, 'Boris Arvatov's Socialist Objects', *October* 81 (Summer 1997), pp. 105-118.
24. Man'kov later became a well-known historian of pre-Petrine Russia. He published, among other things, an acclaimed edition of the 1649 Ulozhenie (*Sobornoe ulozhenie 1649 goda. Tekst kommentarii*, ed. A.G. Man'kov (Leningrad: Nauka, 1987)).
25. A.G. Man'kov, 'Dnevnik riadovogo chelovcka (1933–1934)', *Zvezda* 6 (1994).
26. In his diary, Ivan Sich, a retired schoolteacher of French, also focused on the hardships of everyday life, contrasting them to the ideological proclamations of the Soviet regime. Sich especially made a point of recording the critical views of workers towards Soviet power, to discredit the latter's claims for legitimacy. Unlike Man'kov, however, Sich did not seem to be motivated by a personal vision of a better socialist world (I.I. Sich, 'Fragments du journal inédit d'Ivan Ivanovic Sitc', *Cahiers du monde russe et soviétique* 1 (1987), pp. 75–94; especially entries of 7 Nov. 1929 and 'First days of June (1930)'.
27. Diary of Galina Shtange, in Garros *et al.* (eds), *Intimacy and Terror*, pp. 167-218.
28. Diary of Anatolii Ul'ianov, in Otdel rukopisei Rossiiskoi gosudarstvennoi biblioteki (OR RGB), f. 442, op. 1, ed. khr. 10, entries of 20 May 1933 and 13 July 1933.
29. Diary of A.V. Peregudov, in Rossiiskii gosudarstvennyi arkhiv literatury i iskusstva (RGALI), f. 2211, op. 3, ed. khr. 18, entry of 8 April 1961. Peregudov's diary notes of the 1930s are indeed redundant and shallow, consisting for the most part of weather reports and minute descriptions of the author's activities, particularly the types of food and drinks consumed on a given day ('I slept ... got up ..., drank two cups of tea ..., went to ...').
30. For references to the extensive body of Western travellers' descriptions of the emerging Soviet state, see Paul Hollander, *Political Pilgrims: Western Intellectuals in Search*

of the Good Society (New Brunswick, NJ: Transaction Publishers, 1998); Christiane Uhlig, *Utopie oder Alptraum? Schweizer Reiseberichte über die Sowjetunion, 1917–1941* (Zurich: H. Rohr, 1992); Bernhard Furler, *Augen-Schein. Deutschsprachige Reportagen über Sowjetrußland 1917-1939* (Frankfurt: Athenäum, 1987).

31. Vsevolod Vishnevskii, *Sobranie sochinenii v 5 tomakh*, Vol. 6 *(Dopolnitel'nyi): Vystupleniia i radiorechi. Zapisnye knizhki. Pis'ma* (Moscow: Gos. izd. Khudozhestvennoi lit., 1961).
32. Tikhon Puzanov, '"Zhatva" 33-go goda', *Molodaia gvardiia* 5 (1991), pp. 200–12 (pp. 207–8, entry of 2 April 1933; see also entry of 1 Jan. 1933).
33. Ibid., entry of '6 Jan. 1933, Friday'. The notion of the diary as a work record and expressive medium of self-realization is also present in the journal of the coal miner Vladimir Molodtsov: '29 Nov. 1930. The greatest feeling that I could experience in my short life is the feeling of being conscious of the fact that I am a part of the miners' collective. What a great thing not to notice, not to count the hours of the working day, not to wait for the end of the shift, but instead to strive to prolong it ... and after the shift, to leave as a victor in the fulfillment of the plan! How joyful it is to see oneself ahead of the others' (*Chelovek sredi liudei. Rasskazy, dnevniki, ocherki* (Moscow: Sovetskii pisatel', 1964), pp. 161–91).
34. '1933–1936 gg. v griazovetskoi derevne (Dnevnik A.I. Zhelezniakova)', *Vologda. Istoriko-kraevedcheskii al'manakh*, vyp. 1 (Vologda, 1994), pp. 454–521.
35. Katerina Clark, *The Soviet Novel: History as Ritual* (Chicago, IL: University of Chicago, 1981), Nathan Leites, *A Study of Bolshevism* (Glencoe, IL: Free Press, 1953).
36. Diary of Vera Shtrom, in Tsentr dokumentatsii Narodnyi arkhiv (TsDNA), f. 336, op. 1, ed. khr. 32, entries of 31 July 1930 and 14 Aug. 1930).
37. Ibid., entries of 14 Aug. 1930, 5 May 1931 and 9 July 1931.
38. Diary of Anatolii Ul'ianov, entries of 7 March 1936 and 4 May 1938.
39. *Chelovek sredi liudei. Rasskazy*, pp. 161–91 (entry of 29 Nov. 1930).
40. Diary of Leonid Potemkin, in Garros *et al.* (eds), *Intimacy and Terror*, pp. 251–92 (undated entry following 31 July 1935; see also entry marked 'July 1936').
41. *Chelovek sredi liudei*, p. 171.
42. Hellbeck, *Tagebuch aus Moskau*, p. 147.
43. Ibid., pp. 122–3, 125–6, 154 (entries of 10 March 1933, 1 April 1933, 16 April 1934).
44. Ibid., pp. 95–6, 118, 182, 198, 203–4 (entries of 6 Oct. 1932, 8 Feb. 1933, 27 Dec. 1934, 28 March 1935, 30 Sept. 1935).
45. '1933–1936 gg. v griazovetskoi derevne'.
46. Diary of Aleksandr Afinogenov, in RGALI, f. 2172, op. 3, ed. khr. 5.
47. Werner Hohmann, *Heinrich Vogeler in der Sowjetunion 1931–1942. Daten – Fakten – Dokumente* (Fischerhude: Galerie Verlag, 1987), p. 97.
48. Marietta Shaginian, *Dnevniki 1917–1931* (Leningrad: Izd. pisatelei, 1932); Vera Inber, *Stranitsy dnei perebiraia ...: Iz dnevnikov i zapisnykh knizhek*, rev. edn (Moscow: Sovetskii pisatel', 1977).
49. Manfred Jurgensen, *Das fiktionale Ich: Untersuchungen zum Tagebuch* (Berne/Munich: Francke, 1979), pp. 7–8; Andrew Hassam, *Writing and Reality: A Study of Modern British Diary Fiction* (Westport, CT/London: Greenwood, 1993), pp. 4, 8, 51.
50. Henry J. Koren, *Marx and the Authentic Man* (Pittsburgh, PA: Duquesne University, 1967), p. 114.
51. Diary of Galina Shtange, in Garros *et al.* (eds), *Intimacy and Terror*, pp. 167–218.
52. On the reversal of gender roles in and following the Soviet Revolution, see Elizabeth Wood, *The Baba and the Comrade* (Bloomington, IN: Indiana University Press, 1997).
53. PCCT – the People's Commissariat of Communication and Transportation.
54. This passage, from a speech given by Shtange to the wives of commanders in the Transport Sector, follows her diary entry of 27 Dec. 1936.
55. My view of this diary as a coherent agenda of self-expression departs from the interpretation made by the editors of Shtange's diary, who stress the disparate nature of the various sources – diary entries, newspaper clippings, letters, photographs, etc. – making up this 'diary-herbarium', and who view the actual diary as a composite of

interwoven 'codes in which the subject moves forward and unravels, like a spider that dissolves itself in its own web' (Garros *et al.* (eds) *Intimacy and Terror*, pp. 168–9). In my view, this interpretation overstates the formal differences between the various textual and visual genres involved in the diary, and by the same token it underrates the existential meaning at stake for authors like Shtange in the production of these self-records.
56. See, for example, diary of A. Afinogenov, entry of 29 July 1937 (RGALI, f. 2172, op. 3, ed. khr. 5).
57. Iuliia Piatnitskaia, *Dnevnik zheny bol'shevika* (Benson, VT: Chalidze Publications, 1987), p. 149 (entry of 27 May 1938).
58. See especially Plaggenborg, 'Grundprobleme der Kulturgeschichte'.
59. On the turn towards individuating practices in the 1930s see Vadim Volkov, 'The Concept of Kul'turnost': Notes on the Stalinist Civilizing Process', in Christina Kiaer and Eric Naiman (eds), *Everyday Subjects: Formations of Identity in Early Soviet Culture* (New York: Cornell University Press, forthcoming); Oleg Kharkhordin, *The Collective and the Individual in Russia* (Berkeley, CA/London: University of California, 1999); Vladimir Papernyi, *Kul'tura 'Dva'* (Ann Arbor, MI: Ardis 1985); Raymond A. Bauer, *The New Man in Soviet Psychology* (Cambridge, MA: Harvard University Press, 1968).
60. This insistence on individual participation and, indeed, on individuals cultivating their souls has been completely overlooked even by scholars interested in Soviet ideology because the notion of a soul seemed to contradict orthodox Marxist materialism.
61. The nexus between Stalinist terror and subjectivity is more fully discussed in Hellbeck, *Revolution of the Soul*, Chs 3 and 7.
62. In the context of the historiography of the German Democratic Republic, Alf Lüdtke rightly cautions against a 'blockade theory', that is, an assumption that there existed wholly autonomous alternative languages (used by youth groups, dissidents, etc.), unaffected by 'official' culture. Instead Lüdtke emphasizes the shared valorization throughout East German society, irrespective of political differences, of distinct educational and moral norms (Alf Lüdtke and Peter Becker (eds), *Akten. Eingaben. Schaufenster: Die DDR und ihre Texte* (Berlin: Akademie Verlag, 1997), p. 19).
63. Barbara Engel and A. Posadskaya-Vanderbeck (eds), *A Revolution of Their Own: Voices of Women in Soviet History* (Boulder, CO: Westview, 1998), pp. 101–16, especially 102–3. Berezhnaia also remembered how as a worker/forewoman she tried to raise the morale of her fellow workers by going through the shop and singing them the song, 'All Our Life Is a Struggle'. A photograph of her from 1932, which she showed to her Western interlocutors, bore the dedication on the back: 'A few words to my friend: only by means of persistent struggle and lengthy work on the Self can a person reach the heights of science. It is essential to value life and to know how to extract from it only what is good, uniting that with one's ideals. Then life will be interesting and full of happiness' (ibid., pp. 107–8).
64. Author's interview with L.A. Potemkin, 29 March 1995.

6

On Being the Subjects of History: Nazis as Twentieth-Century Revolutionaries

PETER FRITZSCHE

George Steiner offers a wonderful description of the self-dramatization of Europeans during the French Revolution. 'Wherever ordinary men and women looked across the garden hedge, they saw bayonets passing', he remarks. With the vast mobilization of men during the revolutionary and Napoleonic Wars and the narration of their movements in terms of historical progress, history had become 'everyman's milieu'. 'All human beings were as subject to general disaster or exploitation as they were to disease', explains Steiner about the prehistory of the French Revolution. 'But these swept over them with tidal mystery', and did not fundamentally alter the way people thought about change. 'It is the events of 1789 to 1815 that interpenetrate common, private existence with the perception of historical processes.'[1] This suggests not only that individuals perceived change and did so in historical terms that dislodged them from what was now constituted static 'tradition', but also that they felt the impact of public events in their personal lives and as a result authorized themselves to participate in that eventfulness. In similar fashion, Reinhart Koselleck underscores the new sensibility in which non-élite subjects in the nineteenth century thought of themselves as 'taking part' in history or 'making' revolution.[2] Journalists such as Heinrich Heine and Ludwig Börne wrote of Paris in the decades after the Revolution as the French place where the history that everyone would eventually share was being made.[3] The world view of both the nineteenth-century liberal and the nineteenth-century Marxist are classic illustrations of how history came to define the life philosophies and didactic guides of individual people. A historical sensibility saturates Samuel Smiles's *Self Help*, for example. An invigoration of subjective literary genres such as autobiography, diary and correspondence at the turn of the nineteenth century further indicates the ways in which new forms of political representation prompted explorations in self-expression. From William Wordsworth and Chateaubriand to the writer and journalist Ludwig Börne, who endeavored to escape at once the parochial boundaries of Frankfurt's Jewish ghetto and Germany's reactionary politics, individual subjects came to see their personal development through the lens of abstract, but forceful, historical developments.[4] What defines the historical age in the dozen decades after 1789 is just this: the durability of narratives that see and make sense of change and the consequent authorization of political subjectivity so that private lives could be (re)constituted in remarkably large part by public eventfulness. The result was the quite novel recognition of the possibilities of throwing the Self into the turbulence of politics.

World War I has a special place in this modern history of historical consciousness because it recapitulated in such an intense way the displacements of political revolution, industrial transformation and geographical and social mobility. 'The involvement of every citizen, the unaccustomed collectivities, the emergencies and shock, the loss, the private totems and shared superstitions' of the war, writes Catherine Merridale, left 'indelible prints on the imagination'. For Eugen Weber, it was the mobilization for war more than anything else that effaced regional loyalties and gave France a recognizable national identity. Serving at the front, moving to the big city, working in munitions factories, men and women were relentlessly uprooted from parochial surroundings. Even in death, the nation honored the individual and personal sacrifice of every soldier; World War I was the first war in which the conscripted dead were not buried anonymously.[5] Across the garden hedge, the bayonets of national politics were visibly more ominous than ever before. World War I completed what the French Revolution had begun: the process by which individuals could regard their own lives in terms of national politics and ideological allegiances.

Military mobilization and revolutionary upheaval not only revealed the visceral press of history on individual lives in an age of mass death but indicated as well the fragility of the entire architecture of public order. War, revolution and economic calamity all raised apocalyptic expectations about the end of time. So startling were the rapid-fire events of the years 1914–19 that the remembered past had little to offer in the way of guidance. History had truly become a delinquent. Derailed by war and revolution, it no longer seemed to run along the straight and predictable tracks of the nineteenth century. It was thus with an acute sense of disorientation that contemporaries viewed the bayonets marching past. While this disorientation was distressful, the recognition of what I have called 'the delinquency of history' also dramatized the ways in which individuals were caught in its marauding movements and were the potential subjects of history, and thus made more credible the search for new collective (or, for that matter, individual) identities.[6] The future had never appeared so dangerous or so open-ended as when viewed from among the ruins of the post-war years. Along with Communism, fascism was the classic twentieth-century performance of the consciously held modernist myth that the world was at a critical turning-point, that a new era was about to manifest itself and that individual action was not only urgent but emancipating.[7]

Fascism has generally been regarded as the derivative of political upheaval and economic catastrophe. Without the emergencies of the inter-war years, this common-sense line of argumentation implies, fascist movements would not have been nearly so successful. Both Italian fascism and German National Socialism prospered in conditions of instability, but could not count on genuine support except from a core of true believers, so that, when stability returned, constituents would turn away from revolutionary politics and long for a return of normal conditions.[8] While this argument has the important merit of recognizing the different reasons for the appeal of fascism, it over-emphasizes the functional, material and economic motives behind political involvement. It also tends to regard supporters only in terms of their social and economic origins. What this view obscures is the degree to which fascism was also a cultural movement, which appealed to the senses and emotions and offered a blueprint for regeneration. 'Quite consciously', writes George Mosse, 'fascism addressed people's perceptions of their situation in life and their hopes for the future.' Therefore, he insists, 'it is essential to understand how fascist self-representation was so successful in taking up and satisfying these perceptions if we want to gauge the depth of the movement's appeal'.[9]

Indeed, fascists explicitly characterized their project as one of creating new men and new women who would meet the exigencies and opportunities of the post-war period. What one of the most incisive Nazi intellectuals, the sociologist Hans Freyer, described as 'this masculine, steeled, expansive and industrious century' offered individuals previously unimagined paths to self-development in which the Self fused with the course of history.[10] Fascist activists themselves described their political activity in terms of personal engagement and personal growth. This transformation was no less authentic for being manifestly illiberal. To presume the priority of a liberal self, which is then simply beset and stressed by illiberal calamities, is to misunderstand the nature of ideological allegiances in the twentieth century and the massive calibration of individual citizens with the mechanisms of larger political projects. In a series of remarkable statements made in the mid-1930s,

National Socialist autobiographers reported on their new life, the rejection of the parochial bounds of an older version and the embrace of a newly constituted, historically self-aware revolutionary subjectivity. This new subject position demanded difficult, often incompletely learned commitments which revolved around responsibility to the national collective and to biological hygiene.

Rather than turn to intellectual figures such as Moeller van den Bruck or Ernst Jünger or interrogate the literary production of Nazis such as Goebbels and Hitler, I propose to look at more ordinary political activists in order to probe the extent of fascist subjectivity in the post-war years. The primary source is an extraordinary collection of some six hundred autobiographical essays written in 1934 by Nazi party members under the auspices of Columbia University sociologist Theodore Abel and with the permission of the party. The Nazi party itself undertook two major collections to document its own history. In winter 1934, the party's director of education (*Reichsschulungleiter*) issued an appeal for autobiographical statements about the party's years of struggle. However, specific questions about political enemies, prominent allies and street battles discouraged authors from providing reflective commentary. A more interesting collection was gathered beginning in 1936: the memories of the Nazi old guard, who some party activists felt had been illegitimately pushed to the sidelines once the revolutionary movement assumed power. Written without any guides, these statements were more personal and autobiographical, although they lacked the free style of the Abel responses, perhaps because they were addressed to party officials. Abel also quite explicitly asked for autobiographical 'background' information regarding family, education and career.[11]

I

Central to the new politics of the Self in the fascist revolution was the perception of the massive disruption at work in the twentieth century. This was not the only way to see things, but the historical imagination of the post-war period in both its utopian and nostalgic versions latched on to discontinuity. Although World War I is generally described retrospectively by historians in terms of disastrous immobility – four long years of irresolution, the war of attrition in the trenches, the scarcities on the home front – it cannot be fully understood without taking account of the astonishing mobility on which contemporaries reported: not simply the unprecedented battles beneath the ocean and above ground or even the dramatic movements on the eastern front in 1917–18, but also the extraordinary mobilization of industry, the highly visible role of organized labor, the dramatic rearrangements of the domestic balance of power, the carefully choreographed production of civilian morale, and the production of new kinds of public roles for men and women and new sources of collective intimacy. The catastrophe of the war was the precondition for thought, as Jünger once put it. 'After lying dry for a long time', he explained, 'the once-secure precincts of order explode like gunpowder, and the unknown, the extraordinary, the dangerous become not only familiar but also permanent features.'[12] This catastrophic imagination appeared to reopen the possibilities of history which the 'routinized, bourgeois conduct of political life' had previously foreclosed.[13] The rough politics of the post-1918 years – the technocratic impulses of organized capitalism, the rise of fascism, the insurgency of Communism, and the killing ground of Auschwitz – rested on the dizzying assumption that history was malleable and could be reworked and reshaped in hitherto unimagined ways. Again and again, thinkers on the left as well as the right linked emergency with renewal, and tradition and convention with decadence. Inter-war politics endeavored to apply the newly furnished lessons of the war; these included a pacifist impulse but mostly revolved around notions of collective sacrifice, social justice, and national and economic reorganization.[14]

The prevalent feeling of discontinuity sustained a reckless politics manufactured to meet the challenges and opportunities that crisis seemed to imply. The formulation of Arthur Moeller van den Bruck, a conservative critic who was later posthumously adopted by the Nazis, is apt. He repeatedly referred to the *Revolutionsgewinn*, the revolutionary yield, of the year 1918.[15] Catastrophe had given the Germans the latitude to gamble. After their capitulation on the western front and their humiliation at Versailles, the Germans had become a *Gefahrvolk*, a people of danger, better able to prosper in conditions of extreme peril than the citizens of France or Britain, 'tired, matured' nations whose opportunities and revolutions had long since passed.[16] In so far as Germany embraced the logic of a newly fashioned geopolitical order, or newly available technological possibilities, or newly revealed biological truths – Weimar culture cut innumerable keys to enable national activism – it would emerge as a vitalized nation. Moeller van den Bruck indicated how the conditions of emergency and danger had constituted the revolutionary subject in the twentieth century.

What made post-1918 Germany so revolutionary and so modern was the central role that catastrophe played in cultural apprehensions and political visions. It was the 'modernist nation par excellence of our century', writes Modris Eksteins, because it was 'starkly future-oriented'.[17] The conviction that the grand narrative of 'History' as it had developed over the course of the nineteenth century had been invalidated was allied with a commitment to renovate the body of the nation. Characteristic post-war images of crippled veterans, unemployment lines, tumbledown metropolitan facades and marauding armies all testified to the impermanence of the material world but also to the tractability of its reconstruction. It is the consciousness of radical political subjectivity premised on the alleged disorder of historical process that this chapter will explore by way of an analysis of the rise and appeal of National Socialism. Adolf Hitler himself left an account of his political transformation in *Mein Kampf*. In these 1925 memoirs he recalled the hours he spent on Munich's Odeonsplatz on the day of Germany's declaration of war in August 1914: They were 'like a redemption from the annoying moods of my youth', he wrote. At least figuratively, Hitler fell to his knees and 'thanked Heaven' that he had been granted 'the good fortune of being allowed to live in these times'. What filled this outcast with 'impassioned enthusiasm' was his identification with the cause of Greater Germany. 'In my eyes it was not Austria fighting for some Serbian satisfaction, but Gemany fighting for her existence.'[18]

It was with the declaration of war that Hitler first found a wider meaning to his life and a sense of political purpose. For the rest of his life, Hitler sought to retrieve what he glimpsed in 1914: an unshakeable union based on ethnic-based nationalism and public self-sacrifice. In his eyes, summer 1914 was truly historic because it had created a new historical subject in world history – the German *Volk* – one that was unencumbered by past history and inequities and was finally unified to claim its imperial destiny. The year 1914 introduced a sense of epic time into the flow of German history. After 1933, party rallies and especially their national broadcast in films and newsreels endeavored to achieve the same effect: the insertion of the individual in the frame of the nation. In the end, what Nazi spectacle sought to recreate for every person was the experience of Adolf Hitler when he stepped into the patriotic crowd on Munich's Odeonsplatz and recognized the correspondence of his personal with Germany's national identity.[19] Indeed, Nazi autobiographers often described their own moment of political self-transformation: the first time in uniform, the first march in public, the camaraderie of party activists – small-town versions of August 1914.

The Nazis returned to August 1914 in January 1933. The day after Hitler's appointment as chancellor, the *Völkischer Beobachter* compared the million-headed throng that had rallied the night before on the streets of Berlin with the crowd that had gathered along the same streets on the eve of World War I, in July 1914: 'Then as now', editors commented, 'the blazing sign of a national insurrection. Then as now, resistance has been broken, the dams breached, the people have risen up.'[20] What is the nature of this imaginative leap from 1933 back to 1914? After all, January 1933 is usually paired with November 1918, when military defeat, an onerous peace and an incomplete revolution created the emergency conditions in which National Socialism thrived. That the partisans of 1933 elected another affinity, one with the crowds of 1914, is revealing because it explicitly connects the rise of National Socialism with national renewal rather than with the Weimar crisis, with new time rather than restoration.

For the National Socialists, the attention to 1914 was warranted because it had projected a sense of new or epic time in which political collectivities were suddenly made possible.[21] For all their hardships, the years after 1914 were imagined by Weimar contemporaries as providing the materials by which hitherto unimagined and unrealized national projects could be constructed. The year 1914 stood for the very discontinuities of history – the sudden, often disorienting, invalidation of the past, the invention of alternative, even ominous, futures, the authority in any case of the subjunctive mood – that intensified the individual's awareness of and participation in a dramatic process of destruction and fabrication.

To explore the ways in which, as Jünger put it, catastrophe was the precondition for thought, historians need to recognize the degree to which World War I disrupted individual autobiographies and exposed them to a more delinquent understanding of history. Again and again, witnesses recounted how the war and its aftermath was experienced as a radical break, as 'new time' or 'end time', which old history could not decode.[22] The economic ruin of the post-war period further disrupted autobiographies. During seasons of economic hardship previously secure pensioners had to find manual labor; factory workers sat idle for months, then years; prospective students postponed or abandoned their education altogether.

Since the ruptures of history in war and revolution coincided with the unprecedented engagement of millions of actual individuals, crisis had a remarkable autobiographical aspect. All sorts of documents reveal this personal engagement. During the war, newspapers published hundreds of unsolicited poems every day; one estimate has 50,000 German war poems written on each day of August 1914.[23] Families pasted scrapbooks and ordinary soldiers kept diaries and sent millions of letters home every day. No other war had been depicted in this unmanaged, democratic way. Of course, after the war, the German government and the German army put out official histories of the conflict. Since 1918 there has been a steady stream of history books about major battles and outstanding generals. But this production cannot compare to the letters, poems, songs and newspaper articles written during the conflict itself. This was a war in which most of the histories were written by ordinary people for ordinary people. This archive is not simply a repository for social historians to take measure of wartime experience; its assembly is also evidence of the public sense of being in historical, intimate time.

The people's archive corresponds to the vernacular, almost democratic vocabulary in which the war was discussed. Personal experience rather than official versions became the popular currency in which knowledge of the war was exchanged. Illustrated magazines paid notable attention to the way that the war had changed ordinary lives, following the crowd through the streets of Berlin in July 1914, illustrating the goodbyes in crowded train stations in August, depicting the reading and writing of postcards and letters in the months that followed.[24] From the very beginning of the conflict, Germany's major newspapers published thousands of *Feldpostbriefe* from the front. To be sure, the selection of these letters was often tendentious and reflected literary conventions about honor, bravery and sacrifice. Nonetheless, editors plainly felt the need to insert popular perspectives into overall understandings of the conflict. By the end of the war, over 97 separate editions of war letters had been assembled and published, the most famous of which was Philipp Witkop's 1916 *Kriegsbriefe deutscher Studenten*.[25] The high command eventually acknowledged the power of these completely ordinary, unauthoritative letters and incorporated them into the patriotic 'enlightenment' that the troops received in the last two years of the war.[26] What all this suggests is the degree to which the war was regarded as a distinctively people's war which reflected popular efforts and mass mobilization. It was legitimated in the name of the people rather than of the state or the dynasty, and it dramatized as never before the involvement of the individual subject in the larger movements of history. Both the material disruption and the vernacular representation of the war expressed the new mass scale of political subjectivity. The war thus generated a process of disruption in which individuals were uprooted from pre-war routines and one of reclamation, by which individuals authorized their own vernacular, unofficial versions of the war and, often enough, re-imagined the nation. Without the internalized sense of historical rupture, and the possibilities of re-imagined, more intimate relationships between the individual and the nation, the political radicalism of the post-war period would have been unthinkable.

One of the most powerful collective identities that the war brought to life was the idea of the *Volksgemeinschaft*, the people's community. In the years since 1914 this abstract notion had been made credible by the everyday endeavors and the vernacular representations of millions of Germans. Wartime efforts and suffering reconstituted the nation in populist fashion. Moreover, the losses of the war highlighted the fate of being a German and undoubtedly gave an ethnic slant to national feeling. No newspaper reader or tavern bystander could help but be caught up in a European war that was invariably cast in terms of 'us' versus 'them'. Germany's casualties – missing, wounded or dead – totalled one million by the first Christmas. 'By the end of 1914, virtually every ... family had suffered some bereavement.'[27] Clearly, personal ties as well as abstract expectations connected more and more even working-class Germans to the fortunes of the nation and its armies. The nation mattered more because it had vividly inscribed itself on individual bodies who on the battlefront had been mobilized, captured, maimed and killed, or who on the home front had been pressed into work, separated from their families and made vulnerable to malnutrition and disease.

The striking relationship between the individual body and the national body held for the post-war period as well. The Treaty of Versailles and the creation of the Polish Corridor (1919), the partitioning of Silesia (1921) and the French invasion of the Ruhr (1923) were deeply felt by Germans of all classes: collections were taken up, young children boarded in rural sanctuaries, and town squares filled with angry protestors of all parties, including the Social Democrats. Obsessed with the integrity of the nation that appeared to have been badly damaged, nationalists thought in increasingly exclusive or racial terms. Finally, the effects of the 1922–23 inflation were so sweeping, the pain it inflicted was so general, and its appearance so fused in the public mind with the Treaty of Versailles, that it exposed the national fate shared by all Germans, gave stark expression to national character and suffering, and thereby spurred programs for national salvation. The difficult terms of war and peace imposed what Ernest Renan referred to as the 'daily plebiscite' of nationalism in which the abstract state that raised taxes and enacted laws was re-imagined as a living, breathing, injured collectivity. This nation was at once immediately recognizable in the patriotic efforts invested and the bitter anguish felt by millions of Germans, and concealed by the fragmented means of political representation during the Weimar Republic.

It was in the name of this fragile, intimate political subject that nationalist Germans mobilized in the years after 1918, providing as they did a stark contrast with the republic which did not appeal to citizens on an emotional level and which could not adequately integrate wartime experiences. (And it was not only right-wing or liberal nationalists who mobilized; Social Democrats rallied again and again under nationalist banners.) In the early 1920s, the 'hidden nation' was worked and reworked by the public engagement of millions of men who took up the explicitly gendered task of political soldiering. This mobilization was not a continuation of military or national traditions from the pre-war era: it was very clearly a grass-roots effort that came together from below, involved participation from a relatively broad social context, spoke in an unmistakable anti-élite vernacular and imagined the German future as a work of strenuous, revolutionary engagement in order to bring the collective subject – the people – to life. The myth of palingenesis – the rebirth of the *Volk* – applies to the mobilizing myths of Nazi Germany as much as it does to those of fascist Italy.[28] This was anything but pre-war nationalism, hurrah patriotism or imperial nostalgia. Rather, this rebirth depended on the perceived violence of the war's break with the past, the scope of mobilization the war entailed, and the collective and national nature of the efforts the war demanded.

The fashioning of an intimate relationship between male nationalists and the imaginary, hidden nation is clearly visible in the frantic activity of the Stahlhelm, the Young German Order and a dozen other smaller patriotic associations which dominated post-war social life. In this regard, the National Socialists were not innovators, and many latter-day Nazi activists were veterans of earlier periods of political engagement in the 1920s. Yet it was the Nazis who most closely identified with the not-yet-existent *Volksgemeinschaft*, who claimed the new lineage of the wartime experience, who thus operated most clearly in the subjunctive mood, and who therefore claim our particular attention.

II

Nazi autobiographers rehearsed the new possibilities of history in their liberation of the political self from the past and from the parochial. Making catastrophe the explicit premise of their political practice, Nazis rejected the heritage of the past, manufactured their own historical traditions and imagined their own alternative futures. Again and again, National Socialists staged history as an extreme boundary situation that required uncommon political collaboration and that sought to come to terms with a brand-new world regarded as unstable and dangerous. In the first place, Nazi activists were remarkably conscious of history and the moment of its delinquency. Second, they described their embrace of National Socialism as a political commitment that required both a leave-taking and an advance, at once the repudiation of older loyalties and the acquisition of new ones. This release from older affinities facilitated the articulation of an intimate relationship with the hidden nation. The highly self-conscious transformation of the Self provided the central pivot to privately constituted autobiographical narratives which were later transcribed publicly in response to party appeals or to Abel's essay project. Finally, the new subjects of history elaborated their selves by the practices of racial grooming, especially in the years after 1933.

While a number of historians account for the political universe of the Weimar Republic with repeated references to the fragmentation of the middle-class milieu and the exfoliation of economic interest groups, there was more ideological coherence than these interpretations would suggest. Political mobilization after World War I was intense and far-reaching: every German town boasted paramilitary groups, political clubs and national associations. Quarrels among neighbors over the black–white–red banner of the empire or the black–red–gold flag of the republic consumed public life, so much so that the novelist Ernst Glaeser described the beleaguered young hero of his Weimar-era novel as the 'last civilian'.[29] Political discussions took over taverns, schoolrooms and family circles. The year 1918 prompted garrulous 'political conversations with fathers and brothers'.[30] 'Our class carried on lengthy discussions, some of which went on for hours. Sometimes the discussions became so heated that the teacher had to remind us of his authority to maintain order', recalled one middle-class Nazi about the Weimar years.[31] This ceaseless discussion and also the recollected opposition to 'authority' are indicative of how open-ended the political future appeared in the 1920s.

The ideological tone of even provincial politics is apparent as well in the careful study that political activists made of various ideological programs, seeking as they were the right kind of tools to rebuild the German community. The sense of making history and of fashioning new subjects that Koselleck regards as distinctive to modernity's temporal structure was widespread. Respondents who prepared autobiographical statements in 1934 remembered working through political possibilities ten years earlier. 'World war ... days of revolution ... French occupation ... Spartacists ... inflation' – we 'were already quite interested in why these things had to happen', wrote Hermann Jung.[32] Future party members were often ravenous readers, browsing among newspapers until they reported finally picking up a Nazi edition, or they visited all sorts of political meetings until they were captured by one or another Nazi orator. This stocktaking is evidence of a remarkable visualization of the indeterminate, but sensible forces of history, which were alternatively imagined in Marxist, nationalist or racial terms. Quite a few autobiographers had seriously considered Marxism, or at least well articulated its alleged shortcomings. 'Having thrown aside the Marxist idea long ago, I thought and thought', recalled one miner who eventually 'in 1928–1929 ... read and heard about Adolf Hitler', whose 'words went right to my marrow'.[33] Another worker perused 'Social Democratic and Communist newspapers and pamphlets ... my newspaper at the time was the *Dortmunder General-Anzeiger*', which was Social

Democratic. A few years later, this inquisitive reader came across a copy of the *Völkischer Beobachter*, 'the contents interested me a great deal', he reported: 'What I felt and thought was here expressed in words.'[34] A teacher from Vorsfelde explained that in the 1920s two books stood on his desk: 'Adolf Hitler's *Mein Kampf* and Karl Marx. *Jawohl* Karl Marx! ... Learning, reading, comparing. On top of that the bitter experience of daily life.' The teacher admitted that in time 'Karl Marx disappeared' from his desk.[35] Autobiographers also remembered their keen interest in history, which was frequently a favorite subject in school.[36] The awareness and study of the novel ideological parameters of the post-war years – 'learning, reading, comparing' – is characteristic, suggesting the high degree of self-dramatization in the streams of delinquent history.

This study of the mechanics of political mobilization was particularly appropriate to a period when activists were so aware of the disjunction between past and present and the transitory nature of the present day. The political self was constructed in terms of discontinuities and uncertainties; this historical consciousness was the defining feature of the twentieth century, argued ideologue Hans Freyer.[37] History was visualized in terms of violent beginnings and explosive uprisings, and described as a struggle against the nineteenth century. To account for his journey to National Socialism, an East Prussian farmer began his memoirs with the day 'exactly twenty years ago, when I was only five years old. I first saw field-grey-clad soldiers with sabres and guns, and my own father dressed the same way. My mother watched, serious and worried. War! I heard this word then for the first time, but I soon understood it.'[38] The point is not so much that the war actually germinated national consciousness but rather that autobiographers used the war or other ruptures to narrate their own newly acquired sense of responsibility to the collective: 'For the first time I heard from my *Volk*', reflected Heinz Mai about August 1914.[39] A bank clerk surveyed the post-war years in rapid fire: 'The outward glamor of pre-war days, the outbreak of the war, the invasion of the Russians ... the distribution of provisions during the war ... the breakdown of November 1918, the struggle against the new republican regime, interminable political arguments, battles in lecture halls, political terrorism, the economic difficulties during the inflation and deflation ... all will remain ineffaceable in the memory of the young German.'[40] A sense that an older world had been left behind prevailed: 'My old world broke asunder in my experiences' in the war, recalled one Catholic National Socialist.[41] By the fall of 1918, another Nazi reported, 'everything in the fatherland had begun to stagger'.[42] 'Soon thereafter came the revolution', explained an activist in a breathless, telegraphic style in which the medium is the message: 'it was something new, incomprehensible. For me, something unknown.'[43] By the same token, the discontinuities between the pre-war and the post-war world were also constituted by the widespread recognition that new social relations and collective responsibilities had emerged out of the conflict. Whether in reference to frontline camaraderie, vague notions of socialism or the *Volksgemeinschaft*, revolutionary activists repeatedly identified the powerful, as-yet-unrealized treasures of the world war. They operated in a radical subjunctive mood.

What accompanied this recognition of disjunction was an intense engagement in politics, particularly in the years 1918–23: it is striking how many activists in the last crisis years of the republic were in fact long-term veterans of political struggle. About half of the respondents to the 1934 Abel essay project reported right-wing political activity in the years 1921–24.[44] However black the colors in which the German condition after the war was portrayed, the political self was constituted and came to life by way of the felt discontinuities and the allied sense of possibility. Autobiographers also stressed their active participation in the coming of the Third Reich. 'What was important for me', reported Paul Holzapfel, 'was belonging to a movement that did not just protest, but actively committed itself to fight for Germany.' 'We all helped out, me too', reflected another old fighter. 'I *had* to propagandize', confessed Emil Schlitz after joining the party in 1927, 'wherever I stood and wherever I went, on the street, in the streetcar, in restaurants ... at work.'[45] Indeed, the Nazis, like the Social Democrats and Communists, put great stress on mobilization at the grass roots, and on the efficacy of voluntary action. Popular participation did not, of course, mean that the movement was accountable to its followers, but fascist liturgy gave citizens the 'feeling of participating, of belonging to a true and meaningful community'. Supporters were transformed from 'spectators into participants'.[46] The doom-and-gloom accounts of Weimar's perilous history usually miss the active process by which this political subjectivity was fashioned and a sense of collective responsibility articulated. That autobiographers insisted on their political naivety before committing themselves to National Socialism is important not because the verdict applies but because it dramatizes so well the break with the conventions of an earlier political understanding. This merger of the previously complacent self with the discipline of the political echoes the studied composure, or *Verhaltenslehre,* which Helmut Lethen considers characteristic of Weimar social relations. But whereas Lethen draws attention to the formation of the cold, agile metropolitan type, the political revolutionary adhered to the newly imagined collective and, as will be suggested, to a specifically biological collective. Both, however, left behind the warmth of the traditional, self-enclosed community.[47]

The construction of the political self and the traverse of the open political ground after the revolution corresponded to a rejection of parochial contexts of family and village and to a new affiliation with the hidden nation. Political soldiering in the 1920s was not rooted in obligations to the family or justified in non-political or material terms.[48] Activists reported on the conflict between political soldiering and responsibilities to family, thereby carrying on the destructive work of the war which had claimed so many sons, brothers and fathers for the sake of the nation. 'My father wrote me something like, "Don't bother with all this party rubbish,"' recalled one middle-class Nazi; 'I made up my mind that I would have to choose between politics and family.'[49] 'There was no way of avoiding a fight with my father', wrote Paul Schneider, 'so I left my parents' house and moved in with my oldest, married sister.' Raised by Social Democrats, Karl Mernberger 'left home and found lodging in an SA shelter'.[50] A vintner's son contrasted his own political commitment with the pre-war apoliticalism of his parents and contrasted his Self to the 'old aunties in my family'. While one young clerk cherished his family, he recognized that he had no choice but to leave: 'the experiences of war, revolution and inflation ... we were rudely pushed out of our childhood'.[51] The other possibility was for Nazis to 'nationalize' their families, recruiting younger brothers, but also fathers and occasionally sisters and mothers. In either case, the revolutionary subject compellingly described the disintegration of the folds of private life.

The exit from home was all the more conclusive along the byways of the new politics. Horizons expanded with political activity. 'Almost daily I cycled five miles of bad road into town to listen to a Nazi speech, and then home again alone', recalled one old fighter.[52] 'Night after night, Sunday after Sunday, in wind and rain', activists spread the Nazi word on bicycles and trucks; Werner Goerendt was on his motorcycle 'night and day'.[53] Hiking, bicycling and motoring to the next village, and eventually on to the regional center for larger rallies and to the big city for national events are references that recur repeatedly in Nazi autobiographies and indicate just how non-local the identifications of the new political self had become. Memories of national rallies, whether they were athletic competitions in Munich, glider meets in Gersfeld, Stahlhelm marches in Berlin, Reichsbanner parades in Magdeburg or Nazi days in Nuremberg, punctuate political autobiographies in the Weimar period.[54] The Abel respondents also testified to their explorations of wider, unfamiliar social precincts: 'I walked through the city. I wandered through the Communist district. I talked to the people there a number of times', recalled a young middle-class youth.[55] It was not only workers, but also farmers, artisans and shopkeepers whom Nazi activists engaged. They did so not so much to appeal to specific occupational interests, as some scholars have suggested, but rather to cross social boundaries and to get to know 'the little man', the 'ordinary person', to reconstitute the nation as a collective, integral whole.[56] What Nazi campaigners endeavored to realize was the myth of the trenches, in which soldiers from a variety of social backgrounds allegedly discovered their common German being, or the experience of the Weimar-era *Werkstudent*, the impoverished middle-class students who spent summers working in factories and learning to appreciate the working class.'[57]

The movement away from the past, the family and the home town was experienced as a 'rebirth'. In the Abel autobiographies, the commitment to political soldiering is carefully and dramatically told and was often described as a transition or conversion. Werner Goerendt carefully set the stage:[58]

> Spring 1925. The early evening darkens the streets of the East Prussian capital and a spring shower whips rain into my face. Gas lamps flicker like big bright spots. Shivering, I pull up my collar and think of the Bergstrasse where the trees have long since bloomed and the tender green of the forests gleams. I'm lost in thought as I make my way home. Suddenly I hear the footfalls of a marching column. Reichswehr, I think, or one of the dozens of patriotic troops? The next lantern releases the group from the darkness of the street: brown shirts appear, arm bands glimmer, the flag flutters blood-red, the sharp contours of the swastika contrast with the pale ground. It is only a small troop, not even 20 men: I am completely taken. I can't do anything but turn around and march alongside.

Autobiographical sketches quite explicitly framed the transformative experience of joining the Nazis, bearing the titles: 'How I Became a National Socialist', 'Why I Found the Way to My Führer', 'Why and How I Came to National Socialism', 'My Path to the NSDAP', 'My Life Journey to Adolf Hitler', 'Autobiography of a Hitler German', 'How Did I Become a National Socialist?'[59] 'On the day that I first walked on the street with my brown uniform, I had burned all my bridges behind me', realized one civil servant from eastern Berlin.[60] After that, 'I never took off my brown shirt', remembered the newly initiated Friedrich Kurz; 'wearing brown shirts we felt safe!'[61] Even before Abel encouraged expansive autobiographical statements of this sort in his 1934 essay project, Stahlhelm and Nazi activists frequently worked in an autobiographical genre, giving speeches about their personal entry into politics, sketching out the reasons 'why I became a National Socialist', and thus reproducing in countless vernacular forms Hitler's own literary self-presentation in *Mein Kampf*.[62] In many ways, this practice was a continuation of the nationalized gestures of writing and publishing and otherwise circulating *Feldpostbriefe* during the war. Whether or not the fascist self of the Weimar era produced disproportionately more in the way of autobiographical texts cannot be determined; what might have militated against too much in the way of personal self-reflection is that political activity was directed toward the construction of collective and hierarchical ensembles rather than of the free-thinking individual as was the case during the French Revolution, a period in which political engagement and literary production went more comfortably hand in hand. Nonetheless, when prompted to write autobiographical statements, Nazi activists relied on ready-made narrative structures which choreographed the remaking of the Self and its commitment to the German people and the political mission of National Socialism. By preparing long, detailed and usually hand-written autobiographical statements, activists literally seized their own history. The majority of the sketches are told in the first person, describing a shorter or longer journey to National Socialism, and they are appended with mementoes, photographs, diaries, letters, newspaper clippings that had been collected along the way and which express the deeply personal value put on the newly fashioned political commitment. It is difficult to imagine activists of the middle-class parties maintaining such private archives or photo albums. The impulse both to narrate and archive reveals how ideological and historical parameters contributed to the growth of the revolutionary self.

Finally, I would like to suggest that the revolutionary subject continued to cultivate the Self by strenuously learning the new vocabulary of *Rassenlehre*, the racial teachings, which particularly in their National Socialist reformulation as modern biological science were probably unfamiliar to most activists. But learn them they did, and party members increasingly applied them to decisions in everyday life. Indeed Nazism's eugenic and racial policies are so compelling in this regard because of the way they invited even ordinary (non-Jewish) citizens to regard themselves and act as protagonists and beneficiaries of a qualitatively new, though unprecedentedly demanding epoch in German history.

When the National Socialists came to power in January 1933 they believed they stood at the very edge of history, poised to redirect the nation to fit the grooves of an envisioned Aryan future. The whole previous itinerary of Germany, in which a liberal sphere had been elaborated, in which public claims had been put forward by political parties and interest groups, and in which various ethnic groups, provincial identities and religious communities had survived and commingled, was to come to an abrupt end. From the perspective of the Nazis, the year 1933 marked a sharp break. In place of the quarrels of party, the contests of interest and the divisions of class that had supposedly compromised the ability of the nation to act, the Nazis proposed to build a unified racial community guided by modern science. The biological politics to which the Nazis adhered corresponded to the delinquency of history which visualized grave dangers that imperiled the future of the German people and which also identified strenuous collective efforts that would reclaim Germany's future.

On the one hand, the National Socialists sought to nurture the biological inheritance of Germans by putting in place an elaborate pronatalist social-welfare edifice and refurbishing the workplace in a more rational manner. All the intense efforts to promote family health, to reward parents with tax allowances, to extend young people technical training and to provide workers with vacations and other diversions may at first glance resemble an attractive 'New Deal' but was proposed so that Germans could assume roles as productive members of the national *Volksgemeinschaft*. The emphasis of social policy was always on the enforcement of discipline in the name of the community rather than provision of opportunity for the individual. On the other hand, this constructive program of national health was accompanied by a stern eugenic administration which sought to weed out alleged biological dangers to the German *Volk*. From the very beginning, the regime applied measures to identify, segregate and eradicate supposedly debilitating or foreign matter. The end result of racial nurturing and racial weeding was to be a well-regulated *Völkisch* society, strong and homogeneous enough to prosper in the dangerous era of world wars.

To be a Nazi, then, meant representing the Self as an ongoing biological project. There was an astonishing performative aspect to National Socialism which has scarcely been acknowledged by scholarship. It is worth contemplating the extent to which Nazi activists and sympathizers groomed themselves in the years after 1933. National Socialism put stress on a well-turned public self that revealed the presumption of racial superiority and a keen sense of style. The Nazi-era 'body project' included guidelines on make-up, fashion and hair styling, on callisthenics and exercise, and on a proper diet. It embraced what has become to us the familiar politics of lifestyle, as the Nazi war on cancer so well reveals.[63] The Nazi New Man put great value on mechanical ability; building instruments, repairing a motorcycle or car, or joining a glider team: all these activities calibrated the individual body to the demands of the machine age. In many ways, technical dexterity was a biological attribute.[64] At the same time, Germans learned to coordinate their vocabulary to the biological world view. We know that children came to carry a new stock of Germanic and Nazified names. Autobiographical texts such as family trees, genealogical tables or *Ahnenbücher* projected a new sense of self. The prominent Hessian Nazi Adalbert Gimbel, for example, chaired his extended family's

Familienforschungsverband e. V. Gimbel (Genealogical Research Gimbel) and regularly published the association's *Nachrichtenblatt*.[65] Moreover, as historians of everyday life point out, citizens in the Third Reich reconsidered their relations with friends, neighbors and biological 'others' in light of the regime's racial guidelines. Alf Lüdtke and Ulrich Herbert have shown that German workers increasingly used racial vocabulary to designate differences between Jewish and non-Jewish Germans and between first-class Germans and third-class foreign laborers.[66] This linguistic *Rassenlehre* had become quite prevalent by the late 1930s. A few years later, Wehrmacht soldiers articulated in their letters home a Nazified anthropology to describe the Slavic, Jewish and other non-German populations they were conquering and the demographic policies they were imposing. This folk anthropology authorized various racial hierarchies and enjoined necessarily severe actions that were otherwise inappropriate to 'civilized' groups. War was *Rassenlehre* and German soldiers proved to be quick learners.

It is plausible to suggest that even before 1939 it was precisely the biological terrain that dramatized the presence of mobility in this German revolution and invited activists to link their personal selves to the larger national project by learning and carrying out the practices of racial grooming. It is striking how often biological metaphors were deployed by the Abel respondents to denote the incomplete nature of the revolution and the necessity for vigilance in order to ensure its realization. 'To be sure, several storms still had to shake and shudder the German oak tree in order to clear out both the rotten and the sterile underbrush and to drive the roots deeper', explained one Nazi in 1934. This racial groomsman tried out another image: 'The years of suffering and shame and disgrace removed the healthy core of our people from a degenerate exterior shell.'[67] 'I know that a mature tree is replanted only with difficulty', conceded one Nazi worker; 'I know that the contemporary generation is still infected with the spirit of an age of liberalism, materialism, egoism, class consciousness, etc.'[68] Obviously revolutionary mobilization was an ongoing project. 'Today more than ever we have to bring a National Socialist attitude to every single one of our actions', averred Paul Schneider; 'we are still at the beginning.'[69] The chilling metaphor of gardening that Zygmunt Bauman conjures up in his argument regarding the Enlightenment roots of National Socialism appears in the words of one Nazi artisan: 'As fighting pioneers we are laying the blasting fuses in infertile, alien [*volksfremden*] rock in order to bring it down violently; as fighting gardeners we carefully tend and plant the nascent flower of Germandom.'[70] Young Nazis explicitly invoked the *Volkskörper*, or people's body, that they wished to cultivate and to which they struggled to belong.[71]

Rassenlehre is a terrifying reminder as to how self-conscious Nazi revolutionaries were. They perceived themselves in a historical time whose delinquency and brittleness had authorized their political subjectivity and enabled their political project. Given their acute historical-mindedness, their sense of being cut off from the inheritance of the past, their dramatically charged catastrophic thinking and their invocation of a biological era, the Nazis are misunderstood if the revolution of January 1933 is explained only in terms of economic hardship, social instability and international humiliation. The Nazis constructed themselves as the subjects of history and as such were revolutionary and, operating as they did in the subjunctive poetics of revolution, unmistakably modern. Stanley Payne comments that the Nazis 'carried the modern goal of breaking the limits and setting new records to an unprecedented point. For no other movement', he adds, 'did the modern doctrine of man as the measure of all things rule to such an extent. This "cult of the will" is the very basis of "modern culture".'[72] Modernism, which has usually been conceived in literary or artistic terms, has remarkable social and political implications. It is the apprehension of the malleable: the dark acknowledgement of the fragility and impermanence of the material world along with the conviction that relentless reform could steady collapsing structures. By being reflexive and making instability the explicit premise for its practice, modernism is hospitable not only to anarchic individualism but also to authoritarian design.[73] In my view, it is the premises rather than the attributes of modern projects that need to be examined more closely. What makes the twentieth century so promiscuous is not the content of the identities people have fashioned or the designs they have erected, but the historically self-conscious presumption that contingency abounds and has to be managed, that chaos is about to take over and has to be negotiated, that society can be designed and revolution made. In the end, it is an unsettling but unmistakable self-reflexivity, the bayonets seen across the garden hedge, that distinguishes both the modern and its revolutionaries.

NOTES

1. George Steiner, *In Bluebeard's Castle: Some Notes towards the Redefinition of Culture* (New Haven, CT: Yale, 1971), pp. 12–13.
2. Reinhart Koselleck, *Futures Past: On the Semantics of Historical Time* (Cambridge, MA: MIT, 1985). For more on this temporal revolution, see David Lowenthal, *The Past is a Foreign Country* (Cambridge: Cambridge University Press, 1985); and Georges Poulet, *Studies in Human Time* (Baltimore: Johns Hopkins University Press, 1956).
3. Ingrid Oesterle, 'Der Führungswechsel der Zeithorizonte in der deutschen Literatur. Korrespondenzen aus Paris, der Hauptstadt der Menschheitsgeschichte', in Dirk Grathoff (ed.), *Studien zur Ästhetik und Literaturgeschichte der Kunstperiode* (Frankfurt: P. Lang, 1985), p. 15.

4. See, for example, Mary A. Favret, *Romantic Correspondence: Women, Politics, and the Fiction of Letters* (Cambridge: Cambridge University Press, 1993); Gerald N. Izenberg, *Impossible Individuality: Romanticism, Revolution, and the Origins of Modern Selfhood, 1787–1802* (Princeton, NJ: Princeton University, 1992); Nicola Watson, *Revolution and the Form of the British Novel, 1790–1825: Intercepted Letters, Interrupted Seductions* (New York: Oxford University Press, 1994); and Marilyn Yalom, *Blood Sisters: The French Revolution in Women's Memory* (New York: Basic Books, 1995).
5. Catherine Merridale, 'War, Death, and Remembrance in Soviet Russia', in Jay Winter and Emmanuel Sivan, *War and Remembrance in the Twentieth Century* (Cambridge: Press Syndicate of University of Cambridge, 1999), p. 61; Eugen Weber, *Peasants into Frenchmen: The Modernization of Rural France, 1870–1914* (Stanford, CA: Stanford University Press, 1976); Thomas Laqueur, 'Memory and Naming in the Great War', in John R. Gillis (ed.), *Commemorations: The Politics of National Identity* (Princeton, NJ: Princeton University Press, 1994).
6. See Peter Fritzsche, 'Landscape of Danger, Landscape of Design: Crisis and Modernism in Weimar Germany', in Thomas W. Kniesche and Stephen Brockmann (eds), *Dancing on the Volcano: Essays on the Culture of the Weimar Republic* (Columbia, SC: Camden House, 1994), pp. 29–46; and 'Nazi Modern', *Modernism/Modernity* 3 (January 1996), pp. 1–21.
7. Roger Griffin, *The Nature of Fascism* (New York: Routledge, 1993), p. 35. The argument is made in full in Jochen Hellbeck, 'Laboratories of the Soviet Self: Diaries from the Stalin Era', Ph.D diss. (Columbia, 1998).
8. Even the most far-sighted analysis of fascism, Griffin, *Nature of Fascism*, emphasizes the popular desire for a return to law and order and to normality once the fascist regime is in power and the emergency is over.
9. George L. Mosse, *The Fascist Revolution: Toward a General Theory of Fascism* (New York: H. Fertig, 1999), p. xi.
10. Hans Freyer, 'Das Geschichtliche Selbstbewusstsein des 20. Jahrhunderts', *Vorträge*, Kaiser Wilhelm-Institut für Kunst- und Kulturwissenschaft, Vol. 3 (Rome, 1938), p. 7.
11. See the 1934 appeal by Reichsschulungsleiter Gohdes, Bundesarchiv, NS22/123; and the 1936 appeal of Rudolf Hess to party members with membership numbers below 100,000 in ibid., NS26/532. See also Theodore Abel, *The Nazi Movement* (New York: Atherton Press, 1966).
12. Cited in Martin Meyer, *Ernst Jünger* (Munich: Hanser, 1990), p. 165. See also Stefan Breuer, *Anatomie der Konservativen Revolution* (Darmstadt: Wissenschaftliche Buchgesellschaft, 1992), pp. 14, 45–7.
13. Richard Wolin, 'Carl Schmitt. The Conservative Revolutionary: Habitus and the Aesthetics of Horror', *Political Theory* 20 (Aug. 1992), p. 432. See also Karl-Heinz Bohrer, *Die Ästhetik des Schreckens. Die pessimistische Romantik und Ernst Jüngers Frühwerk* (Munich: Hanser, 1978); Andrew Hewitt, *Fascist Modernism: Aesthetics, Politics, and the Avant-Garde* (Stanford, CA: Stanford University Press, 1993); Peter Sloterdijk, *The Critique of Cynical Reason*, trans. Michael Eldred (Minneapolis, MN: University of Minnesota, 1987); and Fritzsche, 'Landscape of Danger', pp. 29–46.
14. See, for example, Dan S. White, *Lost Comrades: Socialists of the Front Generation* (Cambridge, MA: Harvard University Press, 1992).
15. Arthur Moeller van den Bruck, 'Wir wollen die Revolution gewinnen', *Gewissen* 2 (31 March 1920).
16. Arthur Moeller van den Bruck, *Germany's Third Empire*, trans. E.O. Lorimer (London: Allen & Unwin, 1934 [1922]), p. 17; idem, 'Die Ideen der Jungen in der Politik', *Der Tag*, 26 July 1919.
17. Modris Eksteins, *Rites of Spring: The Great War and the Birth of the Modern Age* (Boston, MA: Houghton Mifflin, 1989), pp. xvi, 73, 119.
18. Adolf Hitler, *Mein Kampf*, trans. John Chamberlain *et al.* (New York: Reynal & Hitchcok, 1940), pp. 210–11.
19. Peter Fritzsche, *Germans into Nazis* (Cambridge, MA: Harvard University Press, 1998), pp. 225–6.

20. Herbert Seehofes, 'Das erwachte Berlin marschiert, *Völkischer Beobachter*, 31 Jan. 1933.
21. On fascism and time, see the innovative work of Roger Griffin: '"Party Time:" Nazism as a Temporal Revolution', *History Today*, Vol. 49, No. 4 (April 1999), pp. 43–50; and '"I am no longer human. I am a Titan. A god!" The fascist quest to regenerate time', Electronic Seminars in History, http://ihrinfo.ac.uk/esh/quest.html.
22. Eric J. Leed, *No Man's Land: Combat and Identity in World War I* (Cambridge: Cambridge University Press, 1979), pp. 1–72; Klaus Vondung (ed.), *Kriegserlebnis: Der Erste Weltkrieg in der literarischen Gestaltung und symbolischen Deutung der Nationen* (Göttingen: Vandenhöck & Ruprecht, 1980); Klaus Vondung, *Die Apokalypse in Deutschland* (Munich: Deutscher Taschenbuch Verlag, 1988); Eksteins, *Rites of Spring*, p. 155.
23. C. Busse (ed), *Deutsche Kriegslieder 1914/16* (Bielefeld: Velhagen and Klasing, 1916), p. vi, cited in Vondung, (ed), *Kriegserlebnis*, p. 13.
24. *Illustrierte Zeitung*, 13 Aug. 1914; 20 Aug. 1914.
25. Jeffrey Verhey, 'The "Spirit of 1914": The Myth of Enthusiasm and the Rhetoric of Unity in World War I Germany', Ph.D diss. (University of California, Berkeley, 1991), pp. 262, 270–1; Philipp Witkop, *Kriegsbriefe deutscher Studenten* (Gotha: F.A. Perthes, 1916). A British version of the expanded German edition appeared as *German Students' War Letters*, trans. A.F. Wedd (London: Methuen 1929). See also Ulrich, 'Feldpostbriefe', in Peter Knoch (ed.), *Kriegsalltag: die Rekonstruktion des Kriegsalltags als Aufgabe der historischen Forschung und der Friedenserziehung* (Stuttgart: Metzler, 1989), p. 40; and Manfred Hettling and Michael Jeismann, 'Der Weltkrieg als Epos. Philipp Witkops "Kriegsbriefe gefallener Studenten"', in Gerhard Hirschfeld and Gerd Krumeich (eds), *'Keiner fühlt sich hier mehr als Mensch': Erlebnis und Wirkung des Ersten Weltkriegs* (Essen: Klartext Verlag, 1993), pp. 175–98.
26. Gunther Mai, '"Aufklärung der Bevölkerung" und "Vaterländischer Unterricht" in Württemberg 1914–1918: Struktur, Durchführung und Inhalte der deutschen Inlandspropaganda im Ersten Weltkrieg', *Zeitschrift für Württembergische Landesgeschichte* 36 (1977), p. 215.
27. Eksteins, *Rites of Spring*, p. 100.
28. On palingenesis, see Griffin, *Nature of Fascism*.
29. Ernst Gläser, *The Last Civilian*, trans. Gwenda David and Eric Mosbacher (New York, R.M. McBride, 1935).
30. Lüttgens, folder 13, Box 1, Theodore Abel Papers, Hoover Institution Archives, Stanford, CA.
31. 'The Story of a Middle-Class Youth', in Abel, *Nazi Movement*, p. 268. See also Hans Haas, folder 52, Box 1, Theodore Abel Papers, Hoover Institution Archives, Stanford, CA.
32. Hermann Jung, 'Erinnerungen aus meiner Kampfzeit', January 1937, Bundesarchiv, NS26/532.
33. Peter Merkl, *Political Violence under the Swastika* (Princeton, NJ: Princeton University Press, 1975), p. 89.
34. Wilhelm Wittfeld, folder 15, Box 1, Theodore Abel Papers, Hoover Institution Archives, Stanford, CA.
35. Rudolf Kahn, folder 31, Box 1, Theodore Abel Papers, Hoover Institution Archives, Stanford, CA. See also Fritz Junghanss, folder 526, Box 7, ibid.
36. Hans Plath, folder 96, Box 2; Ernst Schmitt, folder 265, Box 5; Oskar Klinkusch, folder 349, Box 5, Theodore Abel Papers, Hoover Institution Archives, Stanford, CA; Heinrich Wilkenloh, 'Meine Kampferlebnisse', 31 Dec. 1936, Bundesarchiv, NS 26/531.
37. Freyer, 'Das Geschichtliche Bewusstsein', pp. 5–6, 10–12.
38. 'The Story of a Farmer', in Abel, *Nazi Movement*, p. 289.
39. Heinz Mai, untitled statement, 6 Aug. 1934, Bundesarchiv, NS26/532.
40. 'The Story of a Bank Clerk', in Abel, *Nazi Movement*, p. 275.
41. Merkl, *Political Violence*, p. 53.
42. Ibid., p. 160. See also Heinrich Potz, folder 50, Box 1, Theodore Abel Papers, Hoover Institution Archives, Stanford, CA; Martin Dries, 'Aus Meiner Kampfzeit', 31 Dec. 1936, Bundesarchiv, NS26/529; and Josef Schimmel, 'Meine Kampferlebnisse', n.d. [1937], ibid., NS26/532.

43. Hans Müller, folder 99, Box 2, Theodore Abel Papers, Hoover Institution Archives, Stanford, CA. See also Fritz Schuck, folder 172, Box 3, ibid.
44. Merkl, *Political Violence*, pp. 28, 139, 162, 223, 359–60.
45. Paul Holzapfel, 'Kampferlebnisse des SA-Standartenführers Paul Holzapfel', 27 Jan. 1937, Bundesarchiv, NS26/531; Beickendorf, untitled statement, n.d. [1937], ibid., NS26/532; and Emil Schlitz, untitled statement, 2 Nov. 1936.
46. Mosse, *The Fascist Revolution*, pp. xii, 73. See also Fritzsche, *Germans into Nazis*.
47. Helmut Lethen, *Verhaltenslehre der Kälte: Lebensversuche zwischen den Kriegen* (Frankfurt: Suhrkamp, 1994).
48. This point is also made by Elisabeth Domansky, 'Militarization and Reproduction in World War I Germany', in Geoff Eley (ed.), *Society, Culture and the State in Germany, 1870–1930* (Ann Arbor, MI, 1996), p. 428.
49. 'The Story of a Middle-Class Youth', in Abel, *Nazi Movement*, p. 270.
50. Paul Schneider, 'Bericht über meine Kampfjahre 1925–1933', 16 Dec. 1936, Bundesarchiv, NS26/528; Karl Mernberger, 'Kampferlebnisse vor der Machtübernahme', 6 Dec. 1936, ibid., NS26/530.
51. Merkl, *Political Violence*, p. 236. The original is Hans Plath, folder 96, Box 2, Theodore Abel Papers, Hoover Institution Archives, Stanford, CA.
52. Merkl, *Political Violence*, p. 132.
53. Friedrich Kurz, 'Meine Erlebnisse in der Kampfzeit', 25 Dec. 1936, Bundesarchiv, NS26/529; Werner Goerendt, 'Meine Kampferlebnisse aus der Kampfzeit', n.d. [Jan. 1937], ibid., NS26/530.
54. August [last name illegible], folder 63, Box 2; Hans Plath, folder 96, Box 2, Theodore Abel Papers, Hoover Institution Archives, Stanford, CA. See also Peter Fritzsche, *Rehearsals for Fascism: Populism and Political Mobilization in Weimar Germany* (New York: Oxford University Press, 1990), Chs 9, 11.
55. 'The Story of a Middle-Class Youth', in Abel, *Nazi Movement*, p. 269.
56. Thomas Childers, *The Nazi Voter: The Social Foundations of Fascism in Germany, 1919–1933* (Chapel Hill, NC: University of North Carolina Press, 1983), emphasizes the importance of occupational politics.
57. Kurt Liebert, folder 216, Box 4; Ernst Schmitt, folder 265, Box 5, Theodore Abel Papers, Hoover Institution Archives, Stanford, CA.
58. Werner Goerendt, 'Meine Erinnerungen aus der Kampfzeit', n.d. [1937], Bundesarchiv, NS26/530.
59. Hugo Seiler, folder 43, Box 1; Hilde Boehm-Stoltz, folder 44, Box 1; Fritz Linde, folder 45, Box 1; Hans Haas, folder 52, Box 1; Josef Schemme, folder 146, Box 3; Edmund Schülter, folder 242, Box 4, Theodore Abel Papers, Hoover Institution Archives, Stanford, CA.
60. Georg Witt, folder 579, Box 8, Theodore Abel Papers, Hoover Institution Archives, Stanford, CA. On the distinctive identity lent by the uniform, see also Heinz Horn, 'Abschnitte und Erlebnisse aus meiner Kampfzeit!', 29 Dec. 1936, Bundesarchiv, NS 26/528.
61. Friedrich Kurz, 'Meine Erlebnisse in der Kampfzeit', 25 Dec. 1936, Bundesarchiv, NS26/529.
62. See, for example, Gregor Strasser, 'Wie wird man Nationalsozialist?' based on a 19 Dec. 1927 speech in Munich's Hofbräuhaus and published in *Völkischer Beobachter* 294, 21 Dec. 1927.
63. Robert N. Proctor, *The Nazi War on Cancer* (Princeton, NJ: Princeton University Press, 1999).
64. Peter Fritzsche, *A Nation of Fliers: German Aviation and the Popular Imagination* (Cambridge, MA: Harvard University Press, 1992); and 'Machine Dreams: Airmindedness and the Reinvention of Germany', *The American Historical Review* 98 (1993), pp. 685–709.
65. Gimbel files, Bundesarchiv, NS26/142.
66. Alf Lüdtke, 'The Appeal of Exterminating "Others": German Workers and the Limits of Resistance', *The Journal of Modern History* 64, supplement (Dec. 1992), pp. S46–67; Ulrich Herbert, *A History of Foreign Labor in Germany, 1880–1980: Seasonal*

Workers/Forced Laborers/Guest Workers (Ann Arbor, MI: University of Michigan Press, 1990).
67. Hugo Döll, folder 8, Box 1, Theodore Abel Papers, Hoover Institution Archives, Stanford, CA.
68. Fritz Schulte, folder 22, Box 1, Theodore Abel Papers, Hoover Institution Archives, Stanford, CA.
69. Paul Schneider, 'Bericht Über meine Kampfjahre 1925–1933', 16 Dec. 1936, Bundesarchiv, NS26/528.
70. Heinrich Potz, folder 50, Box 1, Theodore Abel Papers, Hoover Institution Archives, Stanford, CA; Zygmunt Bauman, *Modernity and the Holocaust* (Ithaca, NY: Cornell University Press, 1989), p. 70.
71. The term *Volkskörper* has been used widely by historians in the last ten years, but how widely it circulated in contemporary discourse is not clear. In any case, A. Schranke uses it in his 1934 autobiographical sketch, folder 24, Box 1, Theodore Abel Papers, Hoover Institution Archives, Stanford, CA.
72. Stanley Payne, *A History of Fascism, 1914–1945* (Madison, WI: University of Wisconsin Press, 1995), p. 203.
73. On the reflexivity of modernism, see Anthony Giddens, *Consequences of Modernity* (Stanford, CA: Stanford University Press, 1990), pp. 38–45.

7

Intimacy in an Ideological Key: The Communist Case of the 1920s and 1930s

IGAL HALFIN

Many view the Russian Revolution as a socio-economic upheaval. Following 1917, so the argument goes, Russia transformed itself from a backward, agricultural country into a modern, industrial one. Certainly, profound changes did take place, and Stalin's Soviet Union looked very different from the tsarist state. It would seem, however, that this emphasis on the Revolution as rupturing the material fabric of the past misses what is perhaps its most interesting aspect – the bold effort undertaken by the Bolshevik regime to change not only the social environment but the human soul itself, to revolutionize the very consciousness of man – man's most basic attitudes about himself and others.

The construction of the New Man was at the heart of the Bolshevik Revolution. Only those who identified fully with revolutionary values and were ready to sacrifice themselves for the cause at any time deserved, according to the leaders of the Party, to take part in the future society. Yet it was not easy to determine who was worthy. Hence the prominence in the Bolshevik regime of the 'hermeneutics of the soul' – a collection of enunciations and practices that came to distinguish those who should be admitted to the brotherhood of the elect from those who should be cast aside.

The hermeneutics of the soul ('hermeneutics' because of the attempt to adduce from his outward behavior the essence of man, an essence that supposedly lay underneath and invited decipherment) included not only a set of theoretical positions on the nature of the human psyche but also such important practices as purges, comrade trials and public self-criticisms. A meeting place for the Judeo-Christian view of man and modern psychology, the hermeneutics of the soul sought to establish the departure point of each and every comrade, the point where he was standing at present and the point toward which he was moving – all this from a spiritual point of view. It was crucial to ascertain the sincerity of every comrade – whether he or she had joined the movement out of genuine ideological conviction or out of some secret utilitarian considerations – in order to determine whether he could truly serve the Revolution.

The image of the New Man was central to this hermeneutical investigation: its importance invites a closer look into the Communist notion of the family. It is well known that traditional family values and the notion of intimacy they involved came under severe criticism, not to say ridicule, in revolutionary Russia. The Bolsheviks scoffed at the suggestion of a meaningful distinction between Orthodox, peasant family culture and the 'bourgeois' Western ideal of family life – both were clearly partriarchal, exploitative and based on prejudice. The traditional family structure was presented as a conduit of conservatism, one of the most important the old order used to maintain its hegemony. While one's explicit political orientation was a conscious matter that might be directly repaired, one's mental attitudes (family values were relegated to this category) were considered a deep-seated, subconscious mental stratum, not easily altered.

Communist language hinted at the delegitimization of family relations in their traditional form. 'Bourgeois family loyalties' were thought to separate one from a larger social whole (for example, the productivist cell or the Party organization) that alone embodied true collectivist values. Spouses were customarily referred to by first name and patronymic, thereby leaving the marital connection linguistically invisible; wives did not take their husbands' surnames. Those expressions traditionally invested with reverential filiality came to have a pejorative meaning: 'family ties' (*semeistvennost'*) came to refer to nepotism, 'kinship' (*rodstvo*) to sinister solidarity. 'Why', wondered the Arkhangel'sk NKVD in October 1937, 'would two totally unconnected individuals such as Vezvesel'skii, the son of a gendarme and a recent graduate from the Institute of Red Professors, and Perskii, a non-Party accountant there, correspond with each other?' 'Their rapport', concluded one of its employees, 'can be explained only by the "kinship of alien souls".'[1] Because kinship and family were pejorative, in this context, the direct mention of family relations was avoided in Party protocols.

We shall look now at how Communist ideology regarding the family was disseminated into institutions of higher education as part of the revolutionary project of revolutionizing the human soul. Bolshevized during the Civil War, Soviet universities functioned in the 1920s and the 1930s as the contentious arena for an encounter between the proletariat and its consciousness, a laboratory where new family values were inculcated. Students were always scrutinized by the Party, which established a pervasive presence in the universities to cope with the volatile and unpredictable effects of mental labor. Separated from a healthy industrial environment before their consciousness was fully developed, and exposed to the lifestyle of the reclusive academic intelligentsia, students would surely be tempted by bourgeois individualism and philistinism. Because Bolshevik psychologists and sociologists considered 'student youths' at risk for degeneration, everyday practices in the universities were closely observed. Had not academic cells, more than any other sector of the Party, supported Trotsky in the 1920s? This error of judgement convinced many that the dormitories were breeding grounds for political deviation.

Students could not be regarded as natural Communists in contrast to proletarians working in factory or field. If they could have been, the Party might have relied on objective economic processes to strengthen students' class consciousness. Rather, Communist cells had to ascertain that applicants had a fully articulated proletarian consciousness at the time of their enrollment. Whereas in the case of workers, class consciousness could be implicit, sure to develop later through the influence of industrial labor, in the case of students it had to be explicit and fully articulated. Thus, a paradox emerged: in order to join the brotherhood of the elect, students had to possess the best-articulated Communist consciousness, yet the environment of the students was the most ideologically perilous of all.

THE COMMUNIST NOTION OF 'LOVE'

Despite, or perhaps due to, their ambivalent reputation, Communist students were in the forefront of the project of reshaping personal values. 'Love' – the cement of family relations and a notorious 'bourgeois fetish' – was a widely debated topic in the new universities. The vicissitudes of this notion reflect the ambivalence toward it in Bolshevik thinking. The early Bolsheviks advocated sexual promiscuity because it ensured health and prevented the dyadic attachments which threatened exclusive loyalty to the Party. 'Love always sins', some of them said, in that, absorbing the thoughts and feelings of the 'two loving hearts', it at the same time 'isolates, separates off the loving pair from the collective.'[2] Love was defined as 'egotism for two', a bourgeois aberration whereby 'one member of a collective is preferred over everybody else'.[3] Student questionnaires from the early 1920s had the following to say about love:

> You must realize that love, in the usual sense of the term, does not exist; I do not acknowledge love. It is simply a matter of habit, becoming accustomed to one person.

> I believe that love is a certain psychological condition ... The shape it takes depends on our internal constitution, emotions, mind and ideology in general.

Lass, a sexologist who ran this questionnaire, summarized his findings by noting that 'our student youth often deny love's existence'.[4] The subject provoked a great deal of curiosity among students at Irkutsk State University, for example. These were some of the questions they posed to the Party discussant there in November 1924.

> – Should we recognize pure, Platonic love? Is love a temporary or a lasting emotion? Will Communism be a time of monogamy or polygamy? Is polygamy a sign of the degeneration of the working class?
>
> – What should we do with the knowledge that monogamous marriage separates us from the collective but that polygamous marriage is abnormal from a physiological point of view?
>
> – Which is right, free love or abstinence? If abstinence leads to the degeneration of the working class, should we assign a norm for sexual activity? What should be its minimum and maximum? Is sexual energy not designed by nature to be released through emission? How then can you say that sexual release is harmful?[5]

'In all the questionnaires, base sexual instincts reign supreme', summarized another sexologist, Gel'man, his own set of very similar findings. 'Blind sexual need transports a youngster from one sexual encounter to another.'[6] Here are some notes Gel'man found appended to his questionnaires:

> My sexual life revolves around two girls. Neither knows about the other. Love is something I do not recognize. Excitement is all that I am after.
>
> I mixed the sour with the sweet and had sex with whatever filth showed up.
>
> I acknowledge no limits in sexual life. I have intercourse almost every week, and if the opportunity arises, do it every day, every hour, as long as my energy holds out.

At the early stages of the development of Bolshevik libertinism, 'free love' in the spirit of Kollontai's 'Winged Eros'[7] came to replace 'bourgeois possession of the other'. Quite unlike love, libertine sexual relations invited polygamy and were thus perceived by at least some Bolsheviks as a force that could bond together the members of the collective. Sexual pluralism was ordained because it attested to the worker's willingness not to favor one specific comrade over everybody else.[8]

From the late 1920s on, the notion of love, associated now with at least a modicum of sexual temperance, began undergoing a certain rehabilitation. Sexual promiscuity was denigrated as something that weakened proletarian prowess. Consciousness and the desire to direct proletarian energies toward socialist construction and not waste it on the satisfaction of immediate bodily needs became the basis for a union between 'healthy' and 'class-conscious' proletarians. The famous Bolshevik psychologist, Aaron Zalkind, pontificated:

> Because the difference between the human and the animal lies in the mediation of the physiological by the psychological, that is, in the social ... purely physical sexual attraction cannot be recommended ... More than purely physical contact between organisms of different sexes, the sexual encounter evokes elements of jealousy, hatred, sexual competition – sentiments that can introduce chaos into the working class, fragment its powers and divert some of the class energy away from production and into sexual pursuits, often in glaring violation of class interests.[9]

When he observed that Soviet society was 'ripe for a sexual revolution', what Zalkind meant was not a sexual liberation à la Kollontai but, on the contrary, new restraints on sexuality mediated by the consciousness. Declaring a 'strict proletarian sexual dictatorship' the order of the day, Zalkind hoped that the Soviet Union would become the first society in history to be 'rationally organized'.[10]

Romantic love was brought back into favor. The new orthodoxy maintained that a 'purely sexual act can never gratify a genuinely conscious person'.[11] The updated 'dialectical' view posited that 'love is actually a very intricate complex of conditional reflexes that permits us to derive pleasure from an object'; these reflexes were important because they were 'permanent'.[12] Now it was possible to speak about 'gradations of love', from 'animal' to 'noble', depending on the 'weight of the spiritual element of the sentiment in question'.[13]

If Khokhorin, the villainous student of Gumilevskii's *Dog Alley* (1928), proudly explains that 'love is a bourgeois prank that only spoils things, an entertainment for the jaded', Korolev, the novel's positive character, has other things to say: 'Sexual restraint, a comradely attitude toward the woman one loves – this should be the highest Communist ideal of sexual relations ... Everything that weakens the proletarian will to construct a New World is immoral!'[14]

Blaming the 'self-absorbed' intelligentsia for claiming that 'a worker is a soulless, stern beast that is supposedly incapable of feelings and understanding', Soviet psychologists declared that the true emotional tie between two proletarians was not a blind, instinctual liaison but 'conscious love'.[15] The question of whether love was a 'Platonic idea' or a 'biological need' was fiercely debated.[16] Zalkind posited that 'in order for love to promote happiness, physical attraction and sexual desire had to be coupled with spiritual closeness. No longer an everyday affair, love could only become more precious.' Zalkind objected to frequent changes of sexual partner. 'Constant competition for new love objects consumes a great deal of socially useful energy and separates members of the same class.'[17]

True love was considered possible only between a couple that shared the same level of consciousness. A model proletarian student admitted that: 'Moral considerations led me to pursue sexual partners whose consciousness was equal to mine.'[18] Or, in Zalkind's crass formulation: 'A worker's sexual attraction to a class-antagonistic object is no less depraved than sexual attraction to an orang-utan or a crocodile.'[19]

A good marriage was conceived as a union of two conscious souls; matrimony outside the Party was not advised. When such a 'mishap' did occur, it was the duty of the Communist half not to forget the importance of discretion during pillow talk. Communists who disclosed Party secrets to their uninitiated family members were promptly purged. Instructors at the Institute of Red Professors wondered: 'How could Anis'ia, a housemaid, be among the first to know that Tikhomirov, the institute's Party secretary, had been purged?' And yet, it was she who informed everybody that 'when his Party card was revoked Tikhomirov was so startled that, in fleeing from the district committee office, he left his coat behind'. That a housemaid could obtain 'such sensitive information proves', according to one of the instructors, Basin, 'that even at home, you have to abide by the golden rule that, "Even the walls have ears"'. Basin guessed Anis'ia's source: 'When discussing Tikhomirov's case at Ivashchenko's we were whispering. Aside from Ivashchenko's sleeping wife no one could hear us and tell the news to the housemaid; clearly, our wives divulge plenty of secrets.' The instructors involved agreed that 'we have to be vigilant at home, especially when our wives are not Party members'.[20]

Thus even at home comrades were supposed to be constantly in control of themselves. To be sure, they were expected to love, but they had to love with their minds, not with their instincts or with their bodies. Love was an enhanced affinity between two minds – a rational more than an emotional bond. Within the Communist nuclear unit, consciousness and common political interests were supposed to replace kindred feelings as the source of genuine intimacy.

'LOYALTY TO THE PARTY ABOVE ALL ELSE!'

While the bourgeoisie had idealized the family as a shelter from public interaction, a private, secluded sphere, the Communist home was an important venue for political activity. Permeated with ideology,

Communist intimacy was supposed to be expressed through mutual political education and mutual surveillance. To take part in an intimate relationship meant to engage in constant questioning, to serve as the interrogator and the interrogated at one and the same time. Does my loved one understand the needs of the Revolution? Could my loved one, by any chance, be a Trotskyist? Such were some of the questions that married couples, brothers and sisters, fathers and sons asked themselves.

The hermeneutics of the soul penetrated to the very core of Communist family life. One's political orientation – in the final analysis, a state of the mind, something quite invisible to the eye – was considered private, largely inaccessible, a set of subjective orientations, not overt actions. Lacking what it needed most – the objective criteria that would distinguish true revolutionaries from impostors – the Party drafted family members and put them to work deciphering the souls of their loved ones. Above all the Party longed to know whether a given comrade abided by the Communist ethos in both the public and the private sphere or whether he only outwardly presented himself to the world as a loyal Communist. The latter was the sort of 'two-faced' behavior typical of the opposition. (Trotskyists, for example, were considered a Trojan horse concealed within the Party, ready to launch a surprise attack at a crucial moment, perhaps during the international war then visible on the horizon.) Having declared its interest in not only the conscious but also the subconscious stratum of the human personality, not only in comrades' political thinking but also in their habits, inclinations and moods – in short, having politicized every aspect of everyday life – the Party demanded that the family yoke itself to the Communist project.

Castigating the bourgeois contention that family loyalty ought to take precedence over every other loyalty, the Party warned all conscientious Communists that the enemy might be living in their own houses, and urged them to take advantage of daily contact with their families to get to the bottom of their political personas.[21] If ever the collective sensed that a member's 'sense of kinship' had surpassed his 'loyalty to the Party', a warning was immediately issued.[22] 'Vile sentimentalists' whose 'bourgeois consciences' made them hesitate to condemn their kin were dubbed 'abettors of crimes' or 'denunciation-objectors'.[23]

Party members were expected to proselytize with special zeal within their own families. It was a common practice among Party officials to enquire which family members a Communist had already converted and which clung to their 'retrograde ways'. The Party expected that the younger siblings, assumed to be more open to a Communist lifestyle because of their age, would be persuaded right away. With the older generation, especially mothers and grandmothers (women were regarded as far more obtuse than men), the task could prove to be more difficult, though there was hardly anything a clever Communist plan could not accomplish.

At the Ninth Party Conference (1920), Kotlian declared: 'Hard to believe, but true. We have comrades on board who have been discussing the meaning of true socialism at various meetings and gatherings for a number of years now but these same men are apparently incapable of converting their own wives.' The audience exploded with laughter.[24] When asked during one of his 1936 interrogations by the NKVD why his wife had not joined the Party, Zaidel', a senior Party lecturer in Leningrad, attempted to exculpate himself by saying: 'My wife is ill and she hears poorly. She is also busy with our child.'[25] The protocol does not specify the interrogator's reaction, but we do know that this excuse did not prevent the eventual condemnation of the entire Zaidel' household as 'enemies of the people'.

Family members judged hopelessly unreformable had to be handed over to the authorities. Pavlik Morozov, a peasant boy who denounced his own kulak father in 1932 and paid for this exploit with his life, became a very important role model for Communist youths. Gorky urged the new generation of Soviet men and women: 'Recall Pavlik's heroism, the heroism of a "young fellow" who understood that blood kin can be your worst spiritual enemy.'[26] Stalin taught that the Party, not the family, had to be the primary object of identification: 'Be worthy sons and daughters of our real mother – the Communist Party.'[27]

Alien family background was not an unsurpassable handicap provided it was spontaneously and totally renounced. The Tomsk Technological Institute student, Berman, for example, became a Party member in the mid-1920s despite 'socially incriminating material against him'.[28] Difficulties had arisen as a result of Berman's wealthy background, and the Tomsk district committee rescinded the cell's original decision to enroll this student upon discovering that 'Berman's family owned a spacious house in Chita.' At this point, Berman pleaded that the Party pay attention to that part of his life that he, Berman, had been directly responsible for, and ignore his socio-economic roots. Candidly admitting that his parents were Jewish petit bourgeois, he pointed out that 'since the age of 17 I myself have worked as a hired laborer, a teacher and a cattle procurer'. More importantly, Berman was able to prove that his political development corresponded to his gradual proletarianization. Starting as a member of a Zionist organization (1916), he progressed in a few years to become a Red Army sapper. Incarcerated at one point by Kolchak, Berman presented the six weeks he had spent in a White jail as his conversion experience. The members of the cell were clearly satisfied with the political profile of this student. 'When Berman requested my recommendation I asked him about his social origins', admitted one of the applicant's recommenders. Upon hearing that he was a merchant's son I thought to myself that he was alien to us. On second thought, however, having taken into consideration the four years Berman had dedicated to Party work, I decided to shoulder the responsibility of supporting his Party candidacy.' The cell upheld its previous decision and voted overwhelmingly in Berman's favor. The only dissenting vote belonged to a comrade who clarified that 'I too have no reservations regarding Berman the individual. Since I do not know the applicant well, I felt obliged to vote against him on account of his alien class origin.'

When she applied to become a member of the Party cell at the Tomsk Technological Institute, Bukhareva found her alien class background to be a serious liability.[29] Yet, the source of her trouble was not purely that she was a clergyman's daughter but that her spiritual break with her family apparently had been incomplete. She began quite well. 'The applicant gave exhaustive answers to all queries regarding her social origins.' Although a certain Solonikin voiced some reservations, declaring that 'Bukhareva cannot join the Party because our party is the party of the proletariat', this argument, in itself, did not sway the cell, particularly as the secretary of the institute's Komsomol organization testified that Bukhareva was a conscientious Komsomol member with an adequate social physiognomy and political consciousness. It was the support Bukhareva's detractors received from a certain Dereviagin that tipped the scales against her: 'Though Bukhareva was in the Komsomol from 1919 to 1921 she continued to live with her family.' This meant that Bukhareva's three years in the Komsomol coincided with cohabitation with her clerical father and that they should therefore be ignored.' Bukhareva's clerical origins would not have precluded her from becoming a Communist provided she had convincingly demonstrated that she had overcome them. The trouble with her application was that many in the cell interpreted her participation in the Komsomol as a utilitarian step, the evidence being Bukhareva's inability to renounce her father. Although the case was resolved in Bukhareva's favor, in all likelihood the vote was too close to be ratified by the district committee. (Sixteen were in favor of Bukhareva's admission, ten against, three abstained.)

Students who were reluctant to give up on their ideologically unfit parents condemned themselves to inevitable purging. In 1935, Comrade Bogdanova, an instructor at Leningrad Communist University and an erstwhile Zinov'evist, was asked at a local Party meeting to explain why she maintained some connections with her bourgeois family. Bogdanova began by describing a fragmented family and moved quickly to insist that she had little contact with her parents and brothers. 'My father died when I was a child. I was raised by my brothers. One of them is a journalist in TASS, the other is a poet and a third is a student. Politically, they are not our people. In 1919 another brother of mine was shot by the Cheka ... At fifteen I left my family behind and joined the Komsomol.' When the details of a meeting she had some years earlier in Germany with her 'White émigré mother' and the fact that 'her husband, Churakov, was formerly an active Oppositionist' became known, her other testimony lost all credibility and Bogdanova was quickly purged.[30]

Accused of refusing to take responsibility for the 'political profile [*politicheskoe litso*]' of her arrested father, Gubarina, a colleague of Bogdanova's from the Leningrad Institute of Red Professors, also got into deep trouble. But Gubarina managed to convince her judges that she considered the Party more important than her father. 'I retain no filial feelings toward my father', she claimed. 'If the NKVD has arrested him, they must have had their reasons.' [31] Iakunina, yet another Leningrad student, was purged for stating falsely in her autobiography that her father and mother were poor peasants. But she had her punishment commuted when she showed that it had been she who had denounced her kulak uncle, thus facilitating his arrest.[32]

The Party overlooked filial ties to dubious elements if it found these ties emotional rather than ideological. When a student named Tumasheva was accused in May 1924 of having been financially supported by her bourgeois family, she denied having had any meaningful contact with her kin. Tumasheva admitted that 'I am still in touch with my mother, and she sends me parcels once in a while', but insisted that the mother–daughter bond in question was not ideological: it was 'filial, purely organic – I would say, psychological in its nature'. This argument was accepted and Tumasheva retained her Party affiliation.[33]

In the 1930s Party committees at Leningrad's Communist universities asserted that they were 'entitled to know everything about our students' families'. In 1935, special teams of officials, usually two or three persons, were assigned to investigate comrades with suspicious family backgrounds. Over the next two years the scope of such investigations would widen considerably: many students lost their Party membership because they had failed to alert their committees to the presence of ideological enemies in their family circle.[34]

In January 1936, Gel'man, a student at the Institute of Red Professors, was caught 'misleading the Party about his father's occupation'. Gel'man was the first to admit that he was guilty: 'I know I should have found out what my family was doing as soon as I returned from Palestine.' 'My duty as a Communist', Gel'man now realized, 'was to reveal the fact that my father had kept his business after the 1919 pogrom and pass this information along.'35 It went without saying that Gel'man – a student at an institution that was considered the bastion of Communist education in Leningrad – was not in touch with his bourgeois family (that had remained in Russia all this time, clinging to their old-fashioned Jewish occupations). Nonetheless, as a member of the Communist Party he had assumed a sacred responsibility: he was expected to find a way to go on monitoring his father's actions even from afar.

Parents were also expected to denounce their disloyal children. During one of the Party purges at Communist University, a 66-year-old man named Orlov was accused of shielding his son. According to the NKVD the younger Orlov had planned to assassinate Zhdanov. He was arrested in the summer of 1936 and confessed that 'I received a revolver from a leader of the local Trotskyists and was supposed to assassinate Zhdanov, the head of the Leningrad Party organization, upon his arrival at Uritskii Palace [the location of Communist University]. My arrest foiled this plan.' When the father of the accused testified, he asserted that his son (whom he referred to consistently as 'he') was not as wicked as he seemed:

> I talked to him a number of times and tried to convince him to drop his objections to Trotsky's expulsion. I never read the recantations he made in the past, but I am inclined to think they were two-faced. The more I talked to him, though, the more sincere his confessions seemed to become. Not that his purge is unjust – he failed to learn from recent events – but he did try to make amends. I do not think he is an enemy of the Soviet regime now.

The senior Orlov, who had failed to grasp the severity of the charges against his son, was purged – not for being an enemy himself but for failing to recognize one: 'Instead of decisively condemning his son as an ardent Trotskyist–Zinov'evist, Orlov, who was no longer vigilant, claimed that his son had "lost his way".'36

'Not Every Brother Is a Brother', a chapter title in one of the first biographies of Pavlik Morozov, was one of the great themes of the 1930s.37 At the time of the Great Purge, many students who had failed to denounce their criminal siblings were driven from Leningrad universities. Il'in, Prem's replacement as Party secretary, explained that Katsman, for example, had to be expelled, 'because she never mentioned her Trotskyist–Zinov'evist brother until his arrest ... Now Katsman admits that at one point she shared an apartment with him for six whole months.' Nor could Katsman, according to Il'in, say whether the family reunions at which she and her brother used to see each other were of a 'familial' or a 'political' character. 'Even if we accept the unlikely and assume that she was unaware of her brother's political convictions, we would still have to conclude that she had become less than vigilant.' In this case Il'in was overruled: the district committee reinstated Katsman on the grounds that 'the evidence that links Katsman to her brother is not firm enough'.[38]

When in July 1936 Communist University found out that the brother of the graduate school's deputy director, Narodnitskii, had been an active Oppositionist, charges were brought against the administrator. 'Six of my siblings', explained Narodnitskii, 'are good Communists who occupy responsible positions. Only one brother somehow remained backward. I don't know why he descended into Oppositionism or whether other family members are in touch with him.' Gershfel'd, a teacher of Leninism at the university, voluntarily corroborated Narodnitskii's story: 'I used to work with this brother of Narodnitskii's in a knitting factory in the late 1920s; he is indeed illiterate, psychologically unsophisticated and incredibly obstinate in his Oppositionism.' Gershfel'd swore that he had 'never imagined' that Narodnitskii would fail to reveal his brother's past. 'I cannot forgive myself for having had such faith in Narodnitskii's honesty.' The Party committee proved a bit more forgiving: it concluded that Gershfel'd had 'failed to take the correct Bolshevik line' and limited itself to issuing him a severe reprimand. Narodnitskii, on the other hand, had to be purged; in the words of the rector, Prede, he had 'disingenuously presented his Trotskyist brother as nothing more than a lightweight, one who had ostensibly joined the enemy by accident'.[39]

In some cases, one parent had to ensure that the other had no contact with their child. Buzulevich, an instructor at Communist University, received a letter from his ex-wife informing him that: 'since you must have been close to the university apparatus that turned out to be teeming with Trotskyists, I must ensure that our child has no communication with you'. A distraught Buzulevich insisted on seeing his son. He claimed that he had never been a Trotskyist, but he never questioned the assumption that parenthood was a political matter.[40]

When a child was not separated from its pernicious parents – as was the case when a child accompanied convicted parents to prison camps, for example – there was little chance that the child could ever become a conscientious Soviet citizen.[41] An NKVD officer made this point in 1936: 'It is true that a five-year-old who plays with the children of the decent camp inmates may hear them speak the names of the leaders of the working class ... However, since his mother categorically forbids him to utter those names, a child thus separated from the happy realities of Soviet life is likely to develop into a Trotskyist.'[42] Inspired by this approach to child psychology, the NKVD ordered all children under the age of 8 living in the Belomor camp to be transferred to orphanages.[43]

On 20 May 1937 the NKVD issued a directive entitled 'On the Correct Political Education of Children of Repressed Parents'.[44] A special 'proletarian city' was built so that such disadvantaged youths could be re-educated.[45] Children had to be taught how to distinguish friend from foe as early as possible. Radek was proud of those who showed a precocious interest in political trials. 'When wreckers were pardoned, there was a torrent of indignation among some of the children I met', he recalled. 'They asked me: "How could people who had betrayed their country, who had wanted to condemn workers and peasants to hunger, not be executed?"'[46]

Innumerable schoolchildren were taught to do likewise. Velman, a prisoner in a camp to the north of Leningrad, recalled: 'In the winter of 1937, when our column was moving toward the Kargopol' camp and we were passing a small Archangel'sk village, we saw a young schoolteacher and a class of students by the side of the road. When we drew abreast of them, the teacher commanded: "Three-Four!", and the children rapturously sang out, "Death to enemies of the People!"'[47]

Stories about children who denounced their own parents abounded. During the arrest of Svanidze and his wife, their 8-year-old son yelled: 'You are enemies of the people. I renounce you!'[48] Antonov-Ovseenko's son advocated his father's execution, saying, 'Father is a Trotksyist!'[49] Though she may not have been quite so sure of her parent's guilt, the daughter of Bubnov, also a military man, still believed after her father was arrested that 'No one goes to prison for nothing.'[50] Not all children exhibited such strong faith in the Party. Iura Baranov, a pupil, wrote in his diary in 1937: 'A terrible misfortune has befallen our family: my father was arrested and accused of the worst crime – wrecking. I am convinced, more than convinced, that he is not guilty. Quite the contrary.' Soon after another entry followed: 'That which I have feared more than anything has just happened – my father has been condemned to death.' But the young Baranov remained defiant in his views: 'The guilty verdict does not mean I take back anything I confided to this diary about my father.'[51]

Some children were easier to re-educate than others. In Leninsk-Kuztentsk (Siberia) a children's counter-revolutionary organization was uncovered and its members were tried in February 1938. Led by 10-year-old Vitia Logunov, the conspiracy consisted of 160 pupils involved in 'disseminating seditious leaflets and fascist placards, portraits of enemies of the people' and so on.[52] Children locked away in camps and re-education facilities were supposedly even more prone to sedition. An NKVD directive from 31 March 1938 inaugurated the position of deputy head of the children's colony (a sort of a re-education camp for youngsters) whose principal task was to 'monitor the children's moods'. Generally dissatisfied with the ideological atmosphere in orphanages, state security organs issued a directive on 28 February 1939 in which they warned against 'the activism of the sons and daughters of repressed enemies of the people now living in foundling homes'. A few cases of 'child mutinies' had apparently been reported. The directive demanded the immediate creation of an information network surveying the political attitudes and dispositions of the young.[53]

INDIVIDUAL GUILT? COLLECTIVE GUILT?

Even during the harsh years of the Great Purge, every Party member was still invited to save his good name by cutting himself off from his sinning relatives. That is why the accused talk in the cases examined below – in fact, they do quite a bit of talking. Though in every case someone very close to them – a husband, a brother – had been arrested, they were not reduced to silence and made no attempt to lie low. On the contrary, they speak, complain, explain, expound, digress, rail and fulminate.

Though their loved ones had been kidnapped in the middle of the night, many Soviet citizens continued to see the Party as an arena in which righteous action was possible and in its institutions the prospect – in fact the necessity – of ameliorating the condition of the individual. They were trying to do much more than go underground or flee: they tried again and again to influence their fate and that of others by working from within the system. In their eyes as well as in the eyes of those around them, theirs was a legitimate voice until proven otherwise. If it could be demonstrated, through a correct application of Communist rhetoric (without attempting here to gauge its sincerity), that the accused truly identified with Communist values, this would save him from conviction. This was true even if every person in a Party member's family had already been rounded up, shot or sent to the camps.[54]

If one's family was not exactly one's fate then the interrelation between collective guilt and individual guilt in Communism had to be re-evaluated. Many Soviet citizens resented being blamed for the sins of their family members. Citing one of the clauses in Stalin's recently promulgated constitution, they demanded that they be judged only according to their own actions, not those of their relatives. When the father of a Leningrad worker, Tselmerovskii, was arrested, his son felt it as a massive jolt. 'Father used to tell me about beating the Whites in the north. When Kirov was assassinated his eyes filled with tears', wrote Tselmerovskii. 'It is amazing that a human being can play a part so well.' Tselmerovskii demanded of the authorities that he be considered a legal entity utterly separate from his father. 'If Father is guilty, he should be held responsible. I was schooled by the Soviet system, however, and have no intention of shouldering his disgrace.'[55]

In 1939, a commission headed by Zhdanov and charged with revising the Party regulations (Ustav) received a letter from a man named Karaulov. 'Did not Comrade Stalin say that a son is not responsible for his father? In practice, however, a brother is held responsible for a brother, even when the two lead totally isolated lives. As a result, a Communist with an otherwise spotless record comes to be relegated to the second tier, is never elected to any post, never trusted, always rebuked for the handiwork of his relatives.' Karaulov proposed the following clause for the new regulations: 'A Party member is not responsible for the crimes of his relatives unless his personal involvement is proven.'[56]

Much to the consternation of the petitioners mentioned above and many like them, Soviet law extended guilt to family members during the Great Purge.[57] Molotov explained later that 'it was absolutely self-evident that repressive measures had to be applied to wives and children of the enemies'.[58] From the time of Kirov's assassination, the hunt for the relatives and the next of kin of convicted traitors had been on; it was systematized through a series of secret decisions made by the Central Committee in July 1937. A barrage of administrative measures followed. On 30 July 1937 a key NKVD directive notified provincial authorities that 'relatives of enemies of the people must be registered and their steps closely monitored'. Families considered 'capable of anti-Soviet actions' were to be interned in camps and labor colonies. Additional directives issued between 15 August and 20 September of that year specified further that 'wives of Rightist-Trotskyist spies be subject to internment for five to eight years'. Criminal files were opened on 'each wife and each child older than 15' (younger children were sent to NKVD corrective labor colonies). As a result of these measures large numbers of special camps had to be set up in Siberia and the far north in the late 1930s for what the Soviet bureaucracy called 'family members of traitors to the motherland' (the abbreviation for the Russian term was ChSIR).[59]

At the peak of the Great Purge, affected families from border zones such as Leningrad were exiled to the interior of the country at an astonishing rate. On one, by the standards of the time, not particularly exceptional day, 22 July 1937, a 'Special NKVD Commission for the Eviction of the Families of the Condemned' deported 129 families (215 individuals) from Leningrad. Between 23 July and 2 August, an additional 433 families were evicted (924 individuals); by February 1938, a summary of the operation reported that 1,614 women – wives of enemies of the people – had been exiled from the province.[60]

The letter a certain Antipov wrote to the Central Committee while awaiting deportation at a Leningrad train station on 12 December 1938 gives a sense of how these measures were received. 'To exile ... politically dangerous individuals – this I understand. But to uproot entire families, wives and the elderly included – a wrecker's hand must be enmeshed in this ... Because I am convinced that you are unaware of what is going on I am telling you: Leningrad NKVD employees must have lost all sense of proportion.'[61]

Complaints of this sort abounded. A certain Ivanova wrote to the Central Committee:

> I am writing on behalf of hundreds of women who refer to their Soviet jail as a 'wailing wall'. In these jails young interrogators, hoping to make a career for themselves, humiliate ... the wives of the arrested, trying to prove themselves vigilant in this way. When a wife approaches an investigator to ask: 'What is my husband guilty of?', she usually hears in response: 'He is an enemy of the people, but his specific crime is a secret.' We, Soviet women, demand that the government try our husbands openly so that we can see for ourselves whether they are true enemies. Then we will be able to tear our husbands out of our hearts ... Comrades, look into this! Perhaps we are being mistreated because enemies of the people have penetrated the NKVD![62]

This letter, and many others like it, went unheeded. In December 1937 the Leningrad NKVD confiscated the passport of Emma Aver'ianovna and exiled her to Omsk for five years – she was the wife of Dmitriev, the executed Communist University instructor. Dmitrieva's remonstrations were in vain. 'I and my daughter were crushed under the weight of the stigma we had to carry.' Many years later, in 1955, after she had become a village schoolteacher in the Stalin region of the Ukraine, Dmitrieva petitioned the chairman of the Soviet of Ministers, Bulganin, demanding that her suffering as the wife of an infamous enemy of the people be finally brought to an end. Dmitrieva also asked for help in 'finding my husband, Dmitriev, who was arrested on the night of 29–30 April 1936 ... All of my previous attempts to determine his fate have remained fruitless; the KGB tells me that it has no information about him.' Almost 20 years after her husband's disappearance, Dmitrieva remained uncertain whether he had been shot or was rotting away somewhere in one of the eastern camps. Heartened by Khrushchev's liberalism, the petitioner hoped the authorities would 'find Dmitriev, re-examine his case, and, if there were sufficient grounds, consider his rehabilitation'. The dubious widow did realize that such a rehabilitation might be posthumous.[63]

Did the arrest of the family members of wrongdoers suggest that the state believed that moral faculties were attached not to discrete individuals but to entire communities? Could it be that patterns of collective responsibility and group victimization violate the thesis, presented in the first part of this chapter, that guilt in Communist Russia was individual? If Communist guilt was strictly subjective, what are we to make of Stalin's famous toast made during the celebration of the Revolution's 20th anniversary (7 November 1937): 'We shall hunt down and destroy every single enemy of the people and his kin, his entire family'?[64]

I propose adopting a new perspective on the Communist family. Rather than emphasizing the repressive legislation to which some space has been devoted in the preceding pages, I would like to examine the functioning of mutual surveillance within the primary cell. This will allow me to explain why entire families were rounded up and sent into exile in the late 1930s. Paradoxically, rather than signifying the resurgence of some sort of geneticism, the Soviet focus on family ties will emerge as the pinnacle of Communist individuation.

In the mid-to-late 1930s, the need to judge every soul by its inner worth received a radical interpretation: the individual who fully identified with the brotherhood of the elect had to release himself completely from the emotional grip of his loved ones. Communists were obligated to renounce a traitor spouse. Pochtarenko, whose husband, Otrozhdenov, was arrested in 1935, proved weak-willed. Not only did she try to make illicit deliveries to her husband, she even requested a tête-à-tête with him. When, despite repeated warnings that she should renounce the 'enemy', Pochtarenko appeared at the NKVD offices, 'demanding to join her husband in Iakutsk', the Party organization at her place of work, the Herzen Institute, purged her.[65]

Rafailovich's husband, Sorokin, was also arrested. When she claimed to be evaluating him 'as a Communist, not as a wife', this student at the Institute of Red Professors was clearly making an effort to distance herself from her unreliable mate. 'In conversations with me, Sorokin always identified with the Party', she reported. 'True, he suffered such ill effects of War Communism as leadership-mania [*vozhdizm*]. But I was working hard to reform him. Whether he was faking his emotions I cannot tell, but Sorokin gave the impression of being deeply distressed over Kirov's assassination.' The Party committee was unimpressed: 'Rafailovich contradicts herself: even as she claims that she "cannot distrust the NKVD", she praises Sorokin. Personal feelings must have overshadowed her sense of duty and rendered her class-blind.'[66]

Incidentally, the victimization of 'wives' should not be read as patriarchy pure and simple. Husbands whose wives were found guilty were also punished. Anatolii Isaevich Anishev, the director of a major Leningrad agricultural institute, was, for example, purged from the Party in 1933 for 'corresponding with his exiled wife'. Anishev was not saved by having earlier been characterized as an 'energetic Communist dedicated to the Party line'.[67]

Communists who adopted a 'liberal attitude' toward their arrested spouses put themselves at high risk.[68] Anastasia Koch, the wife of a German immigrant arrested early in 1938, wrote a letter to the heads of the Soviet state that speaks eloquently in this regard. 'I was purged from the Party', Koch complained, 'only because I dared to say that I found it hard to believe that my husband could be an enemy of the people. When he was taken I was presented with the following choice during a Party meeting: "Either you renounce him or we will have you purged". I do not know whether I was correct, but I could not bring myself to accept his guilt, not only because he is my husband but because I had seen no proof. Honestly, you must believe me when I say that to do such a thing would mean to crucify an individual who could have been arrested erroneously.'[69] Koch was expected to dissociate herself from her husband completely and instantaneously. The NKVD order of 11 May 1939 stipulated that 'requests for divorce coming from wives of arrested enemies of the people should be satisfied immediately' – no certificates were demanded.[70]

In order to survive the investigation bound to follow the arrest of one's spouse, it was best to distance oneself from the accused as evidence of his or her guilt was brought forward: the individual under suspicion tried to ascribe to himself or herself as much agency as possible, arguing that the better he or she came to know his or her spouse the less he or she trusted him or her. It was important to show one was not a complete failure as a hermeneut. In March 1936, Communist University discovered that Khudiakova displayed an unhealthy ambivalence about her Trotskyist husband, Chistov. Khudiakova claimed to have learned that Chistov was an Oppositionist only during the 1933 purge, that is, after their marriage. 'As long as there was hope that Chistov could be reinstated', she explained, 'I remained in touch; Chistov was ill and I had to give him succor.' Once the purge was ratified by the control commission, however, 'I took the rector's advice, reconsidered my life with him and informed Chistov that we were finished.' Khudiakova referred to the house she had shared with her husband for two years not as 'our house' but as 'Chistov's house'. She made a point of saying that she talked over personal things not with her husband but with 'Comrade Prede [the rector]'. 'Why', wondered the members of the board charged with purging her, 'does Khudiakova need our advice about her personal life? ... Had she not been sympathetic to Oppositionists she would have severed her ties to Chistov sooner.'[71]

Indeed, Khudiakova was nothing like Zavadovskaia, a student at the Institute of Red Professors, who denounced her husband without hesitation. 'During the nine years we lived together, Zavadovskii was always under my influence. In 1935 I even recommended him for secret work.' In the following year Zavadovskii had an adulterous affair. 'At present', wrote Zavadovskaia, 'we are separated by 10,000 miles and another woman, whose political face I do not know ... Since I know nothing of the influence currently brought to bear on Zavadovskii, I believe it is my duty to withdraw the positive recommendation I gave him earlier (June 1937).'[72]

Zavadovskaia appears to have known what she was doing: the NKVD order announced in the summer of 1937 stated expressly that 'wives who report their husbands to state organs' would not be arrested.[73] Conversely, divorcees who knew of their spouses' counter-revolutionary activities and failed to report them were subject to immediate detainment. If the accusation could be substantiated, a special file was opened; a certificate documenting the counter-revolutionary crime was appended and the case was moved to the NKVD Special Council.[74]

In the Communist universe, family intimacy and surveillance went hand in hand. Consider the case of Miasin, a student at Leningrad's Institute of Red Professors, whose wife, Khutorok, was drummed out of the Party for Trotskyism by the district troika. A letter to the Party committee maintained that Miasin was not behaving as a good Communist should: 'He insists at Party meetings and in private conversations that what happened to Khutorok was "totally unjustified".' Miasin shrugged off the charges but the denouncer, Nekrasova, clung to her story. Had not Khutorok tried to kill herself in 1933? Why did Miasin refuse to acknowledge her true motives for this desperate act? 'Khutorok had grown tired of her life because she was a disgruntled Oppositionist. In the process of sounding me out, she once confessed that she remained loyal to Trotsky. Instead of denouncing his wife's clear opposition to the Party, Miasin managed to obtain a special ration [of food and clothing] for Khutorok from Kirov.' Nekrasova was implying that in taking advantage of Kirov's benevolence Miasin was behaving just like Nikolaev, who had also begged Kirov for assistance, before shooting him in the back.

For a certain period Miasin defended his wife's integrity. As he recalled events which had occurred three years before, he made a real effort to convey her despair: 'Khutorok suffered from a functional disorder of the nervous system. She was in a despondent mood and the doctors told me to watch her carefully.' Once Miasin awoke in the middle of the night to the sight of his wife sitting by the window, scribbling something. 'When I asked what she was doing she suggested I hide the gun from her. Let me emphasize that I heard no Trotskyist complaints from her on this occasion. I knew that Khutorok had supported Trotsky while at Sverdlov Communist University in 1923 and then again before the Fifteenth Congress in Orel [1927]. But though we constantly discussed politics – Khutorok had to reveal her hand during the four years we lived together – I detected no vestiges of Trotskyism in her.'

Charged with 'having invented a theory that distinguished between "good Trotskyists" and "wicked Trotskyists"', Miasin was not disheartened. 'All I can say is that the Party teaches us to approach everyone individually. I believe that Khutorok is a Trotskyist of the Piatakovian sort' – at this date the soon-to-be-arrested Piatakov still served as a symbol of true repentance – 'and that she has the right to appeal her conviction.' Since Khutorok had always socialized with true Communists, it had never occurred to Miasin to compare himself with 'somebody like Rafailovich, whose wife had ties with the Leningrad Center'.

But the possibility that Oppositionists such as Khutorok could have truly repented was now discounted. Those who failed to recognize and bring to justice a traitor they had been living with day in and day out had blundered, and badly. One by one, comrades berated Miasin: 'Didn't it occur to you that there were things you just did not notice? Your failure to see the vestiges of Oppositionism in Khutorok for all these years only deepens your guilt!' And: 'How come you ran to the Party offices three times to make inquiries? Who is supposed to know Khutorok better, you or the Party secretary?' And:

> It is unthinkable that Khutorok did not tell you what she was accused of. She wanted to be let off with rehabilitation and must have consulted you on how to obtain it ... Your insincerity is evident. You speak about Khutorok – an active Oppositionist – in legalistic terms. Familiar with the tactics of the Opposition though you are, you still prefer to question the verdict of the Party instead of your wife!

One of the committee members tersely commented: 'Miasin, you have a philistine attitude toward the institution of the family!' Taking his cue from the rector, who suggested that 'Miasin should take the opportunity presented by his final remarks to offer an honest assessment of Khutorok', Miasin weakly muttered, 'Once the NKVD arrested Khutorok, I understood that I was wrong.' There was no possibility that this lukewarm apology would save him; Miasin was purged as a 'two-faced protector of Trotskyists'.[75]

Not all families were as close as the Miasins and not all spouses were held equally responsible for their mates. Though Rokhlina, an instructor at the Herzen Institute, reported the arrest of her Oppositionist husband,

Bogomol'skii, to her Party cell immediately, she was blamed for resisting the idea that he was guilty. Once she had shown that 'since we were living in different apartments [Bogomol'skii had continued to live with his former family] I could not get to know him well', Rokhlina was granted the benefit of the doubt. Apparently, the committee concluded, Rokhlina had been denied a real chance to peer into the deepest recesses of Bogomol'skii's soul. This example shows that the spouses of enemies of the people were suspected not because of a kinship link, but because they had failed in their hermeneutical duties.[76]

In 1936–37 the families of many students in Leningrad were arrested in massive sweeps. Remaining at large, Baron, an instructor in the Institute of Red Professors suffered the trials of Job. During the 1936 purge her husband was condemned as a Trotskyist. A communiqué from the military academy dated July 1936 stated that 'Dobrov, a Komsomol member in Kiev who actively participated in the Opposition, used to write proclamations demanding that Trotsky be allowed to express himself'. As soon as she got the news, Baron confessed before the Party committee at Communist University (where she worked as a technical secretary): 'A short time ago I received an anonymous letter indicating that Dobrov was a Trotskyist. Only very reluctantly did Dobrov disclose his ties with those people to me, using the pretext that he had not yet given the details to the Party Committee.' As if proving to the authorities that she was not a 'lost soul' (*poteriannyi chelovek*), Baron had decided to seek a divorce.[77]

Though her request that she be allowed 'to remain a Bolshevik' was temporarily granted, Baron's troubles were only beginning. Shortly thereafter she was reprimanded again, this time for 'concealing the fact that her father used to exploit hired labor'. It was now time to renounce her father: 'Yes,' admitted this sedulous Communist, 'I knew that Father owned a knitting shop. This was precisely why I was raised by my older brother, Svetov.'[78] Another month passed and Baron received a letter from her younger brother Maev, informing her that 'our older brother has just been purged as a Trotskyist'. Again she held up her head and marched boldly forward: 'It is my duty to inform the cell', she wrote in March 1937, 'that my older brother, the head of the Ukrainian Glavlit, was just expelled from the ranks of the Party for shielding enemies of the people.'[79]

Sometimes hanging together, at other times acting separately, the Barons were going from bad to worse. When its members learned that Baron's younger brother had also been arrested, the heretofore surprisingly patient university Party organization decided it was time to look more carefully into the matter:

Q: Why do your brothers have different surnames?

A: They were ashamed of having a last name like 'Baron'.

Q: When did you find out that your brothers had been purged from the Kiev Komsomol?

A: In 1928. At that time I also knew that my husband was a member of that Oppositionist organization.

The members of her cell came to believe that 'Baron knew back in 1928–29 that Kievan Trotskyists, her husband and brothers included, were two-faced, but had said nothing'. Three arguments were advanced to show that the accused remained close to her Oppositionist family: 1) Had Baron divorced her husband because, as she alleged, she could not stand his views, 'she undoubtedly would have severed all ties to her Trotskyist brothers as well, something she failed to do'; 2) Baron received news from her Trotskyist brothers 'not through her mother, but directly', which meant that she was still very much in touch with them; 3) Despite being repeatedly told to sever ties with the enemy, 'Baron went to Kiev and met her Trotskyist husband there'. Reconstructed from scratch, Baron's family lineage was depicted as a Trotskyist tree: her father was the root, her husband and brothers the branches. In the resolution ordering that she be purged, the committee offered the following summary: 'Baron's very nature is that of an exploiter. Her consciousness was cultivated by enemies.'[80]

Though her family background was no less problematic than Baron's, Volodarskaia, a history instructor at the Institute of Red Professors, managed to uphold her Communist self by convincing her questioners that her own political record was at odds with the record of her treasonous family. Her difficulties had started when Volodarskaia's husband, Rudnitskii, committed suicide in 1935. An investigation suggested that 'Rudnitskii may have had contacts with counter-revolutionaries; when he saw that he would be unmasked, he decided to avoid responsibility.' Volodarskaia convincingly sketched out a conjugal existence that presented her husband in a different light: 'Rudnitskii and I spent 15 years together. Beyond being simply husband and wife, we were comrades. I never suspected his Party loyalty and always believed in him. When he put an end to his life, it came as a total surprise to me.' Advised 'to be objective and find out the truth about her husband', Volodarskaia made extensive inquiries at the Communist Academy where she was assured by students who knew Rudnitskii that 'his name had never surfaced in connection with enemies of the people'. Remaining suspicions were dispelled when Volodarskaia obtained materials from the military prosecutor diagnosing her husband's suicide as 'motivated by physical illness'.[81]

But a cloud was still hovering over Volodarskaia. In the summer of 1936 she was instructed 'to question in detail all her relatives and acquaintances ... to check whether any of them was ever an Oppositionist'. Volodarskaia took this advice very seriously: 'I started going over my relatives in my head as soon as I got home.' She decided it was best to ask her brothers in writing – after all, there was nothing better than a written statement to show at a Party court. Only her older brother had anything to confess: 'Aleksandr, now an engineer at a Moscow chemical plant, wrote to me: "Yes, I vacillated in 1923; by 1925–27, however, I had mended my ways".'

But this was far from the end of the story. In February 1937 one of Volodarskaia's brothers was sentenced to five years in a labor camp for 'concealing his connection' to Piatakov, a former Trotskyist and recent victim of the Second Moscow Show Trial. Another was described as 'an editor at a polluted journal', and arrested. Old suspicions regarding Volodarskaia were dredged up again. How could she not have known what her brothers were up to? Could she have been hiding something? Her colleague Kulagin did not believe that Volodarskaia could have been unaware of what her brothers were doing. 'I, for example, know everything not only about my relatives but also about my acquaintances.' The Party committee concluded that 'fraternal emotions must have overwhelmed Volodarskaia'.[82] A motion was put forward to purge her. 'Despite the numerous positive traits of this instructor we cannot trust someone whose relatives turn out to be enemies of the people left and right.' Ready to take 'moral' but not 'political' responsibility for their crimes, Volodarskaia declared that 'because my brothers played a very minor role in my life, my Communist identity should not be based on their record'. Finally she obtained a certificate to the effect that 'as a student at the Herzen Institute in 1923, Volodarskaia gave Trotsky's daughter, who used to teach there, hell'. She thereby escaped the axe by the skin of her teeth.[83]

SUMMARY

The Great Purge brought about the collapse of the Communist family. Communist families, however, were not only an object of Party scrutiny and intervention but also its subject: thus, the disintegration of the family was not exclusively a matter of an autocratic regime wreaking destruction in a dictatorial, top-down fashion. Having thoroughly penetrated many families and having succeeded in convincing individuals that the revolutionary movement came before personal happiness, Communist ideology left family loyalty an empty shell, a dated bourgeois value, a regrettable vestige of the past if it existed at all.

The material presented above corroborates what historical scholarship has already known full well – family members usually shared a fate in the 1930s. But the explanation offered here diverges from the accepted interpretation: the victimization of entire families ceases to be the result of a Stalinist rejection of the Christian precept of personal responsibility and has little to do with the pseudo-biological patterns of thought prevalent in the period. In fact, the opposite is closer to the truth: the Stalinist machine set out to realize, not to distort Marx's teachings; it fingered so many relatives not because their genes were tainted but because they failed as hermeneuticists. Who could be so incompetent as to fail to unmask the wicked souls of those with whom they lived intimately? The Communist who reported nothing while perched in such a convenient hermeneutical position was most likely not an innocent, not even an incompetent, comrade but a cunning, wicked enemy deliberately shielding his collaborators.

Thus, many families were wiped out with a single blow during the Stalinist period, but they suffered that fate not as an organism united by strong blood ties but allegedly as a tightly knit counter-revolutionary cell united by a common consciousness. Because participation in the second group was a matter of free will, whereas in the first it was a matter of biological destiny, individuals could always hope to be vindicated. The road to Communist conversion, significantly narrowed during the era of sweeping purges, to be sure, always remained negotiable, though it could be very difficult indeed. The fact that a successful manipulation of the official discourse enabled at least a few to clear their names by distancing themselves from convicted family members points to the importance of the voluntarist kernel in Communism. The right to petition, to write a complaint protesting one's innocence, all this while using public language, did not disappear even during the worst days of the Great Purge. Neither class background nor national origins were an insurmountable obstacle.

Though both Stalin and Hitler destroyed whole families of would-be 'enemies', the most fundamental distinction between Communism and Nazism has been exposed in the preceding pages: biological determinism, the perception of man as fully determined by nature, was alien to the Soviet legal system. Because guilt in the Soviet Union was always a personal concept, the victim died not as an anonymous number but as a concrete individual convicted for specific actions. In this context, the issue of fair or unfair trial is irrelevant. A victim of Stalin, unlike one of Hitler's victims, always left behind a personal file and a verdict pertaining to one unique case. If in Nazi Germany people were sentenced to death exclusively because their blood was of the 'wrong type', in Stalinist Russia the court of the NKVD troika was obliged to prove that the relative of a convicted traitor, even when taken as a discrete moral persona, was also an irredeemable enemy.

NOTES

1. Tsentral'nyi gosudarstvennyi arkhiv istoriko-politicheskikh dokumentov (TsGA IPD), f. 566, op. 1, d. 208, l. 174.
2. H.K. Geiger, *The Family in Soviet Russia* (Cambridge, MA: Harvard University Press, 1968), p. 63.
3. M. Liadov, *Voprosy byta. (Doklad na sobranii iacheiki Sverdlovskogo kommunisticheskogo universiteta)* (Moscow, 1925), pp. 35–7.
4. I. Lass, *Sovremennoe studenchestvo. Byt, polovaia zhizn'* (Moscow, 1926), p. 198.
5. Partiinyi arkhiv Novosibirskoi oblasti, f. 6, op. 1, d. 12, ll. 2–4.
6. I. Gel'man, *Polovaia zhizn' sovremennoi molodezhi. Opyt sotsial'no-biologicheskogo obsledovaniia* (Moscow/Petrograd: Gos. izd., 1923), p. 65; P. Lepeshinskii, 'V vol'no diskussionnom klube', *Molodaia gvardiia*, no. 1 (1923), pp. 96–7; 102–3; L. Vasil'evskii, 'Polovoi byt uchashchikhsia', *Komsomol'skaia pravda*, 19 March 1927.
7. B. Evans Clements, *Bolshevik Feminist: The Life of Aleksandra Kollontai* (Bloomington, IN: Indiana University Press, 1979), pp. 226–7.
8. The love life of students was frequently an object of investigation by the 'comrades' court' (*tovarishcheskii sud*) which was active in every large university. The main purpose of the court was 'to bring to light the socio-political essence of every misdemeanor'. Its judges, not jurists but regular students elected by the Party meeting, pledged 'not to forget for a moment that the university is eager to remove moral illnesses from our lives. [...] Let the student court become the barometer that demonstrates the growth of our self-awareness, temperance, discipline, comradely sensitivity and responsiveness.' The activity of the court, its frame of reference for dealing with issues, shows that the Party tried to regulate students' love lives, imbuing them with Communist consciousness. Early in 1924, Rimma Sruleva Shteinman, a female student at the Leningrad Communist University, handed in a statement to the comrades' court accusing a fellow student, Nikolai Vasil'evich Kuznetsov, of an 'anti-Communist deed', namely raping her on 29 December 1923. The court had the following data on the two students involved in the litigation: 20 years of age, Kuznetsov, a 'worker' by social position, had been a Party member since 19 January 1921; Shteinman, an 'employee' by social position, was two years older (and a member of the Party since 1922).

    A court protocol detailed the conclusions of the case: from the statements of the sides it emerged that the sexual liaison between Shteinman and Kuznetsov was the fruit of a long moral and psychological gestation period; intercourse was said to be the logical outcome of what preceded it and, therefore, could not qualify as rape. Furthermore, the fact that Shteinman was a 'staunch and temperate comrade', that is, that she was mature as an individual and a Communist, suggested that she could not be presented as a passive and helpless victim: she willingly flirted with Kuznetsov and should, allegedly, not have been surprised when he forced himself on her. It is another matter, said the court, that 'frequent cases of drunkenness and rowdy brawls, ties with non-proletarian milieu, and NEP have all corrupted Kuznetsov, spoiling his relations with comrades, many of them offspring of the formerly exploited nationalities [read: Jews]'. Indeed, Kuznetsov's attitude toward Shteinman was 'not Communist in nature. [...] Treating her not as a comrade but as an object of scorn, he displayed a light-hearted attitude to sexual liaison, a fact which proves his non-Communist attitude toward women and toward sexual intercourse.' Furthermore, Kuznetsov was manipulative: 'marrying a girl who is an offspring descended from a noble family, he made simultaneous claims to sexual relations with Shteinman, his "lover" – a fact that characterized his sexual perversity'.

    On 24 February 1924, the comrades' court decided that it was not enough to apply moral pressure on Kuznetsov and resolved to expel him from the university. Clearly, the court distinguished between a low kind of love, grounded in base instincts and self-interest, and Communist love, driven by proletarian consciousness and a deep sense of camaraderie. Shteinman took some criticism of her own along these lines. It was said that she had recently grown 'alienated from healthy proletarian psychology'. Hoping to 'protect Shteinman from anomalous phenomena, strengthen her temperance and resolve, and open a wider field of activity for her', the court decided that only in the factory 'can she eradicate the discrepancies between her words and her deeds, her theory and her practice, temper her will-power and regain healthy aspirations'. In a statement she sent to the comrades' court, Shteinman admitted that she had degenerated: 'My relations with Kuznetsov indeed displayed a certain weakness on my part. My idealization of the notion of a comrade, my desire to show sympathy to his advances even when I did not want them, finally my disinclination to respond with philistine evasions (something I eventually had to resort to) – all these suggest to me I would be better off sent to the factory. Only working on the assembly line can I become a better worker and a better Communist.' Her request was granted. TsGA IPD, f. 197, op. 1, d. 35, ll. 32–3, 35, 37

The so-called Koren'kov Affair, a juicy episode that involved sex and suicide, aroused much discussion in the mid-1920s. These, in a nutshell, were the events: Koren'kov, a Communist student in the Moscow Mining Academy, whose 'free love' drove his wife, Rina Davidson, to suicide, was purged from the Komsomol. The cell justified his expulsion stating that 'individuals who callously tread upon young females and live with three women at once cannot contribute to socialist construction'. During the deliberations on the case, however, many youngsters came to Koren'kov's defence. There are no stipulations against Communists having more than one wife, they argued. Still others pointed out that Davidson, having come from a family of intelligentsia, 'had philistine expectations from life. [...] She was probably a prim lady (*kiseinaia baryshnia*), a student (*institutka*, clearly a pejorative here), in short, a philistine unable to come to terms with the simple 'comradely relations' between the sexes typical of the new, Bolshevik Russia. Blaming Davidson herself for her death, several Komsomol journalists preferred to speak about the Davidson Affair rather than the Koren'kov Affair. Davidson, they claimed, should have appealed to the public against her husband rather than kill herself in order to cast a negative light on him. Eventually the Zamoskvoretsk Party Control Commission decided to retain Koren'kov in the Komsomol 'taking his young age into account'. Before long, Koren'kov was detained by the police for 'robbery and murder' thus vindicating his detractors. This time a harsh sentence was demanded 'so that the honor of proletarian students would be preserved'. The affair was regarded as debunking Kollontai's views on 'free love' and additional proof that the Party should intervene in personal affairs. 'It is much wiser', Smidovich argued, 'to regard "private life" as an inseparable part of a whole that determines what a man is, than to shut one's eyes to private life, assuming that somebody like Koren'kov is indispensable.' The Party, Smidovich concluded, could not neglect the 'social point of view' and leave private matters unattended. L. Sosnovkin, 'Delo Koren'kova'; S. Smidovich, 'O Koren'kovshchine'; and S. Smidovich, 'O Davidsonovshchine'; all reproduced in *Komsomol'skii byt* (Moscow, 1926), pp. 126, 140–4.

9. A. Zalkind, *Polovoi vopros v usloviiakh sovetskoi obshchestvennosti* (Leningrad, 1926), pp. 39, 45–6, 56.
10. Ibid., pp. 39, 45–6, 56.
11. M. Postnikov, 'Polovoi vopros v srede sovremennoi uchashcheisia molodezhi', *Omskii rabfakovets* 2 (1928), p. 53.
12. Val'gard defined love as a 'conditional reflex toward an object which produces pleasure'. S. Val'gard, *O psikhologii polovoi zhizni* (Moscow/Leningrad, 1926), pp. 67–9.
13. A. Lents, 'Ob fiziologicheskoi teorii chelovecheskogo povedeniia', *Priroda* 6–7 (1922), pp. 16–17.
14. Lev Gumilevskii, *Sobachii pereulok* (Riga: Biblioteka noveishei literatury, 1928), pp. 10–11.
15. N. Velt', 'Otkrytoe pis'mo tovarishchu Smidovich', *Komsomol'skii byt* (Moscow, 1926), p. 181.

16. V. Kuz'min, 'O 'molodoi starosti', asketizme i kazenshchine', *Komsomol'skii byt*, p. 206.
17. Zalkind, *Polovoi vopros v usloviiakh sovetskoi obshchestvennosti*, p. 53.
18. Gel'man, *Polovaia zhizn' sovremennoi molodezhi*, p. 75; Gel'man could not decide whether love in the future would be monogamous or polygamous. 'We have to admit', he however noted, 'that monogamy is more suited to the interests of race and society.' Gel'man, *Polovaia zhizn' sovremennoi molodezhi*, p. 130.
19. Zalkind, *Polovoi vopros v usloviiakh sovetskoi obshchestvennosti*, pp. 45–6, 56.
20. TsGA IPD, f. 566, op. 1, d. 276, l. 98.
21. The rise of the idea of the New Man brought with it a critical examination of the idea of family not only in the Soviet Union. No revolutionary ideology could avoid relating to this subject. In socialist Zionism, for example, children were regarded as belonging to the collective; the kibbutz insisted that children sleep together in a children's house – separate from their biological parents. Married members were intentionally assigned to different shifts from those of their spouses in the kibbutz so that their bond would not overshadow relationships with other members of the collective. The Nazis also intervened in the German family: families were destroyed when mixed-race couples were separated. Inversely, new families were constituted on a biological basis. 'Aryan children' were kidnapped in Poland and other countries and handed over for adoption in order to enlarge the genetic pool of the allegedly superior race. Despite the generally conservative orientation of Nazi family policy, procreation within the race was encouraged through such unorthodox measures as creating brothels for SS commanders who were supposed to impregnate as many blonde German women as they possibly could. Y. Talmon, *Family and Community in the Kibbutz* (Cambridge, MA: Harvard University Press, 1972).
22. TsGA IPD, f. 566, op. 1, d. 288, l. 53. M. Burleigh and W. Wippermann, *The Racial State: Germany 1933–1945* (Cambridge, MA: Harvard University Press, 1991).
23. O.V. Khlevniuk, *1937-i: Stalin, NKVD i sovetskoe obshchestvo* (Moscow: Respublika, 1992), p. 182.
24. *Deviataia konferentsiia VKP(b). Stenograficheskii otchet* (Moscow, 1972), p. 171.
25. Documents from the archive of the Leningrad Martyrology, Central Library, St Petersburg, in the personal possession of the author.
26. I. Druzhnikov, *Donoshchik 001* (Moscow, Moskovskii rabochii, 1995), p. 149.
27. *Pravda*, 9 July 1932.
28. Partiinyi arkhiv tomskoi oblasti (PATO), f. 320, op. 1, d. 7, l. 17.
29. PATO, f. 115, op. 2, d. 7, l. 42.
30. TsGA IPD, f. 197, op. 1, d. 725, ll. 270–1.
31. TsGA IPD, f. 566, op. 1, d. 288, ll. 69–70; d. 331, ll. 23–4.
32. Ibid.
33. PATO, f. 17, op. 1, d. 370, l. 54.
34. TsGA IPD, f. 566, op. 1, d. 331, l. 2.
35. TsGA IPD, f. 197, op. 1, d. 992, [1936].
36. TsGA IPD, f. 197, op. 1, d. 982, ll. 209–11; d. 1000, l. 53.
37. P. Solomein, *Pavlik Morozov* (Moscow, Obshchestvennyi Fond 'Glasnost', 1938).
38. TsGA IPD, f. 197, d. 982, l. 316; d. 1131, l. 4; TsGA IPD, f. 197, op. 1, d. 1000, l. 68.
39. TsGA IPD, f. 197, op. 1, d. 982, l. 207; d. 1132, ll. 31, 34.
40. TsGA IPD, f. 197, op. 1, d. 994, l. 1.
41. Iu. Stetsovskii, *Istoriia sovetskikh repressii* (St Petersburg, 1997), Vol. 1, p. 437.
42. *Soprotivlenie v gulage. Vospominaniia. Pis'ma. Dokumenty* (Moscow, Vozvrashchenie, 1992), pp. 150–4.
43. *Gulag v karelii, 1930–1941: sbornik dokumentov i materialov* (Petrozavodsk: Karel'skii nauchnyi tsentr RAN, 1992), p. 72.
44. V. Ivanov, *Missiia ordena. Mekhanizm repressii v Sovetskoi Rossii v kontse 20-kh–40kh gg. (na materialakh Severo-Zapada RSFSR)* (St Peterburg, 1997), p. 165.
45. *Izvestiia*, 4 July 1991.
46. Stetsovskii, *Istoriia sovetskikh repressii*, Vol. 2, p. 215.
47. V. Vel'man, 'Kak torzhestvovala lozh'', *Imet' silu pomnit'* (Moscow, 1991), p. 145.
48. Iu. Drunina, 'Postradavshii ot Stalina Kapler', *Ogonek* 41 (1988), p. 30.

49. A. Antonov-Ovseenko, *Vecherniaia Moskva*, 7 Jan. 1989.
50. S. Mikoian, 'Asketizm vozhdia', *Ogonek* 15 (1989), p. 30.
51. Stetsovkii, *Istoriia sovetskikh repressii*, Vol. 2, p. 245.
52. *Sovetskaia sibir'*, 21 Feb. 1938.
53. Ivanov, *Missiia ordena*, p. 166.
54. The Communist attitude toward women was a thorny issue during the 1930s as well. Politics remained intimately linked with sex, love and marriage. On 17 January 1935, for example, a certain Potapova denounced Drozdov, a student at the Institute of Red Professors, for making anti-Semitic remarks toward his Jewish wife. Reading the paper, he turned to her and said, 'Look how Hitler, that son of a bitch, is dealing with your kind! [*vot Gitler, sukin syn, kak vashego brata kroit*].' Drozdov defended himself: 'True, I did beat my wife from time to time, forgetting at such moments I was a Communist. But I have no idea what basis she has for calling me an anti-Semite – apparently a case of feminine logic.' Clearly, Drozdov was worried his political consciousness might be questioned – that he had not fully rid himself of misogyny was a small matter by comparison. He was reprimanded. TsGA IPD, f. 566, op. 1, d. 255, l. 37.

The related case of Trofimov, a 37-year-old instructor at the same institute, shows how thin the boundary between a crime of love and a political crime was during the 1930s. Political questions were translated into moral terms and vice versa with great ease. Though the litigation involved primarily issues of sex and love, the defendant tried to show that his accusers must have been connected with the enemy. The female complaint was narrated by the Moscow city committee in the following terms: 'Comrade Apelianskaia informed the Komsomol cell in her place of work (a car factory) that Trofimov, when teaching at the Moscow Road Transport Institute, invited her to his apartment, served her wine and took advantage of her, promising to marry her. In the morning he changed his mind, justifying himself on the basis that "she was not a virgin". When he found out that she was pregnant, Trofimov decided to get rid of her using any available means. Using the stationery of the institute's Party committee, he twice sent her certificates, written with his left hand, where she was informed that "Trofimov had left the city". Furthermore, once, when Apelianskaia fainted, he removed his letters from her purse hoping to eliminate all documentary evidence that would link them'.

In the spring of 1937, Trofimov had to answer these charges at the Party meeting of the Leningrad Institute of Red Professors where he was now teaching. 'It is a lie that I took advantage of citizen Apelianskaia', he said. 'She was trying to drag me to the marriage license bureau … Do not believe anything she tells you. If she were to say I was a Trotskyist I would be imprisoned!' Trofimov charged that in daring to denounce a seasoned Communist, Apelianskaia resembled 'terrorist enemies of the people'. In one of his written statements he compared her 'crimes' with the 'crimes of Zinov'ev, an enemy of the people'. But Trofimov's wager on his standing as a Communist backfired. 'Did you sleep with her or did you not?', Efimov asked him point blank. The accused responded, 'I did not know she was in the Komsomol', that is, he was unaware she had to be treated as a comrade. No wonder, Trofimov added. 'Apelianskaia had a permanent wave and she wore lipstick' – she resembled an 'unreliable philistine' more than a conscious citizen. Disagreeing with him for the most part, his peers stated that it was Trofimov 'whose political education turned out to be vulgar'. 'There is not even one drop of Party-mindedness in Trofimov', they noted. According to Shumilev, Trofimov had a 'philistine view of contemporary women: he sends her away, then calls on her to satisfy his animalistic lust, then throws her out again and so on'. 'Apelianskaia saw in Trofimov an older comrade, a Communist', Emdin noted. 'But he tried to push this Komsomol girl into the enemy camp.' Linchik concluded that 'unaware that Stalin's Constitution regards a woman as an equal citizen, Trofimov behaves like putrid scum and not a Communist'. Only Zubarev defended Trofimov: 'The question of everyday life is complex and perplexing. I believe we should approach the issue differently, though I sense the meeting is inclined to purge him. The woman is not naive: she carefully collects documents and so on …Trofimov is a worker by origin, with no Party reprimands – we should not purge him without further investigation'. But this was a

minority opinion. Trofimov was purged and sent to production. TsGA IPD, f. 566, op. 1, d. 277, ll. 43, 46, d. 280, l. 61.
55. *Obshchestvo i vlast', 1930-e god. Povestvovanie v dokumentakh* (Moscow: Rosspen, 1998), pp. 189–90.
56. *Obshchestvo i vlast'*, p. 201.
57. *30-e gody. Vzgliad iz segodnia* (Moscow: Nauka, 1990), p. 94.
58. F. Chuev, *Sto sorok besed s Molotovym, Iz dnevnika F. Chueva* (Moscow: Terra, 1991), p. 415.
59. Stetsovskii, *Istoriia sovetskikh repressii*, p. 437.
60. Ivanov, *Missiia ordena*, p. 167.
61. *Obshchestvo i vlast'*, p. 191.
62. Ibid., p. 186.
63. Documents from the archive of the Leningrad Martyrology, Central Library, St Petersburg, in the personal possession of the author.
64. *Rossiiskaia gazeta*, 22 Dec. 1992.
65. TsGA IPD, f. 1816, op. 2, d. 5091, ll. 23–4.
66. TsGA IPD, f. 566, op. 1, d. 255, l. 53; f. 1816, op. 2, d. 4408, ll. 8–19; d. 509, l. 55, 25 Jan. 1935.
67. *Reabilitatsiia. Politicheskie protsessy 30kh-50kh godov* (Moscow: Izd. Politicheskoi literatury, 1991), pp. 151–2.
68. TsGA IPD, f. 566, op. 1, d. 310, l. 25. Ivashev was purged for 'failing to unmask his wife, Pal'tseva, who was accused of having contact with the enemy of the people Serebriakov'.
69. *Obshchestvo i vlast'*, pp. 188–9.
70. Stetsovskii, *Istoriia sovetskikh repressii*, Vol. 1, p. 421. The marriage/divorce ratio in Leningrad during the Great Purge was 10 to 4. Ivanov, *Missiia ordena*, p. 376, Note 120.
71. TsGA IPD, f. 197, op. 1, d. 982, l. 62.
72. TsGA IPD, f. 566, op. 1, d. 320, l. 14.
73. Stetsovskii, *Istoriia sovetskikh repressii*, p. 437.
74. *Shornik zakonodatel'nykh i normativnykh aktov o repressiiakh i reabilitatsii zhertv politicheskikh repressii* (Moscow: Respublika, 1993), p. 88.
75. TsGA IPD, f. 566, op. 1, d. 255, ll. 63–8; f. 1816, op. 2, d. 5091, l. 35.
76. TsGA IPD, f. 1816, op. 2, d. 5091, l. 55.
77. TsGA IPD, f. 197, op. 1, d. 993, l. 107.
78. TsGA IPD, f. 197, op. 1, d. 1000, l. 18.
79. TsGA IPD, f. 197, op. 1, d. 1132, l. 6.
80. TsGA IPD, f. 197, op. 1, d. 1103, ll. 92, 105–6.
81. TsGA IPD, f. 566, op. 1, d. 309, l. 10; d. 311, ll. 1–13.
82. TsGA IPD, f. 566, op. 1, d. 311, ll. 15–17.
83. TsGA IPD, f. 566, op. 1, d. 280, l. 13.

8

Grigorii Aleksandrov's *Volga-Volga*

KATERINA CLARK

Recent writing on Stalinist culture of the 1930s has tended to see it as 'totalitarian culture', a category that includes, probably most paradigmatically, the culture of Nazi Germany. Yet contemporary studies of Nazi film, such as Linda Schulte-Sasse's *Entertaining the Third Reich* and particularly Eric Rentschler's *The Ministry of Illusion*, have suggested that our sense of Nazi film as heavily ideological – as in the best-known example, Leni Riefenstahl's *Triumph of the Will* – is distorted. Such 'infamous state-sponsored productions', writes Rentschler, '... were the exception, not the rule; they constituted a very small portion of the era's features. Films of the Third Reich emanated from a Ministry of Illusion, not a Ministry of Fear.' Most films made during the Nazi era, he contends, were genre films, citing the figure 941 out of 1,094. Moreover, 'almost half of all features – to be precise, 523 – were comedies and musicals (what the Nazis termed *heitere*, "cheerful" films), light fare directed by ever-active industry pros'.[1] 'Studios were dream factories, not propaganda machines. Goebbels quickly grasped the fact that conveyor-belt, brown-shirt epics were box office poison.'[2] In consequence, he 'eschewed overt agitation'.[3] In 'the vast majority of films made under Goebbels', he observes, 'we encounter neither steeled bodies nor iron wills, no racist slurs, state slogans, or party emblems. [Rather, characters who] dance about with zest, singing of joyful lives without responsibility ...' Here Rentschler cites as an example a snatch of a song from Paul Martin's *Lucky Kids* (*Glückskinder*) of 1936:

> I wish I were a chicken!
> I wouldn't have much to do!
> I'd lay an egg in the morning
> And take the afternoon off![4]

This generalization, however, does not apply to Soviet films of the 1930s, the overwhelming majority of which were undisguisedly ideological: Romm's *Lenin in 1918*, Pyriev's *The Party Card*, the Vasil'ev brothers' *Chapaev* (about the growth in political consciousness of a Soviet Civil War commander), to name but a few of the best known. There is no shortage of steel wills or iron bodies in such works. Another common category was the political allegory using a historical subject (also used by the Nazis as Schulte-Sasse has shown); the only two films Eisenstein was able to complete after the 1920s, *Aleksander Nevsky* of 1938, and *Ivan the Terrible*, Part I, of 1944, fall into this class. Less common, though nevertheless strongly represented, were the comedy and the musical comedy. The first Soviet sound comedies emerged in 1934 (five of them) and from then until the war, between five and 12 were produced annually.[5] However, these also had overt ideological messages. Pure comedies lacking in clear political content were not released for viewing. A fine example of this category would be Boris Barnet's delightful *Old Jockey* (*Staryi naezdnik*) of 1940, written by Nikolai Erdman, the principal scriptwriter for *Volga-Volga*, which was completed in 1938.

Volga-Volga was the third of four musical comedies made by Grigorii Aleksandrov in the 1930s to orders from on high. In August 1932 Aleksandrov had been invited to Gorky's dacha where Stalin, who 'happened' to be visiting, spoke of the need for a new Soviet culture which would be an 'upbeat, joyous art [*bodroe, zhizneradostnoe iskusstvo*], full of fun and laughter'.[6] In 1933 (or the fall of 1932, dates vary) the Party Central Committee called a conference of film people at which they advanced the slogans 'Give Us Comedy' and 'Laughter Is the Brother of Strength', and called on the country's chief film directors to produce comedies. Those assembled were told that viewers' letters were demanding comedies. Eisenstein thereupon produced a comedy script *MMM*, one of his many projects of the 1930s not to reach fruition.[7] These developments coincided more or less with the coining of the term 'socialist realism' (May 1932) and with the attempt by leading figures in Soviet culture and politics in the ensuing months to try to formulate exactly what it might mean. *Volga-Volga*, it should be noted, was described in the standard Soviet book on film comedies of that era (by R. Iurenev, 1964), as a paradigm of socialist realist comic film.[8]

Thus *Volga-Volga* must be seen as a standard Soviet film, an exemplar of socialist realism. Yet it was also one of the most popular films of the Soviet 1930s; throughout the country long lines formed at the box office to see it.[9] Clearly, this was far from the case of one film that had managed to slip through state control and address true mass taste and concerns. In fact, among its most devoted fans was Stalin himself; he even sent a copy to Roosevelt in 1942 for his edification.[10] Stalin apparently had the film screened so often that as he viewed it he would recite many of the jokes before they came up on the soundtrack.[11]

Volga-Volga, then, must be viewed as a genuine Soviet cultural artefact. As such, it illustrates particularly well the hybrid nature of Stalinist culture in the 1930s.[12] As this chapter will show, the film constitutes a politicized parable of subject formation that also promotes some of the political and cultural prejudices of high Stalinism, while still providing rollicking entertainment that seems to have been generated by something comparable to Rentschler's 'Ministry of Illusion'.

VOLGA-VOLGA AS AN ILLUSTRATION OF SEVERAL POINTS IN THE PARTY LINE

Like most musicals, *Volga-Volga* has a love plot at its center. This one follows the vicissitudes in the relationship between Strelka, a mail carrier in the provincial Volga town of Melkovodsk, and Alyosha, a bookkeeper who also conducts the local amateur orchestra. Strelka, too, conducts, but in her case the group is an amateur ensemble which does largely folk musical numbers, dance routines and recitation. All the fun and caper, however, does not fail to make points that reinforce both stock Soviet values and recent developments in the Party line on culture.

The film opens as Strelka and Alyosha kiss in the hay in Melkovodsk's bucolic river setting. She confesses to him that she has composed a song about the Volga. Alyosha dismisses the notion that a mere mail carrier such as she could compose a song. He declares this to be an affront to classical music and calls her a 'silly fool' (*dura*), thus initiating the series of lovers' tiffs and reconciliations that punctuate this film.

Strelka is actually in the process of delivering an urgent telegram from Moscow to Byvalov, the retrograde director of the local musical instrument factory, who essentially presides over the town but who, in fact, is bureaucracy personified. The telegram invites him to send a group from his factory to compete in a Moscow Olympiad for amateur performers, but Byvalov refuses to send a group, claiming that there is no talent in this backwater. Needless to say, the rest of the film proves both Alyosha and Byvalov wrong in their dismissive attitude toward folk endeavor. Strelka, her ensemble and her song overcome great odds to reach the Olympiad and become stars on the Moscow stage.

Most Soviet commentators see the plot as revolving around the conflict that begins with Byvalov's remark and which continues in a series of clashes between Byvalov and Strelka, the bureaucrat and the mail carrier. In this aspect, it is typical of much cultural production under Stalin, which was about the clash between a corrupt, inept, self-seeking or dyed-in-the-wool bureaucrat and one of his subordinates, who is bursting with energy, ideas and enthusiasm for the cause but is obstructed by bureaucratic rigidity and obtuseness.

The film's main plot can also be seen as a version of the standard narrative of the Stakhanovite movement, according to which simple workers defy the caution of engineers about what is feasible in their line of work and outdo production quotas two or three times over. The clash between Strelka and Alyosha has an element of class warfare, in that it is a contest between an orchestra peopled by bookkeepers, clerks and other white-collar semi-professionals and a group of amateur performers whose occupations presuppose – or did at that time, at any rate – very limited formal education: water carrier, mail carrier, fireman, concierge, waiter, cook, driver. Here the field where the heroine excels is, atypically, amateur music rather than industrial production. However, at the time *Volga-Volga* was made the conflict between Strelka and Alyosha-cum-Byvalov over musical styles and musical competence provided a neat illustration of another official policy: in the second half of the 1930s Soviet cultural policy promoted the folk and the amateur.

As Aleksandrov himself characterized the film, it is dedicated to 'the genius of the folk' which must be allowed its full expression. It could be said, then, that the major themes of the film have less to do with Stakhanovism specifically than with Russian appropriations of German Romanticism. Indeed, the shots presented of the local landscape around Melkovodsk reinforce the Romantic bent. In surrounding stretches of the river we are shown virtually a Caspar David Friedrich landscape of conifers and crags. (The actual area filmed, around Yelabuga, was the favorite subject of Russia's best-known kitsch landscape artist, Shishkin whose forest scenes owe much to such sources.)

The implicit claim of the film is that Strelka's amateur ensemble presents a more authentic, Russian, culture than that represented by Alyosha's. As such, however, it is not really folk. As Strelka in Melkovodsk tries in vain to persuade Byvalov that there are talented performers in the town, the numbers that first she alone, and then the ensemble, demonstrate to him come both from the Russian folk tradition and from the Russian classical repertoire of the nineteenth century. For example, the first song she sings to him is Tatiana's aria from Tchaikovsky's *Eugene Onegin*. (Not coincidentally, perhaps, 1937 was the centenary of Pushkin's death, an event celebrated in public ceremonies throughout the year.)

Strelka's preferences for Russian folk and classical music had xenophobic overtones in this time of a rising fascist menace. We should note that the classical composers which her bumbling foil, Alyosha, reveres are all Germanic: Wagner, Beethoven, Mozart and Schubert. Of all the examples of German music played in the film, Wagner's *Death of Isolde* is singled out as totally alien to the truly Russian ear. Aleksandrov has Alyosha play a section of it on the tuba to bring out its unmelodic, dreary tones. Strelka, who as the positive hero must insist on the upbeat at all times, cannot share his enthusiasm.

This caricature of the Wagnerian is, however, less an anti-German gesture than an anti-modernist one, an allusion to another development that had taken place in cultural policy. In a famous episode of January 1936, a year before the film was made, an attack on Shostakovich's opera *Lady Macbeth of Mtsensk District* had been leveled in a *Pravda* article entitled 'Muddle instead of Music'. This article railed not only against the Shostakovich opera, but against 'leftist distortion in opera' in general, which it contended 'stems from the same source as leftist distortion in painting, poetry, education and science'.[13] With this article, and the ensuing 'anti-formalist' campaign, an end was put to all manner of avant-gardism, not just in opera, but in all cultural and intellectual life.

Though the film promotes the anti-modernist cause, most of the leading names working on it had past associations with Soviet avant-garde art of the 1920s. Aleksandrov himself began his Moscow career in the early 1920s working with Eisenstein at the Proletkult Theater, then an enclave of Meyerhold's disciples, and went on to serve as principal assistant to Eisenstein on all his films of the 1920s. He accompanied Eisenstein on his two-and-a-half year trip to Europe, the US and Mexico in the early 1930s. Around the time of his return, Aleksandrov broke with Eisenstein and went on to make his four popular musical comedies, in each of which Liubov Orlova (eventually his wife) was the star. Also notable among the actors was Il'inskii, who played the role of Byvalov and who was most famous for his interpretations in Mayakovsky's plays *The Bedbug* and *The Bathhouse*. Indeed, the figure of Byvalov appears to have been modeled on Pobedonosikov in *The Bathhouse*, the role played by Il'inskii in the original Meyerhold production; even though the two scripts had different authors, several of the lines were similar. The cameraman (and part scriptwriter) for *Volga-Volga* was Vladimir Nielsen, who had also worked on Eisenstein's *October* and *The Old and the New*, and on Aleksandrov's two preceding musicals. The principal scriptwriter was Nikolai Erdman, author of two satirical comedies of the late 1920s produced by Meyerhold (though the second of these productions, *The Suicide*, was shut down by the authorities).

In that, as emerged later, the primary target of the *Pravda* article 'Muddle instead of Music' was not Shostakovich but Meyerhold, one must ask: is this film not an instance of a cautionary tale about avant-garde figures of the 1920s who in the 1930s were reduced by the regime to producing politically correct kitsch? Much Russian and Soviet modernist endeavor in music, opera, theater and even literature and art had been influenced by Wagner (and Nietzsche). Had these avant-gardists of the 1920s sold out in order to continue producing films? This may have been true to some extent, although it is difficult to dismiss such a clever and rollicking production as kitsch.

Several details of the film make an alternative reading possible whereby it is actually defending those old avant-garde ideals. For example, in the scene where Alyosha dismisses the notion that someone like Strelka could compose a song, he labels the work of her group '*balagan*', a word that literally means fairground theater, implying that it is vulgar and lowbrow, but which – and this is surely no accident – also happens to be the term used by Meyerhold when he conducted his experimental theatrical work in the 1910s and 1920s.[14] Another subtle defiant gesture may be found in some of the many arrangements of Strelka's song that come later in the film, which are in jazz form, even though jazz, like Meyerhold, had become problematic from 1936 on.[15]

Much of this inferred defense of 1920s avant-gardism comes from the Erdman text, which is full of verbal humor and innuendoes, most of which are lost in the English subtitles. One should be careful about going to the other extreme and arguing that the entire film represents encoded dissidence. After all, it was precisely in this verbal wit that Stalin reveled.

VOLGA-VOLGA AND THE HOLLYWOOD MUSICAL

It could be argued that the film owed more to popular Hollywood films than to avant-gardism of the Soviet 1920s. Aleksandrov had seen many Hollywood comedies and musicals since he had not only spent some time in America with Eisenstein, but also many Hollywood films had been shown to Soviet filmmakers in the 1930s, though not released to the general public. To some extent, *Volga-Volga* uses several of the trademark gestures and even physical attributes of well-known American comic actors.[16] Moreover, the similarities are not confined to the acting. Even the paddle steamer seems to be a nod to the American comic and musical tradition (albeit the paddle boat, identified as a gift from America, is dilapidated and slow). Possible sources for Aleksandrov's use of the steamboat as a stage for comic effects and for staging musical numbers include not only the different versions of *Showboat* (1929, 1936) but also several Buster Keaton movies, such as *Steamboat Bill Jr.* of 1927; indeed, Keaton, together with Chaplin and Harold Lloyd, were credited at the beginning of the first of Aleksandrov's four musical comedies, *The Happy-Go-Lucky Guys* of 1934, as the film's true heroes.

The appropriations from American comedy and musicals to be

found in *Volga-Volga* are too numerous to cite here but in any case a more telling debt to that genre may be found in the way the overall structure of *Volga-Volga* resembles that of the standard American musical. The most common plot of the American musical, and particularly of its sub-genre, the backstage musical which was particularly fashionable in the 1930s, charts the way of a girl (or, sometimes, a boy) from the provinces, who becomes a star on the New York stage, and culminates when, despite all odds, she brings off a smash hit before a big New York audience;[17] in *Volga-Volga* the provincial, Strelka, does so in New York's Soviet counterpart, Moscow. The love plot of the American musical is essentially subordinated to this goal of stardom. It reaches its resolution, generally, just as the triumphal show is about to begin, or at a critical juncture in the course of the show, after which the show becomes a stupendous success. In *Volga-Volga*, Strelka and Alyosha make up and declare their love just as she is about to be conveyed to the river station stage. In the American musical, in order for the heroine to make it to the big stage, she has to overcome small-town values, a producer/director who refuses to recognize her talent, or a temperamental, imperious and self-seeking star with lesser gifts; in *Volga-Volga*, the figures of Byvalov and Alyosha provide variants of all three.

The battle of the two musical styles that we see in *Volga-Volga* – between Alyosha and his classical orchestra, and Strelka with her amateur folk group – was also fundamental to the American movie tradition. Jane Feuer, in *The Hollywood Musical*, notes that 'the battle between popular and élite art was waged on every front in the musical'.[18] Indeed, 'as early as *The Broadway Melody* (1929), the first original MGM musical and the prototype for the backstage sub-genre, we are shown a fight between the conductor and the director over whether the music for the show should be played in highbrow or lowbrow fashion'.[19] Generally, this battle proceeds in parallel with the love plot; low and high are fused when the couple are finally joined. There are variants on this high/low dichotomy. For example, in the Gershwin musical *Shall We Dance?* of 1937, Ginger Rogers is a tap dancer while Fred Astaire is a ballet dancer who feels constricted in that form and longs to perform tap as well. But his rigid impresario forbids any such devolution from the high art form of ballet, and Ginger is unmoved by Astaire's entreaties to dance with him. When her heart is finally won over enough for her to agree to dance with him (which of course can only happen in New York), they perform numbers which combine ballet and tap.

The typical Hollywood musical generally favors 'the low' in the battle over musical styles, representing it as more spontaneous, more organic to the people. In noting this feature, Jane Feuer concludes that 'the Hollywood musical becomes a mass art which aspires to the condition of a folk art, produced and consumed by the same integrated community'. To this end, she notes the 'enshrining of [pseudo]-spontaneous over-engineered effects, the masking of choreography and rehearsals, the creation of amateur entertainment to cancel professionalism'.[20] Thus, for example, dancers or singers characteristically use props that appear to be 'at hand', and not provided for in the choreography.[21]

The battle of musical genres is a particular variant of what Rick Altman, in his book *The American Film Musical*, sees as the fundamental structure of the American musical and terms the 'dual focus'. By this, he means the dichotomy between two characters, generally the principals in the love plot, each of whom represents a different set of values. The film proceeds by jumping back and forth from one point of focus to the other, generally showing each of the two principals involved in either parallel or contrasting activity.[22] In *Volga-Volga* the dual focus – on Strelka and Alyosha – propels the narrative forward as each sets off with his or her ensemble for the Moscow Olympiad, each on a different form of river conveyance, and each competing to get there first, and to have his/her form of music prevail.

Both kinds of musical project a sense of community centered on an ensemble of performers. Both chart the progressive fusing among members of the ensemble, and its triumph also represents the moment of greatest unity among them. Thus, in projecting a sense of community, they are mediating the transition from a *Gemeinschaft* to a *Gesellschaft*. The hero or heroine comes from the provinces – from small-town America/from Melkovodsk – but on the way to success, because his/her city life is shown largely in terms of an ensemble and its audience, most of the complexity and alienation endemic to the big city are not shown.

Therefore a journey and a symbolic locus characterize both. Of course, there are differences. Moscow is not New York. In the two traditions of the musical, these two cities function as the most representative loci in their respective countries; in each instance, only success in that particular city really counts. Both cities are often used to embody the entire country, but, as such, each city defines the country in a different way. New York may be the premier American city and capital of capitals, while Moscow was the Soviet city and world capital of Communism, but Moscow was also the capital city, as New York was not. Moscow was also the center of an authoritarian state. During the 1930s Moscow was rebuilt, in a sort of Haussmannesque moment. As with Hitler's Berlin and Mussolini's Rome, Moscow was to become a showcase for the nation. The 'new Moscow' was also to be the model for the new socialist society. Once the grandiose plans for rebuilding Moscow were launched, the capital assumed a major role in Stalinist rhetoric as a synecdoche for the state itself. Hence, the journey from Melkovodsk to

Moscow in *Volga-Volga* also represents the conflict between spontaneous self-expression and control.

As with Hitler's grandiose plans for Berlin, however, the design for Moscow was only ever partially realized. Hence in the film, all we actually see of the capital is the newly constructed river station that emerges as a sort of fantastic portal to a fantastic place. As the Melkovodsk group approaches, the expanse of water suddenly widens and the audience feels as if it is approaching what one critic has described as a modern-day Venice.[23] The outside plaza of the river station functions as the end point, the final stage of the performers' journey. Here the Olympiad is held. But this locus of 'totalitarian ritual' bears little resemblance to the Nuremberg arena of Leni Riefenstahl's *Triumph of the Will* – or, for that matter, to the parades on Red Square. At the river station, one finds a surprisingly impromptu event which has the air of an uncoordinated town meeting. Often neither the master of ceremonies, nor any apparent program, dictates what is to be performed on stage.

This seems to be suspension of the reality of a totalitarian state which is typically associated with alienation, regimentation, loss of individuality and powerlessness. Schulte-Sasse makes an observation about Nazi cinema that seems particularly pertinent here. In *Entertaining the Third Reich* she points out that 'what is "going on" in Nazi cinema is to be found not only in its ideological patterns but in a broader social-psychological function that encompasses and transcends ideology ... societies "invent" social fantasies to mask the impossibility of ideals by which they identify themselves'.[24] As with Feuer's account of the Hollywood musical, one should perhaps question the suggestion of conscious agency here – 'societies invent' – however, the element of 'social fantasy' in this film is clear.

Jane Feuer sees the Hollywood musical as a genre which

> perceives the gap between producer and consumer, the breakdown of community designated by the very distinction between performer and audience, as a form of cinematic original sin. The musical seeks to bridge the gap by putting up 'community' as an ideal concept ... The musical ... creat[es] humanistic 'folk' relations in the films; these folk relations in turn act to cancel out the economic values and relations associated with mass-produced art. Through such a rhetorical exchange, the creation of folk relations *in* the films cancels out the mass entertainment substance *of* the films. The Hollywood musical becomes a mass art which aspires to the condition of folk art, produced and consumed by the same integrated community.[25]

If, as in Feuer's account, the Hollywood musical tries to gloss over its profit motive, then it could be said that the Stalinist musical glosses over its power motive. *Volga-Volga* may use many of the strategies and general plot line of the classical Hollywood musical but this is a case of appropriation of a genre rather than one of imitation. In addition to promoting specific items in the current 'Party line', such as the antimodernist campaign, and the advancement of the amateur and folk, *Volga-Volga* provides a parable about the formation of the Stalinist subject, which I have identified as the defining feature of socialist realism.[26] Understandably, being a musical comedy, this film presents a somewhat singular version of this parable.

An unkind joke about Soviet socialist realist culture has it that it is essentially about boy-meets-tractor. Another stereotype, our sense of the Soviet woman formed by Ernst Lubitsch's *Ninotchka* that appeared one year after *Volga-Volga* (1939), is of a sexless, grim, humorless zealot (read non-consumerist woman). Why, then, is this film all about girl-with-song-meets-stage-in-Moscow? Why does Strelka not bring her 'tractor' to Moscow, that is, her production achievement? Why does she not meet Stalin there (as, for example, in Mikhail Chiaurelli's classic of socialist realism, *The Vow* (*Kliatva*), in which the heroes take a tractor to Moscow and, when it breaks down on Red Square, Stalin emerges to fix it), or at least meet some Stalin surrogate in the form of a high official or party leader? And why does she not, as was a convention of socialist realism, have a local mentor, some party official or manager (who is also a party member) to guide her on her way? The two potential surrogates for Stalin in the film, Byvalov as the Melkovosk potentate, and the master of ceremonies of the Moscow Olympiad, are totally inadequate to fulfill these two functions. Is this an example of what Rentschler points to in Nazi film, a recognition of what the box office will not accept?

Arguably, such glaring omissions are not just because Aleksandrov's assigned task was a soft, not a hard, sell of Soviet life and doctrine. His orders were essentially to produce a Soviet variant of the American musical and hence he appropriated, with inevitable modifications, many of its conventions. The plot of *Volga-Volga* reworks the Marxist-Leninist account of historical progress in a way that, as will be shown, fits within the socialist realist tradition but reworks some key paradigms to achieve a parable that represents more fundamental values of Stalinist culture than economic achievement.

VOLGA-VOLGA AS A SOCIALIST REALIST PARABLE

In Soviet history, the 1930s were essentially a time of nation building. It was then that the main legitimizing myths of the Stalinist state cohered in their final form. It was then that Moscow was rebuilt as the grand socialist capital. And it was then that most attention was paid to the formation of citizens for the state. Arguably, *Volga-Volga* is a parable about this process, about state formation presented as entertainment and through entertainment.

The entertainers in the film undertake a highly symbolic journey to Moscow. In this way, as it were, they mediate the gap between the limited consciousness of ordinary Soviet citizens and the state and party-oriented consciousness that characterizes the realization of Communism. Given this mythic dimension to the entertainers' river journey, it is not surprising that the film has a certain fuzziness about space, and especially about calendric time. For example, the telegram from Moscow never specifies the date of the Olympiad. As the paddle steamer sets out, there are indications of a journey scheduled in time. As the paddle turns, titles are superimposed announcing that days one and two of a six-day period have elapsed, but then later the same sequence of dates is repeated, making a mockery of calendric time. Actual time elapsed is otherwise very vague. There seems no need to meet a timetable, only to attain a spatial goal. When the Melkovodsk contingent arrives, after a host of misadventures that delay them, the Olympiad is already in progress and all are waiting for the 'author' of the song.

This haziness about calendric time is possibly due to the fact that the spatial dimension has assumed all the symbolic weight. Although Strelka and Alyosha's journey to Moscow is ostensibly to participate in the Olympiad, its underlying purpose is to mediate spatially the temporal distance between here and now and the Communist future. In the film, as in Soviet rhetoric, Moscow functions as the symbolic locus of the Communist utopia achieved; the provincial town, as its opposite, embodies an earlier stage in historical progression. This is a basic pattern of most of the films and novels of the Soviet era.

The temporal dimension is captured in the names. Melkovodsk – which means literally 'shallow waters' – essentially represents the backward Russia of the pre-revolutionary era which is having trouble crossing into the new era.[27] It is also suggested in the names of the two characters: Byvalov, or 'has-been', versus Strelka, denoting both an 'arrow' – the arrow of time – and an indicator or clock hand. She is moving forward purposefully and at a high speed.

There are essentially three loci in the film that embody three different times, each representing a stage in the Marxist-Leninist account of historical progress. Melkovodsk and the lower reaches of the river where progress is primitive and slow represent old Russia. The second locus, which symbolizes the present with its high technological level, provides a panorama of river banks dotted with giant industrial plants. This serves as a prelude to the Moscow–Volga Canal, which ushers the Melkovodsk group into that wide expanse of water heralding the approaches to Moscow. The river station (Moscow) is already the locus of the future.

Besides this slowing of time, the sort of hard work that seems so central to the Stalinist ethos is markedly downplayed in the film. All is dance and song, even the brief interlude of choreographed work on the timber barge. Of course, this was in the tradition of the musical where, as Feuer remarks, 'At last the world had become a stage.'[28] But the Soviet world was indeed more of a stage.

This tendency to understate work intensifies as the Melkovodsk performers approach Moscow; they also drift out of real time in the sense that they enter more and more into a world of leisure (and luxury). They pass yachts on which sailors are stretched out languidly, and the group are themselves transferred to a truly luxurious cruise boat (Strelka gets a stateroom all to herself). Industrialization and industrial labor which have thus far received only the briefest treatment fade completely. Time has stood still, and the performers have entered a sort of land of Cockaigne.

But this land is not entirely idyllic. Military uniforms are increasingly evident in the landscape. Strelka herself puts on an oversized naval uniform when she gets soaking wet after an adventure in the water, a comic moment making her look like a clown and the military seem benign. Similarly, her song about the Volga, ostensibly an ode to nature, in effect celebrates the Soviet Union's imperial might represented spatially. As is clear at several points in the film, as well as the song, the Volga stands for the nation. Its characterization, contained in a nutshell in the last line of the chorus, comprises three terse adjectives: 'Broad, deep, strong.' These adjectives ostensibly convey physical qualities of the river, but clearly encapsulate the might of the Soviet state. Indeed, the Russian adjective for 'broad' here – *shiroko* – might in this context be translated more accurately as 'vast'. The same adjective opens the theme song for Aleksandrov's previous musical comedy, *The Circus* of 1936, which runs 'Vast is my native land'. This latter song enjoyed the curious distinction of having been one of the greatest hits of the 1930s, while simultaneously functioning as a sort of unofficial second national anthem; the Kremlin chimes which were used like London's Big Ben as Moscow's leitmotif (played each night as the radio signed off) were changed to ring out the tune of this opening line. In both songs, the country's extraordinary physical dimensions are a guarantee of its extraordinary stature as a nation. Yet, as Strelka's song also notes, so many songs about the Volga had been composed but none had done justice to its reality. Thus, the new age and new nation required a new song.

In musicals, song often functions as the cement that bonds a community. As Feuer remarks: 'Often the plots of these backstage musicals take as their theme the need for community within the world of the stage. Within the society of the theatrical company, personal greed (usually embodied in a temperamental star) may stand as an obstacle to the show's success.'[29] In *Volga-Volga*, an analogous role is played by Byvalov as the self-seeking bureaucrat who does not have the collective's best interests at heart; the performers' integration and their adoption of the song represent the consolidation of society at large.

It should be noted that there is nothing intrinsically Soviet about composing such a parable of nation building around a song which is embraced by increasingly wider circles of the populace. Jean Renoir, in *The Marseillaise* made in 1937, demonstrates how in late eighteenth-century France the new revolutionary nation was built out of disparate groups of supporters as the song 'The Marseillaise' somehow emerged from people converging on Paris from disparate regions and backgrounds. In Renoir's film, discussion of the meaning of the Revolution – as shown in a heated debate among the citizenry of Marseilles – can only generate conflict of opinion and cannot effect such a strong sense of bonding among fellow citizens. However, it should be noted that in the Renoir film the song itself is authorless; it appears to well up among the Revolution's supporters.

In most works of socialist realism, as the text or film moves toward its finale, tension mounts over whether, despite all manner of unexpected obstacles, the collective will meet its production or construction goal or, alternatively, whether it can prevail over the enemy in an impending struggle. In *Volga-Volga*, however, the tension leading up to the film's climax is over the true identity of the author of the song about the Volga, and when it will be revealed – even though everyone there is already singing the song and working on their own arrangements of it. The reporters who have come to the Olympiad are all converging excitedly, not, as was more typical, to photograph and interview a Stakhanovite producer, but to see the 'author' (*avtor*) of a song. The trophy of the Olympiad is going not to the best performers, but to the best song.

VOLGA-VOLGA AS A PARABLE ABOUT AUTHORSHIP

Authentic authorship was arguably of greater concern in Soviet culture of the 1930s than even economic achievement. Particularly striking in this film is the extent to which written texts play a crucial role, even though it is ostensibly about the triumph of the folk (meaning the oral tradition).[30] Crucial to authorship in this film – and here it differs from the conventions of the American musical – is recording the composition in writing, an act that leads to the song's broad dissemination.

This is no trivial detail. The Soviet 1930s were an age of letters when writing emerged as one of the most prestigious occupations. Possibly, this was because the country had become literate by then, whereas in the 1920s the masses had still been largely illiterate. Though the increase in literacy was a factor in the emphasis on letters, it was also connected with permanence, rationalization and consolidation (as well as respectability). Foucault and others have pointed to the historical link between power and writing. Angel Rama has argued in *The Lettered City*, drawing on the example of colonial Latin America, that lettered culture, the culture of scribes and literati alike, has often played a central role whenever a state has sought to impose its own single order on a disparate populace. The special role assumed by texts was symptomatic of a new phase of consolidation and legitimization which the regime entered around 1931 after the upheavals of collectivization and the cultural revolution.

The Soviet 1930s were framed and punctuated by the successive publication of authoritative texts, some from the Marxist legacy, others newly generated. (Here one might mention in particular some of the texts associated with Stalin, such as the Constitution of 1936, and the *Short Course of Party History* from 1938.)

In the 1930s, the Stalinist state had a hierarchy based on power over texts. This was reflected in terms of who had, and who had not, access to written documents. Thus, for example, a big Party boss or industrial manager in Siberia would receive weekly dispatches from Moscow which could be read by him alone. He would give a closed-session address to his immediate subordinates based on their content, but they could never read the original. This kind of scenario, which was endemic to Stalinist practice, is parodied early in the film when Byvalov tries to compose a response to his telegram from Moscow and labels it 'completely confidential' – the translation here should perhaps have read 'top secret' – but he is obliged to impart it orally to a large group of townsfolk.

Many of the moments in the plot connected with the question of authorship use motifs that in conventional theater and film are usually found in events in the love plot. For example, the duel between the lovers Strelka and Alyosha is not just over high- versus lowbrow music, as in so many American musicals, but also about authorship. Similarly, Strelka throws herself on to her bed in the stateroom in a highly emotional state, not, as one might expect, because she is rejected in love, but because there is a crisis about her identity as author. And when Strelka wants Alyosha to understand that she is the true author, she changes into (what one presumes to be) her best ruffled dress, which is unlike any outfit she has worn before. In other words, she dresses as if for an important date with her beau; but this act also conveys the social reality that authors in Stalinist Russia were among the privileged élite and she would have had to dress the part to be recognized. It is, moreover, only when Strelka finally reveals to Alyosha that she is the actual author of the song about the Volga that he declares his love for her.

At this point it might be appropriate to examine the question of gender roles in this film, especially in regard to Strelka. As was generally true of the Hollywood musical (with some exceptions such as the films of Fred Astaire), *Volga-Volga* has as its lead a female performer. However, Strelka effectively combines, or more accurately alternates, masculine and feminine roles, a pattern that roughly corresponds to alternating from pants to dress. Even Soviet criticism has noted how a more commanding, masculine self generally took precedence over the feminine: 'Together with a touching naivety, and feminine trust and subordination which we see in the mail carrier from Melkovodsk there is also a feistiness [*aktivnost*] ... She is not intimidated by the shouting of superiors ... She is a person of the new type, she fights courageously and stands up for her opinion to the end, wins out, and exposes the primitive and fatuous nature of Byvalov.'[31]

Strelka not only withstands bureaucratic and physical obstacles, in the best traditions of the socialist realist hero (who, in the 1930s, was almost always masculine), but she also appears larger than life. She can perform the routines of everyone in her group, and she can compose a song that will captivate one and all. Thus, she is essentially a mythological figure; the 'Song of the Volga' speaks of fairy tale becoming real (again, a confusion of the legend and the reality), and in this it prefigures the unfolding of the plot. But Strelka as effective commander of her group is more than just a fairy-tale princess; she is also an author, and in that sense a local version of the great author Stalin. Inasmuch as she provides an example of the way that, in the new society, even the most lowly can become elevated – can become authors – she illustrates the Leninist maxim, 'Every female cook will rule the state.'

It should be noted that neither Byvalov nor Strelka can read or write music. Byvalov is unconcerned about this (another mark of his unworthiness), but Strelka realizes that her song can only be truly legitimate if it can be rendered in written form. She enlists the help of Alyosha's musicians, thus taking a first step toward resolving the conflict between the two performing groups (read, between the intelligentsia and the people – as it were, the 'people' have the inspiration, and the function of the intelligentsia is to be the afflatus of folk creativity). However, disaster strikes when a storm blows all the copies of the song into the river. Strelka is distraught – 'The song is lost', she wails. In reality, of course, the song is not lost since she is its composer and remembers it still. What is lost is the written record of the song, which becomes crucial in determining the future course of events. Copies of it are recovered from the river by a variety of people – a worker hoists it up on the hook of a crane, the people in yachts pluck it casually out of the water, and so on. In this way, the song reaches ever broader circles of the population.

This episode – which might even be called a Gutenberg moment – takes the film into a sort of higher gear, a different spatio-temporal plane. As the crane swings up with its cargo of the text, the camera pans upward to reveal an entire panorama of factories hugging the river's shore, symbolizing the new industrialized and modernized Russia. In other words, the film shifts to the second spatio-temporal plane mentioned earlier. It is also at this point that the entrance of the Volga–Moscow canal emerges and the Melkovodsk performers begin their journey through a great white way that will lead them to the wonderland of Moscow (the third, and ultimate, spatio-temporal plane). As they approach Moscow they are confronted with the results of dissemination of the song's lyrics (of which they had been unaware): on every passing ship groups on deck are singing Strelka's song, but each group uses a different arrangement – jazz, martial and so on.

Literature played a major role in the Stalinist system of the 1930s. In addition to official documents and authoritative historical or theoretical writings, professionally generated literature was used to systematize reality (Bolshevik experience), and also to manufacture subjects for the state – functions it was most explicitly assigned during this period. As Zhdanov, the party spokesman at the First Writers Congress in 1934, put it, writers were to become 'engineers of human souls'. In addition to 'engineering' a transformation in ordinary citizens by means of literary works, those in power tried to 'engineer' this transformation by having ordinary citizens write of their own experiences. However, as Skip Gates has argued in *The Signifying Monkey* for the case of the slave narrative, a text with an analogous function, this kind of writing inevitably involves in large measure inscribing the 'self' into a pre-existing narrative. In the case of these Soviet texts, allegedly based on individuals' experiences, their 'authors' were to be guided in composing them by authorized Marxist and historical writings, on the one hand, and by professional writers on the other. Memory was 'corrected' to conform to the texts.

Byvalov establishes his unworthiness in part by revealing his ignorance of literature. When Strelka tells him how well a local talent recites Lermontov's 'Demon', his immediate response is that you can't say that word in public. Thus this moment serves a dual purpose by exposing his ignorance while simultaneously parodying the mentality of the purge era. This decade was one of textual anxiety in general, of concern for textual purity. Texts played a crucial role in all aspects of purging.

It should be remembered that the two years when this film was made and released (1937–38) mark the worst period of the great purge. Indeed, two of the principal creators of this film themselves fell victim to the purges. The cameraman, Vladimir Nielsen, was not able to see the film through to its completion. He was arrested a few days after returning from shooting in September 1937, and perished in 1942. His name disappeared from the film's credits until he was rehabilitated under Khrushchev in 1956. The principal scriptwriter, Nikolai Erdman, was likewise purged in the late 1930s, though he was able to return in 1942 (the film director Sergei Iutkevich claims he was able to have him brought back to work for his NKVD troupe).

Not surprisingly, in this upbeat comedy the purges do not receive explicit treatment, but there are frequent implicit references among the many puns and quips in Erdman's text, most of which are lost in translation or obscure to the uninitiated viewer. But two aspects are treated obliquely. First, the whole film was essentially commissioned to celebrate the completion of the Volga–Moscow Canal, a massive project connected with the rebuilding of Moscow, which was opened in 1937. Much of this project was built by convict labor. Indeed, in its closing phases the project was supervised directly by the NKVD, and when it was completed many of its top officials received the Order of Lenin for their services.[32]

The 'Gutenberg moment' coincides with the moment when the entrance to the canal comes into view. The work of the NKVD, as it were, channels individuals into proper citizens. The walls on either side of the canal, as it were, guide the steamer along the correct route – or confine it. It is significant how the locks of this canal are presented in the film. As the group's steamer passes through them, the camera focuses on the gates opening for the steamer to enter, as if the canal presents citizens with an opportunity, rather than the gates closing behind them, a gesture with ominous associations. Our two lovers have a privileged view of the canal through a great picture window at the fore of the luxury steamer.

The rhetoric of the purge era urged everyone to look more closely at those around them, to 'tear off each and every mask' in order to reveal the true person concealed beneath; they were to be 'vigilant' in unmasking 'enemies of the people'. The key elements of this scenario have been appropriated for the story of Strelka's song and her relationship to Alyosha. When she decides to reveal her authorship to him and appears in a new dress, she instructs him to 'look closely' (*vnimatel'no*), assuming that he will see the true author beneath. And when she arrives at the Olympiad with the entire audience demanding to know who is the author of the song, she decides to confess that she had lied earlier, and that she is, in fact, the author. 'Don't confess', implores Alyosha, now effectively her fiancé. But she does. 'Do with me what you will', she says, 'but it was I who wrote that song.' Here she parodies that insidious Soviet institution of confessing one's political sins before the collective, but the film's audience knows that, in this case, confession will lead not to punishment, but to just rewards, in fact to acclaim. Thus the act is presented in a favorable light. Strelka, having confessed, then renders the song of the Volga with passion, as if presenting her own defense. In a sense, we have in this scene a true realization of the term 'show trial'.

It should be noted that in the most famous of the show trials, that of Bukharin, Rykov and others held in the same year as the film was made, 1938, the exchange between Bukharin, the chief defendant, and the chief prosecutor Vyshinskii can be analyzed in terms of a debate over the authority for textual exegesis. Here, however, it is no problem. 'Strelka, listen to this', says a mere boy on the Olympiad podium wearing a pioneer's red scarf, and he proceeds to conduct an orchestra which plays her song 'according to my arrangement' (of crashing chords). What follows in the film is largely fun and caper as Strelka disappears under the judges' table to change out of the sailor's suit she had been lent – a touch of levity for which, incidentally, Aleksandrov has been criticized. When a frantic search fails to produce Strelka, the Melkovodsk collective renders the song without her. Byvalov tries to tag along, and even to dominate by stepping forward to perform a section of the song solo, but all he can do is croak. He seems, incidentally, to be the only member of the Melkovodsk group who has no talent for singing, and this lack of merit as a performer seals his fate. 'Clear the decks', one of the group calls, parodying an earlier moment when Byvalov had told Strelka's group they had to get off the steamer before it set out from Melkovodsk for Moscow. But the 'clear' used here (*ochistit'*) has the same root as the word for a purge (*chistka*). And, if we should fail to catch the meaning of that event, the group, once reunited with Strelka, sings an ostensibly playful song that tells the audience the moral of what they have just seen. Fortunately, there are not too many like Byvalov, they say, but if you find one all you need is a broom (to sweep him away). That taken care of, they cluster under the emblem of the Soviet state for a brief final rendition of the song.

This moment corresponds to the finale of the classical American musical when, as Jane Feuer puts it, 'The couple is frozen into an eternal embrace, the show frozen into a perpetually triumphant curtain call.'[33] We should note, however, that in this scene Strelka essentially blends in with the collective; she is not foregrounded as the star, nor does she conduct, nor is she paired with Alyosha as part of the loving couple. This reminds us of a moment slightly earlier. When no one could find Strelka (who was under the table) and the Melkovodsk contingent had to sing the song without her, the master of ceremonies said: 'It is not who wrote the song, but the song itself, that matters.' This remark seems curious in light of all the frantic efforts earlier to establish who the author was. But, essentially, in these closing moments Strelka's image shifts from that of a folk genius – the romantic version – to an earlier model for creativity, that of an afflatus. It matters not who the composer is because the song is already there. It has been composed by true authors. All that remains is for it to be rendered in infinite variations. Spontaneity, or creativity, can thrive in a society governed by a single text. In *Volga-Volga*, progressively more and more of reality is suffused with a single song.

Let us return momentarily to a much earlier moment in the film. When, back in Melkovodsk, Strelka tries to convince Byvalov that the town has talent and, to prove it, sings Tatyana's aria from *Eugene Onegin* as an example of what a particular member of her group can do, Byvalov dismisses her claim saying: 'In order to sing like that, you would have to study for 20 years.' He, of course, appears ridiculous because the song has just been 'sung like that' by an untutored performer, and 20 years sounds like an exaggeration. But it should be noted that in 1937, the year that *Volga-Volga* was filmed, the country was celebrating the 20th anniversary of the Revolution.

In effect, then, the country had been training for 20 years on its citizens' behalf and now they could sing its song so well that all could be 'frozen into a perpetually triumphant curtain call'. In short, *Volga-Volga* was genuinely popular, genuinely great mass entertainment, yet fundamentally ideological in both direct and indirect ways. It was very Soviet, yet drew on the conventions of the American musical comedy, as well as on those of the Russian avant-garde. This poor man's *Showboat* wedded to slapstick comedy was completely Party-line, yet occasional subtle details permit alternative readings.

NOTES

1. Eric Rentschler, *The Ministry of Illusion: Nazi Cinema and Its Afterlife* (Cambridge, MA: Harvard University Press, 1996), p. 7.
2. Ibid., p. 9.
3. Ibid., p. 16.
4. Ibid., p. 100.
5. R. Iurenev, *Sovetskaia kinokomediia* (Moscow: Nauka, 1964), p. 191.
6. G.V. Aleksandrov, *Epokha i kino* (Moscow: Politicheskaia literatura, 1976), p. 159.
7. P.I. Frolov, *Grigorii Aleksandrov* (Moscow: Iskusstvo, 1976), p. 21; Aleksandrov, *Epokha i kino*, p. 163.
8. Iurenev, *Sovetskaia kinokomediia*, p. 5 describes it as a '*blestiashchii primer*' of socialist realist comedy, defined as *sochetanie satiricheskogo otritsaniia s radostnym utverzhdeniem.*'

9. Ibid., p. 445.
10. Aleksandrov, *Epokha i kino*, p. 208.
11. Ibid.
12. The contrasting backgrounds of the husband and wife team of Aleksandrov (director) and Orlova (star) who made all four of these musicals provide a further striking example of this hybridity. Aleksandrov himself was of working-class background from Ekaterinburg (Sverdlovsk) in the Urals, one of many in the arts whose careers were essentially created by the Revolution. Indeed, he was originally sent to Moscow in the early 1920s by the secret police (Cheka), having worked in their cultural club. By contrast, Liubov Orlova, the heart-throb of the 1930s screen, was the offspring of a minor branch of the noble Orlov family. She grew up in the environs of Moscow where her parents moved in intellectual circles and she was given lessons in all branches of the performing arts. A curious detail in one so closely associated with Soviet culture was that Orlova, throughout her life, used the old, pre-Bolshevik calendar for reckoning dates.
13. [Unsigned], 'Sumbur vmesto muzyki', *Pravda*, 28 Jan. 1936, p. 3.
14. One should also note the extent to which circus routines, which Meyerhold and many others in the avant-garde saw as a vital source of 'theatricality', enter into the performances by Strelka's amateur group.
15. F. Starr, *Red and Hot: The Fate of Jazz in the Soviet Union 1917–1991* (New York: Limelight, 1994).
16. For example, the singing waiter in the Melkovodsk restaurant is reminiscent of Charlotte Greenwood, a star of American comedy films. For an account of her and other relevant material, see H. Jenkins, *What Made Pistachio Nuts* (New York: Columbia University Press, 1992), *passim*.
17. This theme, particularly characteristic of the 'backstage musical', is discussed in Jane Feuer, *The Hollywood Musical*, 2nd edn (Bloomington/Indianapolis, IN: Indiana University Press, 1993), pp. 19–20.
18. Feuer, *Hollywood Musical*, p. 55.
19. Ibid., p. 62.
20. Ibid., pp. 3, 15.
21. A particularly good example of this in *Volga-Volga* would be the routines of the staff at the Melkovodsk restaurant.
22. R. Altman, *The American Film Musical* (Bloomington and Indianapolis, IN: Indiana University Press, 1987), esp. pp. 16–58.
23. O.L. Bulgakova, 'Prostranstvennye figury sovetskogo kino 30-kh godov', *Kinovedcheskie zapiski* 29 (1995), p. 57.
24. Linda Schulte-Sasse, *Entertaining the Third Reich: Illusions of Wholeness in Nazi Cinema* (Durham, NC/London: Duke University Press, 1996), p. 6.
25. Feuer, *Hollywood Musical*, p. 3.
26. Katerina Clark, *The Soviet Novel: History As Ritual* (Bloomington, IN: Indiana University Press, 2000).
27. It should also be noted that the progress of the two boats proceeding to Moscow is held up as both hit sandbanks (*meli*).
28. Feuer, *Hollywood Musical*, p. 89.
29. Ibid., p. 17.
30. An obvious example is the '*molniia*', or telegram, that sends the Melkovodsk performers to Moscow.
31. Frolov, *Grigorii Aleksandrov*, p. 85.
32. As mentioned earlier, Aleksandrov first made his mark in Ekaterinburg producing work in the cultural club of the Cheka, the predecessor of the NKVD. Significantly, perhaps, his chief rival as maker of musical comedies in the 1930s, Ivan Pyriev, also worked there.
33. Feuer, *Hollywood Musical*, p. 87.

9

The Symphony as Mode of Production: Shostakovich's Fourth Symphony and the End of the Romantic Narrative

BORIS GASPAROV

Shostakovich completed his Fourth Symphony in autumn 1936, soon after the official denunciation of his opera *Lady Macbeth of Mtsensk District*.[1] As the atmosphere grew increasingly oppressive, and his music was criticized and condemned, the composer eventually decided to withdraw his new symphony from rehearsals; its premiere took place 25 years later, in 1961. Nevertheless, it was the Fourth Symphony that marked, more clearly than any other Shostakovich work of that time, a watershed in his development as a composer. It signified the end of an early period that comprised approximately ten years of Shostakovich's creative work and was characterized by a radical avant-garde style and bold experimentation with genres and musical forms. In particular, the Fourth opened a distinct new period in Shostakovich's symphonic writing, whose chronological boundaries roughly coincided with the epoch of 'high Stalinism'. The last symphony belonging to this line, the Tenth, was completed a few months after Stalin's death, in 1953. While his two previous symphonies, the Second (1927) and the Third (1932), departed radically from the traditional symphonic form (the Second was not even called a symphony in the beginning), the symphonies of Stalin's era (with the exception of the Ninth) clearly rejoined the tradition of the 'grand' symphony, which had been founded by Haydn and Mozart, fully developed by Beethoven, and which continued to evolve throughout the nineteenth and early twentieth centuries. Their expansive contours and many features of their musical form, including the dominance of the first movement, accorded well with this established genre. The first movement – the so-called sonata or symphonic *Allegro* – of Shostakovich's symphonies of his middle period in general, and of the Fourth in particular, will be the subject of this chapter.

The Fourth Symphony opens with a shrill signal – reminiscent of an alarm clock or a factory siren – which proclaims the beginning of a new work day. The sound is rendered by wind instruments playing in unison in the upper register, followed by the rattle of a xylophone. The motif of a siren, whistle or alarm clock to signify the start of a new day became popular in music and literature during the period of industrialization in the late 1920s and early 1930s, supplanting the traditional serenity of romantic dawns. It represented urbanism and industrialization, activity and productive labor and exhorted the newly awakened subject to hasten to meet the challenges of the day ahead. One of the most avant-garde pieces of the young Shostakovich – his Second Symphony written on the occasion of the tenth anniversary of the October Revolution – used an actual factory whistle to signal the beginning of the final apotheosis, which featured Bezymensky's exhortative verses sung by a chorus. Another work by the early Shostakovich, conveying the same motif verbally if not musically, was his famous 'Song about the Counter-Plan' from the film *The Counter-Plan* (*Vstrechnyi*) (Sergei Iutkevich, 1932), which became a musical symbol of industrialization. The song exudes a spirit of energy and optimism with which its protagonists anticipate the labors of the coming day. It features a young worker who teases his female comrade: 'Don't sleep, wake up, curly head / with the toll of its factories / the country is arising joyfully to meet the coming day!' (*Ne spi, vstavai, kudriavaia / V tsekhakh, zveni, / Strana vstaet so slavoiu / Navstrechu dnia!*).

A similar motif appeared in the opening of Valentin Kataev's *Time, Forward!* written in the same year – one of the prototypes of the 'industrial' sub-genre of the socialist realist novel – which will be used in this chapter as the primary literary source. Like the film *The Counter-Plan*, Kataev's novel depicts heroic efforts to fulfill the First Five-Year Plan within four years. The novel commences with the second chapter – a literary device which entailed skipping a conventional opening in order to gain narrative time. It begins as follows:

> The first chapter is omitted for the time being.
> II.
> The alarm clock rattled like a tin of bonbons. The alarm clock was cheap, painted brown, of Soviet manufacture.
> Half-past six.
> The clock was accurate. But Margulies was not asleep. He rose at six, in order to beat the clock.[2]

Margulies, a young engineer at one of the grandiose construction sites of the First Five-Year Plan, had every reason to race with time. The previous evening he had learned that his colleagues at a plant in

THE SYMPHONY AS MODE OF PRODUCTION

Khar'kov had set a new world record: they had produced 306 allotments of concrete during an eight-hour shift; Margulies' team's best result had been 206. The novel describes one day in the life of Margulies and his companions – workers, foremen, scientists, journalists, his girlfriend Shura – spent in a frantic attempt to beat Khar'kov. At the end of the day, they produce 426 allotments of concrete. Completely exhausted, their clothes and the skin of their hands torn to shreds, without having eaten, washed or been to the toilet, they still have to spend a good part of the night extinguishing a fire lit by a saboteur. The last thing Margulies overhears shortly before the dawn, half asleep in Shura's arms, is the latest dispatch about a new record that has just been set in Cheliabinsk: 504 allotments of concrete. And so it continues until the next morning and its alarm clock. The relentless race against time is completely circular.

Kataev's heroes and the subjects of Shostakovich's early music performed their feats amidst great physical hardship, a hectic environment and physical danger. But they seemed to have accepted those adverse conditions as inherent to the new era of industrialization and collectivity, something never reflected upon, let alone protested. Kataev persistently compares the construction site with a battlefield, which makes all the grim and oppressive moments experienced by his characters seem appropriate and even natural. When a young worker's hand is severely injured in an accident, it is presented matter-of-factly: a comrade is wounded, he is given first aid and promptly taken away (time is precious), and is never seen again. Time continues to fly, leaving little opportunity for dwelling on the past. The only follow-up to this episode is Shura's cursory question to Margulies: 'What do you think? Will they be able to salvage his hand?' – to which Margulies replies: 'Don't know.'

In the same vein, the deliberate shrillness and discordant sound of avant-garde music conveyed a mood celebrating the harsh urban or industrial environment. This trait was by no means confined to Soviet avant-garde aesthetics. A composition for orchestra whose cacophonous clash of voices and deafening crescendos recreated the sounds and rhythms of the approaching technological era was a device that had gained considerable popularity since the late 1910s. It was eagerly embraced by by musicians of the Italian futurist school; Luigi Russolo (a painter and amateur musician) advocated 'noises' as the new medium of music[3] and tried, rather naively, to realize his theory in compositions under suggestive titles, such as 'Awakening of a City' (*Risveglio di una Città*), which used altered sounds of musical instruments alongside 'natural' urban noises. Perhaps the most famous example of that genre was Honegger's *Pacific 231*, a piece that recreated, by conventional and some unconventional orchestral means, the sounds of a speeding transcontinental train. Shostakovich's own Second and Third Symphonies belonged to the same genre.

Another archetypal feature of the avant-garde aesthetic was the creation of a compartmentalized, patchwork form which sharply departed from, and even deliberately destroyed, literary and musical narrative principles of the nineteenth century. Characteristic of these principles was an uninterrupted development throughout the whole extended piece, be it a novel or a symphony. The nineteenth-century novel had achieved a unity of form which would have been inconceivable for earlier examples of the genre. The same might be said of the nineteenth-century symphony *vis-à-vis* concerti grossi and suites of the previous century.

The twentieth century witnessed many attempts to overcome this legacy of nineteenth-century aesthetics. Accentuating the patchwork and piecemeal became staples of avant-garde art, emphatically expressed by Stravinsky,[4] Ravel, Bartok, the young Prokofiev and, of course, the young Shostakovich. Experiments with literary form in the 1910s and early 1920s, notably by Andrei Bely, Kafka and Joyce, also proceeded along these lines.

What distinguished the Fourth and all subsequent 'Stalin' symphonies by Shostakovich within this general trend was their profound affinity in rhetorical means to the romantic and early modernist 'grand' symphonies, especially those of Mahler and Tchaikovsky. However, it was precisely this inner resemblance that made Shostakovich's departure from that form particularly dramatic and poignantly revealing. The Fourth Symphony abandoned the more traditional avant-garde mold of a relatively short, programmatically oriented orchestral piece, to which the two preceding symphonies by Shostakovich were closely related. Instead, it incorporated relentless industrial-like sound and episodic, piecemeal development of its musical narrative into a symphonic *Allegro* with an extensive thematic development, which provided a narrative frame typical for the first movement of a traditional 'grand' symphony. This unusual combination of futurist sonorities and traditional large-scale symphonic drama was in a sense more devastating in its effect for the fundamental narrative principles of the previous century than the boldest avant-garde experiments of the preceding two decades.

Let us observe briefly how the musical narrative of the Fourth Symphony's first movement proceeds. The sounds of its opening pages, following the initial 'awakening' theme, once again evoke images of the industrial clatter and relentless rhythms of labor. However, this narrative topos, by that time familiar in avant-garde works, emerged in a different mood. Four years had passed since Shostakovich had produced the blowing cacophony of the Third Symphony and the innocent

THE SYMPHONY AS MODE OF PRODUCTION

exuberance of 'The Song about the Counter-Plan'. One of Shostakovich's official admirers stated in 1937, when the composer had already exculpated himself with his Fifth Symphony, that Shostakovich 'has come through a lot in his life and thoughts' (*'mnogoe perezhil i peredumal'*).[5] Even though when he began his Fourth Symphony he could not anticipate the crushing blow that would soon befall him, the change of mood, compared with earlier compositions, was remarkable. The unabashed optimism of the late 1920s and early 1930s gave way to a somber and sometimes outright ominous tone. The musical narrator of the Fourth Symphony appears to be becoming aware of the horrifying and menacing character of the world he is living in – as if suddenly awakened to its brutality and violence. All the discords of the avant-garde discourse suddenly lose their narcotic effect, laying bare their oppressive and menacing side.

The symphony's initial and main theme of a loosely shaped symphonic *Allegro* proceeds rapidly, in a mechanically persistent rhythm, to everincreasing intensity. New voices are continually added, the aural volume and register swell almost without any respite, eventually reaching piercing heights and deafening lows. The tension culminates in a march, whose relentless pace is even more horrifying than the frantic cacophony out of which it emerged. Throughout the entire extensive exposition of the main theme, as well as in all subsequent episodes in the *Allegro*'s development and recapitulation when it reappears, it never abandons either its compulsive rhythmical pace or the menacing aggressiveness of its sound.

Typically, the second theme displays an entirely different mood and musical language. Suddenly the music becomes muted, its pace slow and vague almost to the point of drowsiness. Solo instruments alternate with lengthy monologues, until a new relentless race, fiercer and more extended than the previous one, erupts, only to give way to another segment of eerie stasis.

One such episode, which follows a second exposition of the main theme, begins deceptively, with an ascending phrase of tremolo strings. The expectation of a lyrical outburst becomes stronger when the phrase quotes a poignantly lyrical passage from Tchaikovsky's *Italian Capriccio*. However, the would-be lyrical breakthrough gets stuck at the very beginning; the string phrase is repeated again and again, with ever-increasing speed, until it erupts into another fit of manic cacophony. Then, without any interlude, the music sinks into a stupor. A slow solo by the bassoon is followed by violas and violoncellos in unison, then first and second violins, then the bass clarinet, punctuated throughout by barely audible pizzicatos of the strings and dreamlike chords of the accompanying harp. Again, the whole protracted segment never deviates from its extremely slow pace, and subdued dynamic, dreamy, even somnolescent sonorities.

Throughout the whole of the first movement, the music vacillates between these two modes which, for all the apparent polarity of their mood and musical texture, resemble each other in their respective homogeneity. The movement proceeds as a chain of sustained episodes, each consistent in character and markedly distinct from the ones that precede and follow it.

Juxtapositioning a dynamic and extroverted main theme with a quieter and lyrical second theme is typical for an *Allegro* of the classical and romantic 'grand' symphony. And yet, the musical narrative of Shostakovich's symphonic *Allegro*, in spite of this outward similarity to the traditional form, departs from its underlying principles. While proceeding largely along the same formal categories that would shape a symphony by Mahler or Scriabin, the musical narrative of the Fourth Symphony undermines fundamental philosophical and psychological premises that underpinned the symphonic, as well as literary, tradition of the previous century.

Highly characteristic for that tradition was a narrative technique that rarely allowed prolonged spans of music homogeneous in mood and texture – at least, not in the first movements, and certainly not in their development. A sustained and lengthy ascendancy to a roaring fortissimo could appear in a scherzo of a symphony, or a sustained cantilena of a solo instrumental voice could take place in a slow movement. But the main feature of the first movement was dynamism and volatility of musical discourse that rendered sustained homogeneous episodes virtually impossible; this feature corresponded well to the *Allegro*'s function as the dramatic core of the whole symphony. The music evolved through continual shifts of texture, volume, intensity, and the number and character of participating voices. Each single episode appeared transient, almost precarious, its borders invaded, its mood undermined by contradictory voices, pushing in different directions, struggling, colliding, chasing each other in a never-ceasing commotion. A beautiful cantilena of first violins could be punctuated by a worrisome ostinato of the basses that eventually pushed its way into the foreground, disrupting the lyrical monologue. Confessionary exclamations of the strings would be haunted by dry-sounding echoes of the winds. A blasting juggernaut of the brass would suddenly appear on a collision course with the rejoicing or lamenting voice of the strings, and so on. Innumerable examples of such and similar rhetorical devices can be found in symphonic scores from the nineteenth and early twentieth centuries, from Beethoven and Schubert, Schumann and Berlioz, to Brahms and Bruckner, Tchaikovsky and Mahler, Scriabin and Sibelius.

THE SYMPHONY AS MODE OF PRODUCTION

This point may be illustrated by a few well-known examples. At the beginning of Beethoven's *Eroica* (1803), the main theme is far from being unequivocally 'heroic' throughout its exposition. Instead, it passes through a complicated and contradictory development, in which different moods and voices interact and struggle to get the upper hand, each receding momentarily and giving way to a competing voice. An initial upbeat introduction of the theme by the violoncellos is interrupted by interrogatory phrases of the violins before reaching a conclusion. The violins, in turn, yield to a pastorale-like echo of the theme played by the winds. Several short remarks from different orchestral groups follow, as if the theme is unsure what character to assume. These hesitant replies are underscored by a succession of chords, which become increasingly more assertive, until they come to the foreground, and finally erupt into the full climax of the initial theme. But even at this point, the theme's heroic simplicity is not permitted to reign supreme; while its diatonic contour is emphatically proclaimed by the brass, it is punctuated and soon overcome by frantic exclamations of the strings. The heroic mood dissipates as quickly as it has erupted, giving way to the second theme, which emerges as a dialogue between the flute, horn, oboe and violins. Although pastoral in its general character, the second theme, due to rapid changes of voice and register, proceeds as an intricate and ever-changing interplay of different moods and colors. All this perpetual whirlwind of ever-changing emotional states and struggling voices barely takes one and a half minutes.

Another example is the main theme of the first movement of Tchaikovsky's Fourth Symphony (1878). The theme begins as a mournful lyrical monologue. Its orchestral color (first violins), slow tempo, subdued dynamic, a long descending pace of the melody punctuated by moaning intonations – every musical means seems to come together to create this image. However, one dissonant element is present: a dance-like rhythmical punctuation of mournful phrases performed by lower string voices. Barely noticeable in the beginning, it becomes more persistent with every new phrase. It sways the first violins from their quietly melancholy course until they give up the theme, which is now continued by the flutes and oboes. The new timbre gives the theme a more frantic character; at the same time, the disturbing rhythmical punctuation, assumed by the first violins, becomes very audible. A clear contest between the monologue and the dance-like movement evolves: the more frantic the former becomes, the more compulsive the latter. Both voices quickly gain in dynamic and pitch to the point that their competition becomes unbearable. Then it erupts in several frantic tutti accords, followed by a dramatically exclamatory concluding reply of the first violins. The implied subject of this symphonic narrative is never left alone with his mournful thoughts. He does not present a statuesque figure like Rodin's *Thinker*. Instead, we witness and become part of his inner struggle, contradictions, frustrations and volatility of thoughts.

Such character of the musical narrative in a traditional symphonic *Allegro* had a profound symbolic value. Its transient, ever-shifting states, its tensions and contradictions corresponded to a spiritual phenomenon that Herzen aptly called 'dialectic of the soul'. The inner life of a subject projected by a symphony by Beethoven, Berlioz, Tchaikovsky or Mahler was similar to that of the heroes of a romantic or realist psychological novel, from Goethe's Wilhelm Meister and Constant's Adolphe to Flaubert's Emma Bovary or Tolstoy's Pierre Bezukhov. This does not mean, of course, that the content of a musical narrative could be compared with situations and characters in a psychological novel. Such attempts to interpret symphonic music – even music to which the author himself attached more or less explicit programmatic indicators – inevitably descends into vulgarity. It is hardly worth arguing that any attempt to reconstruct a 'plot' of a symphony and a 'character' or 'characters', in a manner resembling the plot and characters of a novel, is essentially futile. Perhaps, in the case of a symphony, we should speak of its 'subjectivity' rather than its 'subject': that is, of a dynamic of changing emotional states and modes of expressions that do not coalesce into any congruent character or chain of events. Given all these necessary reservations, however, it seems safe to say that, as far as depiction of human mind and heart is concerned, there are some parallels between the nineteenth-century symphony and the psychological novel. In both cases, emphasis was on the contradictory and volatile nature of individual consciousness, on its unceasing conflicts with itself and with the world around it.

A hero or heroine of a nineteenth-century novel experienced constant, yet ever-changing, tensions between the free flow of his thoughts and emotions and the fixed nature of his status in the world – between what Hegel called 'poetry of heart' and 'prose of social relations'. This tension between the subjective and the objective, between a social drama and psychological landscapes evolving in the souls of its protagonists, can be seen as perhaps the most fundamental common denominator of nineteenth-century aesthetics, both literary and musical. While following the plot of a novel which evolves according to the laws of social causality, the reader at the same time gains access to the minds of the novel's protagonists, whose turmoil defies laws of consistency or causality. A protagonist might be compelled to act in a certain way while experiencing contradictory emotions; the reader, on the other hand, construes action as a result of the interaction between the objective and the subjective. Unlike his numerous predecessors in seventeenth- and eighteenth-century adventure novels, Wilhelm Meister's experiences in his wanderings were punctuated by his conflicting thoughts and feelings, ever-changing hopes, memories, suspicions, desires, fears, joys and regrets. This gave the novel a fluidity that was lacking in a traditional picaresque work. Similarly, Madame Bovary's adulteries did not appear as a succession of episodes glued together in a Decameron fashion, since they interacted with the vicissitudes of her inner life. Likewise, the spiritual world of an implied subject in a symphonic narrative produces tensions similar to those that can be seen in characters of a psychological novel or musical drama. The whirlwind of voices of a symphonic *Allegro* renders the explosive and volatile nature of the inner life, its conflicts with the outer world and with itself, with an unprecedented degree of polyphonic tensions and dynamism.

This fundamental principle of presenting subjectivity in musical or literary works of the late eighteenth to the early twentieth centuries may be termed the 'romantic narrative', since it reflects a new concept of the subject which was introduced by Romanticism. The subject of romantic art, expostulated in theoretical works by Schiller, F. Schlegel and Schelling, and incarnated in such characters as Goethe's Wilhelm Meister, Byron's Childe Harold, Constant's Adolphe and Pushkin's Onegin, becomes acutely aware of his lack of organic wholeness. Besides experiencing an insoluble conflict between his inner world and the world around him, he believes that his inner world is being torn apart by contradictory feelings and thoughts. No matter how he struggles, he can never become a whole man, happily in possession of himself and living in unquestioned harmony with 'objective' existence. This malaise, however, works simultaneously with a creative impulse, since it is his longing for harmony that drives the romantic subject's struggles and actions. In this respect, at least, realism – denunciation of its romantic precursors notwithstanding – could be seen as a continuation of the romantic infatuation with and longing for 'real life'.

Shostakovich's Fourth Symphony, as far as its sophisticated infrastructure of motifs, complexity of form, intricacy of polyphonic and orchestral texture were concerned, could be viewed as a resumption of the great tradition of the 'grand' symphony. These outward musical features, however, stand in stark contrast to the choppy compartmentalization of its narrative, which moves as a chain of successive episodes, each dominated by a single narrative modality, be it a frantic race or somnolent repose. Had Shostakovich abandoned the form of the symphonic *Allegro* altogether, as Stravinsky did in his ballets in the 1910s, or, as he himself did in his Second and Third Symphony, the piecemeal nature of his narrative would not appear so striking. Here, however, within the traditional frame of an extensive symphonic drama, such a violation of one of its fundamental narrative and psychological premises had profound psychological and aesthetic implications.

The subject projected by the Fourth Symphony differs radically from his predecessors', from novels and symphonies written in a more humane age. He seems to be capable of only one emotion or one thought at a time. If he possesses a soul it must be one devoid of Romantic dialectic. The protagonist of the new narrative can be alternately horrified or pacified, frantic or dreamy, hyperactive or lost in thought, but all these states never come together and never interact. The landscape of his soul assumes the laws of the outer world: its different domains each occupy a distinct place in space and time, and come and go in turns. There is no inconsistency, no incompatibility between the subjective and the objective world anymore. This means, in effect, the end of the inner world of a person as it was perceived and portrayed by the art of the previous century. Since the inner state of mind assumes the same successive character as that of the outer realm, the former merely reflects and reacts to the latter.

In this sense, the world of Shostakovich's symphony bears remarkable resemblance to the world projected by the socialist realist novel, whose appearance at the turn of the 1930s also signified a revival of the old rhetorical form of the 'grand' novel of the previous century, after two decades of avant-garde experimentation. Its positive heroes – its Chumalovs, Korchagins or Margulieses – express a wide range of emotions, from enthusiasm to grief and from anger to childish playfulness. In fact, the ingredients out of which their inner life is composed appear no less rich and diverse than those that constituted the character of the hero of a nineteenth-century novel. What distinguishes the new hero from an old one is the fact that his inner states, however varied, rarely concur or struggle with one another. At any given moment, our hero is the whole man, his state of mind entirely focused on the moment he lives in, or on the task ahead.

Typically, it takes a negative hero, a living shadow of the past, to be burdened with memories, torn apart by doubts and lost in conflicting thoughts and emotions. In Kataev's *Time, Forward!* this is represented by Nalbandov, the chief construction engineer – a brilliant, well-educated person and an old Bolshevik. Now, however, he is unable to catch up with Margulies and his friends, and is becoming an obstacle to their leap forward. When speaking with American visitors, Nalbandov seems to be excited by his own rhetoric about the uninhibited pace of progress of the new socialist science that will eventually attain the speed of light and abolish mortality. Yet at the same time Nalbandov has to concede to himself that his opponents are right to be skeptical:

THE SYMPHONY AS MODE OF PRODUCTION

> 'You are a poet,' said Mr. Ray Roupe, smiling.
> 'No, I am an engineer – a Bolshevik,' Nalbandov replied roughly. 'We shall attain the speed of light and we shall become immortal!'
> 'If your poor, earthly human heart can bear it,' Mr. Ray Roupe said with a religious sigh, clasping his hands on his stomach and glancing covertly at Nalbandov.
> He is right, Nalbandov thought to himself, but he said:
> 'It will bear it. You may be sure of that.'

This contradiction between a remembered past enthusiasm and present doubts, between what is said and what is thought, would be typical for a hero of a nineteenth-century novel but becomes the sole prerogative of a negative character in the new narrative.

Positive heroes are free from this disease of Lermontov's Pechorin or Constant's Adolphe. After their record has been set (if only for a few hours), Margulies and Shura engage in the following dialogue:

> 'Have you any children, David?' she suddenly asked, earnestly.
> 'No. As a matter of fact, I don't even have a wife.'
> 'And haven't you ever had one? Well, why not?'
> 'Of course, I had one.'
> 'Where is she now?'
> Margulies waved his arm.
> 'I had one for a while, and now I don't.'
> 'Aren't you ever lonely?'
> 'At times.'
> They walked into the shadow of the warehouse and kissed tenderly.

(Lest the reader suspect that they were tempted to move *into* the warehouse, he is duly informed that a watchman stood there on guard.) This is all that we and the heroine learn about Margulies's past life. Time rushes forward and forward only, and both heroes are concerned only with the next dawn, when they will begin another frantic race for a new record.

Margulies's ex-wife has disappeared into the past and cannot trouble him anymore. Margulies's deputy, Korneev, has a more immediate psychological conflict to resolve. The woman he loves, who has abandoned her husband, child and Moscow apartment to come to live with him, cannot endure the hardships of life at the construction site anymore. Korneev, who dwells perpetually at his working place, receives a note from her in which she threatens to leave that very evening if he does not come to see her. With the note in his pocket, Korneev makes sporadic attempts to concentrate on this personal problem. He fails, however: not for want of love or concern, but simply because at that point his thoughts are focused on preparing the workplace for the record.

Korneev, dropping his eyes, looked at the wheels of the car that flashed by. It reminded him that something unpleasant had happened recently. Something untoward had happened this morning. That unpleasant thing had not been yet disposed of and it would have to be faced ...
    He remembered something strange and unpleasant. But what?
    Yes! Quite right! Klava! She was going away. She had to go home. Perhaps he could still patch things up.
    But how untimely the whole thing was!

Contrary to the conventional image of the hero of a socialist realist novel as schematic and one-dimensional, we see here that he is capable of a full range of thoughts and emotions. The only thing he seems not to be capable of is experiencing them simultaneously. When Korneev recalls Klava, a moment is lost in the race for the new record; the next moment, however, his concentration returns, and Klava vanishes from his thoughts. It is an almost perfect compartmentalization of the hero's mind, rather than a schematic uniformity that characterizes the peculiar world of the novel and its characters.

No matter how much struggle, pain and sacrifice are portrayed in a socialist realist novel of the 1930s, its world is a very happy place. However hectic the circumstances its heroes find themselves in, their lack of memory allows them to enjoy an undisturbed wholeness of self, be it of total happiness or total suffering, at any given moment. Hence the effortlessness with which they shift from excruciating pain to small pleasures, from crushing fatigue to a renewed burst of energy, from the tragic to the jocose. These shifts might seem abrupt to an external observer, yet they appear quite natural under the compartmentalized conditions of human consciousness projected by the novel's narrative.

In Shostakovich's Fourth Symphony, the shining narrative world of the late 1920s to the early 1930s has crumbled like a dream at a rude and sudden awakening. What had sounded and looked to be an exhilarating mode of existence, festive and bursting with energy, turns into a horrifying and menacing cacophony. Perhaps the closest literary analogy to this effect can be found in Platonov's *The Foundation Pit*, another lugubrious travesty of the frenzy of industrial construction. The subject of Shostakovich's symphonic narrative awakens to the existential horror of a world into which he finds himself plunged, and is now overcome with terror and agony. This is all the more acute due to his inability to emancipate his inner self from the world that oppresses it. Having lost the radiant wholeness that guaranteed harmony with the world in which he lived and acted, Shostakovich's lyrical hero does not regain the subjectivity of a nineteenth-century character. The mode of existence of the symphony's subject is purely reactive. All that his inner world is capable of producing is a chain of successive fits of pain and escapes from it into an introspective dreamland.

The Fourth Symphony highlights a paradox concerning the nature of a new artistic trend that had gradually begun to emerge in the late 1920s and was officially proclaimed in 1934, under the name of socialist realism, the all-encompassing and total doctrine of Soviet art. Its conservative, even retrograde, features were quite obvious, especially when contrasted with dominant artistic practices of the preceding period. The return to traditional literary and musical forms, the simplification of artistic means, the drive toward representational objectivity and stylized verisimilitude appeared to be a restoration of many features of nineteenth-century realism, which had been abandoned only recently. At the same time, the formulaic, ritualistic character of the new art evoked precedents from a more distant past – eighteenth-century neo-classicism and a medieval and folklore aesthetic. This big leap backward was clearly caused by the pressures exerted by an increasingly intrusive state and its official ideology.

This chapter has attempted to demonstrate that Shostakovich's works of the mid-1930s, while outwardly turning away from avant-garde practices toward more traditional forms and musical discourses, accomplished a more profound and disturbing demolition of the spiritual fabric of the old world than modernism with its penchant for spectacular escapades from nineteenth-century positivism. What could be seen, from an avant-garde perspective, as a regression, was in fact an innovation so radical that it appeared to have reached a point of no return.

Shostakovich as a composer had developed within the aesthetic and psychological environment of the Soviet and European avant-garde of the 1920s. What distinguished him within that environment was his profound affinity to rhetorical means and the psychological world of the late-romantic 'grand' symphonies. This side of his creative personality emerged under the terrible pressures of the Stalinist mid-1930s. Shostakovich's nostalgia for that world rendered the abyss that separated it from the spiritual realm of the 1930s particularly dramatic and poignantly revealing.

NOTES

1. According to Laurel Fay's well-documented account in her book, at least the third movement of the symphony was written after the debacle (*Shostakovich: A Life* (Oxford: Oxford University Press, 2000), pp. 492–3).
2. Excerpts of Kataev's novel are quoted from Valentin Kataev, *Time, Forward*, trans. Charles Malamuth (Bloomington, IN: Indiana University Press, 1973), p. 3.
3. Luigi Russolo, 'The Art of Noises' in Umbro Appollonio (ed.), *Futurist Manifestos* (New York: Viking, 1973), pp. 74–88.

4. As Richard Taruskin has shown convincingly in his recent book on Stravinsky, the latter's deliberate efforts to make his musical narrative patchwork inconsequential and episodic led to his liberating twentieth-century musical language from 'German' principles of compositional determinism that dominated nineteenth-century music. Moreover, in doing so, Stravinsky highlighted certain features of musical language that were characteristic of the Russian musical tradition in general (Richard Taruskin, *Stravinsky and the Russian Traditions: A Biography of His Works through Mavra*, Vol. I (Berkeley, CA: University of California, 1996), Ch. 16).

5. M. Gromov, 'Zametki slushatelia (o 5-i simfonii Shostakovicha)', *Sovetskaia muzyka* 3 (1938), p. 29, as quoted in Richard Taruskin, *Defining Russia Musically: Historical and Hermeneutical Essays* (Princeton, NJ: Princeton University Press, 1997), p. 516n.

10

Regarding the Modern Body: Science, the Social and the Construction of Italian Identities

DAVID G. HORN

INTRODUCTION: MODERN BODIES AND SOCIAL BODIES

It has been more than a decade since *The Making of the Modern Body*[1] proposed a new acceptance of the historicity of bodies (or at least of Western bodies). Inserting itself at an intersection of social history and cultural anthropology, of feminist studies and the work of Michel Foucault, the volume advised attending to the ways in which 'representations and routines of the body were transformed' in relation to the emergence of 'modern forms of social organization'.[2] The editors of the collected essays were not, of course, the first to offer such advice; but the volume's title was intended as a provocation, and perhaps ought still to disturb us. The very pairing of 'modern' and 'body' appears to challenge any easy recourse to a primordial or else timeless human form – even if we remain unsure precisely how to relate the adjective to the noun (the body in modernity? modernism's body? the body made modern?). The claim that bodies are made and not merely born is, or once was, similarly provocative. And if today invocations of the 'constructed body' scarcely raise eyebrows, we should not forget that this metaphor has enabled a range of contradictory political projects, and remains in tension with an ambition (in feminist studies, sexuality studies, anthropology and history) to take seriously the materiality of the body – its appetites and desires, its states of health and disease, its coming into being and dying.

It is not surprising that in the 1980s a number of studies sought to work out (or work with) these theoretical and political ambivalences by taking as their object the Western body in the period between the two world wars. This was, after all, a period of explicit talk about the making, or rather the remaking, of bodies in relation to particular understandings of 'the modern'. In nations as apparently diverse as the United

States, the Soviet Union, fascist Italy and Nazi Germany, reworkings of the body were tied to the production of new types of male and female citizens, to the elaboration of regional and national identities, and, perhaps most fatefully, to the 'defense' of the health and well-being of the body of society. And in each case, the making of bodies (fertile bodies, energetic bodies, healthy bodies, degenerate bodies) was tied to the elaboration of knowledge: biomedical and social sciences able to diagnose pathologies and identify potential.

In earlier work I explored the constitution of the procreative body as a site of scientific knowledge and technical intervention in 1920s Italy, and in relation to a 'demographic campaign' conceived and waged at the level of the 'population'.[3] Here I move back to the nineteenth century to explore some of the conditions of possibility of this and other inter-war projects. (In so doing I have no wish to minimize the importance of World War I, or to suggest that there was nothing properly 'revolutionary' about fascist engagement of the body.) This historical detour also involves a shift in focus, from the bodies of ordinary Italian women and men, to the bodies of criminals and prostitutes. The 'normal' body and the 'pathological' body have, of course, always been dependent on one another for their existence. But by the end of the nineteenth century there had emerged a growing confidence that both kinds of bodies could be known through science and made objects of rational management. Both kinds of bodies were resituated in the domain of 'the social', were newly invested with anxiety and hope, and were re-articulated with the imperatives of national and biological collectivities.

CRIMINALS AND ITALIANS

In his 1886 *Polemic in Defense of the Positive School of Criminal Anthropology*,[4] Cesare Lombroso struggled to salvage his notion of the 'criminal type' from an international chorus of detractors. In *L'uomo delinquente* (1876), Lombroso had proposed that the bodies of criminals made visible their latent social dangerousness.[5] Yet, by Lombroso's own calculations, some 60 per cent of criminals bore no resemblance at all to the anatomical portraits he had constructed, appearing more or less 'normal' even under the anatomizing gaze of the scientist – a fact that had not escaped the attention of French sociologists of crime.[6] In his *Polemic*, Lombroso responded by pointing hopefully to the 40 per cent of criminals who did possess some elements of the type, by emphasizing the 'invisible passage' from one trait to another that is the hallmark of biological variation among plants and animals, and by highlighting the increased variation among individuals that resulted from the perfection and civilization (*incivilmento*) of the human species. 'Besides', concluded

Lombroso, 'it is unlikely that you could find among one hundred Italians as many as five of the noted [Italian] type (the others exhibit only fractions of it, which do however stand out in comparison to foreigners). And yet it would never occur to anyone to deny the Italian type.'[7]

Reverting to the proverbial and commonsensical (we all know the type when we see it) was something Lombroso had done often in his studies of criminal anatomy. Indeed, as we will see, his scientific 'readings' of the body were in many ways consistent with (and at times dependent upon) folk physiognomies. However, the move in 1886 to shore up the embattled construct of the typical criminal by invoking the typical Italian is at least unexpected. Just 16 years earlier there was no consensus about what it meant to be an Italian: the Risorgimento might have 'made Italy', but it had not yet 'made Italians'.[8] In 1886, even the fabrication of the nation remained in doubt: the Italian state (and Italian identity) remained fractured by differences in language, economy, religion and, as Lombroso would point out, crime. 'Even in evil', he wrote, 'Italy is not unified.'[9]

As Daniel Pick has observed, the political project of making Italy and the scientific project of making criminals were indeed linked for Lombroso. Much of the anthropologist's energy was engaged in making intelligible regional and local differences in criminality – in particular, varied practices of resistance to national unification that ranged from 'anarchy' to 'brigandage'. Lombroso's goal, Pick argues, was to give at least discursive unity to Italy's contradictory social processes, and to provide a rational basis for political inclusions and exclusions: '[Lombroso] desired to unify the dangers, to hold them within a single conceptual model, in order to hold them outside the state, outside the fragile coherence of "Italy"'.[10]

This chapter will examine some of the ironies and unintended effects of a mapping project that assumed the possibility of separating scientifically, and at the level of the body, the criminal from the (normal) Italian population. At first glance, the discourses and practices of criminal anthropology seemed to construct durable and reassuring boundaries around bodies that were 'other'.[11] They promised to make explicit the atavistic and anomalous nature of criminality, and to locate dangerous women and men in relation to children, 'savages' and non-human primates. But here, as in other modern projects of boundary drawing,[12] borders proved permeable, and the scientific efforts to shore them up were further destabilizing. On the one hand, statistical and probabilistic constructions of criminality and bodily difference threatened to collapse the categories of the deviant and the normal.[13] On the other hand, the criminal body was imagined to resist and subvert the exegetical practices of anthropologists: to mask its truths and to seduce its 'readers'.

In the end, I hope to show that what emerged was less the (desired) coherence of the Italian, or the transparent pathology of the criminal, than the barely 'legible' potential dangerousness of normal women and men. Far from isolating the criminal in his or her typicality, criminal anthropology and related sciences worked to make everyone a possible danger to others, or more precisely to the 'body' of Italian society. As a result, not only was the criminal made an object of new practices of surveillance, prevention and punishment, but normal Italians were placed at the center of a whole range of modern discourses and technologies called 'social', ranging from social medicine to social housing and to social work. And by the 1930s, the defense of the Italian stock (*stirpe*) against the dangers posed by its constituent parts would be made the object of both civil and criminal law.[14]

ITALY, MODERNITY AND CRIMINALITY

Italian criminal anthropology constituted itself as a modern, social scientific discourse and practice, with links not only to the evolutionary theories of Darwin (whose works were first translated into Italian in 1864), but also (and perhaps more importantly) to the emergence of the science of statistics, to the 'discovery' of social facts and to the identification of the national population as an appropriate object of scientific knowledge and government.[15] Each contributed in the mid-nineteenth century to the reconfiguration of crime as a 'social problem': a patterned and predictable, if undesirable, consequence of social life, rather than the sum total of individual acts threatening the sovereignty of law or the king. Crime became a 'risk' that criminal anthropologists proposed to know and manage through detailed knowledge of social laws and embodied criminality.

Lombroso's criminology embodied both historical anthropology and a theory of modernity. It sought, among other things, to explain the apparent increases in rates of crime revealed by modern statistics, to trace historical shifts in the nature of crime and criminality, and to locate Italy in relation to other nations in Europe. In a sense, Lombroso imagined that each culture got the crimes it deserved. Lombroso argued that 'violent and bloody offenses [*reati*] predominated exclusively in ancient times and among the least evolved peoples, while those of forgery and fraud prevail among the most modern'.[16] Just as, in matters of property, possession by force of arms had given way to contracts, criminal violence had over time, and through the work of civilization, been displaced by 'trickery'. The increase in crimes against morality (*costumi*) was part of a more general shift, Lombroso argued, away from violent crimes that damaged persons to crimes that damaged 'things'.[17]

At the same time, Lombroso argued that murder among savages was not really a crime at all, but, rather, customary and natural. Crimes were infrequent among 'savages', reasoned Lombroso, because these peoples lacked moral sense.[18] Even among uncivilized Europeans, vendetta killings were duties rather than crimes (*delitti*), while (as the stories of Boccaccio and Sacchetti revealed) adultery, rape and sodomy were almost 'comical transgressions'.[19] According to this relativistic stance, a person could not commit a 'crime' by reproducing the traditions of the population in which he or she lived; the true delinquent in the historical and evolutionary pasts was not the murderer but the violator of 'custom' (*delinquente contro l'uso*).

Thus, 'civilization' could be characterized both by an increase in crime and by a shift in its objects, or rather by the addition of new 'civilized' crimes to those of 'barbaric times'.[20] The increase in crime was facilitated by the introduction of new technologies: not only was train robbery unthinkable without trains, but 'modern' crimes often depended on practices of life insurance, telephones and electricity.[21] Other new crimes, Lombroso suggested, were facilitated by the invention of tunnels, chloroform, lock picks and hypnotism.[22] Fortunately, Lombroso added, new sciences and technologies, including the social technologies of criminology, also made possible a more effective policing of crime.

In some cases, however, an increase in crime could signal something else: social danger. This was the case, Lombroso proposed, in both the United States and Italy.[23] In the United States, the increase was to be explained in large part by the 'colored population' and its inferior stage of *civiltà*.[24] Though Lombroso conceded that blacks had been 'unfairly treated', he went on to decry their lack of foresight (*previdenza*), and noted that black criminals failed to cover their tracks and tended to confess easily. Above all, blacks failed to be modern: 'No matter that he is clothed in the dress and habits of modern civilization, the American black too often retains that disregard for the lives of others, that lack of pity that is common to all savage peoples.'[25]

The problem facing Italy in 1879 was rather different. Again, it was not the numerical increase alone that worried Lombroso: the causes for this could be found in Italy's larger population and in the progressive work of civilization.[26] But in 1878 the increase had been 'all out of proportion',[27] and Italy had not yet experienced the shift away from violent crime (that symbol of barbarity) that had characterized other modern nations, including Italy's neighbors. Much of the violence in Italy was directed, Lombroso further noted, against the nation itself.

Even worse, in fact, was the existence of regional differences in rates of criminality revealed by the collection of statistics. How could the social expert account for the fact that in Cantanzaro there were 14 times more homicides than in Turin, and 20 times more in Naples than in Venice? What sense could be made of the fact that there were 23 times more thefts in Rome than in Florence?[28] The fact that the regions of the south, those that had in the past been 'poorly tamed' (*mal domati*), always 'topped the lists' indicated the presence of a 'profound evil' that required 'serious and energetic measures'.[29] These were regions, Lombroso suggested, where internationalism, organized crime (*camorra*) and 'associations' found a natural home; where 'social hybridity' and poverty created instability; and where weapons and alcohol were too easily available.

But Lombroso also pointed to the poverty of the new nation's social technologies, especially as deployed in the south: the uncertainty and mildness of penalties, delays in punishment, excessive appeals, and an undue reliance on the subjective evaluations of juries. Lombroso was particularly critical of the dispensation of pardons by the king, which 'reproduced one of the effects of religion with which modern criminal law purports to have broken'.[30] Lombroso was not, as will become clear, arguing that all violators of the law should be treated uniformly – far from it. Indeed he suggested that the creation and application of a uniform penal code, which might have been appropriate 'for a people that has reached the acme of civilization', could be disastrous for Italy, 'where in many regions an almost medieval barbarism still reigns supreme'.[31] Lombroso suggested that in regions where 'vendetta homicide is almost a duty, it seems to me a grave error to punish it in the same manner as in regions where it provokes a profound disgust'.[32] As he put it a decade later, 'In order to unify the law, truly and not only on paper, it would be necessary to level customs, birth rates, ages of sexual development, and even climates, soils and farming.'[33]

Underlying all of these critiques was a challenge to prevailing penal theories and their focus on criminal responsibility. In Lombroso's view, the nation needed to substitute strategies of social defense for 'metaphysics', and evaluations of social dangers for determinations of free will and intention. Lombroso's 'positive school'[34] of criminology was distinguished from its predecessor and rival, the 'classical school', by a shift of objects from the crime to the criminal and his or her environment,[35] and by a new anthropology in which 'penal man' (*homo penalis*) gave way to 'criminal man' (*homo criminalis*).[36] The classical school, as Pasquino has noted, had operated around the triangle of law, crime and punishment. The problem was to adjust penalties to offenses; the individual to be punished (*homo penalis*) was interesting only in so far as his or her identity and legal responsibility (the capacity of free will) were at issue.

The new anthropological school socialized crime, and focused instead on the two main poles of the criminal (*homo criminalis*) and society.[37] On the one hand, anthropologists expressed a new concern with statistical regularities (including, as we have seen, regular regional differences). They complained that the classical school had been unable to explain (and indeed had never thought to explain) why there were 3,000 murders every year in Italy, and not 300 or 300,000.[38] On the other hand, the anthropologists argued that it was necessary to take account of the social dangerousness of individual offenders. They proposed replacing the classical school's typology of crimes, which Enrico Ferri termed a 'juridical anatomy' of deeds,[39] with a typology of criminals and, as we will see, an anatomy of deviant and dangerous bodies grounded in scientific measurements. In this way, they sought to break classical theory's link between responsibility and punishment practices. As Lombroso's collaborator Raffaele Garofalo argued, the social dangerousness of an individual might, in fact, be greatest when his or her legal responsibility was least.[40] Indeed, for the first time, one could be a criminal (that is, a danger to society) without having committed a crime,[41] something that had been literally unthinkable for the classical school.

This 'social' construction of the problem of criminality also implied a new regime of governmental practices focused on the prevention rather than the repression of crime. The anthropological problem was to determine 'in what manner and to what degree it is necessary for the health of society to limit the rights of delinquents'.[42] Remedies and penalties were to give way to practices of surveillance, preventive detention and parole, and to proposals for making talented criminals 'serviceable to civilization'.[43] These interventions depended in turn on estimations of the social risk posed by particular kinds of individuals; specific crimes figured merely as 'indications' of dangerousness.[44]

In sum, the unity (and modernity) of Italy were not to be guaranteed by the application of uniform codes linking transgressions and penalties, but by measures of social defense flexible enough to evaluate the potential social dangerousness of individual offenders. In the south, a vendetta homicide might not indicate social danger, while in the north the same act might be an index of something altogether different. In short, building a nation and suppressing crime were both seen to require detailed knowledge about and management of difference. Lombroso's project was to make dangerous difference visible at the level of the body, so that the larger body of Italy might be defended against risks, and made modern.

THE BODY IN THE 'SOCIAL' CONSTRUCTION OF CRIMINALITY

Attention to bodies, Lombroso argued, promised to deliver criminology from the idealism and 'metaphysics' of the classical school. His anthropology shared with other nineteenth-century scientific (and political) projects the assumption that only the body could ground and locate difference.[45] In particular, a science of bodies promised to make intelligible the 'dangerousness' that was the object of the new criminological discourse, but which threatened to remain invisible. Here Lombroso drew on the sciences of physiognomy and phrenology, which purported to find signs of interior intellectual and moral states on the body's surfaces, particularly at the level of the head and face.[46] However, Lombroso rejected what he termed the 'qualitative and deterministic'[47] readings of phrenologists in favor of anthropometry: the precise measurement of the dimensions and relations of parts of the body, a practice that had been joined to social statistics by Adolphe Quetelet.[48] For Lombroso, anthropometry appeared (at least initially) 'an ark of salvation'[49] able to fix bodily difference as deviation from statistical norms.

Anthropometry and other scientific reading practices promised both to make known and to make manageable potential dangers,[50] and to specify the social, historical and evolutionary place of the criminal body. Lombroso argued that the criminal was linked by his abnormal anatomy and physiology to the insane person and the epileptic, as well as to those other 'others' who were constituted as the objects of the social sciences: apes, children, women, prehistoric humans and contemporary 'savages'. For Lombroso, the criminal was, in his body and conduct, an 'atavism' – a re-emergence of the historical and evolutionary pasts in the present. The pederast was tied by his desires to Periclean Athens[51] as surely as the Italian murderer was linked by his violent, bloodthirsty acts to the Australian aborigine.[52] The slang of criminals was said to recall primitive languages,[53] the artwork of criminals to be reminiscent of Australian handicrafts, and the handwriting of criminals to suggest pictography and hieroglyphics.[54] Finally, behaviors such as tattooing and 'sexual excesses', and morphological features such as the slope of the forehead and the shape of the ears, linked criminals to lower forms of animal life, as well as to children and savages. Among the latter, as we have seen, criminal behavior (but not crime) was identified as 'natural', indeed 'normal'.[55]

READING THE BODY: PHYSIOGNOMY AND STATISTICS

Although criminal anthropology privileged the body, and especially the head and face, as indices of social dangerousness, knowledge of deviant bodies was not presumed to be exclusive to anthropologists. Artists, writers, the 'lower classes' (*il volgo*) and even children, according to Lombroso, were aware of and could reproduce in paintings and poems the contours of criminal physiognomy.[56] Folk taxonomies were, in Lombroso's view, rooted in 'natural instincts': honest men and (especially) women were innately repulsed by the ugliness of the criminal type, and the conclusions of 'instinctive observers' had found expression in proverbs, folk songs and jokes. Lay observational practices could, in fact, be put to the test: Lombroso's daughter recounts that her father 'once placed before forty children, twenty portraits of thieves and twenty representing great men, and 80 per cent recognized in the first the portraits of bad and deceitful people'.[57] Even Lombroso's mother, we are told, knew a potential murderer when she saw one.[58] Painters and novelists had also demonstrated a certain knowledge of criminal anatomy and physiognomy. And though Lombroso insisted on the modernity of criminal anthropology, he was also not above calling on 'the ancients', and in particular Homer and Avicenna, to declare that there was nothing new about his criminological claims.[59]

If these folk and non-scientific typologies (which were themselves made objects of anthropological analysis)[60] served to reinforce the findings of the criminologists, they might also have risked calling into question the privileged position of anthropological observers, or (as some critics charged) the scientific status of their theories.[61] However, for Lombroso and his contemporaries, the anthropologist was distinguished from the artist, from the observant folk, from the child (and indeed from the non-anthropological folklorist and the phrenologist) by his specialized techniques for reading the body: by a corporeal literacy that made possible both an exegesis and a diagnosis. As Lombroso put it, what the anthropologist did was not 'guesswork, or a prophecy, but a reading' of the body's forms and gestures.[62] Lombroso, who spent a good deal of time collecting 'prison palimpsests' (the overlaid inscriptions made by prisoners on cell walls, drinking vessels, uniforms and the sands of the exercise yard),[63] identified the body as an 'inverted palimpsest',[64] a partially effaced text which, when read correctly, yielded up its submerged truths: the signs of degeneration and atavism. He advised experts in criminal law not to waste time reading books in libraries, but to read the 'living documents' contained in prisons.[65]

However, it is important to note that, although the criminal's physiognomy was seen to make visible and legible (in a relatively unambiguous, unmediated fashion) the degeneration of the population or race,[66] it was a sign of the individual's social dangerousness only in a statistical, probabilistic sense. As we have seen, according to Lombroso, fewer than 40 per cent of convicted male criminals had any physical anomalies,[67] and still fewer bore the composite of factors (the 'criminal type') that was considered a reliable predictor of dangerous conduct. Indeed, the infinite possible combinations of measurable signs of atavism seemed to frustrate the effort to construct typologies and taxonomies, and Lombroso struggled in his writings to find the appropriate metaphor to capture the relation between physical deviance and dangerousness. At times, Lombroso referred to anomalies as notes in a musical chord: the isolated anomaly had to be taken together with other physical and moral notes for the criminal type to take shape.[68] This musical metaphor was in turn linked to a modern notion of visibility. Lombroso compared patterns of atavism to impressionist paintings: 'examined from up close, they seem shapeless, colored blotches, while at a distance they prove to be wonderful'.[69] A wide (statistical) perspective was necessary for any image of the criminal to emerge.

However, by the time Lombroso published his study of female criminals, *La donna delinquente*,[70] the practice of anthropometry seemed in fact to be experiencing a crisis. During what Elizabeth Fee has called the 'baroque period of craniology',[71] there was an unbounded multiplication of cranial angles and indices, of other anatomical measurements, of mechanical measuring devices, and indeed of the parts of the face and body that could be distinguished as candidates for measurement. However, the significance of the new measurements and correlations was no longer always obvious to those who collected them. Lombroso had earlier regarded anthropometry as 'the backbone … of the new human statue of which he was at the time attempting the creation'.[72] Now, the body threatened to become exhausted as a source of scientific meaning.

This epistemological (and narrative) crisis was reflected in the text of *La donna delinquente* (1893) and its subsequent translations, which presented pages of numbers and statistical correlations without any developed analysis or interpretation.[73] Some correlations might have seemed meaningful in a transparent way, or were made to appear so in the text: for example, the fact that female poisoners (who were said to depend on practices of concealment and distraction) turned out to have the highest cranial capacities, while those women guilty of simple assault or 'assisting in rape' had the lowest.[74] But what, after all, was the criminal anthropologist (or the reader) to make of the fact that the length of the face was greatest among women who had been convicted of wounding others, and least among those guilty of arson?[75] Though, in principle, the undigested numbers of anthropometry lent scientific authority to the text, they also risked being revealed as gratuitous quantification.

As in later editions of his studies of male criminals, Lombroso (here joined by his son-in-law Ferrero) felt obliged to look elsewhere, to turn to anomalies (particularly facial and genital deformations and asymmetries) as well as to other qualitative materials and sources (anecdotes, paintings, folklore) in order to construct a portrait of the criminal.[76] The result was an unwieldy and heterogeneous text, one that moved from discussions of crime among female animals (the alcoholism of ants and the adultery of pigeons) to anthropometry, to folklore, and to vivid accounts of the deeds of prostitutes and monstrous mothers.

Here, as elsewhere in Lombroso's work, the affirmation of the expert reading practices of the social scientist was accompanied by recognition of the difficulty, if not impossibility, of any reliable readings of the criminal body. There was, in the case of women, a layering of uncertainties: the erosion of boundaries and taxonomic categories effected by a probabilistic understanding of criminal dangerousness, and the absence of adequate markers caused by the tendency of women to 'adhere to the norm'[77] were joined by bodily acts of epistemological resistance. Together, these worked to blur the very boundaries between normal and deviant that criminal anthropology sought to draw, and to multiply the possible objects of social scientific concern and technical intervention.

In sum, while the criminal may have had a fixed appearance in popular culture, there were no sure anatomical guides to social dangerousness – that is, to that feature that was placed at the center of anthropological discussions of criminality. In the end, criminal anthropologists made everyone potentially (if not equally) dangerous – just as, to use an analogy favored by Enrico Ferri, Pasteur's studies of disease had made everyone a possible source of microbial contagion.[78] In both cases, science pointed to the need for globalized practices of prevention and social hygiene. And in both cases, a dramatic re-imagining of society was linked to the expanding power of the experts of the social.[79]

The object of the new sciences of the social (sociology, social medicine, social hygiene) was no longer the society envisaged by liberalism: a collection of autonomous individuals, each equipped with free will, and responsible for his or her own actions. Rather, it was a social body with its own laws, regularities and pathologies, which had to be known by new sciences and managed according to new rationalities of government. In this sense, criminal anthropology was linked to the emergence of what Foucault called governmentality: modern forms of power and knowledge concerned with the management of risk, and the promotion of the health and welfare of the biological population.[80]

THE LEGACY OF LOMBROSO: FROM CRIMINAL ANTHROPOLOGY TO SOCIAL DEFENSE

In many respects, Lombroso failed in his effort to draw stable boundaries dividing criminals and Italians. But his work (and that of related experts of the social) was not without its productive effects: it made possible, even urgent, new knowledge about the Italian population, and new methods of policing. Many of the criminologists' recommendations were taken up by reformers of Italy's 1889 penal code. Reform of the code began in 1919, with the creation of a commission charged with constructing 'a more effective and sure defense against habitual delinquency', one that was 'in harmony with the rational principles and methods for the defense of society against crime in general'.[81] The resulting project – a draft for Book I – was directed by Enrico Ferri, a socialist and one of the founders of the positivist school of criminal anthropology.[82] The project did no less than propose a new penal order, based on a new punitive rationality.

The focus of the new code, consistent with positivist criminal anthropology, was no longer the crime but the criminal, not his or her imputability, but his or her 'dangerousness'. In parallel, the code abandoned to a significant extent retributive penalties in favor of preventive measures. The goal of the latter was less deterrence than neutralization of risk and social hygiene: 'the sanctions established for the authors of crimes … must only provide for the most effective social defense against dangerous offenders, and the most rapid and sure redemption and reutilization of less dangerous offenders, who are the most numerous'.[83] This project was never completed, and was abandoned when the fascists came to power in 1922. But the code authored by Minister of Justice Alfredo Rocco eight years later would nevertheless take as its principal object the defense of the body of society against the risks posed by its constituent parts.

The early years of fascism were characterized almost exclusively by acts of repression – of political dissent, journalistic freedom and trade unionism. But by the late 1920s the regime had gradually moved toward a different economy of power that attempted to substitute rigorous and no less harsh practices of prevention for 'excesses' of repressive violence. At one level, this shift was marked by suppression of the violence of fascist squads (*squadrismo*) in 1925 and subsequent regulation of the fascist militia (MVSN) – part of a broader campaign of 'normalization' and a first step in the subordination of the party to the state advocated by Rocco and other nationalists.[84] At another level, this transformation was marked by the elaboration of new techniques of intervention, designed less to penalize than to recognize and contain risks.

For example, the theme of prevention is developed in the 1926 *Testo unico delle leggi di pubblica sicurezza*,[85] which grouped together, under the heading 'Provisions regarding public order and public safety', a series of measures regulating public assemblies, accidents and disasters, and dangerous industries. To be sure, the document gave the police broad powers to repress seditious crimes, public demonstrations and the display of subversive flags. But it also developed a new set of preventive measures focused on 'persons dangerous to society', including juveniles, vagabonds, the mentally ill, former convicts and political opponents of the regime. Perhaps the most important of these measures was internal exile (*confino di polizia*) from one to five years, which could be imposed on anyone deemed to be a danger to society.[86]

As the national police chief Arturo Bocchini explained in a telegram to prefects, the *Testo unico* articulated a new conception of 'public order':

> [I]n the new law, public order does not have the old, merely negative meaning, but signifies undisturbed and peaceful life of the positive political social and economic systems which constitute the essence of the regime. Whoever attacks this peaceful development must immediately be put in the position of doing no harm.[87]

This, the jurist Antonello Caprino argued, contrasted with the liberal conception, according to which guaranteeing the public order meant 'assuring individuals an indispensable minimum of tranquillity in the inevitable conflict of the competing interests of the collectivity'.[88] In fact, the state's action was intended to move beyond prevention; it was now charged with a positive transformation of the social order. Public order was to be assured by 'policing', not merely in the repressive sense, but also in the eighteenth-century sense of a technique for developing the strength and quality of the social body.[89]

The logic of prevention was further, if fitfully, developed in the penal code of 1930. Rocco's code was in many respects much less 'revolutionary' than the project drafted by Ferri in 1921. It constituted a 'compromise' between the classical and positivist schools of criminal anthropology, and, as one commentator put it, between natural and social law.[90] But if Rocco was not prepared to abandon the liberal rationality of punishment completely, his code did mark a dramatic shift toward prevention and social defense. Repression, as Rocco argued in 1925, was clearly 'insufficient' to defend the social organism.[91]

In the new code, delinquency was to be prevented both by the deterrence of penalties – 'a defense against the danger of new offenses committed by the criminal, by the victim and his family members, or by the collectivity'[92] – and by proactive security measures. These included the housing of minors and deaf-mutes in centers for 'education and instruction'; the institutionalization of the dangerous mentally ill; the creation of special asylums for habitual drunks, alcoholics and drug addicts; the opening of confinement camps for habitual or otherwise incorrigible delinquents, and workhouses for loiterers, vagabonds and habitual beggars; the experimental use of parole and probation; and 'special vigilance' of the public security forces.[93] As Rocco explained in his report to the king on the final version of the new code, '[b]y means of such measures ... social defense against crime extends its traditional limits'. In medical terms, he argued, these measures represented 'rather than therapy, prophylaxis, and social hygiene against crime'.[94]

This new penal rationality, an aspect of a broader rethinking of the social, defined not only new measures, but also new targets and goals of intervention. In the name of social defense, the state could now intervene preventively where its actions had previously been limited, including in the domain of reproduction. In both the penal code and in sections of the civil code regulating marriage and the family, being an Italian would be construed as being a constituent part of a larger social organism, whose interests and needs surpassed those of the individual.[95]

As Foucault has argued, the fact that some of the most fundamental theses of criminal anthropologists took hold in penal thought and practices owes little to their 'truth value' or persuasive power. Rather, it was changes surrounding the notions, accidents, risks and responsibility that made possible a new articulation of law and human sciences. I want to suggest, in conclusion, that these are more general features of the modern uses of statistics, which Urla has termed 'a technology for the production of social knowledge and subjectivity'.[96] The rise in Italy of statistical discourses and practices – and of a whole array of sciences of 'the social' – contributed to the fact that, by the 1930s, being an Italian – like being a criminal – had come to mean being a part of a 'population' that was made the object of specific forms of knowledge and specific practices of government.[97] Identity would not, after all, be fixed by the body, but by the common experience of being the object of modern social technologies, from censuses to social work and to practices of penal prevention.

NOTES

1. Catherine Gallagher and Thomas Laqueur (eds), *The Making of the Modern Body: Sexuality and Society in the Nineteenth Century* (Berkeley, CA: University of California Press, 1987), p. vii.
2. Ibid.
3. David G. Horn, *Social Bodies: Science, Reproduction, and Italian Modernity* (Princeton, NJ: Princeton University Press, 1994).
4. Cesare Lombroso, Enrico Ferri, Raffaele Garofalo and Giulio Fioretti, *Polemica in difesa della scuola criminale positiva* (Bologna: Zanichelli, 1886).
5. C. Lombroso, *L'Uomo delinquente* (Milan: Hoepli, 1876).
6. Among Lombroso's fiercest critics on this point was Gabriel Tarde. See, for example, *Criminalité comparée* (Paris: Félix Alcan, 1886). For discussions of the relations among French and Italian criminal anthropologies see Robert Nye, 'Heredity or Milieu: The Foundations of Modern European Criminological Theory', *Isis* 67 (1976), pp. 335–55;

Daniel Pick, *Faces of Degeneration: A European Disorder, c.1848–c.1918* (Cambridge: Cambridge University Press, 1989); and especially Laurent Mucchielli, 'Hérédité et milieu social: le faux-antagonisme franco-italien', in Laurent Mucchielli (ed.), *Histoire de la criminologie française* (Paris: L'Harmattan, 1994), pp. 189–214.
7. Lombroso et al., *Polemica in difesa*, p. 39.
8. D'Azeglio cited in Pick, *Faces of Degeneration*, p. 119.
9. Lombroso, 'L'Italia è unita, non unificata', *Archivio di psichiatria, scienze penali, ed antropologia criminale* 9 (1888), p. 146.
10. Pick, *Faces of Degeneration*, p. 128. As Pick notes, the acts of the first International Congress of Criminal Anthropology were introduced by diagrams of the anomalies of the criminal body, and ended with a series of maps showing the distribution of particular kinds of crime in Italy: 'The maps serve perhaps as a short-hand illustration of how Lombroso's *oeuvre* endeavored to link the body, the nation and history. Criminal anthropology constituted at once a political geography, a conjectural history of civilization, an evolutionary account of organisms and races' (p. 141). For Lombroso's studies of the south see, in particular, *In Calabria, (1862–1897)* (Catania: Arnaldo Forni, 1898).
11. Sander Gilman, *Disease and Representation: Images of Illness from Madness to AIDS* (Ithaca, NY: Cornell University Press, 1988).
12. Donna Haraway, *Primate Visions: Gender, Race, and Nature in the World of Modern Science* (New York: Routledge, 1989).
13. Ian Hacking identifies a fundamental tension (and source of power) in the modern idea of the normal, which can be traced back to Auguste Comte: 'the normal as existing average, and the normal as figure of perfection to which we may progress'. *The Taming of Chance* (Cambridge: Cambridge University Press, 1990), p. 168. Also see Georges Canguilhem, *The Normal and the Pathological*, trans. Carolyn R. Fawcett (New York: Zone Books, 1989 [1978]), pp. 151–79.
14. Horn, *Social Bodies*, pp. 66–94.
15. On statistics and the constitution of the 'social' domain see Jacques Donzelot, 'The Poverty of Political Culture', *Ideology and Consciousness* 5 (1979), pp. 73–86; François Ewald, *L'Etat providence* (Paris: Grasset, 1986); Hacking, *The Taming of Chance*; Horn, *Social Bodies*; Paul Rabinow, *French Modern: Norms and Forms of the Social Environment* (Cambridge, MA: MIT Press, 1989); and Jacqueline Urla, 'Cultural Politics in an Age of Statistics: Numbers, Nations and the Making of Basque Identity', *American Ethnologist* 20 (1993), pp. 818–43.
16. C. Lombroso, *Delitti vecchi e delitti nuovi* (Turin: Bocca, 1902), pp. vii–viii.
17. Ibid., p. 3.
18. Ibid., p. 274. As Lombroso put it, 'Savage ethics is moral madness.' Lombroso et al., *Polemica in difesa*, p. 36.
19. Lombroso, *Delitti vecchi e delitti nuovi*, p. 274.
20. Ibid.
21. Ibid., p. 290.
22. In *Delitti vecchi e delitti nuovi*, Lombroso devoted an entire chapter to bicycle crimes. The roles of bicycles as objects of theft, means to commit crimes and causes of madness were, in the author's view, offset by the bicycle's physical benefits.
23. For Lombroso, early twentieth-century Australia offered the best model for the rational management of social dangers. From Australia 'radiated, as if from an immense lamp, that happy state of civilization that our grandchildren will enjoy' (ibid., p. 29).
24. Ibid., p. 11.
25. Ibid., p. 12.
26. C. Lombroso, *Sull'incremento del delitto in Italia e sui mezzi per arrestarlo* (Turin: Bocca, 1879), p. 3.
27. Ibid., p. 4.
28. Ibid., pp. 5–6.
29. Ibid., p. 6.
30. Ibid., p. 40.
31. Ibid., p. 135.

32. Ibid., p. 138.
33. Lombroso, 'L'Italia è unita', p. 147.
34. Italian criminal anthropology variously described itself as the 'Italian School', the 'Anthropological School', the 'Positive School', the 'Modern School', the 'Scientific School' and the 'New School' (Gina Lombroso-Ferrero, *Criminal Man, According to the Classification of Cesare Lombroso* (Montclair, NJ: Patterson Smith, 1972 [1911]), p. vi). Its members shared no particular disciplinary training, but rather a manner of problematizing criminality and deviance.
35. Enrico Ferri, *The Positive School of Criminology: Three Lectures by Enrico Ferri*, ed. Stanley E. Grupp (Pittsburgh, PA: University of Pittsburgh Press, 1968 [1901]), p. 60.
36. Pasquale Pasquino, 'Criminology: The Birth of a Special Savoir', trans. Colin Gordon, *Ideology and Consciousness* 7 (1980), pp. 19–20; Michel Foucault, 'About the Concept of the "Dangerous Individual" in 19th-Century Legal Psychiatry', *International Journal of Law and Psychiatry* 1 (1978), pp. 1–18.
37. Pasquino, 'Criminology', p. 20.
38. Ferri, *The Positive School*, p. 72.
39. Ibid., p. 71.
40. Lombroso et al., *Polemica in difesa*, p. 197.
41. Robert Fletcher, 'The New School of Criminal Anthropology', *American Anthropologist* 4 (1891), p. 210.
42. Lombroso et al., *Polemica in difesa*, p. 201.
43. Lombroso-Ferrero, *Criminal Man*, pp. 212–16. Vagabonds, Lombroso suggested, might be used to colonize wild and unhealthy regions; murderers might perform surgery or serve in the military; and swindlers might pursue police work or journalism (Cesare Lombroso, *Crime, Its Causes and Remedies*, trans. Henry P. Horton (Montclair, NJ: Patterson Smith, 1968 [1911]), p. 447).
44. Lombroso et al., *Polemica in difesa*, p. 198.
45. George W. Stocking, Jr, 'Bones, Bodies, and Behavior', in George W. Stocking, Jr (ed.), *Bones, Bodies, and Behavior: Essays on Biological Anthropology (History of Anthropology 5)* (Madison, WI: University of Wisconsin Press, 1988), pp. 3–17.
46. See Allan Sekula, 'The Body and the Archive', *October* 39 (1986), pp. 11–12; Barbara Maria Stafford, *Body Criticism: Imaging the Unseen in Enlightenment Art and Medicine* (Cambridge, MA: MIT Press, 1991), pp. 84–129; Robert M. Young, *Mind, Brain and Adaptation in the Nineteenth Century: Cerebral Localization and Its Biological Context from Gall to Ferrier* (Oxford: Clarendon Press, 1970), pp. 9–53. While the focus on the head was in some ways 'commonsensical' and continuous with popular practices of reading faces, Sekula suggests it also worked to 'legitimate on organic grounds the dominion of intellectual over manual labor'. 'The Body and the Archive', p. 12. The anthropology of criminal women also privileged the genitals as loci of deviance.
47. Lombroso et al., *Polemica in difesa*, p. 5.
48. On the links between anthropometry and photography see Sekula, 'The Body and the Archive', pp. 19–23; on anthropometry's relation to racist evolutionary thought see Stephen Jay Gould, *The Mismeasure of Man* (New York: Norton, 1978), pp. 73–122.
49. Cesare Lombroso and Guglielmo Ferrero, *The Female Offender*, ed. W. Douglas Morrison (London: T. Fisher Unwin, 1895), p. 1.
50. On the uses of anthropometry to manage populations in other domains see Claude Blanckaert, 'On the Origins of French Ethnology: William Edwards and the Doctrine of Race', in Stocking (ed.), *Bones, Bodies, Behavior*, pp. 18–55.
51. Lombroso-Ferrero, *Criminal Man*, p. xiv.
52. Alfredo Niceforo, *Antropologia delle classi povere* (Milan: Vallardi, 1910), p. 112. Lombroso claimed to have discovered atavism when, while examining the skull of the brigand Vilella during a post-mortem, he detected a formation typically found in rodents: 'This was not merely an idea, but a revelation. At the sight of that skull, I seemed to see all of a sudden, lighted up as a vast plain under a flaming sky, the problem of the nature of the criminal – an atavistic being who reproduces in his person the ferocious instincts of primitive humanity and the inferior animals. Thus were explained anatomically the enormous jaws, high cheek-bones, prominent superciliary

arches, solitary lines in the palms, extreme size of the orbits, handle-shaped or sessile ears found in criminals, savages, and apes, insensibility to pain, extremely acute sight, tattooing, excessive idleness, love of orgies, and the irresistible craving for evil for its own sake, the desire not only to extinguish life in the victim, but to mutilate the corpse, tear its flesh, and drink its blood.' (Lombroso-Ferrero, *Criminal Man*, pp. xxiv–xxv.) The notion of atavism was rejected by Raffaele Garofalo and Gabriel Tarde who emphasized the social environment. Fletcher, 'The New School of Criminal Anthropology', p. 209; Nye, 'Heredity or Milieu'.

53. Niceforo, *Antropologia delle classi povere*, p. 116.
54. Lombroso-Ferrero, *Criminal Man*, pp. 134–5.
55. Ibid., p. 134. One anthropologist went beyond this relativizing of 'the normal' in an effort to subvert its usual meaning. Paul Albrecht, in a paper read at the 1885 Congress of Criminal Anthropology, defined the modern criminal as 'normal' – that is, like all other animals – and the honest, law-abiding citizen as an abnormal being: 'Abnormal or honest man kills or punishes normal or criminal man because the latter refuses to allow himself to be abnormalized'. Fletcher, 'The New School of Criminal Anthropology,' p. 235.
56. Lombroso *et al.*, *Polemica in difesa*, p. 11; Lombroso-Ferrero, *Criminal Man*, pp. 48–51.
57. Lombroso-Ferrero, *Criminal Man*, p. 50.
58. C. Lombroso, *L'Uomo delinquente, in rapporto all'antropologia, alla giurisprudenza ed alle discipline carcerarie*, 5th edn, Vol. 1 (Turin: Bocca, 1896), p. 310.
59. Lombroso *et al.*, *Polemica in difesa*, p. 42. At the same time, Lombroso contrasted his 'anthropological' colleagues with others who 'follow the latest fad at the Sorbonne' (p. 43).
60. Alfredo Niceforo traced the roots of his 'anthropology of the poor' to the early nineteenth-century work of Cadet-Gassincourt which, basing itself in popular beliefs, had sought to explain the misanthropy of bakers, the cruelty of butchers, the debauchery of hosiers and 'the seditious spirit' of masons and typographers. Niceforo, *Antropologia delle classi povere*, p. 9.
61. Lombroso *et al.*, *Polemica in difesa*, p. 11.
62. Ibid., p. 8.
63. Lombroso, *Palimsesti del carcere* (Turin: Bocca, 1888).
64. Lombroso *et al.*, *Polemica in difesa*, p. 8.
65. Lombroso-Ferrero, *Criminal Man*, p. 302.
66. Lombroso *et al.*, *Polemica in difesa*, p. 6. The degeneration of the race was due, in Lombroso's view, to the action of alcoholic beverages and 'inheritance'. Its effects included sterility, madness and crime, and it manifested itself in anomalies of the ear, the skull and the genitals.
67. Ibid., p. 12.
68. Ibid., p. 38; Lombroso-Ferrero, *Criminal Man*, pp. 48–9.
69. Lombroso *et al.*, *Polemica in difesa*, p. 34.
70. Lombroso turned to the study of criminal women to address an apparent inconsistency identified by his French critics: women, though ostensibly less evolved than men, committed fewer crimes, while the heads and bodies of female criminals present fewer signs of degeneration than those of males. Lombroso and Ferrero, *The Female Offender*, p. 27. The cranial anomalies of male criminals were, by Lombroso's count, three to four times more frequent, and the 'complete criminal type', characterized by four or more atavistic characteristics, could be found in only 18 per cent of female criminals (as compared with 31 per cent of males). Ibid., p. 104; C. Lombroso and G. Ferrero, *La donna delinquente, la prostituta e la donna normale*, 3rd edn (Turin: Bocca, 1915), p. 208. Also see David Horn, 'This Norm Which Is Not One: Reading the Female Body in Lombroso's Anthropology', in Jennifer Terry and Jacqueline Urla (eds), *Deviant Bodies: Critical Perspectives on Difference in Science and Popular Culture* (Bloomington, IN: Indiana University Press, 1995), pp. 109–28.
71. Elizabeth Fee, 'Nineteenth-Century Craniology: The Study of the Female Skull', *Bulletin of the History of Medicine* 53 (1979), p. 426.
72. Lombroso and Ferrero, *The Female Offender*, p. 1.

73. The data presented were the collective production of criminologists working throughout Europe, including Lombroso and his colleagues. Lombroso cited studies of a total of 1,033 criminal women, 685 prostitutes, and 225 normal women in hospitals, as well as studies of 176 crania of deceased criminal women and 30 of normal women. Lombroso and Ferrero, *La donna delinquente*, p. 164.
74. Lombroso and Ferrero, *The Female Offender*, p. 24.
75. Ibid.
76. Lombroso remarked in the preface to *La donna delinquente* that his critics, in any case, attached too much importance to anthropometrical measurements. Lombroso and Ferrero, *La donna deliquente*, pp. 1–2.
77. Horn, 'This Norm Which Is Not One'.
78. Lombroso, *Crime, Its Causes* and *Remedies*, p. 99.
79. As Bruno Latour notes, Pasteur's microbiology 'metamorphosed' the very composition of the 'social context', and endowed Pasteur with 'one of the most striking fresh sources of power ever': 'Who can imagine being the representative of a crowd of invisible, dangerous forces able to strike anywhere and to make a shambles of the present state of society, forces of which he is by definition the only credible interpreter and which only he can control?' Latour, 'Give Me a Laboratory and I Will Raise the World', in Karin D. Knorr-Cetina and Michael Mulkay (eds), *Science Observed: Perspectives on the Social Study of Science* (London: Sage, 1983), p. 158. On Alexandre Lacassagne's use of Pasteur to construct a critique of the Italian school of criminology see Sekula, 'The Body and the Archive', p. 37.
80. Foucault, *The History of Sexuality*, Vol. I, *An Introduction*, trans. Robert Hurley (New York: Pantheon, 1978).
81. Article 1, Royal Decree 1743, 14 September 1919.
82. Ministero della Giustizia, Commissione Reale per la Riforma delle Leggi Penali, *Relazione sul progetto preliminare di codice penale (Libro I)* (Rome: L'Universale, 1921). The outline for Book I was published in four languages: Italian, English, French and German. For a further discussion of the relations between criminal anthropology and the revision of the penal code see Pasquino, 'Criminology'.
83. Ministero della Giustizia, *Relazione*, p. 14.
84. For a discussion of the militia see Alberto Aquarone, *L'organizzazione dello stato totalitario* (Turin: Einaudi, 1965), pp. 65–8, 246 ff. Also see the circulars from the Minister of the Interior Luigi Federzoni concerning fascist 'illegalisms' (pp. 382–5).
85. Royal Decree 1848, 6 Nov. 1926.
86. Ministero dell'Interno, Direzione Generale della Pubblica Sicurezza, *Testo unico delle leggi di pubblica sicurezza* (Rome: Provveditorato Generale dello Stato, 1927). As Aquarone notes, some of these measures dated from the nineteenth century; house arrest (*domicilio coatto*) was introduced by a law dated 15 Aug. 1863, for the suppression of brigandage. *L'organizzazione*, p. 99.
87. Reprinted in Aquarone, *L'organizzazione*, p. 423.
88. Antonello Caprino, 'Ordine pubblico e ordine morale', *Politica sociale* 2 (1930), p. 291.
89. As Johan van Justi wrote in 1768: 'The science of policing consists ... in regulating everything that relates to the present condition of society, in strengthening and improving it, in seeing that all things contribute to the welfare of the members that compose it. The aim of policing is to make everything that composes the state serve to strengthen and increase its power, and likewise serve the public welfare.' Cited in Jacques Donzelot, *The Policing of Families*, trans. Robert Hurley (New York: Pantheon, 1979), p. 7.
90. Silvio Longhi, 'Istituti di prevenzione, di pena, di assistenza nella legislazione fascista', *Gerarchia* 12 (1932), pp. 961–5.
91. Alfredo Rocco, 'Relazione al disegno di legge "Delega al Governo del Re della facoltà di emendere il Codice penale, il Codice di procedura penale, le leggi sull" ordinamento giudiziario e di apportare nuove modificazioni e aggiunte al Codice civile', in *La trasformazione dello stato: Dallo Stato liberale allo Stato fascista* (Rome: La Voce, 1925), p. 216.
92. Alfredo Rocco, 'Sulla delega al Governo del Re della facoltà di emendere il Codice penale, il Codice di procedura penale, le leggi sull'ordinamento giudiziario e di

apportare nuove modificazioni e aggiunte al Codice civile', in *La trasformazione dello stato: Dallo Stato liberale allo Stato fascista* (Rome: La Voce, 1925), p. 269.
93. Rocco, 'Relazione al disegno di legge', p. 222.
94. Rocco, 'Relazione a S. M. il Re del Ministro Guardasigilli', in *Codice Penale* (Rome: Istituto Poligrafico dello Stato, 1930), p. 9.
95. Horn, *Social Bodies*.
96. Urla, 'Cultural Politics in an Age of Statistics', p. 836.
97. On the genealogy of 'population' see Michel Foucault, *The History of Sexuality*, Vol. I; Foucault, 'Governmentality', *Ideology and Consciousness* 6 (1979), pp. 5–21; and Barbara Duden, 'Population', in Wolfgang Sachs (ed.), *The Development Dictionary: A Guide to Knowledge and Power* (London: Zed, 1992), pp. 146–57. On the relations between statistics and identities see especially Ian Hacking, 'Biopower and the Avalanche of Printed Numbers', *Humanities in Society* 5 (3-4) (1982), pp. 279–95; I. Hacking, 'Making Up People', in T. Hellwe, M. Sosna and D. Wellbery (eds), *Reconstructing Individualism* (Stanford, CA: Stanford University Press, 1986), pp. 222–36. On the history of Italian anthropology see Sandra Puccini and Massimo Squillacciotti, 'Per una prima ricostruzione degli studi demo-etno-antropologici italiani nel periodo tra le due guerre', in *Studi antropologici italiani e rapporti di classe: Dal positivismo al dibattito attuale* (Milan: Franco Angeli, 1979), pp. 67–93, 201–39.

11

Bodies of Knowledge: Physical Culture and the New Soviet Man

DAVID L. HOFFMANN

In October 1920, the Soviet government issued a decree entitled 'On the physical upbringing of the juvenile population', which stated, 'it is essential for the laboring population to have physical and mental strengths in order to move forward on the path of socialist construction'. The decree called for physical culture activities in all schools, for extra-curricular athletic programs (including those for pre-school children) and for the overall expansion of physical culture in everyday life.[1] Soviet leaders saw physical culture as an essential element in the construction of socialism and the creation of the New Soviet Man. Between 1917 and 1941 they instituted widespread programs to promote bodily health and fitness. A healthy and fit population represented an important resource in an age of large-scale industrial manufacturing and mass warfare. Physical exercise ensured the labor capacity and military preparedness of Soviet citizens.

Physical culture also served the Soviet government's larger aspiration to restore social harmony and remake humankind. Consider a 1920 Commissariat of Health report entitled, 'The Tasks of Physical Culture'. The report stressed the necessity of physical culture both 'to make the population healthy' and 'to create the harmonious and complete individual [*garmonichnaia i tselostnaia lichnost'*], from which one can expect qualities of the most benefit for the common good'.[2] Soviet officials saw physical culture as something that would create harmonious individuals upon which a collective, socialist society could be built.

In this chapter I will consider both of these tasks of physical culture – the health of the population and the creation of harmonious individuals. State concern with the population's health and physical capacity dated from the seventeenth century, and it grew in both urgency and ambition with the rise of modern medicine in the nineteenth and twentieth centuries. Soviet physical culture may be considered part of what Foucault termed 'anatomo-politics' – government and expert intervention to improve people's bodily health for the sake of economic and political power. The second task outlined above – the creation of a harmonious individual who would contribute to society's overall well-being – also had an important political component. This task was part of the revolutionary endeavor to overcome class animosity and social alienation through the creation of the New Soviet Man.

In addition to discussing the motivations behind the physical culture movement, I will also examine the forms the movement took. Once the Soviet government included physical culture as part of its revolutionary project to remake individuals and society, it launched a myriad of studies and programs focused on bodily health. It first compiled statistics on the population's level of physical fitness – a process that entailed government access to measure and categorize people's bodies. The categories in which this statistical knowledge was assembled in turn influenced Soviet officials' perceptions of their tasks and the programs they initiated. Physical culture initiatives in other countries constituted another influence on Soviet programs. The physical culture movement was by no means limited to the Soviet Union, and by the 1930s the Soviet government was closely monitoring and often imitating physical fitness efforts in other countries. The rising international tensions of the late 1930s impelled Soviet physical culture to assume its extreme militaristic character.

ANATOMO-POLITICS AND SOCIAL HARMONY

According to Foucault, a new form of power over life emerged in the seventeenth century, one 'centred on the body as a machine: its disciplining, the optimization of its capabilities, the extortion of its forces'.[3] This 'anatomo-politics of the human body' stemmed in part from cameralist thought and the realization that economic power depended upon the size and labor capabilities of the population. The rise of social science and modern medicine in the eighteenth and nineteenth centuries magnified the ambitions of state officials, social reformers and medical personnel alike in their quest to solve social problems and ensure the health and productive capacity of the population. Advancements in physiology and epidemiology in particular fueled a sense that state health programs could radically reduce disease and disability and hence guarantee the population's ability to work.

Soviet officials placed special emphasis on labor as a social obligation and means to personal fulfillment, so it is not surprising that they stressed the role of physical culture in expanding people's work capacity. The Commissar of Health, Nikolai Semashko, called physical culture 'one of the principal links to labor and to work ability'.[4] Official reports touted physical culture as a means to teach peasants to work rationally and effectively.[5] Studies on labor productivity showed that workers who did physical exercises at the start of the workday and during breaks were more productive than workers who did not.[6] Labor hero Aleksei Stakhanov endorsed physical culture as something that 'disciplines people, and instills in them new strengths and enthusiasm [*bodrost*]'.[7]

Beyond the practical aim of increasing the population's labor capacity, physical culture offered a means to transform people's attitude toward work. Soviet physical culture pageants sometimes combined labor and sports images in an allusion to Marx's prophecy that work would become pleasurable.[8] Of course Marx's vision of unalienated labor was based primarily upon the fact that workers would reap the benefits of their own work. But it also relied upon a notion of labor as voluntary, recreational and fulfilling. By portraying physical labor as akin to recreational exercise, Soviet authorities sought to instill a new attitude toward work.[9]

The renowned Soviet theater director Vsevolod Meyerhold applied these ideas about labor in his techniques to train actors. In a 1922 lecture entitled 'The Actor of the Future and Biomechanics', Meyerhold argued that the actor would 'be working in a society where labor is no longer regarded as a curse but as a joyful, vital necessity'. Under socialism, workers would no longer avoid labor, as long as they could be revitalized to overcome fatigue. 'Under ideal conditions', according to Meyerhold, 'a rest of as little as ten minutes is capable of completely restoring a man's energy. Work should be made easy, congenial and uninterrupted.' Meyerhold extolled skilled workers for their rhythm, stability and absence of superfluous movements, and declared that 'the spectacle of a man working efficiently affords positive pleasure'.[10]

In order to prepare workers and actors alike for continuous, efficient and aesthetic labor, Meyerhold prescribed the physical perfection of the body. He stated that 'the actor must train his material (the body), so that it is capable of executing instantaneously those tasks which are dictated externally'. In response to his own question, 'How do we set about molding the new actor?' Meyerhold replied, 'If we place him in an environment in which gymnastics and all forms of sport are both available and compulsory, we shall achieve the New Man who is capable of any form of labor.'[11]

Ideas about bodily perfection were also expressed in Soviet poster art. For aesthetic as well as utilitarian reasons, Soviet authorities produced posters that projected images of well-proportioned, vigorous, muscular bodies.[12] The Soviet ideal of the perfect body closely resembled fascist aesthetics of a hard, sculpted body, which was de-sexualized and pure. In Soviet sculpture and posters the body was generally clothed, while Nazi sculpture, following a neo-classical model, presented the body nude.[13] Soviet and Nazi representations of the body also differed in their portrayal of motion. In contrast to Nazi statues of taut and rigidly controlled bodies, Soviet statues and posters presented bodies in motion – especially the bodies of workers building socialism.[14] Despite these variances, Soviet and Nazi representations of the body shared an emphasis on youth, fitness and purity.

The role of physical fitness in the tasks of bodily perfection and labor efficiency was also apparent in the image of the human–machine hybrid. The machine was perhaps the most salient symbol of progress and perfectibility, and for some it became a model for human transformation as well.[15] Some nineteenth-century European thinkers argued that the body, like the machine, was a motor that converted energy into mechanical work. They believed that society should conserve, deploy and expand the energies of the laboring human body, and harmonize its movements with those of the machine. By the 1890s 'the science of work' had emerged as a field, and in the twentieth century this scientific approach to the laboring body pervaded parliamentary debates, sociological treatises, liberal reform programs and socialist tracts.[16]

Soviet leaders, like a range of politicians throughout Europe, adopted the ideal of human beings as machines, whose labor would be deployed rationally in order to maximize the productivity of society as a whole. In 1923, Bukharin urged the creation of 'qualified, especially disciplined, living labor machines.'[17] Aleksei Gastev, the leading Soviet Taylorist, developed even more extensive ideas on human automation. His Central Institute of Labor in Moscow studied the physiological aspects of labor and trained workers to perform more efficiently. Gastev's ultimate goal was the symbiosis of man and machine, in which workers would adopt the rhythm and efficiency of factory equipment and become robot-like producers with perfectly disciplined minds and bodies.[18]

Physical fitness and bodily perfection were also linked to the transformation of consciousness, and had been since before the Revolution. In the first half of the nineteenth century, the social critic Vissarion Belinskii had written that 'the development of mental capacity corresponds to that of the health and strength of the body', and he advocated gymnastics and Russian folk games to develop 'will power, initiative and creativity', as well as 'a harmonious personality'.[19] Nikolai Chernyshevskii, an admirer of Belinskii, emphasized physical fitness in characterizing Rakhmetov, the prototypical New Man of his novel *What is to be Done?* Rakhmetov prepares himself for the revolution with daily gymnastics, heavy physical labor, a diet of raw beef and complete celibacy and sobriety.[20] Rakhmetov served as the archetype for an entire generation of Russian revolutionaries, and embodied the ideal of physical conditioning to develop the mental strength and will-power to create a new world.

Following the Revolution, Soviet leaders continued to stress the transformation of both the body and the mind in the creation of the New Man. In 1924 Trotsky looked forward to a time in the near future when

> the human species ... will once more enter into a state of radical transformation, and, in his own hands, will become an object of the most complicated methods of artificial selection and psycho-physical training ... Man will become immeasurably stronger, wiser and subtler; his body will become more harmonized, his movements more rhythmic, his voice more musical.[21]

Semashko, in less visionary terms, also stressed physical culture's capacity to strengthen the bodily organism, prevent disease and develop well-rounded citizens.[22] Moreover, fundamental to Meyerhold's biomechanical method of training actors was his belief that 'all psychological states are determined by specific physiological processes'.[23]

The creation of the New Man, with a healthy body and pure mind, was intimately connected with the creation of the perfect society, one made up of harmonious individuals. Hence, Soviet government saw physical culture as a means to promote not only mental and physical fitness, but social harmony as well. A 1919 report on children's well-being explained that a healthy body also meant a 'healthy spirit [*dukh*]', and it went on to link a proper physical upbringing with 'the harmonious development of the individual [*lichnost'*]'.[24] In 1920 the Commissariat of Health admitted that 'medicine, with all its scientific discoveries, is not in a position to create the new individual'. It went on to argue that of all means available ('new social conditions, cultural enlightenment work, a new upbringing, sanitary-hygiene measures'), physical culture 'has nearly the most important place' in creating 'an individual with the harmonious development of mental and bodily strengths'.[25]

The concern with shaping a harmonious society had many antecedents in European thought. A variety of nineteenth- and twentieth-century intellectuals, including Marx, Wagner and Nietzsche, abhorred the alienation of the modern world and sought to overcome its fragmentation.[26] To them industrialization and urbanization had destroyed the organic unity and natural rhythms of (pre-modern) society. In place of traditional life, rural purity and social cooperation, they saw urban upheaval, filthy slums and class antagonisms. Some theorists and policy-makers prescribed a return to the (mythical) past; through rural imagery, invented traditions and folklore, they sought to recreate the organic unity of the pre-modern era.

But others sought new, distinctly modern and rational ways to surmount the alienation of the modern world. The ambition to restore social harmony was behind the work of a range of philosophers, artists, architects, city planners and social reformers in the late nineteenth and early twentieth centuries. These people conceived of techniques to transform and integrate a modern world that seemed fragmented and out of sync. In Russia, both before and after the Revolution, a number of thinkers sought ways to overcome social fragmentation and alienation. Pre-revolutionary theater activists, constructivist architects and Soviet efficiency experts alike emphasized rhythm as a way to restore harmony to people's lives and to society.[27] Synchronization of movement, whether in the theater, apartment complex or factory, offered a means to end social friction, and to recreate the unity and harmony lost by the modern world.

State-sponsored physical culture and sports programs in particular emphasized rhythm and group activities for the same reason. All team sports promoted cooperation and solidarity; group gymnastics in particular synchronized the movements of participants and seemed to unify people in body and spirit. Gymnastics programs in many countries had national unity as their explicit goal. Friedrich Ludwig Jahn founded the German gymnastics movement in order to promote German unification.[28] The gymnastics movement in nineteenth-century Germany also combined group exercises with walks in the countryside to recapture the wholeness and purity of rural life and to overcome the alienation and decadence of the city.[29]

Like the German *Turnen* societies, the Czech *Sokol* and the Scandinavian gymnastics movements of the nineteenth century, Russian gymnastics were introduced to enhance national solidarity. The first Russian gymnastics club was founded following the country's defeat in the Crimean War, and in 1874 Petr Lesgaft, the 'father' of Russian gymnastics, instituted a Prussian model of gymnastics training into the Russian military. Also in the 1870s, official school gymnastics manuals were published; these prescribed marching in formation and other exercises to teach unity and discipline.[30]

In a similar way, Soviet physical culture emphasized rhythm, discipline and unity. Rhythmic gymnastics, performed in large groups with synchronized movements, received special attention in Soviet schools and physical culture parades. Team sports also promoted not only healthy individuals but collective activity, cooperation and unity. Soviet leaders were explicit about the goals of unity and political mobilization to be accomplished through physical culture. A Communist Party resolution in 1925 stated,

> Physical culture must be considered not simply from the standpoint of public health and physical education ... It should also be seen as a method of educating the masses (inasmuch as it develops willpower and builds up team work, endurance, resourcefulness and other valuable qualities). It must be regarded, moreover, as a means of rallying the bulk of the workers and peasants to the various Party, Soviet and trade union organizations, through which they can be drawn into social and political activity.[31]

Physical culture, then, was seen as a means to accomplish social unity and political mobilization. Physical culture was also presented as a bulwark against the decadence of modern life. A 1926 Komsomol resolution stressed physical culture as a means to divert young people from the evil influences of alcohol and prostitution.[32] Soviet officials throughout the 1920s expressed enormous concern that the energy of youth was being dissipated in sexual libertinism.[33] Sports and exercise seemed to be a more healthy outlet. One Soviet commentator, after observing sporting exercises, contrasted their 'freshness, vibrancy and healthy strength' to the decadence of 'Americanized dances'.[34] Soviet officials sought to channel the sexual energy of youth toward the tasks of socialist construction. In this discourse, physical culture was presented as pure, healthy and collective, while sex was described as impure, decadent and selfish.

The tasks of physical culture, then, were several. It offered a means to ensure the health and labor capability of the population. It also promoted labor efficiency and, according to some, could transform work into a recreational, fulfilling and joyous enterprise. Physical culture also served the aestheticizing impulse inherent in the ambition to create the New Man. Exercise would result in pure, muscular, healthy bodies, and would instill a sense of rhythm and harmony. Many believed that physical exercise would develop mental as well as physical strength, and would cultivate harmonious individuals, which would contribute to the building of a harmonious society. Group gymnastics received particular attention as a sport that synchronized the movements of individuals and instilled a collective spirit and social unity.

STATISTICAL KNOWLEDGE AND PHYSICAL CULTURE PROGRAMS

It is impossible to comprehend either the concerns about physical fitness or the programs implemented to improve it without considering the bodies of knowledge generated by social scientists and governmental officials. Once physical development became part of the project of creating the New Man and new society, Soviet officials amassed data on the physical state of the population and developed techniques to improve it. The same had been true of tsarist officials prior to the Revolution who, with the much more limited goal of military preparedness, gathered statistics on the physical condition of potential recruits. New goals of government spawned new bodies of knowledge, which in turn influenced both the goals and policies pursued by government officials and medical experts. The ambition to fashion ideal bodies and the knowledge about those bodies, then, developed in tandem, and to understand this process one must examine the production of statistical and bio-mechanical knowledge. Knowledge about the body, while purportedly scientific, was certainly not objective. The categories used in the engendering of this knowledge and the ways in which data were compiled and manipulated were highly normative, and had important ramifications for the policies and programs that resulted.

Seventeenth-century cameralist thought had speculated on the need for a quantitative understanding of the population, but it was only the Enlightenmènt in the eighteenth century that sparked projects, such as those by Condorcet, that statistically represented and analyzed it. By the nineteenth century there occurred an enormous expansion of population statistics, which included the professionalization and regularization of their collection and usage.[35] In addition to large amounts of census data and statistics on fertility and mortality, governments compiled military statistics on the physical characteristics of young men. The tsarist government, for example, in the first half of the nineteenth century, had already begun to gather data and categorize the population.[36]

Following the Revolution, the Soviet government made explicit the importance of statistics to its project of knowing and shaping the population. In an article entitled, 'The Tasks of State Statistics', one Soviet official described statistics as 'a necessary technical apparatus, which will help the new state build the new society'.[37] In addition to national censuses, the Red Army conducted its own censuses that extended beyond recruits to count the entire population. The 1923 Census of the Red Army and Navy, for example, gave the number of people in each province, broken down by age cohort, sex, nationality, family position, social origin, Party membership, literacy and previous military service.[38] The Soviet military also compiled statistics on the height and weight of all recruits, and cross-tabulated these by province of origin, urban versus rural residence, and nationality.[39]

These data in turn influenced how officials conceptualized and acted upon the population's physical condition. For example, statistical categories structured the thinking of officials, who came to see the young men of some provinces as undernourished, the residents of some cities as unhealthy, and the members of some nationalities as physically inferior. Statistics also gave Soviet officials a means to measure the physical improvement of the population and the results of physical culture programs. The head of the Komsomol, Aleksandr Kosarev, cited statistics showing that the average height and weight of 18-year-old males had increased and that the number of illnesses had dropped, and he concluded that 'our youth is growing up stronger and physically more robust'.[40]

Statistical study of the population involved a process of normalization. In the 1830s and 1840s, Adolphe Quetelet had developed the concept of the average man, based upon his discovery that population statistics had a regular distribution around the mean. This step took something abstract – there was no real-life 'average man' – and made it seem real, a postulated reality against which people would be measured.[41] People who fell below this norm were then labeled substandard, or even deviant (a deviation from the norm). The establishment of norms for people's physical development also set a mark for improvement. The founder of eugenics, Francis Galton, classified people in quartiles around a statistical median, and advocated interference in reproduction to make statistical gains in the qualities of a race or population.[42] While Soviet authorities ultimately condemned eugenics as a fascist science, they too paid enormous attention to reproduction and child rearing in an attempt to improve the median physical characteristics of the population.[43]

In addition to statistical knowledge about the population's physical development, Soviet physical culture experts produced knowledge about the most effective means of physical conditioning. The Institute of Physical Culture in Moscow conducted studies and trained instructors in exercise and fitness throughout the 1920s.[44] During the 1930s, laboratory research by physiologists established norms for exercise and leisure. One such study determined that 'active leisure' in the form of rhythmic exercises was the most efficient way to restore the body's energy and labor ability.[45] Research focused particularly on the health and fitness of children. Medical check-ups in schools and statistics on children's health were complemented by studies on the importance of diet and physical exercise to children's physical condition.[46]

As physiological studies and health statistics were compiled, this scientific knowledge in turn prompted the expansion of programs to raise the overall level of physical fitness. Already during the Civil War compulsory physical education had been instituted in schools, and the Central Board of Universal Military Training had taken over and expanded existing gymnastic societies and sport clubs.[47] The October 1920 government decree, 'On the Physical Upbringing of the Juvenile Population', called for the creation of commissions to oversee programs in schools and for the institution of pre-school physical culture programs.[48]

Soviet authorities also founded 'Houses of Physical Culture' – centers that were to promote physical exercise in a 'scientifically instructive' manner, including medically supervised activities, lectures and exhibits.[49] In July 1925 the Central Committee rejected earlier ideas about the development of non-competitive physical culture activities (proposed as a socialist alternative to bourgeois sports) and mandated a more competitive approach to sports and physical culture.[50]

The Soviet government devoted even greater attention and resources to physical culture in the 1930s. In April 1930 the All-Union Physical Culture Council was founded and given executive powers to oversee physical fitness programs throughout the country.[51] The establishment of this central body at least partially resolved the struggle for control of physical culture that had embroiled the military, education, health, Komsomol and trade union bureaucracies.[52] The Council continued to give gymnastics a central place in Soviet physical culture programs. In 1933 a national conference on gymnastics resolved that it should be the basic component of primary and secondary physical education, and a 1936 national gymnastics competition received extensive coverage in the press.[53]

In June 1936 the Politburo approved the formation of the Committee for Physical Culture and Sport under the Council of People's Commissars. This new executive body received even greater financial resources for physical culture.[54] Its establishment also signaled increased attention to competitive sports and sport heroes (in parallel with Stakhanovism in labor). Soccer, basketball and ice hockey, as well as combat sports such as boxing, wrestling and fencing all received heightened priority. The Soviet press also publicized records and record holders in track meets and riflery competitions.[55] All of these measures had military preparedness as a primary objective. As one speaker at a 1936 conference of Moscow physical education teachers stated, 'The preparation of the colossal mass of Moscow students for labor and defense of our motherland depends upon the results of our work.'[56] Moreover, as a report on a physical culture parade in 1938 indicated, 'if war breaks out tomorrow', athletes will quickly become 'tank drivers, pilots, snipers and sailors'.[57]

FOREIGN INFLUENCES AND MILITARIZATION

The physical culture movement in the Soviet Union paralleled developments throughout Europe and around the world. To account for the similarities in physical fitness programs, one should note that the Soviet Union and other countries had common forms of knowledge (statistics on the population's physical development) and common concerns (military preparedness) that informed their policies. But in addition to these shared perceptions and considerations, there were also concrete ways in which information on foreign physical culture influenced Soviet policies. In fact, Soviet officials made a conscious effort to monitor and emulate the physical education initiatives of other countries, especially Germany, and this emulation was one reason for the increasing militarization of Soviet physical culture in the late 1930s.

Already prior to the Revolution, Russian officials borrowed foreign techniques to instill fitness and discipline in young people. One of these techniques was the Boy Scouts, founded by Colonel Robert Baden-Powell to provide physical training and paramilitary skills to British boys. Russian military officers who had trained abroad observed the Boy Scouts in Britain and formed the first scout troop in Russia in 1909. By 1917 there were 50,000 boys and girls in scout troops that existed in 143 Russian towns.[58] After the Revolution, scout organizations were labeled bourgeois and disbanded, but in a sense they were reconstituted with the formation of the Young Pioneers – an organization for Soviet children that taught physical fitness, discipline, patriotism and outdoor survival skills.

Under the Soviet government, the accumulation of data on other countries' physical culture programs became much more extensive and systematic. The Committee on Physical Culture and Sport had an international relations division which researched and wrote regular reports on physical training taking place in Europe, North America and Japan. A report on sports in fascist countries stated that in Nazi Germany 'the entire nation must do physical exercises. The physical perfection of men and women is extremely important to the state, and no one has the right to refuse the obligation to develop their body and fortify their health.'[59] Government reports and articles in the press covered topics such as the administration of athletic clubs in France, training techniques of Japanese swimmers, international cross-country ski races, foreign soccer tournaments and the 1936 Olympic Games in Berlin.[60] These reports kept Soviet officials apprised of the physical and military preparedness of other countries, and also provided ideas and techniques that could be applied in the Soviet Union.

To take one important example, Soviet officials observed and emulated foreign initiatives that promoted physical culture among women. They translated articles from American journals on how to incorporate athletic events into women's higher education.[61] The All-Union Physical Culture Council in 1934 lauded the benefits of physical fitness among German women, and argued that female athletics created 'well-developed young women, who also produce healthy and robust children'. In language that echoed Nazi ideology, it concluded that 'this rapid transformation of the [German] race, without a doubt, must be attributed to physical education ... The German government is occupied by a concern to create a robust people. They have understood that only physical culture may sustain and increase the capital of the health of the nation.'[62] Within two years the Soviet government had convened a conference that launched new programs to promote physical culture among women.[63] It is also noteworthy, however, that the aims of Soviet programs differed from Nazi programs. Unlike the essentialist Nazi gender order which assigned women the single role as mothers of the next generation, the Soviet gender order stressed women's roles as both mothers and workers, and cultivated their physical fitness to enhance their performance in both roles.[64]

In addition to highlighting the physical benefits of athletic programs, Soviet reports on physical culture abroad stressed its disciplinary and patriotic aspects. One report on Germany stated that 'only physical education can bestow the following qualities proclaimed by National Socialism: a sense of discipline, order and subordination; a sense of solidarity, courage, decisiveness, and the ability to make quick decisions when circumstances demand it; endurance and readiness for self-sacrifice'. The same report noted that the German government focused on young people, and oriented them toward self-discipline and 'the spirit of Adolf Hitler'.[65]

Soviet officials were also very aware that other countries used physical culture as military preparation. In 1934 they cited a German article on how gymnastics 'galvanizes patriotic energy', and concluded that German physical culture programs had created a new spirit of militarism.[66] A 1938 report of the Committee on Physical Culture and Sport stated that under the Nazi dictatorship 'sport has become an integral part of preparation for war'.[67] An article in the Soviet press noted that the development of alpinism in Germany had allowed the rapid formation of mountain troops during World War I, and concluded that 'alpinism has for us [the Soviet Union] enormous military significance'.[68]

Soviet commentators' attention to the military aspects of physical culture abroad focused on the training of youth. Describing military instruction in schools and the military agenda of the Hitler Youth organization, the head of the Komsomol warned in 1936 that fascist governments in Germany, Poland, Italy and Japan had conducted 'an intensified militarization of youth'. Based on these assessments, he called on the Komsomol to prepare young people to defend their country.[69] In a 1937 speech to leading members of the Komsomol at the Dynamo Sports Club, an official of the Committee on Physical Culture and Sport criticized the lack of attention to military aspects of sport. Taking the example of automobile and motorcycle racing, he said that 'it is no secret that motor sports are a means of mass preparation of reserves for motorized divisions of the Red Army'. He went on to point out that Germany had over a million motorcycles while the Soviet Union had only eight thousand. He also called for gymnastics that were less like ballet and more like military training.[70]

In the years leading up to World War II, Soviet physical culture indeed took on an increasingly militaristic character. Already in 1935 a civil defense pamphlet stated that 'to be prepared for defense means to be physically healthy', and it emphasized the importance of shooting contests, gymnastics, swimming and cycling, as well as training in the use of gas masks and bayonets.[71] A Politburo resolution in November 1939 created a new organization, 'Prepared for Labor and Defense of the USSR'. The organization was to develop additional physical education programs in schools, physical culture centers and prizes, instructional manuals and films, and medical supervision to maximize the health benefit of exercise and activities.[72] Articles in the Soviet press continued to promote sports and stressed 'military physical education' and the importance of physical culture to master military skills.[73]

The Soviet government placed special emphasis on militaristic physical culture parades. Soviet journals heralded these parades as indicators of the importance of physical education and 'the discipline of physical culture participants'.[74] In the summer of 1937, the Politburo ordered that a physical culture parade be held on Red Square with over 40,000 participants, including delegations from each republic and record holders in a number of sports.[75] An article about this event, entitled 'The Parade of the Powerful Stalin Breed [*plemia*]', included photographs of gymnastic teams and stressed the unity of all the nationalities of the Soviet Union.

> The living poem created on Red Square by Russian, Ukrainian ... [lists the nationalities of all 15 republics] physical culture participants proclaims in a loud, sonorous voice, which echoes around the entire world, the blood brotherhood and indissoluble friendship of the peoples which populate the broad expanse of the country of Soviets; ... and [declares] that the brave, strong Soviet youth are an inexhaustible reserve for our powerful Red Army.[76]

This quotation demonstrates that physical culture parades were more than just a display of discipline and potential military strength. Parades symbolized the unity of Soviet society. In them, all nationalities and social groups were symbolically united as they marched and performed synchronized exercises in perfect unison.

Physical culture parades were a type of theater or spectacle, and, as such, were characteristic of the mass politics of the modern era. In an age of popular sovereignty and mass warfare, the participation of thousands of citizens in theatricalized rituals of unity and strength were important mobilizational mechanisms. Meyerhold in 1929 had predicted that the 'theater of the future' would have 'theatricalized sporting games' staged on a mass scale.[77] In a similar vein, Wagner and Nietzsche had both seen theatrical space as a remedy to the alienation of modern society. As Katerina Clark has pointed out, these thinkers had championed theater as a means to unite previously unsynchronized individuals and social groups.[78] In this sense, participation in mass theatrical spectacles was intended not only to symbolize unity but to transform and integrate the participants.

While participatory, physical culture parades were not democratic. As was true of fascist spectacles and marches, parades on Red Square were conducted under the paternal gaze of leaders, who stood atop Lenin's mausoleum. Physical culture parades symbolized not simply unity, but unity behind Stalin and other Communist Party leaders. Their character was quite different from that of the early Soviet mass spectacles, which, while also choreographed, celebrated the spontaneity of the masses and incorporated revolutionary iconoclasm and the carnivalesque.[79] Throughout the 1920s, spectacles and parades had become more ceremonial and patriotic, and by the 1930s they were rigid and militarized.[80] Physical culture parades in particular emerged as rituals of discipline, controlled movements and homage to Party leaders.[81]

CONCLUSION

For Soviet authorities, physical culture represented an important component in their attempts to create the New Soviet Man. They sought to shape the body as well as the mind, and in fact believed that physical exercise was essential to mental health and the transformation of consciousness. Physical culture, according to Soviet experts, was a means to perfect the body and ensure the harmonious development of the personality. Harmonious individuals would contribute to a collective society, one in which the alienation and antagonisms of the past might be overcome in favor of an organically whole, unified community. Gymnastics emerged as a favored form of physical culture precisely because it taught not only discipline and control, but also synchronization, through group exercises believed capable of integrating and uniting individuals.

The population's physical well-being also served state interests in cultivating a healthy and productive labor force. This type of anatomopolitical thinking both prompted and was reinforced by bio-mechanical studies designed to optimize the body's productive potential. Added to these studies were social science and medical research that shaped the perceptions and programs of Soviet authorities. When masses of statistics were gathered and processed on the physical state of the population, Soviet experts perceived a need to improve people's physical characteristics, particularly of those nationalities and social groups that fell below newly created averages and norms.

Concerns about the physical capacity of the population and programs designed to improve it were in no way unique to the Soviet Union. Indeed, Soviet authorities obtained many of their ideas about the importance of physical culture from reports on fitness initiatives throughout Europe and other parts of the world. In the late 1930s, physical culture in Nazi Germany came under particular scrutiny, and Soviet athletic programs replicated its militarism. Physical culture was seen as having an enormous role in preparing the population for war. Athletic programs were believed not only to strengthen the body and prepare it for combat, but to teach discipline, patriotism and unity. Physical culture parades became a symbol of this unity and received enormous attention in the years leading up to the war.

While Soviet physical culture resembled foreign (especially Nazi) programs, it had important differences as well. Soviet efforts sought to unite all nationalities, in stark contrast to the racially exclusionary and ultimately genocidal policies of the Nazis. In comparison with the democratic countries of Europe, which also had social thinkers who advocated physical fitness and social harmony, the Soviet Union possessed a revolutionary ideology which greatly heightened the sense that the world and human beings could be entirely remade. This sense both induced and justified the extreme forms of state intervention in an entire range of areas, including physical culture and the body. Also significant was the lack of any legal protections to prevent this type of government intrusion. The Soviet system was born at a moment of total war when the mobilizational and defense priorities of the state took precedence over everything else. It is therefore not surprising that physical culture programs, which were seen as having a crucial part in preparation for war and in unification of the country, were rigorously imposed upon schools, factories, communities and individuals throughout the country.

NOTES

1. GARF (Gosudarstvennyi arkhiv Rossiiskoi Federatsii [State Archive of the Russian Federation]), f. A-482, op. 11, d. 58, l. 19.
2. GARF, f. A-482, op. 11, d. 58, l. 8.
3. Michel Foucault, *The History of Sexuality*, Vol. I, trans. Robert Hurley (New York: Vintage, 1990), p. 139.
4. N.A. Semashko, *Novyi byt i polovoi vopros* (Moscow/Leningrad: Gos. izd., 1926), p. 15.
5. GARF, f. A-482, op. 11, d. 58, l. 9.
6. *Gigiena i sotsialisticheskoe zdravookhranenie* 4/5 (1932), pp. 27–30.

7. *Gimnastika na predpriiatiak i proizvoditel'nost' truda* (Moscow: OGIZ-Fizkul'tura i turizm, 1936), p. 5.
8. Toby Clark, 'The "New Man's" Body: A Motif in Early Soviet Culture', in Matthew Cullerne Bown and Brandon Taylor (eds), *Art of the Soviets: Painting, Sculpture and Architecture in a One-Party State* (New York: Manchester University Press, 1993), p. 40.
9. Soviet musical films of the 1930s portrayed smiling peasants who sang while working in the fields and factory workers who swung their hammers in time to music; see the documentary, 'East Side Story', dir. Dana Ranga (Germany, 1997).
10. Vsevolod Meierhold, 'The Actor of the Future and Biomechanics', in Edward Braun (ed. and trans.), *Meyerhold on Theatre* (London: Methuen, 1969), pp. 197–8.
11. Meierhold, 'The Actor of the Future and Biomechanics', p. 200.
12. Victoria Bonnell, *The Iconography of Power* (Berkeley, CA: University of California Press, 1997), p. 41.
13. Analyzing the work of Nazi sculptor Arno Breker, George Mosse writes that 'the nude body is not merely symbolic of true beauty and nature, but also points backward to Paradise as the paradigm of a healthy world before the onset of modernity'. George L. Mosse, *Nationalism and Sexuality: Middle-Class Morality and Sexual Norms in Modern Europe* (Madison, WI: University of Wisconsin Press, 1985), pp. 172–3.
14. Bonnell, *Iconography of Power*, p. 41; Barbara Keys, 'Totalitarian Corporealities: Educating the Body under Nazism and Stalinism', Paper presented at the AAASS conference (September, 1998), p. 24.
15. Clark, 'The "New Man's" Body', p. 36.
16. Anson Rabinbach, *The Human Motor: Energy, Fatigue, and the Origins of Modernity* (New York: Basic Books, 1990), pp. 2–8.
17. As quoted in Clark, 'The "New Man's" Body', p. 36.
18. Richard Stites, *Revolutionary Dreams: Utopian Vision and Experimental Life in the Russian Revolution* (New York: Oxford University Press, 1989), pp. 152–4; David L. Hoffmann, *Peasant Metropolis: Social Identities in Moscow, 1929–1941* (Ithaca, NY: Cornell University Press, 1994), pp. 78–9. See also Kendall E. Bailes, 'Alexei Gastev and the Controversy over Taylorism in the Soviet Union, 1920–1924', *Soviet Studies* 3 (1977).
19. V.G. Belinsky, *Izbrannye pedagogicheskie sochineniia*, Vol. II (Moscow/Leningrad, 1948), p. 76, as quoted in James Riordan, *Sport in Soviet Society: Development of Sport and Physical Education in Russia and the USSR* (New York: Cambridge University Press, 1977), p. 43. In nineteenth-century England the field of psychophysiology also stressed the link between the physical and mental condition. See Bruce Haley, *The Healthy Body and Victorian Culture* (Cambridge, MA: Harvard University Press, 1978), p. 23.
20. Nikolai Chernyshevsky, *What is to be Done?*, trans. Michael R. Katz (Ithaca, NY: Cornell University Press, 1989), pp. 278–83.
21. Leon Trotsky, *Literature and Revolution* (Ann Arbor, MI: University of Michigan Press, 1966), pp. 254–6.
22. N.A. Semashko, 'Fizicheskaia kul'tura i zdravookhranenie v SSSR', (1927) *Izbrannye proizvedeniia* (Moscow: Gos. izd. meditsinskoi literatury, 1954), pp. 263–5. See also Stefan Plaggenborg, *Revolutionskultur: Menschenbilder und kulturelle Praxis in Sowjetrussland zwischen Oktoberrevolution und Stalinismus* (Cologne: Bohlau, 1996).
23. Meierhold, 'The Actor of the Future and Biomechanics', p. 199.
24. GARF, f. A-482, op. 11, d. 19, l. 77.
25. GARF, f. A-482, op. 11, d. 58, l. 8.
26. Katerina Clark, *Petersburg: Crucible of Cultural Revolution* (Cambridge, MA: Harvard University Press, 1995), pp. 80–1.
27. Clark, *Petersburg*, p. 260.
28. Mosse, *Nationalism and Sexuality*, p. 78.
29. Ibid., p. 50.
30. Riordan, *Sport in Soviet Society*, pp. 19–20. The Russian *Sokol* gymnastics movement that arose in the 1880s was modeled on the Czech movement and had an explicit pan-Slavist ideology; see Riordan, *Sport in Soviet Society*, p. 35.
31. *Izvestiia tsentral'nogo komiteta RKP(b)*, 20 July 1925, as quoted in Riordan, *Sport in Soviet Society*, p. 106.

32. Riordan, *Sport in Soviet Society*, p. 107.
33. See Eric Naiman, *Sex in Public: The Incarnation of Early Soviet Ideology* (Princeton, NJ: Princeton University Press, 1997).
34. A. Gvozdev, 'Postanovka "D. E." v "Teatre imeni Vs. Meierkhol'da"', *Zhizn' isskustva* 26 (24 June, 1924), p. 6, as cited in Clark, *Petersburg*, p. 162.
35. Paul Rabinow, *French Modern: Norms and Forms of the Social Environment* (Cambridge, MA: MIT Press, 1989), p. 59; Ian Hacking, *The Taming of Chance* (New York: Cambridge University Press, 1990), pp. 2–3.
36. Peter Holquist, '"To Remove" and "To Exterminate Totally": Population Statistics and Population Politics in Late Imperial and Soviet Russia', Paper presented to 'Empire and Nation in the Soviet Union', University of Chicago, Oct. 1997.
37. P. Popov, 'O zadachakh gosudarstevennoi statistiki', *Vestnik statistiki* 1 (1919), p. 31.
38. RGAE (Rossiiskii gosudarstvennyi arkhiv ekonomiki [Russian State Archive of the Economy]) f. 1562, op. 21, d. 356.
39. RGAE, f. 1562, op. 21, d. 434.
40. A. Kosarev, *Otchet TsK VLKSM desiatomu vsesoiuznomu s"ezdu Leninskogo Komsomola* (Moscow: Molodaia gvardiia, 1936), p. 21.
41. Hacking, *The Taming of Chance*, pp. 107–9.
42. Ibid., pp. 168–9; Rabinow, *The Taming of Chance*, p. 327.
43. David L. Hoffmann, 'Mothers in the Motherland: Stalinist Pronatalism in its Pan-European Context', *Journal of Social History*, Fall (2000), pp. 35–54.
44. GARF, f. A-482, op. 11, d. 58, l. 27.
45. *Gimnastika na*, p. 25.
46. A.V. Mol'kov (ed.) *Shkol'naia gigiena* (Moscow/Leningrad: Gos. izd. biologicheskoi i meditsinskoi literatury, 1937), pp. 360–71.
47. Riordan, *Sport in Soviet Society*, pp. 69–76.
48. GARF, f. A-482, op. 11, d. 58, ll. 19–20.
49. GARF, f. A-482, op. 11, d. 40, l. 81.
50. Robert Edelman, *Serious Fun: A History of Spectator Sports in the USSR* (New York: Oxford University Press, 1993), p. 34.
51. Riordan, *Sport in Soviet Society*, p. 122.
52. Keys, 'Totalitarian Corporealities', pp. 11–12.
53. Riordan, *Sport in Soviet Society*, p. 137; *Fizkul'tura i sport* 1 (1937), pp. 4–5.
54. RTsKhIDNI (Rossiiskii tsentr khraneniia i izucheniia dokumentov noveishei istorii [Russian Centre for the Preservation and Study of Documents of Contemporary History]) f. 17, op. 3, d. 978, l. 130.
55. *Fizkul'tura i sport* 1 (1937), pp. 6–15; Riordan, *Sport in Soviet Society*, pp. 127, 140.
56. TsMAM (Tsentral'nyi munitsipal'nyi arkhiv Moskvy [Central Municipal Archive of Moscow]), f. 528, op. 1, d. 383, l. 46.
57. *Izvestiia*, 26 July 1938, as cited in Edelman, *Serious Fun*, p. 44.
58. Riordan, *Sport in Soviet Society*, pp. 35–6. See also Josh Sanborn, 'Empire, Nation, and the Man: Conscription and Political Community in Russia, 1905–1925' (dissertation, University of Chicago, 1997), Ch. 5.
59. GARF, f. 7576, op. 2, d. 153, ll. 2–3.
60. GARF, f. 7576, op. 2, d. 245, ll. 2–6; *Fizkul'tura i sport* 1 (1937), p. 14; 2 (1937), pp. 4, 12; 13 (1937), p. 15; GARF, f. 7576, op. 2, d. 183, l. 117.
61. See for example GARF, f. 7576, op. 2, d. 210, ll. 1–10.
62. GARF, f. 7576, op. 2, d. 153, l. 5.
63. GARF, f. 7576, op. 14, d. 2, l. 1.
64. For further discussion, see Keys, 'Totalitarian Corporealities', p. 16.
65. GARF, f. 7576, op. 2, d. 153, ll. 3–4. The report also paraphrased a German article that claimed Hitler had 'restored the pride of the German people', and that gymnastics societies had helped develop this pride.
66. GARF, f. 7576, op. 2, d. 153, l. 4.
67. GARF, f. 7576, op. 2, d. 201, l. 64.
68. *Fizkul'tura i sport* 3 (1937), pp. 8–9.
69. Kosarev, *Otchet TsK VLKSM*, pp. 28–34.

70. TsKhDMO (Tsentr Khrgneniia dokumentov molodezhnykh organiszatsii [Center for Preservation of Records of Youth Organizations]) f. 1, op. 23, d. 1268, l. 3.
71. M. Likhachev, *Byt' gotovym: Rabota oboronnoi sektsii sel'soveta* (Leningrad: Izd. Lenoblispolkoma i Lensoveta, 1935), pp. 26–8. The pamphlet's preface explained that fascist Germany planned a 'crusade' against the Soviet Union and that Japanese fascists conspired to grab territory in eastern Siberia; p. 3.
72. RTsKhIDNI, f. 17, op. 3, d. 1016, ll. 37, 79–80.
73. *Komsomol'skii rabotnik* 6 (1941), p. 1; 11 (1941), p. 1.
74. *Gimnastika* 1 (1937); *Partiinoe stroitel'stvo* 15 (1939), p. 28.
75. RTsKhIDNI, f. 17, op. 3, d. 987, l. 91. See also GARF, f. 3316 sekretnaia chast', op. 64, d. 1651, ll. 5–7, for the detailed plans behind a 1935 physical culture parade.
76. *Fizkul'tura i sport* 13 (1937), pp. 4–5.
77. Cited in Clark, *Petersburg*, p. 254.
78. Clark, *Petersburg*, p. 80.
79. The mass spectacles of 1920, for example, ridiculed foreign leaders and included a re-enactment of the storming of the Winter Palace; Stites, *Revolutionary Dreams*, pp. 94–6.
80. In the early 1930s, parades still stressed the egalitarian character of physical culture, but by the late 1930s participation was restricted to those who had earned 'Prepared for Labor and Defense of the USSR' medals; Edelman, *Serious Fun*, p. 42.
81. For further discussion see Stites, *Revolutionary Dreams*, p. 228, and Clark, *Petersburg*, p. 306.

12

Discourse Made Flesh: Healing and Terror in the Construction of Soviet Subjectivity

ERIC NAIMAN

In 1932–33, Klara Zetkin, suffering from the heart problems that would soon lead to her death, required doses of camphor to raise her blood pressure. On one occasion, as the medical personnel prepared to inject this stimulant into her left buttock, Zetkin told them to find another site: 'That one', she explained, 'belongs to Dr Zamkov.'[1]

In a society in which the ownership of property did not convey the same status as in the capitalist West, ownership of the left (or even the right) buttock of one of the most prominent figures in the history of the world Communist movement may have been the equivalent of quite a few liquid or immovable assets. And Dr Aleksei Zamkov's list of patients was not limited to infirm and elderly foreign Communists. His career was powerfully furthered by another patient, Maksim Gorky, and among others he numbered influential members of the Bolshevik hierarchy, including Valerian Kuibyshev, a Politburo member and the chairman of the State Planning Commission, as well as leading figures in the Moscow cultural establishment, such as the star ballerina Marina Semeneva and the novelist Marietta Shaginian (author of the production novel *Hydrocentral*), who in 1935 helped him place an article about his research in the country's leading cultural journal *Novyi mir*.[2]

Equally important as this anecdote about Zetkin's buttock, however, is the identity of the person who related it. It forms part of the still-unpublished autobiographical reminiscences of Zamkov's wife, Vera Mukhina, as set down in a surprisingly candid series of interviews with the writer Aleksandr Bek in late 1939 and early 1940. Mukhina, the creator of what is probably the most ideologically important sculptural work of the Soviet period – the tremendously resonant *Rabochii i kolkhoznitsa* ([Male] Worker and [Female] Collective Farmer) which originally crowned the Soviet pavilion at the 1937 international exhibition in Paris – played a major role in the elaboration of the ideal Soviet, or Stalinist, body. Today her name and that sculpture, which was subsequently enshrined in the Soviet iconic pantheon at the entrance of the Exhibition of the Achievements of the National Economy of the USSR – has become emblematic of socialist realism and the system of aesthetic representation of the Stalinist period. Her husband, an endocrinological therapist and, in the 1930s, a giant in the prestigious Soviet-championed field of 'experimental biology', is virtually forgotten today,[3] but he had an important function in the production *from the inside* of the Stalinist body, a body capable of working tremendously long shifts, a body in a nearly perpetual state of élan, a body that would not be weakened by infection, stress or even fear. Trying to describe to Bek why she had fallen in love with her husband, Mukhina summed up his attraction for her in two words: '*vnutrenniaia monumental'nost*' (internal monumentality) adding that she loved the way he combined 'external coarseness with great spiritual fineness'.[4] In telling this story about Zetkin's reliance on Zamkov, Mukhina was in her own way attempting to do what Zamkov had sought for a decade – to stake the equivalent of a copyright claim on their era's emblematic body of power.

The study of Soviet subjectivity is a field in which exciting work is just getting under way. For a long time, scholarship on the Soviet Union was dominated by a Cold War model of a subject formed through external coercion, one in which the subject either resists or submits to the demand for ideological conformity, or manages both, through a split between public conformity and private resistance, between the 'false', public identity of the mask and the 'true', private identity of the face. More recently, social historians have focused on questions of demographic and class identity, asking which groups benefited and thus were likely to have supported or welcomed the Stalinist transformation of Soviet life.[5] In the last few years, partly as a result of the opening of Russian archives, scholars have begun to approach subjectivity from the perspective of rhetoric, analyzing the expressive forms of ideology and the attempts of individuals to master them. Seen from this perspective, Soviet subjectivity becomes a matter of mastering a new language of power, a language that not only empowers an individual, creating access to positions of influence and material goods and offering protection from the often-lethal consequences of lack of such access, but also transforms the speaker desirous of talking herself (in both senses of this expression) into membership in the Soviet community.[6]

The study of Soviet ideology has recently moved from the analysis of concepts to the analysis of discourse; scholars are beginning to accept the notion that ideology is a text to be read. The gap between this text and 'real life', however, has remained the Achilles heel of discourse analysis; attempts to patch it up with memoirs and reminiscences are an unsatisfactory way of approaching the issue of what subjects thought or desired at a given time. One approach is to examine how the ideological text was read and absorbed by its consumers. How did contemporaries process this material in the construction of their own identities? Of course, here, too, we can only act as readers of texts, but these 'secondary' texts offer a more promising nexus between public discourse and subjective identity; they provide a glimpse at the process by which individual subjects were shaped and by which official discourse transformed and was transformed by individual bodies and minds. This chapter will explore this question of ideological incarnation by describing Dr Zamkov's practice and inquiring into the desires of his patients.

Aleksei Andreevich Zamkov was born in 1883 in Borisovo, a village in the Moscow Guberniia. He was part of a large peasant family; his grandfather had been a serf and herded cattle. In a 1908 autobiography, written when the 25-year-old Zamkov was preparing himself for medical school, he recalled this period in vivid if rather clichéd sentimental terms:

> Family arguments and squabbles were ordinary events. I frequently found myself an involuntary witness to oppressive and unpleasant scenes. They have forever clouded my childhood memories. In the summer my mother worked in the field, and in the winter she took care of the cattle and little children, of which she had 14. I grew up not knowing her caresses and was left entirely to myself.[7]

Zamkov went to a parish school before attending, for four years, the local *uezdnoe uchilishche* (upper school), to which he walked five kilometers every day. When he was 15 his father insisted that he be sent to Moscow, where he worked hauling barrels and sacks in the customs office. After several years of this labor, he began to attend night school at the Moscow Society for Commercial Knowledge, studying bookkeeping, calligraphy and German and eventually earning qualification as an accountant. Zamkov worked for seven years in the Moscow bank of the Mutual Credit Society, at first as an errand boy, and then as a bookkeeper. During this period he may have become active in revolutionary activity, although in this matter it is difficult to separate fact from family myth.[8] In 1906 Zamkov began to put aside the money that he would need to prepare for examinations for the *attestat zrelosti'* – the matriculation certificate required for entrance to a university. In his 1908 autobiography, apparently written as an assignment for one of the preparatory courses, he explains that he took the decision to study further because 'I dreamed of knowledge, dreamed of conscientious work for the good of society'.[9] He related that he barely had time to sleep, was eating very little and had become isolated from most of his family, which disapproved of any further education: 'Only my 90-year-old grandpa was on my side and gave me his blessing. He used to tell me that everything in life can collapse, everything can betray a person, knowledge is the only thing that won't.'[10] Zamkov passed the exam for the certificate on his second attempt and enrolled in the medical school of Moscow University. In 1913 he served as a medical assistant at a Yalta hospital; the following year he received his medical degree with distinction and was immediately sent to the front.

Zamkov returned to Moscow seriously ill with typhus in 1915. Upon recovering he began to work as a surgeon in a series of Moscow hospitals, at one of which he re-encountered Vera Mukhina, whom he had first met in 1914. A wealthy young sculptress who had trained in Paris, Mukhina was now working as a nurse in Moscow hospitals; when she fell ill with trichinosis, she was treated by Zamkov. The two married in 1918 and their survival during the next two years was largely facilitated by Zamkov's Sunday practice in Borisovo, his native village, where he treated peasants who paid him in produce.[11] Their only child, Vsevolod, who became a physicist, was born in 1920. During the 1920s, as Mukhina slowly made a name for herself in various competitions, Zamkov worked as a surgeon in several Moscow hospitals and was affiliated with the treatment center at a large factory; he also began to serve as a consultant at the Moscow Regional Clinical Institute, in particular, for its therapeutic clinic headed by Dmitrii Pletnev, one of the most respected figures in the Soviet medical establishment.

Zamkov grew bored by surgery and offered his services as a volunteer researcher to Nikolai Kol'tsov, the director of the Institute of Experimental Biology. Trained as a zoologist and with impressive credentials as a political progressive, Kol'tsov had founded the institute with his own money in 1916, and after the Revolution he had forged strong relationships with leading Bolshevik intellectuals and guided the institute to prominence as a flagship of revolutionary, future-oriented science, including eugenics, a field that would eventually prove his undoing. Kol'tsov was fascinated by the so-called rejuvenation operations developed in Austria and France by Eugen Steinach and Sergei Voronoff and practiced by various physicians across Europe. Steinach, who earlier in his career had experimented with the use of hormones to produce 'a wide range of hermaphroditism' in rats, promoted the idea of tying the vas deferens (a procedure already in use for sterilization) to transform the testes into an organ of heightened internal secretion for the revitalization of the entire organism.[12] In Voronoff's case these experiments involved grafting materials from the sex glands of animals on to various organs of human patients, a procedure that supposedly restored vitality.[13] Over the course of the mid-1920s, Zamkov performed over 500 of these grafting operations, but was dissatisfied with the results, since the rejuvenation effect seemed short-lived.

Zamkov was not alone in his fascination with the Steinach and Voronoff treatments, which produced a great deal of resonance in the Soviet press. In fact, Zamkov's interest in this area may well have been a response to the prominence enjoyed by endocrinology in Soviet popular science during the 1920s. The old belief in 'the sovereignty of the brain' had been displaced by new knowledge about hormones, the true 'builders of the living body' (*stroiteli zhivogo tela*).[14] The knowledge that in Russia endocrinology was – albeit largely by dint of historical coincidence – primarily a post-revolutionary, and thus distinctly Soviet, science may account for the politically charged language that informs accounts of the glandular system's challenge to the nervous system's rule.[15] In at least one version, hormones emerge as a kind of corporeal proletariat that has finally thrown off the brain's domination and serves as the 'voice' (*golos*) of cells situated throughout the entire body.[16] Some popular science writers used the endocrine system to explore the real meaning of the term 'soul'[17] or to speculate about the feasibility of human immortality;[18] some seized upon hormonal research and hormonal manipulation as proof that God did not exist.[19]

In about 1928 Kol'tsov asked Zamkov to try to replicate the experiments of two German gynecologists (Bernhard Zondel and Selmar Aschheim) who had developed the first pregnancy test based on urine samples. Urine was injected into sexually immature female mice. If the donor was pregnant, the German physicians claimed, the young mice would rapidly become sexually mature. Zamkov confirmed that the test was accurate, and he was particularly intrigued because some of the effects noted in the injected mice resembled the physical changes produced by Voronoff's sex grafts. In the grand tradition of charismatic endocrinological research, Zamkov first injected himself with sterilized urine from pregnant women to make sure there were no toxic effects; he then began to experiment by intramuscularly injecting sterilized urine from pregnant women into women with endocrine disorders or psychological disturbances attributed to improper ovarian functioning. Coining the term 'gravidan' (from the Latin word for pregnant), Zamkov began expanding the scope of the filtered urine's application, claiming that it was a non-specific therapeutic agent that could produce positive effects on a wide variety of conditions. He published his research on gravidan in the influential journal *Klinicheskaia meditsina*, directed by Pletnev,[20] and he delivered a paper on the subject at the Moscow

Therapeutic Society, which was also headed by Pletnev. After this paper, Zamkov later claimed, Pletnev came up to him and proposed that they work together on gravidan: 'You'll do the experiments, Aleksei Andreevich, and I'll write.' Zamkov coyly responded that he could manage to do both himself, and this, he claimed, was the origin of his decade-long feud with Pletnev.[21]

During 1929, Zamkov's experiments raised a great deal of interest. Gorky invited him to his home and soon was helping him to secure the white mice necessary for his experiments. At some point, Gorky became a patient. On 22 March 1930, however, the tide turned. *Izvestiia* published a letter signed by 13 researchers at Kol'tsov's institute.[22] They accused Zamkov of uncontrolled, non-clinical testing, of improper treatment – at home – of private patients with materials obtained at the institute, and thus of private 'speculation'. They thus linked Zamkov to the therapeutic equivalent of the kulak in the furious campaign against private medical practice that had been raging for several months. The journal *Voprosy zdravokhraneniia* (Questions of health care), which changed its name to *Na fronte zdravokhranenii* (On the health care front) during the campaign, reported that 40 per cent of all those engaged in 'free professions' in Russia were doctors and dentists, not including doctors with private practices who also worked in government institutions.[23] Class warfare in medicine and the evolution of a medical establishment with the correct world view supposedly depended on the eradication of private practitioners, who were allegedly exploiting members of the working class. (In part this was a guise for an anti-abortion campaign, because 61 per cent of the 1.9 million private visits to doctors in Moscow involved gynecological consultations, most frequently for abortions; and 40 per cent of Moscow abortions were performed in private practices.[24]) Zamkov's private practice was apparently booming; on the average a private practice doubled a doctor's income, from 100–150 to 200–300 rubles a month.[25] Before he began treating patients with gravidan, private practice already accounted for about half of Zamkov's reported income; if he was less than truthful on his tax declarations it accounted for much more.[26]

Even though he retained Kol'tsov's support, Zamkov's life at the institute was made miserable, his experiments were sabotaged and his lab animals killed. Moreover, his status as one of Kol'tsov's protégés may have hurt him. In 1928 the All-Union Association of Workers of Science and Technology for the Facilitation of Socialist Construction in the USSR had been formed for the purpose of introducing ideological order into scientific research institutes. These institutes had been sundered from universities and other teaching facilities earlier in the decade, on the basis of the German system of organization for scientific research, the difference being, in Loren Graham's pithy formulation, that 'while the Germans feared the effects of mass education on science, the Soviet authorities feared the effects of bourgeois scientists on mass education'.[27] The All-Union Association saw as its mission the 'bolshevization' of the leadership of medical institutes and resolved 'to compete with the OGPU' (secret police) in the unmasking of wreckers.[28] Kol'tsov, a representative of pre-revolutionary as well as Soviet science, was selected as a target, and his genetics laboratory (his own particular area of specialization) was particularly hard hit. Zamkov's class origin would seem to make him an unlikely victim of this campaign, but he may have suffered as a Kol'tsov surrogate.

Late in the spring, panic and despair about the future of his work led Zamkov to decide to flee to France, where he had professional contacts. After securing false passports, he and his family began a circuitous journey to the Persian border. They were pulled off a train by the NKVD in Khar'kov but received a rather light punishment: exile from Moscow for three years with official – but in actual fact, only partial – confiscation of all their property.[29] (This detail of her attempt surreptitiously to cross the Soviet border is missing in all of Mukhina's biographies.) Zamkov and Mukhina chose Voronezh, an industrial city 330 miles south of Moscow, where Zamkov had at least one well-placed colleague.

In Voronezh Zamkov worked at the clinic attached to the Dzerzhinskii Locomotive Factory, a big enterprise with nearly 10,000 employees. Zamkov noted that many of the workers were exhausted and in poor health. He convinced the Party officials in the factory that gravidan might be useful to them: 'I'll fix the workers, you fix the trains.'[30] He soon had the reputation of a miracle worker. Although Mukhina told Bek that she disliked actors because she found the idea of playing a part thousands of times inherently insincere, she described her husband's fame in Voronezh in terms of a theatrical career: 'His success was enormous. It was simply a triumph [*triumf*]. Every dog in Voronezh knew him.'[31] She recalled that eager potential patients lined up to catch him when he went to the outhouse at 6 a.m. Zamkov, who proudly told Bek how Stanislavskii, whom he had met in Yalta in 1913, had pressed him to abandon medicine for acting because 'you could play Napoleon without any make-up', also recounted the Voronezh chapter in dramatic terms, stressing in particular a meeting called by the town's medical establishment to criticize him. Workers stood up in the audience and attested to their miraculous cures; former cripples danced *prisiadki*.

The local health authorities set up a lab for Zamkov, but meanwhile Kol'tsov's institute had been receiving requests for gravidan from hospitals all over the country, including, Kol'tsov wrote, the one servicing the Kremlin.[32] Kol'tsov himself had been under fierce attack from within and without his institute for alleged philosophical deviations, but, on 13 May 1932, Gorky, who was still commuting between Sorrento and Moscow and whom Stalin was courting as a permanent symbol of Soviet culture, personally handed Stalin an appeal for help from Kol'tsov. The next day, Kol'tsov wrote to Gorky, 'the Commissar of Public Health visited the Institute, re-established the absolute authority [*edinonachalie*] of the director and eliminated a series of vexing trifles which had been rendering my existence absolutely impossible'.33 The following day, Zamkov and Mukhina returned to Moscow, although they had only completed half of their term of internal exile, and on the subsequent day, the Politburo resolved to create a laboratory of 'urogravidanotherapy', with Zamkov as its director.34 Zamkov later recalled how he had learned the news from Gorky, in whose rooms he and Kol'tsov had drunk tea and waited while Gorky attended the decisive Politburo meeting.35

Throughout the year, articles appeared regularly in *Izvestiia* reporting in glowing terms on gravidan and its rural applications – injections of gravidan increased the weight of pigs and rabbits, raised piscine egg production and brought libidinally recalcitrant livestock into heat on a collective farm run by the Commissariat of Internal Affairs.36 On 21 August of the following year, Zamkov's laboratory was transformed into a scientific research institute.37 The institute received an official monopoly on the production of gravidan, production was ordered to remain secret, and discussions were instituted with the Commissariat of Foreign Trade for gravidan's export. Press reports continued to be positive; Zamkov was hailed as the director of the 'Institute of Audacity', working boldly and tirelessly to bring health and productivity to the populace.38

By 1934 at least 15,000 people had been treated with gravidan throughout the Soviet Union.39 In 1935, 4,868 more patients were treated at 160 treatment 'locations' (hospitals, clinics) in the USSR. By late 1937, the number of facilities using gravidan had grown to 345, but the number of people taking gravidan had grown at a much faster rate, because beginning in 1936 gravidan was sold in Soviet pharmacies and thus consumed outside of the institution's auspices. The collection of urine, the raw material essential for the production of gravidan, did not pose a problem. Prenatal care had always been a top priority of the Soviet Commissariat of Public Health, and even more attention was devoted to this area in the 1930s, when natalist concerns, relatively absent in the 1920s, took hold and resulted in an array of measures, ranging from the eventual banning of abortion to directives that doctors pay more attention to easing pain during delivery. The attention to prenatal care enabled Zamkov to tap into a steady supply of urine from pregnant women; healthy mothers were given kits and were paid for supplying their urine at various periods of their pregnancy.[40]

The boom in gravidan production was accompanied by triumphant claims about the scope of its efficiency. According to the institute, about 80 per cent of patients showed significant improvement when treated for a variety of conditions that ranged from disorders of the nervous, circulatory and endocrine systems to eye disease, mental illness, gastro-intestinal ailments, post-surgical infections, gynecological problems and even cancer. In the institute's first bulletin, published in 1935, research studies were published showing that gravidan had a remarkable impact on glaucoma, endocrine disorders, pathological lactation, schizophrenia, whooping cough, bovine endometriosis and the speed of trotters at the Moscow hippodrome. Most important, though, was the fact that treatment with gravidan raised the 'general tone' of the organism.[41]

It is this last point that deserves the greatest stress. Zamkov's institute flourished in an ideological climate that emphasized the importance of raising economic productivity. Central to Soviet ideology in the 1930s was the celebration of the heroic deeds of Stakhanovites, enthusiastic, exemplary workers who dramatically raised production norms and were rewarded with new suits, record players, trips to Moscow and a material lifestyle that was supposed to one day become universal but remained disconcertingly distant for the vast majority of Soviet citizens. Medical journals applied the ominous term of 'wrecking' to claims that the phenomena of shock-work and 'socialist competition' between factories and among brigades were detrimental to the health of workers.[42] Reports on gravidan therapy in the popular press invariably mentioned its impact on production. The Krasnyi Bogatyr factory in Moscow reduced its output of defective boots from seven to one per week.[43] Gravidan enabled people, so the press claimed, to work better and feel better. 'Is not a smile on the face of yesterday's psychosthenic not as telling as a (medical) document?'[44] began a report in *Vecherniaia Moskva*. The case histories described in Zamkov's work nearly always emphasize the number of workdays performed by his patients, who were near death when he begins treating them. Some rise from their deathbeds to enter collective farms. In a book *Ia byl svidetelem chudes* (I Was a Witness to Miracles), written by the journalist V. Pavlovich in 1937 but which became unpublishable after the closure of Zamkov's institute a year later, Zamkov recounts a series of similar narratives. Patients with mental ailments are transformed by treatment from shaggy, non-productive recluses into productive, well-dressed and well-groomed inventors – the bearers of the Stalinist principle of *kul'turnost'* (cultured living). Some of the stories are particularly poignant reminders of the time. Pavlovich's book, in which Zamkov and the author sit on a bench at a

Black Sea resort, chatting as they watch happy children treated by the doctor splash in the water below, includes the following episode, which Pavlovich says especially etched itself on his mind:

> My attention was directed at a girl of about 22 years of age. She had developed a strong nervous condition because her fiancé, whom she loved very much, had for some reason been exiled. She loved him, as they say, to the point of madness, and, in fact, she did indeed lose her mind. Her relatives put her in a home for the mentally ill. Her disease was serious: for three years she did not utter a single word. She refused to accept food and had to be fed artificially. She did not dress herself, did not bathe and lost human form. I endeavored to treat her and began to give injections. After the sixth injection, she began to menstruate, something she had not done for two years. That was already a victory; the girl's organism had awakened. She began to feel herself a woman. I continued the injections. And she got better.
>
> The doctor fell silent and then added: 'Within a year she had married ... married another man. She has a child and is now completely healthy.'
>
> 'So, gravidan can cure someone even of an unhappy love? (*izlechivaet i ot nechastnoi liubvi*)' I asked jokingly.
>
> 'Yes, so it would appear', the doctor answered and smiled.[45]

This episode, as are others in the manuscript, is chilling in that the 'cure' worked by gravidan entails the restoration of a woman to a happy society in which the repressive cause of trauma has been elided. Of course, Stalinist society is the only one to which this woman could be restored – there was, obviously, no other option – yet here we have an arrest replaced by the clichéd sentimental formula of 'unhappy love'. Gravidan not only awakens this young patient – as in a fairy tale – it virtually creates her as a female subject for the new society, enabling her to speak and to consume and endowing her with adaptive 'human form'.

It is instructive to compare the treatment narratives provided by Zamkov and his patients to the 'rejuvenation' accounts contained in the books by Steinach and Voronoff. The case studies adduced by Zamkov's predecessors in the field of hormone treatment focused on overcoming the debility of age, and they were frequently accompanied by before and after photographs, a necessary generic feature of endocrinological narrative. Zamkov's accounts focus more often on psychological and emotional transformation; they depict the attainment of the ideological enthusiasm and general merriment that the press portrayed as a defining feature of the Soviet subject, whose absence was evidently interpreted by some Soviet citizens as individual pathology. The hundreds of letters from Zamkov's patients preserved in the institute's archive reinforce this impression of gravidan therapy as a kind of coping mechanism, a drug that overcomes the depressing or terrifying consequences of insight into ideological contradictions and allows patients to continue living the Stalinist dream: 'After one injection I experience a feeling of rejoicing [*otrada*], which can be compared with the feeling of a person who has just received joyous news ... [*radostnoe izvestie*] My nervous system has grown stronger, obsessive thoughts return much less frequently. I have become more life-affirming and gayer, have become more capable of work ... It is as if I have been reborn.'[46] One patient whom unfounded accusations and arrest had deprived of all will to work or to live noted a complete change of attitude after gravidan injections: 'Suddenly I felt a surge of buoyancy, my gloomy mood and obsessive thoughts vanished; now there was a desire to live and engage in scientific work. My sleep has improved significantly.'[47] Zamkov's patients credited gravidan with enabling them to work shifts of 12 or even 13 hours for years on end without a single vacation; it helped them feel that they were capable of meeting the miraculous 'norms' being raised all around them and of living the Stalinist dream.

The letters from Zamkov's patients demonstrate how in the 1930s political repression worked hand in hand with psychological repression. When we speak of 'Stalinist repression' we should bear in mind not only the destruction of, or practice of violence against, concrete individuals but also the discourse – or representational system – that facilitated that violence by *not* speaking about it. The study of Stalinist repression should entail the analysis of rhetorical practice by which certain things were not looked at. Using gravidan, Zamkov's patients 'succeeded' in coping with the stressful demands of ideological and political pathology by viewing that pathology as situated within their own bodies. They survived as Soviet subjects by seeking medical rather than political relief. Zamkov's favorite motto was '*ne ubivat', a lechit' nado*' (It is not necessary to kill, but to heal),[48] but the tragedy of his humanitarian efforts is that killing and conscientious curing could work toward the same ends, rather than at cross purposes.

The tales of Zamkov's patients suggest a paradoxical effect of the workings of ideology in Soviet society. Ideology has been defined in a number of ways,[49] two of which seem particularly relevant to the question of Soviet subjectivity. The first derives from the work of Marx: ideology is the set of ideas that renders a given reality 'natural' and thus impervious to intellectual challenge by the subject under its sway. According to Marx, ideology is essentially a negative concept, one that papers over contradiction and naturalizes inequality and exploitation.[50] The Russian Revolution wrought a fundamental transformation of the social and psychological function of ideology. Among the changes introduced into Russian life by the triumph of Bolshevism, one of the most profound (and historically underappreciated) was the bringing of ideology to consciousness. Neither governments nor political élites in Western democracies talked much about 'capitalist ideology' because the ideology was so embedded that it did its work without being named, while the Soviets explicitly placed ideology at the center of all their programs. But this was ideology in the sense of a second, perhaps more common, definition adopted in Russia, and, in particular, by Lenin: ideology as the ideas that express a particular class, or the political consciousness of classes – bourgeois ideology proletarian ideology, and eventually Bolshevik ideology. Here, ideology is conscious, and can, in theory, be consciously self-imposed. In Soviet Russia, ideology no longer served as the vehicle that prevented exploited subjects from perceiving the extent and conditions of their exploitation. Rather than an unconscious mechanism that had to be transcended by the enlightened, ideology became something to be mastered, something that could be acquired by speaking, thinking, acting and feeling in a specific, studied way. In linguistic terms, ideology was transformed from a native to an acquired tongue, a language of which there were no native speakers, since its grammarians were the 'vanguard' of future subjects, as yet unborn, who, untainted by the capitalist past, would eventually speak this language virtually from birth.[51]

The explicit entry of ideology into public discourse was defining of Soviet modernity in both its liberating and its terrifying features. Ideology, in its traditional, naturalizing, unconscious function, may have been the handmaiden of exploitation, but it also allowed subjects to cope with the conditions of their exploitation. It prevented the alienated worker from perceiving the extent of his alienation. When ideology was wrenched by the Bolsheviks from the unconscious to the conscious, alienation became a much more conscious phenomenon. As they sought to master the new Soviet ideology, Soviet citizens were made aware of the extent to which that mastery was either beyond their reach or ever in danger of slipping from their grasp;[52] the result – probably anathema for some historians – may have been anxiety over the extent to which the individual was alienated from an ideal community of Soviet subjects. The penetration to consciousness of ideology held enormous potential, seeming to promise individuals a magical and scientific key to mastering their own destiny as they overcame the forces of oppression, yet the very consciousness of ideology made alienation far more palpable. Alienation was no longer a condition with which the unconscious subject could 'naturally' cope. In effect, the coming to consciousness of ideology de-familiarized many aspects of daily life and significantly narrowed the scope of the non-problematic, 'everyday' sphere; life became increasingly *unnatural*.

Part of this dynamic involves the relation of language (and ideology is as much a discourse susceptible to poetic analysis as it is a set of concepts) to experience. In nineteenth- and twentieth-century Russia, an ideological premium was placed on language. Its esteemed status can be attributed to the social and spiritual prominence of literature in a society in which opportunities for political expression and opposition were drastically curtailed. Literature served 'as a replacement for those political, social, legal and even economic phenomena that could not develop fully in Russian society'.[53] As a result, the political and social stakes of language were more consciously apparent than in other, less discursively deprived societies. This emphasis on the power of language emerged with particular force in the early twentieth-century Russian symbolists' and futurists' interest in spells and incantations; language does not just reflect, it creates, conjures a world into being and is a primary sphere of voluntaristic endeavor that is at least complementary to scientific knowledge.[54] The Bolsheviks, although they would never have acknowledged Belyi or Khlebnikov as their avatars,[55] were equally enamored of the potential for charismatic intervention in the workings of the world and with the notion of a prophetic, privileged volunteerism; they saw the Party's role as one of active intervention, yet this was to a great extent *speech* activity in so far as it entailed the bringing of the masses to consciousness. Stalin's speeches, which became the authoritative documents by which ideological affinities were measured, are striking in the tremendous importance they accord to language itself: 'Everyone is *talking* about the successes of Soviet power in the area of the kolkhoz movement ... What does this all *say*?'[56] For Stalin, events were primarily discursive and metadiscursive, often to a dizzying degree: 'Remember the latest events in our Party. Remember the latest *slogans*, which the Party has put forward lately in connection with the new class shifts in our country. I am *speaking* about *slogans*, such as the *slogan* of self-*criticism*, the *slogan* of heightened struggle with bureaucracy and the purge of the Soviet apparatus, the *slogan* of organization, etc.' The transition from slogans to events is almost a matter of synonymity in Stalin's representation of Soviet realia.[57] (In other words, the place of language and of speaking in Soviet *dictatorship* has far more than etymological relevance.) Essentially, one can see the entire premise of socialist realism, that 'the engineers of human souls' should show life in its 'revolutionary unfolding' and thus expedite the inevitable future by portraying it as if it currently existed, as a form of incantation.

Stalin's speeches provided much of the specific language for the incantatory discourse; particularly important was his pronouncement in 1935 that 'Life has become better, more cheerful.' The press and cinema of the 1930s were replete with a rhetoric of mirth and an iconography of merriment. The texts produced by these media should not simply be dismissed as empty expression – as evidence of the great Soviet divide between ideological fantasy and everyday experience, between ideological representation and reality. On the one hand, ideology was grounded in reality for its speakers, in that learning how to speak ideologically had consequences for one's education and career. Speaking ideological words influenced everyday life; they were the mark of Soviet subjectivity. It would be a wild exaggeration – and Marxist blasphemy – to say that language determines consciousness, although this does seem to be the tenor of much Stalinist discourse. But language certainly has effects for consciousness, and one of these effects may have been the insecurity occasioned by a perceived gap between incantational promise and corporeal sensation. If verbal enthusiasm was a principal marker of Soviet subjectivity, corporeal frustration may have been one of its principal effects. Gravidan seems to have been used by at least some to overcome this frustration, to absorb ideological discourse, to internalize it and somatically reproduce it. An ideological placebo, gravidan may have worked in part because it provided discourse with an unmediated, physical vehicle for incorporation.

Stalinist ideology was not the only discursive thread in the language used by journalists and patients to describe gravidan: it competes with Christian images and the language of heroic positivism that, to be sure, went hand in hand with the rhetoric of 'scientific Communism'. The adjective *chudesnyi* – miraculous – was routinely applied to Zamkov's work; letters from patients and inscriptions in books by patient-authors repeatedly refer to him as a miracle worker, or *chudodei*.[58] Gravidan therapy was proclaimed a scientifically documented miracle, and one which was surrounded by the ideologically requisite mix of cheerfulness and awe. One of Zamkov's patients even devoted to gravidan a *poèma* of several hundred lines in which the hormones of pregnant women are portrayed as dramatically overfilling nature's plan as they produce a surplus of hormonal vitality that the fetus alone cannot absorb but that medicine can tap into:

> No ch'ia zh ona?
> Takaia divnaia mocha!
> Pora davno nam znat';
> Ee daet beremennaia mat'.
> [But whose is it, this marvelous urine? / It is high time that we knew / A pregnant mother gives it.][59]

Zamkov himself cultivated this aura of scientific cheerfulness. When describing in the 1930s the effect he had experienced when he had first injected himself with gravidan, he likened his sensations to the intoxicating kick of a glass of champagne –'*pod'em kak ot bokala shampanskogo*' – with the difference that this burst of enthusiasm had been economically productive and had lasted for the next ten days.[60]

Zamkov does not seem to have regarded his project as ideological; rather he viewed his work as being within the framework of medicine's traditional humanitarian mission. If any ideological discourse colored the way he spoke about his work, it was Christian. The verb *spasti* (to save) continuously surfaces in his and Mukhina's description of his work. As far as I have been able to determine, Zamkov never signed any petition in support of the purge trials; at home, he criticized the wave of arrests in the years 1936–38 as 'made-up trials',[61] and he showed great loyalty to friends and patients who were repressed: when the writer Galina Serebriakova was under house arrest after the arrest of her husband (the former finance commissar), Zamkov and Mukhina were among the few to visit her at home.[62] Zamkov was an outstanding diagnostician whose substantial personal charisma inspired belief in his patients, but, whatever he might have intended, that belief had to correspond with the discursive environment in which his patients lived.

Zamkov's miraculous therapy was seen by some of his admirers as concordant with other miraculous events of the day. Here is a letter written to him in the mid-1930s by a certain Ol'ga Sotnik.

> Si la vieillesse pouvait
> Si la jeunesse savait
> an old and sad French saying

Comrade Zamkov!
Imagine this:
A woman – a gynecologist – is pregnant. She doesn't want the baby. She loves one old man passionately – it doesn't matter if he is her husband, maybe he isn't. Gretchen in *style moderne* or a new Maria from Pushkin's *Poltava*.

Perfectly acquainted with the process of pregnancy, having studied all its subtleties, she has something like Dneprostroi [the Dnepr Hydroelectric Power Station, the largest power station in Europe and an emblem of Stalinist achievement] in her blood-bearing arteries. She constructs a unique kind of dam and succeeds in allowing only an insignificant part of the enormous strength of maternity to be transmitted to the child; with the will of a stubborn, audacious woman she directs the rest, that is, the chief, dominant part of this strength, to the old man. Injections, blood transfusions, whatever.

The result of the pregnancy is the following: A child is born – a monster, a mutant, a kikimora [folk goblin], something inhuman, weak, sickly, monstrous, a being absolutely unfit for life. It dies an hour after birth.

But on the other hand the old man is full of strength, life, vitality. The old man has been transformed into a handsome youth with a rosy face, a burning gaze, with the mind of a wise man and the spark of youth.

A fantasy:
Yes?
A monstrous one?
No, why?
It is an idea inspired by you. By your gravidan.
It might seem monstrous only at first glance. But if you think about how many abortions occur in our land ... the monstrosity disappears.

In fact, your gravidan, if it might be sought not in the urine but in the blood, perhaps in the excretions of some sort of glands in a pregnant woman, might multiply by ten, by a hundred times its invigorating rejuvenating strength.

This fantastic thought has come to me, a poorly educated, poorly trained woman.

I am a dreamer and constantly think about the future.
This thought has amazed me, has taken deep root, and will probably give birth to other shoots.

But my mind is not developed. I know nothing. But you? You have worked a great deal – if not in this then in a closely related area. How can one know?

We live at a time when fairy tales are being transformed into life, day-dreams into reality, fantasy into fact.

I am not imposing anything on you. I simply entrust my fantasy, my dream to a profound specialist.

I will not drop my tasks onto others' shoulders. I will work. I will study, search. Myself. The problem of age is infinitely dear to me. It torments me. But if I find a response in you, perhaps you will succeed sooner; that about which I write is sought not only by me but by all proud, unbowed, rebellious, revolutionarily inclined grey humanity [*vse gordoe, ni pered chem ne prekloniaiushchee golovu, buntarskoe, revoliutionno nastroennoe, sedoe chelovechestvo*].

Write to me.

I will be happy, if my thought even slightly appeals to you. And if, having considered it, having studied, having conducted experiments on animals, under your wise guidance and with your help as a man of science, I, a woman, with the strength of the maternity of my body, can smooth someone's wrinkles, restore confidence and cheerfulness to someone's ageing and death-anticipating eyes, once more color elderly, sad hair which has been rendered colorless by gray, I will call myself happy.

Write.
Respond.
Ol'ga Sotnik[63]

Sotnik's letter is not a typical document in the Zamkov archive, and yet it is perhaps characteristic in that it reveals most clearly strains sounded less exuberantly in many of the letters from Zamkov's patients. Sotnik not only reveals a nearly Fedorovian belief in the transformative, immortalizing powers of science, she implicitly realizes that Zamkov's work is of a piece with the ideology of heroic labor, grand, transformative projects and charismatic leadership that was typical of the day. Her letter, like those of other patients, bespeaks a desire to absorb those projects into the writer's body, to incarnate in the individual subject discourse that on its own was still painfully lacking in physical conviction. Mukhina, too, processed her husband's work into compelling physicality. Her reference to Zamkov's internal monumentality implicitly links her husband's work to the ethos of the day and to the spirit of her own work, but there were additional dimensions to this connection: Zamkov brought her high-placed patients with interesting profiles to sculpt; Mukhina regularly injected herself with gravidan during intensive periods of work. While her famous worker and collective farmer was being cast and assembled, she took constant doses to enable herself to withstand the grueling, nearly round-the-clock pace of work.[64]

The issue of gender never surfaces in the accounts of Zamkov or of his patients. There was absolutely no expression of doubt that female urine should be given to male patients. The absence of this issue is rather extraordinary, given the importance of sexual difference to early hormone therapies in western Europe. Throughout the 1920s, European endocrinologists largely accepted Steinach's model of hormonal 'sex antagonism': healthy masculinity was deemed to be the product of male hormones alone, while healthy femininity was seen as the result of female hormones. Over the course of the 1930s, endocrinologists gradually moved away from this position and accepted that healthy men *and* women produced the hormones that came to be known as androgens and estrogens. They still adhered rigorously, however, to an insistence on the relation of sex hormones to gender: feminine men and masculine women were thought to have unusually high proportions of the other sex's hormones. Perhaps most important, though, female sex hormones were used to treat women and male hormones were used to treat men; there was very little use of 'paradoxical' hormone therapy, the exception being the treatment of men for enlarged prostates and some psychological conditions. Existing networks of prenatal care made women's urine far cheaper for doctors and pharmaceutical companies to procure; the result, in the judgement of one of the most thorough scholars of endocrinological research at this time, was that hormone therapy became largely therapy for women, and women were 'hormonalized' in the medical and popular imagination.[65]

Why was the question of gender so unproblematic in Russia? Discussions of rejuvenation operations in the 1920s focused mostly on male patients, in part because ovarian grafts were more invasive than testicular ones and in part because Steinach's procedure (ligature) does not seem to have been contemplated for women. Zamkov's treatment would appear to represent a dramatic shift from male to female specificity. Yet there were other factors at work. The first is that the female body, a site of ideological anxiety in the 1920s, when it had been represented as corrupted by centuries of economic exploitation and had served as shorthand for the notion of egotistical, capitalist desire run wild,[66] was reclaimed by ideological discourse in the 1930s.[67] Soviet posters and cinema begin to highlight the female form; the bust, in particular, comes to serve in the 1930s as a sign of health rather than a source of ideological temptation.

The campaign for collectivization enabled the countryside to serve as a location for uplifting ideological narratives; previously, only the factory had played this role. The 'success' of collectivization was figured by amazing displays of agricultural fecundity; the celebration of Stalinist society's achievements at times seems to blur into the celebrations of a fertility cult. Finally, 'socialist paternalism' (or parentalism) has been proposed by Katherine Verdery and others as the dominant model for state–citizen interaction in Russia and the East Bloc.[68] According to this model, the economy of shortage strengthened the Party by allowing it to serve as a distributional source and as the addressee of appeals for material goods; the Party's centrality to material well-being was concomitant with its role as the source of all ideological pronouncements. In this context, we might describe the psychological power of Zamkov's treatment as residing in its appeal to a mass infantilization of the population; injecting gravidan, Soviet citizens were in effect re-establishing a kind of umbilical rapport to health.

Many of Zamkov's patients provide their narratives within the context of the socialist paternalist model: they report the miracles of their treatment to their doctor in the same communication in which they ask him to send them more gravidan. If one wants to adopt a gendered model of analysis, one might observe that the maternal function (here, as with the state and its 'Father of Nations') has been paternalized, both in its co-option by a charismatic, masculine man (who could play Napoleon without make-up) and to the extent to which one might see gravidan therapy as a kind of impregnation by ideological Logos.

Pursuing a symbolic reading of the significance of gravidan in Stalinist culture, we might want to consider briefly the relationship between utopia and human waste. Zamkov's patients seem beset by an awareness that they are in danger of being left behind, tossed on to the trash heap of history. Gravidan may have represented a symbolic promise of recycling, redeeming human waste in a utopian economy. Andrei Platonov, a writer who had his finger on the pulse of Soviet ideology, and whose work often engaged in a sort of literalizing deconstruction of socialist realist tropes, wrote a novel called *Happy Moscow*, which remained unpublished for nearly 60 years. One of the novel's heroes is a surgeon, Sambikin, who seeks the source of all life – the soul – in the intestines, in the small gap between food and feces. More important for our purposes, the entire novel is a kind of lament for all who have been left behind by the Stalinist utopia, and the text attests to its love and pity for this human refuse by its attention to the process of excretion. The heroine, named Moscow, walks with an engineer, Sartorius, to the outskirts of the city, where they will make love. 'If Moscow had squatted down to pee, Sartorius would have burst into tears ... He could have looked at the waste products of her body with the greatest of interest, since they too had not long ago formed part of a splendid person.'[69] Later, in despair, a man living near a communal toilet cries out in the middle of the night, begging God for something real in a world of discourse run amok. He can only do this, however, with the words that he knows, and those words have already been colonized by the ideology from which he tries hopelessly to escape: 'Remember me, Lord ... give me something factual [*dai mne chto-nibud' fakticheskoe*], I implore you.' Not real, not genuine, but the beloved Stalinist word 'factual'.

Bodily waste is nothing if not factual, and urine and feces serve Platonov as a touchstone for reality, a sign of biological community for grown-up Communist infants. It would not be surprising to see excrement used in a distopian or satirical narrative – this is precisely what the Russian writer Vladimir Sorokin does in a recent novel, *The Norm*, where each participant has to ingest a packet of excrement.[70] In such cases, a focus on waste is the equivalent to writing 'shit' on a Party poster. What Platonov's novel shows us, and what may have accounted for some of the success of gravidan, is that waste may also be the symbolic key to the redemption of the failed individual in the glorious collective. Mikhail Bakhtin's celebrated book on Rabelais, a product of the same era, may also be read within this paradigm. The public exercise of body functions and the revelry in language about physiological processes serve Bakhtin as evidence of the overcoming of proto-bourgeois egoism and antisocial individuality.[71]

Despite his status as director of a scientific institute and his rather high salary of 1,500 rubles a month, Zamkov's life during the mid-1930s was fraught with tension and frustration. The Scientific Research Institute of Urogravidantherapy never had adequate space. Most of its researchers were employed at other institutes and hospitals around the country; they signed contracts with the institute that contained research and treatment plans. (The contracts stipulated that the doctors would receive a free supply of gravidan, in exchange for their agreement to provide the institute with detailed results and to publish findings in the institute's bulletin.[72]) The institute itself moved from one location in Moscow to another, yet it was always trying to squeeze its clinic and gravidan production center into two or three rooms in buildings belonging to various subdivisions of the Commissariat of Public Health.

Although its production reached 200 litres or 40,000 doses a month, its collection and distribution efforts were hampered by its never having been allocated a truck.[73] The institute's material problems reflect the conditions of medical research in the Soviet Union, where market forces did not prevail. The institute was funded by the government, gravidan was provided free of charge to medical practitioners, and the sale of gravidan in pharmacies – probably at cost, as was the case with most other goods in the Soviet economy – does not appear to have generated any revenue. Unlike in the West, where the pharmaceutical industry was a driving force in endocrinological research,[74] in Russia a laboratory's success depended on channels of patronage through influential political figures. Zamkov might well have remained in exile in Voronezh had his cause not been championed by Gorky; Zamkov himself frequently referred to his institution as having sprung from 'a special Politburo resolution' and reminded the Commissariat of Health, the source of virtually all his institutional funding, that his work enjoyed 'the care and support of the Central Committee of our Party'.[75]

In addition, Zamkov had competitors. Pletnev, who by this time had become director of a new research center of his own, the Scientific Research Institute for Functional Diagnostics and Experimental Therapy, had to be cautioned several times from packaging and even exporting his own gravidan; eventually he began to produce and distribute a urine-based product called 'uro-gormon', and he took every opportunity as editor of *Klinicheskaia meditsina* to publish material critical of Zamkov's work.[76] Letters from Zamkov's patients – some of which are written on the institute's stationery – provide testimony to the high quality of Zamkov's filtered urine – and to the necessity of distinguishing it from other ideologically beneficial potions: 'I know the worth of your gravidan and only your gravidan. Two years ago I injected myself with Dr Shmulevich's gravidan 47 times, but there was no result, while after 35–36 injections of your gravidan I was strong, enthusiastic, hardworking, merry, slept miraculously and completely lost the propensity to catch cold.'[77] Although Pletnev was a powerful competitor, Zamkov's nemesis proved to be Nikolai Adol'fovich Shereshevskii, the director of the All-Union Institute of Experimental Endocrinology. Shereshevskii was appointed to several commissions in the 1930s that audited or investigated the work of Zamkov's institute. The second, which was headed by Kol'tsov and reported in March 1936, concluded that gravidan was an extremely important therapeutic agent for the treatment of hormonal insufficiency, and for all cases in which raising the general tone of an organism was deemed necessary. This commission recommended that Zamkov's institute be furnished with a large quantity of beds in a hospital or clinic so that it could better follow up its patients.

But it also removed from Zamkov responsibility for the production of gravidan; this job was transferred to the Factory of Endocrinological Preparations, headed by S.B. Katkovskii, perhaps not coincidentally another member of the second review commission.

In June 1937, Pletnev was suddenly catapulted into national fame when he was accused by *Pravda* of sexually assaulting and even crippling a female patient (by biting her breast), a gesture that may be read as an assault on the very symbolic logic that underlay the success of gravidan: the ideological cathexis of fertility as the rhetorical model for Stalinist paternalism.[78] The initial report in *Pravda* unleashed a virtual frenzy on the part of Soviet medical clinicians, some of whom charged that Pletnev's anti-Soviet character had long been evident in the manner in which he had relentlessly pursued therapists who disagreed with his methods.[79] *Pravda*'s campaign was soon followed by the intervention of Andrei Vyshinskii and the Soviet prosecutorial apparatus; Pletnev was arrested and a month later convicted of rape, for which he received a two-year suspended sentence.[80] Pletnev's fall was hardly a blessing for Zamkov, because it came as part of a campaign against medical research 'fiefdoms' and 'princes' of the medical establishment; even the jubilee ritual of celebrating 'x' number of years in the profession was attacked as bourgeois and inefficient.[81] Soon the Soviet Commissar of Health, Grigorii Kaminskii, who had been a friend and supporter of Zamkov, was charged with anti-Soviet activity, and a purge swept through the medical establishment, with poor sanitary conditions in hospitals being attributed to both conscious and unconscious wrecking. Additionally, in the mid-1930s, many of Zamkov's most prominent patients died or were purged; their disappearance deprived Zamkov of channels for effective appeals for resources.

January 1938 saw the birth of a new medical newspaper, *Meditsinskii rabotnik*, which set as its task the elimination of the consequences of wrecking, and of the 'feudal princedoms' in which wrecking often occurred. The newspaper specialized in the genre of investigative denunciation; unfortunately for Zamkov, its offices were located in the same building as his clinic, and during the course of the first few months of 1938, with the blessing of the Commissariat of Health, the paper began to take over room after room. On 15 February it published an article entitled 'Ignorance or Charlatanism'. Accompanied by a caricature of Zamkov selling 'sure-fire remedies for mice, epilepsy and earthquakes', the article accused Zamkov of peddling a panacea; its author professed to be particularly disturbed by the manner in which rumors of Zamkov's miraculous curative powers had spread from mouth to mouth, an uncontrolled 'legend' whose communication was apparently worse than that of a disease.[82] Five days later a new commission headed by Shereshevskii was established to investigate the Institute of Urogravidan therapy.

Meditsinskii rabotnik kept up its attacks; the reputation of Zamkov's institute was likened to a 'mass psychosis' and readers were reminded that the great nineteenth-century writer Nikolai Gogol had been killed by a charlatan. This reference to a writer was not coincidental, for Gorky's death was now deemed a homicide and attributed to ideological sabotage. Two weeks later the case of the Anti-Soviet Bloc of Rights and Trotskyites opened in Moscow; Pletnev was in the dock accused of complicity in the murder of Gorky and Kuibyshev, both of whom Zamkov had also treated. Also on trial, along with Nikolai Bukharin, Aleksei Rykov and other more internationally prominent defendants, was Ignaty Kazakov, who had pioneered his own patented brand of treatment, lysotherapy, in which patients at his own research institute were injected with protein compounds or 'lysates'.[83] Testifying at the trial as a member of a special medical commission was none other than Shereshevksii. (It is curious that Zamkov himself was virtually the only expert in his field of experimental endocrinology who did not participate in the trial as either a defendant or an expert witness. Zamkov's son recalls that his father was asked several times to provide testimony against his former rivals but he always refused.[84] This relatively courageous act of omission may have played a role in Zamkov's personal downfall.) The transcript has its ironic dimensions; the commission of medical experts, which on one hand had as its professional agenda to prove that lysate therapy was a total fraud with no effect whatsoever, had nevertheless to agree that lysates were powerful enough to kill a patient when administered with murderous intent. It hedged its bets by stating that Kazakov had killed his famous patients by administering lysates in combination with foxglove.[85] The prosecutor, Vyshinskii, on several occasions had to rein in Pletnev and Kazakov, who were, understandably, more eager to promote their therapeutic methods than to implicate themselves in a heinous anti-Soviet conspiracy.

The conviction and sentencing of Pletnev and Kazakov – to 25 years' imprisonment and execution, respectively – marked not only the apogee of the show trials and a remarkable instance of virtually literal cut-throat competition among medical specialists, but also the enshrinement of internal, non-specific therapy as the branch of medicine most central to Soviet ideological discourse.[86] The almost unlimited scope of therapeutic cures trumpeted by the directors of medical scientific research institutes proved to be a reversible discourse; a force harnessed by charismatic healers for unbounded good could easily be portrayed as capable of achieving unlimited evil. The artistic mastery of internal secretions and diabolically clever, seditious conspiracy were quite easily linked.

As for Aleksei Zamkov, the simultaneous presence of Shereshevskii on both the judicial commission and the committee investigating gravidan was obviously not a good omen. To compound his problems, *Meditsinskii rabotnik* was stepping up its attacks, some of which bordered on advertisements for competitors' products. Thus one Honored Man of Science (*zasluzhennyi deiatel' nauki* – a title conferred upon scientists by the Soviet Union and its republics) declared that the trial showed how keeping formulas for medications secret inexorably led to the utilization of those medications with criminal, wrecking ends. Gravidan therapy was valuable for gynecological disorders, this clinical expert maintained, but 'the primitive method of its preparation practiced by Dr Zamkov does not satisfy me. I prefer the preparation of Dr Artynov's product, urogomon.'[87] On 26 March the Shereshevskii Commission recommended that Zamkov's institute be closed; it concluded that although gravidan therapy was often useful, the scientific studies conducted under the institute's auspices were poorly formulated and that it was ridiculous to have an institute devoted to the administration of a single medicine. *Meditsinskii rabotnik* took over Zamkov's clinic's space; Shereshevskii's Institute of Experimental Endocrinology inherited Zamkov's institute's library and all of its patients.[88] Zamkov himself had three heart attacks in fairly rapid succession and died in October 1942.

Although the period of Zamkov's disgrace coincided with that of Mukhina's greatest fame, during the 1930s both played sustaining roles in the formulation of the Stalinist notion of corporeality. Their different professional fates may have much to do with the circumstances in which they practiced their arts. Pletnev, the leading figure in medical therapy, was a confirmed empiricist, and he stressed time and again that the therapist, like a great artist, operated largely on the basis of intuition.[89] Zamkov's miracles were, likewise, 'triumphs' on the ideological stage, and it was his success in manufacturing gravidan by mixing batches of urine from women in various stages of pregnancy that served as the proof of a uniquely medical brand of charisma that, he and his patients contended, could not be reproduced by doctors without his unquantifiable skills. Both Zamkov's and Mukhina's activities were highly prized by the organs of ideological discourse; both were continually evaluated by governmental organs bent on ideological control. Yet a crucial difference probably inheres in the essentially public nature of monumental sculpture; the site of the medical examination and medical treatment was too private, too apt to escape the sort of transparency that affected all other areas of Soviet life. The persecution of Zamkov for private practice in 1930 had its analog in the attacks of 1938 on the private, secret nature of the production of materials that had sustained (or allegedly undermined) the public bodies for which doctors had served as visible but vulnerable trustees.

The claims of Zamkov and Kazakov for the efficacy of their secret formulas may strike us today as so incautious and ambitious as to have invited the fates inflicted upon them. Certainly, their attitude toward their 'patented' treatments contrasts sharply with that of Western endocrinological researchers, who tempered their claims out of a strong sense of medical ethics and, Nelly Oudshoorn suggests, in part out of the fear of the charlatan label.[90] (Western physicians, Adele Clarke notes, were wary of clinical endocrinology, which was extremely lucrative but professionally disreputable because of its association with 'quackery'.[91]) But we should appreciate the different cultural context and institutional pressures in Russia. First, after the Revolution the status of doctor ceased to carry its pre-revolutionary weight. The profession was somewhat tarnished as bourgeois, and doctors may have felt that recuperation of their status depended on the adoption of the Bolshevik ideology's Promethean attitude toward the laws of nature which – Engels notwithstanding – existed to be understood and overturned. Second, Zamkov was operating in a nation that was largely rural and where industrialization and the urban proletariat went back just one or two generations. Certain aspects of faith healing were not as out of place in the Soviet Union as they would have been in Holland or Germany.[92] We can see the appeal of Zamkov's pre-modern method of treatment – the use of urine in folk medicine – as a miracle of medical modernity. Finally, in the climate of Stalinist science, institutional survival depended far less on the extent to which products were practically efficacious than on the extent to which they were ideologically spectacular. Holland's pharmaceutical firm Organon could be satisfied with the treatment of endocrinological complaints because there was tremendous economic demand in Europe for products aimed at and limited to those problems. In the Soviet Union, the alleviation of menopausal problems (one of Organon's areas of concentration) would not have put a doctor in the pages of *Izvestiia, Nashi dostizheniia* or *Novyi mir*. A fundamental difference between capitalist and Communist endocrinology may well have been that, in the Soviet Union, women were not 'hormonalized', because such a strategy would not have been profitable: economic (consumer) demand was irrelevant, and women – for all the importance of fertility as an ideological theme – had minimal political power, the only kind that counted.

To conclude: in the rise and fall of gravidan, we see the potential for both conflict and complementarity between the organic and symbolic realms, between language and flesh. We also see the risks inherent in a proprietary therapeutic relationship with physical bodies of power.

The product of a therapist's art – a healthy body – is less like a work of sculpture, which can last for years on the grounds of the Exhibition of the Achievements of the National Economy of the USSR, than it is like a play – something quintessentially ephemeral, the beauty of which, moreover, cannot be demonstrated by the display of an image but must be attested to by transmission from mouth to mouth. The display of a healed body must be accompanied by a narrative about its miraculous production; otherwise, there is no way to distinguish a healthy body from a healed one. Even accompanied by a medical provenance, however, bodies eventually decay; they cannot continue to perform like statues. When bodies of power decay, the fault must lie in their maker, custodian or trustee. Immortality, the anti-utopian Russian philosopher Vasilii Rozanov insisted in a Schopenhauerian mood (and in the face of greater opposition than such a view would probably face in any other European country), is in the life cycle rather than in a single individual's physical immortality or continued growth to gigantic proportions.[93] Ultimately, Aleksei Zamkov's downfall was that there can be no such thing as internal or organic monumentality; the very idea entails something of a contradiction in terms. In the ideological climate of the 1930s Aleksei Zamkov's undoing may have been that, pursuing a track parallel to his wife's, he was simply unable to turn the body into steel or stone.

Unlike a name or a text, a living body exhibits a stubborn reluctance to be entirely absorbed into the realm of discourse. Yet the ultimate point of this part of the story may lie less in Zamkov's fate than in his meaning for his patients, who used gravidan to establish a complementary relationship betwen organic and symbolic spheres, emphasizing these spheres' capacity for interpenetration as well as their points of mutual resistance. After all, like today's scholars of Soviet discourse, Zamkov's patients suffered from and tried to assuage the pain of the gap between speech and physical reality, between the reality of their everyday lives and the socialist realist reality unfolding 'revolutionarily' in the discourse surrounding them. In their letters to their doctor, we see an at least temporarily successful search for a magic wand that would seamlessly relate ideological poetry to everyday prose and confer a secure sense of Soviet subjectivity by turning the ideological word into individual flesh.

NOTES

1. L. Toom and A. Bek, *Zapisi s besed s V. I. Mukhinoi (1939–1940)* (notes from conversations with V.I. Mukhina), p. 104, private archive of V.A. Zamkov.
2. A. Zamkov, 'Gravidan v meditsine' (Gravidan in medicine), *Novyi mir* 8 (1935), pp. 190–212. See Shaginian's letter to Zamkov, RGAE (Russian State Economic Archive), f. 9457, op. 1, ed. khr. 88 and also a copy of her book, *Dnevnik deputata mossoveta*

(The diary of a Moscow council deputy), which she gave to Zamkov with the inscription: 'To Dear Dr Zamkov, my constant, reliable and best helper in life – in those difficult days when nothing and nobody [else] provides any help' (RGAE, f. 9457, op. 1, ed. khr. 93). None of the case histories kept by Zamkov's institute identify famous patients. A letter from N.K. Kol'tsov, Zamkov's friend and mentor, mentions Gorky's interest in gravidan (RGAE, f. 9457. op. 1, ed. khr. 99) and one file contains Zamkov's medical notes about the conditions of Zetkin's health (RGAE, f. 9457, op. 1, ed. khr. 21), which confirms that he was at least partly responsible for her care. In her memoirs, the author Galina Serebriakova describes seeing Zamkov inject gravidan into Gorky, who introduced him to her as a 'mighty healer' (*moguchii istselitel'*). *O drugikh i o sebe* (Moscow: Sovetskii pisatel', 1971), p. 330. According to his son, Zamkov's patients also included Ia.K. Berzin, the head of Soviet military intelligence, and A.N. Poskrebyshev, Stalin's personal secretary. Conversation with V.A. Zamkov as recorded by E. Naiman (1996). For the assertion that Kuibyshev was a patient of Zamkov and 'believed in gravidan', see Toom and Bek, *Zapisi besed*, p. 104.
3. The sole works to discuss Zamkov in substantive detail are M.A. Zolotonosov, 'Masturbanizatsiia: erogennye zony sovetskoi kul'tury 1920–1930-kh godov' (Masturbanization: the erogenous zones of Soviet culture in the 1920s and 1930s), *Literaturnoe obozrenie* 11 (1991), pp. 93–9, and A.I. Kremneva, *Gravidan – dolgaia doroga k zhizni* (Gravidan – the long road to life) (Ivanovo: Talka, 1993).
4. Toom and Bek, *Zapisi besed*, p. 62.
5. Sheila Fitzpatrick's work inaugurated and has continued to be exemplary of this scholarly movement. See, *inter alia*, her collection of essays *The Cultural Front: Power and Culture in Revolutionary Russia* (Ithaca, NY: Cornell University Press, 1992).
6. A founding contribution in this area was the publication of *Intimacy and Terror*, a collection of diaries from the 1930s collected by Véronique Garros, Natalia Korenevskaya and Thomas Lahusen, trans. Carol A. Flath (New York: The New Press, 1995). This collection was closely followed by Jochen Hellbeck's edition of Stepan Podlubnyi's extensive diaries, *Tagebuch aus Moskau 1931–1939*, ed. Jochen Hellbeck (Munich: Deutscher Taschenbuch Verlag, 1996). The primary materials in these two books show in raw, fascinating terms the role of ideology in the formation of private identity. An extensive investigation of the concept of Soviet subjectivity will be provided in a forthcoming collection of essays on everyday life edited by Christina Kiaer and myself. Several of the theoretical formulations in this chapter have been taken from our joint introduction to that collection.
7. RGAE, f. 9457, op. 1, ed. khr. 2; Russian State Archive for Literature and Art (RGALI), f. 2326, op. 1, ed. khr. 457.
8. In the autobiography written in 1908, Zamkov – not surprisingly – does not mention any revolutionary activity in 1905. In an autobiography from the late 1920s, Zamkov used entire paragraphs from this earlier autobiography unchanged, but he inserted a new section devoted to 1905: 'The Revolution of 1905 not only fascinated me; it caught me up completely. I devoted to it all the ardor of my young soul. Revolutionary assemblies, meetings, conversations, lectures significantly broadened my mental horizon. I broke out of a stagnant environment on to a new path that led to a new conscientious life. In 1906, 1907, 1908 I covered my tracks and fervently prepared for my secondary education certificate.' This passage is so formulaic and vague that it leads one to suspect that Zamkov's revolutionary activity was minimal.
9. RGAE, f. 9457, op. 1, ed. khr. 2; RGALI, f. 2326, op. 1, ed. khr. 457.
10. Ibid.
11. Toom and Bek, *Zapisi besed*, p. 56. Conversation with V.A. Zamkov.
12. Paul Kammerer, *Rejuvenation and the Prolongation of Human Efficiency: Experiences with the Steinach Operation on Man and Animals* (New York: Boni and Liveright, 1923), p. 52. See also Eugen Steinach and Joseph Lobel, *Sex and Life: Forty Years of Biological and Medical Experiments* (New York: Viking, 1940). A recent article goes so far as to claim that the operation had a salutary effect on the poetry of William Butler Yeats. See Stephen Lock, '"O that I were young again": Yeats and the Steinach Operation', *British Medical Journal* 287 (1983), pp. 1964–7.

13. Serge Voronoff, *Rejuvenation by Grafting*, trans. Fred F. Imianitoff (New York: Adelphi, 1925 [1924]). Voronoff was a colorful figure who made a fortune with his grafting operations, for which he charged $5,000 at his clinic in Southern France. According to one undocumented account, published after his death, Voronoff's use of monkey glands resulted in the infection of many of his patients with syphilis (P. McGrady. *The Youth Doctors* (New York: Coward-McCann, 1968)).
14. Nik. Perna, *Stroiteli zhivogo tela. Ocherki fiziologii vnutrennei sekretsii* (Builders of the living body. Sketches of the physiology of internal secretion) (Petrograd: Seiatel', 1924), pp. 7–9.
15. See V.A. Oppel', 'Endokrinologiia, ili osnova sovremennoi meditsiny' (Endocrinology: the foundation of contemporary medicine), *Leningradskii meditsinskii zhurnal* 1926: 3, pp. 3–18; D.M. Rossiiskii, *Ocherk istorii razvitiia endokrinologii v Rossii* (A historical sketch of the development of endocrinology in Russia) (Moscow, 1926). In Western Europe and the United States, too, endocrinology posed a challenge to the physiological, disciplinary dominance of work on the nervous system, although this challenge does not seem to have undergone the symbolic, rhetorical politicization that one observes in Russia. See Adele E. Clarke, *Disciplining Reproduction: Modernity, American Life Sciences, and 'the Problems of Sex'* (Berkeley, CA: University of California Press, 1998), p. 48.
16. Perna, *Stroiteli zhivogo tela*, p. 9
17. A.V. Nemilov, 'Uznaem li my kogda-nibud' chto takoe "dusha"?' (Will we ever know what the soul really is?), *Chelovek i priroda* 4 (1924), pp. 321–8.
18. N.K. Kol'tsov, 'Vvedenie: smert', starost', omolozhenie' (Introduction: death, old age, rejuvenation), in *Omolozhenie* (Moscow and Petrograd, 1923), pp. 1–28.
19. Ts. Perel'muter, *Nauka i religiia o zhizni chelovecheskogo tela* (Science and religion on the life of the human body) (n.p., 1927).
20. A.A. Zamkov, 'O primenenii mochi beremennykh s lechebnoi tsel'iu' (On the use of urine from pregnant women for healing purposes), *Klinicheskaia meditsina* 12 (1929).
21. Conversation with V.A. Zamkov; 'My ne Gerakly' (Reminiscences of V.A. Zamkov/We are not Hercules), p. 5, unpublished manuscript, private archive of V.A. Zamkov.

    Pletnev would prove a powerful enemy. A consultant at the Kremlin hospital and one of the most sought-after diagnosticians in the Soviet Union, his patients included Ivan Pavlov and, at Lenin's personal directive, the ageing anarchist Petr Kropotkin, as well as foreign dignitaries such as Romain Rolland. Pletnev was on the editorial boards of at least eight medical journals and the first edition of the *Large Medical Encyclopedia* and was hailed in the Soviet press as 'a shock worker on the front of public health'. A dozen years older than Zamkov, Pletnev had little in common with him personally. A member of the aristocracy, Pletnev had graduated from medical school at a young age, trained in Germany (he was known for his ability to quote Goethe and Schiller in the original) and made a name for himself in several fields of internal medicine. (Today he is recognized as the founder of Soviet cardiology.) A former student recalled him as impeccably dressed, perfumed and eternally surrounded by a bevy of attractive young women. His lectures 'were brilliant improvisations' performed by 'an artist in the best sense of the word'. V.I. Borodulin and V.D. Topolianskii , 'Dmitrii Dmitrievich Pletnev', *Voprosy istorii* 9 (1989), pp. 36–54. Zamkov resembled Pletnev only in that he wore his class origins quite literally on his sleeves: he rarely wore a suit and tie, preferring instead the pseudo-military attire favored by many cultural figures of the time as a sign of ideological commitment.
22. K. Konova *et al.*, 'Protiv spekuliatsii na nauke' (Against speculation in science), *Izvestiia*, 22 March 1930, p. 5.
23. V. Korneev, 'K voprosu o chastnom sektore v dele zdravokhraneniia' (On the question of the private sector in health care), *Voprosy zdravokhraneniia* 2 (1930), p. 9.
24. Ibid. See also L. Bronshtein, 'O chastnom kapitale v dele zdravokhraneniia' (On private capital in health care), *Voprosy zdravokhraneniia* 2 (1930), p. 2.
25. Korneev, 'K voprosu o chastnom sektore v dele zdravokhraneniia', p. 5.
26. RGALI, f. 2326, op. 1, ed. khr. 462, ll. 113–14.

27. Loren R. Graham, 'The Formation of Soviet Research Institutes: A Combination of Revolutionary Innovation and International Borrowing', *Social Studies of Science* (1975), p. 322.
28. V.V. Babkov, 'N.K. Kol'tsov: Bor'ba za avtonomiiu nauki i poiski podderzhki vlasti' (N.K. Kol'tsov: the struggle for the autonomy of science and the search for the support of power), *Voprosy istorii estestvoznaniia i tekhniki* 3 (1989), p. 8; Nikolai Krementsov, *Stalinist Science* (Princeton, NJ: Princeton University Press, 1997), p. 40.
29. Toom and Bek, *Zapisi besed*, pp. 92–3; conversation with V.A. Zamkov.
30. Toom and Bek, *Zapisi besed*, p. 93.
31. Ibid, p. 92.
32. RGAE, f. 9457, op. 1, ed. khr. 99.
33. V.V. Babkov, 'N.K. Kol'tsov', p. 12. Babkov portrays this incident as a (short-lived) triumph of academic freedom over ideological persecution, but we should note that Kol'tsov is celebrating the perpetuation in his institute of a Stalinist model of management.
34. RTsKhIDNI (Russian Center for the Preservation and Study of Documents of Contemporary History – formerly the Communist Party Archive), f. 7, op. 3, d. 884. Protocol No. 100, meeting of 16 May 1932. Members present were Voroshilov, Kaganovich, Kalinin, Kuibyshev, Ordzhonikidze and Stalin.
35. Toom and Bek, *Zapisi besed*, pp. 96–96a.
36. 'Endokrinnye preparaty na sluzhbu krolikovodstvu i rabochemu khoziaistvu' (Endocrine preparations in service of rabbit breeding and the workers' economy), *Izvestiia*, 20 June 1932.
37. Resolution of the Council of Commissars No. 1804/395, 21 August 1933. RGAE, f. 9457, op. 3., ed. khr. 42a, l. 36.
38. Nik. Atarov, 'Gravidan', *Nashi dostizheniia* 3 (1934), p. 78.
39. Ibid.
40. Conversation with V.A. Zamkov.
41. *Urogravidanoterapiia*, Vol. 1, 1935, pp. 1–80.
42. E.I. Tsukershtein, 'Pis'mo tov. Stalina v readaktsii zhurnala *Proletarskaia revoliutsii* i nashi zadachi' (Comrade Stalin's letter to the journal *Proletarian Revolution*, and our tasks), *Klinicheskaia meditsina* 1 (1932), p. 3.
43. I. Al'pir, 'Institut derzanii' (Institute of audacity), *Vecherniaia Moskva*, 14 Jan. 1934, p. 3.
44. Ibid.
45. RGAE, f. 9457, op. 1, ed. khr. 102.
46. RGAE, f. 9457, op. 3, ed. khr. 14, l. 64, 92, 171. Here Zamkov's treatment is portrayed as the ideological equivalent of finding Christ; cf. Luke's *'ne boites'; ia vosveshchaiu vam velikuiu radost'* (Fear not. I bring you tidings of great joy.)
47. RGAE, f. 9457, op. 3, ed. khr. 14, l. 105.
48. Conversation with V.A. Zamkov.
49. For a summary of these ways and their history, see Terry Eagleton's *Ideology: An Introduction* (London: Verso, 1991), pp. 1–31.
50. For an overview of Marx's evolving notion of ideology, see Jorge Larrain, 'Ideology', in Tom Bottomore (ed.) *A Dictionary of Marxist Thought* (Cambridge, MA: Harvard University Press, 1983), pp. 219–23.
51. This discourse on ideology and alienation in the early Soviet Union owes its formulation to discussions with Christina Kiaer and is elaborated in our joint introduction to the forthcoming collection of essays mentioned above.
52. Podlubnyi's diary is a striking example of this phenomenon. See Hellbeck, *Tagebuch aus Moskau*, and Garros *et al.*, *Intimacy and Terror*.
53. Boris Gasparov, 'Introduction', in Alexander D. and Alice Stone Nakhimovsky (eds), *The Semiotics of Russian Cultural History* (Ithaca, NY: Cornell University Press, 1985), p. 13.
54. The ultimate verbalist manifesto of the pre-revolutionary decade is probably Andrei Belyi's 'The Magic of Words', in *Simvolizm kak miroponimanie* (Moscow: Respublika, 1994), pp. 131–42.

55. See Trotsky's hostile comments in his *Literatura i revoliutsiia* (Moscow: Politicheskaia literatura, 1991 [1923]), pp. 49–54, 107–8.
56. I.V. Stalin, 'Golovokruzhenie ot uspekhov' (Dizzy from success), *Sochineniia* (Moscow: Gosudarstvennoe izdatel'stvo, 1949), Vol. 12, p. 191.
57. In Stalin's attack on Bukharin at the Party plenum in 1928, the latter's chief fault was his failure to grasp the Party's slogans; a major error of Bukharin and his followers was that they *talked* about the wrong things. *Sochineniia*, Vol. 12, pp. 10–11.
58. See, *inter alia*, the inscription made by the writer M. Rykachev in a copy of one of his books, a gift to his physician: 'To my Doctor-Miracle Worker'. RGAE, f. 9457, op. 1, ed. khr. 94. The presence of this competing, religious discourse at one point posed difficulties for Zamkov; in the late 1920s he was visited by the NKVD after one of his patients was heard to refer to him as 'Saint Aleksei'.
59. RGAE, f. 9457, op. 1, ed. khr. 83. The author is identified by his name, or, more probably, his pseudonym: Luchezarov, a name formed from words signifying 'dawn' and 'a ray of light'.
60. V.A. Zamkov, 'U Kol'tsova', personal archive of V.A. Zamkov.
61. Conversation with V.A. Zamkov.
62. Serebriakova, *O drugikh i o sebe*, p. 336.
63. RGAE, f. 9457, op. 1, ed. khr. 83.
64. Conversation with V.A. Zamkov.
65. This brief summary of the history of endocrinology in western Europe and the United States is based on the account by Nelly Oudshoorn in *Beyond the Natural Body: An Archeology of Sex Hormones* (London: Routledge, 1994). For a more traditional medical history, see V.C. Medvei, *The History of Clinical Endocrinology* (Carnforth: Parthenon, 1993). Oudshoorn's book is brilliant in its interpretive sensitivity to gender, but oddly oblivious to the impact of other ideological influences. The book's discussion of the marketing of hormone treatment in Germany in the 1930s is curiously unconcerned with the fascist preoccupation with gender and health, and Oudshoorn's analysis may demonstrate the extent to which gender theory has difficulty gaining analytical perspective, or, as Bakhtin would have it, the necessary 'outsideness' on a phenomenon in which gender is so explicitly present from the start.
66. See, for instance, the claim by the rector of Sverdlov Communist University that non-seasonal sexual desire and, implicitly, menstruation, were the products of capitalism. M.N. Liadov, *Voprosy byta* (Moscow: Kommunisticheskii universitet, 1925), p. 30.
67. See Elizabeth Waters, 'The Female Form in Soviet Political Iconography, 1917–32' in *Russia's Women: Accommodation, Resistance, Transformation*, ed. Barbara Evans Clements, Barbara Alpern Engel and Christine D. Worobec (Berkeley and Los Angeles, CA: University of California Press, 1991), pp. 225–42; Zolotonosov, 'Masturbanizatsiia'; and Victoria Bonnell, 'The Peasant Woman in Stalinist Political Art of the 1930s', *American Historical Review* 98 (1993), pp. 55–82.
68. Katherine Verdery, *What Was Socialism, and What Comes Next?* (Princeton, NJ: Princeton University Press, 1996). See Lewis Siegelbaum's survey of the variations in this model in his '"Dear Comrade, You Ask What We Need": Socialist Paternalism and Soviet Rural "Notables" in the Mid-1930s', *Slavic Review* 1 (1998), pp. 107–9.
69. Andrei Platonov, 'Schastlivaia Moskva', in *'Strana filosofov' Andreia Platonova: Problemy tvorchestv*a (Moscow: Nasledie, 1999), vyp. 3, p. 44.
70. Vladimir Sorokin, *Norma* (Moscow: Tri kita, 1994).
71. Mikhail Bakhtin, *Rabelais and His World*, trans. Hélène Iswolsky (Cambridge, MA: MIT Press, 1968).
72. This was a testing (and marketing) strategy pursued by pioneering endocrinologists in the West, including Claude Brown-Sequard and Ernst Laqueur. See Merriley Borell, 'Brown-Sequard's Organotherapy and its Appearance in America at the End of the Nineteenth Century', *Bulletin of the History of Medicine* 3 (1976), p. 313, and Oudshoorn, *Beyond the Natural Body*, pp. 90–1.
73. Zamkov, 'My ne Gerakly', p. 13.
74. Oudshoorn, *Beyond the Natural Body*, pp. 65–111.
75. The quotation comes from a speech read to the State Scientific Council of the Commissariat of Public Health in the summer of 1935. RGAE, f. 9457, op. 1, ed. khr. 85.

76. See the articles by D.D. Pletneva, G.P. Artynov, B. Mogil'nitskii, I. Zhdanov, K.F. Mikhailov, L.M. Izhevskii, G.E. Rikhter and N.A. Mel'nikov, *Klinicheskaia meditsina* 23–24 (1933), pp. 1206–32.
77. RGAE, f. 9457, op. 1, ed. khr. 57 (letter from the writer Altaeva-Iamshchikova).
78. 'Prestuplenie Prof. Pletneva' (The crime of Prof. Pletnev), *Izvestiia*, 9 June 1937, p. 4; 'Professor – nasil'nik, sadist' (The professor is a rapist and a sadist), *Pravda*, 8 June 1937, p. 3. The account in *Izvestiia* is striking in its peculiarly Soviet representation of the crime's monstrosity, where the more traditional loss of virtue is replaced by its Marxist equivalent: 'Fearing that this repulsive crime would be revealed, Pletnev himself treated the wound, although the treatment of such a disease was not at all within his medical expertise. In the end the disease assumed a grave, chronic form, and Citizen B. (the victim) *lost the ability to work*.'
79. 'Rabotniki meditsiny kleimiat prestupleniia sadista Pletneva' (Workers from the field of medicine express their outrage at the crimes of the sadist Pletnev), *Pravda*, 9 June 1937, p. 3.
80. Pletnev was not free for long. He was rearrested within several months and charged with anti-Soviet conspiracy and complicity in the 'murder' of Gorky. Testifying the following year as a co-defendant in the Bukharin trial (see below) Pletnev begged to be spared so that he could continue his research, noting that while incarcerated he had managed to write 'a monograph ten or twelve signatures long'. *Report of Court Proceedings in the Case of the Anti-Soviet 'Bloc of Rights and Trotskyites'* (Moscow: People's Commissariat of Justice of the USSR, 1938), p.788. For a recent examination of the circumstances 'behind' the case, see Borodulin and Topolianskii, 'Dmitrii Dmitrievich Pletnev'.
81. 'Protiv bespechnosti. Za bol'shevistskuiu samokritiku' (Against carelessness. For Bol'shevik self-criticism), *Klinicheskaia meditsina* 8 (1937), pp. 561–6.
82. M.P. Konchalovskii, 'Nevezhestvo ili sharlatanstvo?' (Ignorance or charlatanism), *Meditsinskii rabotnik*, 15 Feb. 1938, p. 2.
83. I.N. Kazakov, 'Lizoterapiia', *Izvestiia*, 4 and 5 Nov. 1932; I.N. Kazakov, 'Lizoterapiia', *Vecherniaia Moskva*, 9 May 1934.
84. Conversation with V.A. Zamkov.
85. *Report of Court Proceedings in the Case of the Anti-Soviet 'Bloc of Rights and Trotskyites'* pp. 608–9, 618–22.
86. Pletnev was 66 or 67 years old at the time of his trial, but in fact his sentence proved to be one of death rather than life imprisonment. Imprisoned in the city of Orel, he was executed, along with all others incarcerated for crimes against state security, when the Soviet Army abandoned the town to the Germans in September 1941. Borodulin and Topolianskii, 'Dmitrii Dmitrievich Pletnev', p. 51.
87. M.S. Malinovskii, 'Protiv "zasekrechennykh" metodov lecheniia' (Against 'secret' methods of treatment), *Meditsinskii rabotnik*, 10 March 1938, p. 4.
88. Order No. 473 of the People's Commissariat of Public Health of the Russian Federation, 29 July 1938, RGAE, f. 9457, op. 3, ed. khr. 42a, l. 35.
89. D.D. Pletnev, 'Problemy sovremennoi kliniki' (Problems of the contemporary clinic), *Klinicheskaia meditsina* 19–20 (1930), pp. 1067–70.
90. Oudshoorn, *Beyond the Natural Body*, pp. 99–100, 109.
91. Clarke, *Disciplining Reproduction*, p. 143.
92. It is to this peasant strain in Soviet culture that Mikhail Zolotonosov attributes Zamkov's 'success' during the 1930s. 'Masturbanizatsiia', pp. 95–6. Recall Mukhina's comment that Kuibyshev '*believed* in gravidan'.
93. V.V. Rozanov, *Liudi lunnogo sveta: metafizika khristianstva* (People of the lunar light: the metaphysics of Christianity) (St Petersburg, 1911), p. 77.

13

Death in Auschwitz as 'Ugly Death'

BOAZ NEUMANN

This chapter tries to face a difficult topic: death in Auschwitz. Auschwitz should be considered as three camps in one. It was a labor camp, a concentration camp and an extermination camp. The number of labor camps located around Auschwitz I and II reached 27. The largest labor camp was Buna-Monovich (Auschwitz III), which manufactured synthetic rubber. The main extermination camp was Birkenau (Auschwitz II) where the four main crematoria were located. Therefore, in order to say anything about death in Auschwitz, we must first define the level we are discussing. The historical literature has dealt with three levels.[1] It has depicted the horrifying labor conditions in Auschwitz and death caused by such conditions (Auschwitz as a labor camp). It has considered death caused by mental and physical abuse (Auschwitz as a concentration camp). It has traced the industrial process of killing (Auschwitz as an extermination camp). However, appalling labor conditions, mental and physical abuse, torture and systematic murder, terrible as they were, do not constitute the essence of Auschwitz. The focus upon Auschwitz as a labor/concentration/extermination camp was not only a historical but mainly a conceptual one as far as it concerned the meaning of death. The victim has always been presented in the historiography as having been 'killed'/'executed'/'murdered'/ 'exterminated' in a physiological manner, with no regard to whether his death was caused by labor conditions, mental and physical abuse or a gas chamber. Such a concept of death, as an ending of physiological life, is the prevalent one and is defined as such in the *Oxford English Dictionary*: 'Death: the final cessation of vital functions in an organism; the ending of life.'

Descriptions of Auschwitz as a place of 'total extermination through gas',[2] as a place of 'mass extermination of millions of people'[3] and as a 'Nazi killing machine',[4] even if they strive to depict Auschwitz as a death camp, have failed in my opinion because they have not made the notion of death in Auschwitz itself an issue for historical investigation. Therefore they have not been able to transcend the common physiological meaning of death. Not a single attempt to distinguish between the way the victim died in Auschwitz as a death camp, on the one hand, and the way he died in Auschwitz as a labor/concentration/extermination camp, on the other hand, has transcended the positivistic/quantitative features of death, i.e., numbers of bodies, killing techniques, capacity of the gas chambers, the speed of trains, the victims' identity and so on. But Auschwitz functioning as a labor/concentration camp was not the same Auschwitz functioning as a death camp. Practices such as 'labor' and 'concentration' belong to the social/political sphere. They represent ways of organizing or controlling society. As such they are not relevant to death camp Auschwitz. Auschwitz as a death camp was not the same Auschwitz in which food was 'organized', in which underground movements operated and from which people tried to escape. All these events belong to the social/political sphere. Nor did Auschwitz as a death camp have much in common with Auschwitz as an extermination camp. In Auschwitz the extermination camp the Nazis aimed at ending people's 'lives'. As such, it was assumed that the victims had 'life' before it was taken away.

The common assumption we find in the literature dealing with the Holocaust in general and with Auschwitz in particular conceives death as an end result of implementation of force which can be articulated through ideological or bureaucratic power. We find this inherent assumption in both intentionalist and functionalist perspectives. The intentionalist perspective represents death in Auschwitz as caused by Hitler or another central figure or combination of figures who used force against the Jews on the basis of an anti-Semitic position.[5] The functionalist perspective represents death in Auschwitz as a result of bureaucratic processes which executed death orders directed against the Jews, in an effort to provide a bureaucratic solution to a given problem.[6] In general, death has been understood as inflicted by one side (Hitler, SS guard, bureaucrat) against the other (Jew, Gypsy) by implementing force (beating, rape, torture, shooting, operating gas chambers) from a given ideological or mental position (anti-Semitism, hatred, indifference, discipline). Lucy Davidowicz has called it a 'war';[7] yet, what are we to make of episodes such as that described by Yehiel Dinur, who wrote under the pseudonym, Ka-Tzetnik.

> Shaking, I raise my eyes to see God's face in all its splendor, and there I see the face of an SS man standing in front of the truck. He is still very tired. The dawn is cold, his hands are in his black military coat. Before him – a river of skeletons streams silently by from the block entrance to the truck. And then, his mouth opens widely in a huge yawn.[8]

DEATH IN AUSCHWITZ AS 'UGLY DEATH'

Here we do not find one side using force against another. There is no murderer – merely a yawning SS guard; nor is there any murdered subject – the river of skeletons streams quietly. We do not hear the protest of any victim. Even if the people, streaming like a river of skeletons, faced their physiological death from inhaling poison gas, this physiological death only finalized the fact that they were already dead before entering the gas chamber. In other words, I would claim that the victim's physiological death in death camp Auschwitz would seem to be the least relevant aspect of his death: 'their death had begun before that of their body. Weeks and months before being snuffed out, they had already lost the ability to observe, to remember, to compare and express themselves.'[9]

In order to comprehend death in death camp Auschwitz we will refer to an ontological death. Ontology is the branch of metaphysics dealing with the nature of Being. An ontological perspective of death will conceive it as a certain mode of Being. I will try to show that this was the case in death camp Auschwitz.

One of the survivors, Dr Golse, wrote that Auschwitz was a place where one 'has to die' (*il faut mourir*).[10] If in any other place one 'had to live', including Auschwitz as a labor/concentration camp, one 'had to die' in Auschwitz the death camp. Even in extermination camp Auschwitz, in contrast to death camp Auschwitz, one had to live first, in order to be murdered later. If in any other place life was a normative value while death was a diversion, in death camp Auschwitz death became a normative value, a kind of regulative idea, and life became anomaly.[11] 'The business of Auschwitz was death' (Elisabeth Leitner).[12] Ludwig Wörl, a German prisoner in Auschwitz, distinguished between the various death orders in the camp in a similar way:

> The Jews had to die, the Poles were supposed to die, and the Germans were allowed to die.[13]

Auschwitz inverted the ontological order first articulated by the Greek philosopher Parmenides in which Being is and Nothing is not. Life supposedly means being/existing. Death supposedly means non-being/non-existence. Until Auschwitz, life meant existing until existence ended and became non-existence/death. In the world of Auschwitz in which one 'had to die', a world in which one was ontologically dead before being physiologically killed/murdered/executed/exterminated, 'Being' became 'non-Being'. To be in death camp Auschwitz was actually not to be. To live in death camp Auschwitz was precisely to be dead. Any living figure in Auschwitz was 'a dead man on holiday'.[14] For this reason we should not refer to Auschwitz as an 'extermination camp' but rather as a 'death camp'. Ontologically, it was not a place in which people were exterminated, but a place where people were always already dead. The following chart summarizes the distinction between the three spheres and practices of killing which existed in Auschwitz:

labor/concentration camp	political sphere	killing, dying
extermination camp	biological sphere	exterminating
death camp	ontological sphere	death

This ontological reverse of death camp Auschwitz is to be found in many memoirs and testimonies – not only in conceptual categories but also as a description of daily life experience. The individual in death camp Auschwitz was not a living slave/prisoner who died (Auschwitz as a labor/concentration camp) nor a living human being who was exterminated (Auschwitz as an extermination camp). He was a dead being who by chance was still physiologically alive.

> in the end there is no difference between the living and the dead ... indeed, the difference is minor! We are skeletons, still moving, and they are frozen and paralyzed skeletons. But there is a third type: these, the ones that were disintegrated without any ability to move, and they are still breathing ... the others expect them to die and make room ... is it a wonder that they are considered dead and that one begins to make errors while counting? ... the corpses stay on the beds: live, dead, half dead ... The barriers are destroyed between these and those. The borders are blurred almost totally.[15]

In death camp Auschwitz no victim died, for death was a mode of Being. No victim passed from one physiological state (life) to another (death). No force was implemented in this process. As Vladimir Yankelevitch argued, Auschwitz was a 'catastrophe in itself' (*catastrophe en soi*).[16] Thus we cannot refer to the acts committed by the Nazis in Auschwitz as being altogether a 'death policy'. That death camp Auschwitz was not the historical or conceptual paramount of power, but its failure, is best illustrated in Ka-Tzetnik's description presented above. Paradoxically we can conclude from the ontological reverse in Auschwitz that the individual achieved his proper state of Being only with his death: 'To be a (living) Jew is to be dead.'[17]

Halina Birenbaum, who was sent in one of the selections to the crematoria, was saved at the last minute by the selector who ordered her number to be erased from the list. 'Life was given to us! Life!' she exclaimed.[18] By saying this, she articulated the ontological reverse of the victim's state of Being. When the selector erased her name from the death list he did not 'save her from death' but gave her (temporary) life. Her ontological condition in Auschwitz was always that of death.

With death in Auschwitz we pass from one ontological state in which both murderer and prisoner were alive, to a certain point in which the murderer caused death to the victim and made him pass from one physiological state of life (prisoner, *Häftling*) to another physiological state of death (victim), and then to a new ontological state in which the murderer was ontologically alive and the prisoner, alive or dead physiologically, but always ontologically dead. Therefore we cannot refer to the victim in Auschwitz as a 'human being', a 'person' or a 'prisoner' before Auschwitz, or a 'survivor' after Auschwitz. As ontologically dead, he was, he is and he will be a 'victim' – before, during and after Auschwitz.

If the victim was not sent directly to the crematorium he was a combination of physiological life and ontological death in one body:

> Again it was not an ordinary death, it was Auschwitz death. There is Auschwitz life and there is Auschwitz death. This [death in the crematorium] was death of life in Auschwitz. Everyone here was used to ordinary death. Piled high, they are lying behind the gates of the blocks. The dead are lying. The hanged – hanged. But dead standing and watching you with open, living eyes?[19]

The 'dead standing and watching with open, living eyes' is an expression for the ontologically already-dead victim who was still physiologically alive. It may be that he was kept alive due to a technical malfunction of the system. In a death camp, in contrast to the labor/concentration/extermination camp, there was no place for an intermediary state between life and death, for example a state of being incarcerated or punished: 'Here there is no place for sick people. There are only living people and dead ones.'[20]

Even a death certificate, when it was still issued, was signed when the selected victim was still alive. The moment of physical killing by means of gas in the gas chamber and the actual physiological death were no more than a symbolic gesture. That moment merely sealed the fact that the person never really existed.

The combination of ontological death and physiological life created what could be termed 'the living experience of death'. This experience of death while still alive caused the victim to face death repeatedly. This was the victim's nightmare. He died not only once. He had to live and relive his death over and over again. 'I want to die once, only once because it will be the only one ... everyone dies thousands of times his own death.'[21] The victim in death camp lived/experienced his death while still alive without traversing the line between life and death.

> ... experiencing the essence of evil was actually experiencing death ... I say 'experience' deliberately ... for death was not something we slightly touched or were saved from, as after an accident which one survives with no injury. We lived it ... We are not survivors but ghosts ... It is incredible, one cannot share it with others, it is almost incomprehensible, for death, rationally thinking, is the only event we cannot experience individually ... the only event one cannot conceive but through dread ... as a *futur antérieur* ... and still, we experienced this experience of death as a collective experience ... as a *Mit-sein-zum-Tode*.[22]

Death experience, according to Jorge Semprun, was like an experience of an 'anterior future', that is, an experience that refers to a future event that has already come to pass. The victim was always in an 'anterior future' time frame *vis-à-vis* his own death. He was always dead even if he was still not dead. In other words, he experienced in the present his future death. In Semprun's view this death experience proved Ludwig Wittgenstein's mistake. According to 'that silly man': 'Death is not an event that belongs to life. No one experiences death [*Der Tod ist kein Ereignis des Lebens. Den Tod erlebt man nicht*].'[23] In the camps, Semprun claimed, one could indeed experience one's own death:

> Actually I did not quite survive. I was not a real survivor for sure. I traversed death, it was a life experience of mine. There are certain languages which have a special word for such an experience. In German one says *Erlebnis* ... life as something that experiences itself.[24]

One can contrast between the Nazi ideal of life experience in the 'living space' (*Lebensraum*) and death experience in the 'death space' (Auschwitz). Death experience in a death camp was supposed to be the counter-experience to that of life in the *Lebensraum*. Whereas in the *Lebensraum* the Nazis decreed that Aryans experience life as a 'living life' (*erlebtes Lebens*),[25] this decree reversed itself in death camps, where one was commanded to experience one's own death.

How can one experience one's own death? In order to experience something one has to be alive. The only way to resolve this paradox of being able to experience one's own death, as reported by survivors, is to understand death as experiencing itself through human being. In death camp Auschwitz, I will argue, human beings did not die; rather death knew or articulated itself through them. Death in death camp Auschwitz was not a syndrome. A syndrome is defined as a state which appears through other 'parasitic' elements, for example, AIDS. People do not die from AIDS but from diseases that the AIDS syndrome facilitates. In the same way we can argue that death is a syndrome. No one dies of death but of diseases. Normally, the moment of death never consists of 'death' itself. Death does not present itself at the actual moment of death. In other words, death itself is not a phenomenon. What is remarkable in death camp Auschwitz is that death did appear in a concrete way, articulated in human beings. The victim did not die of mental or physical abuse, of hunger, sorrow, lack of information concerning the destination of a train, from being Jewish or from being Gypsy. This death etiology belongs to Auschwitz as a labor/ concentration/extermination camp. The cause of death in death camp Auschwitz was death itself. Isabella Leitner made this the epigraph of her memoir: 'You don't die of anything except death. Suffering doesn't kill you. Only death.'[26]

Death in Auschwitz was not an act of killing or of negation of life because the victim was always already ontologically dead. Death in Auschwitz was therefore the negation of death itself. Death took the possibility of dying from its victim. Thus we find many utterances concerning the victim's craving and yearning for death. 'Dying, it must be beautiful, but living here, it's horrible! ... Days of execution are days of fête for us. Dying in Birkenau is not a punishment.'[27] '[In Auschwitz] only death could bring deliverance, the final rest, oh, rest.'[28]

Anyone who speaks about death as a wonderful thing, as a cause for celebration, as a kind of deliverance, as a final rest, is one who was deprived of death. Outside the death camp death is regarded as a part of life. Death frees man from his life. But death in a death camp has no meaning of freedom. 'Due to overcrowding in the gas chambers victims remained standing after their death.'[29] Every individual who 'survived' Auschwitz was therefore not one who was saved from death but one who earned it. He could return at last to his proper state of Being/ontology, that is, he could finally die. 'In the camps death has a novel horror; since Auschwitz, fearing death means fearing worse than death.'[30] Since Auschwitz, being afraid of death means being afraid of being dead while still alive, only the 'death of death' is worse than death itself. '

An ordinary act of killing assumes that the victim was alive before the act of killing actually took place. As such, the act of killing was an act of destruction. An act of killing in the style of Auschwitz took place on the premise that the victim was already dead before being killed/murdered/exterminated. As such, this was a therapeutic act – the removal of dead parts from the body of the German *Volk* (*Volkskörper*) or from the *Lebensraum*. Killing was an act of creation.

Historical proof of the therapeutic character of death in Auschwitz can be found in the euthanasia project initiated by the Nazis at the beginning of the war which aimed at purifying society of ailing elements.[31] Extermination in Auschwitz, like the euthanasia project, divided society into two main categories – those whose life was 'worth living' and those whose life was 'not worth living' (*Lebensunwertes Lebens*). Extermination in Auschwitz as an extension of the euthanasia project aimed at a hygienic, therapeutic and creative extermination – to clean, purify and create life through the removal of infectious, afflicted and dead elements. If in 1919 Hitler blamed the Jews for carrying tuberculosis, in 1930 they became a 'cancer'. The first metaphor led to moderate treatment. Tuberculosis is cured by sending the patient to a sanatorium – the Jews would be expelled. A tumor must be removed from the body through a more aggressive surgical procedure – the Jews would be 'treated' by means of the crematoria.[32] In Greek, euthanasia is 'the beautiful death' or 'the worthy death'. Auschwitz was the forbiddance of euthanasia. It was an ugly death.

This ontological reverse that occurred within the borders of Auschwitz had an effect on the outside world. 'No one must leave here and so carry to the world, together with the sign impressed on his skin, the evil tidings of what man's presumption made of man in Auschwitz.'[33]

Auschwitz revealed death – not a physiological cessation of life, but knowledge of the existence of an ontological death – that death can become a mode of existence or a way of life. The 'survivor' of Auschwitz is a carrier of this knowledge and as such he is in a position of an Other in the post-Auschwitz society. The 'survivor' decrees to humanity the impossible: know what happened in Auschwitz even though you can never know what happened in Auschwitz.[34]

If death in Auschwitz was conditioned by an ontological gap between the murderer and the victim, how could any contact occur between them? The French philosopher Jean François Lyotard has conceptualized this gap between the SS guard and the Jew as the difference between an 'aristocrat' and a 'farmer'. Himmler himself emphasized more than once the obligation of the SS guard to be a 'gentleman'. Two SS soldiers who cannot agree between themselves at court, he argued, should resolve their differences in a duel. Only one feature, according to Himmler, distinguished between the old aristocracy and new SS aristocracy. Whereas the old aristocrat was told, 'You must marry this or that one' (*Du mußt die und die heiraten*), the SS aristocrat is told, 'You cannot marry this or that one' (*Du darfst die und die nicht heiraten*).[35] One should bear in mind that the idea of aristocracy is based on blood like the Nazi racial concept. As an aristocrat, Lyotard argues, the SS guard could not acknowledge or accept anyone as a subject but himself or other aristocrats like him. As an 'aristocrat' the SS guard could not command or inflict death on the victim. Such an act would have infected his 'aristocratic' hands with the blood of the 'farmer'. Such an act would create an unbearable and impossible situation in which the living contacted the dead. The SS guard could command or inflict death only upon himself, i.e., commit suicide, or on his peers, i.e., on other SS guards.[36] The only solution that the SS guard could suggest concerning the 'farmer' was a 'final solution' (*Endlösung*) that would resolve once and for all the problem of 'Being'. It could not be a 'final-goal' (*Endziel*), an expression which appeared in an order issued by Reinhard Heydrich to the Einsatzgruppen in September 1939, because a 'goal' is something that can be achieved or not. Nor could it be a 'general solution' (*Gesamtlösung*), an expression which appeared in an order issued by Hermann Göring to Heydrich in July 1941, because 'general' refers to the sum of all parts of a problem at a given time but not to the solution of the problem once and for all. A 'final solution', by contrast, offers a solution to a problem by eliminating the problem itself and destroying all the possible solutions to it.[37] Only a 'final solution' could put an end to the abnormal existence of the 'farmer' in the 'aristocrat's' world. It was indeed the way the Nazi thought and acted.

At the end of August 1942 a typhus plague broke out at the 'hospital' in Auschwitz. All prisoners, sick and healthy, were sent to the crematorium. No one considered dealing with the plague itself.[38] The SS guard could not command the victim – 'Die, I decree it' (*Meurt, je l'édicte*), according to Lyotard, because this would be an acknowledgement of the Other which is ontologically impossible. The death formula in Auschwitz had to be 'That he dies, I decree it' (*Qu'il meurt, je l'édicte*) in which there was no contact or acknowledgement between them.[39] In such a formula death was not positioned in a causal relation to the order of death. Death was caused by a third, anonymous element – 'That he dies'. It is not initiated by the statement of the SS guard – 'I decree it.' The impersonal functioning of the death machinery in Auschwitz aimed at preventing any contact between executioner and victim. The 'aristocrat' inflicting death on the 'farmer' did not have to be afraid of contaminating his hands with the victim's blood. Contamination in such a context can be understood on three levels. On the first level the murderer could be stained by the victim's blood. In such case water would be sufficient in order to cleanse himself. On a second level contamination could be caused by mixing Aryan and Jewish blood. In such a case water would be insufficient. A blood regulation was demanded (Nuremberg laws). On a third level contamination was caused by penetration of a dead person's blood into the blood circulation of a living one. This penetration was conceived by the Nazis as possible also on the level of the 'people's body' (*Volkskörper*): '300,000 Jewish-Germans' bastard blood in our "people's body" (*Volkskörper*) – a very sad record. This is a racial disgrace.'[40] On all three levels we deal with the fear of being soiled, contaminated or killed due to uncontrollable streams of blood.[41]

The impersonal method of killing in Auschwitz which will be described below enabled the SS guard to protect himself from being contaminated by the victim's blood on all three levels. This impersonal death machinery provided him with the other, anonymous faculty that created the gap between his death decree ('I decree it') and the victim's death ('That he dies'). It will also enable us to see how death presented itself as a phenomenon, how death articulated itself in human beings. I will focus on four elements that together constructed Auschwitz as death camp, as a place ruled by death. These elements were: technology, impersonal relations between the SS guard and the victim, the industrial character of the extermination process and the negation of the acts of birth and suicide in the camp.

TECHNOLOGY

Death technology in Auschwitz was an end product of a process which roughly included two technological stages. The first was an extermination process based on the 'special squads' (*Einsatzgruppen*). These units accompanied the German army invading the Soviet Union. The *Einsatzgruppen* used to concentrate their victims where they lived or in nearby forests and execute them. This phase was characterized by a process of bringing the extermination system to the victim. The second stage of extermination was extermination in camps. This phase brought the victim to the extermination system.

Two traditional explanations are usually given for this change of extermination strategy – from *Einsazgruppen* to extermination camps. The first one, the so-called psychological explanation, focuses on the moral and psychological difficulties that confronted the killers while executing their victims – they were killing in a direct manner and in large numbers. The extermination camp based on a gas chamber was a more sterile method with which to solve these issues. A second explanation, the so-called functional one, focuses on the logistic and functional problems resulting from the first stage. Execution units, however efficient they may have been, could not execute millions. According to the functional explanation, extermination camps were set up to resolve this problem. As Adolf Eichmann said to Rudolf Höss, the commander of Auschwitz:

> Only gas was suitable since killing by shooting the huge numbers expected would be absolutely impossible and would also be a tremendous strain on the SS soldiers who would have to carry out the order as far as the women and children were concerned.[42]

In contrast to the intentional/psychological or functional explanations, I suggest reading this change of strategies as an essential feature deriving from the new ontology. The Nazis developed an extermination system in which they, as 'aristocrats', would be exempted from any contact with their victims, whose existence was conceived of as 'death'. It was already in the first stage of extermination that the Nazis improved the execution methods so that no connection would be established between them and the victim. This was accomplished mainly by standardization of execution methods.

In the development of the *Einsatzgruppen*'s execution techniques one can already identify the tendency toward impersonal killing methods which would reach their highest level of perfection in the extermination camp. The use of machine-guns or rifles to shoot the victim in the neck, carried out by 'neck shooting specialists' (*Genickschußspezialisten*), relieved the executor from having to make any eye contact with the victim. Certain commanders demanded that the shooting range be increased even if it meant inability to hit the neck. Another impersonal killing method was the 'sardine method' (*Ölsardinenmanier*) in which the victims were compelled to lie in deep trenches heads facing the same side. After they were shot, a second layer was put into the trench with their heads to the other side, facing the legs of the first group. In that manner the executor could avoid any eye contact with the victim.[43] The most conspicuous qualitative change toward total separation between executioner and victim was introduced at the end of 1941 in the first experiments with gas trucks in which any sensory contact between the two sides was eliminated.

These experiments with gas trucks had tremendous effects on the death procedure in Auschwitz. As described through the eyes of its chief commander, Rudolf Höss:

> The extermination process in Auschwitz took place as follows: Jews selected for gassing (*Die zur Vernichtung bestimmten Juden*) were taken as quietly as possible to the crematories ... After undressing, the Jews went into the gas chamber, which was furnished with showers and water pipes and gave a realistic impression of a bathhouse ... The door would be screwed shut and the waiting disinfecting squads (*Disinfektoren*) would immediately pour the gas [crystals] into the vents in the ceiling of the gas chamber down an air shaft which went to the floor. This ensured the rapid distribution of the gas. The process could be observed through the peep hole in the door ... After twenty minutes at the most no movement could be detected.[44]

Rudolf Höss is the murderer, but he does not present himself as such. He does not present the victim as his victim but as a victim of a third, anonymous faculty (*die zur Vernichtung bestimmten Juden*). The gas chamber technology enabled him to present death as inflicted not by him. Who is the murderer in this description? According to Höss he is none other than a 'sanitary officer' whose job was to throw gas crystals into the chamber. The description of the Nazi as such proves that killing was not conceived by him as an act of destruction but as an act of creation. A gas mask or a peep hole through which he could look at the victim, if he was at all interested, separated the murderer and the victim. Death could have occurred even while the murderer drank a cup of coffee.

> Death occurred in the crammed full cells immediately after the gas was thrown in. Only a brief choking outcry and it was all over ... I must admit openly that the gassings had a calming effect on me, since in the near future the mass annihilation of the Jews was to begin ... Now we [Eichmann and Höss] had discovered the gas and the procedure. I was always horrified of death by firing squads, especially when I thought of the huge numbers of women and children who would have to be killed. I had had enough of hostage executions, and the mass killings by firing squad ordered by Himmler and Heydrich. Now I was at ease. We were all saved from these bloodbaths, and the victims would be spared until the last moment. That is what I worried about the most.[45]

Death from the murderer's perspective was a 'bloodbath that has been spared' rather than a bloodbath. The murderer did not murder the victim but 'spared' him. Death became a kind of favor. A gesture. A real 'aristocrat' killing a 'farmer' would never do it out of resentment toward him, for then contact between them would be established. An act of killing coming out of such a sentiment would prove the 'farmer's' ability to influence the 'aristocrat' emotionally – making him hate him, causing him to be afraid of him or making him want to seek revenge. A real 'aristocratic' act of killing cannot be derived from any feeling toward the 'farmer'. It was probably this that Himmler had in mind when he argued that the SS guard should not be a sadist nor someone who is praying for the victim's sake or empathizes with him. The SS guard, as part of an 'aristocracy', must be able to remove the 'pest' (*Schädling*) from the community while remaining 'decent' (*ständig*). The SS guard must never torture the victim: 'A master-people must be able to shoot also when the pest [*Schädling*] runs away; he must be able not to curse him. It would not be decent, because he could not protect himself.'[46] And Rudolf Höss again:

> The door was opened half an hour after the gas was thrown in and the ventilation system was turned on. Work was immediately started to remove the corpses. There was no noticeable change in the bodies and no sign of convulsions or discoloration. Only after the bodies had been left lying for some time – several hours – did the usual death stains appear where they were laid. Seldom did it occur that they were soiled with feces. There were no signs of wounds of any kind. The faces were not contorted.[47]

DEATH IN AUSCHWITZ AS 'UGLY DEATH'

Höss's description of the dying victim resembles more that of a person going to sleep. Ontologically the victim was always dead and the gas chamber enabled the murderer to kill the victim without getting him dirty or injured, without even a convulsion on his face. Sometimes the victims died while holding hands.[48] That is the worthiest way for a dead person to die. Any injury or wound on the victim's body or any spasm on his face would have been a proof of the existence of a situation of struggle for life before death. But someone who is already dead in his life cannot die while struggling. That is the reason for the cleanness and sterility of the death procedure. Observing Adolf Eichmann's conduct throughout his trial, Hannah Arendt noticed that the only time he exploded was when he was charged with beating a child to death. The fact that he was accused of being responsible for killing millions did not affect him at all. Arendt interpreted that reaction in her 'banality thesis'. But Eichmann was not a 'desk killer'. He was no killer at all. He was an 'aristocrat' and as such he wouldn't have bothered to beat the 'farmer' or his children. All the more so to kill them and infect his hands with their blood. As far as Eichmann was concerned, the accusation of beating a child to death was absurd – for no one can kill someone who is already dead.

IMPERSONAL RELATIONS BETWEEN THE SS-GUARD AND THE VICTIM

The impersonal death technology described above was backed and completed by an impersonal relationship between murderer and victim. In every point along the extermination process in which contact between murderer and victim could occur, from the moment the victim got off the wagon until his ashes were removed, the victim himself was exploited as the 'death agent'. The Kanadakommando was established to deal with confiscation of the victim's goods – confiscating the property on the ramp, organizing it in the 'Kanada' depot and shipping it out of the camp. The Sonderkommando was established to deal with the victim himself. Its role was to lead him into the crematorium, to make sure that he got undressed while deceiving him about his real destiny, to sort his clothes and belongings, to clean the cloakroom and prepare it for the next transport, to clean the gas chamber and to remove the bodies from the gas chamber to the ovens. The Sonderkommando staff were the paradigmatic expression of the clear-cut distinction created between murderer and victim and the process of transforming the latter into a murderer. 'Conceiving and organizing the squads was National Socialism's most demonic crime ... This institution represented an attempt to shift onto others – specifically, the victims – the burden of guilt, so that they were deprived of even the solace of innocence.'[49]

Any contact between the Sonderkommando staff and the Nazis was forbidden and was established through the Kapo in charge. Joseph Sacker claimed that as a Sonderkommando staff member he never spoke with any German in the camp. The order to start moving into the gas chamber was indeed given by the Nazis but it was a Sonderkommando member who instructed the victim to move forward and enter the chamber. Physical contact between murderer and victim occurred rarely. The only function that was left to the Nazis was to shut the door of the gas chamber and to throw the gas can inside.

The victim was forced to take active part in the maintenance of the camp, thus becoming an organ in a self-extermination system. He took part in constructing both camp and extermination facilities. He also participated, for example, in laying the train tracks and constructing the crematoria. The construction units were called 'Arbeitskommando Krematorium'. The victim also took part in the dismantling process of camp and extermination facilities and in removing any evidence of his own extermination. The Sonderkommando staff led the victim to his death while eating food that was left behind in the cloakroom. They were drafted into the special unit from among the newcomers and after a short period of time were exterminated by others who replaced them. By forcing the victim to participate in his own extermination process and in the process of eradicating the extermination process the Nazi could enable himself to extricate himself from the process and to reduce the level of contact with the victim to a minimum. After closing the doors, the last battle of the victim began.

> The bodies were not lying here and there throughout the room, but piled in a mass to the ceiling. The reason for this was that the gas first inundated the lower layers of air and rose but slowly toward the ceiling. This forced the victims to trample one another in a frantic effort to escape the gas. Yet a few feet higher up the gas reached them. What a struggle for life there must have been! Nevertheless it was merely a matter of two or three minutes' respite. If they had been able to think about what they were doing, they would have realized they were trampling their own children, their wives, their relatives. But they couldn't think. Their gestures were no more than reflexes of the instinct of self-preservation. I noticed that the bodies of the women, the children, and the aged were at the bottom of the pile; at the top, the strongest.[50]

The victim was fighting his last moments trying to reach higher ground. His last battle therefore was not against the murderer but against his fellow victims.

Despite the efforts to refrain from any contact with the victim, such contact could not be avoided. Contact could occur through corruption, such as stealing property from the victim, or out of pure sadism. These two phenomena were considered by the Nazis as detrimental to camp activity. Himmler, for example, forbade any act of stealing. Every SS guard risked the death penalty even if he was stealing one Reichsmark from a Jew.[51] Sadism was also considered a dangerous phenomenon which interfered with the systematic extermination activity in the camp. The ban on corruption and sadism in the camp can also be explained psychologically and functionally. Corruption, from a functional point of view, could harm the efficiency of the extermination process. It could be expressed, for example, through blackmailing the victim. Sadism, from a functional perspective, was also an inefficient killing method unsuited to handling masses of people. Psychologically, sadism was regarded as an expression of sentiment toward the victim. This sentiment might subsequently develop into a sense of compassion or pity. A third explanation for proscribing corruption and sadism is derived from the Nazi ontology. Both corruption and sadism demanded a certain degree of physical/emotional contact between the murderer and the victim which controverted the ontological difference between them.

This contact between murderer and victim was avoided by a chain of role bearers such as the Stubenälteste, Blockälteste, Lagerälteste in administration, by the Kapo in maintaining law and order in camp, by the Kanadakommando in regard to property and by the Sonderkommando in the extermination process. In May 1944, while the transports from Hungary were being shipped to camp, an order had been issued concerning Jewish property. The document includes the following paragraph: 'I am aware and today I have been instructed to this effect that I shall be punished by death should I make an attempt to appropriate any Jewish property.'[52]

Occasionally, SS guards were sent to the ramp where the transports arrived to make sure that no one stole property. The camp commanders issued orders forbidding beating – let alone killing – prisoners such as the one issued in autumn 1943. The interdiction was renewed from time to time. It was forbidden to hit a prisoner even if he committed an offense. In such cases one was supposed to press charges against him. Anto Gläser, a guard in Auschwitz, was put on trial at a police court in Breslau on charges of killing 20 prisoners who tried to escape. He had 20 bullets missing from his cartridge.

Two judges dealt on a regular basis with corruption and murder cases in Auschwitz. Gerhard Wiebeck investigated 'corrupt practices and acts by SS men outside the general scope – such as, for example, 'independent killings', as he put it.[53] In the second half of 1943 a special committee was established to investigate corruption cases concerning stolen property by SS members. It was headed by SS Major Konrad Morgen. Morgen began his investigation in Auschwitz after an SS guard sent his wife a package containing gold. The guard received a 12-year prison sentence. During his inquiries Morgen discovered, among other things, that women prisoners were used as whores and that personal lockers of SS guards were filled with stolen diamonds and other goods. The committee he headed investigated murder attempts against prisoners, as well. Overall, more than 700 SS staff members were fired or sent to prison. The highest-ranking officer to be put on trial was Maximilian Grabner, the head of the political department in Auschwitz. He was charged with corruption and murder of non-Jewish prisoners and was tried at the SS court in Weimar in October 1944. Grabner was accused of arbitrarily selecting 2,000 prisoners in order to execute them, as well as of executing prisoners to alleviate the lack of space and recording a false cause of death. In summer 1944 Wiebeck and Morgen arrived at Auschwitz to investigate an affair in which Rudolf Höss, the camp commander, was involved. He was suspected of having had an affair with a prisoner named Elinor Hodis. While this investigation produced no evidence, the fact that it took place is indicative of the effort invested in trying to separate victim from murderer.

INDUSTRIAL CHARACTER OF THE EXTERMINATION PROCESS

A third element that enabled the total separation between murderer and victim during extermination was the industrial nature of this process. The timing of death was not contingent upon the murderer's decision regarding the act of killing, but on the movement of the line at the entrance to the crematoria or on the transports. During extermination of transports from Hungary, thousands stood in line. Wagons used to stand one after the other in a line going into Birkenau. The line was so long that the last wagons reached the ramp at Auschwitz I, located three kilometers away: 'Anyhow we are not with the living. We are nothing but numbers who still exist due to technical reasons.'[54] The administration of death depended on three main factors: technical issues, the use of victims for building, maintaining and operating the camp and exploitation of the labor force.

Extermination tempo was influenced by the rate of transports rolling into camp. When the latter was reduced, so too was the tempo of extermination. The decision on the numbers to be sent to the crematorium did not depend only on the victim's actual physical condition – whether he was healthy or ill, whether or not he was able to work – but also on the density of population in the camp. When the density increased, more victims were sent to death in order to clear the way for the newcomers. When SS doctors decided on selection quotas in advance in order to dilute population or due to a surplus in the labor force, a situation could occur, as in one of the selections at the end of February 1943, in which healthy victims were sent to the crematorium along with some of the prisoner-doctors and nurses. Death was the result of an a priori decision on numbers. This is best illustrated by Joseph Keller's habit of rounding the numbers upward during selection because he preferred round numbers. If he discovered that the number of 'selected' was not to his liking he used to fetch more victims from the camp hospital.

When there was no need for labor it could happen that whole transports were sent to cremation including those who could still be physically exploited. In a situation of *Druck* (pressure), a term used by the Sonderkommando to describe pressure at work in the crematorium as a result of a high rate of transports, additional 'jobs' were created in which the victim could find temporary shelter from extermination. This phenomenon was most conspicuous during the arrival of massive transports from Hungary in which many victims were drafted to different tasks concerning the extermination process. Halina Birenbaum, for example, was recruited to the task force which extended the railroad up to the new ramp.[55] The Sonderkommando as well as the Kanadakommando were reinforced. The former was increased from 224 members to 884; the latter up to 2,000 and more.

Inversely, reduction in transport tempo was followed by respective reduction of the extermination rate, thus creating a new situation of 'unemployment'. To be 'unemployed' in Auschwitz meant death. The victim did not die because of any personal reason. Death occurred with no reference to him. After the huge wave of transports from Hungary had gone in September 1944, almost the entire Sonderkommando staff was exterminated. When the 'Kanada' site was evacuated in autumn 1944 along with the deconstruction of the camp, most of the Kanadakommando labor force was sent to death.

One of the most notorious examples of the impersonal death procedure in Auschwitz, as a result of the impersonal character of the killing process in Auschwitz, which derived from its industrial character, can be found on those occasions in which the victim was close to death but was kept alive due to technical problems or a lack of space in the gas chambers. A striking example can be found in Block 25 in Auschwitz. The women who were in line for execution but still could not be sent to the crematorium were concentrated in this block, which was separated by high fences from the rest of the camp. They remained there for a period of time that ranged from several days up to several weeks. In another example, Otto Wolken already stood in front of the gas chamber, that is, he was about to enter the gas chamber, when he was suddenly taken back to camp with the rest of the transport. Later he found out that the bodies from a French transport which had arrived the night before had not been evacuated.[56] Franz Ruprecht was sent to Auschwitz in August 1942. He and 2,000 other victims waited for hours in front of the crematorium until they were finally sent back to camp. Later they found out that the crematorium had been full of victims from a Dutch transport and so, he claimed, 'they had no place for us'.[57] The return of transports to camp due to lack of space was a common occurrence during the extermination of Hungarian Jews. Even the ovens could not always handle the high rate of gassing. Occasionally bodies were burned in piles near the crematoria, in a nearby forest or, as in the Hungarian case, in huge ditches dug near the crematoria.

The extermination system did not fail because it did not function; it 'got stuck' due to its inability to keep up with its own high rate of 'production'. Through this impersonal death situation the 'aristocrat' could detach himself from the victim. There was really nothing personal between them.

NEGATION OF THE ACTS OF BIRTH AND SUICIDE

The fourth and final element that will be discussed here which contributed to separating the murderer from the victim and creating the impersonal death was the negation of any autonomous act of giving life (birth) or of taking life away (suicide). The victim could not bring a child with him into the camp nor bring a newborn into the world, nor could he put an end to his own life in an autonomous way, i.e., by committing suicide: 'the harsh Birkenau day acknowledged neither birth nor death, only silence and obedience to its pitiless laws.'[58]

If the victim was ontologically always 'dead', he could consequently not create life nor take it away. It was not only that the 'aristocrat' did not kill the 'farmer', he denied him the privilege of taking his own life – an act which would have enabled him to define himself as a person responsible for both his life and his death – or, in existential terms, as a 'Being' and 'Being-toward-Death' at the same time. With the prohibition on creating life, the victim was deprived of his 'Being' and was left only as a 'Being-toward-Death'. With the prohibition on the act of suicide, he was deprived of his 'Being-toward-Death' and was left only as a 'Being'. In no place could the victim be both 'Being' and 'Being-toward-Death'.

In the course of the 'Final Solution' 228,000 Jewish children under the age of 17 were exterminated in Auschwitz. Every pregnant woman and every woman accompanied by a child was sent to the crematorium. On 26 March 1942 a women's camp was erected in Birkenau, enabling women in early stages of pregnancy to enter the camp and even to give birth to a child. Until mid-1943 no list of babies was kept. Women who were found to be pregnant were executed at the 'hospital' by phenol injections. Others underwent abortions in 'medical experiments'. During these same experiments women were sterilized as well. Children born in camp were drowned in water buckets or put to death with phenol injections. Others died as a result of 'objective' conditions of malnutrition, disease and cold weather. The family camp at Auschwitz, populated with families from the Theresienstadt ghetto, was an exception – it was the only place in which children were allowed to stay alive. In June 1943 the process of executing non-Jewish children came to a halt. The first baby registered in camp was born on 18 September 1943. The first Jewish baby to be registered was born on 21 February 1944. In all, 650 babies were born in camp and registered; the births of only eight Jewish children were registered. The negation of every element of new life in Auschwitz was thus a result of deprivation of the possibility of bringing new life into the world (through execution of pregnant women, forced/voluntary abortion, sterilization) and eliminating life that had already been created (through extermination of children arriving at the camp or born in it).

The act of 'creating life' was made impossible. So was the act of autonomous 'ending of life'. Suicide in the death camps in general, and in Auschwitz in particular, was a rare phenomenon when compared to suicide rates in other stages of the extermination process.[59] As I tried to show above, the victim in Auschwitz was exterminated impersonally. The victim's only refuge from such an impersonal death was to take his own life, thus giving some meaning to his death. In an act of suicide the victim takes responsibility for his death (and life) and endows it with the character of a 'beautiful death' or a 'worthy death' (euthanasia). As I will show, he was deprived of this possibility as well.

I will suggest three explanations for the low rate of suicide in death camp Auschwitz. The first will focus on the Nazis' attempts to prevent the act of suicide; the second on the victim's physical and mental condition, which did not enable him to commit the act; the third will attribute it to the very essence of Auschwitz as a 'death camp' in which death became a mode of Being.

The act of suicide is an act of death which is derived from an individual's will. It is not carried out by the official extermination system. As such it is an act which did not meet the order and efficiency standards of the extermination machine and was therefore perceived as a punishable act of sabotage. Punishments for attempted suicides varied from 25 strokes to a public death sentence intended as a deterrent. The Nazi effort to prevent the victim from committing suicide was most conspicuous in the signs that were hung on the camp's electrified barbed-wire fences which showed a skull and read: 'Warning. Danger of Death'.[60] A similar sign appeared on the outside doors to the gas chambers: 'High Tension – Lethal Danger' (*Hochspannung–Lebensgefahr*).[61] We can explain these signs from a functional point of view. When someone committed suicide by throwing himself against the fence he had to be removed from it.[62] In order to do so the electric current had to be cut off. Such an act disturbed the normal proceedings of the camp. Shutting down the electric current increased the chances of escape from camp. A dead person on the barbed-wire fence could also inspire others to acts of suicide or resistance. The sign on the fence also served to warn the victim not to go near it, thus preventing him from establishing any contact with the outside world, and perhaps warning newcomers who were on their way to the gas chambers.[63] Above all this sign epitomized the essence of the ontological death in Auschwitz as I have depicted it. The Nazis 'warned' the victim of mortal danger and actually tried to 'save' him. Death in Auschwitz had to be caused impersonally and anonymously. The sign presupposed that death could not be caused by the SS guard, for it was he who cautioned the victim 'Attention! Danger of Death', nor could it be caused by the victim – after all he had been warned not to commit suicide. The warning on the sign suited the victim's ontological state. No one could cause death to someone who was ontologically dead and anyone who was already dead could not commit suicide.

The negation of the act of suicide not only derived from the Nazi's prohibition of it, but also from the victim's physical and mental condition. An act of suicide supposes some minimum level of physical and mental ability which the victim allegedly lacked. Freddie Hirsch, for example, the head of the Maccabi youth movement in Prague and one of the leaders of the family camp in Auschwitz, decided to commit suicide after he had been informed by a Sonderkommando who had sneaked into the camp that everyone was destined for extermination. He had to decide between two options. The first was to lead the whole camp to resistance. The second, to continue as if nothing had changed. After considering the two options and understanding that both meant extermination in one way or the other he decided to commit suicide.[64] This act of suicide was contingent upon the fact that he was capable of weighing possibilities and of physically and mentally executing them. The relatively good conditions in the family camp served as the backdrop against which he was able to execute the suicide option. Most of the victims in the camp lacked the physical and mental conditions required to carry out the act. Most of all they lacked the minimal energy that was crucial to fulfill it. Primo Levi wrote that the vitality with which he was left in his daily existence in Auschwitz enabled him to overcome starvation and cold, but was insufficient for him to complete the act of suicide: 'I am not even alive enough to know how to kill myself.'[65] He also argued that suicide was an act of a human being while they in Auschwitz were merely animals.[66]

Extermination camp Auschwitz was a death camp in which death had become a normative value. In a world in which death had become the norm, the act of suicide lost its attraction. The questions 'Did you hear that X decided to commit suicide?' or 'Did you hear that X took his own life?' had no meaning in death camp Auschwitz, just as the questions 'Did you hear that X decided to live?' or 'Did you hear that X is alive?' had no meaning in the outside world. In a normal world, based on a norm of being alive, one may escape life through death by suicide. In the Auschwitz world, based on a death norm, one escaped death through life, i.e., survival.[67] Survival in a death camp was a much harder act than suicide and was a greater challenge. The act of survival in Auschwitz took the place of suicide as an act of self-sacrifice. Life in Auschwitz became a heroic act while death/suicide became a conformist one.[68] In a world in which death became a mode of Being people committed suicide just by remaining alive.

NOTES

1. See for example Yisrael Gutmann and Michael Berenbaum (eds), *Anatomy of the Auschwitz Death Camp* (Bloomington/Indianapolis, IN: Indiana University Press, 1994); Hermann Langbein, *Menschen in Auschwitz* (Vienna: Europa Verlag, 1972); Anna Pawelczynska, *Values and Violence in Auschwitz – A Sociological Analysis* (Berkeley, CA: University of California Press, 1979).
2. Yisrael Gutmann, *Anashim Vaefer: sefer Oshvits-Birkenau* (Men and Ashes: The Story of Auschwitz-Birkenau) (Merkhavia: Sifriat Hapoalim, 1957), p. 87.
3. Ota Kraus and Erich Kulka, *Beit hacharoshet lamavet: Oshvits* (Death Factory: Auschwitz) (Jerusalem: Yad Vashem, 1960), p. 118.
4. Gutmann and Berenbaum, *Anatomy of the Auschwitz Death Camp*, p. vii.
5. See for example Eberhard Jäckel, *Hitler's World View – A Blueprint for Power* (London: Harvard University Press, 1981).
6. See for example Karl Schleunes, *The Twisted Road to Auschwitz* (Urbana, IL: University of Illinois Press, 1970).
7. Lucy Davidowicz, *The War Against the Jews, 1933–1945* (New York: Bantam Books, 1986).
8. Ka-Tzetnik 135633, *Tsofen edma: masa ha-garin shel Oshvits* (Tel Aviv: Hakibbutz hameuchad, 1987), p. 5.
9. Primo Levi, *The Drowned and the Saved* (New York: Summit Books, 1988), p. 84.
10. Dr Golse, 'Birkenau en 1943', in *Témoignages sur Auschwitz* (Paris: Edition de l'Amicale des déportés d'Auschwitz, 1946), p. 104.
11. Désiré Hafner, 'Birkenau', in *Témoignages sur Auschwitz*, p. 59.
12. Isabella Leitner, *Fragments of Isabella – A Memoir of Auschwitz* (New York: Thomas Y. Crowell, 1978), pp. 36–7.
13. Ludwig Wörl, 'Testimonies of the Witnesses', in Brend Naumann, *Auschwitz – A Report on the Proceedings Against Robert Karl, Ludwig Mulka and Others before the Court at Frankfurt* (New York: Praeger, 1966), p. 116.
14. Jean Amery, in Levi, *The Drowned and the Saved*, p. 128.

15. Levi Hass, 'Hunger – Terror – Typhus – Decay – Death', in E. Tsanin (ed.), *Kakh ze kara*, (Tel Aviv: Irgun Shearit Hapleta Mehaezor Habriti, 1987), pp. 144, 150.
16. Vladimir Yankelevitch, 'Pardonner?' in Vladimir Yankelevitch, *L'imprescriptible* (Paris: Seuil, 1986), p. 30.
17. Jean Amery, *At the Mind's Limits – Contemplations by a Survivor on Auschwitz and its Realities* (Bloomington, IN: Indiana University Press, 1980), p. 86.
18. Halina Birenbaum, *Hachayim ketikva* (Hope is the last to die) (Tel Aviv: Beit Lochamei Hagetaot and Hakibbutz Hameuchad, 1989), p. 98.
19. Ka-Tzetnik, 'In Line to the Crematorium', in Gutmann, *Anashim Vaefer*, p. 261.
20. Robert Antelme, *The Human Race* (Malboro, VT: Marlboro Press, 1992), p. 21.
21. Charlotte Delobo, *Aucun de nous ne reviendra* (Paris: Berg International, 1970), pp. 106, 176.
22. Jorge Semprun, *Haktiva o Hakhayim* (Writing or life) (Tel Aviv: Sifriat Hapoalim, 1997), pp. 85-6.
23. Ibid., pp. 15–8, 176.
24. Ibid., p. 128.
25. See A. Robert Pois, *National Socialism and the Religion of Nature* (New York: St Martin's Press, 1986), pp. 118–19.
26. Leitner, *Fragments of Isabella*, p. 1.
27. Désiré Hafner, 'Birkenau', in *Témoignages sur Auschwitz*, pp. 71, 74.
28. Tadeusz Stabholz, *Shiva medore gehenom* (Tęl Aviv: Misrad habitachon, 1992), p. 108.
29. Shlomo Dragon, in Gideon Greif, *Wir weinten Tränenlos – Augenzeugenberichte der jüdischen 'Sonderkommandos' in Auschwitz* (Cologne/Weimar/Vienna: Bohlau Verlag, 1995), p. 67.
30. Theodor Adorno, 'Meditations on Metaphysics', in *Negative Dialectics* (London: Routledge & Kegan Paul, 1973), p. 371.
31. Henry Friedlander, *The Origins of Nazi Genocide. From Euthanasia to the Final Solution* (Chapel Hill, NC: University of North Carolina Press, 1995).
32. Susan Sontag, *Illness as Metaphor* (London: Penguin, 1983), pp. 85–6.
33. Primo Levi, *If This Is a Man* (London: Orion Press, 1959), p. 58.
34. Maurice Blanchot, *L'écriture du désastre* (Paris: Gallimard, 1980), pp. 130–1.
35. Heinrich Himmler, *Geheimreden 1933 bis 1945 und andere Ansprachen*, ed. Bradley F. Smith and Agnes F. Peterson (Frankfurt am Main: Propyläen Verlag, 1974), pp. 78–9, 82.
36. Jean François Lyotard, *Le Différend* (Paris: Minuit, 1983), pp. 149–51.
37. Berl Lang, *Act and Idea in the Nazi Genocide* (Chicago, IL: University of Chicago Press, 1990), pp. 85–6.
38. Stanislaus Glowa, 'Testimonies of the Witnesses', in Naumann, *Auschwitz*, p. 184; Kraus and Kulka, *Beit hacharoshet lamavet*, p. 77.
39. Lyotard, *Le Différend*, pp. 149–51.
40. Ernst Dobers, *Die Judenfrage – Stoff und Behandlung in der Schule* (Leipzig: Julius Klinkhardt, 1938), p. 35.
41. Klaus Theweleit, *Male Fantasies* (Cambridge: Polity Press, 1989).
42. Rudolf Höss, *Death Dealer* (New York: Da Capo Press, 1996), p. 28.
43. Raul Hilberg, *The Destruction of European Jews* (London: W.H. Allen, 1961), p. 209.
44. Höss, *Death Dealer*, pp. 43–44.
45. Ibid., pp. 156–7.
46. Himmler, *Geheimreden 1933 bis 1945*, pp. 32, 45.
47. Höss, *Death Dealer*, p. 44.
48. Joseph Sacker, in Greif, *Wir weinten Tränenlos*, p. 37.
49. Primo Levi, *The Drowned and the Saved* (New York: Summit Books, 1988), p. 53.
50. Miklos Nyiszli, *Auschwitz. A Doctor's Eye-Witness Account* (London: Panther Books, 1962), p. 49.
51. Himmler, *Geheimreden 1933 bis 1945*, pp. 78, 169, 170–1.
52. Andrzej Strzelecki, 'The Plunder of Victims and Their Corpses', in Gutmann and Berenbaum, *Anatomy of the Auschwitz Death Camp*, pp. 256–7. Cf. ibid., p. 264, Note 24.
53. Gerhard Wiebeck, 'Testimonies of the Witnesses', in Naumann, *Auschwitz*, p. 259.

54. Kraus and Kulka, *Beit hacharoshet lamavet*, p. 14.
55. Birenbaum, *Hachayim ketikva*, p. 90.
56. Otto Wolken, 'Testimonies of the Witnesses', in Naumann, *Auschwitz*, p. 88.
57. Franz Ruprecht, 'Testimonies of the Witnesses', in Naumann, *Auschwitz*, p. 208.
58. Liana Millu, *Smoke over Birkenau* (Philadelphia, PA/New York/Jerusalem: The Jewish Publication Society, 1991), p. 88.
59. Hannah Arendt, *The Origins of Totalitarianism* (London: Allen & Unwin, 1966), p. 455n; Eli Cohen, *Human Behavior in the Concentration Camps* (New York: The Universal Library, 1953), p. 15; Levi, *The Drowned and the Saved*, pp. 75–6; Langbein, *Menschen in Auschwitz*, pp. 144–9.
60. Elie Wiesel, *Night* (New York: Hill and Wang, 1960), p. 49.
61. Franciszek Piper, 'Gas Chambers and Crematoria', in Gutmann and Berenbaum, *Anatomy of the Auschwitz Death Camp*, p. 162.
62. Stabholz, *Shiva medore gehenom*, p. 114.
63. Kraus and Kulka, *Beit hacharoshet lamavet*, p. 54.
64. Sinai Adler, *Begai Hamavet* (In the Valley of Death) (Jerusalem: Yad Vashem, 1979), pp. 10–11; Kraus and Kulka, *Beit hacharoshet lamavet*, pp. 160–1.
65. Levi, *If This Is a Man*, p. 169.
66. Levi, *The Drowned and the Saved*, p. 76.
67. Cohen, *Human Behavior in the Concentration Camps*, pp. 161–2; Victor Frankl, *Man's Search for Meaning* (Boston, MA: Beacon Press, 1962), pp. 16–17.
68. Levi, *The Drowned and the Saved*, p. 76; Edith Wyschogrod, *Spirit in Ashes: Hegel, Heidegger and Man-Made Mass Death* (New Haven, CT/London: Yale University Press, 1986), p. 22; Blanchot, *L'écriture du désastre*, p. 130.

14

A French Great Man's Last Rites: The National Funeral of Léon Gambetta and the Transfer of His Heart to the Panthéon

AVNER BEN-AMOS

The moment of death is usually considered to be a time propitious for a balanced overview of the deceased person's life. At this moment he is no longer capable of changing the course of life, and this 'frozen' chain of events easily lends itself to a summary that attempts to give it a sense of coherence. This is the impression that one gets from reading numerous funerary eulogies of politicians, in which their lives seem to have been organized around a single political principle from beginning to end.[1] However, when one goes beyond these short narratives, to a thorough biographical investigation, one often finds a complex and even inner-contradictory life that cannot be reduced to a unique formula.

The case of Léon Gambetta was no exception. Although, from a political point of view, there were several distinct Gambettas, the formal image of the republican leader represented at his national funeral was one-dimensional. The first Gambetta was a young politician, a popular opposition leader, who made his name as the defense lawyer in the Baudin trial of 1869.[2] More importantly, he was elected that year to the National Assembly as a deputy of the working-class Belleville quarter, after presenting his famous radical platform, the Belleville Plan. Gambetta was a politician who emphasized social and economic reforms, opposition to the authoritarian regime of the Second Empire, and representing the humble workers.[3]

The second Gambetta was the devoted patriot, who, as a member of the National Defense government of autumn 1870, organized the armed resistance against the invading German army. Elected in February 1871 to the National Assembly, he chose to represent the department of the Lower Rhine, in order to demonstrate his sympathy with the population of the departments occupied by the Germans. A third Gambetta, who complemented the patriotic one, was the moderate republican who, during the 1870s, became the 'traveling salesman of the Republic', criss-crossing the country to persuade the people of the advantages of the new regime. He advocated reforms that were more political than social, promoting the 'new strata' – the various components of the middle classes – as the foundation of the Republic, thereby distancing himself from the workers.

A fourth Gambetta, who emerged during the same period, was the anticlerical politician. For the republican anticlerics, the alliance between the Church and the anti-republican forces, first during the Second Empire, then under the Moral Order, turned the Church into a 'natural' enemy, which had to be fought in the political as well as in the educational arena. In their efforts to deflect the minds of the French away from the teachings of the Church, the republicans considered secular education as the key to their success. Gambetta, with his famous phrase 'clericalism – this is the enemy!' was among the leaders of this struggle, and his radical position *vis-à-vis* the Church helped to compensate for his moderation in social matters. A fifth Gambetta emerged only after the rise of the republicans to power in the Third Republic. A strong, authoritarian figure, who, as the head of the short-lived 'Great Ministry',[4] tried to introduce far-reaching constitutional reforms, he ruled for only 67 days, beginning on 14 November 1881, and was forced to leave office when a coalition of the Right, the extreme Left and moderate republicans – irritated by his style of leadership and his policies – was assembled against him. This is, of course, only a schematic representation of a very complex political biography, but it gives an idea of his multifaceted personality.

Of these major aspects of Gambetta, the first and the last had no place at his national funeral. It was a patriotic, anticlerical and, above all, republican event, serving the young regime as a focal point around which it attempted to unify and mobilize the entire population. Such an effort created countermoves of the opposition forces, on both the Left and the Right of the regime, but these did not manage to diminish the impact of the funeral. This can be explained, in part, by the nature of the ceremony: it was a gargantuan affair, which took place not only in streets, cemeteries and railroad stations, involving huge crowds every step of the way, but also in the nascent mass media, thus reaching even larger segments of the population, both in Paris and in the provinces.[5] Gambetta's image was duplicated and spread, appearing in newspapers, on song-sheets, cartoons, posters and various souvenirs that were manufactured especially for the occasion. The opposition could not compete with such an avalanche, part of which was orchestrated by the regime and its supporters. Public, urban space was controlled by the government, and the opposition's leaflets were meager in comparison with those that extolled Gambetta.

The reasons for effacing the memory of the radical, Bellevillois Gambetta during the funeral are not difficult to determine. The republican regime, led by the Opportunist faction, owed its success to its moderate, socially conservative image, and it seemed inexpedient to remind the people of the radical origins of the dead leader. In addition, the figure of a strong and controversial head of government who tried to impose his will on parliament could not be represented in a funeral, which was supposed to be an educational and unifying event. Authoritarian figures were anathema to the republicans, who feared the return of the likes of Napoleon III, against whom they had fought in the Second Empire. With the elimination of these facets of his character, the path was cleared for representing Gambetta as a republican Great Man. This was an updated version of the Great Men of the French Revolution: a pillar of the regime, a believer in science, reason and progress, patriotic and anticlerical, and a model for his fellow citizens.[6] More difficult to explain, however, is how the desired meaning of the national funeral was conveyed, especially when we consider that it is, fundamentally, a personal rite of passage.

The fact of its being the final rite of passage in a man's life might offer the beginning of an explanation. The republican regime, one of whose principles was separation between the person and the public function that he occupied, was averse to any form of personality cult. This antipathy was even more accentuated in the Third Republic, which, as noted above, arose in opposition to the Caesarean rule of Napoleon III. On many occasions Gambetta himself warned his supporters against bestowing too many public honors upon men of power.[7] Yet, after his death, the Great Man no longer constituted a threat to the republican regime, and the door was open to a majestic celebration of his merits.

The national funeral was also a form of civic festival. The Third Republic had revived the tradition of celebrating major republican holidays, begun in the French Revolution, and turned these festivals into informal educational activities that complemented the formal education offered in the new, secular state schools. In addition to 14 July, first celebrated as a national holiday in 1880, the regime publicly marked such events as anniversaries of births and deaths of Great Men, unveilings of monuments, and provincial visits of presidents of the Republic.[8] The national funeral constituted a particular genre of civic festival, being a personal rite of passage as well as a commemorative ceremony. The emotional power created by the death of a republican Great Man together with the established form of a state funeral produced a powerful ceremony that did not fail to move the people.

A colossal event, a rite of passage, a civic festival, a commemorative ceremony – the national funeral of Gambetta was all of these combined, and the whole was greater than its parts. It was not, however, Gambetta's last appearance on the public scene. His memory was kept alive ceremoniously through annual pilgrimages to his house and unveilings of monuments dedicated to him. The climax of this series of events came in 1920, with the transfer of his heart to the Panthéon on the occasion of the 50th anniversary of the Third Republic. This chapter, then, is a study of the two funerary rituals that shaped the image of Gambetta and transformed him into a model of a republican Great Man. It is concerned with the public face of Gambetta, yet it is important to remember that, under the republican regime, the private aspect was never totally separated from the public.

DEATH AND THE NATIONAL FUNERAL

Léon Gambetta's death was sudden and premature. He died on the last day of 1882, at a relatively young age (44), of an intestinal infection, the result of a wound caused when he was accidentally shot. The suddenness of his death produced a wave of rumors that claimed the shot was the consequence either of his stormy relationship with his mistress, Léonie Léon, or of his secret ties with Bismarck.[9] However, his premature passing also turned him into a tragic figure – one whose political career was cut short before he could attain his rightful position of leadership. This made his death especially shocking and poignant, and partly explains the strong emotions provoked by the news, which was reported by the police even among the workers of Belleville.[10] As Ludovic Halévy wrote in his journal on 1 January 1883: 'Gambetta is dead. The year begins with thunder.'[11]

At the time of his death Gambetta had not occupied any official function, having been a simple deputy to the Chamber. After the short episode of his 'Great Ministry', which ended on 27 January 1882, he became less involved in politics, but his career was far from over. It was clear that the Opportunist government, headed by Duclerc, would not organize an ordinary state funeral. Such a funeral was accorded, for example, to Louis Blanc, on 12 December 1882, and to General Chanzy, on 8 January 1883:[12] both were termed 'funerals at the expense of the state', and each received a budget of 10,000 francs. For Gambetta, in contrast, the government proposed on 2 January to arrange – the term had never been used before – 'a national funeral', with a budget of 20,000 francs. The reasons for such an exceptional honor, which were formulated at Duclerc's formal behest, were an indication of the future characteristics of the funeral. First came Gambetta the patriot, who 'during the most difficult days ... bore the flag of occupied France' and 'at least saved the honor of the *patrie*'. Second was Gambetta the republican, who worked indefatigably 'during the arduous period of the foundation of the Republic' and contributed to its victory.[13] It was as though Gambetta's public career began in September 1870, with the establishment of the National Defense government, and ended in October 1877, with the republican electoral triumph.

While the government was busy planning the funeral, Gambetta's modest house at Ville-d'Avray, near Paris, where he had died and where his body was on display, had already become a pilgrimage site. In addition to friends and close collaborators, such as Joseph Reinach, Paul Bert, Eugène Spuller, Arthur Ranc and René Waldeck-Rousseau, there was a continuous procession of deputies, senators and state functionaries, as well as ordinary citizens, including students of the Ecole Polytechnique and visitors from Alsace and Lorraine. It was the crowd's first contact with Gambetta's body: in the following two days, about 8,000 people filed past the coffin, many of them signing books of condolences. On the morrow of his death the first steps were also taken toward diffusion of the image of the illustrious deceased among the masses. Léon Bonnat, Bastien-Lepage and Antonin Proust drew his portrait, while he lay in his deathbed; Alexandre Falguière made a death mask; and Étienne Carjat took his photograph. The products of their efforts quickly became the basis for numerous illustrated magazine covers, special supplements and pictures sold before, during and after the funeral. The Gambetta portrayed in almost all these pictures was similar – private, unfamiliar, serene, with 'a youthful face'[14] – as though remote from the political quarrels that characterized his final years, and ready to assume another role, that of a respected forefather.

Mass-producing the portrait was only one of the means by which the press played its usual, dual role in such momentous events – reflecting the events, while at the same time amplifying and, to a certain extent, creating them. All the republican newspapers appeared with their front pages framed in black, as a sign of mourning, and some, like Gambetta's newspaper, *La République française*, continued to appear in the same manner until the funeral. Moreover, daily information concerning the preparations for and descriptions of the funeral occupied numerous columns of the front pages of journals of all inclinations, of the Parisian as well as the provincial press. Thus, whatever journal one was reading, one could not avoid the event, at least during the week that passed between the news of his death and the funeral.

Planning the event was no easy matter, considering the republican tradition of respecting the will of the family in matters concerning the organization of a state funeral. The family was represented by Gambetta's father, a shopkeeper of Italian origin, who insisted that the funeral take place in Nice, where the family had settled, and where Gambetta's mother and aunt were buried. Since this could have seriously jeopardized the republican plans for a grand state funeral, the government persuaded the father to agree to a ceremony conducted in Paris that would terminate with a temporary burial at Père-Lachaise cemetery, after which the body would be transferred for final burial in Nice.[15] The success of the Parisian ceremony and the large crowd that visited Gambetta's provisional grave made the government reconsider its position. 'Gambetta belongs to Paris', proclaimed *Le Voltaire*'s headline after the funeral, arguing that the body should remain in the capital instead of being shipped to 'a city that has the characteristics of a winter resort, frequented by many strangers, for whom the tomb would become simply a destination for day trippers'.[16] In addition, Nice had been annexed to France only in 1860 as a reward for Napoleon III's aid to the Italian liberation, and was not yet considered 'French enough'. The government intensified its pressure: it proposed to the father that a magnificent family tomb be built in Paris at the expense of the state, and, when he refused, sent a special delegation to try to convince him to change his mind, with the help of a letter from Victor Hugo.[17] In it, Hugo begged the father: 'Think of the memory of Léon Gambetta; leave your son in Paris; he deserves it, as an illustrious figure'. In another letter to Juliette Adam, who supported the father, he wrote: 'Madame, you were right and so was I. You were for the family; I was for the *patrie*.'[18] The terms of the conflict were presented, then, as a confrontation between private wishes and public needs, but the latter were never clear: was it the republic or the *patrie* – or maybe both – that needed the body? Whatever the identity of the claimants, in the end the father had the upper hand, and the body was finally buried in the family tomb in Nice.

On the other hand, although the government's preference was for a Parisian burial, it certainly did not wish to give Gambetta the supreme republican honor of a burial in the Panthéon, although the idea was floated in the press.[19] Gambetta was too controversial for such a measure and, besides, desacralizing the church of Sainte-Geneviève was too bold a move for the prudent Opportunists. The Panthéon had to wait two more years, for the death of Victor Hugo, before it opened its gates to a republican Great Man as in the times of the French Revolution.[20] Thus, Gambetta's funeral could only be a civil one, and such a ceremony was bound to cause discord. The ceremonies surrounding death were one of the arenas in which the conflict between the Church and the

Republic was most acute,[21] and a state civil funeral for such a prominent figure as Gambetta was an affront to Christian France, especially as it was scheduled for the day of Epiphany. The Catholic press did not hesitate to attack, interpreting Gambetta's premature death as a punishment for his anticlericalism, and accusing the Republic of confiscating the body against the wishes of his father, in order to conduct a civil funeral.[22]

Gambetta's moderate political position ensured that the opposition to his planned grandiose funeral would not be confined to the Right. Louise Michel, the famous ex-communard, and Joffrin, the socialist deputy to the Parisian municipal council, jointly held a public meeting of the Socialist Revolutionary Committee on 3 January 1883, at which they declared that the people should not come to the funeral of the politician who had betrayed them. At the end of the meeting, they sold a brochure entitled *Gambetta, King of Charlatans, faces the People's Justice*.[23] Although Gambetta had voted for the 1880 amnesty for the communards, this gesture did not redeem him in the eyes of the socialists and the anarchists, who continued to regard him as an ally of the bourgeoisie.

Meanwhile, in a reflex action typical of times of trouble, the republicans closed their ranks. All the republican groups of the Chamber held separate meetings concerning the funeral, and decided to convene in order to appoint a common speaker at the cemetery. The exception was the group of the extreme left faction, some of whose members abstained, while others such as Clemenceau and Lockroy participated in the meeting on an individual basis – a sign that the group could not reach a consensus about its position regarding the funeral. At the meeting of 4 January, the deputies unanimously chose Henry Brisson, the president of the Chamber who had replaced Gambetta, to speak in their name.[24]

By this time, the details of the funeral had already been determined. The body of Gambetta was to pass several stations before reaching Nice, its final destination. Since a republican Great Man needed the sanctification of the French people no less than that of the government, the choice of the stations, and the itineraries between them, ensured that the largest crowds possible were able to come into contact with the body. After its semi-private display at Gambetta's house, les Jardies, it was to be solemnly transferred to the Palais Bourbon (the Chamber of Deputies), where the public would be allowed to file past it for two days. The funeral procession on Saturday 6 January would bring the body to Père-Lachaise cemetery, where it would remain for six days in a provisional tomb. Then it would journey to Nice by train, stopping on its way in several major cities, before the burial, which would take place on 14 January. Thus, for two weeks, from the moment his death was announced to the final burial, the country would be immersed in details of the funeral – as well as in the life of Gambetta.

However, in order to enhance the stature of the Great Man, it was not enough just to exhibit the body. It had to be shown amidst magnificent decorations that would distinguish it from bodies of ordinary citizens, and fill the spectator with awe. Hence the complete transformation of the festival hall of the Palais Bourbon where Gambetta's body lay in state, into an imposing mortuary chamber. This was done by several eminent artists, some of whom had already drawn his portrait: Jules and Emile Bastien-Lepage, Charles Garnier, Bonnat, Falguière, Chaplin and Becker, all working under the direction of Antonin Proust, the minister of arts in the Great Ministry. The effect created was described as 'breathtaking' and 'majestic':

> The ceiling is concealed by black voile and the walls are covered with black tissue laminated with silver. The doors are hung with black drapes with silver selvages, raised by pegs of the same metal. At the base of and around the pedestals is a mass of verdure. Higher on the drapes are vessels filled with tricolor flags and laurel branches. The coffin is placed in the catafalque that served Thiers, from which the religious emblems were removed. It is a magnificent catafalque that has four black columns with capitals and bases of silver, and is surrounded with steps covered by black drapes laminated with silver. A tricolor flag veiled with black crepe covers the coffin. Eight lamps illuminate the area around the corpse: four at the catafalque's columns, and four at the pedestals. The catafalque is hidden under a mass of wreaths and bouquets of natural flowers, immortelles and jet. The flowers and the wreaths sent by Alsace and Lorraine are numerous, and those of Strasbourg, Metz, Colmar and Mulhouse are especially noticeable.[25]

Tens of thousands of people filed past the body daily, including Victor Hugo, who well understood the educational nature of the event. He came with his two grandchildren, Jeanne and Georges, to whom he said, while indicating the coffin: 'There lies a great citizen.'[26]

The funeral began on Saturday morning in front of the Palais Bourbon, which was also transformed for the occasion: 'The exterior facade of the legislative palace was covered with black drapery, on which were mounted bundles of flags, and a great black canopy was hanging over the colonnade, following the suggestion of Mr Bastien-Lepage.'[27] The long and varied procession, and the huge crowd that filled the pavements, the windows, balconies and any other viewing post, were a most impressive sight, which left its mark on contemporaries, including the historian Gabriel Hanotaux, who wrote: 'Among the many solemn funerals I have attended, I have not seen anything more poignant.'[28]

The procession's most salient characteristics were its patriotism and its anticlericalism, but while the former was expressed positively (with numerous references to Alsace-Lorraine), the latter was expressed mainly negatively (by the absence of the clergy and of any Christian signs). After the Prussian annexation of Alsace and Lorraine in 1871, the two regions ceased to be simple geographical concepts, and became complex symbols of painful defeat and the hope of revenge. Although geographically situated on the periphery, they found themselves at the heart of French patriotism, which the republicans had claimed to represent ever since their stubborn resistance to the Prussian invasion.[29] As Jules Ferry wrote in a letter following the ceremony: 'The extraordinary funeral that France has just organized for its hero serves as proof for Alsace that it should not despair of the *patrie*. It is such a powerful, profound and sincere upsurge of patriotism that it makes one believe in the future.'[30]

In a study of the ways through which the memory of these regions was evoked in French education, Mona Ozouf remarked that it appeared in many places, mainly in unexpected contexts, such as mathematical exercises and grammar lessons, and always indirectly and in a non-threatening way. Gambetta's funeral cannot be described, however, as an 'unexpected context'. Although he advocated an active colonial policy, which would deflect France from revenge (*revanche*), he remained until his death associated with the amputated provinces, and with the maxim that had guided the republican policy since the defeat: 'Always think about it; never talk about it.' Nonetheless, the motif of Alsace-Lorraine permeated the funeral to no less a degree than it did republican school manuals.

The references already began to appear in les Jardies: when the body was laid in the coffin, Paul Déroulède put a silver medal of the League of Patriots beside it, representing the allegorical figure of Alsace; and, when the coffin was closed, a medallion of the sculptor Mercié, bearing the same representation, was placed on the lid. At the Chamber, the wreaths sent by organizations from Alsace and Lorraine were highly visible on the catafalque, and the last wake was conducted by representatives of the two regions. These representatives also published a manifesto in the newspapers, claiming the honor of erecting a monument on Gambetta's tomb, and they were involved in efforts to convince the father to let the body remain in Paris. In the procession, the delegations from Alsace and Lorraine, which constituted the first unofficial group of visitors and school battalions,[31] also had a prominent place. A single wreath from an Alsatian village was placed, exceptionally, on the hearse, carrying, like most other wreaths, the inscription: 'To the Great Patriot'. The wreath of Louis-le-Grand high school was even more explicit, having been dedicated 'To the Man of Revenge'. On its way to the cemetery, the coffin passed by, in the Place de la Concorde, the statue representing the city of Strasbourg, veiled in black, and the song-sheets that were sold along the route mourned Gambetta with lines such as: 'O patriot! fear of our conquerors / You, who dreamed of imminent revenge / In the name of Alsace and Lorraine / We bring flowers to your grave.'[32]

At the cemetery, by the graveside, a representative of Alsace and Lorraine declared: 'A great citizen, a great patriot, a great friend of Alsace and Lorraine, our force, our hope was taken from us; but France, our beloved fatherland, is here alive, valiant, ready to answer the call of its glorious destiny.' The other nine speakers also evoked, each in his own way, Gambetta's patriotism, and even Métivier, the representative of Belleville, dedicated his speech more to the leader who tried to save Alsace and Lorraine than to the radical politician. Finally, a sachet containing the soil of Lorraine was placed on the coffin when it was lowered into the temporary grave at Père-Lachaise.[33]

But even in this 'loquacious' ceremony, it seems that attempts were made to observe Gambetta's maxim. The lost provinces were constantly evoked, but seldom directly, and the idea of military revenge was never officially mentioned. The organizers were careful not to do anything that might have seemed bellicose, and they rejected a suggestion to put the coffin on a gun carriage together with Mercié's sculpture *Gloria Victis*. Instead, they opted for a traditional hearse, which was used also for Thiers's funeral and was especially reconstructed by Charles Garnier to create a grandiose effect. Nevertheless, evoking Alsace and Lorraine in such a public ceremony was bound to be more stimulating than in the classroom, and the enthusiasm of the crowd whenever the lost provinces were evoked indicated to the journal *Paris* that the people 'have forgotten nothing, that they know, that they contemplate, and that they are ready'.[34] Keeping the memory of these provinces alive was the essential condition of getting them back, and the funeral was an excellent occasion for remembrance.

While Germany was the unnamed external enemy, the Church, by its very absence, was the undeclared domestic antagonist of the funeral. Camille Pelletan, a radical deputy, wrote triumphantly after the ceremony that it was 'a secular funerary celebration, greater than the most splendid Catholic ceremonies. No Christian symbol was in evidence, not a priest, nor a whisper of a prayer. And all official France was there, taking part in this funeral which belonged entirely to the freethinkers ... The Catholic Church yesterday lost something of its power.'[35] The fact that such an important state ceremony took place without the participation of the Church was in itself a strong anticlerical statement, and the presence in the procession of a large and distinct group of Freemason delegations – Gambetta himself was a Freemason – underlined the civil aspect of the funeral. The radical *La Lanterne* proudly declared: 'If the absence of cult did not diminish the magnitude, nor the splendor of the ceremony, the absence of religious sentiment, far from reducing its moral character, gave it an incomparable moral force.'[36]

The itinerary of the procession further accentuated the anticlerical nature of the event. The traditional itinerary for major state funerals included the *grands boulevards*, but, because of the abundant commercial activity there due to the New Year celebrations, the organizers decided to avoid them. However, the boulevards were also considered part of a conservative neighborhood, and the alternative route had a different image. On its way to Père-Lachaise cemetery the procession passed through Rue de Rivoli, Boulevard de Sébastopol, Place de la République, Boulevard Voltaire and Rue de Charonne – which included working-class neighborhoods, the strongholds of anticlericalism. Moreover, an almost identical route was used in the civil funerals of Ferdinand Hérold, the anticlerical prefect of the Seine (4 January), and Louis Blanc.[37]

The Catholic adversaries of the Republic regarded the civil nature of the event as blasphemous and scandalous. *L'Univers* called the funeral 'a Masonic apotheosis', which celebrated 'the rotten corpse of the aggressor of Jesus Christ', who had finally got his due punishment.[38] Yet even they had to admit that it was a splendid spectacle, and, in a curious reversal of roles, contrasted it with the modest religious state funeral of General Chanzy, the republican collaborator of Gambetta during the 1870 war, which took place in Châlons-sur-Marne on 8 January. 'The funeral of Chanzy was not an "apotheosis" like that of Gambetta, but how much more genuine was the sorrow!'[39] In the same vein, Léon Bloy, the sharp-tongued Catholic writer, described in his novel *Le Désespéré* (1887) the procession of Gambetta's funeral as 'three hundred thousand human heads of cattle, accompanying the putrefied Xerxes of the majority to his underground residence, while parade wagons went rolling by'. His hero Marchenoir compares this 'false burial' with the 'true funeral' of an anonymous monk that he encountered in a humble snow-covered cemetery, which seemed to him greater than the 'dictator's inhumation'.[40] These attacks against such a godless republican funeral were motivated also by a fear that the phenomenon might be contagious. According to the calculations of Father Léonce Raffin, the highest percentage of civil funerals in Paris was in the years 1883–85, which he attributed to the examples of Gambetta's and Hugo's national funerals.[41]

If the spiritual qualities of the funeral were the source of a bitter debate, its enormity was something that no one could deny. The number of participants in the procession, composed of more than 2,000 delegations from all over the country, was estimated at 200,000, and the number of spectators at a million.[42] *Le Figaro* compared the funeral, disapprovingly, with the recently established national festival of 14 July: 'The same eager and curious crowd, the same peddlers selling bunches of immortelles instead of tricolor rosettes, the same commerce in places, chairs and benches'.[43] It is possible that many of those who came did so, as *Le Figaro* argued, in order to watch the spectacular procession of army units, flower wagons, famous politicians and various delegations marching behind the coffin. However, the smaller number of spectators at other events of this kind testified to the fact that this explanation did not suffice, and that many people in the crowd came to mourn Gambetta and demonstrate their support of the Republic.

But which Gambetta did they mourn? And what Republic did they support? *L'Illustration*'s shrewd commentator, observing the composition of the procession, noted, first:

> the preponderant role of the provinces, and the nature of the considerable 'clientele' that was profoundly attached to Gambetta. There were no workers' organizations, but all the democratic organizations of the *petite bourgeoisie* took part. The workers' syndicates that might have come were absent because the procession had an official and governmental character. In contrast, the provincial societies were willing to come precisely because the government's participation guaranteed the moderate nature of the event. What it proves is that Gambetta's constituency was profoundly modified. It was no longer, as before, a constituency of resistance and opposition, comprising all the republican nuances in a powerful but non-homogeneous coalition. After the final victory of the republican party, all the intransigent, opposition and revolutionary factions left Gambetta. On the other hand, a considerable portion of the bourgeoisie, recognizing in him a governmental power, rallied and adhered to his politics and his person.[44]

An analysis of the identity of the non-official groups that composed the procession indicates, indeed, a massive presence of representatives of the 'new strata', including those of the provinces, whom Gambetta had insistently wooed, and the absence of official workers' delegations.[45] Their Gambetta, then, was the moderate republican, the patriot and the anticleric, who embodied the promise of social advancement. However, in order to complete the picture one should look also at the spectators. Since many businesses were closed for the event, the workers came in large numbers to watch the procession, and they were especially numerous in the lower-class eastern quarters of the city. In addition, the huge crowd, estimated at 200,000, which made a Sunday pilgrimage to Gambetta's temporary grave in Père-Lachaise, was composed mainly of working-class families, who continued to come in even larger numbers each day until 13 January, when the body was transferred to Nice.[46] Many of the workers came, no doubt, out of curiosity, and others came because of their attachment to *la patrie*, but they all paid their respects to Gambetta and, through him, to the Republic. Even if Gambetta was no longer their political hero, he still retained an important place in the popular imagination.

The republicans' reading of the funeral was not, in principle, different from that of their adversaries. They were not ashamed to compare it with a festival, but their preferred analogy was with the 1790 Federation Festival,[47] alluded to in Gambetta's journal *La République française*, which also referred to the procession as 'triumphal', and in Brisson's funerary oration.[48] More explicit was Pierre Laffitte, who dedicated his Sunday class of positivist sociology in the Sorbonne to Gambetta and his funeral, and who likened the republican leader to Danton and Hoche.[49] The comparison with the 1790 Federation Festival was not merely a nod in the direction of the French Revolution, in whose shadow the leaders of the Third Republic wished to bask. Unlike the storming of the Bastille, which was a violent act whose memory divided the country, the peaceful assembly in Paris of Frenchmen from all the provinces symbolized the unity of the nation. This was also the reason why the national festival of 14 July was officially declared as a double commemoration of both events: it attenuated the extremist image of the first by the moderation of the second.[50] The issue behind the comparison was, therefore, whether the republicans could claim after the funeral to represent the entire nation, or only a part of it.

The figure of Gambetta, in whom it was impossible, according to *La République française*, 'to separate the republican from the patriot and the patriot from the republican',[51] well suited the attempt of the regime to close the gap between the Republic and the Nation, hence the declaration of the funeral as 'national', and the accent put on the patriotic elements of the ceremony. *Le Voltaire* summed up the republican view of the funeral when it wrote: 'It was not only a splendid funeral, but also a national demonstration. Never was a supreme farewell addressed by mourners with such unanimity.'[52] But this very republican claim to represent the entire nation was contested fiercely by the opposition. Paul de Cassagnac, the Bonapartist deputy and journalist, recognized the republicans' right to honor Gambetta with a magnificent ceremony, but objected to their assertion that 'it was not the Republic, but France which conducted the funeral'. He then added the mordant question: 'How many, among these soldiers whom you have dragged to the civil and republican funeral of Gambetta, would not want to die for the Republic, but would happily die for France?'[53] The massive and popular attendance at the funeral testified to the success of the regime in marrying the Republic with the *patrie*, but there were still many for whom the marriage was unacceptable. The cry of Brisson at the end of his funeral oration, 'Long Live France! Long Live the

Republic!' showed that the republicans, too, knew that the two entities could not yet be considered one and the same.

If the Parisian funeral was meant to close the gap between the Republic and *la patrie*, then the funeral in Nice should be seen as part of the republican effort to close the gap between the center and the periphery. Although the choice of Nice as a final resting place was made, as indicated above, only because of the insistence of Gambetta's father, the government used the coffin's journey to the south as another stage in the funeral ceremony. It was a golden opportunity to actively involve the population of the provinces in the cult of Gambetta, and bring them into direct contact with the body.

After a farewell ceremony at the Lyon railroad station, attended by a large crowd, a special train departed on the morning of 13 January 1883, with the coffin on board, in a wagon decorated as a mortuary chamber, including tricolor flags sent by the city of Strasbourg. It was accompanied by a special delegation of deputies to the Chamber, members of the Republican Union, who wanted to take part in the funeral at Nice, but who also served as honorary guards during the voyage. The train made stops at Tonnerre, Dijon, Mâcon, Lyon, Valence, Avignon, Marseille and Toulon, and in each of the cities the train station hosted an official ceremony, with the participation of the local authorities, various delegations and huge crowds.[54] Arriving at Nice the next morning, it was received at the station with another official ceremony, and then a procession was formed to the local cemetery. Except for the presence of the family, immediately behind the coffin, it was a local and smaller replica of the Parisian procession. It had the same official character, with local authorities, army units and numerous delegations, including those of Freemasons' lodges, patriotic societies and schoolchildren, all headed by representatives from Alsace and Lorraine. The funerary orations in the cemetery were also patriotic: General Carré de Bellemare concluded his with a 'farewell to the great patriot' and the prefect of the department of Alpes Maritimes, Lagrange de Langres, evoked the period of 1870, when he worked together with Gambetta, and heard from him the timeless words, 'Think of France, always France, and nothing but France!'[55]

The burial in Nice, then, was not the antithesis of the Parisian funeral, but its echo. These two ceremonies, and those that took place at the railroad stations along the route, enabled the provinces to take part in the posthumous apotheosis of Gambetta the Great Man, and concretized the connection between the center and the periphery. They were meant to reinforce the unity of the nation, without diminishing provincial identity, and corresponded to the vision of the founding fathers of the Third Republic, who saw no contradiction between the political centralism of the Republic and a degree of local autonomy, represented by an elected mayor.[56] The power of the regime was based, according to this vision, on the multiplication of local, republican centers of power, which would jointly create a united nation without suppressing its inner diversity. As Jean-François Chanet pointed out, republican education was aware of the need to create first of all an attachment to local culture, as a necessary condition for arousing patriotic sentiments.[57] 'The love of the small *patrie* leads to the love of the great *patrie*', wrote Louis Pasteur, expressing a common view that saw no contradiction between loving one's small corner and admiring the *patrie* as a whole.[58]

THE HEART GOES TO THE PANTHEON

In the absence of a Parisian tomb, Gambetta's house of les Jardies, at Ville d'Avray, which was donated by the family to the state in 1887, became the center of the posthumous cult of Gambetta which lasted well into the twentieth century. The cult was maintained by his friends and collaborators, who together constituted an influential group of politicians that played an important role in the Third Republic.[59] They established a Gambetta Society, and organized annual pilgrimages to the house, in the course of which a small ceremony usually took place, including a speech by a prominent politician. The cult was given an important boost by the erection near the house of a monument to Gambetta built by Auguste Bartholdi, and financed by a campaign of public donations launched at the initiative of a committee of Alsaciens-Lorrains. The monument was inaugurated at a ceremony filled with patriotic fervor in November 1891, during which Paul Bert's widow rendered up Gambetta's heart, which her husband had kept after the autopsy of the body. The heart, contained in a small casket, was placed inside the monument, which thus became also a huge reliquary.[60]

The pilgrimages continued uninterrupted until the Great War, and, when the cult resumed, after the war, it was 'upgraded' with the transfer of the heart to the Panthéon on 11 November 1920. The transfer was made as part of a dual ceremony, commemorating both the 50th anniversary of the proclamation of the Third Republic (1870) and Armistice Day (1918), during which the body of the Unknown Soldier was buried under the Arc de Triomphe. This 'marriage', in the same ceremony, between a relic of the body of Gambetta, whose name was associated with the fight for Alsace and Lorraine, and the body of a soldier who symbolized the fallen and the return of the lost territories to French sovereignty, seemed at the time quite natural, although it was a decision taken at the last moment. Likewise, the delicate 'division of labor' between the Panthéon and the Arc de Triomphe, the one receiving the heart of Gambetta and the other the body of a simple soldier – the *poilu* – was achieved only after a heated political debate.

The efforts to find the best way to commemorate the fallen had begun already during the Great War, and the figure of the Unknown Soldier had been raised in this context. On 20 November 1916, N.F. Simon, the president of the French Memory of Rennes association, proposed during a military funeral to transfer the body of an unidentified soldier to the Panthéon, and to inscribe on his tomb the words: 'A Soldier'.[61] During the war, the Temple of Great Men still seemed for the republicans the only monument suitable for an official, central act of war commemoration. On 14 December 1917 a large group of deputies from across the political spectrum proposed placing in the Panthéon a golden book containing the names of all the soldiers who had 'died for the fatherland', including those who had had only 'an immense and anonymous tomb – French soil'.[62] This suggestion was replaced on 19 November 1918 by a bill suggesting a more 'corporeal' act: to transfer to the Panthéon the body of an unidentified French soldier and to inscribe on his tomb, in a paraphrase of the Panthéon's inscription: 'To the *Poilu*, the Fatherland is Grateful'.[63] The victory parade of 14 July 1919, at which a temporary cenotaph commemorating the fallen, placed near the Arc de Triomphe, was immensely popular, further advanced the initiative.[64] Before its dissolution on 12 September 1919, the Sacred Union Chamber of Deputies voted to accord an anonymous soldier the honor of a national funeral, and to transfer his body to the Panthéon in an act intended to symbolize 'both the victory that saved the world and the heroism of the citizen who died for the fatherland'.[65] While the funeral was an act of mourning, the transfer to the Panthéon, where the soldier would join the company of Great Men, signified glorification.

The approaching 50th anniversary of the Third Republic added another event to the commemorative calendar of the regime, although the exact dates of the commemorations were far from determined. The election of 16 November 1919, the first since the beginning of the war, produced a *bleu-horizon* Chamber, with numerous veteran deputies – whose uniforms gave it its name – and a center-right majority of the new National Bloc coalition. The most conservative chamber since 1876 was thus in charge of celebrating the republican anniversary. Millerand's government, which wished to continue the tradition of the moderate Republic, envisaged an act for the anniversary that had already become a republican custom: pantheonization. The choice obviously fell on Gambetta, as the heroic founding father of the regime who incarnated the spirit of revenge; however, in view of the circumstances that surrounded the burial in Nice, it was impossible to transfer his body to the Panthéon. The government decided therefore to transfer the heart, which became a synecdoche of the body, on the anniversary of the proclamation of the Republic, 4 September 1920.[66] The republicans were thus following the medieval Church tradition of using saints' relics for the propagation of the faith, but this fact did not deter them. They knew how efficient the Church was in using symbols and rituals for its own ends, and were ready to emulate it if it suited their purpose.[67] The use, in the 1883 funeral (after removing the Christian signs), of the catafalque and the hearse that had already been used for Thiers's religious funeral, was another example of such an imitation.

The transfer ceremony was also to include the inauguration of a commemorative plaque in the Panthéon honoring the soldiers of 1870–71, with a special mention of two republican generals, Chanzy and Faidherbe, who had already been given state funerals.[68] To revive the cult, and as a prelude to pantheonization, President Paul Deschanel visited les Jardies on 28 March 1920, to mark the anniversary of the birth of Gambetta. He was accompanied by the 1870 army flags returned by the Germans, and declared in his speech that 'the minister of 1870 carried in his soul the victories of 1918'.[69]

However, celebrating the anniversary of the Republic on 4 September was inconvenient. It was too close to the anniversary of the defeat at Sedan, and the royalists of the *Action française* movement, who led a campaign against it, claimed that the Republic was actually celebrating a German victory. In addition, it fell during the summer vacation, which meant a smaller crowd and no possibility of parallel educational programs at school. Moving the celebration to 11 November and turning it into a national holiday avoided these inconveniences, and had the advantage of making the day of the French victory also a republican anniversary. A circle would thus be closed: the Republic, which was born out of defeat, had fulfilled its sacred mission and regained the lost territories. It was a victory for France as well as for the regime, and, by celebrating both, the government symbolically closed another circle: the Republic could justifiably claim at last that it was synonymous with the Nation. Gambetta himself, who had hoped to create a 'great, national republican party that had no other ambition than securing the union of all Frenchmen',[70] could be evoked as representing the Republic and the Fatherland at the same time. The inscription that was to be placed on the Arc de Triomphe summarized this vision: '4 September 1870 – Proclamation of the Republic; 11 November 1920 – Return of Alsace and Lorraine to France'.[71]

The original plan for the celebration of 11 November 1920 included only one transfer to the Panthéon – that of Gambetta's heart – but the memories associated with that date, and the old plans concerning the commemoration of an Unknown Soldier, created a climate that was favorable for adding to the ceremony the transfer of the *poilu* as well. The government gave in to the pressure, and a week before Armistice Day it was ready to ask the two Houses, which had returned from the summer recess, to ratify the plan for the ceremony: both Gambetta's heart and the body of the Unknown Soldier would be brought separately to Port Maillot, to the west of Paris, from where they would be borne in a unique procession to the Arc de Triomphe and then, following the itinerary of Hugo's funeral, to burial in the Panthéon.[72]

But the war veterans, who felt that the government and the country were not paying them due respect, were already leading an aggressive campaign against the pantheonization of a dead comrade-in-arms. The Temple of Great Men was a closed, somber and rarely frequented monument, where the Unknown Soldier would be one among many, sometimes second-rate, figures. This unique war hero deserved to rest alone under the Arc de Triomphe, an open and elevated structure that dominated Paris, situated in the heart of a busy and modern part of the city, where his memory would be kept alive.[73] The government yielded and introduced a bill on 8 November proposing to bury the Unknown Soldier in the Arc de Triomphe, with a demand for an urgent discussion. The result was one of the most tumultuous sessions that the Chamber ever knew.

The choice between the two monuments was not politically untainted. While the Panthéon was considered to be representative of the Left, especially since the burial of Emile Zola in 1908, the Arc de Triomphe, with its Bonapartist and militarist connotations, was considered to belong to the Right.[74] Their location, in quarters that had clear political identities on, respectively, the Left and the Right banks of the Seine, reinforced this image. Leaving Gambetta's heart behind in the Panthéon, and proceeding to the Arc de Triomphe as the government had planned, the body of the Unknown Soldier seemed to be distancing itself from republican tradition. The presence in the Chamber of deputies who had fought in the war or had lost family members made the issue of the burial even more sensitive, but, in the end, the liberal Catholic Marc Sangnier succeeded in calming the atmosphere with a conciliatory and eloquent discourse. He reminded his audience that the anonymous *poilu* might have been a royalist as well as a socialist, but that he was above all a patriot, and, since part of the nation was alienated by the Panthéon, his place should be in the Arch. Finally, the bill passed without an official count.[75] Afterwards, in the Senate, which was more radical than the Chamber, the discussion was quieter. Since the Arch by then constituted the supreme national apotheosis, the radical senator Paul Strauss, an ex-Gambettist, demanded and obtained a modification of the plan from the government: Gambetta's heart would proceed together with the body of the Unknown Soldier and pass under the Arc de Triomphe, after which it would return to the Panthéon.[76] Thus both the unified anniversaries and the single itinerary signaled the unity of the Republic and the Nation. Nonetheless, the almost clandestine, nocturnal transfer of Gambetta's heart from the Arch back to the Panthéon testified to the temporary nature of that unity.

On the eve of the ceremony, the two relics arrived separately in Paris. Gambetta's heart was brought from les Jardies by car in a solemn, official procession, headed by André Lefèvre, the minister of war. The body of the Unknown Soldier, chosen ceremoniously among several unidentified bodies, was brought from Verdun by train, accompanied by André Maginot, the minister of pensions. Both were placed in a chapel of rest at Place Denfert-Rochereau, facing the statue of the Lion of Belfort, a site that was chosen because of its association with the French resistance to the German invasion of 1870, and its closeness to the Panthéon. That was to be the point of departure of the procession, whose itinerary would recreate the historical development of the Third Republic: from its birth amidst heroic fighting, through the republican intellectual and moral revival (the Panthéon), to the magnificent victory of the Great War, which effaced the shameful defeat of its beginning (the Arc de Triomphe).

In the morning, the coffin, covered with a silk tricolor affixed with military decorations, was placed on a 155mm gun carriage, and the urn containing the heart was put on a sumptuous hearse built especially for the occasion, decorated with the arms of French cities associated with French military glory and with Gambetta, such as Verdun, Strasbourg and Nice.[77] Both relics were carried to the Panthéon in a unique, military procession, marked by the inclusion of 700 flags of all the French regiments. The procession included elements that represented both the victory and the price that was paid for it: on the one hand, the old French flags of 1870–71, returned by the Germans, and a group of Alsatians, in their regional costumes; on the other hand, a delegation of invalid war veterans, and a symbolic widow and orphan, who followed the coffin of the Unknown Soldier.

At the Panthéon, after a recitation of Victor Hugo's *Hymne*, President Millerand made a speech celebrating the republican victory, which he regarded as the triumph of republican education. If 1870 meant the victory of the Prussian teacher, then 1918 signified the victory of Jules Ferry, minister of education in the 1880s, who was the hero of the speech. Only the republic, the regime that had built a modern, patriotic school system, was capable of the task of revenge, and for that it had deserved a 'title of nobility'. The ceremony, itself an educational act, continued with a procession that passed through rue Soufflot, boulevard

Saint-Michel, boulevard Saint-Germain, place de la Concorde and up avenue des Champs-Elysées, in the opposite direction of the itinerary of Victor Hugo's pantheonization and of segments of the 1919 Victory Parade. Whereas the closed ceremony at the Panthéon was a republican celebration, the open parade in the streets had national and military overtones. No one in the crowd cried 'Long Live the Republic!' but many mentioned France, the army, the *poilu* and the names of the marshals who walked in the procession, in their cries. The film that was made on the occasion corroborates the newspaper reports concerning the huge size of the crowd, which lined the sidewalks and filled every observation point, and its diversity, composed of people of all classes of the population.[78] At noon, the coffin and the urn arrived at the Arch, where the Archbishop of Paris blessed the body in a short religious ceremony. Both relics stayed there side by side, the crowd filing past them, until they were separated in the evening: the body of the Unknown Soldier was placed in a chamber at the top of the monument, awaiting its final burial, and Gambetta's heart was returned to the Panthéon and remained there, in a simple wooden case, until November 1921. Its transfer to a magnificent urn of porphyry took place 'at dawn, with no spectators, no official attendance, at the time of executions'.[79]

The ceremony was presented by the government as mainly a victory celebration of France and the Republic, and an expression of the nation's gratitude to the heroic and anonymous soldiers who fought and fell in the war.[80] The organizers also tried to strike a balance, through the planning of the itinerary, the decorations and the procession itself, between the victorious and funerary aspects. In this formula, Gambetta belonged to the side of victory, his premature death no longer a source of sorrow, and the outcome of the war was portrayed as the fulfillment of his dream. Yet, at its essence, the event was a sad, mournful commemoration, since the memory of the fallen was still fresh, casting a dark shadow over any attempt to turn 11 November into a joyful celebration. Gambetta and the Unknown Soldier shared the same place of honor in the procession, but the latter was the true hero of the day. Whereas the urn containing the heart was half-forgotten in the Panthéon, the tomb of the Unknown Soldier, with its flame, became a popular place of pilgrimage during the inter-war period, both for simple, bereaved families and for state functionaries, who integrated it into their official ceremonies.

However, Gambetta himself was not entirely forgotten in that period. The fiftieth anniversary of his death (31 December 1932) and the hundredth anniversary of his birth (7 April 1938) turned les Jardies again into a site of official commemorative ceremonies, organized by the Gambetta Society, which tried to keep the cult alive. The final passage of Gambetta from the domain of politics to the domain of history occurred after World War II, as demonstrated by two learned exhibitions that were organized around his figure in 1982–83 and 1996–97.[81] Each additional war that separated the French from their heroic stance in 1870–71 made his patriotism seem less relevant. It is, then, Gambetta the republican that the French must resurrect if they wish to bring him back to the political arena.

NOTES

1. For a detailed analysis of the narrative structure of eulogies made at state funerals, see Avner Ben-Amos, *Funerals, Politics and Memory in Modern France, 1789–1996* (Oxford: Oxford University Press, 2000), Ch. 12.
2. A trial, organized by the government of Napoleon III, of republican leaders who began a campaign of public donations to erect a funerary monument on the grave of Jean Baudin, a republican deputy in the Chamber. Baudin died on a Parisian barricade on 3 December 1851, fighting against the coup d'état of Napoleon III.
3. For the changing relationship between Gambetta and the electorate of Belleville, see Gérard Jacquemet, *Belleville au XIXe siècle: du faubourg à la ville* (Paris: Editions de l'EHESS, 1984).
4. A government headed by Gambetta, between 14 November 1881 and 21 January 1882, which included young and little-known politicians; Gambetta had to resign since the majority of the republican deputies were apprehensive of his 'dictatorial' tendencies.
5. See Pierre Nora, 'Le Retour de l'événement', in Jacques Le Goff and Pierre Nora (eds), *Faire l'histoire* (Paris: Gallimard, 1974), Vol. I, pp. 210–27.
6. For the concept of the Great Man see Jean-Claude Bonnet, *Naissance du Panthéon: Essai sur le culte des grands hommes* (Paris: Fayard, 1998); Mona Ozouf, 'Le Panthéon: L'Ecole normale des morts', in Pierre Nora (ed.), *Les lieux de mémoire* (Paris: Gallimard, 1984), Vol. I, *La République*, pp. 139–66.
7. See Yves Déloye, 'Le charisme contrôlé. Entre grandeur et raison: la posture publique de Léon Gambetta', *Communication* 69 (2000), pp. 157–72.
8. For the civic festivals of the Third Republic, see Olivier Ihl, *La fête républicaine* (Paris: Gallimard, 1996).
9. For the gunshot episode, Gambetta's illness and death, and the rumors that circulated around it, see J.P.T. Bury, *Gambetta's Final Years: The Era of Difficulties, 1877–1882* (London: Longman, 1982), pp. 343–5; James R. Lehning, 'Gossiping about Gambetta: Contested Memories in the Early Third Republic', *French Historical Studies* 1 (1993), pp. 237–54; Anne Rasmussen, 'Science et croyance: Les récits de la mort de Gambetta', in Jacques Julliard (ed.), *La mort du roi: Essai d'ethnographie politique comparée* (Paris: Gallimard, 1999), pp. 169–96.
10. Archives de la Préfecture de Police – Ba-92, daily report of 1–2 Jan. 1883.
11. Ludovic Halévy, *Trois dîners avec Gambetta* (Paris: Grasset, 1929), p. 95.
12. Louis Blanc was a socialist politician, a member of the temporary government that was set up after the 1848 Revolution, and a member of the National Assembly elected in February 1871, after the country's defeat by Germany. General Chanzy was a republican general who fought in the 1870–71 war against Germany.
13. *Journal Officiel de la République Française, Chambre des Députés, Documents Parlementaires (JOC)*, 18 Jan. 1883, p. 131.
14. *La République française*, 1 Jan. 1883.
15. *La France*, 3 Jan. 1883; *Le Voltaire*, 4 Jan. 1883.
16. *Le Voltaire*, 9 Jan. 1883.
17. *La République française*, 12 Jan. 1883.
18. Victor Hugo, *Oeuvres Complètes, Correspondance* (Paris: Ollendorff, 1952), Vol. IV, p. 82.
19. *Paris*, 5 Jan. 1883; *Le Voltaire*, 16 Jan. 1883.

20. See Avner Ben-Amos, 'Les funérailles de Victor Hugo: Apothéose de l'événement spectacle', in Nora, *Les lieux de mémoire*, I, pp. 473–522.
21. See Jacqueline Lalouette, *La libre pensée en France 1848–1940* (Paris: Albin Michel, 1997), pp. 333–67.
22. *Le Pays*, 3 Jan. 1883; *L'Univers*, 4 Jan. 1883; *Le Gaulois*, 4 Jan. 1883.
23. Archives de la Préfecture de Police, Ba-92, daily report of 4 Jan. 1883.
24. *Le Voltaire*, 6 Jan. 1883.
25. Ibid.
26. *La République française*, 4 Jan. 1883.
27. Ibid., 7 Jan. 1883.
28. Gabriel Hanotaux, *Mon Temps* (Paris: Plon, 1938), Vol. II, pp. 326–7.
29. For the place of Alsace and Lorraine in the national culture of the period 1871–1914 see Jean-Marie Mayeur, 'Une mémoire-frontière: l'Alsace', in Nora, *Les Lieux de mémoire*, II-2 (1986), pp. 63–95; Mona Ozouf, 'L'Alsace-Lorraine, mode d'emploi: La question d'Alsace-Lorraine dans le *Manuel général*, 1871–1914', in *L'Ecole de la France: Essais sur la Révolution, l'utopie et l'enseignement* (Paris: Gallimard, 1984), pp. 214–30; Claude Digeon, *La Crise allemande de la pensée française 1870–1914* (Paris: PUF, 1959).
30. Jules Ferry, *Lettres de Jules Ferry 1846–1893* (Paris: Calmann-Lévy, 1914), Lettre à Edouard Ferry, 8 Jan. 1883, p. 330.
31. Units of schoolchildren aged 12–14 who received basic military training and used to participate, with wooden rifles and uniforms, in official republican ceremonies symbolizing the patriotism of the regime.
32. Villemer-Delormel, *L'Alsace-Lorraine au Tombeau de Gambetta: Chant Patriotique*, Bibliothèque Municipale de Cahors, Gr. Fol. 38459.
33. For the details of the preparation for and the conduct of the funeral, see *La République française*, 1–8 Jan. 1883, and *Le Voltaire*, 6–8 Jan. 1883. For the funerary speeches see Léon Gambetta, *Discours et Plaidoyers Politiques* (Paris: Charpentier, 1885), Vol. XI, pp. 254–78.
34. *Paris*, 8 Jan. 1883.
35. *La Justice*, 8 Jan. 1883.
36. *La Lanterne*, 8 Jan. 1883.
37. For Hérold's funeral, which was an important precedent, see Louis Capéran, *Histoire contemporaine de la laïcité française* (Paris: Marcèle Rivière, 1957), Vol. I, pp. 250–2.
38. *L'Univers*, 7 Jan. 1883.
39. *L'Univers*, 10 Jan. 1883.
40. Léon Bloy, *Oeuvres* (Paris: Mercure de France, 1964), Vol. III, *Le Désespéré*, p. 124.
41. See Jacqueline Lalouette, 'Les Enterrements civils dans les premières décennies de la Troisième République', *Ethnologie française* 2 (1983), p. 116.
42. Based on estimates of *La Presse Illustrée*, 14 Jan. 1883; *Paris*, 7 Jan. 1883; *Le Temps*, 7 Jan. 1883; *Le Voltaire*, 8 Jan. 1883.
43. *Le Figaro*, 7 Jan. 1883.
44. *L'Illustration*, 13 Jan. 1883.
45. One of Gambetta's aims in founding his journal *La République française* was to reach a large provincial audience. See Claude Bellanger et al., *Histoire générale de la presse française* (Paris: PUF, 1972), Vol. III, pp. 222–3.
46. *La République française*, 9–13 Jan. 1883.
47. A revolutionary festival that took place in Paris on 14 July 1790, commemorating the first anniversary of the storming of the Bastille, and symbolizing the unity of the country through the numerous provincial delegations that had arrived at the celebration.
48. *La République française*, 8 Jan. 1883.
49. *La Ville de Paris*, 9 Jan. 1883; *Paris*, 9 Jan. 1883.
50. Christian Amalvi, 'Le 14 Juillet', in Nora, *Les Lieux de mémoire* I, p. 426.
51. *La République française*, 8 Jan. 1883.
52. *Le Voltaire*, 8 Jan. 1883.
53. *Le Gaulois*, 6 Jan. 1883.
54. *Le Voltaire*, 14–15 Jan. 1883.

55. *La République française*, 14 Jan. 1883.
56. Mona Ozouf, 'Jules Ferry et l'unité nationale', in *L'Ecole de la France*, pp. 400–15. See also Alain Corbin, 'Paris-Province', in Nora, *Les Lieux de mémoire*, III-1 (Paris, 1992), p. 805; Maurice Agulhon, 'Le Centre et la Périphérie', in ibid., p. 838.
57. Jean-François Chanet, *L'Ecole républicaine et les petites patries* (Paris: Aubier, 1996).
58. Quoted in ibid., p. 129. In a similar manner, the United States used the 1865 train journey of Abraham Lincoln's coffin across the country, from Washington, DC, where he was assassinated, to his burial place in Springfield, IL, in order to reinforce the unity of the nation. See Barry Schwartz, 'Mourning and the Making of a Sacred Symbol: Durkheim and the Lincoln Assassination', *Social Forces* 2 (1991), pp. 343–64.
59. See the doctoral thesis of Odile Sassi, 'Léon Gambetta: Destin et Mémoire, (1838–1938)', University of Paris III, 1999.
60. *Léon Gambetta: Un saint pour la patrie?* (Paris, Caisse Nationale des Monuments Historiques et des sites, 1996), pp. 114–15.
61. Marcel Dupont, *L'Arc de Triomphe de L'Etoile et le Soldat Inconnu* (Paris: Editions françaises, 1958), pp. 15–16.
62. *JOC* (14 Dec. 1917), p. 1978.
63. Ibid. (19 Nov. 1918), p. 1823.
64. See K.S. Inglis, 'Entombing Unknown Soldiers: From London and Paris to Baghdad', *History and Memory* 2 (1993), pp. 7–31; Annette Becker, 'Du 14 Juillet 1919 au 11 Novembre 1920: Mort, où est ta victoire?', *Vingtième siècle* 49 (1996), pp. 31–44.
65. *JOC* (12 Sept. 1919), p. 2706. This demand was renewed at the Chamber on 31 July 1920. See *JOC* (31 July 1920), pp. 2252–3.
66. *JOC* (26 July 1920), p. 3034.
67. See, for example, the words of a republican municipal counselor of Paris: 'It is important to satisfy the needs that too often lead children and parents to religious festivals by establishing civic festivals', quoted in Rosemonde Sanson, *Les 14 juillet, fête et conscience nationale 1789–1975*, (Paris: Flammarion, 1976), p. 47.
68. A third general, Louis d'Aurelle de Paladines, was later added to the plaque.
69. *JOC* (1 April 1920), p. 5210.
70. From a speech by Chabrun, the reporter of the committee of Education and Arts, on the law proposing the transfer of Gambetta's heart to the Panthéon, *JOC* (31 July 1920), p. 3330.
71. *JOC* (4 Sept. 1920), p. 12926.
72. *Le Temps*, 4 Nov. 1920.
73. See Dupont, *L'Arc de Triomphe*, pp. 16–17; Antoine Prost, *Les Anciens Combattants et la Société Française 1914–1939* (Paris: FNDSP, 1977), Vol. III, pp. 36–7.
74. For the relation between these monuments and Parisian symbolic geography see Avner Ben-Amos, 'Monuments and Memory in French Nationalism', *History and Memory* 2 (1993), pp. 50–81.
75. *JOC* (9 Nov. 1920), pp. 3178–83.
76. Ibid., pp. 1740–2.
77. For a description of the ceremony see *Le Temps*, 12–13 Nov. 1920, *L'Illustration*, 20 Nov. 1920.
78. *Les Fêtes du cinquantenaire de la Troisième République*, Musée Albert-Kahn, 1992.
79. Paul Léon, *Du Palais-Royal au Palais-Bourbon: Souvenirs* (Paris: Albin Michel, 1947), p. 206.
80. The city of Paris organized another republican celebration for the afternoon in Place Hôtel de Ville, where the Republic was proclaimed in 1870, and which was a joyous event. The decoration included the statue *Victory* by Duret, a statue of Gambetta, and banners carrying an incongruous collection of names, a sort of posthumous Sacred Union: Thiers, Gambetta, Déroulède, Ferry, Waldeck-Rousseau, Jaurès, de Mun, Carnot, Hugo, Berthelot, Pasteur, Galliéni and Courbet. The ceremony began with speeches and ended with torch parades and illuminations (*Le Temps*, 12–13 Nov. 1920).
81. See the catalogs of the exhibitions: *Hommage à Léon Gambetta* (Paris: Musée du Luxembourg, 1982) and *Léon Gambetta: Un saint pour la patrie* (Paris: Caisse Nationale des Monuments Historiques et des Sites, 1996).

15

Enshrined Oblivion: The POW Memorial Church in Bochum, Germany

ELISABETH DOMANSKY

On 9 March 1958, an unusual procession took place in the city of Bochum, which is situated in Germany's highly industrialized Ruhr valley. After attending a devotional service at a Catholic church in one of Bochum's suburbs (Bochum-Stiepel), a group of men, women and children, led by several clergymen, proceeded to a construction site in a neighboring suburb (Bochum-Weitmar). Prominent in the procession was a group of 20 men wearing prisoner-of-war uniforms. Some of them wore Italian forage caps, others old German military coats, yet others Russian fur caps and padded jackets. Their different attire notwithstanding, all of them were recognizable as former prisoners of war in Soviet camps, although only some of them bore on their left sleeves what contemporary newspapers described as the degrading 'cloth badges with the Russian initials VP' (*Voina pleny* or POW).

When the procession reached the construction site, a consecration ceremony took place, in the course of which the 20 men broke ground on the spot where a new church was to be built. As the prominent role of former POWs in the ceremony seemed to indicate, this church was meant to be unique in West Germany. First, it was to serve as the parish church of a newly created parish (Weitmar-Neuling Mark). At the same time, it was planned as a war memorial of an unusual kind. Its construction was seen as an expression of gratitude that former POWs were paying to God for having rescued them – physically and spiritually – from war and imprisonment. This tribute, which was to be become manifest in the construction process of the church as well as in its architecture and interior decoration, was addressed not only to God, but to all those – including contemporary and future generations – who had not personally experienced war or imprisonment. For them, this church was to guarantee, 'for ever', as one of the priests put it in his address during the ceremony, 'the remembrance of unspeakable suffering'.

Locating remembrance of the war in the very heart of communal parish life allowed for a joint venture of a special kind. Members of the local parish-to-be and of the regional dioceses, as well as former POWs from all over Germany and even some who had emigrated to other countries after the war, helped fund, build and decorate the church, which thus provided a public space of remembrance to virtually all – at least all German – former POWs.

The church's double function also informed the choice of the parish's and church's patron saint. Rather than choosing an individual saint, church officials opted for the Holy Family – and a special event in that family's history at that. The official name of both parish and church was 'The Holy Family's Return from Egypt' (*Heiliger Familie Rückkehr aus Ägypten*). Quite unintentionally, the name's stylistic awkwardness also contributed to anchoring remembrance of the war in everyday parish life: the church was and is to this day usually known as *Heimkehrer-Dankeskirche* (POW Thanksgiving Church) rather than by its official name. More importantly, the equation between the Holy Family's and the POWs' exile integrated, as the church's stained-glass windows do, the profane historical war experience of the POWs into the sacred Christian history of salvation.

Remembrance of the war was not simply embodied in the history of the church's construction nor in its architecture and interior decoration. From the beginning, the crypt was reserved as a space for a permanent exhibit of memorabilia from POW camps in which German soldiers had been interned all over the world. Thus, this church also served as a war museum. Not only did it contain and preserve objects of secular history in a space which is usually reserved for sacred relics and remnants, but regular services took place both in the main church and in the crypt, thus blurring distinctions between the profane and the sacred in yet another way. Shortly after its consecration, this church–memorial–museum also became the site of the annual meetings of former POWs – Catholic and Protestant – organized by the local and regional chapters of the national interest organization of war veterans, the Association of Former POWs (*Verband der Heimkehren*). Thus, the church also provided a space for post-war special-interest politics.

The POW Memorial Church constitutes a unique *lieu de mémoire*. Remembering – as well as its counterpart forgetting – is, as Maurice Halbwachs and others have argued,[1] a process in which collective memories, or 'milieus of memory', as they are formed in families, classes, neighborhoods or national communities, support, suppress, distort or even destroy the potential of other collectives and individuals to remember. The church allows us to study this complex and complicated process on various levels. First, it enables examination of one of the major agencies of remembering/forgetting in post-war Germany, the Catholic Church. While its role, as well as that of the Protestant Church during the Third Reich, has been the subject of major critical studies, the contribution of the Church to the reconstruction of West German society and to its politics of memory has not yet elicited much scholarly interest, although the Protestant and Catholic Churches played key roles in the formation of public narratives about the past in the post-war era. This is particularly true of the Catholic Church which, in the era of Christian Democratic governments in the 1950s and 1960s, obtained a previously unparalleled level of political influence.

Second, memory is certainly embodied in memorial sites. Yet memory is of a rather fluid nature and subject to change over time. An examination of the POW Memorial Church as an edifice as well as a site of religious and secular rituals will allow for an integration of written, iconographic and ritual narratives that inform constructions of memory as well as their change over time. Third, since the construction and use of this church was and is the result of a combined effort of various individuals and groups, this focus will also further an examination of the interaction of various levels and agents in official and vernacular culture which participate in the constructions of 'milieus of memory'. In this chapter I will first characterize the general milieu of memory regarding World War II in the Federal Republic in the 1950s and 1960s, before examining more closely the history of the church's construction, its aesthetic message and the language of rituals performed in it. This will lead, it is hoped, to a better understanding of the POW Memorial Church's role in the post-war creation of narratives of remembrance.

REMEMBERING AND FORGETTING WORLD WAR II IN POST-WAR WEST GERMANY

The Second World War engendered politics of memory that were markedly different from those following World War I.[2] Throughout the Weimar Republic a majority of German society, its internal political differences notwithstanding, seems to have been obsessed with 'making sense' not simply, and not even primarily, of Germany's defeat but rather of the war experience itself. Due to the quantitative and qualitative scale of destruction, the war had profoundly traumatized hundreds of thousands of individual soldiers as well as the belligerent nations as a whole.[3] As a result, former soldiers as well as civilians seem to have been unable to 'let go' of their dead. Large numbers of bereaved widows, parents, sisters or children turned toward occult practices in order to communicate with the dead. War monuments were erected in large numbers, and numerous attempts were made to establish a national day of mourning (*Volkstrauertag*). In addition, the media, the arts and the public in general engaged in ceaseless efforts to explore the meaning of the war. It is quite telling that many of the post-war monuments, novels, poems, paintings, films and the numerous war-related devotional articles that were sold expressed the idea that the fallen were not really gone, but dwelt among the living as the often-quoted 'army of the dead'.

This obsession with the war certainly cannot be read in just one way.[4] Post-World War I German society's excessive mourning clearly showed symptoms of what Freud defined as melancholy: the narcissistic identification with the lost object of love that prevents a 'working-through' of one's loss and thus prevents one from forming other meaningful relationships.[5] While this was certainly the case for many of the bereaved, there were others whose focus on the war cannot be explained so easily by referring to war-induced pathologies. Rather, despite the war's all-encompassing and traumatizing effect, there seems to have been still enough hope left in order to enable many other people to view it as meaningful. For some, especially those in newly emerging ultra-reactionary movements, such as the German Fatherland Party (*Deutsche Vaterlandspartei*), this war was the first stage of a future, larger battle that would purge the world of evil. Others, however, saw World War I as a lesson to ensure that war would never happen again.[6]

One of the earliest expressions of National Socialist politics of memory regarding war was the implementation, in 1934, of a national day commemorating the dead of World War I. This day which was to be observed on the fifth Sunday before Easter, was called Heroes' Commemoration Day. The name as well as the rituals developed for the day's celebration constituted a clear departure from Weimar attempts at establishing a single national day of mourning. On Heroes' Commemoration Day, the dead of World War I were not to be mourned but rather celebrated as role models especially for the younger generation. In addition, the heroes who were to be commemorated on this day also included those 'fighters' who had sacrificed their lives for the cause of National Socialism during the Weimar Republic. Shortly after the outbreak of World War II, Heroes' Commemoration Day was expanded to include also the dead of the ongoing war, thus integrating the history of World War I, the inter-war years and World War II into the heroic prehistory of National Socialism's ultimate fulfillment of its historical and, at the same time, historic mission. Thus, the Third Reich's politics of memory were linked to the Armageddonist fantasies that the World War I pro-war movement had developed. Accordingly, the 'ideas of 1914', i.e., the German commitment to true spirit, were to replace the empty French universalist ideas of 1789. This mission was to be achieved by the Third Reich with the help of death-defying, hardened fighters who would not only be willing to endure pain and death themselves but would conduct, without flinching, atrocities in the name of their cause.

The complete defeat of Nazi Germany in 1945 led to the dismantling of its politics of memory: Nazi monuments were destroyed, streets and town squares renamed, and Allied re-education politics were aimed at 'enlightening' (*aufklären*) the German population in various ways about the criminal nature of National Socialist politics.[7] Such attempts, however, did not result in a completely 'new beginning' in German history, as later myths about 'Zero Hour' (*Stunde Null*) would have it. Rather, as Jeffrey Herf has demonstrated in his painstakingly researched book *Divided Memory*,[8] political and social reconstruction was, during the first two decades after 1949, conducted under the aegis of politicians who had been politically socialized in the Weimar Republic. This situation resulted in attempts at reconstructing continuity between Weimar political values and the new political systems, even if such attempts were often expressed in the desire 'to learn from the Weimar Republic's political mistakes'.

It would seem, initially, that a similar approach was taken regarding the politics of memory of World War II in West Germany. Heroes' Commemoration Day was de-Nazified into a national day of mourning and, in order to break even more clearly with Nazi traditions, the day was moved, in 1952, from the fifth Sunday before Easter to the second Sunday before the first Sunday of Advent. Of course, this day was no longer devoted to mourning the inter-war 'fighters for National Socialism'. However, while for obvious reasons it broke with this National Socialist tradition, another tradition was continued. The dead of *both* world wars were still remembered, as if those wars had not been fundamentally different in nature. In addition, included in the commemoration ceremonies of the National Day of Mourning were now also 'all victims' of National Socialism, as if there were no difference between perpetrators and victims. However, contrary to the practices of the Third Reich, the Federal Republic distanced itself from the two world wars and was reluctant to construe them as part of its prehistory. Rather than returning to Weimar practices of mourning, the Nazi taboo on mourning the dead of both world wars was clearly extended into the Federal Republic.

Regarding the First World War, we may explain this taboo against mourning by reference to that war's temporal distance from the history of the Federal Republic, although we know that collective mourning does not depend on individual loss. And indeed, the history of remembrance in many other countries, such as France, Great Britain, Australia,

New Zealand, etc., shows that the Great War seems, to this day, to force every new generation to 'work it through' again. Be that as it may, temporal distance is certainly no justification for not mourning, at least not publicly and openly, the dead of World War II in Germany. In many cases, the names of soldiers were simply added to existing World War I memorials, and the ruins of bombed buildings, which effectively constituted mass graves for many people, were quickly dismantled and replaced. In fact, West German architecture and city planning in the 1950s and 1960s may be regarded as major contributions to forgetting the war and its dead. The dead were certainly not invited to dwell among the living but, rather, quite literally buried under the asphalt and concrete of the 'modern' German cities of the 1950s and 1960s.

There are many reasons for this exclusion of the dead from post-1945 German society. First, World War II traumatized many more people than World War I, because it reached German territory. Consequently, psychic numbing affected many more people than before. Second, war neuroses themselves seem to have been different from those of World War I. While First World War I produced hysterical symptoms – usually called shell-shock – on a large scale, the second one seems to have created psychoses that expressed themselves in apathy. Psychic numbing and apathy are both symptoms that indicate a separation from one's own emotions. Consequently, individual mourning, which is a process that requires being in touch with one's own emotions, was severely hampered.

While these were effects produced by the war itself, the complete breakdown of National Socialist ideology magnified such symptoms to the extreme. This is the famous 'inability to mourn' that A. and M. Mitscherlich described so poignantly in the late 1960s as West Germany's pervasive pathology.[9] While they attributed this inability to mourn to the loss of Adolf Hitler and the Nazi ideology, I would argue that we are probably dealing with a double loss. First, the breakdown of the Nazi ideology constituted, for many people who had grown up in this society and accepted the values of National Socialism, a severe loss of identification. In addition, this loss affected their ability to make sense of other losses of human lives, relationships and homelands.

However, I would caution against a completely medicalized interpretation of post-war German politics. There were also strong political reasons for forgetting Germany's role in World War II. When West Germany became firmly integrated into the alliance structure of its former enemies as a result of the ever-more-escalating Cold War, forgetting their own dead may have seemed to be a small price to pay for being able to pursue revisionist foreign politics. It was also part of the price paid in order to forget the Holocaust. It is true that West Germany accepted, albeit under considerable pressure from its Western allies, its obligation to pay 'restitution' to the State of Israel. However, this acceptance was a kind of ransom money that German society in the 1950s and 1960s paid – not to remember but precisely in order to forget the Holocaust.

These official policies of 'organized oblivion'[10] could neither completely suppress individual and collective memories of World War II, nor eliminate the need for mourning. Instead, remembering and mourning were transferred on to the Cold War. Not long after the conclusion of World War II, Germany's 'unjust' and 'unjustified' division and loss of territories came to be seen in West Germany, as well as by some of its Western allies, as the result not of World War II but of the Cold War. Even the last POWs to return from the Soviet Union in 1955 were welcomed home more as prisoners released from POW camps of a war still raging than of World War II. The transference and displacement of memory from World War II to the Cold War became most obvious in the West German government's choice, in 1953, of 17 June as an official national holiday and in the commemoration practices attached to that day.

This was supposed to be a day of public, collective and individual remembering and mourning. There were ceremonies and speeches in parliament and in every school, as well as conventions of refugee and deportee organizations. Citizens of major German cities participated in silent marches (*Schweigemärsche*) and torchlight processions, and lit memorial fires (*Mahnfeuer*) – especially on the border between East and West Berlin. Certainly, it was Cold War revisionism that provided the impetus and framework for the choice of this national holiday. Its celebration, however, bore a striking resemblance to memorial services.

Those who were to be commemorated and mourned were the ones who had lost their lives in 1953 trying to fight Communist dictatorship. 'Our brothers and sisters' in the 'Soviet occupation zone', who, though still alive, nevertheless saw their lives fading away under the yoke of political oppression, were also to be included in one's thoughts. In addition, West Germans were to remember all those who had lost homelands to which they longed to return. It is not difficult to discern beneath this veneer an image of German society during the Third Reich, painted collectively during the 1950s and 1960s by German politicians, historians, writers and journalists. It was the image of a nation which, conquered and occupied by invading National Socialists, had found its life ruthlessly consumed by this brutal 'alien' dictatorial regime, while longing for the return of its homeland, the 'true Germany'. Such fantasies were most clearly expressed in the concept of 'inner emigration' (*innere Emigration*), in which so many Germans claimed to have lived during the Third Reich.

Even more evocative of commemorations of the dead, however, was a practice recommended for remembering the 'brothers and sisters' in the East on Christmas Eve. Three days before Christmas Eve, 1952, West Berlin's Mayor Ernst Reuter appealed to all of the city's citizens to display a lighted candle in one of their windows on the holiday eve. This candle was intended to serve as a remembrance of 'the POWs who had not yet returned and of all those between the Elbe and the Oder who were being held prisoner by an inhuman regime in its KZs [concentration camps] and prisons'. In 1959, this practice was extended to all of West Germany. This lighting of candles is strikingly reminiscent of the Catholic custom of celebrating All Saints' Day. On this day, votive candles are lit on the graves of deceased family members and friends. In the 1950s and 1960s, West German society replaced the image of Germans in the Third Reich in public commemorative ceremonies and practices with the image of East Germans living in a state that was considered to be a gigantic concentration camp and prison, and substituted its own losses – of actual lives, of years in the lives of those who survived the war and of 'home' – with the losses of East Germans and the loss of East Germany. By so doing, West German society engaged in an act of displacing and displaced memory and mourning.[11]

This is the predominant milieu of memory that dominated West German society in the 1950s and 1960s. An examination of the POW Memorial Church in Bochum will demonstrate how the general 'climate' of memory influenced the Catholic Church's narratives about the past. At the same time, this climate was itself shaped by Christian narratives about the meaning of war.

SHRINE TO THE LIVING

The original St Francis parish had already felt the need to create a new parish after World War I. However, financial issues as well as the lack of a suitable location and, then, World War II, had led to postponement of these plans until the 1950s. There can be no doubt that the new parish would have been created in any event and that a parish church would have been built, even if Chaplain August Halbe (1912–1974) had not been assigned to it in 1950. However, the fact that a POW memorial church was planned and then built was largely attributable to him.

Halbe, who was born in 1912, studied Catholic theology in Paderborn and Bonn from 1934 to 1940. About three months after having been ordained as a priest in February of that year, he was drafted into a medical corps of the Wehrmacht on the eastern front. In 1944, he was captured in Romania and sent to various Soviet POW camps. After his release in 1949, he returned to his home town. A short while later, when offered by his bishop the choice between a parish in the countryside, in a medium-sized town or in a larger city, he opted for a city, because of his war experience. In a posthumously published interview, he explained to his bishop at the time: 'I have spent about ten years among soldiers and POWs, and I got along with them in good and in bad times. I can imagine that I would be suited to spiritual work in a working-class parish, perhaps in the area of the Ruhr.'[12]

Shortly after his arrival in the parish of St Francis, he was given the responsibility of pursuing the planning and construction of a new church. In another interview, Halbe explained that the construction of a church that was at the same time a war memorial was inspired by two factors: First, he had heard of a German women's initiative after World War I to build a so-called peace church. Second, his own survival of the war and, subsequently, of Soviet POW camps, which he ascribed to God's mercy, also induced him to pursue a project that would relate the new church to World War II. Apparently, from the beginning, he received great support for his idea of creating a *Heimkehrer-Dankeskirche* by members of his parish as well as by officials in his diocese. They pooled together to purchase the land on which the church was constructed and were offered generous loans. In 1955, Halbe first called upon former POWs to endorse his plan as a sign of their gratitude for their 'rescue', and they responded enthusiastically: he immediately received monetary, as well as material, donations from former POWs, families of former POWs and even war widows. Some sent money; others sent memorabilia of their own times in POW camps; still others promised to contribute to the interior decoration of the church, once it was built. Although, as articles in the local press tirelessly repeated, donations came from all over Germany and even from foreign countries, they did not suffice to cover the costs of the church's construction, which were estimated to be about half a million German marks.

Halbe, who seems to have been quite an inspiring character, also had a considerable talent for fundraising. Together with another former POW/priest he called for a thanksgiving pilgrimage of former POWs to a church in Bochum in 1956 in order to promote the idea of the POW Memorial Church, and hundreds of former POWs and their families actually came to Bochum in the summer of that year. On the occasion of this pilgrimage, Halbe and other supporters of his project decided that they needed a more organized and structured effort to raise the funds that were still lacking. They formed a committee to pursue the project, and decided to launch a press campaign in various religious papers, as well as in the main publication of the Association of Former POWs. In addition, they sold so-called building blocks, that is, postcards featuring a painting of the Madonna of Stalingrad, and Halbe donated the income from the very successful sales of the memoirs of his POW years to the construction fund.

The campaign went very well. The committee received monetary contributions from individuals as well as from businesses, notably the coal mining enterprises in the region; in addition, architects, civil engineers, artisans and artists, most of whom had been POWs themselves, donated their time and skills to designing, constructing and decorating the church. Within less than two years, in the early spring of 1958, the ground-breaking ceremony took place. In October of that same year, the foundation stone of the church was laid during a similar ceremony, and on 12 December 1959, the church was consecrated in the presence of representatives of the high clergy of the diocese, of the city of Bochum and a large crowd which included many of the donors to the church.

Before proceeding to a description of the church's architecture and interior decoration, it is worth pointing out some of the narrative structures of the history of erecting the church. As noted above, combining a parish church with a memorial site offered former POWs a public space of remembrance. At the same time, it inscribed the war in the everyday life of a religious community, albeit in a specific way. It was not the war dead whose memory this church served. Rather, it was those who had been rescued or saved and whose memory was inscribed in the heart of this parish. Thus, the POW Memorial Church definitely constitutes a shrine to the living, an aspect that will be returned to below. While all former POWs were said to be included in this project, the construction history of the church clearly shows that former POWs of Soviet camps were the main group who were addressed.

The ground breaking was not the only event which highlighted Soviet POWs; the ceremonies of laying the foundation stone and of consecrating the church were replete with verbal and visual references to Soviet POW camps. Many prominent members of the local and regional clergy who were present at these ceremonies had themselves been in Russian POW camps, thus embodying this experience in a very literal way. In addition, the images in the addresses that were given on these occasions were almost exclusively references to Soviet camps or Soviet landscapes. Pictures that had been drawn in Soviet camps, especially the 'Madonna of Stalingrad' and a picture of Jesus, occupied prominent places during those ceremonies, and, as mentioned previously, income from the sale of Halbe's memoirs of his years in Soviet POW camps and of 'building blocks' featuring the 'Madonna of Stalingrad' constituted major contributions to the church's construction funds. In addition, in all verbal and visual images, the years in POW camps were completely disconnected from the war: how and why anyone had got to be in those camps was never mentioned.

There is, of course, an obvious explanation for this equation of POW camps with Soviet POW camps. The last POWs from Soviet camps had just returned when Halbe first called upon former POWs to support his project in 1955. In addition, POWs had spent many more years in Soviet camps than in others, and thus their suffering was much more vivid. However, these obvious reasons do not suffice to explain the POW Memorial Church's almost exclusive focus on Soviet camps. In my view the emphasis expresses a radical reinterpretation of the war from which these POWs were rescued. This was not Hitler's racist war against the world but Communism's war; and not simply against the Western World as in other Cold War memory strategies but against Christianity. This becomes even clearer when we analyze the church's interior decoration.

Of particular interest are the large stained-glass windows that were designed by Willem de Graaf, an artist from Duisburg who had also been a POW. These windows, which are located in the upper third of the church walls, depict scenes of war in vivid colors. While, at first glance, they appear to be mostly abstract, we can distinguish target markers, rockets, fires and a scythe severing the threads of life. Fire is descending from the sky, and what appears to be a river of blood is moving through the windows on the right wall of the church and re-appearing again on the left wall in the last window before the main window next to the altar, which is a window that brings the narrative threads of the other windows together and gives the iconographic narrative a closure.

While the other windows evoke connotations of the apocalypse, the main window's theme is the physical or spiritual rescue from trials and tribulations as a result of unwavering faith. The window's center is occupied by the scene from the book of Daniel of the three youths in the fiery furnace, who refused to pray in front of the king's golden idol and who survived through their steadfastness. Above this scene we see an image of the Trinity, and, on the right and left side, as well as in two smaller windows below, the three youths are surrounded mostly by other biblical figures who either overcame initial religious skepticism (Jonah, St Christopher) or died as martyrs.

The 'comment' of this window upon the others in the church interprets World War II as a war that was not the work of man; rather it constituted a divine trial that human beings had to undergo; they could survive, with God's help, if they remained steadfast in their faith. This interpretation removes the war from the context of secular history, as does the church's name, and transports the war into the sacred history of salvation, thus delivering soldiers from responsibility and guilt. At the same time, it allows them to see themselves not as victims but as martyrs, and hence as Christian heroes.

There is yet another aspect to this displacement of World War II into the Christian history of salvation. It also constitutes a Christian comment on the Holocaust. The permanent exhibit in the crypt confirms this interpretation. First, its design is a combination of church, chapel, museum and memorial shrine, mingling the secular and the profane in a way which clearly inscribes the years in POW camps with notions of sacrificial martyrdom. Second, it constitutes a muted 'response' to, or 'dialogue' with, concentration camp sites. On the one hand, the names of all the POW camps for German prisoners are displayed on clay tablets on a wall, expressing the imperative 'never forget!' On the other hand, the Holocaust and the war's connection with it are completely ignored. The only reference to the Holocaust can be found in a small display case in the back of the exhibit where newspaper clippings about 'Catholic Jews' (*sic!*), such as Edith Stein, are on display as examples of 'millions who died in concentration camps'.

The POW Memorial Church indeed constitutes a unique *lieu de mémoire*. While clearly influenced by overall German strategies of forgetting the war dead, it nevertheless adds its own interpretation of the Cold War, not simply as a war between two antagonistic ideologies but as a war against Christianity.

NOTES

1. Maurice Halbwachs, *La Mémoire collective* (published after his death by Jeanne Alexandre, née Halbwachs) (Paris: Presses Universitaires de France, 1950).
2. On the differences in remembering the two world wars in Germany see Jay M. Winter, *Sites of Memory, Sites of Mourning: The Great War in European Cultural History* (Cambridge/New York: Cambridge University Press, 1995); James M. Diehl, 'Germany in Defeat, 1918 and 1945: Some Comparisons and Contrasts', *History Teacher* 4 (August 1989), pp. 398–409; and Gottfried Niedhart and Dieter Riesenberger (eds), *Lernen aus dem Krieg?: Deutsche Nachkriegszeiten 1918 und 1945* (Munich: Verlag C.H. Beck, 1992).
3. On the impact of traumatic experiences on remembering WWII in Germany see Annemarie Tröger's excellent case study, 'German Women's Memories of World War II', in Margaret Randolph Higonnet, Jane Jenson, Sonya Michel and Margaret Collins Weitz (eds), *Behind the Lines: Gender and the Two World Wars* (New Haven, CT: Yale University Press, 1987), pp. 285–99. See also Martin Bergmann and Milton E. Jucove (eds), *Generation of the Holocaust* (New York: Basic Books, 1982); Barbara Heimannsberg and Christoph J. Schmidt (eds), *The Collective Silence: German Identity and the Legacy of Shame* (San Francisco: Jossey-Bass, 1993); Judith Lewis Herman, *Trauma and Recovery: The Aftermath of Violence – From Domestic Abuse to Political Terror* (New York: Basic Books, 1992); Bessel A. van der Kolk, 'The Body Keeps the Score: Memory and the Evolving Psychobiology of Posttraumatic Stress', *Harvard Review of Psychiatry* 1 (Jan.–Feb. 1994), pp. 253–65.
4. On the obsession with remembering, mourning and explaining WWI in post-WWI France, Britain and Germany – to name only the European examples – see Winter, *Sites of Memory*; see also Michael Jeismann and Rolf Westheider, 'Wofür stirbt der Bürger? Nationaler Totenkult und Staatsbürgertum in Deutschland und Frankreich seit der französischen Revolution', in Reinhart Koselleck and Michael Jeismann (eds), *Der*

politische Totenkult: Kriegendenkmäler in der Moderne (Munich: Wilhelm Fink Verlag, 1994), pp. 23–50, esp. pp. 28–50.
5. See Saul Friedlander, 'Trauma, Transferrence and "Working Through" in Writing the History of the Shoah', *History & Memory* 4 (1992), pp. 39–59.
6. This narrative of a heroic new beginning by no means reflects an actual reality. To be sure, the cessation of armed conflict was greeted with great relief by most Germans. The immediate post-war years were, for many Germans, years of worse suffering, hardship and chaos than the war years had been. See Terry Chapman, *The German Front 1939–1945* (London: Barne & Jenkins, 1989); Christophe Klessman, *Die doppelte Staatsgründung: Deutsche Geschichte 1945–1955* (Göttingen: Vandenhoeck & Ruprecht, 1991), pp. 39–41, 42, 44–53, 354–57; G.C. Paikert, *The German Exodus: A Selective Study on the Post-World War II Expulsion of German Populations and Its Effect* (The Hague: Martinus Nijhoff, 1962), pp. 1–3; Hilde Kammer and Elisabeth Bartsch (eds), *Nationalsozialismus: Begriffe aus der Zeit der Gewaltherrschaft* (Hamburg: Rowohlt, 1992), p. 28; S.P. McKenzie, 'The Treatment of Prisoners of War in World War II', *Journal of Modern History* 66 (1994), pp. 487–520; Martin K. Sorge, *The Other Price of Hitler's War: German Military and Civilian Losses Resulting from World War II* (New York: Greenwood Press, 1986); Gregory Schroeder, 'The Long Road Home: Evacuees, Postwar Victim Identities and Social Policy in the Federal Republic' (Ph.D. dissertation, Indiana University).
7. On re-education and de-Nazification, see Karl-Ernst Bungenstab, *Umerziehung zur Demokratie?* (Düsseldorf: Bertelsmann Universitätsverlag, 1970); Klessmann, *Die doppelte Staatsgrundung*, pp. 87–99; Lutz Niethammer, *Entnazifizierung in Bayern: Säuberung und Rehabilitierung unter amerikanischer Besatzung* (Frankfurt/M.: S. Fischer, 1972); Jutta-B. Lange Quassowski, *Neuordnung oder Restauration? Das Demkratiekonzept der amerikanischen Besatzungsmacht und die politische Sozialisation der Westdeutschen: Wirtschaftsordnung, Schulstruktur, politische Bildung* (Opladen: Leske und Budrich, 1979).
8. Jeffrey Herf, *Divided Memory: The Nazi Past in the Two Germanies* (Cambridge, MA: Harvard University Press, 1997).
9. Alexander and Margarete Mitscherlich, *The Inability to Mourn* (New York: Grove Press, 1984).
10. This is Vaclav Havel's term for the politics of memory in totalitarian states. Quoted from Claudia Koonz's brilliant essay 'Between Memory and Oblivion: Concentration Camps in German Memory', in John Gillis (ed.), *Commemorations: The Politics of National Identity* (Princeton, NJ: Princeton University Press, 1994), p. 258.
11. On remembering in East Germany see Andreas Dorpalen, *German History in Marxist Perspective: The East German Approach* (Detroit, MI: Wayne State University Press, 1985); Eve Rosenhaft, 'The Uses of Remembrance: The Legacy of Communist Resistance in the German Democratic Republic', in Francis R. Nicosia and Lawrence D. Stokes (eds), *Germans against Nazism: Nonconformity, Opposition and Resistance in the Third Reich. Essays in Honour of Peter Hoffman* (New York: St. Martin's Press, 1990), pp. 369–88. George Mosse arrived at the conclusion that the 'German Democratic Republic had faced the problem of honoring the fallen and had *displaced* it onto the victims of National Socialism', George Mosse, *Fallen Soldiers: Reshaping the Memory of the Two World Wars* (New York: Oxford University Press, 1990), p. 214. East Germany had to forget not only its involvement in WWII but also many of its experiences under Soviet occupation. See Norman Naimark, *The Russians in Germany: A History of the Soviet Zone of Occupation, 1945–1949* (Cambridge, MA: Belknap Press of Harvard University Press, 1995).
12. *Westfalenpost*, 20 June 1987.

16

Varieties of Interpretation: The Holocaust in Historical Memory

DAN DINER

It is commonly accepted that history, on the one hand, and memory on the other, offer opposing conceptions in narration and representation. Indeed – and according to the legacy of his craft – the historian strives to attain a high level of universalization and objectivity, which he achieves with the help of the trustworthy tools of source-critique, methodological competence and epistemological awareness. However, memory still obtains its specific impact on the art of writing history. Like a hidden hand, it succeeds continuously in counteracting and in reducing the objectifying pretensions of history, by making the effects of experience and recollection thoroughly visible. Moreover, what seems to be persuasive concerning the writing of history in general becomes even more compelling in the case of an event so insurmountable in its extreme as the Holocaust, which is still in search of its place in Clio's realm.

This chapter will elaborate on the continuous influence exercised by memory in representing the Holocaust. For this, different and memory-bound traditions in historiography will be evaluated in order to relate them to particular existential experiences – the Jewish, the German and, more peripherally, the Polish experience. This axis of presentation will allow us to unfold implicitly the subject: the Holocaust in history. However, for methodological reasons the discussion on memory, historical experience and historiographical tradition concerning the Holocaust will begin with an assessment from a more remote perspective – which I dare to generalize as British or, using the broader, continental term, Anglo-Saxon.

In his major oeuvre *Europe since 1815*,[1] Gordon A. Craig, the Nestor of English-speaking historiography on Germany, surprisingly makes no mention of the Nazi Final Solution – the Holocaust. No chapter is dedicated to the event, no paragraph – not even a single word. Such an omission requires explanation. After all, Craig does not side with those of his colleagues who seek to avoid the Holocaust by all means; in fact, the opposite is true. On a number of occasions he examines themes closely related to this very issue, such as Jewish emancipation and its ambiguities, as well as the destructive distortions of anti-Semitism. And yet, in his fundamental study on European history of the Modern Age, he enigmatically passes over the Jewish catastrophe without a mention.

How can this striking phenomenon be understood? Is it mere oversight, simple thoughtlessness, an indisposition that can and should be overlooked? Let me make it clear from the outset that I intend neither to scandalize this omission in Craig's synthesis of European history, nor to speculate on, or insinuate, hidden motives on the author's part. Rather, I shall reasonably assume that the striking exclusion of the Holocaust from his historical survey seems to be rooted in much more fundamental questions – concerning previous systematic decisions taken by the historian – including the choice of perspective, the means of periodization, the general methodological approach and, last but not least, the structure of narration.

Indeed, narration and narrativity seem to be key indicators for the construction of historical images and proto-historical patterns of interpretation – which, in fact, extend into the realm of historiography proper. In brief, Craig's treatment of the nineteenth and twentieth centuries in European history strongly conforms to a pattern of historical systematization which corresponds to Anglo-Saxon experience, tradition and, finally, its respective memory.

Naturally, such a provocative finding calls for further explanation, which may be found in the notorious conditioning of historical writing by means of periodization and perspectivity. Does this mean that Anglo-centric experience and tradition make it difficult to incorporate systematically the subject of the Holocaust – and not exclusively as far as moral judgement is concerned? This difficulty manifests itself through Craig's unique periodization: namely, embracing the nineteenth and twentieth centuries as a *single* epoch.

Indeed, bracketing the two centuries together as one period would hardly occur to historians of continental tradition. From their perspective and in terms of continental historical experience the two centuries diverge dramatically. In fact, in light of the catastrophic *saeculum* that followed, the nineteenth century appears to be the epitome of historical optimism. The eminent British historian James Joll, for instance, was aware of this variance in approach. He explains it by referring to differing experiences: British legacy is characterized by continuities; continental history, by ruptures and cataclysms. The respective distance from the continent and its upheavals seems to have been safeguarded by naval power and, politically, by the guiding principle of the *balance of power*.

This tendency is reflected in historiography – generating patterns of interpretation with similar paradigmatic effect. It finds its expression both in methodology and in choice of subject matter. This is true mainly in regard to the classical British school of historiography, which stresses narratives of a political, diplomatic and military nature. Long-term continuities, their perspectives and periodizations have so far influenced their perception of European history. Based on the concept of balance, these continuities extend at least from the Napoleonic Wars and the political order subsequently imposed by the Congress of Vienna, through the distortions arising out of the foundation of the German Reich, 1870–71, followed by the Great War, and right up to Hitler's claim to supremacy on the continent. Along this line of interpretation the integration of the Holocaust becomes, by virtue, systematically difficult.

In conformity with the perception of historical continuities embedded in the perspective of balance of power, British understanding of Nazi Germany was by and large governed by an image of the militarist Prussian *Machtstaat* inherited from the nineteenth century. According to this legacy, the 'Third Reich' was perceived *primarily* as a hegemonic continental power of the traditional type – albeit a particularly aggressive one. It is metaphorically interesting that the dissolution of Prussia by Allied decree in February 1947 was part and parcel of this quite belated tendency to perceive Nazi Germany as the immediate continuity and the mere executor of its supposed Prussian testator. But when one attaches to Nazi crimes the importance of a core historical event, long-drawn-out lines of historical continuity lose their explanatory power.

Examples of such a necessarily skewed perception are legion – during the war and afterwards, for instance, Britain's tragically low opinion of the Prussian military opposition to Hitler within Germany. Elements of perception based on historical continuity found their way into the realm of semantics as well – such as denominating the war in purported continuity of the Great War as the 'Second World War', insinuating a mere prolongation of the common European power struggle that had expanded worldwide. Crimes committed by Nazi Germany *outside* the military sphere were overshadowed by past experience. The fact that Auschwitz escaped bombardment was due not least to such historically inherited filters of perception. True, the fate of European Jewry lay hidden beyond the logic and the language of warfare, a perspective that remained dominant until immediately after Germany's surrender, when the war became a subject for juridical inquiry. Initial concern at Nuremberg was far more with penalizing the initiators of a war of aggression than punishing German war crimes and crimes against humanity. Systematic persecution and genocidal crimes committed against the Jews as Jews and against other victims that were perpetuated *outside* the realm of war had yet to penetrate general awareness. The impact of reality's past became history's legacy.

It required the distance of years to recognize the mass extermination of the Jews of Europe as an exceptionally radical phenomenon of Nazism and its very core – and to highlight it as such. Gordon A. Craig's ultimate *Europe since 1815*, of course, follows a tradition of systematization and narration – in perspective as well as in periodization – alien to continental tradition, which leads simply to the surprising omission of the Holocaust. But, above all, this phenomenon indicates, methodologically, how knottily historical tradition and memory are interrelated, both of which are part and parcel of a mutual and prior structure of narrativity.

Is historical writing indeed memory-bound, and thus quite particularistic in nature? I am not entirely convinced that this is the case. It would be a grave distortion to diminish the validity of historical narrations for collective affiliations – and by this to construe them in terms of ethnic memory and tradition. The prerequisites of systematic approaches to history and the standards of historical scholarship as a discipline are far too complex and universal in character to be reducible to the mere effects of collective memories and the type of narratives peculiar to them. On the other hand, simple inversion of that proposition would be no less problematic and extremely rationalistic, since it would ignore accumulated traditions and the impact of memory, as well as presupposed structures of narration in their effect on how history is written. In order to continue our inquiry into the impact of memory on historical writing concerning the Holocaust, we will turn from the more remote British perspective to that of the main protagonists, the German and the Jewish.

As far as so-called German and so-called Jewish narratives regarding the Holocaust are concerned, a common and simultaneously contradictory impulse of memory can be identified: both narratives follow a juridical, or judicial, pattern (*gerichtsförmig*). This judicial pattern of interpretation finds itself rationalized historiographically. It becomes a dominant layer in reconstruction and interpretation. True: judicial patterns of interpretation are not unique to narratives of the Holocaust. They basically underlie historical narrations as such. However, given an event as extreme as the Holocaust, this tendency naturally undergoes a certain qualitative intensification.

Examining, first, the wider meaning of the judicial pattern of historical narrativity, we find that what is significant for the judicial discourse in general and the discourse of the courtroom in particular is the contentious juxtaposition of long-term versus short-term memory spans. The fact that the memory of the plaintiff usually goes back further than the defendant's more restricted faculties in this respect is something that the courts themselves and the rules of legal procedure take into account. Peter Burke[2] stresses the judicial nature of historical memory with reference to the institution of the remembrancer. In early modern Britain, the remembrancer was a communal official whose job was to remind the debtor continuously and repeatedly to pay off his dues. His task was to ensure that outstanding debts did not suffer social oblivion. In much the same way as individual memory, collective retention of memory is also subject to varying rates of decay. Burke distinguished nations with short-term memories from nations with long-term memories. The Irish, the Poles, the Serbs and the Jews, for example, are generally reckoned to possess significantly long historical memory spans. The British, the French and the Germans, on the other hand, are blessed with shorter memories. However, the differences between individual and collective memory notwithstanding, it seems clear that at the level of specific collective 'we' experiences, too, friction exists between the creditor's claim and the delaying reaction of the debtor. Thus debts and claims from distant or less-distant pasts devolve upon the present through the medium of memory and the praxis of commemoration.

How do these juxtaposed perspectives affect writing the history of the Holocaust? It is common knowledge, but escapes awareness, that the investigation of the mass crimes committed by Nazi Germany began with a trial. And the proceedings at Nuremberg evidently had an impact on historiography. The collection of documents, the structure of arguments and the presentation of the narratives necessarily followed the lines of juridical confrontation between prosecution and defense. Taking the establishment of mere facts for granted, the prosecution attempts to prove culpable conduct, while the defense rests and, so to speak, pleads negligence.

On the one hand, there is a *negligence* and on the other a verdict of guilt. True, the criminal qualification inherent in distinctive judgements concerning the respective extent of culpability may shed some light on historical controversies in regard to Nazism and the Holocaust. Certainly, subtexts as well as the structure of historical argumentation reveal the fact that the different approaches in historical interpretation closely correspond to thoroughly judicial rules of procedure – resting on contrary recollections: the memory of the plaintiff and the memory of the defendant. What are the implications of this understanding? Does it mean, for example, that so-called German memory concerning the writing of the Holocaust uses a different construction and follows a different systematization than so-called Jewish memory – and this along the lines of judicial discourse?

With all due skepticism, the juxtaposition and rivalry of academic schools in the reconstruction and interpretation of Nazism and the Holocaust actually reflect the judicial nature of historical discourse. Therefore it is plausible that the so-called internationalist school in Nazi and Holocaust research – while arguing for deliberate action in the extermination of the Jews – complies more closely with the memory of the victims. Although both schools pretend to explain *why* the Holocaust became possible and ultimately occurred, the direction of their questioning differs fundamentally. In epistemological terms, internationalism implies the question of *who* – who were the victims? – and reconstructs through this the story of the Holocaust. The so-called structuralist, or functionalist, school, on the other hand, is much more determined by the question of *how* – how, and in what way, did the mass extermination become possible? Concerning the judicial juxtaposition of negligence and guilt, this school in Holocaust historiography tends heavily toward leniency over the question of responsibility and culpability. The structuralist approach seems to conform more closely with the memory of the Germans and their experience. Yet, above all, this approach attracts much wider support because of its allegedly universalizing and generalizing explanation for the Holocaust – a universalization and anthropologization, *nota bene*, at history's expense.

These opposing schools of historical reconstruction and interpretation of the Holocaust reflect respective narratives alongside the patterns of judicial inquiry and its proper discourse. Finally, this discourse is initiated by questions of collective responsibility and individual guilt. The reason for such evocations are obvious. A crime such as mass extermination which was perpetrated not solely (as Daniel Goldhagen has actually shown[3]) but largely in an administrative and industrial manner, involving a high degree of division of labor, leads to massive dissociation on the part of the perpetrators, a full-blown denial, so to speak, of all traces of responsibility and culpability that were felt, or at least might have been felt, by those embroiled in the act. This reaction, a kind of mental 'alienation', produced by the perpetrators in relation to their own actions, knowledge or suspicions, is wholly and fundamentally denied by the existential experience of the victims. They were directly and without mitigation subjugated to the death machine. The monstrosity they encountered was thus not a historical construction. It was literally and absolutely real.

Concerning the different and even antagonistic patterns of interpretation and their judicial nature, the following conclusion can be drawn. The crime of mass extermination almost inevitably falls into two different, indeed conflicting, worlds of experience: banality on the side of the perpetrators and, as a result of the complex way in which the

Holocaust was administratively carried out, monstrosity on the side of the victims, exposed as they were to the full impact of the crime. This rift in experience generates massive problems for historical representation that are not easily overcome.

All in all, the so-called German perspective – which might be termed a micro-perspective (discussed more extensively below) – claims negligence at the level of judicial discourse. The so-called Jewish perspective, based on the experience of monstrosity, adheres to the macro-level of explanation, and pleads by this, and because of intention, guilty. The narration for pleading, however, stretches back and beyond the very delimitations of the subject proper in space as well as in time; in fact, the history of the Holocaust falls on its real, or allegedly real, prehistory: the history of anti-Semitism.

Indeed, anti-Semitism and its enormous effect as the real or allegedly real cause for the Holocaust is undoubtedly the core ingredient of the pattern of historical narrative that comes closest to the comprehension and affectability of the victim's legacy. After all, the long-term Jewish experience of incessant hostility enfolds a layer of interpretation of such density that escaping its narrative impact on consciousness is almost impossible. Thus Jewish history written after the Holocaust becomes somehow teleologically directed toward the catastrophe. This perspective is hardly avoidable because of the tremendous impact of the event on consciousness. By and large it follows, up to the notorious nationality question in the period in between the two world wars, the patterns of narration so typical for the east European Jewish experience, in which everyday anti-Semitism, rooted in religious aversions and social rivalries, play a major role. This understanding is expressed for instance in Celia Heller's book on Polish Jewry entitled *On the Edge of Destruction*,[4] which describes the fate of Polish Jewry before the German invasion as somehow becoming fused with the events to come. Once I suggested the metaphor of 'compressed time' for such a phenomenon because prehistories are drawn massively into the historical narration of the Holocaust in order to make it tellable or at all recountable.[5] Finally, we are dealing with an extremely brief period of time compared to the enormous impact of the event. Moreover, the patterns of such a narration are of a conspicuous east European gestalt.

Mostly, because of prior experience and the respective narratives related to foregone pasts, as well as the Jewish experience during the war, the relationship between Poles and Jews has become heavily affected by the crimes committed by Nazi Germany. Sometimes the story is even told as one of collaboration and strife, such as can be witnessed on occasions of commemoration and symbolization of the Holocaust. Here Polish and Jewish memories seem fundamentally opposed – and this beside and beyond all historically traceable factitiousness. True, Polish self-perception is committed to the distinctive elevation as Christ's chosen people, that is to say, a martyrological self-understanding, which competes with the much more durable antiquity of Jewish memory and Jewish victimization. This pattern of rivalry can be traced into the realm of historiography. Studies on relations between Poles and Jews during the Holocaust, carried out by Jewish historians, on the one hand, and by historians of non-Jewish memory, on the other, already bear signs and symbols of rivalry in their very title. For instance the fundamental study on Polish–Jewish relations during World War II by Israel Gutman and Shmuel Krakowski is called *Unequal Victims*, while Richard C. Lukas and Norman Davies' book on Poland under Nazi occupation is entitled *The Forgotten Holocaust*.[6] In any event, with anti-Semitism at its core, Jewish memory demands that the history of the Holocaust be told. And however the impact of anti-Semitism on the Holocaust may be assessed, this kind of interpretation is entirely in line with the judicial approach in narration, which argues in support of deliberate intention, culpability and therefore of guilt. But this is not the dominant tendency in historiography any more. Today one can detect more and more approaches in historical reconstruction and interpretation which take us a long way from the Jewish victims as Jews. Accordingly, rather than the centrality of anti-Semitism in the Nazi *Weltanschauung*, various circumstances apparently led to the crime – while the Jews as victims of a deliberate act find themselves increasingly sidelined, as does intentionality, that is, the Holocaust committed on purpose. Such tendencies, represented in the past by the functionalist school, notably Martin Broszat, and today by Hans Mommsen and Goetz Aly, assign only peripheral importance to anti-Semitism.[7] Instead they stress the supposedly chaotic nature of Nazi administrative behavior – euphemistically, but quite seriously, characterized as 'incompetence', and even 'dilettantism'. By this they mean apparent disordered behavior, which forced the different German agencies into alleged impasses that could only be overcome by further radicalization. This perspective places negligence at the forefront of interpretation, and therefore ignores the fact that, at each stage of radicalization, mainly, or even exclusively, the Jews were affected by the most extreme measures undertaken. In the well-known debate with Martin Broszat, Saul Friedlander hints at this fact – that German historians are no less caught up in the structural givens of collective experience, appropriate memories and the kind of narrative that goes with them – an argument that Broszat sought to bestow on his Jewish counterpart.[8]

It may be concluded that layers of memory have a strikingly significant impact on the construction of historical narration, and this beyond mere faculty. They are indeed of epistemological and even methodological importance. True, questions of continuity and causality tend to lead to historiographical controversies. Recollections that champion the life-and-death experience of the victims will essentially focus on immediate or allegedly immediate causalities between expressed intentions of extermination and such measures undertaken by Nazi German agencies that *actually* led to extermination. Other circumstances evoked by and emanating from comparably unpredictable circumstances are too easily overlooked. These might have even contributed more to the immediate realization and execution of the crime than foregrounded intentions documented in the incriminating sources. Reality was much more advanced than political or administrative directions as laid down in key Nazi documents – although such sources became icons of historiography. One might mention *Euthenasie-Erlass,* issued by Hitler and dating back to 1 September 1939; or the letter formulated by Eichmann at Heydrich's order, and signed by Goering on 31 July 1941, empowering the head of the SD (Sicherheitsdienst [Security Service]) of the SS with the Final Solution in all territories under German domination; or the protocol of the Wannsee Conference, and even the conference as such. It should be borne in mind that on 20 January 1942 the Final Solution was already in full swing. Even the planning of the death camps, later known as Aktion Reinhard, was already in progress. As a meeting where the implementation of the Final Solution had to be *decided* on, the Wannsee-Konferenz has no proper meaning.

In short, the widely accepted tendency to overestimate the importance of allegedly key documents concerning the implementation of the Final Solution are the unavoidable result of a specific understanding of the Nazi regime as a government, where administrative acts proceeded rationally and where there was a clear allocation of responsibility. Such a view largely ignores the complex combination of anti-Jewish measures and actions, the impact of anti-Semitic ideology deriving from the Nazi *Weltanschauung,* eugenics and euthanasia, anti-Bolshevism, ethnic cleansing – and finally the systematic murder of the Jews. According to this perspective, the Holocaust is evaluated as the result of an apparently direct line drawn between declarations of intent and the crime itself. For the sake of this immediacy, different historical phenomena were construed into a single chronology, insinuating instantaneous causalities: the discrimination practiced against the German Jews in the 1930s; its intensification, caused conspicuously by the Anschluss of Austria, and accompanied by compulsory emigration and forced expulsions; ghettoization in Poland and the first massacres by mobile SS-Einsatzgruppen and police reservists in the east – as an appendage to the brutal war of *Weltanschauung* against an allegedly Jewified Soviet Union – right up to the negative apotheosis of systematic, industrialized extermination in the death camps in Poland.

Although anti-Jewish actions had already begun in Germany in 1933, the mass extermination began under cover of war against the Soviet Union in the east, and were intended to move in the opposite direction to the original German expansion – from east to west, instead of from west to east. There is nothing paradoxical about the fact that German Jews – the first victims of Nazi measures – had to wear the yellow badge only from autumn 1941. How should the Holocaust be told? From the perspective of an average German Jew, a former civil servant, for instance, who was dismissed from office in 1933, fell under the consequences of the Nuremberg Laws in 1935, became gradually deprived of his means, was arrested during Kristallnacht in November 1938, beaten up in a concentration camp and then released, a man who suffered continuous and increasing discrimination during the war years – and was finally deported in autumn 1941 to Kovno, and executed in the notorious fort? Or, in an effort to avoid overextended lines of continuity, should the story be told from the angle of a common German? German memory and perception would probably incline by and large toward modes of explanation which underscore first and foremost elements of contingency and chance, that is, chaotically improvised operations of state and party agencies, their perpetual disputes over competencies and authority, which may have brought about further radicalization – in short, negligence. The Jewish issue in the whole story is in steady decline. The importance of the Jews, and hence the weight of anti-Semitism, would be interpreted not as a genuine cause – an intention – but as a kind of political currency in a continuous struggle for power within the Nazi hierarchy. And the significance of the anti-Semitic W*eltanschauung* of the Nazis as a precondition for the legitimacy of anti-Jewish actions would be immediately refuted by the fact that mere anti-Jewish feelings or even open hatred of Jews was not as universal in Germany as generally believed. Paradoxically there is some truth in this. But what may have been disregarded in this argument is the fact that anti-Semitic policies and *actions* were not necessarily accompanied by anti-Jewish *sentiments*.

The question of anti-Semitism in relation to the Holocaust and the significance of Jewish victims as Jews, is closely related to the question of the universalization of the event. Were the Jews put to death as Jews or just as human beings? Was the murder directed against humanity or against the Jewish people? *If* universalization is understood in such a way, it will not lead very far. It will just lead to the abandonment of the complex trail of history in order to join the decidedly blurred and sociologically generalizing philippic against modernity. Evidence in experimental psychology such as the Milgram test[9] only tries to impress with anthropological truisms. What is significant about such a universalizing and generalizing approach is the fact that it deals less with past historical *reality* than with future *possibilities* of large-scale mass crimes, apparently inherent in human nature and civilization.

Particularity versus universality. This dualism in narration and interpretation of the Holocaust calls to mind idiosyncratic layers of religious origin still active in secularized memory. It brings to mind classical discourses shaped alongside theological disputes between Christians and Jews, between a universalized Judaism as Christianity, on the one hand, and a more particularistic understanding of God's own people, on the other – that is, between the Jewish claim to election and its Christological denial.

Still, the notion of universality concerning the Holocaust remains even then of importance, when repeatedly applied wrongly or even ideologically misused. The notion of universalization is in fact of epistemological importance, in cases where the historian deals, for example, with complex and painful issues concerning Jewish behavior under Nazi domination, such as those relating to the *Judenrat* or to the question of Jewish resistance – armed or otherwise. Then the Holocaust discloses its universal as well as its particular nature. Its universal nature derives from the notion that all human beings, regardless of their collective belonging, would have reacted the same way in such an extreme plight, including going beyond the realm of purposive rationality, as for instance the *Judenrat* did. The Jewish councils were subservient to a reality in which rationality of action aimed at self-preservation was transformed into self-destruction.

Because this inversion became a reality it is not only part of a specific Jewish experience but should be regarded as a practical negation of the basic assumption of the civilizing power of rational judgement as such. Only in this regard – pertaining to the Jews as human beings – does Auschwitz become a universal experience. But the Nazis' choice to make the Jews their main victims makes the event again extremely particular in nature.

Finally, the Holocaust was a historical event of an extraordinary existential nature, not only out of sheer moral considerations, but particularly because of the limits of comprehension which emanate from the very event and its core: the extermination was above and transcended all extreme experiences of persecution and violence ever suffered – human beings condemned to death *without* any recognizable rational meaning – contrary to a supposedly universally valid meaning of utility, and contrary to the Nazis' own interest in self-preservation. Such an event may be characterized as a 'rupture in civilization' (*Zivilisationsbruch*), based on the horrifying encounter with something that might be characterized as *counter*-rationality, and experienced by the victims, that is, the destruction of purposive rationality as a guideline in human behavior – even behavior based on common evil, which is committed neither out of passion nor for one's own advantage. As Hannah Arendt once put it, this is the striking universal negativity of the Holocaust and the main core of its singularity.

In conclusion, the attempt at historical reconstruction and representation of the Holocaust is by no means situated beyond the craft and the capacity of the historian. The historical elucidation of the Final Solution does not in principle call for any different methodological and theoretical skills than are generally required for historical research. Granted, the exceptional radical nature of the object demands a great deal of introspection and self-reflection, which extend into methodological questions. Indeed, memory is increasingly acquiring an epistemological meaning. And while 'Jewish' memory relates to the Holocaust through major political and dramatic events and their proper symbolization in narration, a historical attempt corresponding to a German context of experience and memory would seek above all to focus on the everyday, the trivial, the accidental and the banal – in short, it would stick to the less dramatic aspects of the historical picture. Jewish memory symbolizes the Holocaust via incisive events in order to constitute its appropriate narrative. Its focus is situated at a certain distance from the unlimited variety of facts symbolizing reality, in order to rationalize them in correspondence with the devastating events consciousness experienced. Therefore the perception of the Holocaust qualified as 'Jewish' may be reflected quite adequately by a macro-perspective. The accentuation of sharp incisions such as high-level decisions, the announcement of major ideological projects and political declarations hinting at extermination offers a much more plausible symbolization in representing major historical disruptions. The 'German' perspective, or related views, on the other hand, may be qualified as a microperspective. By getting excessively close to the historical image of the Holocaust, this perspective is inclined to dissolve the entire picture into its apparently trivial components. Thus, the experiential contexts of the past – monstrosity versus banality – recur in choice of angle and perspective, transforming them into opposites: culpability and guilt versus negligence, and, historiographically, intentionalism versus functionalism. Thus memory – like Clio's invisible hand – turns out to be highly relevant to the historian's craft generally, but especially in the case of the history of the Holocaust.

THE HOLOCAUST IN HISTORICAL MEMORY

NOTES

1. Gordon A. Craig, *Europe since 1815* (New York: Holt, Rinehart & Winston, 1961).
2. Peter Burke, 'Geschichte als soziales Gedächtnis', in Aleida Assmann and Dietrich Harth (eds), *Mnemosyne: Formen und Funktionen kultureller Erinnerung* (Frankfurt am Main, 1991), pp. 289–304.
3. Daniel Goldhagen, *Hitler's Willing Executioners: Ordinary Germans and the Holocaust*, (New York: Knopf, 1996).
4. Celia S. Heller, *On the Edge of Destruction : Jews of Poland Between the Two World Wars* (Detroit, MI: Wayne State University Press, 1993).
5. Dan Diner, 'Gestaute Zeit: Massenvernichtung und jüdische Erzählstruktur', in Dan Diner, *Kreisläufe: Nationalsozialismus und Gedächtnis* (Berlin: Berlin Verlag, 1995), pp. 123–39.
6. Shmuel Krakowski and Israel Gutman, *Unequal Victims: Poles and Jews during World War II* (Washington, DC: U.S. Holocaust Memorial Museum, 1988); Richard C. Lukas and Norman Davies, *The Forgotten Holocaust: The Poles Under German Occupation 1939–1944* (Lexington, KY: University of Kentucky Press, 1986).
7. See for example Hans Mommsen, *The Legacy of the Holocaust and German National Identity* (NY: Leo Baeck Institute, 1999); Hans Mommsen: 'Die Realisierung des Utopischen: Die "Endlösung der Judenfrage" im "Dritten Reich"', *Geschichte und Gesellschaft* 3 (1983), pp. 381–420; Goetz Aly and Susanne Heim, *Vordenker der Vernichtung. Auschwitz und die deutschen Plane für eine neue europäische Ordnung* (Frankfurt: Fischer, 1993); Goetz Aly, *'Endlösung'. Völkerverschiebung und der Mord an den europäischen Juden* (Frankfurt: Fischer, 1995).
8. See Martin Broszat and Saul Friedlander, 'A Controversy about the Historicization of National Socialism', in Peter Baldwin, *Reworking the Past: Hitler, the Holocaust and the Historians' Controversy* (Boston, MA: Beacon Press, 1990).
9. Stanley Milgram conducted a series of experiments on obedience to authority at Yale University in 1961–62. He found, surprisingly, that 65 per cent of his subjects, ordinary residents of New Haven, were willing to give apparently harmful electric shocks of up to 450 volts to a pitifully protesting victim, simply because a scientific authority commanded them to, and in spite of the fact that the victim did not do anything to deserve such punishment. The victim was, in reality, a good actor who did not actually receive shocks, and this fact was revealed to the subjects at the end of the experiment.

Notes on Contributors

DAVID ANDRESS is Senior Lecturer in Modern European History at the University of Portsmouth, England. His research interests lie in the area of the French Revolution, and range from Parisian popular politics to the wider political culture of the 1780s and 1790s. His most recent publications include *Massacre at the Champ de Mars: Popular Dissent and Political Culture in the French Revolution* (2000), and *French Society in Revolution, 1789–1799* (1999). He is currently writing a history of popular life during the Revolution.

AVNER BEN-AMOS is Senior Lecturer and Head of the Department of Educational Policy and Organization, School of Education, Tel Aviv University. A historian of education, he is the author of *Funerals, Politics and Memory in Modern France, 1789–1996* (2000) and numerous articles on French collective memory and Israeli civic education.

KATERINA CLARK is Professor of Comparative Literature, and of Slavic Languages and Literatures at Yale University. She is the author of *The Soviet Novel: History as Ritual* (1981; 3rd edn, 2000), *Mikhail Bakhtin* (with Michael Holquist, 1984) and *Petersburg, Crucible of Cultural Revolution* (1995).

DAN DINER is Professor of History at the Hebrew University of Jerusalem and Director of the Simon Dubnow Institute for Jewish History and Culture, University of Leipzig. He is the author of numerous publications on Weimar Germany and the Nazi period, the history of law, Jewish history, the history of the modern Middle East and the history of international relations. Among his recent books are *Hans Kelsen and Carl Schmitt, A Juxtaposition* (edited with Michael Stolleis) (1999), *Das Jahrhundert verstehen. Eine Universalgeschichtliche Deutung* (1999) and *Beyond the Conceivable; Studies on Germany, Nazism and the Holocaust* (2000).

ELISABETH DOMANSKY was Professor of History at Indiana University, Bloomington, from 1994 to 1997. She subsequently served as a visiting fellow at the Institute for Advanced Study in the Humanities, Essen. She has done pioneering work in the field of memory of the world wars in Germany.

PETER FRITZSCHE is Professor of History at the University of Illinois at Urbana-Champaign. A former Guggenheim fellow, he is the author of numerous books, including *Germans into Nazis* (1998) and *Reading Berlin 1900* (1996). He is currently working on memory and ethnographies of the past, and is completing a book on memory and nostalgia in the modern world.

BORIS GASPAROV is Professor of Slavic and General Linguistics and Russian Literature at Columbia University. He is the author and editor of over 20 books, among them: *Poetics of The Tale of Prince Igor's Campaign* [in Russian] (Vienna, 1984; 2nd edn, Moscow, 2000); *Pushkin's Poetic Language in the History of Russian Literary Language* [in Russian] (Vienna, 1992; 2nd edn, St Petersburg, 1999); *Language and Memory* [in Russian] (1996); co-editor of: *Christianity and Eastern Slavs*, Vols 1–3 (1990–92); and *From the Golden Age to the Silver Age: Cultural Mythologies of Russian Modernism* (1988).

IGAL HALFIN is a Lecturer in the Faculty of History, Tel Aviv University. He is currently engaged in a study of the Great Purge in Leningrad. His book *From Darkness to Light: Class Consciousness and Salvation in Revolutionary Russia* was published in 2000.

JOCHEN HELLBECK is Assistant Professor of History at the University of Giessen, Germany. He is the author of *Revolution of the Soul: Soviet Diaries from the Stalin Era* (forthcoming).

DAVID L. HOFFMANN is Associate Professor of History at Ohio State University and co-editor of *The Russian Review*. He is the author of *Peasant Metropolis: Social Identities in Moscow, 1929–1941* (1994), and co-editor of *Russian Modernity: Politics, Knowledge, Practices* (2000).

NOTES ON CONTRIBUTORS

PETER HOLQUIST is Assistant Professor at Cornell University. He received his PhD. from Columbia University in 1995. His forthcoming book, *Making War, Forging Revolution* examines the Russian Revolution within the context of the broader European crisis of World War I. With David Hoffmann, he is publishing *Sculpting the Masses*, a study of the Soviet Union as one particular form of the emergence of 'the social' in inter-war European states.

DAVID G. HORN is Associate Professor in the Department of Comparative Studies at Ohio State University. He is the author of *Social Bodies: Science, Reproduction, and Italian Modernity* (1994), and is completing a volume on the criminal body and nineteenth-century human sciences.

BORIS KOLONITSKII is a Senior Researcher at the Institute of History of the Academy of Sciences in St Petersburg. He is co-author with Orlando Figes of *Interpreting the Russian Revolution: The Language and Symbols of 1917* (1999) and the author of *Pogony i bor'ba za vlast' v 1917 godu* (Epaulets and the struggle for power in 1917) (2001) and *Simvoly vlasti i bor'ba za vlast': K izucheniiu politicheskoi kul'tury Rossiiskoi revoliutsii 1917 goda* (Symbols of power and the struggle for power) (2001).

ERIC NAIMAN is Associate Professor of Comparative Literature and Slavic Languages and Literatures at the University of California, Berkeley. He is the author of *Sex in Public: The Incarnation of Early Soviet Ideology* (1997), and, more recently, of the introduction to Andrei Platonov's *Happy Moscow* (2001).

BOAZ NEUMANN is a Lecturer in German History at Tel Aviv University. His most recent publications include *Good Soldier* [in Hebrew] (2001) and *The Nazi Weltanschauung: Space, Body and Language* [in Hebrew] (2001), which won the Bahat Prize for non-fiction. His current research concerns early Zionist political thought and the history of disillusionment in the Weimar Republic.

MARK D. STEINBERG is Associate Professor in the Department of History and Director of the Russian and East European Center at the University of Illinois. He has previously taught at Harvard and Yale universities. Recent publications include *Voices of Revolution, 1917* (2001), *The Fall of the Romanovs: Political Dreams and Personal Struggles in a Time of Revolution* (with Vladimir Khrustalev, 1995), *Cultures in Flux: Lower Class Values, Practices and Resistance in Late Imperial Russia* (with Stephen Frank, 1994), and *Moral Communities: The Culture of Class Relations in the Russian Printing Industry, 1867–1907* (1992).

Index

Abel, Theodore, 164, 170, 173, 174, 175, 178
Adorno, Theodor, 28, 323
Aleksandra (Tsarina, wife of Nicholas II), 59, 63, 65, 73, 81
Aleksandrov, Grigorii, 215–34
Aleksandrovskii, Vasilii, 110, 113, 114, 115, 117, 120, 127
All-Great Don Host, 83, 87, 92, 94, 96, 97, 98, 99, 103
Alsace-Lorraine, 345, 348, 349, 350, 354, 355, 357
Altman, Rick, 222
anti-Semitism, 68, 318, 380, 385, 386, 388
Astaire, Fred, 221, 229
Auschwitz, 8, 20, 165, 317–39, 381, 389
Austria, 387

Babel, Isaak, 136
Bakhtin, Mikhail, 126, 305, 315
Baranov, Iura, 197
Barnet, Boris, 216
Bartholdi, Auguste, 355
Bartok, Bela, 238
Bastien-Lepage, Emile, 345, 348
Bastien-Lepage, Jules, 348
Baudin, Jan, 341, 361
Bauman, Zygmunt, 124, 178
Becker, Adolf von, 348
Beethoven, Ludwig von, 218, 235, 240, 241, 242
Belleville Plan, 341
Bely, Andrei, 238
Berlioz, Hector, 240, 242

Berman, Marshall, 124
Bismarck, Otto von, 57, 344
Black Hundreds, 50, 67–8
Blanc, Louis, 344, 351, 361
Blok, A.A., 51, 77
Bloy, Leon, 351
Bocchini, Arturo, 261
Bochum, 21, 365–77
Bogdanov, Aleksandr, 125
Bolshevik Revolution (*see* October Revolution)
Bolsheviks, 73, 84–96 *passim*, 115, 186, 187, 188, 298, 299
Bonnat, Léon, 345, 348
Bourdieu, Pierre, 29
Brahms, Johannes, 240
Broszat, Martin, 386
Bruckner, Anton, 240
Bukharin, Nikolai, 232, 272, 308
Byron, Lord (George Gordon), 243

Calinescu, Matei, 105, 123
Caprino, Antonello, 261
Carjat, Etienne, 345
Chanzy, Antoine Eugene, 344, 351, 357, 361
Chaplin, Charles, 348
Chaplin, Charlie, 220
Chernyshevsky, Nikolai, 272
Chiaurell, Mikhail, 224
Christianity, 3, 7, 19, 21, 66, 375, 376, 389
Church (*see also* POW Memorial Church), 3, 8, 20–1, 30, 342, 346, 350, 357

cinema, Soviet, 14, 50, 62, 215–34, 300, 304
Circle for the Salvation of the Don, 85, 93, 94, 98, 102, 103
Civil War (Russian), 5, 10, 11, 102, 115, 136, 138, 186, 277
Cold War, 288, 370, 371, 375, 376
commemoration, 20, 21, 353, 356, 357, 360, 365–77, 383, 385
communism, 6, 7, 8, 11, 12, 13, 21, 26, 188, 198, 201, 208
Communist Party of the Soviet Union, 6, 12, 140, 147, 185–213, 216, 293, 299, 304; IXth Party Conference (1920), 192
Cossacks (*see also* All Great Don Host; Court for the Defence of the Don; Don Congress of Soviets), 10, 83–103; ethnic distinctions among, 100; impact of land decree on, 86, 100
Court for the Defence of the Don, 95, 98
Craig, Gordon A., 379, 380, 382
criminology, 16, 249–67

Davidowicz, Lucy, 318
de Cassagnac, Paul, 353
de Saussure, Ferdinand, 24
Denmark, 7
Déroulède, Paul, 349
Derrida, Jacques, 24
Deschanel, Paul, 357
Diderot, Denis, 33, 34, 42, 44
Dinur, Yehiel (Ka-Tzetnik), 318, 320
Dmitrii Pavlovich Grand Duke, 58, 65, 68
Don Congress of Soviets (First), 92
Duclerc, Charles, 344, 345

Eichmann, Adolph, 326, 328, 329, 387
Eidinova, V., 122
Eisenstein, Sergei, 216, 219, 220
Eksteins, Modris, 165
Elizaveta Fedorovna, Grand Duchess, 70
Engels, Friedrich, 7, 147, 310
Enlightenment, 6, 28, 29, 35, 178, 276
Erdman, Nicolai, 216, 219, 220, 231
Eroshin, Ivan, 114

Falguière, Alexandre, 345, 348
fascism (*see* Italy, Germany)
February Revolution (Russia), 47–74 *passim*, 80
Ferri, Enrico, 255, 259, 260, 261
Ferry, Jules, 349, 359
Feuer, Jane, 221, 223, 226, 232
Final Solution (*see also* Auschwitz, Holocaust), 334, 379, 387, 390
Flaubert, Gustave, 242
Foucault, Michel, 14, 16, 17, 18, 45, 228, 249, 259, 262, 269, 270
France, 1, 3, 5–6, 20, 27–46, 54, 56, 71, 227, 279, 290, 293, 341–63, 369; Moral Order, 342; Second Empire, 341, 342, 343; Third Republic, 20, 342, 343, 344, 353, 354, 355, 356, 359
French Revolution, 2, 4, 5, 8, 9, 20, 27–46, 71, 85, 161, 162, 176, 343, 346, 353; Girondins, 39, Great Fear/Reign of Terror, 40–3, 85; Jacobin Republic, 42; Jacobins, 39, 43; Montagnards, 39
Freud, Sigmund, 25, 368
Freyer, Hans, 163, 172
Friedlander, Saul, 386

INDEX

Furet, François, 36
futurism, 237, 238

Galton, Francis, 277
Gambetta, Leon, 341–63
Garnier, Charles, 348, 350
Garofalo, Raffaele, 255, 264
Gastev, Aleksei, 112, 113, 120, 122, 272
Gates, Skip, 230
Gavriil Konstantinovich, Grand Duke, 67
Gerasimov, Mikhail, 113, 118, 120, 121, 122, 125
Germanophobia, 68, 69, 70
Germany, 6–7, 14, 16, 17, 20, 21, 25, 54–73 *passim*, 194, 274, 280, 350; defeat of, 369; Nazi, 6, 7, 13, 161–83, 208, 211, 215, 223, 250, 279, 317–39, 367, 368, 369, 371, 372, 381, 383, 385, 388; postwar, 365–77; West, 365, 370, 371
Gimbel, Adalbert, 177, 178
Gippius, Zinaida, 59, 63
Glaeser, Ernst, 171, 331
Goebbels, Joseph, 6, 164, 215
Goethe, Johann Wolfgang von, 242, 243
Golubintsev, General, 90, 96, 97
Gorky, Maksim, 147, 192, 216, 287, 292, 294, 306, 308, 312
Great Britain, 7, 369
Great Purges (*see* purges, Stalinist)
Gypsies, 8, 318, 323

Halbe, August, 372, 373, 374, 375
Halévy, Ludovic, 344
Hanotaux, Gabriel, 348
Haydn, Franz Joseph, 235
Hérold, Ferdinand, 351
Herzen Institute, 201, 204, 207

Heydrich, Reinhard, 325, 328, 387
Himmler, Heinrich, 324, 328, 331
Hitler, Adolf, 6, 7, 8, 12, 13, 17, 164, 166, 171, 172, 175, 208, 223, 280, 286, 318, 324, 370, 375, 381, 387
Holocaust, 21, 22, 318, 370, 376, 379–91
Honegger, Arthur, 237
Horkheimer, Max, 28
Höss, Rudolf, 326, 327, 328, 329, 332
Hugo, Victor, 346, 348, 351, 358, 359, 360

Ianov, Georgii, 93
Illiodor, Hieromonk (*see* Trufanov)
Institute of Red Professors, 186, 190, 194, 201, 203, 205, 206
Italy, 16, 17, 249–67, 280; fascist, 17, 163, 170, 250
Iusupov, Feliks, 65
Iutkevich, Sergei, 231, 236

Jahn, Friedrich Ludwig, 274
Japan, 279, 280
Jews (*see also* Auschwitz, Final Solution, Holocaust), 5, 6, 8, 66, 73, 318, 319, 320, 324, 327, 328, 331, 334, 376, 382–9; Polish, 385
Joyce, James, 238
Jünger, Ernst, 164, 165, 167

Kadets (Constitutional Democrats), 72, 73, 87
Kafka, Franz, 238
Kaminskii, Grigorii, 307
Kataev, Valentin, 236, 237, 244
Kazakov, Ignaty, 308, 310
Keaton, Buster, 220

Kerenskii, Aleksandr, 47, 52, 56, 57, 62, 65, 69, 70, 73
Khrushchev, Nikita, 200, 231
Kirillov, Vladimir, 111, 113, 115, 116, 117, 125, 126, 127
Kirov, Sergei, 156, 198, 199, 201, 203
Kol'tsov, Nikolai, 290, 291, 292, 293, 294, 306, 312
Komsomol, 137, 142, 145, 193, 194, 205, 206, 275, 277, 278, 280
Kosarev, Aleksandr, 277
Koselleck, Reinhart, 161, 171
Krasnov, Petr, 85, 87, 88, 93, 94, 97
Kshesinskaia, Matil'da Feliksovna, 63, 75
Kudinov, Pavel, 83
Kuznetsov, Nikolai Vasil'evich, 119

Lacan, Jacques, 24, 25
Laffitte, Pierre, 353
Lebedev-Polianskii, Pavel, 109, 125
Lefebvre, Georges, 85
Lenin, V.I., 62, 73, 108, 113, 145, 231, 282, 298
Leningrad Communist University, 193
Léon, Léone, 344, 345, 346
Lesgaft, Petr, 274
Lethen, Helmut, 173
Levi, Primo, 319, 320, 324, 329, 336, 337
Liashko, Nikolai, 119, 121, 126
liberalism, 3, 18, 42, 43, 178, 200, 259
Lloyd, Harold, 220
Lombroso, Cesare, 249–67
Louis XVI, 9
Lubitsch, Ernst, 224

Lucas, Colin, 37
Lüdtke, Alf, 159, 178
Lyotard, Jean François, 324, 325

Mahler, Gustav, 238, 240, 242
Marie Antoinette, 9, 71
Martin, Paul, 215
Marx, Karl, 13, 37, 141, 147, 172, 208, 271, 273, 297
Marxism, 3, 13, 108, 124, 171
Mashirov, Aleksei, 120
Mayakovsky, Vladimir, 219
Meister, Wilhelm, 242, 243
Mel'gunov, S.P., 50, 59, 71
Mensheviks, 76
Meyerhold, Vsevelod, 219, 220, 234, 271, 273, 282
Miasoedov, S.N., 52, 61, 69, 75
Mikhail Aleksandrovich, Grand Duke, 68
Milgram, Stanley, 389, 391
Miliukov, Pavel, 54, 69, 72
Millerand, Alexandre, 356, 359
Mirabeau, Honoré Gabriel Riqueti, 32
Moeller van den Bruck, Arthur, 164, 165
Molotov, Viacheslav, 199
Montesquieu, Charles de Secondat, Baron de, 38, 45
Morozov, Pavlik, 192, 195, 211
Moscow, 222, 225
Mosse, George, 163, 377
Mozart, Wolfgang Amadeus, 218, 235
Mukhina, Vera, 19, 287, 288, 290, 293, 294, 301, 303, 309, 311

Napoleon III, 343, 346
Nazism (National Socialism) (*see also* Germany, Nazi), 3, 6, 7, 8, 12, 13, 21, 26, 161–83, 208, 280, 329, 368, 369, 382, 383,

384; and physical culture, 279, 280, 384
Nechaev, Egor, 120
New Man, 3, 5, 8, 10, 14, 15, 16, 23, 137, 185, 186, 211; Soviet, 269–86
New Zealand, 370
Nicholas II, Tsar, 51, 57–69 *passim*, 75
Nielsen, Vladimir, 219, 231
Nietzsche, Friedrich, 220, 273, 282
Nikolai Nikolaevich, Grand Duke, 64, 68
NKVD, 8, 14, 135, 138, 186, 192–204 *passim*, 208, 231, 234, 293

Obradovich, Sergei, 115, 116, 120
October Revolution (1917), 4, 10, 105, 106, 127, 136, 137, 139, 144, 145, 185, 236, 297
Oreshin, Petr, 120
Organon (Holland), 310
Orlova, Liubov, 234
Oudshoorn, Nelly, 310, 315
Ozouf, Mona, 37, 349

Payne, Stanley, 179
Pelletan, Camille, 350
Piatakov, Iurii, 204, 207
Pick, Daniel, 251
Platonov, Andrei, 122, 123, 136, 246, 304, 305
Pletnev, Valerian, 119, 290, 291, 292, 306, 307, 308, 309, 313, 316
Poland, 7, 280, 379, 385, 386, 387
Poletaev, Nikolai, 114, 115
POW Memorial Church, 365–77
POWs (prisoners-of-war), 20–1, 55, 67, 365–77; Association of Former, 366, 373

Prokofiev, Sergei, 238
Proletcult, 109, 110, 111, 114, 119, 120, 121, 125
Proust, Antonin, 345, 348
Prussian War (1870–71), 20
purges, Stalinist (1937–38), 8, 185, 195, 198, 199, 205, 207, 208, 213, 231; Second Moscow Show Trial, 207
Purishkevich, V.M., 66, 67
Pushkin, Aleksandr Sergeevich, 218, 243, 301

Quetelet, Adolphe, 256, 277

Radek, Karl, 197
Raffin, Léonce, 351
Rama, Angel, 228
Rasputin, Grigorii, 9, 49–77 *passim*
Ravel, Maurice, 238
Red Army, 16, 91, 95, 138, 192, 276, 281
Red Guard, 84, 85, 87, 90, 96, 97, 100
Renoir, Jean, 227
Rentschler, Eric, 215, 217, 224
Restif de la Bretonne, Nicolas Edme, 33
Reuter, Ernst, 372
Riefenstahl, Leni, 215, 223
Robespierre, Maximilien, 8, 28, 40, 41, 42
Rocco, Alfredo, 260, 261, 262
Rodin, Auguste, 242
Rodzianko, M.V., 54, 62, 63, 70
Rogers, Ginger, 221
Roosevelt, Franklin Delano, 216
Rousseau, Jean Jacques, 6, 8, 32, 34, 38, 40, 41, 42, 45
Rozanov, Vasilii, 311
Russia (*see also* Civil War, February Revolution, October

Revolution), 18, 21, 91; tsarist, 10, 47–81
Russian Revolution (*see* October Revolution)
Russian Civil War (*see* Civil War)
Russolo, Luigi, 237
Rykov, Aleksei, 232, 308

Saint Just, Antoine Louis Léon de Richebourg de, 8, 42
Sangnier, Marc, 358
Schelling, Friedrich Wilhelm Joseph von, 243
Schiller, Friedrich, 243
Schlegel, Karl Wilhelm Friedrich von, 243
Schneider, Paul, 174, 178
Schubert, Franz, 218, 240
Schulte-Sasse, Linda, 215, 216, 223
Schumann, Robert, 240
Scriabin, Alexander, 240
Sedaine, Michel Jean, 33
Seifrid, Thomas, 122
Semashko, Nikolai, 270, 273
Serebriakova, Galina, 301, 312
Shereshevskii, Nikolai Adol'fovich, 306, 307, 309
Shliapnikov, Aleksandr, 111
Shostakovich, Dmitrii, 14–15, 219, 235–48
Sibelius, Jean, 240
Sieyès, Abbé, 38, 41
Socialist Revolutionaries (SRs), 86, 347
Sorokin, Vladimir, 305
Soviet Union (*see* communism, Communist Party, Russia – revolutionary, Stalinism/Stalinist era)
Stahlhelm, 170, 174, 175
Stakhanov, Aleksei, 271
stakhanovites, 218, 227

Stalin, Iosif, 6, 7, 8, 12, 13, 17, 74, 145, 192, 198, 199, 201, 208, 216, 217, 220, 224, 228, 229, 235, 238, 282, 294, 299
Stalinism/Stalinist era (*see also* purges), 7, 12–19 *passim*, 23, 135–59, 185, 215–34; 208, 247, 287–316 industrialization campaign, 137, 140, 236, 237, 273, 310; labour camps, 18
Stein, Edith, 376
Steiner, George, 161
Strauss, Paul, 358
Stravinsky, Igor, 238, 243, 248
Sukhomlinov, V.A., 52, 61, 63, 69, 72, 74, 75, 81
Sverdlov Communist University, 204

Tchaikovsky, Petr, 218, 238, 239, 240, 241, 242
Theresienstadt ghetto, 335
Third Reich (*see* Germany, Nazi)
Tolstoy, Lev, 242
Treaty of Versailles, 169
Trotsky, Lev, 73, 187, 195, 203, 204, 205, 207, 273
Trotskyists, 13, 191, 195, 196, 199, 202, 203, 204, 205, 206, 207, 212, 308
Trufanov, S., (Illiodor, Hieromonk), 49, 50, 61, 67

Ulrich, Herbert, 178
United States, 16, 250, 253

Verdery, Katherine, 304
Volga-Volga, 14, 215–234
Vostokov, V.I., 66
Vyrubova, Anna, 51, 52, 60, 75, 77

Wagner, Richard, 218, 220, 273, 282

INDEX

Wannsee Conference, 387
Weber, Eugen, 162
Weimar Republic, 165, 167, 169, 171, 173, 174, 175, 176, 332, 367, 368, 369
Wilhelm, Kaiser, 67
Witkop, Philipp, 168
World War I, 13, 47, 64, 68, 74, 94, 99, 102, 162, 164, 166, 167, 171, 250, 280, 355, 356, 359, 367, 368, 369, 370, 372, 373, 381; Nazi attitude towards, 368
World War II (*see also* Auschwitz, commemoration, Germany – Nazi, Holocaust, Nazism, POWs), 20–1, 24, 25, 281, 367–76 *passim*

Yankelevitch, Vladimir, 320
Young German Order, 170
Young Pioneers, 279

Zalkind, Aaron, 189, 190
Zamkov, Aleksei, 19, 287–316
Zhdanov, Andrei, 195, 199, 230
Zinov'ev, Grigorii, 212